THE OEDIPUS PAPERS

Classics in Psychoanalysis

Edited by
George H. Pollock, M.D., Ph.D.
Chicago Institute for Psychoanalysis

Monograph 6

THE OEDIPUS PAPERS

edited by
George H. Pollock, M.D.
and
John Munder Ross, Ph.D.

International Universities Press, Inc.
Madison Connecticut

This collection of classic papers that comprises Monograph 6 of the *Classics in Psychoanalysis* monograph series is presented here with only minor alterations, i.e., Americanized spelling and punctuation. We have not tried to reconcile the differing styles and usages of the original works.

LIBRARY OF CONGRESS
Library of Congress Cataloging-in-Publication Data

The Oedipus papers / edited by George H. Pollock and John Munder Ross.
p. cm. — (Classics in psychoanalysis : monograph 6)
Consists of articles reprinted from various sources.
Includes bibliographies and index.
ISBN 0-8236-3730-1
1. Oedipus complex. 2. Oedipus (Tale) I. Pollock, George H.
II. Ross, John Munder. III. Series: Classics in psychoanalysis : monograph no. 6
[DNLM: 1. Psychoanalytic Theory—collected works. W1 CL122D no.
6 / WM 460 028]
BF175.5.033032 1988
150.19'5—dc19
DNLM/DLC
for Library of Congress 88-2760
CIP

Manufactured in the United States of America

Contents

Interpretations of the Myth After 1970

Clinical, Cultural, and Developmental Implications

Contributors

Norman B. Atkins, M.D. — Training and Supervising Analyst, Los Angeles Psychoanalytic Society and Institute; Associate Clinical Professor of Psychiatry, University of Southern California School of Medicine; Member of Attending Staff, Department of Psychiatry, Cedars Sinai Medical Center, Los Angeles.

Gertrude Blanck, Ph.D. — President, Blanck Institute for Research in Ego Psychology, New York; Past-President, Institute for Psychoanalytic Training and Research; Former Curriculum Director, Institute for the Study of Psychotherapy.

Michael Bross, Ph.D. — Associate Professor, Department of Psychology, Concordia University, Montreal; Member, Canadian Psychological Association; Member, American Psychological Association.

George Devereux (1908-1985) — Formerly Consultant in Ethnopsychiatry, Maison des Sciences de l'Homme, Paris; Professor Emeritus, Ecole des Hautes Etudes en Sciences Sociales.

Erik H. Erikson — Senior Consultant in Psychiatry, Mount Zion Hospital, San Francisco; Professor Emeritus, Human Development, Harvard University; Former Member, Senior Staff, Austen Riggs Center, Stockbridge, Massachusetts.

Luis Feder, Psy.D. — Training and Supervising Analyst, Asociacion Psicoanalitica Mexicana; Professor, UNAM, Mexico; Coordinator-in-Chief, Indice Bibliografico Acumulativo Psicoanalitico de America Latina (IBAPAL).

Sandor Ferenczi, M.D. (1873-1933) — Hungarian psychoanalyst; founder and co-editor of the *Internationale Zeitschrift für Psychoanalyse.*

Sigmund Freud, M.D. (1856-1939) — Austrian neurologist; founder of psychoanalysis.

Erich Fromm, Ph.D. (1900-1980) — German-American psychoanalyst and social philosopher.

Béla Grunberger, M.D. — Training analyst, Paris Psycho-analytical Society.

James M. Herzog, M.D. — Director of Training in Child Psychiatry, Childrens Hospital Medical Center, Boston; Coordinator, Human Development Curriculum, Boston Psychoanalytic Society and Institute.

Mark Kanzer, M.D. — Clinical Professor of Psychiatry Emeritus, State University of New York (Downstate); Past Director, Division of Psychoanalytic Education, State University of New York (Downstate).

Robert Michels, M.D. — Barklie McKee Henry Professor and Chairman, Department of Psychiatry, Cornell University Medical College; Psychiatrist-in-Chief, Payne Whitney Clinic and Westchester Division, The New York Hospital; Training and Supervising Analyst, Columbia University for Psychoanalytic Training and Research.

George H. Pollock, M.D., Ph.D. — President, Institute for Psychoanalysis, Chicago; Professor of Psychiatry, Northwestern University; President, Center for Psychosocial Studies, Chicago.

Otto Rank, Ph.D. (1884-1939) — Austrian psychologist and psychoanalytic psychotherapist; Editor of *Imago*.

Arnaldo Rascovsky, M.D. — Professor of the Psychology Doctorate, University of Belgrano, Buenos Aires; Honarary President of FEPAL (Federation Committee of the Latin American Psychoanalytic Organizations); Founder and ex-president of the Argentine Psychoanalytic Association; Founder and ex-president of the Argentine Scoiety of Medical Psychology, Psychoanalysis and Psychosomatic Medicine; National Honorary Member and Professor of the Argentine Medical Association; Founder and President of FILIUM, Interdisciplinary Association for the Study and Prevention of FILICIDE: Founder and ex-Director of the Argentine Psychoanalytic magazine; Didactic Member and Professor of the Psychoanalytic Institute of Buenos Aires.

Matilde Rascovsky — Member of the Argentine Psychoanalytic Association; Member of the International Psychoanalytic Association; Didactic member and Professor of the Psychoanalytic Institute of Buenos Aires; Honorary member of the Argentine Psychoanalytic Group Association.

Theodor Reik (1888-1969) — Austrian-American psychoanalyst; Founder, National Psychological Association for Psychoanalysis.

Henry Rosner, M.D. — Medical Director, Well Baby Center, New York; Clinical Associate Professor of Psychiatry, New York University School of Medicine; Former Lecturer in Child and Adolescent Psychiatry, Columbia University School of Social Work.

John Munder Ross, Ph.D. — Faculty, Psychoanalytic Institute at New York University Medical Center; Clinical Associate Professor of Psychology in Psychiatry at Cornell Medical College; Former Editor-in-Chief, *International Journal of Psychoanalytic Psychotherapy.*

Paul Schwaber, Ph.D. — Professor of Letters, Wesleyan University; Instructor, Western New England Institute for Psychoanalysis.

Melford E. Spiro, Ph.D. — Presidential Professor of Anthropology, University of California, San Diego.

Samuel Weiss, M.D. — Training and Supervising Analyst, Institute for Psychoanalysis, Chicago; Clinical Associate Professor, University of Illinois College of Medicine.

Acknowledgment

Above all, the editors would like to acknowledge and thank Keith W. Bradley for his invaluable contribution in tracking down manuscripts and obtaining authors' approvals. His enthusiasm for the project was all encompassing. We would also like to take note of the encouragement and helpfulness of Dr. Nathaniel Ross who died on November 29, 1986. His inspiration and teaching was invaluable to all. Finally, we would like to thank Katherine Ball Ross for her helpful and welcome editorial suggestions.

Introduction

For the last two decades, much of the psychoanalytic literature has been given over to debates between proponents of "classical oedipal" and "revisionist preoedipal" points of view. On the one side, theoreticians and practitioners have argued that the Oedipus complex and the conflicts to which it gives rise remain the cornerstone of the psychoanalytic perspective on human development, motivation, and therapy. On the other, attempts to modify and in some instances discard its centrality have been made for various reasons. Some assert that an exclusive stress on oedipal issues bespeaks an intransigence that ignores the wealth of observational and clinical data accumulated over the years, thereby restricting psychoanalytic understanding and effectiveness. Internal object relations, rooted in the preverbal interactions of infant and toddler with significant caretakers, contribute to ego strengths and deficits, which can have fateful consequences in later life and which may not be accounted for on the basis of oedipal dynamics alone. Now and then there is an attempt to steer between the shoals of the controversy, to synthesize and balance the opposing orientations.

We recognize that scientific theories often are simplifications that do not take into account diversity, complexity, and comprehensiveness. Yet we must begin somewhere, and data from clinical and observational settings provide evidence that allows us to confirm hypotheses and to raise new questions for further study. Nor should we discard the data discovered when psychoanalytic inquiry ventures outside the consulting room. Applied analysis has been with us since our beginnings.

Before there was an oedipal debate, there was an Oedipus—Freud's Oedipus, psychoanalysis's Everyman. It was sometime in the early fall of 1897 that Freud discovered his classic hero. In the midst of personal turmoil and professional soul-searching, he encountered Sophocles' play. That October, just about one year after his father's death, he wrote to Fliess, sharing a remarkable insight into the relationship between the ancient work and the symptoms, associations, and dreams of both his patients and himself. The significance of the tragedy lay in its cathartic rendering, to its audience, of universal childhood wishes of a parricidal and incestuous nature. The horror of these wishes was not at all mitigated by the fact that they were confined, in most cases, to the realm of fantasy. Quite to the contrary, their unreality seemed to intensify the individual's guilt, especially if it were not worked through. Parents could no longer be totally inculpated in neurosogenesis, as they were in the seduction theory Freud had developed the preceding year to explain his patients' (and his own) apparent recollections and recitations of childhood seductions. In the mind's eye, in the unconscious that is, no distinction was to be made between the imaginary and the real. *Oedipus Rex,* Freud maintained, dramatized the process of psychoanalysis itself, illustrating our reluctance to accept the intrapsychic nature of our conflicts, desires, and fantasies, and therefore our individual responsibility for them.

When Freud remarked that the death of a father is the most important event in a man's life, he may have been alluding to the presence of oedipal death wishes. Jacob Freud's death, in October 1896, had brought his son grief and neurotic suffering, but also independence of mind. In the myth, Oedipus, years after his unwitting slaying of Laius, the biological father unknown to him, recoils still from the prophecy of parricide which has dogged him from cradle to grave. King Oedipus is relieved to learn of the natural death, in another city, of Polybus, the man he believes to be his father. Hitherto the devoted son to his (adoptive) father, nonetheless he finds himself not grief-stricken but grateful. The release is indeed transient. Ultimately and ironically, the news, exciting self-interest, serves as a link in the inexorable chain of revelations leading to Oedipus' realization of his deed, his criminal guilt, and his transcendent status as self-reflective hero.

It is in midlife, moreover, that both Freud's and Oedipus' dramas reach their climax—a fact overlooked in the modern debate. As the riddle of the Sphinx intimates, the narrative of Oedipus, from womb to tomb and beyond (but culminating in the choices of adulthood), is a lifelong story. Finding Oedipus within himself, Freud uncovered both the childhood genesis of man's effort to contend with the collision of fate and free will and, with this appreciation of ontogenesis, the timelessness of the unconscious. Oedipus is at once babe, child, man, and myth.

In any case, it was myth and literature, peopled with imaginary characters who are emotionally real, that enabled Freud to look ever more deeply into his soul and those of his patients. Freud described the universal Oedipus complex, lending a certain tragic dignity to a core motive from everyone's childhood history and imprinting in our memories a developmental predicament we might otherwise repress and deny.

Moved by many of the questions and controversies raised in the current oedipal debate, the editors of this volume revisited Oedipus and Freud's remarkable encounter with him (see Chapters 19, 21). They found that many psychoanalysts had inquired of the oracle before them.

Some, like George Devereux and Mark Kanzer, had carefully examined the origins of the myth. They had found many Oedipuses—fragments of epics, variants of the myth, and other dramas, some overlooked by Freud in his focus on a single plot line of the Sophoclean version. Each depicted different stories with new characters, and each yielded further psychological and sociohistorical information and insights.

Other writers returned to the drama or the myth with a more pragmatic agenda, whether theoretical or clinical, seeking answers to the psychoanalytic riddles of their day. In the Delphic spirit, they left puzzled, having retrieved from their researches only further enigmas. As with Freud, so with Ferenczi, Rank, Fromm, and others, one is impressed over and over again by the novelty of what has been noted and then somehow forgotten, "repressed" perhaps, only to be rediscovered.

Freud had been preoccupied with Oedipus the child, and Sophocles' play served as a metaphorical and almost ritual enactment of the sins of the heart of all sons and daughters. For Freud, Oedipus' lot, appreciated just as he modified his seduction theory, was paradigmatic of a universal psychic reality wherein the forces of morality and the repugnant "wishes of childhood forced upon us by nature" clashed, giving rise to internal conflict and various attempts at compromise and mastery. The myth dramatized the basic principles of psychoanalysis: the unconscious, psychic reality, childhood determinism, and intrapsychic conflict.

With further study and research, Oedipus no longer was seen simply to wage a solitary war with the clashing forces of private internal morality and unknown instinctual desire. The parents—Jocasta and Laius, Merope and Polybus—came under scrutiny, as did the history and prehistory of the Athenian cultural explosion that had given the protean legend its final shape. Most who investigated the mysterious story retained a Freudian, indeed an oedipal, focus. For them, in the Aristotelian spirit, tragic man was by definition "guilty man." Nonetheless, Oedipus could no longer be thought of as alone responsible for the social and familial horror whose central themes were parricide, maternal incest, and intergenerational tragedy.

The drama of Oedipus was set in the context of a family history—a cast of characters, each with unconscious imperatives, entangled in a web of manifest and latent communications and conflictual relationships. Some authors underscored the filicidal precondition of the oedipal situation (Devereux, Ferenczi, Pollock, Rascovsky). In this vein, the dictates of generational ascendancy were seen to hold sway, demanding the submission of young to old (see Ross, Chapter 19). This behavior, viewed as an attempt, in Freud's terms, to secure the protection of the father and of society, as well as the father's love, lent itself to a fuller appreciation of "negative" oedipal yearnings (Weiss) in addition to the "positive" heterosexual ambition of the Oedipus complex. Countertransference issues were set against the backdrop of the complete myth (Atkins, Grunberger), the archetypal dialogues of parent and child finding their way into the analytic situation.

In summary, then, the interpretations included here have supplemented the central tenets of psychoanalysis by placing greater stress on unconscious communication, social environment, the age-specific conflicts and crises of adulthood, and the interpersonal and generational dialectic (Erikson). Read in sequence, the papers in this volume tell a remarkable story—the history of psychoanalysis's struggle to comprehend the meaning of humanity's paradoxical choices and destiny, and to chart a viable and ethical course amid the forces of instinct, necessity, and the frailty of mortal vision. We have chosen 1970 as a watershed demarcating "early" and "later" contributions. Several papers included here appear in print for the first time. We have concentrated on reevaluations of the myth, but have selected some articles dealing with the complex apart from its literary and historical context (Blanck, Herzog, Michels). Our aim has been to demonstrate the dynamic and evolving complexity of psychoanalysis as its students return repeatedly to ponder the mysterious allegory that has served it as perhaps its most important paradigm. Like Freud and like Oedipus—"mental conquistadors," personifications of a collective ego ideal—analysis at its most intensely inquisitive remains at once steadfast and open-minded in its relentless search for truth. We may not have resolved all the "oedipal conflicts" here, but hope to give the scholar, teacher, student, researcher, and clinician a greater appreciation of Oedipus and the complex that bears his name.

INTERPRETATIONS OF THE MYTH BEFORE 1970

1

from *The Interpretation of Dreams*

SIGMUND FREUD

[1900]

In my experience, which is already extensive, the chief part in the mental lives of all children who later become psychoneurotics is played by their parents. Being in love with the one parent and hating the other are among the essential constituents of the stock of psychical impulses which is formed at that time and which is of such importance in determining the symptoms of the later neurosis. It is not my belief, however, that psychoneurotics differ sharply in this respect from other human beings who remain normal—that they are able, that is, to create something absolutely new and peculiar to themselves. It is far more probable—and this is confirmed by occasional observations on normal children—that they are only distinguished by exhibiting on a magnified scale feelings of love and hatred to their parents which occur less obviously and less intensely in the minds of most children.

From *The Interpretation of Dreams* by Sigmund Freud. Translated from the German and edited by James Strachey. Published in the United States by Basic Books, Inc. by arrangement with George Allen & Unwin Ltd. and the Hogarth Press Ltd. Reprinted by permission.

This discovery is confirmed by a legend that has come down to us from classical antiquity: a legend whose profound and universal power to move can only be understood if the hypothesis I have put forward in regard to the psychology of children has an equally universal validity. What I have in mind is the legend of King Oedipus and Sophocles' drama which bears his name.

Oedipus, son of Laius, King of Thebes, and of Jocasta, was exposed as an infant because an oracle had warned Laius that the still unborn child would be his father's murderer. The child was rescued, and grew up as a prince in an alien court, until, in doubts as to his origin, he too questioned the oracle and was warned to avoid his home since he was destined to murder his father and take his mother in marriage. On the road leading away from what he believed was his home, he met King Laius and slew him in a sudden quarrel. He came next to Thebes and solved the riddle set him by the Sphinx who barred his way. Out of gratitude the Thebans made him their king and gave him Jocasta's hand in marriage. He reigned long in peace and honour, and she who, unknown to him, was his mother bore him two sons and two daughters. Then at last a plague broke out and the Thebans made enquiry once more of the oracle. It is at this point that Sophocles' tragedy opens. The messengers bring back the reply that the plague will cease when the murderer of Laius has been driven from the land.

> But he, where is he? Where shall now be read
> The fading record of this ancient guilt?[1]

The action of the play consists in nothing other than the process of revealing, with cunning delays and ever-mounting excitement—a process that can be likened to the work of a psychoanalysis—that Oedipus himself is the murderer of Laius, but further that he is the son of the murdered man and of Jocasta. Appalled at the abomination which he has unwittingly perpetrated, Oedipus blinds himself and forsakes his home. The oracle has been fulfilled.

[1][Lewis Campbell's translation (1883), line 108 f.]

Oedipus Rex is what is known as a tragedy of destiny. Its tragic effect is said to lie in the contrast between the supreme will of the gods and the vain attempts of mankind to escape the evil that threatens them. The lesson which, it is said, the deeply moved spectator should learn from the tragedy is submission to the divine will and realization of his own impotence. Modern dramatists have accordingly tried to achieve a similar tragic effect by weaving the same contrast into a plot invented by themselves. But the spectators have looked on unmoved while a curse or an oracle was fulfilled in spite of all the efforts of some innocent man: later tragedies of destiny have failed in their effect.

If *Oedipus Rex* moves a modern audience no less than it did the contemporary Greek one, the explanation can only be that its effect does not lie in the contrast between destiny and human will, but is to be looked for in the particular nature of the material on which that contrast is exemplified. There must be something which makes a voice within us ready to recognize the compelling force of destiny in the *Oedipus*, while we can dismiss as merely arbitrary such dispositions as are laid down in [Grillparzer's] *Die Ahnfrau* or other modern tragedies of destiny. And a factor of this kind is in fact involved in the story of King Oedipus. His destiny moves us only because it might have been ours—because the oracle laid the same curse upon us before our birth as upon him. It is the fate of all of us, perhaps, to direct our first sexual impulse towards our mother and our first hatred and our first murderous wish against our father. Our dreams convince us that that is so. King Oedipus, who slew his father Laius and married his mother Jocasta, merely shows us the fulfilment of our own childhood wishes. But, more fortunate than he, we have meanwhile succeeded, in so far as we have not become psychoneurotics, in detaching our sexual impulses from our mothers and in forgetting our jealousy of our fathers. Here is one in whom these primaeval wishes of our childhood have been fulfilled, and we shrink back from him with the whole force of the repression by which those wishes have since that time been held down within us. While the poet, as he unravels the past, brings to light the guilt of Oedipus, he is at the same time compelling us to recognize our own inner minds, in which those same impulses, though suppressed, are still to be found. The contrast with which the closing Chorus leaves us confronted—

. . . Fix on Oedipus your eyes,
Who resolved the dark enigma, noblest champion and most wise.
Like a star his envied fortune mounted beaming far and wide:
Now he sinks in seas of anguish, whelmed beneath a raging tide . . .[2]

—strikes as a warning at ourselves and our pride, at us who since our childhood have grown so wise and so mighty in our own eyes. Like Oedipus, we live in ignorance of these wishes, repugnant to morality, which have been forced upon us by Nature, and after their revelation we may all of us well seek to close our eyes to the scenes of our childhood.[3]

There is an unmistakable indication in the text of Sophocles' tragedy itself that the legend of Oedipus sprang from some primaeval dream-material which had as its content the distressing disturbance of a child's relation to his parents owing to the first stirrings of sexuality. At a point when Oedipus, though he is not yet enlightened, has begun to feel troubled by his recollection of the oracle, Jocasta consoles him by referring to a dream which many people dream, though, as she thinks, it has no meaning:

[2][Lewis Campbell's translation, (1883) line 1524 ff.]

[3][*Footnote added* 1914:] None of the findings of psycho-analytic research has provoked such embittered denials, such fierce opposition—or such amusing contortions—on the part of critics as this indication of the childhood impulses towards incest which persist in the unconscious. An attempt has even been made recently to make out, in the face of all experience, that the incest should only be taken as 'symbolic'.—Ferenczi (1912) has proposed an ingenious 'over-interpretation' of the Oedipus myth, based on a passage in one of Schopenhauer's letters.—[*Added* 1919:] Later studies have shown that the 'Oedipus complex', which was touched upon for the first time in the above paragraphs in the *Interpretation of Dreams,* throws a light of undreamt-of importance on the history of the human race and the evolution of religion and morality. (See my *Totem and Taboo,* 1912–13 [Essay IV].)—[Actually the gist of this discussion of the Oedipus complex and of the *Oedipus Rex,* as well as of what follows on the subject of *Hamlet,* had already been put forward by Freud in a letter to Fliess as early as October 15th, 1897. (See Freud, 1950*a*, Letter 71.) A still earlier hint at the discovery of the Oedipus complex was included in a letter of May 31st, 1897. (Ibid., Draft N.)—The actual term 'Oedipus complex' seems to have been first used by Freud in his published writings in the first of his 'Contributions to the Psychology of Love' (1910*h*).]

Many a man ere now in dreams hath lain
With her who bare him. He hath least annoy
Who with such omens troubleth not his mind.[4]

To-day, just as then, many men dream of having sexual relations with their mothers, and speak of the fact with indignation and astonishment. It is clearly the key to the tragedy and the complement to the dream of the dreamer's father being dead. The story of Oedipus is the reaction of the imagination to these two typical dreams. And just as these dreams, when dreamt by adults, are accompanied by feelings of repulsion, so too the legend must include horror and self-punishment. Its further modification originates once again in a misconceived secondary revision of the material, which has sought to exploit it for theological purposes. (Cf. the dream-material in dreams of exhibiting, p. 243 f.) The attempt to harmonize divine omnipotence with human responsibility must naturally fail in connection with this subject-matter just as with any other.

REFERENCES

Ferenczi, S. (1912), The symbolic representation of the pleasure and the reality principles in the Oedipus myth. In: *Sex in Psycho-Analysis.* New York: Basic Books, 1950, pp. 253–269. Chapter 2, this volume.

Freud, S. (1910*h*), A special type of choice of object made by men. *Standard Edition,* 11:165–175. London: Hogarth Press, 1957.

_______ (1912–1913), Totem and taboo. *Standard Edition,* 13:1–161. London: Hogarth Press, 1955.

_______ (1950), *The Origins of Psycho-Analysis.* New York: Basic Books, 1954.

[4][Lewis Campbell's translation, (1883) line 982 ff.]

2

The Symbolic Representation of the Pleasure and Reality Principles in the Oedipus Myth

SANDOR FERENCZI

[1912]

Schopenhauer writes: "Every work has its origin in a happy thought, and the latter gives the joy of conception; the birth, however, the carrying out, is, in my own case at least, not without pain; for then I stand before my own soul, like an inexorable judge before a prisoner lying on the rack, and make it answer until there is nothing left to ask. Almost all the errors and unutterable follies of which doctrines and philosophies are so full seem to me to spring from a lack of this probity. The truth was not found, not because it was unsought, but because the intention always was to find again instead some preconceived opinion or other, or at least not to wound some favorite idea, and with this aim in view subterfuges had to be employed against both

---

From *Sex in Psycho-Analysis* by Sandor Ferenczi, pp. 253–269.

other people and the thinker himself. *It is the courage of making a clean breast of it in face of every question that makes the philosopher. He must be like Sophocles' Oedipus, who, seeking enlightenment concerning his terrible fate, pursues his indefatigable enquiry, even when he divines that appalling horror awaits him in the answer. But most of us carry in our hearts the Jocasta, who begs Oedipus for God's sake not to enquire further; and we give way to her, and that is the reason why philosophy stands where it does* [italics mine]. Just as Odin at the door of hell unceasingly interrogates the old prophetess in her grave, disregarding her opposition and refusals and prayers to be left in peace, so must the philosopher interrogate himself without mercy. This philosophical courage, however, which is the same thing as the sincerity and probity of investigation that you attribute to me, does not arise from reflection, cannot be wrung from resolutions, but is an inborn trend of the mind" (Schopenhauer, 1815).

The deep and compressed wisdom of these remarks deserves to be discussed, and to be compared with the results of psychoanalysis.

What Schopenhauer says about the psychical attitude requisite for scientific (philosophical) production sounds like the application of Freud's formula about the "principles of psychical happenings" (Freud 1912a, S.1) to the theory of science. Freud distinguishes two such principles: the pleasure principle, which in the case of primitive beings (animals, children, savages), as in that of the more primitive mental states (in dreams, wit, fantasy, neurosis, psychosis) plays the leading part and allows processes to come about that only strive for the shortest way of gaining pleasure, while the psychical activity of acts that might create feelings of unpleasantness (*Unlust*) is withdrawn (repression); then the reality principle, which presupposes a higher development and growth of the psychical apparatus, and has as its characteristic that "in place of the repression, which excluded a number of the incoming ideas as creative of unpleasantness (*Unlust*), impartial judgment appears, which has to decide whether a given idea is true or false, i.e., in harmony with reality or not, and which decides by comparison with the memory traces of reality."

Only one kind of thought activity remains free from the tests of reality, even after the inauguration of the higher principle, and subject solely to the pleasure principle, namely, fantasy, while it is science that is most successful in overcoming the pleasure principle (Freud 1912a, S.4).

Schopenhauer's opinion, quoted above, on the mental disposition requisite for scientific activity would therefore run somewhat as follows if converted into Freud's terminology: the thinker may (and should) give his fantasy play, so as to be able to taste the "joy of conception"—new ideas are of course not to be had in any other way (see Robitschek 1912)—but in order that these fantastic notions may evolve into scientific ideas they must first be submitted to a laborious testing by reality.

Schopenhauer recognized with acute perception that the greatest resistances raised against unprejudiced testing of reality, even in the case of a scientist, are not of an intellectual, but of an affective nature. Even the scientist has human failings and passions—vanity, jealousy, moral and religious bias tending to blind him to a truth that is disagreeable to him—and he is only too inclined to regard as true an error that fits his personal system.

Psychoanalysis can only complement Schopenhauer's postulate in a single point. It has found that the inner resistances may be fixed in the earliest childhood and may be completely unconscious; it therefore demands of every psychologist who enters on the study of the human mind that he should thoroughly investigate beforehand his own mental constitution—inborn and acquired—down to the deepest layers and with all the resources of the analytic technique.

Unconscious affects, however, may falsify the truth not only in psychology, but also in all other sciences, so we have to formulate Schopenhauer's postulate as follows: Everyone who works in science should first submit himself to a methodical psychoanalysis.

The advantages that would accrue to science from this deepened self-knowledge on the part of the scientist are evident. An enormous amount of power for work, which is now wasted on infantile controversies and priority disputes, could be put at the disposal of more serious aims. The danger of "projecting into science as a generally valid theory peculiarities of one's own personality" (Freud 1912b) would be much less. The hostile manner also in which, even nowadays, new unusual ideas or scientific propositions are received when put forward by unknown authors, unsupported by any authoritative personality, would give way to a more unprejudiced testing by reality. I will go so far as to maintain that, if this rule of self-analysis were observed, the development of the various sciences, which today is an endless series of energy-wasting revolutions and reactions, would pursue a much smoother, yet a more profitable and accelerated course.

It cannot be regarded as chance that the Oedipus myth immediately occurred to Schopenhauer when he wished to illustrate by a simile the correct psychical attitude of the scientist in mental production and the inner resistances that arise against this correct way of working. Had he been—as we analysts are—convinced of the strict determination and determinability of *every* psychical act, this thought would surely have made him reflect. For us, who are the fortunate possessors of the Freudian psychology (which like a mental Dietrich provides a ready key to so many locks that have till now been considered impossible to open), it is not at all difficult to retrieve this piece of analysis. This idea that occurred to Schopenhauer indicates his unconscious perception of the fact that of all inner resistances by far the most significant is the resistance against the infantile fixation on hostile tendencies against the father and on incestuous ones toward the mother.

These tendencies, which through the civilized education of the race and of the individual have become intensely disagreeable, and have therefore been repressed, draw with them into the repression a large number of other ideas and tendencies associated with these complexes, and exclude them from the free interchange of thought, or at all events no longer allow them to be treated with scientific objectivity.

The "Oedipus complex" is not only the nuclear complex of the neuroses (Freud); the kind of attitude adopted toward it also determines the most important character traits of the normal man, and in part also the greater or lesser objectivity of the scientist. A man of science who is prevented by the incest barrier from admitting to himself nascent inclinations of love and disrespect toward blood relations will—so as to assure the repression of these inclinations—also not want, nor be able, to test in their reality with the impartiality demanded by science the actions, works, and thoughts of other authorities as well as the paternal one.

To decipher the feeling and thought content that lies behind the wording of the Oedipus myth was thus beyond even the power of a Schopenhauer, otherwise so discerning. He overlooked the fact—as did the whole civilized world until Freud—that this myth is a distorted wish fantasy, the projection of repressed wish-excitations (father-hate, mother-love) with an altered pleasure-prefix (abhorrence, shuddering awe) onto an external power, "fate." This reconstruction of the real meaning of the myth, its interpretation as a "material phenomenon" (Silberer), was thus alien to the philosopher. While writing this letter he was himself dominated—so I believe—by affects that would have debarred this insight.

The actual occasion that led Schopenhauer to choose this comparison of himself with Oedipus may be divined from the other parts of the letter. The neglected philosopher saw himself recognized for the first time by a man of Goethe's greatness and standing. He answered him with expressions of gratitude that we are not accustomed to from the proud, self-confident Schopenhauer: "Your Excellency's kind letter has given me great pleasure, because everything coming from you is for me of inestimable value, a sacred possession. Further, your letter contains the praise of my work, and your approval outweighs in my estimation that of any other."

That sounds absolutely like the enthusiastic gratitude of one man to an older respected one in whom he hopes to find the long-sought protector, i.e., to find again the father. Besides God, King, and national heroes, heroes of the spirit like Goethe are also *"revenants"* of the father for countless men, who transfer to them all the feelings of gratitude and respect that they once showed to their bodily father. The subsequent quotation of the Oedipus myth, however, may well have been an unconscious reaction against this—perhaps rather extravagant—expression of gratitude toward the father, a reaction that allowed some display of the hostile tendencies that go to make up the fundamentally ambivalent feeling-attitude of a son toward his father. In favor of this view speaks the fact that toward the end the letter becomes more and more proud and self-confident. Schopenhauer there asks Goethe to secure the publication of his chief work (*Die Welt als Wille und Vorstellung*), and now speaks to him as to an equal; he lays a eulogizing emphasis on the unusual value of his book, the remarkable nature of its contents, and the beauty of its style, closing with a few cool, businesslike lines, which might perhaps be called brusque. "I will ask you please to give me a quite decisive answer without delay, because in case you do not accept my proposal I will commission someone who is going to the Leipsig fair to seek a publisher there for me."

Perhaps it was just the aid of the attention that had been deviated from the concrete meaning that enabled Schopenhauer to decipher in this letter the "functional symbolism" (which for some time escaped even psychoanalysts) of certain details of the Oedipus myth.

Silberer gives the name of functional symbol-phenomena to those pictures occurring in dreams, fantasies, myths, etc. in which not the content of thought and imagination but the way of functioning of the mind (e.g., its ease, difficulty, inhibition, etc.) is indirectly represented.[1]

If we allow Schopenhauer's comparison and translate it into analytical-scientific language, we have to say that the two chief personages of Sophocles' tragedy also symbolize the two principles of mental activity. Oedipus, "who, seeking enlightenment concerning his terrible fate, pursues his indefatigable enquiry, even when he divines that appalling horror awaits him in the answer," represents the reality principle in the human mind, which permits none of the emerging ideas, even those that produce pain, to be repressed, but bids all to be equally tested as to their intrinsic truth. Jocasta, "who begs Oedipus for God's sake not to enquire further," is the personification of the pleasure principle, which, regardless of objective truth, wants nothing else than to spare the ego pain, to gain pleasure wherever possible, and, so as to reach this goal, bans to the unconscious whenever possible all ideas and thoughts that threaten to set free pain.

Encouraged by Schopenhauer's interpretation and its striking analytical confirmation, I venture to go a step further and to raise the question whether it is pure chance that in both the Oedipus myth and the Edda Saga, also cited by our philosopher, the reality principle is represented by men (Oedipus, Odin) and the pleasure principle by women (Jocasta, Erda). The psychoanalyst is not accustomed to fly hastily to the idea of "accident," and would incline rather to attribute

[1]Cf. Silberer's throughout original and pregnant works on symbolism, especially Silberer (1909, 1910, 1912a,b,c).

to the Greek and Teutonic peoples, as well as to Sophocles and Schopenhauer, an unconscious knowledge of the bisexuality of every human being. Schopenhauer actually says that most human beings carry in them Oedipus and Jocasta. In accord with this interpretation is the observation of daily experience that in general in women the tendency to repression—the pleasure principle, therefore—prevails; in men the capacity for objective judgment and for tolerating painful insight—the reality principle, therefore.

An eye made keen by individual-psychological experience will certainly be able to discover and solve many more significant symbols in Sophocles' tragedy. I will only point out two very striking ones, both of the category of "somatic symbol-phenomena" (Silberer), in which, therefore, bodily states are mirrored. To start with, there is the name of the tragic hero Oedipus, which in Greek means "swell-foot." This apparently senseless and odd denomination at once loses this character when we know that in dreams and jokes, as well as in the fetishistic worship of the foot or in the neurotic dread of this member, it symbolizes the male organ.

The fact that this member is described in the hero's name as swollen is sufficiently explained by its erectibility. It cannot surprise us, by the way, that the myth completely identifies with a phallus the man who achieved the monstrous feat of sexual intercourse with the mother, a feat no doubt conceived as superhuman.

The other somatic symbol-phenomenon is Oedipus' self-blinding as a punishment for his unconscious committed sins. It is true that the tragedian gives the explanation for this punishment: "For why was I to see, When to descry no sight on earth could have a charm for me?" (Young, 1906) he makes Oedipus (not quite unequivocally) cry out. But certain psychoanalytical experiences, in which the eyes regularly have to be interpreted as symbols of the genital organs, give me the right to interpret the self-blinding as a displacement of the really intended self-castration of Oedipus, the talion punishment more comprehensible in this connection. To the horrified question of the Chorus, however—

> Rash man, how could'st thou bear to outrage so
> Thine eyes? What Power was it, what wrought on thee?

—the hero answers:

Apollo, Apollo fulfils,
O friends, my measure of ills—
Fills my measure of woe.

In other words, it was the sun (Phoebus Apollo), the most typical father symbol (Freud, 1912c); the hero was no longer to look him in the eyes, a consideration that may have given a second determining factor for the distortion of the castration punishment to blinding.[2]

If we have once assimilated these interpretations, it must amaze us to see how the folk soul should have managed to fuse together in this myth the knowledge (distorted, it is true) of the most significant content, the nuclear complex of the unconscious (i.e., the parental complex), with the most general and comprehensive formula of mental activity. Our amazement gives way to understanding, however, when we have learned from Otto Rank's fundamental mythopsychological works to grasp the way in which the creative folk soul works. Rank showed in a beautiful example (Rank 1912a) that the individual poet "by means of his own complex tones succeeds in clarifying and emphasizing certain attributes of a transmitted material," but that the so-called folk productions are also to be regarded as the work of numerous or countless individuals, who originate, transmit, and decorate the tradition. "Only in this case," he says further, "the story goes through a series of similarly disposed individual minds, each of which works in the same direction, at the production of general human motives and the polishing of many disturbing accessory works."

After the double interpretation of the Oedipus myth we may imagine the crystallizing process of our myth, described by Rank, somewhat as follows:

[2]These symbol interpretations will be at once evident to the practised psychoanalyst, since he can find them confirmed in his dream analyses countless times. While reading through this article, however, I received from Dr. Otto Rank the information that the correctness both of the interpretation of the name Oedipus here attempted and that of the sexual-symbolic explanation of self-blinding could be determined with certainty from comparative mythological studies. In his work that has just appeared, "Das Inzest-motiv in Dichtung und Sage," these interpretations are substantiated with a rich collection of facts, which makes it possible for the nonanalyst also to accept them.

Significant but unconscious psychical contents (aggressive fantasies against the father, sexual hunger for the mother with erection tendencies, dread lest the father avenge the sinful intent with the punishment of castration) procured, each for itself, indirect symbolic representatives in the consciousness of all men. Men with special creative capacities, poets, give expression to these universal symbols. In this way the mythical motives of exposure by the parents, victory over the father, unconscious intercourse with the mother, and self-blinding, might have arisen in individuals independent of one another. In the course of the passage of the myths through countless poetic individual minds, one that Rank has made probable, condensation of the separate motives led secondarily to a greater unity, which then proved to be durable and which was fashioned anew in much the same form by all peoples and at all times (see Rank 1909).

It is probable, however, that in this, as also in every other myth, and perhaps indeed with mental productivity in general, parallel with the tendency to give expression to psychical contents there is also an unconscious aim at bringing to presentation the mental ways of functioning that are operative in mastering these contents.[3] Only this latter fusion then yields the perfected myth, which without forgoing any of its effect on men is transmitted unchanged for hundreds of years. So was it with the Oedipus myth, in which not only the most deeply repressed feeling and thought complexes of mankind are represented in images, but also the play of the mental forces that were operative in the attempt to master these contents, differing according to sex and individuality.

For the correctness of this interpretation let some passages from the tragedy itself bear witness:

> *Oedipus*: And how can I help dreading
> My mother's bed?
> *Jocasta*: But why should men be fearful, . . .
> O'er whom Fortune is mistress, and fore-knowledge
> Of nothing sure? *Best take life easily*,[4]

[3]Silberer, to whom we owe the formulation of the idea of functional symbolism, cites a long series of myths and fairy-tales that can be resolved into both material and functional symbol-phenomena (Silberer, 1910).

[4]The passages in italics are not underlined in the original.

As a man may. For that maternal wedding,
Have you no fear; for many men ere now
Have dreamed as much; but he who by such dreams
Sets nothing, has the easiest life of it.

. . . .

Jocasta (*to* Oedipus, *who, enquiring after the frightful truth, summons the only witness of the crime*):
Why ask who 'twas he spoke of?
Nay, never mind—never remember it—
'Twas idly spoken!
Oedipus: Nay, it cannot be
That having such a clue I should refuse
To solve the mystery of my parentage!
Jocasta: For heaven's sake, if you care for your own life,
Don't seek it! I am sick, and that's enough!

. . . .

Jocasta: But I beseech you, hearken! Do not do it!
Oedipus: I will not hearken—not to know the whole.
Jocasta: I mean well; and I tell you for the best!
Oedipus: What you call best is an old sore of mine.
Jocasta: *Wretch, what thou art O might'st thou never know!*

. . . .

Oedipus: *Break out what will, I shall not hesitate,*
Low though it be, to trace the source of me.

. . . .

Shepherd (who was ordered to kill the new-born Oedipus, but who exposed him to the open):
O, I am at the horror, now, to speak!
Oedipus: And I to hear. But I must hear—no less.

"The Jocasta in us," as Schopenhauer says, the pleasure principle, as we express it, wishes thus that a man "should best take life easily, as a man may," that he "set no store by" (suppresses) the things that disturb him, e.g., that with the most superficial motivation he should refuse to accord any significance to fantasies and dreams about the death of his father and sexual intercourse with his mother, pay no attention to disagreeable and dangerous talk, and not search after the origin of things, but above all it warns a man against recognizing who he is.

The reality principle, however, the Oedipus in the human soul, does not allow the seductions of pleasure to keep him from penetrating into even a bitter or a horrible truth, it estimates nothing so lowly as to be not worth testing, it is not ashamed to seek the true psychological nucleus of even superstitious prophecies and dreams, and learns to endure the knowledge that in the inmost soul aggressive and sexual instincts dwell that do not pause even at the barriers erected by civilization between the son and his parents.

REFERENCES

Freud, S. (1912a), Formulieringen über die zwei Prinzipien des psychischen Geschehens. In: *Jahrbuch für Psychoanalytische und Psychopathologische Forschungen,* Vol. III, ed. E. Bleuler und S. Freud Leipzig: Franz Deuticke. pp. 1-8. [Formulas on the two principles of psychical happenings. In: *Yearbook for Psychoanalytic and Psychopatholgic Research.*]

________ (1912b), Ratschläge für die Ärzte bei der psychoanalytischen Behandlung Zentralblatt für Psychoanalyse, Jahrgang II, Lizen znachdruck der Ausgabe. Wiesbaden: J.F. Bergman, [Amsterdam: E.J. Bonset, 1964, pp. 483-489.]

________ (1912c), Nachtrag zu dem autobiographisch beschriebenen Falle von Paranoia (Dementia paranoides). In: *Jahrbuch für Psychoanalytische und Psychopathologische Forschungen,* Vol. III, ed. E. Bleuler und S. Freud, Leipzig: Franz Deuticke. pp. 588-590. (Nachtrag zur Analyse Schrebers) [Supplement to the Autobiographical Writings—Condition of Paranoia (Paranoid Dementia) (Supplement to the Schreber Analysis).]

Rank, O. (1909), *Der Mythus von der Geburt des Helden* Leipzig/Vienna: Franz Deuticke. [*A psychological interpretation of mythology* Authorized translation by F. Robbins and Smith Ely Jelliffe. New York: The Journal of Nervous and Mental Disease Pub. Co., 1914; *The Myth of the Birth of a Hero,* ed. Philip Freund. New York: Vintage Book, 1960.]

________ (1912a), Der Sinn der Griselda-Febel In: Imago, Vol. I, ed. O. Rank and H. Sachs Leipzig/Vienna: Hugo Heller & Cie, pp. 34-48 [The Meaning of the Griselda Fable.]

________ (1912b), *Das Inzest-Motiv in Dichtung und Sage* Leipzig: Franz Deuticke. [Incest in Literature.]

Robitschek, A. (1912), Symbolisches Denken in der chemischen Forschung In: Imago, Vol. I, ed. O. Rank and H. Sachs Leipzig/Vienna: Hugo Heller & Cie. pp. 83-90. [Symbolic Thoughts in Chemical Research.]

Schopenhauer, A. (1815), *Gesammelte Briefe Herausgabe von Arthur Hübscher.* Bonn: Bouvier Verlag Herbert Grundmann 1978, pp. 18-23.

Silberer, H. (1909), Bericht über eine Methode, gewisse symbolische Halluzinations—Erscheinungen hervorzurufen und zu beobachten. In: *Jahrbuch für* Psychoanalytische und Psychopathologische Forschungen, Vol. II, ed. E. Bleuler und S. Freud. Leipzig/Vienna: Franz Beuticke, pp. 513–525. [Report on a Method, truly symbolic hallucinations—Phenomena Evoked and Observed].

——— (1910), Phantasie und Mythos, In: *Jahrbuch für Psychoanalytische und Psychopathologische Forschungen,* Vol. II, ed. E. Bleuler und E. Freud. Leipzig/Vienna: Franz Deuticke, , pp. 541–622. [Fantasy and Myth].

——— (1912a), Symbolik des Erwachens und Schwellensymbolik überhaupt. In: *Jahrbuch fü Psychoanalytische und Psychopathologische Forschungen,* Vol. III, ed. E. Bleuler und S. Freud. Leipzig/Vienna: Franz Beuticke, pp. 621–660. [Symbols of Awakening and Growing Symbols in General].

——— (1912b), Uber die Symbolbildung. In: *Jahrbuch für Psychoanalytische und Psychopathologische Forschungen,* Vol. III, ed. E. Bleuler und S. Freud. Leipzig/Vienna: Franz Beuticke, pp. 661–723 [On Symbol Formation].

——— (1912c), Uber die Behandlung einer Psychose bie Justinius Kerner. In: *Jahrbuch für Psychoanalytische und Psychopathologische Forschungen,* Vol. III, ed. E. Bleuler und S. Freud. Leipzig/Vienna: Franz Beuticke, pp. 724–729. [On the Handling of a Psychosis of Justinius Kerner].

Young, G. (1906) Oedipus tyrannus, In: *Sophocles,* ed. Ernest Rhys. London: J.M. Dent & Co.; New York: E.P. Dutton & Co., pp. 128–173.

3

Oedipus and the Sphinx

THEODOR REIK

[1920]

. . . Behold, this is Oedipus
Who unravelled the great riddle . . .
—*Sophocles*

1. Introduction

The reader of *Imago* will find on the cover of the volume containing this essay a little drawing which, in response to the proposal of Otto Rank, will adorn all the publications of the International Psychoanalytical Press. It represents Oedipus, gazing fixedly and unafraid at his terrible adversary, the Sphinx.

Ferenczi (1912) has alluded, in an interesting article, to a passage in Schopenhauer's letters, in which the philosopher praises this hero as the pattern of the serious investigator, who seeks the truth regardless of his own welfare.

From *Dogma and Compulsion: Psychoanalytic Studies of Religion and Myth.* New York: International Universities Press, 1951, pp. 289–332.

Psychoanalysis, which, regardless of the ancient and cherished prejudices of civilized humanity, has indicated the nature of the profoundest psychic impulses, has also revealed the obscure but universal human significance of the Oedipus myth. It has shown us that in the ancient saga the two potent and pristine wishes which are of decisive importance in the development of the individual, as of the peoples, appear to achieve fulfillment.

It seems to us that the picture of Oedipus, the unraveler of riddles, and the Sphinx—a picture so rich in associations—may justly adorn the achievements of psychoanalytic research; especially as a constant warning that we must never be content with what has been attained.

Now, perhaps, is the very time to remind ourselves that the Sphinx itself, that winged monster, is still an enigma to us. But now we shall exchange our roles; we shall ask questions, and the Sphinx, albeit reluctantly, will surrender her secret.

2. The Origin of the Sphinx

The Sphinx of Oedipus, which we see in the little drawing to which I have referred, is a late-born sister of innumerable similar figures which came out of the Near East in prehistoric times. If we wish to learn what she really is we may choose between two methods of inquiry: we may seek to divine her true significance from the context of her setting in the Oedipus legend, or we may look for the solution of the riddle of her existence—and that of her relatives—in the ancient East. The first way is by far the more convenient; it seems to lead directly to the goal, and it has often been followed. Inviting as it may be, we shall avoid it; for the example of so many unsuccessful predecessors warns us that it leads to a very inadequate explanation. The investigators assure us that the story of the Sphinx is a late interpolation in the Oedipus saga—and the Sphinx herself is not autochthonous in Greece—so that we are in danger of taking a frequently reinterpreted and secondary figure of late origin for the original figure. The second way is the more difficult, and it leads us, to begin with, a surprisingly long way from our saga, into the dark regions of primitive religion and mythology, without giving us any assurance that we shall find our way back to the Sphinx of Oedipus. Difficult problems of the evolutionary history of human thought and belief, which would call for more exhaustive treatment, will confront us and threaten to bar the way. Nevertheless, this is the path we shall pursue.

We shall first turn our attention to the early type of the enigmatic being, as revealed by excavation. The Sphinxes of Egypt are lions with human heads, closely akin to the other fantastic hybrid creatures of antiquity—Sirens, Harpies, Gryphons, Cherubim. Wundt speaks of the Sphinx "as indeed the most expressive and therefore the most enduring of the double forms ever produced by art." The Sphinxes represented by the ancient arts of the Near East, of which all these fantastic beings were native, include both male and female forms of the monster. In the early period the female form is rare; according to the experts it first acquired its peculiar importance in Greece,[1] though we know of many female Sphinxes from the Middle and Late Kingdoms of Egypt and the adjacent countries. Many Sphinxes, like that of Aegina (about 460), show women's faces of seductive charm, while others reveal masculine features. Their solemn and rigid gaze, and their noble tranquillity, give the observer a peculiar feeling if he gazes at them for long. But even the Sphinxes which possess the face and the shoulders and breasts of a woman seem, as a rule, strangely alien to the modern European. He may perhaps recall Mephisto, who had to confess to his partner in the classic Walpurgisnacht: "Above the waist your looks are most inviting,/But lower down I find the beast affrighting!"

The poses of the Sphinxes are greatly varied; they show them standing, sitting, crouching, reclining. Many have wings, but many are wingless.[2] One can almost follow the development of the Sphinx, which was originally based on realistic animal images, but which, as time went on, departed farther and farther from its prototypes, becom-

[1]Cf. Ilberg in Roscher's (1909–1915) "The animals are generally male; female specimens are occasional variants of the male types, but the Greek influence first made them an individual form." In the female Sphinxes a lion's body is surmounted by a woman's head; they rarely have nipples; the woman's breasts were a late addition. In such hybrid forms as the Gryphon and the Criosphinx the female does not occur.

[2]In the Egyptian Sphinxes wings are exceptional; in Greece they are the rule. At first the wings were folded; later on they were raised and outspread.

ing more and more richly decorated. Even in the late Egyptian examples the lion's tail ended in a serpent, while in still later statues of the Roman period the Sphinxes had become composite creatures whose bodies were admixtures of many different animals.

We find Sphinxes as statues, in the bas-reliefs on the friezes of temples, on household furniture and utensils, on ornaments and gems, their dimensions varying, with the nature and function of such articles, from the colossal—for example, the Sphinx of Giza—to the tiny and delicate.[3] We know of many isolated representations of the Sphinx, but Sphinxes often occur in pairs. In the avenues leading to the ancient temples they are often seen lying at intervals of a few yards, their faces turned toward the thoroughfare. In Thebes and elsewhere there may have been hundreds of these colossal images on the processional streets. Many representations show them erect, overthrowing their adversaries with their paws, or tearing at them; but more frequently one sees them on guard before the temples. Later on they adorned, and always guarded, tombs.

3. Theories as to the Meaning of the Sphinx

In descriptions of the different forms of the Sphinx we often encounter expressions of amazement at the vast number of variants of this monster, which can look back on a history of many thousands of years. Numerous contradictory features, which refuse all attempts to unite them in a whole, threaten to bewilder us and to baffle all explanation. There is no doubt that many Sphinxes are intended to represent the king or the queen; this is proved not only by the facial similarities, but also by the inscriptions and the insignia of the sovereign. On the other hand, it is equally obvious that many Sphinxes represent divinities; of this there is abundant evidence. Moreover, it is not unusual for one of these singular figures to have between its forepaws a statuette which may be identified as the portrait of an individual Egyptian sovereign. Further, as many inscriptions inform us, single Sphinxes were stationed before temples and palaces, where they acted as guardians.

[3]The Sphinx of Giza is 65 feet in height and 185 feet in length, while many minute Sphinxes appear on decorated vessels, diadems, bracelets, and ornaments.

We may think that even the few dates relating to the Sphinx which have hitherto been noted will have told us how many enigmatical features the monster exhibits—features which should prove equally interesting to the psychologist, the archaeologist, the historian, and the student of aesthetics. There has been no lack of attempts to solve the problems with which the Sphinx confronts us by the mere fact of her existence; but a brief selection of the suggested explanations, which makes no pretension to completeness, will show how little they explain, and how far they are from reconciling, all the contradictory facts.

Classical tradition knows the Sphinxes as images of the gods.[4] In Plutarch they appear as symbols of wisdom (Parthey 1850). Clemens Alexandrinus (Stromata 1906–1909) regarded them as emblems of power, because they possessed a lion's body, and of intelligence, because they had a human face. According to Champollion (1923) the Sphinx is an embodiment of the Sun-god. Mariette-Bey (1893) thinks the king himself keeps guard before the throne which he has erected. Ilberg's (1912; Roscher 1909–1915) view is that the true Sphinx, as distinct from the Gryphon (the lion with a falcon's head) and the Criosphinx (the lion with a ram's head) represents the king. He assumes that only the Sphinxes with animal heads are to be regarded as personifications of the god whose head they bear. He correctly points out that the Egyptians appear to have interpreted one and the same type of relief differently at different periods.

While we find no agreement in the interpretations of the Egyptian Sphinx, and while the explanations provided by historical research entirely fail to unify the many contradictory motives, we are even more surprised at the conceptions of the Sphinx in the Oedipus legend: The old euhemeristic interpretation saw the monster as an audacious robber, while another regarded her as a soothsayer.[5]

Another interesting euhemeristic interpretation makes the

[4]Wilkinson, (1841), Wiedemann (1890) cited from Roscher's (1909–1915), parts 66/67, #1296, Leipzig, 1913. From this instructive article of Ilberg's I take most of the footnotes included in this article.

[5]Schol. Hesiod. Theog. 326, et al., cited by Ilberg (1912).

Sphinx[6] an Ethiopian species of ape, which many geographers declare that they have seen! Modern scholars have agreed with the allegorical interpretations of the ancients. Bötticher (1854), for example, sees in the Sphinx "a very ancient symbol of the wise, pondering intelligence, concealed within the human head." Interpretations of the Sphinx as a natural force are extremely popular; among other things the Sphinx is supposed to be the all-embracing Helios or Aether, the symbol of the East, the giver of light, the solar zenith, the sunset, the waning moon, and Sirius. Gerhard (1843–1867) counts the Sphinx among the powers of the underworld, while Bréal (1877) sees her as a symbol of the rain cloud, and Forchhammer (1875) as the demon of the winter frost. For Schroeter (1876) too she is a wintry demon, conquered by the vernal hero, Oedipus. Keller (1889) regards her as the destroying angel of the plague in the region of the Boeotian lakes.

If we now survey this long series of explanations, we have to admit that it passes with suspicious rapidity from heaven, through the earth, to hell. It would be unreasonable to expect that one poor creature should have even further simultaneous meanings.

In conclusion, it should be mentioned that psychoanalysis has turned its attention to the Sphinx. Rank (1920) attempts to explain the figure of the Sphinx, in connection with other ancient myths, as indicating the identity of the human and mammalian mother. At the same time he points to the fact that the Sphinx combines the upper part of a woman's body with an animal's hindquarters, which are provided with male genitals. He refers to the infantile conception, which often recurs in dreams, according to which all human beings, including women, possess a penis, and he rightly concludes that there is a concealed homosexual aspect of the meaning of the Sphinx in the Oedipus myth, from which he derives the affect of anxiety. According to this the Sphinx would be a subsequent duplication of the mother; a theory repeated by Schmidt (1877), who identifies the Sphinx with Jocasta. It should be mentioned that Laistner, in his well-known work, *Das Rätsel der Sphinx* (1889), agrees with Rank as regards the genesis of the anxiety dream, and equates the Sphinx with the incubus

[6]According to Agatharchides (*Across the Red Sea*), and in other works of the kind. Fully discussed in Ilberg's article, # 1375.

or nightmare. C. G. Jung (1912) seeks to interpret the Sphinx by his theory of the theriomorphic representation of the libido: for him the Sphinx is a half-theriomorphic representation of the "mother imago," which may be described as the imago of the "terrible mother," of whom numerous traces may be found in mythology. The libido thus theriomorphically represented would be the repressed "animal sexuality." From this root Jung derives the theriomorphic attributes of deity. Thus, according to this explanation the Sphinx is an "anxiety animal," which clearly reveals the characteristics of a mother derivative, and represents an original incestuously toned charge of libido, due to a cleavage of the relation to the mother. We shall recur later on to these attempted explanations.

4. One Method of Analytic Interpretation

Any satisfactory explanation should meet two requirements. In the first place, it ought to make all the prominent and essential features of the Sphinx intelligible, however contradictory they may appear; and in the second place, it should show a natural connection between the Oriental type of Sphinx and the Sphinx of the Greek legend. It obviously will not suffice to give an interpretation which would apply to the one type only, or which would elucidate only one general and essential characteristic of the Sphinx, while ignoring all the mutually contradictory details. On the one hand, then, we maintain that the Sphinx of Giza, as a representative of the ancient Sphinxes of the Near East, is closely related to the Sphinx of the Oedipus saga as represented—let us say—on the cinerary urns of the Etruscans. It is probable that the one form developed out of the other, and it will be part of our task to follow this development and explain it psychologically; but it is impossible that the two forms are *toto genere* different. The mere similarity of shape tells us that; and in our attempt at interpretation we shall proceed from the external form. We hold the opinion that the Sphinx herself must enable us to form conclusions as to her nature on the strength of her outward appearance. As a creation of the human imagination she is an authentic child of Nature, and we believe with Goethe that Nature has neither kernel nor husk: "She is everything at one and the same time."

But first we must ask ourselves how anyone ever forms the conception of such fantastic animals. It is not an idle question, for we know that the imagination is incapable of creating anything absolutely new; it can only combine, transform, and recreate fragments of reality. But this it does in accordance with certain eternal and unchanging rules, which are followed by the artist of the age of cave dwellers no less than by the most recent of Expressionists and Dadaists. The man of antiquity, despite all our knowledge of him, is so remote from our mental and emotional life that our intuition of his feelings will always be imperfect and uncertain. Yet even we, the children of an age which has achieved such wonderful things, know psychic states in which we think and feel approximately as did the men of bygone periods of culture. Psychoanalysis has taught us that our dreams revert to such an archaic mental structure.

One of the principal devices of dream work, through whose operation the understanding of the dream thoughts is made so difficult for us, is *condensation*, in which we must include the production of collective or mixed persons. We believe that this peculiar method of combining a number of features, often mutually contradictory, to form a unity which already exists in the dream material or is newly created, can furnish an adequate explanation of the psychic mechanisms which are operative in the formation of such figures as the Sphinx. The singular composition of the Sphinx's body should disturb us as little in our task of interpretation as the apparently meaningless and unintelligible formation of certain hybrid persons in our dreams. For example, in a dream we often see X, whom we know, sporting a beard like Z's, together with a woman's hat and a silk blouse such as Mrs. Y might wear, and in the dream this does not trouble us in the least. We may be sure that the ancient Egyptians were as little astonished by the Sphinx. We see psychic creations resembling the dream in structure in the hallucinations of persons suffering from psychosis, in which it is not unusual for imperfect or composite creatures to appear, and we know that psychoanalysis is able to reveal their significance. Those who are familiar with the technique of psychoanalysis have shown that the images which seem so absurd have really a meaning. Owing to the special character of the psychotic disorder—namely, the rupture of all relations with the environment—it may be impossible to make a complete analysis; yet psychoanalysts are agreed that the hallucinatory figures are determined in every feature, and that their production can be explained by the emergence of affectively toned recollections of certain experiences and impressions. It is possible to understand such images only if we realize that they must be granted a definite place in the structure of the psychosis; and if we place ourselves on the same footing as the patient, refusing to take exception to the absurdity of the hallucinatory images. A woman patient of Dr. Bertschinger's (1911), who drew the hallucinatory pictures that passed before her, furnished explanations of the images which gave one an excellent notion of the way in which they were produced. Twofold creatures appeared with especial frequency; she might see a stag with the upper part of a human body, or even with two human torsos; a horse's body with a human head; a spotted hyena with the head and shoulders and bosom of a woman; a crocodile, which in addition to its own head displayed the head of a man, etc. The individual components of these compositions proved to be determined by the patient's reminiscences. For example, she saw a spotted hyena, and on the following day she offered this explanation: she had compared a wardress who had annoyed her to a spotted hyena because she had such wicked green eyes, and wore a spotted blouse. At the same time the hyena was a young woman who resembled the wardress; the patient had recollected this young woman, and remembered that when she was eleven she had a particularly painful experience in connection with her. The image of a billygoat with a human head was intelligible when one learned that as a little child she had been the unwilling witness of an act of coition, when she compared the man to a billygoat. But this picture too was overdetermined, for during a holiday in the country she had seen for the first time the erect penis of a goat. In the same way analytic investigation traced every individual hallucination back to certain memories. Stimulated by recent impressions which suggested comparisons, the imagination kept on returning to certain affectively toned events of the past. The hallucinations which often occurred at such times presented persons or thoughts in a peculiarly compressed form, unintelligible to the normal mind. If the patient had at some time compared someone to an animal he now actually appeared as the animal. Another person, associated with the first through some real or imagined connection, was blended with the first in the hallucinated image, or was represented by a human head set upon an animal body, while a specific quality was symbolized by a physical attribute, etc. In every case it could be seen that the hidden meaning of the hallucination could be made intelligible only by the adoption of a historical perception, which went back from recent events to the events of early childhood. At the same time, as in solving a picture puzzle, one had to consider the components of the vision singly, and only to survey their combination when each isolated portion had been understood.

If now we return to our consideration of the Sphinx, profiting by the analytic experience of interpreting the mixed beings in dreams and the hallucination of the psychotic, we shall have to confess that every portion of the portrayals of the Sphinx, and every attribute of the Sphinx has been separately explained, and that an interpretation en bloc must necessarily miscarry. Further, the high degree of condensation of the image makes it necessary carefully to remove stratum after stratum; for the recollections of the individual, in superimposed layers, which are drawn upon in creating the dream, correspond with the sedimentary deposits of the experiences of successive generations in the formation of the mass psyche. Thus the historical or rather the genetic standpoint must supplement the psychological in a survey which proceeds from the consideration of the individual components of the figure of the Sphinx. As in the analysis of a dream, we shall for the time being disregard contradictions between the individual elements; in this case, as in that, we shall finally recognize, if our interpretation is correct, a latent connection, which will show even the apparently absurd to be necessary and significant.

5. The Sphinx as the Belated Representation of a Totemic Animal

The most conspicuous motive in the personification of the Sphinx is the blending of a human and an animal body. The individual analogy of this phenomenon in the dream and the hallucination tells us how we are to understand it; there a man was represented as an animal because the patient had likened him to an animal. The similarity or identity was expressed by replacing one object by the other, to which it had been compared. In this way the dream also represents similarity and correspondence. Here one may recall the grimacing animals of Rodin, and the works of Ibsen's sculptor Rubek, whose genesis he himself explains.

The ethnopsychological analogy leads us back to an age when man did not yet arrogantly point to the distance that divided him from the animals; indeed, he was peculiarly impressed by the animals, and felt the comparison with an animal to be not an insult, but an honor. Many evidences of prehistoric culture tell us that there was once a time when in primitive conceptions the bridge between animal and man was not so completely broken down as it is today. Even our children hurry swiftly across it, without any special effort; they find no difficulty in assuming that the person whom they know as an uncle is also a lion. Just recently I saw a little boy, who had been crawling on all fours and baying at his playfellows, run to his mother and inform her, with every indication of terror: "Max is a wolf and wants to eat me!" Protected by his mother, he shouted to his little playfellow, of whose identity he was absolutely positive: "Max, are you a boy again yet?"

The totemic system is based on such a primeval outlook. We have heard that in the opinion of many scholars the Sphinxes were originally personifications of the king, and later on were interpreted as symbols of divinity. We, however, shall be more inclined, proceeding from the animal body of the Sphinx, to assume a development in the reverse direction, which in broad outline we should describe as follows:

The first comprehensive religion of mankind, totemism, regarded the animal as divine. Many thousands of years later the totem god was transformed into an anthropomorphic god; or, remembering the original prototype of deity, the father of the primal horde, we might say that it was changed back into an anthropomorphic god. Nature, who does not take sudden leaps, makes no exception in respect of the evolutionary processes of human thought; the progress of culture is infinitely slow; for thousands of years the image of the animal god must have held its own beside that of the new god in human form, and when at last, after many vicissitudes, the anthropomorphic god advanced into the foreground, there remained, simultaneously with feelings of aversion, the memory, associated with powerful affects, of the important part which the animal had once played in religious worship. The figure of the Sphinx must be regarded as a *very late* reminiscence of the primary totemism, for the god of the dim primeval era reappears in the animal body, while the anthropomorphic deity of a later age is reflected in the Sphinx's countenance. We are therefore inclined to say that the archetype of the Sphinx is not the king, but a powerful animal, probably the lion, which had once been the god of human beings. Let us recollect the lion-headed gods of the Egyptians—Hathor, Neith, and Bast—apparent relics of totemism in Egypt, in which the lion figures as a totemic animal. In our opinion the images of animals—of lions, for example—which were cherished and regarded as sacred in the Egyptian city of Leantopolis, were the immediate prototypes of the Sphinx. There may well be a single long line of development from the crude animal drawings in the caves of the Aurignacian era to the Sphinx of Giza and her contemporaries. The human head which the Egyptian Sphinx so often displays would thus be of late appearance, determined by the anthropomorphization of the gods, and replacing an original animal head. The combination of man and animal is a token of identity; but it tells us that a historical process has preceded it, whose traces we see before us. The psychic process which led to this mode of representation is entirely analogous to the process of condensation in the dream; here too we see, combined in a single image, elements which are to be conceived as a unity, although to our consciousness they are separate; the idol of a primitive age which one knows is superseded, and that of the present day, which cannot deny its relationship to the former.

The difference between the psychic activities of the individual and the collectivity is clearly indicated by the fact that in the dream persons in actual existence are condensed and combined with persons taken from our childish memories, whereas prehistoric art combines in a single structure creatures from bygone stages of evolution with those which are now attracting its attention. The representation of the two historical aspects of the diety, the animal and the human, compressed into a single form,[7] seems absurd to us, and if we are to credit the psychology of dreams, we must assume that such representations conceal a trace of unconscious derision. But it would be quite erroneous to associate such a feeling with the conquest of "animal" sexuality—nothing could be more alien to ancient Egypt—or with any sort of contempt of the animal. The originally high estimation of the animal may, in the course of the gradual evolution of culture, under the influence of many motives, have been followed, at last, by a diminished estimation, which in historical times could lead to a symbolical representation in the manner of C. G. Jung. But as regards the early period which we are considering such an anagogic conception, which might be called the repetition of a fragment of evolution rather than its explanation, is quite out of the question.

From the manner in which the images of the Sphinx originated in totemism[8] one might regard the further development of the type as

[7]A few references supplementing the above definition may be welcome here. In some of the Sphinxes of the Twelfth Dynasty the face is still surrounded by a huge lion's mane. M. Hoernes (1915, p. 58) gives a similar explanation of the origin of hybrid forms: "Plastic art is a firm anchor of religious ideas. Absolute conceptions also are fixed by art, yet even though obsolete and belonging to the past they continue to be current. They enrich the present with the memory of the bygone, and still find a fitting place for the latter in the artistic expression of ideas. This explains the origin of the oldest hybrid figures, the oldest group formations." The interpretation of the Sphinx as a deity is entirely in harmony with the oldest traditions, which assert, with curious persistence, that the Sphinx of Giza represents the Sun-god; but they also insist on the analogy to the meaning of the Gryphon and the Criosphinx; for the Falcon is sacred to Horus as the Ram to Ammon. This explains, also, the many representations of the Sphinx with the statuette of a king between her paws; she is the king's guardian. When she appears before the temples as a guardian it must be remembered that in this late form she figures as a kind of degraded divinity, having become a servant of the godhead. Only in this sense is it understood that the god himself is guarding his temple. It is evident that the Sphinx, in her function as doorkeeper, is closely related to the hybrid creatures of the Assyrio-Babylonian culture, the lions in the palaces of Sargon, Sanheribs, etc. Such guardian lions and bulls are seen not only by the doors of ancient palaces; for the cathedrals of Ferrara and Spoleto, and the palaces and *piazze* of Venice and many other Italian cities show similar animals. Even the monsters that stretch their necks from the gables of our churches are reminiscent of these ancient and originally totemistic animals.

[8]The well-known American expert, Morris Jastrow, has expressed the opinion that "this same factor of resemblance between men and animals in conjunction with the ignorance as to the processes of nature led to the belief in all kinds of hybrid creatures, composed of human and animal organs" (1914, p. 79). He is inclined to

an ever more and more fantastic production of derivative forms. Factors of a different kind may have cooperated in the final product; among them tendencies making it unintelligible, and lastly the erroneous comprehension of obsolete configurations of the Sphinx by later generations. At the same time, a fragment of the political and national history of the Egyptian people may be reflected in the evolutionary history of the Sphinx. The Egyptians of the earliest period, according to the Egyptologists and other experts, were by no means a homogeneous unity, but a mixture of various peoples.[9] Further, we know how many heterogeneous elements were absorbed and assimilated by the primitive population of Egypt. The tribal organization and the local distribution had for the peoples of the ancient East, who were comparatively late in forming States,[10] a special significance in respect of religion. We see, for example, in the history of Babylon, that it repeatedly happened that with the prolongation of the political and cultural supremacy of a particular tribe all sorts of religious transformations occurred; one god would be assimilated by another, various features of the prevailing religion would be condensed, and a divine would attribute be replaced by quite a different attribute. Such hap-

derive from this belief, in connection with the Babylonian doctrine of birth-omens, the fabled creatures of the ancient religions of the Near East and also those of the Greek, Egyptian and Indian mythologies, insofar as they represent such hybrid creatures. Similar views are expounded by Professor Friedrich Schatz (1901) and Dr. Bab (1906 pp. 209–311). These theories alone do not provide an adequate explanation, although they elucidate many individual features.

[9]Cf. F. Hommel (1887), pp. 108–129; A. Wiedemann, (1906), p. 482. That the Egyptian people consists of an admixture of many different peoples and racial remnants is indicated not only by skeletal remains (Cf. Kollmann, 1902, pp. 119–126), and the illustrations of types from the earliest period (cf. J. de Morgan, 1896–1897), but also by the examination of the ancient Egyptian language. This proves to be a mixed language, comprising various African and Asiatic components. According to the researches of A. Erman (1900, pp. 317–353) and Graf Schack-Schackenburg (1902, pp. 209 ff.) and the anthropological discoveries of von Luschan, one may assume that the primitive population of Egypt consisted of African peoples which at a very early period were subjugated by Semitic Bedouins.

[10]The wars of the different city kings of Babylon were concluded in the third century B.C. by the formation of the kingdoms of Sumu and Akkad; not until the latter part of the predynastic period of Egyptian history were the northern and southern provinces of the country combined to form two larger kingdoms, although the provincial organization was not abandoned (about 3400).

penings, in the phase of totemism, led to mixed formations of different kinds; combinations of the totemic animal of one tribal group with that of another might have been formed as the result of the prolonged juxtaposition of several totems. As such evidences of conflict and compromise between old and new, between the conquered and the conqueror, between different tribes, we may note such creatures as the Criosphinx, the Gryphon, etc., which preceded the creation of the Sphinx with a human head. This form was the last of a long series, whose progress we cannot exactly follow.[11]

The historical mode of consideration, if we combine it with the psychoanalytic method, is to understand why in the image of the Sphinx one sees not only the god, but the king; for to the ancients the difference between god and ruler was conceived as vaguely as it is

[11]The above schematic and simplified account can give the reader no idea of the multifarious events which led to the developments that occurred within totemism, but can do no more than hint at a few possibilities out of many. However, it may be noted that many obscure passages of the Bible can be explained by the connection of the tribes with their totems inside the larger political union. A grasp of the subject is even more important in respect of the much-debated question, whether monotheism or polytheism lies at the origin of religious evolution. Andrew Lang (1887, 1901, 1909) and the Viennese priest, Wilhelm Schmidt (1912) are of the opinion that a monotheistic form of belief preceded all other and cruder forms of religion; they are definitely opposed to the majority of investigators in this field, who regard polytheism as the more primitive form. If with Freud we regard totemism as the first comprehensive religion, we come to the conclusion, after a conscientious survey of the ethnological and historical material, that there is a great deal of truth in the opinions of both of the above investigators. It is not correct insofar as it holds that monotheism (the exclusive belief in *one* god) is the primary religion, but henotheism may claim such precedence over other forms of religion. The tribe which traces its descent from a totemic animal, which it worships, is first and foremost an exclusive whole. Its connection with other tribes, which takes the form of a peaceful union, or the subjugation of one or several tribes by an alien tribe, first introduces the possibility of a change of totem, and the more important possibility that new totems shall be valued and worshiped together with the old. In conjunction with other motives, this may be regarded as decisive for the development of polytheism from a primitive henotheism, but for the later development of a primitive monotheism, which has to contend with the older multiplicity of gods, the factor of the racial or tribal organization must be regarded as especially effective and explanatory. Thus, the suppression of the Elohim by Jahveh on Sinai seems to be codetermined by the prolongation of the hegemony of the tribe to which Moses belonged. An exhaustive treatment of the relevant problems will have to be reserved for a separate volume.

among the modern primitives.[12] The kings of antiquity were accustomed to being honored as gods, and their statues were accorded divine honors. Thus, the Babylonian sovereigns, from Sargon I to the Fourth Dynasty of Ur, laid claim to the statue of gods: Indeed, the monarchs of this dynasty had temples built in their honor, and commanded the people to bring offerings to their images. The Egyptian kings were deified during their lifetime and were reverenced as gods in special temples, by a special priesthood. By the people the king was regarded as "the great god," "the golden Horus," and especially as "the Son of the Sun-god Ra." He was addressed as "the Sun, Lord of Heaven and Earth," as "Creator and Shaper of mankind, Life of the great world," etc. The history of Egyptian culture explains how the Sphinx came to signify not only the god but also his human incarnation. As tokens of their divine nature the prehistoric kings wrapped themselves, just as the chieftains of savage peoples do today, in the pelt of the totemic animal. The rulers of prehistoric Egypt wore the skin of the lion long after the totemistic religion had been replaced by a religion of a higher order.

6. The Sphinx as Sun-god

The interpretation of the Sphinx as the Sun-god takes its appropriate place in the development we have sketched; she has indeed some claim to be regarded as a secondary divinity.

We cannot here discuss the psychic hypotheses on which the astral conception of the gods was based, or how this conception came to be entertained, or to what actual and psychic necessities it owed its continued significance. The researches of Otto Rank have corrected and modified the theories of the astral mythologists in essential details, and have demonstrated their value within certain limits; but in these pages—at the risk of exceeding the limits of our subject—we shall do no more than briefly indicate the evolution of the astral mythology. I think we may be certain that the astral religion evolved

[12] J. S. Frazer, (1911) gives numerous examples of such "incarnate human gods" from all parts of the world; and also of the divine states of the ruler in ancient Babylon, Egypt, Peru, Mexico, and China, and he explains this by the evolution of kingship.

from the totemistic philosophy, and that the gods were relegated to the heavens under the combined impression of natural events, psychic revolutions, and changes in the conditions of human life. It may be assumed that the Zodiac, in its very composition, bears witness to the totemistic origin of astral mythology and astral religion. The promotion of the gods to the heavens reveals itself by many indications as a more highly developed and loftier phase of religious evolution. It exiles the gods from their home, the earth, where they originated, and where in the beginning they peopled forest and brake. Primeval humanity, like the child in its first years, took no interest in the heavens and the heavenly bodies; the appointment of the upper regions as the dwelling place of the gods is a sign of the advanced spiritualization of religion.[13] This becomes possible only where man has lifted his gaze from the earth to the heavens.

The projection of the totem upon the heavens was the typical method of disposing of them; it happened at a time when the evolution of religion had already advanced beyond the totemistic idea of the god to higher conceptions; so that now the totem, being of no further service, could be relegated to the celestial lumber room. In this connection it should perhaps be noted that this kind of disposal finally became a euphemistic representation of death, and that it recurs in dreams, in poetry, in folklore, and in the formation of myths. One is reminded of a dream cited by Freud (1900), in which a child of four saw her playmates put on wings and fly away.

This ascension of the god signifies, in this sense, not only a promotion, but also, unconsciously, a banishment, a sort of latent dispossession. In this new religious conception the old psychic mechanisms which were at work in the formation of religion are still conspicuous; respect and esteem for the god have increased to the maximum, but in the same degree the unconscious revolutionary wishes that aspire to his removal to a distance assert themselves. This expression of an intensified ambivalence—for as such we must regard the relegation of the gods to the heavens—was repeated when the status of the anthropomorphized deities was imperiled. The ancients

[13]There are still skeptics who profess their lack of interest in the heavens and their divine inhabitants: "The heavens we resign/To angels and the sparrows" (Heine).

could still allow the gods to wander about the world and die a physical death; but later on they were made immortal and had to dwell in heaven. The effects of unconscious hostile tendencies and reactively reinforced love and reverence are clearly perceptible in this religious conception.[14]

[14]The reference in the text of the astral cult to the projection of gods, first animal and then human in shape, upon the heavens, calls for a more exhaustive consideration. Insofar as this projection was part of a more comprehensive and primitive process, that made use of psychic paths which were already conditioned, it is a subject of extraordinary interest, which should be examined from other aspects. In this connection I will add only a few supplementary remarks, whose fragmentary character is obvious. In connection with the above exposition they may perhaps help to exhibit the astral mythology and religion of the Near East as of secondary importance. The Babylonian cult of the seven planetary gods, Sin (Moon), Sumas (Sun), Nabû (Mercury), Ishtar (Venus), Nergal (Mars, or Saturn), Marduk (Jupiter), Kaimanû (Saturn, or Mars), shows, by the very names of the planets, that these were identified with the gods. We know that the names given to the stars and planets by the Babylonians were retained by the Greek astronomers. As to how the gods became stars, we can only make assumptions on the basis of certain indications in the religions of antiquity and in those of modern savages. The Egyptian deities were mortal, but when their bodies lay swathed and bandaged in their earthly tomb, their souls shone as brilliant stars in the firmament. The soul of Isis shone in Sirius, that of Horus in Orion, that of Typhon in the Great Bear (Frazer, 1912, p. 5). The primitive peoples of today see in the stars either demons or the souls of the departed. It seems to me that this is an advanced phase, in which the gods of old appear as demons. (Example in Frazer, 1912 pp. 61 ff.) A star makes its original appearance when a great man dies; the heroes of Greece and Rome were set in the skies as stars by the gods, in reward for their achievements. Compare the words of Caesar's wife in Shakespeare: "When beggars die there are not comets seen,/The heavens themselves blaze forth the death of princes."

The same motive appears otherwise expressed, in the numerous sagas of primitive peoples in which God, discontented with conditions on earth, takes refuge in the heavens. The existence of the twelve signs of the Zodiac can be traced to the middle of the second millennium B.C. in Babylon (Schrader-Winckler-Zimmern, 1903, p. 627). It has been noted that the boundary stones or "landmarks" mentioned in the text, which display emblems of the Zodiac, the better-known Babylonian-Assyrian deities are indicated; "in the planets of the Zodiac they have, so to speak, their abiding manifestations." The nature of this relation remains obscure; it becomes clearer if we recollect that even the planetary gods were originally totems. This conception of the Zodiacal circle as a gradually emerging pantheon of the totems of different tribes, which finally assumed a permanent form, would be consistent with Peiser's bold interpretation of a passage in Psalm XII (Peiser, 1910, #5). According to Peiser, Psalm XVI, 4, should read: "Other Baals are many/wandering on the wall of the Zodiac;/ Their blood-offerings I will not bring to them/nor take their names upon my lips."

The significance of this interpretation becomes apparent if we compare it with estimation of totemism by the astral-mythological school may be judged from a

The Sphinx must have participated in the long evolution of the deity from the animal on earth to the animal in the heavens, to which in the last resort we owe the nomenclature of the Zodiac, in a definite form. As Horus, from being a totemistic deity, became a solar god, so his plastic representation, the Sphinx, may have become a solar symbol. Other attributes of the solar deity were allotted to her in a secondary degree, and subsequently many functions were ascribed to her which were not consistent with her original character as the image of a totem.

But we are constantly astonished by the fact that what we perceive as the consecutiveness of a very long and gradual evolution of culture appears to be a simultaneousness in the figure of the Sphinx; the past does not wholly disappear, although new and important conceptions assert themselves. It is as though the unconscious mind of the peoples was incapable of completely discarding its outworn and obsolete ideas and feelings. The unconscious mind of the mass is equally indestructible and immortal, and withdrawn from the influences of victorious innovations.

---

passage by Prof. F. Boll (1919): "The discoveries of the last few years have shown that zodiacal research is dealing with one of the most important fossil indications of the ancient cultural stream which is proceeded from the great central point of the spiritual life of the ancient world. In correspondence with the notion that the earth and earthly life are a copy of the greater life of the heavens the human world has been divided from the astral standpoint. Thus, the Peruvian capital of Cuzco was build as a zodiacal monument. Further, the tribe was everywhere divided into groups which were subordinated to the animals of the Zodiac. It was thus that totemism arose, which from this time onward was no longer regarded as a universal and independent phase of human evolution, but as a derivation from the cultural circle which derived from the Zodiacal circle." In opposition to this view, we believe that the form thus described represents an end product which the history of totemism explains; it corresponds to a retroactive projection of the zodiacal emblems upon the earth. We cannot here explain what consequences for the development of astrology and astronomy have resulted from this derivation; but it should be emphasized that in antiquity, and throughout a great part of the Middle Ages, the dominating position of astrology, and the kind of relation which it establishes between the constellations and human destiny, is explained by the religious significance which was originally attributed to the stars.

7. The Wings of the Sphinx

The evolutionary history of the celestial deity may have covered a thousand years, and it may have been extremely complicated; but all the indications seem to show that the removal of the god to the heavens was gradual, and that it took place, according to the views of the prehistoric East, as in those of the primitive peoples of today, in a perfectly natural and obvious manner. Tree totemism and the cult of mountain peaks represented definite evolutionary stages in this important cultural, historical, and religious process, in which the bird plays a part of special significance.

Here we come to a conspicuous attribute of the Sphinx—its possession of wings—which seems inconsistent with its lion's body. The interpretation of this quality as a sign of speed is, of course, reasonable enough, but it needs supplementing in many important respects. It is evident that the wings, with which the religion and mythology of antiquity endowed not only the mixed animal deities, but also such deities as were human in form, as Mercury, and such messengers of God as cherubim, seraphim, and angels, were taken from man's natural environment.

The task we have set ourselves in these pages allows us only to touch upon the significance of the bird in respect of religious conceptions; but we may be sure that a more special treatment of the problem would lead to interesting and valuable conclusions. Here we can do no more than give a few indications. In the final development of the totemistic system the vulture, eagle, or other such bird must have been adopted as a totem at certain definite points, which would be different in the case of the individual peoples. The swiftness of the bird may have impressed the primitive mind, just as the overcoming of gravity, and the ability to disappear and reappear in the ether, might perhaps at a later period serve as the criteria of the omnipresence and omniscience of the gods. There is no possible doubt that at one time the bird was regarded by men as a god; the later conception of the bird-soul must, I think, have developed from the fact that birds alighted upon the corpses of the beloved dead, ate of them, and flew away again. It is probable that the totemistic significance of the bird appertains to a later religious development; the bird then becomes the being that flies to the astral deity, the Father-Sun, representing the soul, and its flight becomes the symbol of the translation and resurrection of numerous heroes, from Moses and Elijah to Jesus.

For the time being we cannot precisely determine the point when the bird was introduced into the totemistic form of religion, but it seems as though it had been totemistically adapted at a time when totemism was already disappearing—that is, that its function and its task were described in totemistic language. It may be for this reason that it afterward became one of the totemistic incarnations of the Savior, and an emblem of the hero. The sparrow-headed and vulture-headed gods of the Egyptians, the doves of Aphrodite, the raven of Wotan, the vulture that devoured Prometheus' liver, the cranes of the Ibykus, the birds whose flight all the peoples of antiquity regarded as an oracle, the vulture which appeared when Abraham offered up a sacrifice, the doves sent forth by Noah, and the dove which plays its part in the Annunciation to Mary—all these birds were originally gods, who subsequently became the auxiliaries and the messengers of anthropomorphic deities. Thus the Sphinx also, from being a deity, became a winged guardian in the service of God, like other familiar figures. She too had at first a place in the pantheon, before she became a mediator between Jahveh and mankind; I mean the angels who bore wings, and whose originally totemistic character we still perceive in the Old Testament descriptions of their predecessors, the cherubim.[15]

Here again it should be noted that the oldest Sphinxes known to us have no wings, and that the Sphinx was first generally represented as winged by the Greeks.

8. Male and Female Sphinxes

We had perforce to trace the far-flung and hardly recognizable paths which were followed by the primitive society before it reached the religious stage at which we find it in early antiquity. We were able to detect traces of this evolutionary progress in the form of the Sphinx;

[15]Among such forms we include the colossal winged and human-headed bulls of the late Assyrio-Babylonian period.

for like the annual rings of a tree, the bygone phases of her development have impressed themselves upon her shape. Owing to the remarkable conservatism of primitive cultures, the ancient characteristics did not disappear when the new arrived, but, mingled with the new, they survived to serve modified purposes, long divorced from their original significance. All progress, in the religion of antiquity—and not only there—occurs, in a similar fashion, through the transformation and the reinterpretation and assimilation of inherited forms. This fact may throw some light on that peculiar form of the Sphinx which we can only describe as hermaphrodite. We know that in Egypt, in very ancient times, the male Sphinxes were in the great majority; later on female Sphinxes appeared with increasing frequency beside the male Sphinxes, until in Greece they completely superseded the male forms. How far is the female form consistent with our explanation of the totemistic derivation of the Sphinx? If we remember that in the early period the female Sphinx was rare, and that later on both male and female forms appeared, it seems obvious that we may accept a historical development which replaced the original male by a female form. The penis which the female Sphinx bears would thus be a relic of her original masculine form. It seems that we have now to enhance the probability of this hypothetically accepted development by facts relating to the prehistory of humanity. We know that the present form of the family was preceded by the matriarchate, in which the members of the horde were grouped about their natural center, the mother. The relics of the matriarchal organization, as we find them in certain very primitive tribes, as well as traces in the organization of the ancient peoples of the East,[16] give us, even when we consider the numerous alterations which have occurred in thousands of years, an approximate picture of that first, primitive group organization. It is difficult to establish the influence of the matriarchal system on religion, if only because we have no direct access to the prehistoric stage of human development. Freud assumed that the great mother divinities may in general have preceded the father-god in the course of evolution. There are two facts in particular which support

[16]Cf. especially Frazer (1907, pp. 382 ff.) and also the older works of Bachofen (1861), Dargun (1892), etc.

this opinion: the relatively late character of totemism, which, by reason of its source, presupposes that a more complicated form of family preceded the fraternal class, and the improbability that the libido-cathected figure of the Mother, which was for so long the center and head of the family, had not been previously raised to the divine status in the primitive philosophy. Nevertheless, one must observe a certain caution in assuming the existence of an original mother religion; we know that the cults dedicated to the mother deities of the Orient—Isis, Ishtar, Cybele, and other embodiments of the Mater Magna—were originally of a very different character from the father religion; they were characterized especially by their emphasis on the sexual factors, their celebration of fertility in man and in Nature, in contrast to the father religion, which kept the social motives in the foreground and created a sort of social anxiety in the consciousness of guilt. Even if we regard these ancient cults as late developments we must nevertheless agree that their characteristic features were already contained in their prehistoric and preliminary stages; indeed, we shall rather be inclined to assume that they appeared there in cruder and less inhibited forms, unaffected by external cultural progress.[17]

It is, of course, only a question of nomenclature if we regard religion as existing in this or that stage of human evolution, or if we date it from another stage, but it seems to me that two of the essential and indispensable motives of the formation of a religion are precisely the social nexus, and with it the powerful agency of the consciousness of guilt. Consequently, though the veneration of the mother in the age of the primitive matriarchate may seem religious in its sincerity, we cannot really speak of religion in this case, since the essential characteristics are lacking.[18] The Mother of the matriarchal era was worshiped with all the signs of the overestimation of sex, as she brought to

[17]One cannot agree with the theory that the difference of the cults of male and female deities rests on externalities, that are the indelible and indestructible signs of a profound difference rooted in the instinctual life.

[18]In order to avoid misunderstanding it should be expressly stated that the above roughly indicated scheme refers to a period prior to any historical experience; the mother cults of the early East, compared with this, belong to one of these phases, divided by thousands of years. In them a genuine mother religion, capable of development, already makes its appearance. It is naturally impossible to say anything definite regarding their development.

a head the object choice of the anaclitic type; for a long while she was undoubtedly the object to which the libido of primitive man was chiefly dedicated; she became his idol, mainly in consequence of the urgent power of the heterosexual instinctual components. Here, through the factor of the first, elementary erotic choice and the overestimation of sex, the difference between the original veneration of the mother and the primitive father religion is clearly demonstrated. If the mother of the first organization of the matriarchal epoch became an idol, as many discoveries relating to the late quarternary seem to indicate was the case in an earlier phase, so the father of the primitive horde subsequently became the father ideal of the members of the fraternal clan. But in the contrast between the *mother idol* and the *father ideal* we find, in addition to an essential trait of the attitude of primitive man to the archetypes of his religion, an indication of the kind of object choice which provides the basis for later and highly significant developments. It has already been noted that the object choice of the primeval era, of which we find indications in the matriarchal period, is mainly of the anaclitic type, whereas later on the object choice of the narcissistic type moves into the foreground. The libidinous veneration of the mother, which was connected with the glorification of the crudely sexual, could of course become subsequently, in a more or less sublimated form, a religious cult, but first of all the god must exist as such, and the father religion, in the form of totemism, must make its entry into human history.

In accordance with the pattern of the father religion the Mother was subsequently deified. She now appeared as a rival beside the father-god, but the right to function as a religious creator was reserved to the father as the prototype of every god, and was bound up, not with the elementary and unbroken power of the first libidinal cathexis, but with the reactively enhanced and perpetuated power of paternal yearning.[19]

[19]The features of the mother and the beloved, united in the first libido object, are still united in the form of the original female deity. Later on the maternal character is more and more strongly emphasized, while the sexual motive recedes into the background or appears only in the more spiritual form of mercifulness and love of humanity or womanly kindness. But even the most advanced development cannot quite exclude it; the female divinities are always the guardians of love and wedlock. The Gretchen of the Faust tragedy who turns to Mary in her sorrow is only a modern

The matriarchate undoubtedly gave an impetus to many significant developments in human society, but it did not give birth to religion as such. In the contrast between the mother idol and the father ideal, which we construed as the preliminary to the divorce between mother divinity and father-god, those motives are already latent which were afterward, with their progressive intensification, to become so important. The cult of the mother divinity led to the excessive glorification of sexuality, and only very much later did it achieve a partial sublimation, such as we perceive in the cult of the Madonna; but it was always responsible for encroachment upon the prescribed though unwritten laws of the father religion, because it was constantly receiving reinforcements from the depths of the eternal powers of the instincts. The strength of Antaeus was renewed when he touched the Mother.

But the father ideal, which had become a god, now became the secret lawgiver of mankind, its personified conscience and its protector against the instinctual assaults that threatened to disintegrate the social order. Within the compass of this work, which has other aims in view, we cannot attempt to gauge the importance of these mutually conflicting principles, which continue to play a significant part in the evolution of religion. We can do no more than observe that one of the most important points of the irruption of sexuality into the social institution of religion may be found here, and that the conflict between mother religion and father religion corresponds with the lifelong hesitation between masculine and feminine object choice in the individual. Further, it must be emphasized that the exhaustive psychoanalytic, religious and historical evaluation of this important

---

embodiment of innumberable sisters in the ancient world who in similar situations sought the help of the local goddesses. The witty Anatole France tells in *La pierre blanche* of a lovely maiden who addresses the Mother of God in the following delightful prayer: "Holy Mother of God, you who conceived without sin, grant me this favor that I may sin without conceiving!" This contrast reminds us of the time when even the mothers of gods conceived in the earthly fashion—for as yet it was not sinful to do so. Another anecdote of the French skeptic's recalls the same epoch of mundane divinities: An Italian, whose wish Jesus had not granted, despite his fervent prayers, returned to the chapel where the image of the Madonna and her child was displayed, and cried: "I am not speaking to you, son of a harlot, but to your sainted mother!"

theme is still in arrears. It would constitute one of the most important and informative additions to and continuations of Freud's introduction to the birth of religion.

The excursion, which, by the hypothesis of the subsequent deification of the Mother, maintained that the totemistic father religion was the first and most primitive religious creation, was only apparently superfluous, for without considering the course of evolution, as we have sketched it in broad outline, it is impossible to understand how the Sphinx should be represented as female as well as male. As we have said, the mother divinities were created after the pattern of the father: and only so can we understand how the god—for the Sphinx was originally a god—should now appear as a woman. The attempt has been made to associate the female form with the victory of the anthropomorphic embodiment of divinity, on the assumption that it was the female form which first and most powerfully impressed the primitive believer when the totemic god came to be replaced by a human god. The process by which god became man, one of the most tremendous events in world history, is still unknown to us as regards its most important psychic conditions; and it is not impossible that it was precisely here that the image of the mother goddess first made its appearance. However, the female form of the Sphinx is secondary, for totemism—and it is to a very late recollection of totemism that we owe the figure of the Sphinx—was purely a father religion and a creation of societies of men. The first prototype of God, the father of the primitive horde, was a strict, powerful, terrifying chieftain; the totemic animal which the primitive regarded as a god must have had a similar character. To no being of milder nature would the primitive savage have bowed; and even the Jahveh of the Bible is a terrible and vengeful god. The transference of such traits to a mother divinity was possible only when profound changes in the relation of prehistoric man to woman, and in the mutual relations of the sexes, had made themselves felt. The image of the "terrible Mother" constructed by C. G. Jung—even if we ignore his anagogic interpretation—is by no means primary, and it presupposes definite changes in the psychic relation to the mother. Tremendous revolutions must have occurred, attributable perhaps to a decisive modification of living conditions and their repercussions on the primitive human family, resulting in a radical transformation of domestic emotions, before the image of the loved and cherished mother could change into the terrifying figure evoked by Jung. In the psychical productions of neurotics we have valuable indications as to the processes which led to this result: I mean those unconscious processes which led to the transformation of the positive into the antithetical Oedipus complex. To those whose attitude toward the mother may be so characterized she appears as a terrible and hateful female; often indeed as a persecutrix and a tyrant. It can be demonstrated by analysis that this particular psychic attitude is a late transformation of the original positive relation, which occurred under the compulsion of certain psychic necessities. But among the motives which condition a disturbance of the original relation to the mother we must include the paternal policy of sexual intimidation and the fear of castration as especially effective. Sexual intercourse with the mother, so ardently though unconsciously desired, resulted for the child in the loss of the cherished member, so that the beloved mother became the dreadful mother, an object of terror.[20]

If we now turn back to the products of the mass psyche we shall surmise that the stern prohibitions of the father generation, in respect of incest, representing or taking the place of actual castration, which were first impressed upon the young generation from the outside, and later on became part of their psychic property, afford a good analogy to every individual evolution. The creation of the mother divinities was in itself an attempted irruption on the part of those impulses which were urgent toward the practice of incest. It was only partially successful, for simultaneously with the deification of the first libido object that seemed to encourage the actual realization of those infantile wishes there emerged unconsciously the prohibition of incest received by many generations, which changed the beloved object into an object of anxiety, all contact with which threatened disaster. To the primitive mind, the result of this complicated process of transformation could be imagined only by giving the mother image the features

[20]It goes without saying that the events which had the effect of altering the conditions of life would also have changed the relation of the mother to her sons, and must have led to the development of the feminine character in a definite direction.

of the father; the prohibition came from the father, and its effectiveness depended mainly upon the unconscious homosexual tendency toward the fathers. But when the father god in animal form was blended with the image of the mother goddess, this was likewise a sign that the homosexual tendencies which played so decisive a part in the evolution of religion had frustrated the irruption of the incestuous impulses; that the attempt to replace the terrible image of the totemic god by the more kindly image of the mother and wife had failed, for the taboo of the incestuous object was inextricably bound up with the mother imago, even though this became a goddess. The victory of the homosexual impulses, which was so plastically manifested in the animal hinder parts of the Sphinx and so disturbingly in the addition of the penis, could not, of course, be enduring; from the very first it was not undisputed, and later on the penis often disappeared from the representations of the Sphinx, whose femininity became ever more pronounced; so that the Greek Sphinxes have gracious and comely faces, far removed from the gloom and the grave virility of the Egyptian Sphinxes.[21] Nevertheless, they retained the animal body as the permanent sign of their descent and a warning of their perilous nature.

What have we gained from this genetic survey? I think we have obtained several interesting results. It has explained the contradiction between the female sex of the upper portion and the male sex of the lower portion of the Sphinx's body. At the same time it must be emphasized that the formation of the lower portion of the body, like that of the most attractive portion of the mother image, has masculine characteristics, so that here also the process of repression of the heterosexual object by an object of the same sex in a later stage of development is most vividly manifested. We have come to understand why the representations of the Sphinx should be now male and now female, and we know that this fact is related to the religious development. In this connection, I believe, we have reason to correct the opinions hitherto held concerning the Sphinx, and not only those which are beyond the scope of psychoanalysis. In the ingenious interpretation of

[21]Siegfried Bernfeld (1928), in discussing this lecture, pointed to the fact that the emphatically feminine form of the Greek type of Sphinx corresponded with the temperament of the Greek people.

the Oedipus legend given by Rank in his work on the incest complex he refers to the infantile sexual theory mentioned by Freud, according to which women as well as men possess a penis. Rank explains the theory by the homosexual anxiety dream. Without prejudice to the correctness of this explanation, our historical interpretation of it may claim to have contributed to the understanding of the psychic processes in the formation of the figure of the Sphinx.

Our interpretation, however, requires a more radical modification of Jung's conception of the Sphinx. A critical examination of Jung's arguments will reveal the inadequacy of the superficially symbolical interpretation of the Swiss author; as in the analysis of individuals, so in the theological field, Jung makes no attempt to go back to the earliest developmental stages of psychic formations. It is highly probable that at some time the Sphinx, in a very late and culturally advanced period, became a theriomorphic representation of libido, and that she must be regarded as the half-animal representation of that mother imago which was described as the terrible mother. But we do not see that this symbolical representation explains anything. It does not enable us to understand how such a figure as the Sphinx was ever conceived; and the interpretation of the Sphinx as an incestuous libidinal charge derived from the relation to the mother will satisfy neither the psychoanalyst nor the inquirer into the evolution of religion and culture. While this kind of interpretation—in the sense of our modern sublimated symbolism—contributes nothing to the explanation of the figure of the Sphinx as represented in early antiquity, it rightly and instinctively refrains from entering into the many mutually contradictory motives of such representations or considering them in detail.

We will conclude by a summary of all the various features of the Sphinx of the Near East, features which are often so mutually contradictory: the ancient conception of the Sphinx as god, as king, as guardian of the sanctuary;[22] her half-animal, half-human form, now male, now female.

[22]The Sphinx's function as guardian signifies that the god guards his own sanctuary. As a matter of fact the situation is even more complicated; for if we consider that the temple of a god is originally part of the god himself, an enlargement of the divine personality, then the Sphinx is really guarding herself. This peculiar situation is intelligible only if we associate the twofold presence of the god—as in the analysis of the ritual of sacrifice—with the course of religious evolution.

9. The Sphinx of Oedipus

Unless we are greatly mistaken, we should now, in the light of our recent discoveries, be justified in returning to the consideration of the legend of Oedipus and the Sphinx, and in anticipating, from their application to the ancient myth, fresh explanations as to the still hidden meaning of this episode. In our opinion the unity of the Sphinx may be accepted, and we do not think that even the legendary monster which oppressed Thebes can have been so remote from its original stock that the results obtained there can be without bearing upon the interpretation of the mysterious part which it played in the destiny of Oedipus.

But before we attempt to wrest from the Sphinx of Oedipus the secret of its nature, we must first of all clearly understand which features of our legend are accepted by the mythologists and philologists as primordial, and which they have regarded as subsequent expansions, embellishments, variants, or what not. No complete reconstruction of the original version is practicable; but the scholars tell us that the legend must once have existed in a much cruder form, and that originally the slaying of the father must have been followed immediately by the violation of the mother, who was present at his murder. The notion of a marriage, which continued for several years, was first introduced by the tragic poets. According to Gruppe, the episode of the Sphinx was first included in the myth where a fresh justification for the marriage was adduced: "Inasmuch as the old romantic motive was exploited, according to which the hand of a king's daughter was won by the conquest of a monster, this terrible creature, which the legend has localized in Boeotia, presented herself as a matter of course." Further, according to Bethe the original form of the Sphinx legend is that in which the Sphinx was put to death by Oedipus without any previous solving of a riddle. Hesiod knew nothing of any riddle.[23] A red-figured Attic lecythos in the Boston Museum (Robert 1915, p. 49) shows the Sphinx (without wings) with forepaws uplifted, like a cat preparing to strike, on the point of attacking Oedipus, who is named in an inscription. The hero's right

[23]H. von Hofmannsthal (1906) omits the riddle in his tragedy.

hand holds the club with which he is about to strike a deadly blow. Robert has justly observed that there can have been no question here of solving a riddle either before or after the encounter, but rather of a fight like that of Hercules with the Nemean lion. Robert also argues, with much ingenuity, that the Sphinx began to ask riddles only in her later history, and that the intellectual contest cannot have been the original form of the monster's encounter with the hero. One should have realized that a creature represented as having a lion's body and a lion's talons must originally have been conquered, not by the ingenuity of a solver of riddles, but by the physical strength of a hero (p. 49). "It seems to me that the notion of turning a man-killing monster into an ingenious riddler of riddles, who could be overcome only if confronted by her intellectual equal, can hardly be of earlier date than the period when the poetical enigma was the fashion in Greece" (p. 57). A gem illustrated in Furtwängler's (1900, Plate XXIV, 21, 22) monograph on gems shows, like one of the Boston vases, that the version in which the Sphinx, when her riddle is solved, flings herself from her rock, can have nothing to do with the original content of the legend: Oedipus, standing behind the Sphinx, plunges the sword into her breast. Perhaps the story of the Sphinx's suicide originated in a late assimilation of the fate of the Sphinx with that of the traditional Lucasta. Many pictures show the hero killing his adversary with his sword. It is our belief that the version of the legend in which nothing is said of any riddle, but in which a terrible monster, which is laying the country waste, is killed by the hero Oedipus, must be regarded as the oldest accessible form of the Oedipus legend. But now the question arises as to the relation of this part of the legend to the myth as a whole. Is it really an episode, a late addition, without any close relation to the essential content, as it may seem at the first glance, and as the majority of the philologists believe? Robert gives an excellent summary of the difficulties of incorporating the episode of the Sphinx in the legend of Oedipus. He suggests that the Sphinx is not unconnected with the fate of Laius—and the legend itself seems to hint at some such relation, but its exact nature is very obscure (p. 63). "If one sought to introduce her as avenging the murder of Laius, as his Erinys, in a manner of speaking, it would be absurd that his murderer should also kill the avenger of the murder, without suffering any harm himself. If one imagines her as a punishment for a crime committed by Laius himself, it would be absurd that she should not appear until after his death, so that Laius himself did not suffer at her hands, but only his innocent subjects. Thus, nothing remains but to conceive her as an instrument of the decree of Fate, and to ascribe her dispatch to the god who emitted this decree, or else to seek a motive for her appearance unconnected with the Oedipus myth." Robert, things being as they were, thinks it unnecessary to look for a motive; the monster was there, and to ascribe her appearance to human guilt was a later and secondary notion.

We think, however, that the author has resigned himself too soon. The ancient legend speaks of a mysterious relation between Laius and the Sphinx, and psychoanalysis tells us that such relations have a psychic—that is, a real—motivation. If we do not perceive its nature we must wait patiently until we find it; at all events we must not simply deny its existence. Even the parallelism between the slaying of Laius and the slaying of the Sphinx seems to indicate that the two figures are somehow related.

Perhaps we shall find an explanation of the relationship if we consider the result of one analysis of the Sphinx. The Sphinx, a late development of the divine totemic animal, confronts the young Oedipus. He fights and kills her, and the city is his reward. If we accept the results obtained by the analysis of the origin of totemism we must assume that in the last resort the Sphinx is equivalent to Laius, the father of the young hero, so that her slaying repeats the murder of the king. But through the symbolism of dreams and myths and poetry and wit we have learned that the significance of the city, and of the country, is, in the unconscious, woman. Moreover, we recognize in this disguise a repetition of the great event which constitutes the kernel of the human, all-too-human story of Oedipus: the slaying of the father and the seizure of the mother.

If we accept this interpretation we are again confronted by difficult questions which have to be answered. Which form of the legend is the original one, and why is its content repeated in a different form? How did it come about that the earlier, male figure of the Sphinx was translated into a female figure? What psychic motives determined the change, and through what psychic mechanism was the transformation effected?

The Oedipus myth hands down to us in its antique forthrightness and simplicity a theme whose emotional content is so universally human that as psychoanalysts we are accustomed to cite it as typical of the strongest unconscious wishes of childhood. But the very naiveté of the Greek tradition, which develops this theme in historical time, in all its crudity, before the eyes and ears of the auditor, should give us cause for reflection. One should always be distrustful when a myth openly relates crudely sexual themes; almost invariably the myth conceals other significant motives, and the emphasis laid on the one sexual subject often serves to conceal other fragments of sexual or innocuous themes.[24]

If we omit the oracle, the episode of the Sphinx, and other specific mythological features of the Oedipus myth, what is left? The life and the actions of a criminal, a patricide and an incestuous son, for whom we cannot even feel compassion, a man whose destiny strikes no profounder note of tragedy. We should not understand why this particular criminal was chosen by so many of the Greeks to be immortalized as a tragic hero, and why for him especially the tribunal should become the stage.

Reflection, as well as the particularly crude form of the tradition, the obscure connection between the role of the Sphinx and the fate of Laius, and its mythological significance—all these motives justify our assumption that the Sphinx legend is not a later interpolation, as the majority of mythologists believe, but is one of the most essential components of the original myth. But if this be so, the question of the relation of one part of the legend to another, which repeats the same story on another plane, now becomes urgent. We will answer it briefly thus: The Sphinx plays much the same part in the life of Oedipus as the Ghost in the tragedy of Hamlet.[25] The episode of the Sphinx is older than what we may call the human legend of Oedipus in its present form. There, in the description of the death of the Sphinx, the typical event of the Oedipus legend occurs in its first, elementary, terrible force; in later versions the superhuman crime has become a

[24]This may best be illustrated by the analysis of the biblical legend of the Fall.

[25]This comparison is not merely superficial. The following inquiry will show us what close relations exist between the theme of Oedipus and that of Hamlet—themes whose unconscious significance Freud justly compares.

deed that rids the country of a monster. But the motive—the fact that the action was that of a young hero, and the victim a late representative of the ancient totemic animal, of the inviolable god—reveals it in all its tragic momentousness, and its true significance, which far exceeds the fate of the individual. Here, in the murder of Laius, all happens, so to speak, within the setting of private life and the ambit of a legal code; but as regards the slaying of the Sphinx, from which the action subsequently received the strongest subterranean repercussion, it is obvious that the exploit of the young savior Oedipus was a crime against deity, since the god was its victim. The human actions and mundane events of the legend now appear in the light of higher powers. The tragic note is greatly enhanced by the fact that Oedipus has not only offended against the transitory morals and questionable customs of mankind, but that he has violated the sacred and eternal laws decreed by the gods. Oedipus has not only slain his father, but in his father he has struck at the supreme authority, the God himself.[26]

[26]In this connection it should be noted that Robert (1915), holds that the oldest form of the legend is that in which the hero goes from Eteonos to the Phix mountain, where he slew a monster which had its lair there, and was devastating the countryside; thus becoming the savior of the country (p. 58). Proceeding from other points of view, the writer comes to the conclusion already reached by E. Meyer (1884–1902, pp. 2, 101, 103, 167), that the Oedipus myth had originally a religious significance. Meyer rightly sees in Oedipus a figure like that of Heracles: one of the great gods in whose life the cycle of Nature finds expression. Oedipus, who weds his mother, the earth, but is then blinded and dies, may have derogated to the rank of hero, of whose remarkable vicissitudes the poets had much to tell. Robert regards Oedipus as a chthonic hero from the Demeter cycle—the Earth-goddess is originally his mother: "Where the Earth, the divine, primal being, is the universal Mother—as she certainly is among all the Greek tribes—her sons are naturally at the same time her husbands" (p. 44). Here our interpretation is consistent with the symbolical role of the country (Thebes). How far Robert, despite his discernment, has diverged from the original meaning of the myth may be judged from the following passage: "The child of Mother Earth originally needed no father. If he had a father, that father, according to the Nature religion, could only be a being like himself—the ancient god of the year, whom he had to slay in order that he himself might become the king of the year, even as Zeus dethroned Kronos. . . . So every year he was given the prophet-god Laius for his father. Every year he slew Laius, and every year he married his mother. *There can hardly have been a causal connection between the parricide and the slaying of the Sphinx*" (italics mine). The author adds that here we have the most difficult problem in the poetical form of the Oedipus myth, and that all attempts to establish such a connection have failed.

One may indeed say that it was just because the terrible gravity of Oedipus' crime was concealed by the story of the Sphinx that it was possible to represent his action as that of an ordinary human being, and to describe it without disguise. We should then assume that the Oedipus of an earlier form of the legend killed the divine totemic animal and had to pay dearly for his crime. Subsequently the original slaying of the totem was no longer recognized in its momentous real significance by the Greeks, who had progressed to the creation of anthropomorphic deities. The totemic animal, degraded by progress to the status of monster, was retained in the very late transformation of the legend as the Sphinx; and the killing of the totem was likewise retained; but now, by a conversion of affect, it acquired a meritorious character.[27]

The whole event was thus misunderstood owing to the influence of the tendencies of a more highly cultured period. We must not forget that the gods had already assumed human form, that religious feeling had become more sensitive and refined, and had suppressed, even though unconsciously, any impulse of sympathy with the monstrous act of deicide. But then another crime offered itself as a substitute for this unique act: a crime grievous enough, and resembling the other, but without the character of a violent insurrection against the deity. This crime was parricide.

However, we do not believe that the choice of this substitute was directed by chance. Let us consider what the substitution of the father for the totem meant: The totemic animal itself had been a primeval substitute for the Father, and the slaying of the totem revived memories of the murder of the chieftain of the primeval horde. If the legend now made Oedipus kill his father, what it recorded was a form of the primitive legend not uninfluenced by the anthropomorphization of the gods, and adapted to the later cultural standards of the period. If we consider this process of evolution, which started from a primitive era that had no conscious memory of the actual event, that found a late echo in the Oedipus myth, and which in the slaying of the totemic animal revealed the act in its religious significance, and later on,

[27]The new interpretation resembles that which was effected in the tradition of the shattering of the Golden Calf by Moses (Reik, 1919).

compelled by the impatience of the repressing forces, allowed it to be replaced by the parricide, we then have the following aspect of the matter: *The myth as we know it does not reflect the primary content of the legend, but already represents a late recurrence of the repressed matter.* An episode broadly resembling the present events of the Oedipus legend may have formed the content of the original nucleus of the legend.

We may understand why this myth, as one of the few of which we have any knowledge, has told us what it has to say in such a crude and naked form. We must not ascribe this peculiarity to its primitive character; we must rather regard it as due to an irruption of repressed material after thousands of years of repression. Disregarding all such considerations as might on principle apply to this example of myth formation, we will confine ourselves to establishing the fact that here, as in other myths, the first form of this imaginative production to reach us already bears traces of religious elaboration and interpretation. Nowhere can we find the prereligious myth in its pure form; but where the divinities, the demons, and the rest of the *personae* of the ancient religions do not occur we can at least envisage a newer form of the myth, which has grown out of the religious phase, and which must not be confused with the primary form, with its animistic associations. Noting that here we are faced with the difficult problem of the relation between myth and religion, we return to the story of the Sphinx.

We have realized that in the Oedipus legend, side by side with the more recent form, the older version of the story of the Sphinx persists, erroneously conceived and interpreted; and further, that the chief emphasis, which formerly rested on the story of the Sphinx, is now transferred to the fate of Oedipus, struggling against a human father. Such a displacement of accent is not unknown to us in the psychic field; in dreams also what was once the kernel makes its appearance as the shell.

Hitherto we have disregarded, with intention, the motives that seem to assign the maternal character to the Sphinx. Rank's view of the meaning of the episode is that the Sphinx and the mother originally coincided; that is, the introduction of the Sphinx should be regarded as the isolation of certain obnoxious features of the mother.

But after the introduction of the Sphinx her proper maternal character was effaced by subsequent waves of repression. The original violation of the mother was replaced by a conflict with the Sphinx, and only in later versions was this transformed into an intellectual contest. The Sphinx mother—formerly the violated mother—asks the youth who is struggling to understand the sexual problem a sexual riddle regarding the nature of man, and only when the hero has solved the riddle—that is, "only after the violation of the mother in the original version"—can he consummate the marriage. According to Rank the Sphinx episode represents a "doubling" of the rape of Jocasta, introduced in the course of repression and mythic stratification. But Rank, sagaciously realizing that this interpretation is inadequate, has adduced the story of Chrysippus, associated with the figure of Laius, whereupon the homosexual significance of the figure of the Sphinx becomes apparent.

It now appears possible to reconcile Rank's interpretation with our own. The one supplements the other; Rank's hypothesis, in our opinion, suggesting a later version. The Sphinx, as a duplication of the mother, has interposed herself before the more primitive image of the totemistic father substitute, concealing it, even as the simply human form of the Oedipus myth has interposed itself before the heroic-religious form. The slaying of the Sphinx is originally the killing of the totem; but it is equally certain, as Rank has explained, that it afterward became the rape of the mother. Then, were duplications of the father imago and the mother image combined in the figure of the Sphinx? As a matter of fact, they were, as another consideration tells us: the human Oedipus legend, which as a recurrence of the primitive legend reflects all the essential details of the latter in a more civilized form, has evolved from the Sphinx legend by a process of humanization and cleavage, so that the essential and significant elements of the later stratum must already have existed in the tale of the Sphinx. We thus arrive at the assumption that in the Sphinx legend as we have it now a wholesale condensation is concealed, the work of many generations, which has compressed the slaying of the father and the violation of the mother into the single act of which the Sphinx is the victim. Homosexual and heterosexual, sadistic and masochistic emotional trends overlap, inextricably blended. The psychic processes which psychoanalysis has detected in the individual provide us an explanation of the situation. The child who observes the sexual intercourse of adults identifies himself not only with the father, but also with the mother; he not only wishes to have sexual intercourse with the mother, as does the father, but he also wishes to be treated by the father as the mother is treated in coitus. This sadomasochistic fantasy corresponds with the first heterosexual and homosexual associations of the child. The infantile-sadistic notion of coitus makes it seem a conflict in the eyes of the child; so it is possible that the child, following the misunderstood example of the father, may wish to overthrow and wound the mother. The transference of this experience to folk psychology draws our attention to the alternate rise and fall of homosexual and heterosexual waves in the life of peoples. Love for the father may coincide with unconscious hatred for the mother, and vice versa. We may now perceive the Sphinx as an embodiment of these two primeval, powerful, and antithetical trends, since Oedipus accompanied parricide with the violation of the mother, and yet in violating the mother made the father the object of his love.

If we now try to elucidate the historical sequence of the predominance of these libidinal trends, we shall realize that the slaying of the father, of the totemic animal, *seems* to have preceded the violation of the mother, who appears in the more nearly human form of the Sphinx. But the components of the hybrid form, in which the male, animal hinder quarters are apparently the older elements, and the human, female features the more recent, gives us reason to suspect that here, as in the whole legend, we have a recurrence of an ancient repressed theme. The condensation of the slaying of the father and the sexual relation with the mother, which is divided in the Oedipus legend into two separate actions, is in our opinion a throwback to a primeval state of humanity when the erotic choice of youth did not declare itself so decisively for the woman as it does today, but also when erotic play and erotic conflict were not so sharply separated as they are today; to a phase which would be analogous to the sadistic-anal period in the libidinal evolution of the individual. If the possibility of return to this atavistic evolutionary phase of instinctual development is the precondition of the existence of condensation, we shall have to assume that the first impetus toward the creation of the

Oedipus myth was the fantasy of (sadistically colored) sexual intercourse with the mother, an obstacle to which was the sexual intercourse of the father. Like the primal form of every myth, this is no more than the objectified hallucination of fulfilled wishes. We know from individual analysis that this formula corresponds with the biogenetic law that the child originally fulfills, by way of hallucination, the wishes whose fulfillment is denied to him by reality. If we have thus traced the Oedipus myth back to its first germ, the fantasied, violent sexual union with the mother, it will not surprise us if we find, in one of its latest forms, and in a significant position, a sign of this derivation; I mean the dream chosen by Freud as the starting point of his analysis, the dream of which Jocasta speaks in Sophocles' tragedy: "Many a man ere now has seen himself in a dream/Mated with his mother. . . ." So that Freud is justified in his assertion that the legend of Oedipus is derived from dream stuff of great antiquity, as we think we have proved by the historical and psychological reconstruction of the later form of the legend. The universal incest fantasy of the mass of humanity is threatened by an obstacle to its formation and hallucinatory fulfillment in the anticipated intrusion of the father. The tremendous event of the father's murder casts its shadow before it, in the form of the picture which emerges in the dream of the forcible removal of the intruder. The possession of the mother is so closely associated with the condition of parricide, the fulfillment of the instinctually rooted wish is so impossible without the removal of this chiefest hindrance, that the one event can be regarded as representative of the other. This psychic constellation later on, in combination with the motives already mentioned, provides the possibility of the condensation to which we have pointed in the legend of the Sphinx.

This possibility could first be realized when the psychic reactions to the actual deed of the father's murder had long been established and when a primal myth had already taken shape. The rape of the mother, as manifested in the subduing of the Sphinx and the slaying of the totemistic father, would be equated with the recurrence of the wish which provided the impetus for the creation of the myth. The possibility of condensation was increased by the reactively enhanced affection for the father and the hostility toward the woman, which after each act increased the originally sadistic component of the incest fantasy. In the duplication of the Oedipus legend, by which the figure of the Sphinx is again divided into the figures of Laius and Jocasta, the hostile and affectionate tendencies in the young hero's relations to his father and mother reemerge separately as before. As in the legend of the Sphinx, sexual intercourse and murder synchronize in one act, affecting one object, so they coincide in our version of the pre-Sophoclean tragedy of Oedipus, when Oedipus, having slain his father, takes his girdle and his sword.[28] The ungirt body is a familiar erotic symbol in Greek antiquity, and the taking of the sword is a symbolic substitute for castration, so that here also, in diachronic action, we have the successive expression of affectionate and hostile emotions in respect of the same object.

We can understand how, under cover of this homosexual motivation, the hybrid figure came into existence. The Sphinx is both man and woman, because both were desired as sexual objects; she is killed, and sexually enjoyed, because for the child both actions coincide in the sadomasochistic, infantile notion of sexual intercourse, as they possibly did in reality, in the earliest period of the differentiation of the sexes in the evolution of the human organism.

We have already stated that the absurd hybrid forms, like that of the Sphinx, which occur in dreams suggest that the dreamer feels derision or contempt for the object represented. If we transfer this rule to the creations of the mass psyche we may assume that in the curious mixed creations of primitive art certain tendencies express themselves whose direction is analogous to that of these emotions. One might perhaps maintain that the hybrid form of man plus animal in the Sphinx corresponds with the unconscious resistance to the superseded totemistic divinities in a culturally advanced period which was already familiar with human divinities. The synthesis of the Sphinx, with her male and female components, would thus reflect an uncon-

[28]Another association, of later date, leads once more to the condensation which we have noted in the legend of the Sphinx; the Sphinx, according to Peisandros's account, was sent by Hera as a punishment, because Laius, the father of Oedipus, had kidnapped the handsome Chrysippus. According to the legend Oedipus, homosexually inclined, killed his unknown father on account of Chrysippus, whom he also loved. We shall not be unduly venturesome if we see in Chrysippus himself a duplication of Oedipus. Thus, legend records the murder of the father out of homosexual jealousy, as well as from motives of heterosexual desire.

scious hostility to the father-god, an impulse of repudiation which directs the heterosexual libidinal tendencies against the religion based on homosexual associations. We should compare this aggressive trend with a repression which set in during the period of late antiquity, and a modified judgment of homosexual practices, whose last remnants we see in the derision of homosexuality by the Greek and Roman satirists.[29] Yet this remains only an assumption, no more probable than another in respect of a period so alien to us in feeling as the prehistoric Orient.

10. The Religious Significance of the Oedipus Myth

I do not know how far I have succeeded in giving the reader of the foregoing pages a notion of the great importance of the Oedipus myth in the religious life of the Greeks, and of the close and cryptic relation of the performance of the *Oedipus* to the religious ritual of Hellas. The profound and lasting influence of the Oedipus legend in antiquity must, I believe, be ascribed to the religious motive which revealed the instinctual life of men in conflict with the laws of the gods. For here, as in the Dionysian games, and the ritual of Attis, Adonis, and Osiris, a young revolutionary savior was represented, rebelling against the old and powerful father-god and suffering a terrible punishment for his offense. I believe the influence of these performances may be compared with that of the ecclesiastical Passion play on the faithful in the Middle Ages, for it depended on the same psychic precedents. The prehistory of Christ is not unlike that of Oedipus. It should be emphasized that in the Oedipus myth, as we now have it, the profoundest psychic motives, which led to the formation of religion, though unrecognized by the auditors, were nonetheless plastically represented, and that here an unconscious sense of guilt was evoked.

Elsewhere I shall try to show that the hidden kernel of this myth is the same as that which underlies the story of original sin in the biblical narrative, on which the sense of guilt of the masses was fixated for hundreds of years. Here we will only note that in Assyrian and

[29] I think the story of Chrysippus and the punishment of Laius by the Sphinx is not unconnected with this change.

Babylonian paintings and reliefs, on cylindrical seals and the like, Sphinxes, Gryphons, and similar winged animal forms are seen to be guarding the Tree of Life. Everyone knows that in the story of the Fall of Man a cherub, whose original animal form we find in the visions of Ezekiel, stands beside the Tree of Life as the Sphinx lies before the Egyptian temples, and as the leonine or tauriform guardians keep watch before the palaces of Assurbanasirpal and Sanherib. All these guardian animals are late descendants of totemistic deities. Further, it can be shown that in the tradition of the Tree of Life precisely the same condensation has occurred as in the Sphinx episode of the Oedipus myth, and that in the biblical narrative the Tree plays the same apparently subsidiary role as the Sphinx in the Greek legend. Recent research has convinced me that the Oedipus myth might be called the Hellenic version of the legend of the Fall.[30]

However, we must not forget that what was struggling for expression in the religiously emphatic form of the *Oedipus*, and what thrilled and moved the Greek auditors, and moves us even today, was just those decisive psychic impulses whose operation first provided the impetus toward the formation of religion. In this sense also the Oedipus legend is a creation which reveals the recurrence of repressed material.

We have intentionally excluded from this interpretation, as a secondary feature, the riddle propounded by the Sphinx. On this occasion we are more concerned to solve the riddle of the Sphinx herself. Or rather, one of her riddles. For these are many, and they still challenge our endeavors to solve them.[31]

This sends us back to the little drawing of which I spoke in the introduction: a sketch which the analyst may regard as a token of what has been achieved, but also as a constant encouragement to further research.

[30]By this I do not intend any reference to the still unsolved and complicated problem of the relations between the Semites and the Greeks.

[31]The position of the riddle in the Oedipus myth corresponds with the place which the knowledge of good and evil occupies in the legend of the Fall of Man. (Reik, 1928).

REFERENCES

Agatharchides, Periplus Rubri Maris (Across the Red Sea). Interprete Laurentio Rhodomanno. In: *Geog. Vet. Script. Gr. Min. Hudson,* Vol. 1, 1698 (Greek and Latin).

Bab, H. (1906), Geschlectsleben, Geburt und Missgeburt in der asiatischen Mythologie, *Zeitschrift Für Ethnologie* 38:269-311. Berlin: Behrend & Co.

Bachofen, J. J. (1861) *Mutterrecht und Urreligion; eine Auswahl,* ed. von Rudolf Marx. Leipzig: Alfred Kroener, 1936

Bernfeld, S. (1928), *Sisyphos; oder Die Grenzen der Erziehung,* 2nd ed. Wien: Internationalischer Psychoanalytischer Vertag.

Bertschinger, H. (1911). Illustrierte Halluzinationen, In: *Jahrbuch für Psychoanalytische und psychopathologische,* Vol. 3. ed. E. Bleuler and S. Freud, Leipzig: Deuticke, P. 69-100.

Bethe, E. (1891), *Thebanische heldenlieder; untersuchungen über die epen des thebanisen-argivischen sagenkreises.* Leipzig: S. Hirzel.

Boll, F. (1919) *Sternglaube und Sterndeutung; die geschichte und das wesen der astrologie,* Leipzig/Berlin: B. G. Teubner

Bötticher, K. (1854). *Berichte der Kgl. Säches, Gesellschaft der Wissenschaften,* No. 6, pp. 53ff.

Bréal, M. J. A. (1877), *Mélanges de mythologie et de linguistique,* Paris: Hachette, pp. 163ff.

Champollion, J. F. (1823). Le Pantheon Égyptien, Collection des Personages Mythologiques de l'Ancienne Égypte, d'aprés les Monuments avec un Texte explicatif, No. 24E.

Clemens, Titus Flavius, Alexandrinus (1906-1909), *Stromata* hrsg. von O. Stählin. Leipzig: J. C. Hinrichs.

Dargun, L. (1892) *Studien zum ältesten Familienrecht. Teil 1, Mutterrecht und Vaterrecht.* Leipzig: Duncker & Humbolt.

de Morgan, J. (1896-1897), *Recherches sur origine de l'Égypte,* Paris.

Erman, A. (1900), *Die Flexion des aegyptischen Verbums.* Sitzungbericht, Berlin: Verlag der Koniglichen-Preussischen Akad. der Wissenschaften, pp. 317-353.

Ferenczi, S. (1912), Symbolishe Darstellung des Lust und Realitätsprinzipes im Oedipus Mythus, In: *Imago,* Vol. I, ed. O. Rank and H. Sachs. Leipzig/Vienna: Hugo Heller et Cie.

Forchhammer, P. W. (1875), *Daduchos, Einleitung in das verstaendniss der hellenischen mythen, mythensprache und mythischen fanten.* Keil: P. Toeche, p. 84ff.

Frazer, Sir J. S. (1907) Adonis, Attis, Osiris: Studies in the History of Oriental religions; In: *The Golden Bough,* 3rd Ed. Part 4. London: Macmillan & Co.

Frazer, Sir J. G. (1911). The magic art and the evolution of kings, In: *The Golden Bough,* Part 1. London: Macmillan & Co.

Frazer, Sir J. G. (1912), The dying god, In: *The Golden Bough,* Part 3. London: Macmillan & Co.

Freud, S. (1900), The interpretation of dreams, *Standard Edition,* 4 & 5. London: Hogarth Press, 1953.

Furtwängler, A. (1900), *Die antiken gemmen; geschichte der steinschneidekunst im Klassichen altertum,* Vol. 3. Leipzig, Berlin: Giesecke & Devrient. p. 43.

Gerhard, E. Ed. (1843-1867), Griechische mythologie, In: *Archaeologische Zeitung,* Vol. 1 Jahrg. Berlin, p. 581.

Gruppe, O. (1897–1906), *Griechische mythologie und religionsgeschichte.* Müchen: Beck.
Hoernes, M. (1925), *Urgeschichte der bildenden Kunst in Europe von den anfangen bis um 500 vor Christi.* Wien: A. Schroll & Co., p. 58.
Hommel, F. (1887), *Abriss der Geschichte des alten Orients.* Nördlinger: C. H. Beck, pp. 108–129.
Ilberg, J. (1912) *Der ägyptische Sphinx* (ungedr. Ms. 38 BL); see also Roscher (1909–1915).
Jastrow, M. (1914), *Babylonian-Assyrian Birth-Omens and Their Cultural Significance.* Giessen: A. Töpelmann, p. 79.
Jeremias, A. (1907), *Die panbabylonisten, der alte Orient und die aegyptische religion.* Leipzig: J. C. Hinrichs.
Jung, C. G. (1912), Wandlungen und Symbole der Libido. In: *Jahrbuch fur Psychoanalytische und Psychopathologische,* ed. E. Bleuler and S. Freud. Leipzig: F. Deuticke, Vol. 3, pp. 120–227; Vol. 4, pp. 164–464.
Keller, O. (1889), *Tier-und pflanzenbilder auf münzen und gemmen des klassischen Altertums,* von Imhoof-Blumer und O. K.; Leipzig: B. G. Teubner, pp. 182ff.
Kollmann, J. (1902), Die Gräber von Abydos, *Korrespondenzbl. Deutsch. Gesell. Anthropol., Ethnol., Urgesch.* 33:119–126.
Laistner, L. (1889). Das Rätsel der Sphinx. *Grundzüge einer Mythengeschichte,* Bd 1–2. Berlin: W. Hertz, p. 61.
Lang, A. (1887), *Myth, Ritual and Religion.* London: Longmans, Green.
——— (1901), *Magic and Religion.* London: Longmans, Green.
——— (1909), *The Making of Religion,* 3rd ed. London: Longmans, Green.
Mariette-Bey, A. (1893), *Voyage dans la Haute-Égypte,* Vol. 2. Paris: Boussod, Valadon, p. 9.
Meyer, E. (1884–1902), *Geschichte des Alterthums,* Vols. 1–5. Stuttgart: Cotta.
Parthey, G. F. C., Ed. (1850), *Plutarch über Isis und Osiris, nach neuverg Lichenen handschriften mit übersetzung und erläuterungen,* ed. von Gustav Parthey. Berlin: Nicholaische buchhandlung, p. 175.
Peiser, F. E., Ed. (1910), *Orientalische Litteratur-Zeitung,* Vol. 5.
Rank, O. (1912), *Das Inzest-motiv in Dichtung und Sage.* Leipzig: F. Deuticke, pp. 266ff.
Reik, T. (1919), *Probleme der Religionpsychologie,* Part I. Vienna/Leipzig: Internationaler Psychoanalytischer Verlag.
Reik, T. (1928), Die Erbsünde, In: *Probleme der Religionpsychologie,* Part II. Vienna/Leipzig: Internationaler Psychoanalytischer Verlag.
Robert, C. (1915), *Oedipus, geschichte eines poetischen stoffs im griechischen altertum.* Berlin: Weidemann, pp. 49, 57, 63.
Roscher, W. H. (1909–1915), Sphinx, In: *Ausführliches lexikon der griechischen und römischen mythologie.* Leipzig: B. G. Teubner.
Schack-Schackenburg, H. (1893–1902), *Aegyptologische Studien,* Vol. 5. Leipzig: J. C. Hinrichs, pp. 209ff.
Schatz, F. (1901), *Die grieschischen Götter und die menschlichen.* Missgeburten, Wiesbaden: J. F. Bergmann.
Schmidt, B. (1877), *Griechische Märchen, Sagen und Volkslieder.* Gesammelt, übersetzt, und erlautert. Leipzig: B. G. Teubner, p. 143.

Schmidt, W. (1912-55), *Der Ursprung der Gottesidee; eine historisch-kritische und positive Studie.* Münster: W. Aschendorff.

Schrader, E., Winckler, H., Zimmern, H., (1902-1903), *Die Keilinschriften und das Alte Testament,* 3rd Ed., Berlin: Reuther & Reichard, p. 627.

Schroeter, R. (1876), *De draconibus graecarum fabularum,* Particula I. Vratislaviae: Behmer and Minuth.

Stucken, E. (1907), *Astralmythen.* Religionsgeschichtliche von E. Stucken. Leipzig: E. Pfeiffer.

von Hofmannsthal, H. (1906), *Oedipus und die Sphinx. Tragedie in drei Aufsagen.* Berlin: S. Fischer.

Wiedemann, A., Ed. (1890), *Herodots Zweites Buch,* Leipzig: B. G. Teubner, pp. 598-602.

Wiedemann, A. (1906), *Agyptische religion, Archiv für Regligions-wissenschaft,* 9:481-499. Leipzig: B. G. Teubner.

Wilkinson, Sir J. G. (1841), *Manners and Customs of the Ancient Egyptians,* 2nd Series, 3 Vols. London: T. Murray, p. 302.

Wundt, W. (1904), *Volkerpsychologie,* Vol. III, 2nd ed. Leipzig: W. Engelmann, pp. 521f.

4

from *Beyond Psychology*

OTTO RANK

[1941]

Unaware of such irrational determinants in our most common concepts, many anthropologists and sociologists, indeed, even our modern psychologists, seem to take their obvious meaning for granted. They tacitly assume that the family unit existed from the very beginning for the benefit of its members, and, since they could not find such a pleasing "tableau" in the history of the past, they naively projected their own conception into it. Freud, when he had to supplement his psychology of the individual by the social aspects of personality development, even went so far as to reinterpret primitive anthropological material in the light of our present-day family organization. In his sensational interpretation of the Greek Oedipus saga we find the social significance of a collective myth explained in terms of the highly individualized psychology of modern neurotics. In pointing out the *social* significance which this tradition had for the Greeks themselves, I found (Rank, 1932) that this story epitomizes the transition from a more archaic form of social life to the later family organization. Greek tradition reflects the struggle between individualism and socialization in the rebellion of the self-sufficient hero not only against the power of the gods but also against the new laws of man encroaching upon his freedom of action. The Oedipus tradition, in particular, gives us an idea of the tremendous resistances on the part of the individual who at that stage felt that he lost his freedom through the family as we may now feel deprived of our liberty by the state.

As is well known, the story tells of King Oedipus, who was exposed as a child because of the warning given his father by an oracle that his son was destined to kill his own father and marry his widowed mother. Freud thought to have found the explanation for these "horrible crimes," which the hero unknowingly commits, in the unconscious wish of every son to kill his father in order to have intercourse with his mother. If, however, we consult the scholarly analysis of the Oedipus material by Carl Robert (1915) we realize that there is a much more primitive basis to the Oedipus tradition of the Greek drama corresponding to the creation rite. The Oedipus of the primitive seasonal myth was originally a phallic vegetation spirit, an offspring of the earth-mother, whose son was also her husband. "The child of the mother earth," says Robert, "needed no father in the beginning; and if it should acquire one then this according to primitive cult could only be an identical one, the old Year-god whom the son must kill in order to become the Year-king himself." Here we realize that the Greek Oedipus tradition simply represents a reinterpretation of the creation rite in which the father is substituted for the brother (and the mother for the sister). In other words, what we have here in terms of Greek civilization amounts to a further sexualized version of the creation ceremony, transposed into the framework of the father-centered family. The two kings, the old and the new self, originally conceived of as twin brothers, appear here as father and son. The killing, although conceived of in terms of the struggle between generations, has the same ritual meaning. The incest likewise has the ritual meaning of self-perpetuation transposed from the magical to the sexual plane. Whereas Freud saw in it an instinctual (unconscious) desire of the son to have sexual intercourse with his mother, the tradition actually reflects the transition—accomplished in Greek civilization—from heroic self-perpetuation to man's reluctant acceptance of his biological role as father and his perpetuation through the generations. The resistance which both Oedipus' father and the hero himself show to accepting their respective roles in the human drama of family relations really makes it a *drama of fatherhood* clad in the typical vestige of "the myth of the birth of the hero," who is not born a son nor does he become a father. The killing of the twin brother, this typical motif symbolizing the hero's immortal self, appears projected back into Oedipus' childhood—where another newly born is killed in his stead—as if to indicate that this heroic double belongs to a remote past which the highly sophisticated Greek playwrights seem eager to recapture—in vain. At this time when our present family organization was just in the making, man from the threshold of the heroic age was enviously looking back into the past stage of heroic self-perpetuation epitomized in the creation rite. The heroic self rebelling against his biological successor was given the name "Oedipus" and invested with the old incest ritual, because the latter formerly had been the symbol of heroic self-perpetuation which had given way to the acceptance of biological procreation.

In this sense, the Greek Oedipus saga, in which Freud saw only the rebellion of the son, proves in the light of social developments a heroic defense on the man's part against his role of father. The father of Oedipus, Laius, clearly represents the type of man rejecting sexual procreation. According to the tradition, he abstained from intercourse with his wife because he was told his son would be a mighty hero and overthrow his reign. When the child, conceived by accident, was born, the father, not wanting any son to succeed him, ordered his death. In the incest of Oedipus with his mother, the tradition symbolizes this universal desire to be one's own successor. Hence, Oedipus himself becomes a representative of the father who does not care to have children (the two sons whom he begets with his own mother kill each other according to ritual tradition in fratricide). This compromise to beget himself, as it were, as his mother's son and be reborn by her must fail tragically. This—not that he slew the father and took his place with the mother—is the veritable sin of Oedipus. For as little as the father wants to continue his existence in his son, just as little is the son inclined to play the part of successor to his father. In this sense,

Oedipus rebels alike against the role of son and of father, not as son against father. This double conflict in the individual himself, who wants to be neither father nor son, but simply *self*, is portrayed in the Greek tragedy, which epitomizes the struggle of the immortal heroic self against the racial self of sexual procreation manifested in marriage and children. The inner resistance of man to his ephemeral racial role, be it that of father or son, is represented in the Oedipus drama as an external strife between father and son. However, the two do not recognize each other when they meet and fight, since in King Laius Oedipus does not kill his biological father but revolts against the father principle as such. In this sense, the father-son relation is from the beginning a generative, not a personal one, that is to say, a clash between two world views at the transitional stage of development from the heroic to the social self, personified in the father- and son-type.

With the dawn of the patriarchal ideology, the child is no longer the bearer of collective immortality in the meaning of the old soul belief, but as the individual successor to his father he becomes a personification of the latter's immortality. Thus the conception of the son-type was first derived from the social ideology of fatherhood and only much later appears in biological terms of the mother-relationship. Against this denial of his own individuality, the son has rebelled from the time when man accepted fatherhood as a symbol of the social self. From then on, we see in the history of mankind the grandiose duel of those two principles personified in the father- and son-type, manifesting itself in social, political, and religious strifes. The Greeks perished in that struggle of the prefamily self, the hero, against the emergence of the social self epitomized in the family types of father and son. Roman civilization, on the other hand, was built up on a further socialization of this new father principle. Just as the ritual marriage ceremony between brother and sister was gradually adopted by the common man in order that he might benefit vicariously from such magical participation, so Roman civilization enabled the average citizen to participate in the advantages of socialized fatherhood. Every freeborn citizen had by the very fact of his political status the right to be a father, that is, to have legitimate children over whom he legally ruled. This right to social fatherhood, which proved identical with being a Roman citizen, was denied the class of slaves whose children were not sons or daughters of their fathers or mothers but merely slaves of their masters. Besides and above this general Oriental distinction between rulers and slaves, Roman civilization for the first time developed a definite class consciousness and with it political class struggle between ruling groups. The right of every citizen to social fatherhood meant no right for the son except the one to become a father in his turn, that is, a social type prescribed by this first totalitarian state. Since the legal power of the father over his sons was equivalent to his power over his slaves (the word "family" is derived from "famulus"—servant, slave) we can justly say that the sons dominated by legalized fatherhood actually were the first "have-nots." Not that the slaves had more, but they had no hope and hence no real desire to demand or take what the "haves" possessed. It was different with the sons, who, despite their lack of legal rights, were brought up with the idea of promotion—provided they behaved—from the "have-not" into the "have" group. Hence, they could easily form the nucleus of a rebellious class striving to overthrow the ruling class of fathers. At the same time, there existed an equally strong rivalry between the members of the ruling class as to who was the strongest and thus entitled to rule the rulers.

At the height of the patriarchal rule in ancient Rome, the father had become invested with a power derived from the magic self of the hero in whose image civic fatherhood was created as a social type. Paradoxically enough, it seems that Freud's "primitive dominance of the father" who ruled tyrannically over the "herd of brothers" only existed politically in the highly organized Roman state at the peak of its power. In this light, psychoanalysis, centered around the father psychology, appears as a last stand of the crumbling patriarchal ideology which collapsed together with imperialism in the World War. For a while, the outlived father principle found refuge in an individualistic psychology which explained the father-son relation on the basis of personal, more specifically sexual rivalry between two individuals within the same family. On the basis of its patriarchal ideology, psychoanalysis had to explain the Oedipus saga in terms of the Decalogue and thus appears as the last bulwark against the decadence of the bourgeois family structure as it grew out from socialized fatherhood in Roman law. This collapse of the ideology on which the social structure of Western civilization was built occurred simultaneously in the political, economic, and psychological sphere. The breakdown of the institution of kingship in the World War, followed by class struggle and disintegration of the family, led to the present chaos with its moral bewilderment and economic insecurity.

Although it may be tempting to draw a prophetic parallel between the instability of our own civilization and the collapse of the Roman Empire (see Haskell, 1939), the difference between the two situations is nevertheless sufficiently striking to obviate any such easy historization of our problem. The struggle in the Roman Empire signifies the beginning of a social movement through the end-phase of which we seem now to be laboring. The proverbial diseases of children and the natural decay of old age are sufficiently distinct as to cause and symptoms not to be treated in the same way, although both may be fatal. The common assumption that history repeats itself seems to spring more from our emotional need for likeness than from factual observation. Far from repeating itself, history does not even seem to move in evolutionary cycles but rather manifests itself in and through crises. What does repeat itself, though, is a traditional pattern handed down in ritual cult and mythological tradition; a pattern which, clashing at different times with different realities, produces new and unique events.

The task in which Roman civilization ultimately failed was to apply an ideology of magic origin which had worked socially in creating a new type of citizen, to the final test of establishing economic equality. Contrary-wise, the problem of today's economic crisis is to find a new ideology after Western civilization has failed to maintain this universal type of citizen promoted by Christianity. When the church lost this cultural function, psychology had to divert the failure of establishing economic equality into an attempt for political equality stated in terms of the democratic type of man. Whereas in Roman times it was the first democratic government which had failed in its ultimate application, it now is the democratic type who resists his democratic government's carrying his ideology of equality too far into realistic achievement. In this sense, it is true that fascism and communism are the result of unfulfilled promises of democracy (see Ascoli and Feiler, 1938). If a too liberal government carries the democratic ideology beyond the endurance of the democratic type, then there appears the paradox of the individual feeling forced—"governed"—by a government which he himself created as an expression of his type.

Here we are reminded that government—of any kind—originated in kingship, which, under the name of monarchy, has survived as the most popular form of regime. Indeed, it has been argued that any one-man rule as opposed to government by a group or class is monarchic in principle, whether it sails under the flag of fascism, communism, or so-called democracy (Belloc, 1938). Such a political conception gains momentum from the emotional fact that the people themselves are inclined to conceive of their government in terms of a "governor," whether or not he be autocratic. When, for example, the president of the United States has been mockingly made responsible even for bad weather, we see in such a "joke" more than an echo of the "primitive's" belief in the rainmaker.

REFERENCES

Ascoli, M., & Feiler, A. (1938), *Fascism for Whom?* New York: Norton.
Belloc, H. (1938), *Monarchy*. London: Cassell.
Haskell, H. J. (1939), *The New Deal in Old Rome*. New York.
Rank, O. (1932), *Modern Education*. New York: Knopf.
Robert, C. (1915), *Oedipus*. Berlin: Weidemann.

5

The "Passing of the Oedipus Complex" in Greek Drama

MARK KANZER

[1948]

I

The attention focused by Freud on Sophocles' *Oedipus Tyrannus* has not been transferred, strangely enough, to the sequel, *Oedipus at Colonus,* which is integrally related to the problems of the earlier play. Whereas *Oedipus Tyrannus* confronts men with the disastrous results of their fundamental unconscious drives, *Oedipus at Colonus* depicts the process of restitution and social application of the same forces in a manner which anticipates and closely resembles Freud's own formulations as to the passing of the Oedipus complex through superego development.

The career of Oedipus did not end when he blinded himself after discovering that he had inadvertently carried out the prophecy that he would murder his father and marry his mother. He later went into exile from Thebes, the city he had ruled, and for twenty years (a generation!) wandered miserable and homeless through many lands, accompanied only by his daughter Antigone. *Oedipus at Colonus*

Reprinted with permission from *International Journal of Psycho-Analysis,* vol. 29, pp. 131–134.

deals with the refuge and peace which he finally found, and with his death.

At the beginning of the play, Oedipus and Antigone rest momentarily in a grove at Colonus, outside Athens. The natives warn them that they have committed sacrilege in entering the holy place of the Eumenides and are completely horrified when they discover that the stranger is the notorious Oedipus. The exiled king feels, however, that his accidental intrusion into the haunts of the Fates, or Eumenides, is a signal which he has awaited from the gods that his trials are over, and implores the alarmed populace to summon the Athenian king, Theseus. While awaiting Theseus, a second daughter of Oedipus, Ismene, arrives with the message that oracles have recently proclaimed that the grave of Oedipus will have great powers and that consequently rival disputants for the throne of Thebes will seek to gain possession of him. Oedipus rejoices that "the gods who overthrew him now sustain him" but entertains only bitterness to the Thebans who drove him into exile. When Theseus arrives and shows himself well disposed, Oedipus offers him the promised power of his grave if the Athenian king will provide him refuge and protection the remainder of his days. Theseus agrees and the stage is set for two dramatic interviews with the contending rulers of Thebes.

The first encounter is with Creon, maternal uncle and ancient enemy of Oedipus. When his blandishments fail to win over his blind nephew, he seizes the daughters and lays hands upon Oedipus himself. Theseus intervenes in time and drives off Creon ignominiously. Then Polynices, a son of Oedipus, arrives to beg his father's aid. In the dramatic highpoint of the play, Oedipus rebukes his son for his previous indifference and, in a violent diatribe, curses Polynices and his brother Eteocles as undutiful sons and predicts their death in battle at each other's hands.

Lastly, a thunderstorm arises and Oedipus senses a message from the gods that his time has come. He summons Theseus for the third and last time and grants him alone the privilege of witnessing his last moments and final resting place on earth. Then the old hero disappears in a mysterious manner and Theseus, guarding the secret, assumes the obligations of a father to the bereaved daughters.

II

The grove of the Eumenides as the scene of the action is of key importance. As Oedipus himself points out, his wandering to this spot is an omen that the gods are ready to grant him forgiveness and peace. The Eumenides are the Furies, who in Greek mythology are older and stronger than the gods. They are female spirits, representative of the prehistoric matriarchy and the savage customs of an earlier period. The rise of the father state was paralleled by the evolution of a hierarchy of gods who symbolized the need for reason and discipline so characteristic of the later Greek culture. Throughout the patriarchal period, however, secret cults dedicated to the more primitive gods continued to flourish. The sins of Oedipus in killing his father and committing incest with his mother were crimes against the two most fundamental taboos of the tribe, and his punishment and sufferings were regarded as sentences executed upon him by the Furies, who torment the violators of family morals. Polynices, subtly hinting at his spiritual as well as biological relationship to his father, declares, "I believe that the Furies that pursue you were indeed the cause (that I too was driven from my native city and have become a wanderer, inasmuch as I have forfeited the right to dwell within the family)."

The question then arises as to why Oedipus felt that his entrance into the holy place of the Furies was a sign of the end of his torments. Here we must recall the special history of the Furies in the mythology of Athens and their role in the Greek drama of the period. Aeschylus had recorded the sufferings of Orestes, who had killed his mother for instigating the murder of his father. Although the deed of Orestes was approved by the gods of the father state, the Furies pursued him with merciless ferocity, which could not be averted by the gods themselves. Finally, a trial was held at Athens in which the Furies were persuaded to reconcile themselves with the rule of the gods, in token of which their names were flatteringly changed to "The Eumenides," or "The Gentle Ones." This superb repressive mechanism did not change the dread in which these powerful and passionate spirits were held, and in *Oedipus in Colonus* they are referred to as "most feared daughters of darkness and mysterious earth" and the grove into which Oedipus has wandered as "the inviolate thicket of those whom it's futile to fight, those whom we tremble to name. When we pass we avert our eyes, close our eyes, in silence without conversation, shaping our prayers with our lips." The Furies evidently represent the dread forces of the unconscious, which must be appeased by the reasonable mind and, in the imagery of Sophocles, have their abode in the womb of the mother. That Oedipus dares to enter the forbidden region is indeed the characteristic of Oedipus; but why should this action now be in accord with the divine will and not an affront to the gods, as on the previous occasion? His blindness cannot be the extenuating circumstance, since his earlier incestuous deed had been carried out unwittingly and even in accord with the prophecies of the oracles.

The difference between the two occasions must be inferred as the drama proceeds. First we find Oedipus, the proud and arrogant, paying obeisance at this spot to the rightful king, Theseus, and obtaining his permission to dwell here with his daughter Antigone until his death. In this act we may see a familiar rite of homage of vassal to sovereign, duplicating the dutiful relationship of the son to the father. In this traditional ceremony, the subject places his life and all his property at the disposal of the king and at once receives them again at the hands of the benevolent ruler. What Oedipus receives from Theseus is analogous to the real meaning of the ritual of homage, namely forgiveness for rebellion and the right to a partial satisfaction of his desires so long as he accepts the laws of the community. Through his acknowledgment of Theseus as his ruler, Oedipus undoes the crime of parricide and restores to life the figure of the father. He has been freed of the first of his two sins. As a reward for giving up his independence, which has long since lost its attractions, he is granted protection, a home, and security for his daughter Antigone.

The figure of Antigone requires our study. We recall that after the blinding and exile of Oedipus he wandered over the earth shunned by all men and accompanied only by this faithful daughter. There is here a complete allegorical account of a neurosis following a traumatic experience. In giving up his kingdom and his eyesight, Oedipus renounces the gratification of his drives in the outer world and, dominated by feelings of shame and guilt, regresses to a more infantile relationship to the mother. The self-inflicted blindness by the man who solved the riddle of the Sphinx, namely the mysteries of intercourse and birth, points to a primal scene which gave him knowledge and instigated his desires. In yielding his power of sight, Oedipus subjects the memory of the primal scene to infantile amnesia and to a dwelling place in the unconscious, as do countless children who have repeated his experiences in more attenuated form in real life. Antigone here plays the role of the mother—a familiar distortion of the unconscious. In the period of expiation which corresponds to his neurosis, Oedipus has clung to incestual satisfactions with all the more vigor for the disguise, just as symptoms regularly embody the return of the repressed in the measures of defense.

In *Oedipus at Colonus*, we see the basic drives of Oedipus repeating themselves as they do in every neurosis, in an effort to master the original trauma. Again he horrifies the populace, by wandering with his mother-daughter into a sacred region which symbolizes her genitals. His blindness reverses the original deed, which was visual, just as the father-daughter relationship reverses the original family ties. The act is a signal that the good will of the gods is in store for him instead of their displeasure, and is to be followed by a treaty of friendship with the father instead of deadly combat. The psychopathology of this process is closely allied to the normal passing of the Oedipus complex into the latency phase.

Secure in the pact with the father, Oedipus can confront a repetition of the old traumatic experiences. Creon himself appears, his mother's brother and the very man who had played such a vital role in exposing and punishing Oedipus on the occasion of his earlier transgression. Again Creon seeks to separate him from a mutual female relative, now Antigone instead of Jocasta, and to drive him forth from a home which he has found. In Creon's determination to seek "the power of his grave" may be found a death threat with implications of castration. The situation now terminates differently; it is Creon who is convicted of behavior offensive to society and who is driven off. That Oedipus summons Theseus for this task shows that he no longer depends upon the infantile omnipotence of earlier days but has delegated his powers to the father, as the child ordinarily learns to do in his latency period. Social implications of this action relate not only to the course of the individual with respect to the authority of the community but, in the specific sense of the Athenian drama, with the triumph of the father state, represented by Theseus, over the supreme authority of the matriarchy, the mother's brother Creon.

The appearance of Polynices at this point provides the cue to the supreme emotional climax of the play, the curse of Oedipus upon an undutiful son. The undoing of the crimes of Oedipus reach a culmination when he can only defend himself against his former accuser, Creon, but sits in judgment himself upon the man who is guilty of his own sins. In Polynices, Oedipus confronts the projected image of his former self, and the merciless hatred which he pours forth is a reaction-formation which shows how far he has gone in the identification with his father. Oedipus as guardian of family morality has proceeded still further along the road of undoing his evil deeds. He has accepted completely the customs and interests of the father and, in Freudian terminology, has formed a superego.

Creon and Polynices provide two great tests of the pact between Theseus and Oedipus. He has refrained from the use of his infantile omnipotence in his dealings with Creon, and has renounced his former goals in his rejection of Polynices. The third and last manifestation of his loyalty to Theseus is in his complete surrender of individuality by death and transmission of his powers to the king. The ensuing drama of the passing of Oedipus is obviously a puberty rite in which father and son each renounce their death wishes against each other, and only one man emerges from the ceremony. The mysterious burial place and powers of Oedipus are in Theseus, who "alone has witnessed the secret passing of Oedipus" and who now addresses Antigone as "my daughter." Symbolically, Theseus, who represents the reason and culture of Athens, has mastered but still bears within himself the passions of a more primitive phase of development. Oedipus will still provide him with powers in critical times; where reason finds its limits, the driving force and prophetic insight derived from the forgotten oedipal experiences will still be of service.

On the stage at the end are Theseus and Antigone, and now the last meaning of the drama reveals itself. The puberty rites and the identification of father and son have terminated in a wedding ceremony. The setting at the entrance to the womb has been robbed of its terror by the purifying action of the drama. On the stage, throughout the play, at the opening of the grove has been the equestrian statue of Colonus, ancestor of the natives. The totemic significance of the figure has been borne out throughout the drama by repeated reference to the horses and olive trees for which Colonus is famous. These emblems of male and female fertility, animal and vegetable, flourish in this region, which had long been a sacred spot marked by many temples and altars. Colonus, "the white columns," derives its name from its setting on two white hills which guard the road into Athens. Poseidon, the god of horses, and Athena, goddess of olives, were supposed in Greek mythology to have contended for possession of the place. Theseus and Polynices both appear upon the stage after having made sacrifices to Poseidon. The wedding ceremony requires that the man shall be freed of his Oedipal guilt. It is the sanctified Theseus, not the youth of unbridled passions, who may be the bridegroom. And for Antigone, the site is a reminder of how the untamed female spirits here became the "gentle ones" and thrived and were honored in the form of the goddess of spinning and domestic arts. Antigone, "daughter" of Theseus, and Athena, daughter of Zeus, reincarnate the conditions of marriage in the patriarchy, where the women shall take the dependent role and yield to men the precedence they enjoyed when they were mothers.

III

Oedipus at Colonus is regarded as the last of Sophocles' plays, written when he was eighty-nine years old. There is a legend that the aged man was once haled before a tribunal by his son, Iophon, on the ground of mental incompetence and the need for a guardian for himself and his estates. Iophon, a tragedian like his father, is said to have been jealous of the preference which the old man showed for an illegitimate son. At a hearing before the court, Sophocles defended himself solely by reading portions of the *Oedipus at Colonus,* which he was then writing and was acquitted without further dispute. This tale, which is reported in Cicero's *De Senectute,* has been regarded as of doubtful validity, but shows a remarkable resemblance to the action of the play.

Certainly the picture of Oedipus finding peace and death at the end of his journey would serve as an appropriate valedictory from Sophocles and the imagery of resurrection and reunion with the ancestors would be in a fitting vein. The locale of the drama, Colonus, was actually the birthplace of Sophocles, and as such provides a natural "unity in place" for a play whose "unity in time and action" is a sweeping survey of life and death expressed in symbols which condense and integrate all the stages of existence. How aptly the oedipal theme may represent the problems of each phase of development: the infantile omnipotence, the latency period, puberty, and marriage rites; the characteristic perpetuation in the mature man through preference for the daughter and hostility to the son; and finally, even at the brink of the grave, in reincarnation and perpetuation in the successor.

Not that Oedipus would ordinarily come to mind as the prototype of Sophocles, who was known rather as "The Serene." His entire life seems to have been marked by success and serenity and he was famed for his pleasant disposition. The character in the play who really resembles the dramatist is Theseus, the temperate and cultured Athenian. Perhaps in the metaphor that Theseus "knew the final resting place of Oedipus" is to be found the hidden source of the drives and insight which found their sublimation in the tragic plays in which Sophocles gave play to his imagination. We are given pause by the casual comment placed in the mouth of Jocasta, that "many men dream that they have slept with their mothers." Plato quotes Sophocles as welcoming old age because it gave him freedom from the passions—a statement that does not accord with the traditional picture of serenity. Perhaps it is not without significance that it was the aging dramatist, presumably rejoicing at his liberation from physical drives, who created the *Oedipus Tyrannus* with the violent and tragic conflicts of the hero who is forced by fate to renounce his sexual life.

Finally, the political situation in Athens was certainly not without its influence on the Oedipus plays. *Oedipus Tyrannus* was written soon after Athens had begun her long and disastrous war with Sparta, and the theme of the play is primarily political: how has this evil befallen our state and what sins have our rulers committed that the gods should punish us in this way? *Oedipus at Colonus*, conceived during the final decline of Athens, invokes the spirit of her ancestral hero, the victorious Theseus, and annihilates with imprecations the foes of the city. His last play contains the parting message of the oracle: "Those who come to terms with Oedipus will triumph; the others will be doomed by their guilt."

6

The Oedipus Trilogy

MARK KANZER

[1950]

In Sophocles' drama, *Oedipus Tyrannus,* Freud found support for his concept that the drives to kill the father and commit incest with the mother constitute the basic repressed wishes of men (Freud, 1900). The name Oedipus thus became momentously linked with the complex which Freud found dominating the stage of phallic libidinal development. He cited the passage from the play which states the frequency of incestuous dreams among men, and compared the action of the tragedy to the processes of psychoanalytic investigation. In the "riddle of the Sphinx," which Oedipus solves, Freud saw the perpetual search of the child for sexual information, thereby elucidating this age-old enigma.

In the ample literature on the Oedipus complex, the trilogy of Sophocles has often been used to confirm or dispute Freud's discoveries. Among those who explored the Greek legend were Ferenczi (1912), Jung (1912), Reik (1920), Abraham (1923), and Róheim (1934, 1946). Rank (1912), after valuable initial researches in support of Freud,

---

Reprinted with permission from *Psychoanalytic Quarterly,* vol. 19, pp. 561–572.

evolved his own theories of psychodynamics and used them for a reinterpretation of the Oedipus dramas (1932). Fromm (1949) has discussed the plays in terms of their sociological background and has also arrived at conclusions different from Freud's.

A review of the psychoanalytic literature on the Oedipus trilogy was recently published by Mullahy (1948), but it is strangely incomplete, failing to take note of the writings of Ferenczi, Reik, Abraham, and Róheim on this subject. A reading of the plays also reveals much material that has not yet been evaluated psychoanalytically. The intrinsic interest of the dramas as psychological and sociological documents, and the special role which must be accorded them in the history of psychoanalysis, make them worthy of detailed study.

I

Oedipus Tyrannus, the first drama of the trilogy, presents the hero-king of the Thebans confronted with a plague which has afflicted his land. A messenger sent to consult the oracles to determine the cause and remedy of this catastrophe returns with word that the unknown criminal who killed the land's former king, Laius, must be discovered and brought to justice if the plague is to cease. It is in the search for this evildoer that the history of Oedipus' misdeeds comes to light. He had been unconsciously guilty of killing his father and wedding his mother. In so doing, he fulfilled prophecies made before his birth which he and his parents vainly sought to avert, a detail which corresponds to the fact that each man is destined to struggle against his oedipal strivings. At the end of the drama, Jocasta, the queen and mother-wife, hangs herself, whereupon Oedipus tears out his own eyes (interpreted by Ferenczi as symbolic castration).

In the course of the developments which lead to this tragic climax, we learn that Oedipus has won the throne and the widowed queen of Laius by solving the riddle of the Sphinx. This monstrous creature, whose upper portion is that of a human female and whose lower parts are those of a lioness, sat upon a rock and questioned all passersby, slaying those who could not solve the problem she propounded. Only Oedipus understood the riddle. According to the version of the legend used by Sophocles, he then slew her; according to another, she threw herself in mortification into the sea and was killed.

The riddle of the Sphinx is evidently an allegory of the problems presented by female sexuality. A full-breasted woman above, a lioness below, she combines the beloved and dreaded aspects of femininity which the boy must reconcile in order to achieve genital potency. Freud (1905) emphasized the relationship of the Sphinx to the mysteries of childbirth. The legend of Oedipus and the monster also belongs among many others—Perseus and the Gorgon, Theseus and the Minotaur, the countless legends of the dragon-slayers—which symbolically depict the dangers that the young man must overcome before he may attain his sexual partner. In these menacing antagonists, components of both parents may be detected; the father, who would keep the son from women, and the mother, whose very fulfillment of sexual desires would bring disaster. The Sphinx is such a combined parental figure. Jung saw in her the "terrible mother"; Rank, Reik, and Róheim have described her variously as the phallic mother, the symbol of the parents in intercourse, or as a disguised homosexual representation of the father. In the riddle which she propounds—"What has first four legs, then two, then three?" (the correct answer being "Man" during the stages of maturation)—there are apparent allusions to the appearance of the limbs during intercourse, to the additional "limb" which distinguishes the male, and perhaps also to pregnancy: "that which is first two becomes three."

It is our conclusion, from a study of the play, that the precipitating cause, the "catastrophe which threatens the land" and leads to the undoing of Oedipus, is the pregnancy of the mother-wife, Jocasta. The birth of a son renews the father's oedipal conflicts. The drama states that a plague "blights the fruitful blossoms of the land" and causes the women to suffer "barren pangs" (all quotations from Sophocles are from the edition of Oates and O'Neill, 1938). The symbols of birth are represented through opposites—"sterile blossoms," "barren pangs," maternal death—the hostile and negating images corresponding to a neurotic denial of the actual event. Such reactions are appropriate to the child in the oedipal phase, anticipating the birth of a sibling, or to the expectant father who has not resolved his infantile fixations.

If this surmise as to Jocasta's impending delivery is correct, then we find that the Sphinx has reemerged from the repressed with the old riddle in a new form; for if the *Oedipus Tyrannus* exposes clearly the parricidal drives of the son, it deals no less unambiguously with the counteroedipal determination of the father to rid himself of the rival son. Laius had sought as unsuccessfully to evade the foreordained parricide as had Oedipus, and had tried to kill his child in infancy. The great cycle of the generations thus completes itself with Oedipus as an expectant father who is destined to seek the destruction of the fruit of his wife's womb. The mature man is able to cope with paternity, but not the neurotic whose wife is also his mother. Oedipus never worked through the relationship to his father, which is necessary for adjustment to reality. He never accepted him, never identified with him, as is necessary in superego formation, but merely encompassed his death. There was no identification with the parental role; in the hero the child was preserved unchanged. Oedipus, the arrogant, quick-tempered, arbitrary monarch accustomed to homage, incorporates the infantile fantasy of omnipotence.

Such immaturity must be reflected in the sexual relationship to the mother, and as to the details, a psychoanalytic interpretation of the play leaves little doubt. This mother is assuredly the full-breasted Sphinx, bestial and terrifying below the waist. The chorus refers to her as "the maiden with crooked talons who sang darkly," thus placing her in the category of the phallic mother, the woman with the dentate vagina, and all the other terrifying images of the castrating female. The "dark songs" are a link to the Sirens, dangerous seducers of men. In the relationship of Oedipus to Jocasta, there is no simple erotic drive, as Freud originally postulated, but also the anxieties and hostilities aroused by the preoedipal "bad mother" (Klein, 1928). In the great climax of the play, the sex act is depicted symbolically when the king rushes into the room where the body of the mother is hanging (the womb), seizes the golden brooches from her garments, and repeatedly and passionately stabs his eyeballs, from which the blood flows "not with a few slow drops, but all at once in a dark shower." In this fantasy of coitus and orgasm, the sexual act is depicted as a sadistic and castrating attack from the maternal phallus. The brooches of Jocasta are another version of the talons of the Sphinx; in the earlier and more successful encounter, Oedipus had taken the active role and stabbed her with his sword.

The action of the play, as a whole, is a repetitious depiction of the duel between Oedipus and the Sphinx. In the presence of her true form, the mother, he again carries on a remorseless inquiry into his origin. The tormented queen, foreseeing the disastrous outcome, seeks vainly to divert him. Oedipus takes a peculiarly stubborn and obtuse attitude until the riddle of his birth is solved; then Jocasta kills herself, as had the Sphinx. The core of this mighty tragedy is the determined boy plying his reluctant mother with embarrassing questions.

The legend of the Sphinx casting herself into the sea is another familiar symbol of childbirth, a condensation of sexual surrender and pregnancy. Oedipus, emerging from the death room of the mother, blind, wailing, and helpless, presents an unmistakable representation of rebirth. The religions of the East are pervaded with the fantasy of the mystic identity of father and son. It is the father who enters the womb (funeral chamber) and the son who emerges in a repetitive cycle, as in the advent and the wane of the seasons. In this fantasy of rebirth, the neurotic father finds satisfaction. He averts the threat of the new rival by identifying with him and regressing to infancy. Oedipus, who took his father's place, will now take his son's. The past repeats itself when he is cast from the city by his uncle Creon, just as his father Laius had expelled him after he was born. His only companion and comforter in exile is to be his daughter, Antigone, who will take the place of the mother.

II

The two remaining plays of the Oedipus trilogy seek a more satisfactory solution to the problem of man's relationship to parents and children. Success can be achieved, we know, only by maturation of the ego, which devolves on the formation of the superego and abandonment of infantile fantasies of omnipotence.

The third drama of the trilogy, *Antigone,* was the first to be written, but belongs psychologically in an intermediate position. It deals with the civil war between Polynices and Eteocles, sons of

Oedipus, after his death, in which both lose their lives. Antigone, their sister, and Creon, maternal uncle and king, are depicted as at odds over the disposition of the corpse of Polynices, which lies outside the city. Here Creon decrees that the body of the rebel shall remain unburied and unsanctified. Antigone defies these orders and inters her brother with her own hands. This is clearly a continuance of the oedipal theme. Polynices, as Oedipus, finds no forgiveness from Creon, the father substitute. Antigone displaces her loyalty from her father to her brother.

Antigone is sentenced to death by Creon. She is to be shut up in a stone vault with a small quantity of food. After this judgment has been executed, Creon, disturbed by the pleas and resentment of his son Haemon, who was betrothed to Antigone, and by the warnings of the seer Teiresias, is moved to release his niece. When the tomb is opened, it is found that Antigone has hanged herself. Haemon, who had secretly found his way to her side, slays himself with his own sword. Creon, grief-stricken and penitent, emerges only to find that his wife, Eurydice, has killed herself upon hearing of the death of her son.

The tragic ending of Antigone and Haemon clearly repeats, almost in exact detail, the catastrophe of Jocasta and Oedipus. The Sphinx is thus thrice destroyed. The slayer now is Creon, a new guise for Oedipus. If in the first play the husband-king solves his conflict by identification with the newborn babe, in the second he achieves the alternate solution of identification with the father. He is now Creon, the banisher and destroyer of infants. He emerges from the tomb, reborn, while the sons—Haemon, Polynices, and Eteocles—have all been destroyed.

Oedipus and Creon are complementary: the parricidal son, and the castrating father. Oedipus was rejected at birth by his father, Laius, and in his partial identification (superego) with him can become only a rejecting father. This is the problem inherent in the *Antigone*. It corresponds to a stage in the normal development of the superego in which the boy experiences hostility toward his father, and in retaliation, through projection of his own aggression, fears castration by the father. It is the force of this castration anxiety, effecting the resolution of the Oedipus complex, which is the unconscious content of the *Antigone*. The boy is faithful to his mother, conspiring with her against his father; but Creon triumphs over Antigone. The son, ashamed of his mother's weakness, thenceforth transfers allegiance to his father. The third play of the trilogy, *Oedipus at Colonus,* is the consummation of this process. The relationship between son and father is not one-sidedly hostile, but has the elements of sympathy and love which are indispensable components of the superego.

This theme may be traced in the action of *Oedipus at Colonus.* The now aged hero, after years of bitter exile, arrives at Colonus, where he is kindly received by the enlightened ruler, Theseus, with whose aid he defeats Creon's efforts to separate him from Antigone. Oedipus dies mysteriously, leaving his blessing and the custody of Antigone to his benevolent protector, Theseus, who inherits some strange and undescribed power from the grave of the hero. This unknown resting place of Oedipus is within Theseus himself (Kanzer, 1948). He is the good father who shelters the son, and it is in this guise that Oedipus is finally presented: the superego, "which is the heir of the Oedipus complex" (Freud, 1923), has completed its development in him. The tired exile has given up his battle against the taboos of mankind; his wounds and defeats have taught him to bow to the reality principle; he cannot stand alone but must accept his status as son, brother, and father among men. In the character of Theseus he discovers the rewards for surrendering the infantile illusion of omnipotence. A king again, he is now a wise and benevolent ruler. The "custody" of Antigone which he achieves is the possession of the woman he loves, but without violating the social taboos which protect the wife and her children from the unrestrained passions of the Sphinx-killer.

Each play of the trilogy resolves a conflict by the symbolic rebirth of the hero. Oedipus, Creon, and Theseus are the successive avatars the maturing man must assume in his persisting endeavors to answer the riddle of the Sphinx.

III

The Oedipus trilogy is a product of Athenian culture, conceived in the mind of one of its most typical representatives, the dramatist

Sophocles. The religious and political traditions of the city bore witness to a profound psychological conflict over adherence to male or female divinities. Studies of mythology and custom suggest that the goddesses had been the objects of ancient worship and had gradually been supplanted by male deities (Engle, 1942). Typical were the legends about Athena, patroness of the great city, who was the daughter of Zeus, ruler of the gods, and had sprung fully grown from his forehead—symbolizing the intellectual superiority of the male. Her shield bore the head of Medusa, the Gorgon, whose terrible visage turned men to stone. Originally warlike, Athena became patroness of the domestic arts, of spinning and the cultivation of the olive, and was also a symbol of wisdom. The Gorgon-Athena, like the Sphinx, represented the destructive potentialities to the male of female sexuality, but after the triumph of men she was shorn of her warlike attributes. The head of Medusa (Freud, 1933) on her shield is a remnant of her former power which is left to her, and is also the basis for the new order of things: it is the incest taboo which must be respected if the dangerous Sphinx is not to be reawakened in all her dreaded might.

Not only is the Oedipus legend a version of this revolution in the relations between men and women, but also such typical Athenian legends as the conquest of the Amazonian warriors by Theseus, who took their queen Hyppolita in marriage, and the tale of Orestes, the matricide, who received protection in the city after pursuit by the avenging female goddesses, the Furies. In the time of Sophocles, these myths appealed greatly to the imagination of the people and provided themes for many great plays and works of art of the age. It is noteworthy that in the dramas of Sophocles and his great contemporaries, Aeschylus and Euripides, these legends were used for probing into the moral relationships among men and women within the family and the state. The *Antigone,* for example, explores the conflict between love of family (Antigone), and duty to the government (Creon). Primary allegiance to the family is doomed with the death of Antigone; however, the ruler also learns that he must not be harsh and autocratic, and suffers personal injury when he fails to respect the ties within the family.

Bachofen (1861), reviewing the Greek myths, concluded that

earlier matriarchal forms of society had existed and then yielded to masculine rule. This hypothesis seems reasonable but has little actual historical evidence. Such myths could also be accounted for on the basis of the experiences of each generation of men in giving up the ways of childhood, dominated by the relationship to the mother, and assuming the inevitable duties and responsibilities of adult masculinity. A more serious objection, however, must be made to a second hypothesis of Bachofen. He believed that in the matriarchy, maternal love and natural ties prevailed, while in the patriarchy there was stern authoritarianism. Evolution from matriarchy to patriarchy was brought about not by economic or military necessity, but by the triumph of masculine reasoning over feminine feeling. This theory, which bears the impress of the author's mid-Victorian background, is not substantiated by modern sociological observations (Zilboorg, 1944). In contrast may be cited the Trobriand matriarchy, where the men maintain friendly relations with each other but show fear and hostility toward women; or the polyandrous Marquesans (Kardiner, 1939) whose dread of wild female spirits suggests the terror in which the Furies, Gorgons, and similar ferocious goddesses were held in Greece.

It is noteworthy that two psychological studies of the Oedipus trilogy (Rank, 1932; Fromm, 1949) which reproach Freud for lack of sociological orientation lean heavily on the antiquated views of Bachofen. Rank, developing his thesis from his conception of the central significance of the birth trauma, sees in Oedipus the struggle of men to retain their individuality in the face of the demands made upon them to submit to the authority of the state. The individualist finds difficulty in accepting the role of father or son. This conflict was intensified during the Hellenic period of Greek history, when patriarchy flourished. The incestuous element in the Oedipus myth is explained not as a result of sexual attraction but as an attempt to insure personal immortality by achieving psychological rebirth from the mother, thereby eliminating both father and son. Psychoanalytic interpretation arrives at some of the same conclusions but sees the struggle of the ego for mastery (Rank's goal of individualism) as inherently linked with infantile libidinal and aggressive aims.

Fromm's "sociological" approach to the Oedipus complex (1949) is illustrated by his solution of the riddle of the Sphinx. The question about the number of limbs, he maintains, has no significance except to elicit the answer, "Man." In this response, he sees the implication that the solution to the riddle of man is himself and that in the matriarchal state, represented by Oedipus, the dignity of man is more assured than in the patriarchy. This questionable assumption is rendered even more dubious by the fact that the Sphinx herself has a better claim to representing the matriarchy than has Oedipus (Reik, 1920) who in overthrowing her begins the process of patriarchal dominance. The emotional and dramatic values of the plays most clearly show the limitations of Fromm's concept. It is difficult to believe that in the life and death encounter between Oedipus and the Sphinx the monster was moved to throw herself into the sea by an exposition on sociology.

Psychological knowledge that reveals to us, as do the constructions of Freud, the intimate and hidden views of men of Athens two thousand years ago on childbirth, sexual intercourse, and family relationships, obviously provides tools of great value. What sidelights are thrown on the intangibles of history when we learn that phrases of Sophocles' Creon seem to have been borrowed from Pericles, contemporary ruler of Athens (*Encyclopaedia Brittanica*), or that the crisis which precipitated the downfall of Oedipus—the plague that afflicted his state—presumably mirrored the anxieties and self-searchings of the Athenians after the outbreak of the disastrous Peloponnesian War! Social forces impinge upon and are transmuted into the idiom of individual experience. It is the unique contribution which psychoanalysis makes to sociology that it can illuminate and decipher this process. In this work of interpretation, the social elements are crystallized from the psychological, just as the events of the day emerge in new significance from the analysis of the dream. A valid psychology is the indispensable prerequisite for any "sociological approach" to such great human documents as the Oedipus trilogy.

REFERENCES

Abraham, K. (1923), Zwei Beiträge zur Symbolforschung. *Imago,* 9:122–126.
Bachofen, J. J. (1861), *Mutterrecht und Urreligion.* Leipzig: Alfred Kroener, 1926.
Engle, B. S. (1942), The Amazons in Ancient Greece. *Psychoanal. Quart.,* 11:512–554.

Ferenczi, S. (1912), The symbolic representation of the pleasure and reality principles in the Oedipus myth. In: *Sex in Psycho-analysis.* New York: Basic Books, 1950, pp. 253-269. Chapter 2, this volume.

Freud, S. (1900), The Interpretation of Dreams. *Standard Edition,* 4/5. London: Hogarth Press, 1953.

_______ (1905), Three essays on the theory of sexuality. *Standard Edition,* 7:130-243. London: Hogarth Press, 1953.

_______ (1923), The ego and the id. *Standard Edition,* 19:12-66. London: Hogarth Press, 1961.

_______ (1933), New introductory lectures. *Standard Edition,* 22:5-182. London: Hogarth Press, 1964.

Fromm, E. (1949), The Oedipus complex and the Oedipus myth. In: *The Family: Its Function and Destiny.* Vol. V, The Science of Culture Series, ed. R. N. Anshen. New York: Harper, pp. 334-358.

Jung, C. G. (1912), *Wandlungen und Symbole der Libido.* Vienna: Deuticke.

Kanzer, M. (1948), The "passing of the Oedipus complex" in Greek drama. *Internat. J. Psycho-Anal.,* 29:131-134. Chapter 5, this volume.

Kardiner, A. (1939), *The Individual and His Society.* New York: Columbia University Press.

Klein, M. (1928), Early stages of the Oedipus conflict. In: *Love, Guilt and Reparation and Other Works: 1921-1945.* New York: Delacorte Press/Seymour Lawrence, 1975, pp. 186-198.

Mullahy, P. (1948), *Oedipus—Myth and Complex.* New York: Hermitage Press.

Oates, W. J., & O'Neill, E., Eds. (1938), *The Complete Greek Drama.* New York: Random House.

Rank, O. (1912), *Das Inzestmotiv in Dichtung und Sage.* Leipzig: Deuticke.

_______ (1932), *Modern Education.* New York: Knopf.

Reik, T. (1920), Oedipus and the Sphinx. In: *Dogma and Compulsion: Psychoanalytic Studies of Religion and Myth.* New York: International Universities Press, 1951, pp. 289-332. Chapter 3, this volume.

Röheim, G. (1934), *The Riddle of the Sphinx.* London: Hogarth Press.

_______ (1946), Teiresias and other seers. *Psychoanal. Rev.,* 33:314-334.

Encyclopaedia Britannica. Sophocles. 11th ed. Vol. 25/26.

Zilboorg, G. (1944), Masculine and feminine. *Psychiat.,* 7:257-296.

7

Why Oedipus Killed Laius: A Note on the Complementary Oedipus Complex in Greek Drama

GEORGE DEVEREUX

[1953]

It is striking to note that psychoanalytic theory pays exceedingly little attention to certain complexes which, in a very genuine sense, complement the Oedipus complex. In particular, even though occasionally reference is made to the tender and even to the erotic components of what may be called the Laius complex and the Jocasta complex (Ferenczi, 1949), the sadistic (and homosexual) components of these complexes are, generally speaking, ignored by psychoanalytic writers.[1] Indeed, there exist certain Greek traditions regarding Laius

[1]Offhand, the writer can think of only one author who devoted considerable attention to the Jocasta complex, and that author was not a psychoanalyst but an anthropologist (Raglan, 1933).

Reprinted with permission from *International Journal of Psycho-Analysis*, vol. 34, pp. 132–141.

which suggest that the complementary oedipus complex, even in its homosexual and sadistic phases, was close enough to the threshold of consciousness to receive at least a mythological expression. Yet even Rank (1912), who specifically discusses these traditions, fails to stress that they provide us with a highly specific and "historical," rather than only a general and "paleopsychological," explanation of Laius' behavior toward the infant Oedipus.

It must be assumed that this continued scotomization of the complementary Oedipus complex is rooted in the adult's deep-seated need to place all responsibility for the Oedipus complex upon the child, and to ignore, whenever possible, certain parental attitudes which actually stimulate the infant's oedipal tendencies. This deliberate scotoma is probably rooted in the authoritarian atmosphere characteristic of nineteenth-century family life. This interpretation is supported by the history of Freud's thoughts on the subject of the etiology of hysteria. At first, Freud accepted as genuine the seduction stories narrated by his patients. When he discovered that these tales merely expressed certain fantasies and wishes, he made the necessary revisions in his theory of the etiology of the neuroses. Unfortunately, from that time onward he also began to ignore fairly consistently the very genuinely seductive behavior of parents,[2] perhaps because the concept of the Laius and Jocasta complexes was even more ego-dystonic and culturally objectionable than was the theory of the Oedipus complex, which, in a sense, merely confirmed the nineteenth-century adult's low opinion of children in general.[3] In certain later writers the scotomization of the Laius and Jocasta complexes appears to have led to the need to develop an elaborate, and not overconvincing, theory of a phylogenetically determined infantile fantasy life. This theory predicates that, regardless of how loving and humane the

[2]This development led to a shift toward greater conservativeness in matters pertaining to the ethics of sexual acts, and also to the theory of the death instinct, or primary self-aggression, which psychoanalytically well-informed theologians have sometimes compared to the doctrine of original sin.

[3]This outlook—represented, e.g., by such attitudes as "spare the rod and spoil the child," or "children should be seen and not heard"—had as its complement the conception of the "angelic" nature of children. Similar institutionalizations of ambivalence toward children also occur in primitive society (Devereux, 1941).

father may be, the infant will nonetheless view him primarily as a monster, because of instinctually determined and phylogenetically anchored fantasies of its own.

The trend away from the recognition of the seductive behavior of adults, which was bolstered not only by Freud's genius and prestige, but also by social pressure and by the analyst's own need to scotomize this anxiety-arousing idea, was too strong to be reversed even by the findings of Ferenczi (1949) and of certain of his students, who stressed that, presumably by means of the "dialogue of the unconscious," children recognize the true instinctual roots of the tenderness which adults display toward them (Rotter, 1933).

Actually, it is a matter of common experience that in sexual relations between adults and children—which are far less uncommon than one would like to believe—it is usually the adult who takes the initiative. Only in rare instances are the children the actual seducers (Devereux, 1950).

The great popularity of Sophocles' Oedipus trilogy also tends to support this interpretation. It must be assumed that many members of the Greek audience found the play of absorbing interest precisely because they successfully—though perhaps unconsciously—identified themselves with the problems of certain major characters.[4] Alice Balint's analysis of the irrational and primitive aspects of the mother-child relationship (1939) also lends plausibility to our inference that the women in Sophocles' audience must have had at least an unconscious empathy with Jocasta's problems. By extension, the male audience must likewise have felt a certain carefully repressed kinship with Laius, who, as we propose to show, was not a mere puppet of Fate, but a psychologically consistent and plausible person, whose character structure provides us with the true explanation of his destiny.

[4]Licht (1932) records that a rather cynical and hedonistic defense of incest—in terms of the thesis that whatever gives pleasure is good—occurring in one of Euripides' plays was hooted by the audience so violently that the line had to be changed to an admission that whatever is dishonorable *is* dishonorable, regardless of how pleasant it may be. Of course, in this instance, the incest enacted on the stage was that of a brother and a sister, which was both psychologically and economically unacceptable to parents in the audience.

The Character of Laius

Laius' early life is vaguely reminiscent of that of Oedipus. King Labdacus of Thebes died when Laius was but a year old. A nobleman named Lykos (Wolf) usurped the throne, and grievously wronged his niece Antiope. Later on, Antiope's sons conquered Thebes, slew Lykos, and banished Laius, who only regained his throne after the death of Antiope's sons. At the time of his restoration to the throne Laius was already burdened with a curse, which he had brought on himself through an act of homosexual rape. It was this curse which eventually culminated in the Oedipus tragedy (Rose, 1928).

Numerous Greek sources and fragments[5] reveal that Laius was deemed to have been the inventor of pederasty. In his early manhood, long before he married Jocasta and fathered Oedipus, Laius fell violently in love with Chrysippus, son of King Pelops. Instead of courting and winning the handsome youth, in a manner which the latter-day Greeks would have deemed proper, he chose to kidnap him during the sacred Nemean games, without seeking to obtain the consent of King Pelops, which, Licht (1932) intimates, would probably have been forthcoming. The enraged Pelops therefore laid upon Laius the curse that his own son should slay him and then marry his own mother. According to a later version it is the Delphic oracle which informs Laius of Zeus' decision that Laius' son would kill him in retribution for the rape of Chrysippus. This curse seems to suggest that the Greek mind linked Oedipus with Chrysippus—an inference which is further substantiated by still another version of this myth, according to which Hera was so greatly angered by the rape of Chrysippus that she sent the Sphinx to ravage Thebes, in order to punish the Thebans for having tolerated Laius' homosexual escapade (Rank, 1912). The *Oidipodeia* is even more specific in conjoining the fates of Chrysippus and of Oedipus. According to this epic, Oedipus was exposed as a propitiatory sacrifice, in order to appease Hera's wrath over the Chrysippus incident (Rank, 1912). In other words, Hera

[5]According to Licht (1932), these sources include: the epic *Oidipodeia,* Praxilla, a fragmentary play by Euripides, a fragmentary play by Aeschylus, and some other fragments.

caused Laius to lose not only his youthful bedfellow Chrysippus, but also his son Oedipus.[6]

In this context it cannot be stressed strongly enough that after the imposition of the curse, and especially after the birth of Oedipus, almost nothing further is heard of Chrysippus, until the moment of the fatal encounter between Laius and Oedipus. At that point several sources once more bring Chrysippus into the plot, it being alleged that Laius and Oedipus fought each other because they were rivals for the love of Chrysippus. Yet, significantly, Chrysippus himself was not present during this combat, while, according to some sources, Jocasta did witness the death of Laius. Be that as it may, various versions of this myth clearly represent this combat as a homosexually motivated encounter. After this episode Chrysippus once more disappears, for all practical purposes, from the rest of the Oedipus myth. The overall impression created by these various accounts is that, psychologically at least, Chrysippus is, in a sense, the representative of Oedipus' own passive homosexual characteristics, which were brought into being, or were at least aroused, by Laius' aggressive and homosexual impulses toward his son.

Regardless of whether this curse was uttered by Pelops in person, or by the Delphic oracle, it made a considerable impression upon even so impulsive a man as Laius. According to sources cited by Rank (1912), Laius (self-castratively) refrained from cohabiting with Jocasta for several years, in order to avoid the risk of procreating a son.[7] However, on a certain occasion, when Laius was either drunk, or else unable to resist Jocasta's seductiveness, he succumbed to temptation and knowingly procreated a son, even though he well knew what

[6]Hera's anger over this incident is, in itself, a problem of some magnitude, which can only be partially understood in terms of her position as the custodian of family life and in terms of her own experiences with Zeus' various heterosexual and homosexual loves. Her choice of the Sphinx—whom Rank (1912) views as a phallic woman—as the special instrument of her further retribution is equally perplexing. Unfortunately, lack of space prevents us from discussing this matter in detail, and forces us to content ourselves with pointing out the existence of this interesting mythological problem.

[7]Some aspects of the problem of chastity in marriage were discussed in another essay (Devereux, 1951b) in connection with certain ancient Indian traditions regarding two kings, each of whom killed a father figure at the very moment when the latter was engaging in marital relations.

calamities the birth of an heir would entail for him. Thus, after a period of self-restraint, Laius' self-destructive impulsiveness once more got out of hand, only to be followed by another futile (self-castrative) attempt to ward off the consequences of his second hasty sexual act by exposing the infant Oedipus.

Laius appears to have retained throughout life a propensity for unconsidered violence. This is clearly shown by his wanton aggression against the wayfarer Oedipus, which caused the latter to slay him.

This, however, is not the whole story. Indeed, there exist several versions of this incident, the best known being the story that Oedipus and Laius quarreled over the right to *pass first* over a certain *narrow road.* This incident appears to be a somewhat bowdlerized and symbolic version of certain far more explicit accounts of Laius' death. Rank quotes a series of sources, according to which Oedipus and Laius did not quarrel over even so symbolic a trifle as the right to pass first over a narrow road. Indeed, Praxilla affirms that not only Laius but Oedipus himself was also in love with Chrysippus, and the scholium to Euripides' *Phoenissae* is even more explicit, in that it states outright that Oedipus killed Laius in a quarrel over Chrysippus.

In apparent contradiction to this homosexual motive, various sources quoted by Rank allege that the combat took place in the presence of Jocasta. For example, Nikolaos Damaskenos stated that incest between Oedipus and his mother occurred immediately after the combat while still another source stresses that Oedipus *knowingly* raped his mother. Furthermore, the *Oidipodeia* specifies that, after killing Laius, Oedipus deprived him both of his sword (castration) and of his belt. The latter deed suggests the feminization of Laius, since, in ancient Greece, the undoing of a woman's belt was a preliminary to intercourse. If this inference is correct, Oedipus did more than kill his father and marry his mother, in token of his heterosexual maturity. He also turned the tables on his homosexual father, by castrating (sword) and feminizing him (belt), as he himself had once been castrated and feminized (pierced ankles) by Laius. If this be so, then cohabitation with Jocasta was not only cohabitation with the mother as a woman, but also with the mother as the representative of the now feminized homosexual paternal ogre.

This latter inference gives added meaning to Gruppe's opinion

(1897-1906), cited by Rank, that Oedipus originally bested the Sphinx—who, according to Rank, is a phallic mother—in physical combat.[8] If Rank's inference is correct, then Oedipus' triumph over the phallic mother—whose phallus, needless to say, was derived from the father—represents both a heterosexual and a homosexual victory and gesture of triumph. Since this latter meaning of incest with the phallic mother—i.e., the combination of heterosexual relations with the mother and of symbolic active homosexual relations with the father—is a relatively novel inference, it is offered here only as a tentative conclusion, and as a problem which may well deserve further study.[9]

The important point in all these considerations is the fact that our sources emphasize primarily the homosexual element in the causation of Laius' death, and only bring in the incest with Jocasta more or less as an afterthought, e.g., as the link which couples the tragedy of Laius with the latter fate of Oedipus Rex. Thus, it may not be too farfetched to suggest that cohabitation with Jocasta should be viewed primarily as a homosexual and only epiphenomenally as a heterosexual act, Oedipus' true love-hate object being the now feminized homosexual ogre Laius.

In this context it is important to remember that Greek mythology, which, after all, is our real authority in regard to the problem of Oedipus, did not derive Oedipus' hostility to Laius from heterosexual, but from homosexual sources. Indeed, Oedipus is not even described as having been particularly fond of his foster mother, Queen Merope, while all accounts of his early life emphasize his devotion to his savior and foster father, King Polybus, who apparently represented the "good father" in Oedipus' unconscious. What we do find in Greek

[8]If the Sphinx was killed in a physical combat, then its death was, in a sense, similar to the death which Laius brought upon himself. If the Sphinx killed itself after Oedipus guessed its riddle, the suicide of the Sphinx approximates to that of Jocasta. These seemingly divergent versions of the same plot-element therefore actually converge and further support the thesis that Jocasta, when 'raped' by Oedipus, represented both herself and the castrated and feminized Laius.

[9]A Hungarian military joke specifically describes an incident in which adultery with the wife is at the same time represented as anal cohabitation with the woman's husband, thus further substantiating well-known theories of paranoid jealousy.

accounts is an explanation of Oedipus' aggression against Laius in terms of Laius' character structure: his propensity for homosexual rape, and for unconsidered, injudicious violence and overbearingness ("hybris").[10] Indeed, Laius is presented to us as a pederastic ogre—as a homosexual rapist, rather than as a seducer—even before Oedipus was born. Licht (1932) also adds that when Laius married Jocasta he was deprived both of his real love-object Chrysippus, and of the hope of an heir. After the birth of Oedipus, Laius made himself guilty first of attempted infanticide and, later on, of an attempt to kill his adult son in the course of a quarrel which the overbearing old man had wantonly started with the peaceful wayfarer Oedipus.

Be that as it may, Laius' character, as depicted by Greek mythology and tragedy alike, is not an attractive one, and corresponds rather closely to what clinical psychoanalysis found to be the small boy's conception of his father. Indeed, unlike many other tragic figures of Greek drama, Laius is not presented to us as a good man caught in the toils of fate, and having "an appointment in Samarra" with death, but as a violator of good manners, which the Greeks deemed more important than good morals. In brief—and despite Oedipus' possible rivalry with Laius for the love of Chrysippus—Laius' death was not caused primarily by Oedipus' own incestuous impulses, but by Laius' character, which included both "hybris" and a tendency toward homosexual and other violence.

Despite the rivalry over Chrysippus, it is not asserted that Oedipus himself was not partially motivated also by the violent impulses connected with the normal Oedipus complex. We simply suggest that, according to Greek data, Oedipus' murderous and incestuous wishes were neither purely heterosexual nor truly spontaneous ones, but were induced by the behavior of his father Laius. In fact, it may even be tentatively suggested that Oedipus' partly heterosexual attraction to Jocasta was to a certain extent motivated by his desire both to escape and to gratify indirectly his own sadomasochistic and homosexual

[10]Only rarely—and then primarily in those versions which attribute Laius' death to a quarrel over the right of way—is there any mention of Oedipus' own proneness to violence, which, it is specified, *is similar to that of Laius.* In other words, even where impulsiveness is attributed also to Oedipus, this character trait of the son is derived from, or correlated with, the father's character structure.

wishes, which had been stimulated by his father's behavior. At the same time, Oedipus' marriage to Jocasta may also represent an unconscious attempt at restitution, since he took Laius' place at Jocasta's side,[11] and provided further heirs for the kingdom of Thebes.[12] Conversely, it may be permissible to suggest, at least tentatively, that aggressively homosexual paternal attitudes toward the child may represent—in part at least—a defense against murderous impulses elicited by the sight of the nursing infant, whose very existence interferes with the formerly close relationship between husband and wife.[13]

Our central thesis—that Oedipus' own impulses were stimulated by the behavior of his father—appears at least plausible in the light of the preceding considerations. However, in order to render this thesis even more convincing, and worthy of being taken into account in actual clinical work, it is necessary to examine rather closely the real, albeit unconscious, causes of King Pelops' extreme wrath, and the motives which impelled him to utter *precisely* and *specifically* the rather unusual curse that Laius' son should kill his father and wed his mother.

Pelops, Oedipus, and Electra

According to Licht (1932), Pelops' wrath over the abduction of Chrysippus should be understood as follows:

> The father (Pelops) is not driven to the curse because Laius loved a boy and was intimate with him, consequently not by the "unnatural nature" of his passion . . . but simply and solely because Laius steals the boy, and abducts him against his father's wish: it is not the perverted direction of the impulse that makes Laius guilty, but the violence employed by him. . . . Laius

[11]In certain primitive societies the murderer is adopted as a replacement for the murdered kinsman (Devereux, 1942).

[12]The providing of heirs is analyzed elsewhere (Devereux, 1951b).

[13]In many primitive societies cohabitation is prohibited during the long period of lactation. This situation, as it pertains, e.g., to the Sioux Indians, has been discussed elsewhere (Devereux, 1951c).

> becomes a curse-laden man in consequence of an offence against conventional form; he thought he might be allowed to abduct the boy, when he could have sued for the beautiful prize freely and openly.

In other words, Laius is guilty of a breach of manners, rather than of morals, in a context—pedophilia—in which the Greeks manifested that "poetic chivalrousness" which the knights of the feudal period manifested toward women. Laius' behavior toward Chrysippus is, thus, an unusually clear-cut expression of "hybris"—excess and overbearingness—which, in Greek tragedy, is the cause of man's ultimate downfall.

These considerations refer, however, only to the conscious causes of Pelops' reaction to the rape of Chrysippus. On a deeper level the psychological problem of Pelops' wrath has an even more significant connection with the fate of Laius and of Oedipus.

More even than Oedipus himself, Pelops was familiar with the potential cruelty of fathers and father figures. Pelops was the son of the evil King Tantalus, who, from sheer overbearingness, wished to test the omniscience of the immortals, whom he presumed to invite to his palace as his guests. He therefore had young Pelops slain and served to the immortals as the *pièce de résistance* of the feast he gave in their honor. Fortunately the gods discovered the deed, but not before Demeter, still distressed by Persephone's loss, had absentmindedly eaten the dismembered Pelops' shoulder. At the request of the immortals, either Rhea or else Clotho, one of the Fates, cast Pelops' remains into a cauldron, from which he reemerged alive, but with an ivory shoulder. The cannibalistic impulses of Tantalus are further underscored by the fact that his eternal punishment in Hades consisted in being "tantalized" by food and drink, and in his being in constant fear of death. Despite these evil deeds, Greek legends stress that Pelops honored his deceased cannibalistic father devoutly.

If we take into account only the best-known version of the Feast of Tantalus, it is hard to understand why Pelops should display such filial piety toward his brutally egotistical and cannibalistic father. Indeed, such devotion would be understandable only if, by some twist in his unconscious fantasy life, Pelops managed to construe this cannibalistic act as a token of love. This startling inference is strikingly confirmed by Pindar's First Olympian Ode, which Bunker (1952) interprets *primarily* as a bowdlerized version of the original cannibalistic feast. According to Pindar, the Feast of Tantalus never took place at all. He assures us, instead, that the story of that feast was hollow gossip, and that, in reality, Poseidon had abducted Pelops, with whom he was in love, and had taken him to the abode of the immortals, just as Zeus brought Ganymede to Olympus. On the basis of the contrast between the original myth of the Feast of Tantalus and Pindar's version of Pelops' disappearance, Bunker concludes that the Feast of Tantalus is a disguised description of initiation ceremonies.

However, Pindar's version is not *simply* a bowdlerization of a cannibalistic myth which originated in ruder days. Rather does it enunciate the self-same theme as the original myth, but in a language and by means of symbols which pertain to a *different stage* of psychosexual development. Specifically, the fate of Pelops which, in the earlier version, is told in the language of the oral stage, and represents the anxiety-laden and yet pleasurable fantasy experience of being devoured, appears in Pindar's version as an experience pertaining to the second phase of the Oedipus complex, and is presented to us as erotized submission to a divine homosexual father figure, Poseidon.

When seen in this light, Pelops' filial piety toward his ogre-like father Tantalus no longer appears to us as a paradox, but only as the one-sided—and highly erotized—expression of the positive component of Pelops' ambivalence toward his father, whose idealized representative is Pelops' homosexual divine lover Poseidon.

Yet Pelops could not have accepted without ambivalence his passive role either in the Feast of Tantalus, or in his abduction by Poseidon, which so startlingly duplicates the abduction of his son Chrysippus by Laius. We must examine therefore also the manner in which Pelops expressed the hostile component of his ambivalence toward Tantalus. This was accomplished by means of a displacement of his hostility from its initial object Tantalus to Pelops' murderous father-in-law, King Oenomaus, ruler of Elis. Oenomaus had a daughter, Hippodamia, of whom it was prophesied that she would be married on the day her suitor slew her father.[14] Being cognizant of this prophecy, Oenomaus tried to fend off his daughter's suitors, by proposing to them a chariot race. If the suitors lost, the king was at liberty to slay them, and, until Pelops arrived to sue for Hippodamia's hand, the king had always succeeded in his designs. However, Pelops asked Oenomaus' coachman Myrtilus, son of Hermes, to replace the linchpin of his master's chariot with a waxen one. To pay for this treachery, he promised that Myrtilus would be permitted to share Hippodamia's favors (Rose, 1928).[15] The king pursued Pelops and Hippodamia, and almost won the race, when his sabotaged chariot disintegrated and he was killed. Then, in order not to have to pay Myrtilus the promised bribe, Pelops drowned his accomplice.

From the sociological point of view, this peculiar courtship episode is understandable in terms of Sir J. G. Frazer's discussion of the transmission of kingly powers in early Greek society (1951). Apparently such powers were transmitted from the present king to the king's son-in-law. Hence, in permitting his daughter to marry, the king automatically created a rival for his throne, exactly as Laius provided a future king for Thebes by fathering Oedipus. In this system, in which power was transmitted from mother to daughter, although the exercise of power was delegated to the spouse—a mechanism characteristic of matri*liny* as distinct from matri*archy*—the same effect could be achieved by marrying either the mother or the daughter. Thus, Oedipus married Jocasta, as Pelops married Hippodamia, in order to be elevated to the throne. The fact that Oedipus obtains Jocasta after mortal combat, while Pelops obtains Hippodamia by means of a (murderous) race, is fully explained by Frazer's proof that athletic competitions for the bride were but attenuated latter-day representations of earlier mortal combats. The fact that Hippodamia rode in Pelops' chariot is reminiscent of the practice of bride theft.

From the psychoanalytic point of view, even if we disregard the

[14]In this connection too Pelops' fate is similar to that of a personage in the Oedipus myth. Just as Laius had to protect his life against his son Oedipus, so Oenomaus stood in danger of death from his daughter's suitor Pelops.

[15]According to another version Pelops' victory was due to the direct intervention of Pelops' erstwhile lover Poseidon, who, at the crucial moment, caused the wheel of Oenomaus' chariot to become detached (Schwab, 1946).

obvious symbolism of the chariot race, the sexual bribe offered to Myrtilus, and the fact that he was killed so that the bribe (*ius primae noctis?*) need not be paid, clearly suggests that—psychologically speaking—King Oenomaus and his unfaithful coachman Myrtilus are one and the same person in the eyes of Pelops, and that Oenomaus' murder was oedipally motivated. At the same time Myrtilus is perhaps also a part of Pelops himself, who, after profiting by the treachery, kills his accomplice. These deeds caused a blood-guilt which gave rise to the tragedy of Pelops' sons and also to that of Electra.[16]

Indeed, Tantalus seems to have been psychologically reincarnated in Pelops' vicious sons, Atreus and Thyestes. The latter seduced his brother's wife Aerope, and stole a marvelous golden ram given to Atreus by the gods, in token of sovereignty over Mycenae.[17] Atreus first banished Thyestes, then feigned to be reconciled with him, and set before him *a dish made of the flesh of Thyestes' own children.* Thyestes then departed, but first placed a curse upon his brother Atreus. This curse eventually caused the tragedy of Electra, precisely as the curse of Pelops caused the tragedy of Oedipus. Indeed, Thyestes soon discovered that he could be avenged on his brother *by cohabiting with his own daughter, Pelopia.*[18] The son born of this union, Aegisthus, is the killer of Agamemnon and the lover of Clytemnestra, who is then slain by Orestes and Electra—a deed which, to psychoanalysts, is the prototypal expression of the Electra complex. These events confirm the validity of our thesis that the legend of the Pelopids is intimately connected with that of the house of Laius. It will be sufficient, however, if, in this context, we summarize only King Pelops' connections with the death of Laius.

[16]A note on unconscious insight may not be out of place in this context. Professor Rose (1928), whose style is usually of exemplary clarity, at this particular point failed to make it clear whether the blood-guilt which Pelops had to shoulder was for the death of Oenomaus or for that of Myrtilus. Since Professor Rose was not an analyst, his slip is of special interest, in that it reveals his unconscious insight into the identity of Oenomaus and Myrtilus. Correctly stated, the myth records that the blood-guilt fell upon Pelops as a result of the murder of Myrtilus.

[17]Compare here the story that Tantalus concealed a golden dog, sacred to Zeus, which had been stolen by a thief from Zeus' shrine.

[18]In one of the Bantu tribes a man setting out to hunt a dangerous beast first commits incest, so that his terribleness shall match that of the hunted beast.

The legend of Pelops—who was both cannibalized and homosexually raped by his father, respectively by the father figure Poseidon, and who nonetheless devoutly revered his father even though he slew his father-in-law, explains precisely why Pelops was so enraged by Chrysippus' abduction, and why he chose to curse Laius in so highly distinctive a manner. The chief features of Pelops' conflict may be summarized as follows:

1. Pelops behaves toward Chrysippus as a fond father should behave. In doing so he performs a highly complex action, since, on the one hand, he shows Tantalus how he *should* have treated him, and, on the other hand, shows Poseidon how he should *not* have treated him.

2. Laius' deed enraged Pelops beyond all measure, probably because Laius, in raping Chrysippus, acted out one of Pelops' own most severely repressed impulses, and at the same time reawakened Pelops' own passive homosexual conflicts.

3. The curse which Pelops laid on Laius is quite clearly rooted in Pelops' own conflicts: Oedipus is to slay his father Laius and then marry his mother Jocasta. This curse gives us the true unconscious meaning of Pelops' killing his father-in-law on the very day on which he married Hippodamia, these deeds reflecting the displacement of his oedipal homosexual hostility from Tantalus and Poseidon to Oenomaus and Myrtilus.

Character and Fate in Greek Drama

The analysis of Laius' character, and of the character and curse of Pelops, casts a great deal of doubt upon the validity of the traditional conception of Greek tragedy as an account of man's helplessness in the face of undeserved Fate. Laius' death at the hands of Oedipus is not the trigger-event which sets in motion the millstones of the gods. Rather is it a rigidly determined consequence of Laius' own character structure, just as the nature of the curse laid upon him is an unavoidable consequence of Pelops' own passive homosexual conflicts and of his repressed murderous hatred of his father Tantalus, which was displaced to, and then acted out in, the killing of Oenomaus and of Myrtilus. Thus, in a very genuine sense, we must credit the Greek poets and dramatists with more psychological acumen than we have so far done. What they called Fate was merely the personification of man's character structure, and of his need to act out those of his intrapsychic conflicts which determine the course of his life. The role which the Greek tragedians assigned to the character trait "hybris," as a determinant of man's tragic fate, at once confirms this view, and casts a vivid light upon the social psychology of Greek society, in which a character structure involving hybris was the one least well adapted to the demands of society. At the same time the need to manifest overbearingness and excess must have been very strong indeed in a society which professed to follow the path of the "golden mean" (which is the true meaning of the constantly misused term "aurea mediocritas"). This subjective need to escape the bounds of the golden mean explains why the Greek dramatists not merely condemned but also admired and pitied those whose hybris brought about their downfall.[19]

In brief, Greek drama is not a tragedy set in motion by a fate external to man, but by man's character structure and latent conflicts, witness the adage that whom the gods wish to destroy they first render mad. If we replace "the gods" with parental figures, this adage confirms our interpretation of the characterological and conflictual sources of Greek tragic destinies. This fact was simply obscured by the Greeks' habit of personifying character structure as Fate, and also by the fact that the dramatist dealt with well-known mythical personages, whose background and early history were expected to be familiar to the audience. In other words, it is very much to be doubted whether the intelligent Greek attending the representation of Sophocles' Oedipus trilogy was unaware of Laius' character and early history, and accepted the thesis that Laius' death was predetermined by Fate in

[19]The psychological situation obtaining in Pueblo Indian society is very much the same. These tribes profess to follow a way of life which Ruth Benedict (1934) has characterized as Apollonian. Yet we do know that underneath this peaceful facade there bubbles a witch's cauldron of hate which finds expression in constant panicky preoccupation with witchcraft (Simmons, 1942; Devereux, 1951c). As regards the tendency to condemn with admiration those guilty of violating the social norm, we learn that in Central Australia those guilty of incest are "condemned with admiration" (Róheim, 1932). The same attitude also prevails in at least one of the Moi tribes of French Indo-China (Devereux, n.d.).

the literal sense. It must be presumed that he accepted this thesis simply as a poetically appropriate allegorical reference to Laius' personality, since at that time—and until very recently—explicit "psychologizing" was not considered to be a poetical or even a literary device. The dramatist was therefore compelled to achieve plausibility—both psychological and other—by means which the society from which his audience was recruited was culturally conditioned to accept as "literary plausibility."[20] It might also be added that these considerations further justify the psychological and psychoanalytic interpretation of nominally nonpsychologically formulated narratives and myths.

Concluding Hypotheses

The following remarks, and in particular the remarks which pertain to clinical problems, are offered in a very tentative manner. They should be viewed not as conclusions in the strict sense of this term, but as attempts to indicate the location of certain problem areas in psychoanalytic theory, which deserve to be explored further. The fact that they have been expressed in the form of simple declarative sentences should not be taken as an indication that they represent statements of fact, or time-tested theoretical insights. We have used simple declarative statements solely because we did not wish to encumber our statements with monotonous and repetitive warnings that all our remarks are highly tentative and stand in need of a great deal of further confirmation.

This being said, the material presented in the preceding pages suggests that the following hypotheses stand in need of further study:

1. History of Psychoanalysis

Culturally determined scotomata may be responsible for the tendency to minimize the significance of the Laius complex and of the Jocasta complex, which complement the Oedipus complex.

[20]The problems of the cultural and psychological formulation of the criteria of literary plausibility are discussed elsewhere (Devereux, 1948).

2. Metapsychology

An analysis of the Oedipus myth does not seem to support the thesis that biological and/or phylogenetic factors are *primarily* responsible for the Oedipus complex. The notion that the child's psyche is a "chamber of horrors" for *biological* reasons is also contradicted by Freud's thesis (1925), further elaborated by the writer (1951c), that instincts become luxuriant and monstrous *only as a result of repression.* As suggested elsewhere (Devereux, 1951a, 1953) it may be necessary to assume that the child's sensitiveness even to minimal aggression may be epiphenomenal to its sensitiveness to minimal tokens of love, since the latter appears to be one of the child's chief psychic homeostatic mechanisms.

3. Psychosexual Development

The Oedipus complex appears to be a consequence of the child's sensitiveness to its parents' sexual and aggressive impulses. Homosexual conflicts may play a greater role in the genesis and development of the Oedipus complex than has hitherto been suspected.

4. Clinical Implications

It may be worthwhile to investigate to what extent heterosexual impulses directed to the parent of the opposite sex include and/or disguise also homosexual impulses directed to the parent of the same sex. Genitality seems to mean more than the attainment of heterosexuality pure and simple. In the case of males it also seems to require a shift from sublimated passive to sublimated active homosexuality, and, in the case of women, a shift from sublimated active to sublimated passive homosexuality. It may even be possible to assume that "activity" and "passivity" in the sexual sphere may be derived from homosexual rather than from heterosexual sources, since these attitudes are closely related to aggression, which belongs to the pregenital stage of psychosexual development.

5. Applied Psychoanalysis

a. The Oedipus myth. The early history of Laius seems to provide us with data which are fundamental for the understanding of the entire Oedipus myth. These data appear to express the Greeks' insight into the external and realistic sources of the male child's tendency to view his father as a homosexual ogre, and of his desire to exchange roles with the father also in this respect.

b. Greek literature. A study of the problem of Laius suggests that, especially in Greek drama, Fate is actually a personification of character structure.

c. Mythology. We found that whenever there exist divergent and even seemingly contradictory versions of a given mythical episode, these variants not only do not contradict each other psychologically, but actually supplement each other, and help us obtain a deeper insight into the latent nuclear meaning of the basic theme, motif, or plot element. For example, we found that the bowdlerized explanation of the causes of the quarrel between Laius and Oedipus not only repeats in a symbolic form (narrow road) the sexual theme which is explicitly mentioned in other sources, but also helps us obtain a deeper insight into Laius' character structure, which is of paramount importance for the understanding of the entire Oedipus myth.[21] Furthermore, the various unexpurgated versions, some of which highlight the role of Jocasta, while others highlight that of Chrysippus, enable us in turn to discover the combined heterosexual and homosexual undercurrent in the male child's struggle against his father and in his love for his mother. As regards the legend of Pelops, the striking contrast between the traditional version of the Feast of Tantalus and Pindar's theory that Pelops was abducted by Poseidon amounts to little more than the presentation of the basic theme—erotized passivity in the face of aggression—in, respectively, oral and homosexual oedipal terms. This suggests that a given theme has an inherent and

[21] It is of considerable interest that Laius' character structure, i.e., his proneness to unconsidered violence, is put in relief more strikingly in the bowdlerized than in those unexpurgated versions of this incident, in which the grosser instinctual elements are more prominent. This is not surprising, since character formation results from attempts to cope with the instincts and with unmanageable external stimulation.

specific latent significance which no amount of voluntary or involuntary, or else conscious or unconscious, distortion can obliterate. In fact, such distortions serve only to highlight certain additional psychological implications of the basic theme. Thus in mythology, as in dream-work, we seem to be constantly confronted with the basic fact that *plus ça change, plus c'est la même chose.* This finding may have an important bearing not only upon the study of dreams, fantasies, and mythology, but also upon such everyday matters as false perception, the embellished and distorted rumor, deliberate lying, false evidence in courts of law, etc., all of which, though being distortions of the manifest content, probably adhere rather closely to the latent content. Finally, this inference also has a bearing upon those clinical psychological tests in which the subject is expected to repeat a story told to him, as well as upon such partially structured projective tests as the Rorschach, the TAT, and probably also the Draw-a-Man Test.[22] Needless to say, these suppositions are fully compatible with classical psychoanalytic theory.

The one conclusion which we can offer with any degree of confidence is that, as long as there are human beings, the task of psychoanalytic research will never be finished.

REFERENCES

Balint, A. (1939), Liebe zur Mutter und Mutterliebe. *Internationale Zeitschrift für Psychoanalyse und Imago,* 24:33–48.

Benedict, R. (1934), *Patterns of Culture.* London: Routledge.

Bunker, H. A. (1952), The feast of Tantalus. *Psychoanal. Quart.,* 21:355–372.

Devereux, G. (n.d.), *Moi field notes.* Unpublished manuscript.

________ (1941), Mohave beliefs concerning twins. *Amer. Anthropologist* n.s., 43:573–592.

________ (1942), Social structure and the economy of affective bonds. *Psychoanal. Rev.,* 29:303–314.

________ (1948), Mohave coyote tales. *J. Amer. Folklore,* 61:233–255.

________ (1950), Status, socialization and interpersonal relations of Mohave children. *Psychiat.,* 13:489–502.

[22]These considerations seem to provide a theoretical basis for an interesting idea advanced by Professor Ralph Linton (personal communication). He suggested that divergent versions of primitive tales may represent a kind of cultural Thematic Apperception Test, in which the basic plot—corresponding to a TAT picture—is subjectively elaborated by various tellers of tales.

——— (1951a), Cultural and characterological traits of the Mohave related to the anal stage of psychosexual development. *Psychoanal. Quart.*, 20:398–422.
——— (1951b), The oedipal situation and its consequences in the epics of ancient India. *Samiksa: J. Ind. Psycho-Anal. Soc.*, 5:5–13.
——— (1951c), *Reality and Dream: The Psychotherapy of a Plains Indian.* New York: International Universities Press.
——— (1953), The technique of analyzing occult occurrences in analysis. In: *Psychoanalysis and the Occult*, ed. G. Devereux. New York: International Universities Press, pp. 391–417.
Ferenczi, S. (1949), Confusion of tongues between the adult and the child. *Internat. J. Psycho-Anal.*, 30:225–230.
Frazer, J. G. (1951), The succession to the kingdom of ancient Latium. In: *The Golden Bough.* London: Macmillan.
Freud, S. (1925), Repression. In: *Collected Papers*, Vol. IV. London: Hogarth.
Gruppe, O. (1897–1906), *Griechische Mythologie und Religionsgeschichte.* 2 vols. Munich: Beck.
Licht, H. (1932), *Sexual Life in Ancient Greece.* London: Routledge.
Raglan, L. (1933), *Jocasta's Crime.* London: Methuen.
Rank, O. (1912), *Das Inzestmotiv in Dichtung und Sage.* Leipzig: Deuticke.
Róheim, G. (1932), Psycho-analysis of primitive cultural types. *Internat. J. Psycho-Anal.*, 13:1–224.
Rose, H. J. (1928), *A Handbook of Greek Mythology.* London: Methuen.
Rotter, L. K. (1933), A nöi genitalitás pszichológiájáról. In: *Lélekelemzési Tanulmáyok* (Ferenczi Memorial Volume). Budapest: Somlo.
Schwab, G. (1946), *Gods and Heroes.* New York: Pantheon.
Simmons, L. W., Ed. (1942), *Sun Chief.* New Haven: Yale University Press.

8

Symbolic Language in Myth, Fairy Tale, Ritual, and Novel

ERICH FROMM

[1957]

The myth, like the dream, offers a story occurring in space and time, a story which expresses, in symbolic language, religious and philosophical ideas, experiences of the soul in which the real significance of the myth lies. If one fails to grasp the true meaning of the myth, one finds oneself confronted with this alternative: either the myth is a prescientific, naive picture of the world and of history and at best a product of poetically beautiful imagination, or—and this is the attitude of the orthodox believer—the manifest story of the myth is true, and one must believe it as a correct report of events which actually happened in "reality." While this alternative seemed inescapable in the nineteenth and the beginning of the twentieth centuries in Western culture, a new approach is taking place gradually. The emphasis

Reprinted with permission from *The Forgotten Language: An Introduction to the Understanding of Dreams, Fairy Tales and Myths.* New York: Holt, Rinehart & Winston, pp. 195–231.

is put on the religious and philosophical meaning of the myth, and the manifest story is viewed as the symbolic expression of this meaning. But even as far as the manifest story is concerned, one has learned to understand that it is not just the product of fantastic imagination of "primitive" peoples, but contains cherished memories of the past. (The historic truth of some has been established by many findings from excavations in recent decades.) Foremost among those who have paved the way for a new understanding of the myth are J. J. Bachofen and Sigmund Freud. The former, with an unsurpassed penetration and brilliance, grasped the myth in its religious and psychological as well as its historical meaning. The latter helped the understanding of the myth by inaugurating an understanding of symbolic language on the basis of his interpretation of dreams. This was more of an indirect than a direct help to mythology, because Freud tended to see in the myth—as in the dream—only the expression of irrational, antisocial impulses rather than the wisdom of past ages expressed in a specific language, that of symbols.

The Oedipus Myth

The Oedipus myth offers the outstanding illustration of Freud's method of myth interpretation and at the same time an excellent opportunity for a different approach, one in which not sexual desires but one of the fundamental aspects of interpersonal relationships, the attitude toward authority, is held to be the central theme of the myth. It is at the same time an illustration of the distortions and changes that memories of older social forms and ideas undergo in the formation of the manifest text of the myth.[1]

Freud (1900) writes:

> If the *Oedipus Rex* is capable of moving a modern reader or playgoer no less powerfully than it moved the contemporary Greeks, the only possible explanation is that the effect of the Greek tragedy does not depend upon the conflict between fate and

[1]The following interpretation is taken from Fromm (1948).

human will, but upon the peculiar nature of the material by which this conflict is revealed. There must be a voice within us which is prepared to acknowledge the compelling power of fate in the Oedipus, while we are able to condemn the situations occurring in *Die Ahnfrau* or other tragedies of fate as arbitrary inventions. And there actually is a motive in the story of King Oedipus which explains the verdict of this inner voice. His fate moves us only because it might have been our own, because the oracle laid upon us before our birth the very curse which rested upon him. It may be that we are all destined to direct our first sexual impulses toward our mothers, and our first impulses of hatred and violence toward our fathers; our dreams convince us that we are. King Oedipus, who slew his father Laius and wedded his mother Jocasta, is nothing more or less than a wish-fulfillment—the fulfillment of the wish of our childhood. But we, more fortunate than he, in so far as we have not become psychoneurotics, have since our childhood succeeded in withdrawing our sexual impulses from our mothers, and in forgetting our jealousy of our fathers. We recoil from the person for whom this primitive wish of our childhood has been fulfilled with all the force of the repression which these wishes have undergone in our minds since childhood. As the poet brings the guilt of Oedipus to light by his investigation, he forces us to become aware of our own inner selves, in which the same impulses are still extant, even though they are suppressed. The antithesis with which the chorus departs:

> . . . Behold, this is Oedipus
> Who unravelled the great riddle,
> and was first in power,
> Whose fortune all the townsmen
> praised and envied;
> See in what dread adversity he sank!

. . . this admonition touches us and our own pride, us who since the years of our childhood have grown so wise and so powerful in our own estimation. Like Oedipus, we live in ignorance of the desires that offend morality, the desires that nature has forced upon us and after their unveiling we may well prefer to avert our gaze from the scenes of our childhood. [p. 308]

The concept of the Oedipus complex, which Freud has so beautifully presented, became one of the cornerstones of his psychological system. He believed that this concept was the key to an understanding of history and of the evolution of religion and morality. His conviction was that this very complex constituted the fundamental mechanism in the development of the child, and he maintained that the Oedipus complex was the cause of psychopathological development and the "kernel of neurosis."

Freud referred to the Oedipus myth in the version of Sophocles' tragedy *King Oedipus*. This tragedy tells us that an oracle has told Laius, the King of Thebes, and his wife, Jocasta, that if they have a son this son will kill his father and marry his own mother. When a son, Oedipus, is born to them, Jocasta decides to escape the fate predicted by the oracle by killing the infant. She gives Oedipus to a shepherd, who is to abandon the child in the woods with his feet bound so that he will die. But the shepherd, taking pity on the child, gives the infant to a man in the service of the King of Corinth, who in turn brings him to his master. The king adopts the boy, and the young prince grows up in Corinth not knowing that he is not the true son of the King of Corinth. He is told by the oracle in Delphi that it is his fate to kill his father and to marry his mother. He decides to avoid this fate by never going back to his alleged parents. On his way back from Delphi he engages in a violent argument with an old man riding in a carriage, loses his temper, and slays the man and his servant without knowing that he has slain his father, the King of Thebes.

His wanderings lead him to Thebes. There the Sphinx is devouring the young men and women of the city, and she will cease doing so only if someone will find the right answer to a riddle she asks. The riddle is this: "What is it which first goes on four, then on two, and eventually on three?" The city of Thebes has promised that anyone who can solve the riddle and thus free the city from the Sphinx will be made king and will be given the king's widow for a wife. Oedipus undertakes the venture. He finds the answer to the riddle—which is *man,* who as a child walks on all four, as an adult on two, and in his old age on three (with a cane). The Sphinx throws herself into the ocean, the city is saved from calamity, and Oedipus becomes king and marries Jocasta, his mother.

After Oedipus has reigned happily for some time, the city is ravaged by a plague which kills many of its citizens. The seer Teiresias reveals that the plague is the punishment for the twofold crime which Oedipus has committed, patricide and incest. Oedipus, after having tried desperately not to see this truth, blinds himself when he is compelled to see it, and Jocasta commits suicide. The tragedy ends at the point where Oedipus has suffered punishment for a crime which he committed unknowingly and in spite of his conscious effort to avoid committing it.

Was Freud justified in concluding that this myth confirms his view that unconscious incestuous drives and the resulting hate against the father-rival are to be found in any male child? Indeed, it does seem as if the myth confirmed Freud's theory that the Oedipus complex justifiably bears its name.

If we examine the myth more closely, however, questions arise which cast some doubts on the correctness of this view. The most pertinent question is this: If Freud's interpretation is right, we should expect the myth to tell us that Oedipus met Jocasta without knowing that she was his mother, fell in love with her, and then killed his father, again unknowingly. But there is no indication whatsoever in the myth that Oedipus is attracted by or falls in love with Jocasta. The only reason we are given for Oedipus' marriage to Jocasta is that she, as it were, goes with the throne. Should we believe that a myth, the central theme of which constitutes an incestuous relationship between mother and son, would entirely omit the element of attraction between the two? This question is all the more weighty in view of the fact that, in the older versions of the oracle, the prediction of the marriage to the mother is mentioned only once in the version by Nikolaus of Damascus, which according to Carl Robert (1915) goes back to a relatively new source.

Furthermore, Oedipus is described as the courageous and wise hero who becomes the benefactor of Thebes. How can we understand that the same Oedipus is described as having committed the crime most horrible in the eyes of his contemporaries? This question has sometimes been answered by pointing to the fact that the very essence of the Greek concept of tragedy is that the powerful and strong are suddenly struck by disaster. Whether such an answer is sufficient or whether another view can give us a more satisfactory answer remains to be seen.

The foregoing questions arise from a consideration of *King Oedipus*. If we examine only this tragedy, without taking into account the two other parts of the trilogy, *Oedipus at Colonus* and *Antigone*, no definite answer can be given. But we are at least in a position to formulate a hypothesis, namely, *that the myth can be understood as a symbol not of the incestuous love between mother and son but of the rebellion of the son against the authority of the father in the patriarchal family; that the marriage of Oedipus and Jocasta is only a secondary element, only one of the symbols of the victory of the son, who takes his father's place and with it all his privileges.*

The validity of this hypothesis can be tested by examining the whole Oedipus myth, particularly in the form presented by Sophocles in the two other parts of his trilogy, *Oedipus at Colonus* and *Antigone*.[2]

In *Oedipus at Colonus* we find Oedipus near Athens at the grove of the Eumenides shortly before he dies. After having blinded himself, Oedipus had remained in Thebes, which was ruled by Creon, his uncle, who after some time exiled him. Oedipus' two daughters, Antigone and Ismene, accompanied him into exile; but his two sons, Eteocles and Polynices, refused to help their blind father. After his departure, the two brothers strove for possession of the throne. Eteocles won; but Polynices, refusing to yield, sought to conquer the city with outside help and to wrest the power from his brother. In *Oedipus at Colonus* we see him approach his father, begging his forgiveness and asking his assistance. But Oedipus is relentless in his hate against his sons. In spite of the passionate pleading of Polynices, supported by Antigone's plea, he refuses forgiveness. His last words to his son are:

[2]While it is true that the trilogy was not written in this order and while some scholars may be right in their assumption that Sophocles did not plan the three tragedies as a trilogy, the three must nevertheless be interpreted as a whole. It makes little sense to assume that Sophocles described the fate of Oedipus and his children in three tragedies without having in mind an inner coherence of the whole.

> And thou—begone, abhorred of me, and unfathered!—begone, thou vilest of the vile, and with thee take these my curses which I call down on thee—never to vanquish the land of thy race, no, nor ever return to hill-girt Argos, but by a kindred hand to die, and slay him by whom thou hast been driven out. Such is my prayer; and I call the paternal darkness of dread Tartarus to take thee unto another home,—I call the spirits of this place,—I call the Destroying God, who hath set that dreadful hatred in you twain. Go, with these words in thine ears—go, and publish it to the Cadmeans all, yea, and to thine own staunch allies, that Oedipus hath divided such honours to his sons. [Oates and O'Neill, 1938; all subsequent quotations from this edition]

In *Antigone* we find another father-son conflict as one of the central themes of the tragedy. Here Creon, the representative of the authoritarian principle in state and family, is opposed by his son, Haemon, who reproaches him for his ruthless despotism and his cruelty against Antigone. Haemon tries to kill his father and, failing to do so, kills himself.

We find that the theme running through the three tragedies is the conflict between father and son. In *King Oedipus*, Oedipus kills his father Laius, who had intended to take the infant's life. In *Oedipus at Colonus*, Oedipus gives vent to his intense hate against his sons, and in *Antigone* we find the same hate again between Creon and Haemon. The problem of incest exists neither in the relationship between Oedipus' sons to their mother nor in the relationship between Haemon and his mother, Eurydice. If we interpret *King Oedipus* in the light of the whole trilogy, the assumption seems plausible that the real issue in *King Oedipus*, too, is the conflict between father and son and not the problem of incest.

Freud had interpreted the antagonism between Oedipus and his father as the unconscious rivalry caused by Oedipus' incestuous strivings. If we do not accept this explanation, the problem arises as how otherwise to explain the conflict between father and son which we find in all the three tragedies. One clue is given in *Antigone*. The rebellion of Haemon against Creon is rooted in the particular structure of Creon's relationship to Haemon. Creon represents the strictly authoritarian principle both in the family and in the state, and it is against this type of authority that Haemon rebels. An analysis of the whole Oedipus trilogy will show that the struggle against paternal authority is its main theme and that the roots of this struggle go far back into the ancient fight between the patriarchal and matriarchal systems of society. Oedipus, as well as Haemon and Antigone, is representative of the matriarchal principle; they all attack a social and religious order based on the powers and privileges of the father, represented by Laius and Creon.

Since this interpretation is based on Bachofen's analysis of Greek mythology, it is necessary to acquaint the reader briefly with the principles of Bachofen's theory.

In his *Mutterrecht* (Mother Right), published in 1861, Bachofen suggested that in the beginning of human history sexual relations were promiscuous; that therefore only the mother's parenthood was unquestionable, to her alone could consanguinity be traced, and she was the authority and lawgiver—the ruler both in the family group and in society. On the basis of his analysis of religious documents of Greek and Roman antiquity, Bachofen came to the conclusion that the supremacy of women had found its expression not only in the sphere of social and family organization but also in religion. He found evidence that the religion of the Olympian gods was preceded by a religion in which goddesses, motherlike figures, were the supreme deities.

Bachofen assumed that in a long-drawn-out historical process men defeated women, subdued them, and succeeded in making themselves the rulers in a social hierarchy. The patriarchal system thus established is characterized by monogamy (at least so far as women are concerned), by the authority of the father in the family, and by the dominant role of men in a hierarchically organized society. The religion of this patriarchal culture corresponded to its social organization. Instead of the mother-goddesses, male gods became supreme rulers over man, as the father was the supreme ruler in the family.

One of the most striking and brilliant illustrations of Bachofen's interpretation of Greek myths is his analysis of Aeschylus' *Oresteia,* which according to him is a symbolic representation of a last fight between the maternal goddesses and the victorious paternal gods.

Clytemnestra had killed her husband, Agamemnon, in order not to give up her lover, Aegisthus. Orestes, her son by Agamemnon, avenges his father's death by killing his mother and her lover. The Erinyes, representatives of the old mother-goddesses and the matriarchal principle, persecute Orestes and demand his punishment, while Apollo and Athena (the latter not born from woman but sprung from the head of Zeus), the representatives of the new patriarchal religion, are on Orestes' side. The argument is centered around the principles of patriarchal and matriarchal religion, respectively. For the matriarchal world there is only one sacred tie, that of mother and child, and consequently matricide is the ultimate and unforgivable crime. From the patriarchal point of view, the son's love and respect for the father is his paramount duty and therefore patricide is the paramount crime. Clytemnestra's killing of her husband, from the patriarchal standpoint a major crime because of the supreme position of the husband, is considered differently from the matriarchal standpoint, since "she was not related by blood to the man whom she killed." The murder of a husband does not concern the Erinyes, since to them only ties of blood and the sanctity of the mother count. To the Olympian gods, on the other hand, the murder of the mother is no crime if it is carried out as revenge for the father's death. In Aeschylus' *Oresteia,* Orestes is acquitted, but this victory of the patriarchal principle is somewhat mitigated by a compromise with the defeated goddesses. They agree to accept the new order and to be satisfied with a minor role as protectors of the earth and as goddesses of agricultural fertility.

Bachofen showed that the difference between the patriarchal and the matriarchal order went far beyond the social supremacy of men and women, respectively, but was one of social and moral principles. Matriarchal culture is characterized by an emphasis on ties of blood, ties to the soil, and a passive acceptance of all natural phenomena. Patriarchal society, in contrast, is characterized by respect for man-made law, by a predominance of rational thought, and by man's effort to change natural phenomena. Insofar as these principles are concerned, the patriarchal culture constitutes a definite progress over the matriarchal world. In other respects, however, the matriarchal principles were superior to the victorious patriarchal ones. In the matriarchal concept all men are equal, since they are all the children of mothers and each one a child of Mother Earth. A mother loves all her children alike and without conditions, since her love is based on the fact that they are her children and not on any particular merit or achievement; the aim of life is the happiness of men, and there is nothing more important or dignified than human existence and life. The patriarchal system, on the other hand, considers obedience to authority to be the main virtue. Instead of the principle of equality, we find the concept of the favorite son and a hierarchical order in society. The relationship, Bachofen (1926) says,

> through which mankind has first grown into civilization which is the beginning of the development of every virtue and of the formation of the nobler aspects of human existence is the matriarchal principle, which becomes effective as the principle of love, unity, and peace. The woman sooner than the man learns in caring for the infant to extend her love beyond her own self to other human beings and to direct all her gifts and imagination to the aim of preserving and beautifying the existence of another being. All development of civilization, devotion, care, and the mourning for the dead are rooted in her.
>
> The motherly love is not only more tender but also more general and universal. . . . Its principle is that of universality, whereas the patriarchal principle is that of restrictions. . . . The idea of the universal brotherhood of man is rooted in the principle of motherhood, and this very idea vanishes with the development of patriarchal society. The patriarchal family is a closed and restricted organism. The matriarchal family, on the other hand, has that universal character with which all evolution begins and which is characteristic of maternal life in contrast to the spiritual, the image of Mother Earth, Demeter. Each woman's womb will give brothers and sisters to every human being until, with the development of the patriarchal principle, this unity is dissolved and superseded by the principle of hierarchy. In matriarchal societies, this principle has found frequent and even legally formulated expressions. It is the basis of the principle of universal freedom and equality which we find as one of the basic traits in matriarchal cultures. . . . Absence of inner disharmony,

> a longing for peace . . . a tender humaneness which one can still see in the facial expression of Egyptian statues penetrates the matriarchal world. . . . [pp. 14-16]

Bachofen's discovery found confirmation by an American scholar, L. H. Morgan (1871, 1877), who entirely independently came to the conclusion that the kinship system of the American Indians—similar to that found in Asia, Africa, and Australia—was based on the matriarchal principle and that the most significant institution in such cultures, the gens, was organized in conformity with the matriarchal principle. Morgan's conclusion about principles of value in a matriarchal society were quite similar to Bachofen's. He proposed that the higher form of civilization "will be a repetition—but on a higher level—of the principles of liberty, equality, and fraternity which characterized the ancient gens." Both Bachofen's and Morgan's theories of matriarchy were, if not entirely ignored, disputed by most anthropologists. This was also the case with the work of Robert Briffault (1927), who in *The Mothers* continued Bachofen's research and confirmed it by a brilliant analysis of new anthropological data. The violence of the antagonism against the theory of matriarchy arouses the suspicion that the criticism was not entirely free from an emotionally founded prejudice against an assumption so foreign to the thinking and feeling of our patriarchal culture. There is little doubt that many single objections to the matriarchal theory are justified. Nevertheless, Bachofen's main thesis, that we find an older layer of matriarchal religion underneath the more recent patriarchal religion of Greece, seems to me to be established by him beyond any doubt.

After this brief survey of Bachofen's theory we are in a better position to take up the discussion of our hypothesis that the hostility between father and son, which is the theme running through Sophocles' trilogy, is to be understood as an attack against the victorious patriarchal order by the representatives of the defeated matriarchal system.

King Oedipus offers little direct evidence except in some points which will be mentioned presently. But the original Oedipus myth in the various versions which existed in Greece and upon which Sophocles built his tragedy gives an important clue. In the various formulations of the myth, the figure of Oedipus was always connected with the cult of the earth-goddesses, the representatives of matriarchal religion. In almost all versions of the Oedipus myth, from parts which deal with his exposure as an infant to those which are centered around his death, traces of this connection can be found (see Schneidewin, 1852). Thus, for instance, Eteonos, the only Boeotian city which had a cult shrine of Oedipus and where the whole myth probably originated, also has the shrine of the earth-goddess Demeter (Robert, 1915, p. 1). At Colonus (near Athens), where Oedipus finds his last resting place, was an old shrine of Demeter and the Erinyes which had probably existed prior to the Oedipus myth (Robert, 1915, p. 21). As we shall see later, Sophocles has emphasized this connection between Oedipus and the chthonic goddesses in *Oedipus at Colonus.*

Another aspect of the Oedipus myth—Oedipus' connection with the Sphinx—seems also to point to the connection between Oedipus and the matriarchal principle as described by Bachofen. The Sphinx had announced that the one who could solve her riddle would save the city from her wrath. Oedipus succeeds, where everyone else before him had failed, and thus becomes the savior of Thebes. But if we look at the riddle more closely we are struck by the insignificance of the riddle in comparison with the reward for its solution. Any clever boy of twelve might guess that that which goes first on four, then on two, and eventually on three is man. Why should the right guess be proof of such extraordinary powers as to make their possessor the savior of the city? The answer to this question lies in an analysis of the real meaning of the riddle, an analysis which must follow the principles of interpretation of myths and dreams as they were developed by Bachofen and Freud.[3] They have shown that often the most important element in the real content of a dream or myth appears as a much less important or even insignificant part of the manifest formulation, whereas that part of the manifest formulation which has the main accent is only a minor part in the real content.

[3]Their interpretation of the Sphinx myth, however, differs from the one which follows here. Bachofen emphasized the nature of the question and stated that the Sphinx defines man in terms of his telluric, material existence, that is, in matriarchal terms. Freud assumed the riddle to be the symbolic expression of the child's sexual curiosity.

Applying this principle to the Sphinx myth, it would seem that the important element in the riddle is not the part which is stressed in the manifest formulation of the myth, namely, the riddle itself, but the answer to the riddle, *man*. If we translate the Sphinx's words from symbolic into overt language, we hear her say: He who knows that the most important answer man can give to the most difficult question with which he is confronted is *man himself* can save mankind. The riddle itself, the answer to which required nothing but cleverness, serves only as a veil for the latent meaning of the question, the importance of man. This very emphasis on the importance of man is part of the principle of the matriarchal world as Bachofen described it. Sophocles, in *Antigone*, made this principle the center of Antigone's as against Creon's position. What matters for Creon and the patriarchal order he represents is the state, man-made laws, and obedience to them. What matters to Antigone is man himself, the natural law, and love. Oedipus becomes the savior of Thebes, proving by his very answer to the Sphinx that he belongs to the same world which is represented by Antigone and expressive of the matriarchal order.

One element in the myth and in Sophocles' *King Oedipus* seems to contradict our hypothesis—the figure of Jocasta. On the assumption that she symbolizes the motherly principle, the question arises why the mother is destroyed instead of being victorious, provided the explanation suggested here is correct. The answer to this question will show that the role of Jocasta not only does not contradict our hypothesis but tends to confirm it. Jocasta's crime is that of not having fulfilled her duty as a mother; she had wanted to kill her child in order to save her husband. This, from the standpoint of patriarchal society, is a legitimate decision, but from the standpoint of matriarchal society and matriarchal ethics it is the unforgivable crime. It is she who by committing this crime starts the chain of events which eventually lead to her own and to her husband's and son's destruction. In order to understand this point, we must not lose sight of the fact that the myth as it was known to Sophocles had already been changed according to the patriarchal pattern, that the manifest and conscious frame of reference is that of patriarchy, and that the latent and older meaning appears only in a veiled and often distorted form. The patriarchal system had been victorious, and the myth explains the reasons for the downfall of matriarchy. It proposes that the mother by violating her paramount duty brought about her own destruction. The final judgment, however, whether this interpretation of Jocasta's role and of *King Oedipus* is correct must wait until we have analyzed *Oedipus at Colonus* and *Antigone*.

In *Oedipus at Colonus* we see the blind Oedipus accompanied by his two daughters arriving near Athens, close to the grove of the goddesses of the earth. The oracle has prophesied that, if Oedipus were to be buried in this grove, he would protect Athens from invasion by her enemies. In the course of the tragedy Oedipus makes known to Theseus the word of the oracle. Theseus gladly accepts the offer that Oedipus become the posthumous benefactor of Athens. Oedipus retreats into the grove of the goddesses and dies in a mysterious way not known to anybody but Theseus.

Who are these goddesses? Why do they offer a sanctuary to Oedipus? What does the oracle mean by telling us that Oedipus in finding his last home in this grove reverts to his role of savior and benefactor?

In *Oedipus at Colonus* Oedipus implores the goddesses, saying:

> *Queens of dread aspect,* since your seat is the first in this land whereat I have bent the knee, show not yourselves ungracious to Phoebus or to myself; who, when he proclaimed that doom of many woes, spake of this as a rest for me after long years—on reaching my goal in a land where I should find a seat of the *Awful Goddesses,* and a hospitable shelter—even that there I should close my weary life, with benefits, through my having dwelt therein, for mine hosts, but ruin for those who sent me forth—who drove me away. [my italics here and in subsequent quotations]

Oedipus calls the goddesses "Queens of dread aspect" and "Awful Goddesses." Why are they "dreadful" and "awful," since to him they are the goddesses of his last resting place and those who will give him peace eventually? Why does the chorus say:

> A wanderer that old man must have been—a wanderer, not a dweller in the land; else never would he have advanced into this

> untrodden *grove of the maidens* with whom none may strive, *whose name we tremble to speak,* by whom we pass with eyes turned away, moving our lips, without sound or word, in still devotion.

The answer to this question can be found only in that principle of interpretation, valid for both myths and dreams, which has been recognized by Bachofen and Freud. If an element appearing in a myth or in a dream belongs to a much earlier phase of development and is not part of the conscious frame of reference at the time of the final formulation of the myth, this element often carries with it the quality of dread and awfulness. Touching upon something hidden and taboo, the conscious mind is affected by a fear of a particular kind—the fear of the unknown and the mystifying.

Goethe, in one of the least understood passages of *Faust,* has treated the problem of the dread of the mysterious mothers in a spirit very similar to that in Sophocles' *Oedipus at Colonus.* Mephistopheles says:

> Unwilling I reveal a loftier mystery—
> In solitude are throned the *Goddesses,*
> No space around them, Place and Time still less;
> *Only to speak of them embarrasses;*
> *They are the Mothers!*
> *Faust* (terrified): Mothers!
> *Mephistopheles: Hast thou dread?*
> *Faust:* The Mothers! Mothers!—a strange word is said.
> *Mephistopheles:* It is so. Goddesses, unknown to ye,
> The Mothers, named by us so unwillingly.
> Delve in the deepest depth must thou, to reach them:
> It is thine own fault that we for help beseech them.

Here too, as in Sophocles' tragedy, the feeling of dread and terror is bound up with the mere mentioning of the goddesses, who belong to an ancient world which now is banned from the light of day, from consciousness.

As we see from this short passage, Goethe anticipated Bachofen's theory; according to Eckermann's diary (January 10, 1830), Goethe mentioned that in reading Plutarch he found "that in Grecian antiquity the Mothers are spoken of as Goddesses." This passage in *Faust* has appeared enigmatic to most commentators who tried to explain the mothers as a symbol of Platonic ideas, the formless realm of the inner world of spirit, and so forth. Indeed, it must remain an enigma unless one understands it in the light of Bachofen's findings.

It is in the grove of these "awful" goddesses where Oedipus, the wanderer, at last comes to rest and finds his real home. Oedipus, although himself a man, belongs to the world of these matriarchal goddesses, and his strength lies in his connection with them.

Oedipus' return to the grove of the goddesses, though the most important, is not the only clue to the understanding of his position as representative of the matriarchal order. Sophocles makes another and very plain allusion to matriarchy by having Oedipus refer to Egyptian matriarchy[4] when he tells about his two daughters. This is the way he praises them:

> O true image of the *ways of Egypt that they show in their spirit and their life! For there the men sit weaving in the house, but the wives go forth to win the daily bread.* And in your case, my daughters, those to whom these toils belonged keep the house at home like girls, while ye, in their stead, bear your hapless father's burden.

The same trend of thought is continued by Oedipus when he compares his daughters with his sons. Of Antigone and Ismene he says:

> Now, these girls preserve me, these my nurses, *these who are men not women,* in true service: but ye are aliens, and no sons of mine.

We have raised the question whether, if incest was the essence of Oedipus' crime, the drama should have told us that he had fallen in

[4]Sophocles probably refers here to a passage from Herodotus, II, 35.

love with Jocasta unwittingly. In *Oedipus at Colonus,* Sophocles has Oedipus himself answer this question. The marriage to her was not the outcome of his own desire and decision; instead, she was one of the rewards for the city's savior.

> Thebes bound me, all unknowingly, to the bride
> that was my curse.

We have already pointed to the fact that the main theme of the trilogy, the conflict between father and son, finds its full expression in *Oedipus at Colonus;* here the hate between father and son is not, as in *King Oedipus,* unconscious; indeed, here Oedipus is very much aware of his hate against his sons, whom he accuses of having violated the eternal law of nature. He claims that his curse is stronger than the sons' prayer to Poseidon, "if indeed Justice [Dike, the *Goddess* of Justice, who protects the eternal law of natural bonds and not the man-made rights of the first-born son], revealed of old, sits with Zeus in the might of eternal laws." Simultaneously he gives expression to his hate against his own parents, accusing them of their intention to sacrifice his life. There is no indication in *Oedipus at Colonus* that the hostility of Oedipus' sons against their father has any connection with the incest motif. The only motivation we can find in the tragedy is their wish for power and the rivalry with their father.

The end of *Oedipus at Colonus* clarifies still further the meaning of Oedipus' connection with the goddesses of the earth.

After the chorus has prayed to the "Unseen Goddesses," "the Goddess Infernal," the messenger reports how Oedipus died. He has taken leave of his daughters and—accompanied only, though not guided, by Theseus—walks to the holy place of the goddesses. He seems to need no guidance, since here at last he is at home and knows his way. The messenger sees Theseus

> . . . holding his hand before his face to screen his eyes, as if *some dread sight had been seen,* and such as none might endure to behold.

We find here again the emphasis on something awful and terrifying. The line following the ones just quoted makes it very clear how the remnants of the matriarchal religion are blended with the ruling patriarchal system. The messenger reports that he saw Theseus

> . . . salute the earth and the home of the gods above, both at once, in one prayer.

The end of the description of Oedipus' death shows the same blend of the patriarchal and matriarchal systems. The messenger goes on:

> But by what doom Oedipus perished, no man can tell, save Theseus alone. No fiery thunderbolt of the god removed him in that hour, nor any rising of storm from the sea; but either a messenger from the gods*, or the world of the dead, the nether adamant, riven for him in love,* without pain; for the passing of the man was not with lamentation, or in sickness and suffering, but, above mortal's wonderful. And if to any I seem to speak folly, I would not woo their belief, who count me foolish.

The messenger is puzzled; he does not know whether Oedipus was removed from the earth by the gods above or by the gods below, by the world of the fathers or that of the mothers. But we can be certain that, in a formulation written centuries after the mother-goddesses had been conquered by the Olympian gods, this doubt can only be the expression of a secret conviction that Oedipus was brought back to the place where he belonged, to the mothers.

How different is the end of *Oedipus at Colonus* from that of *King Oedipus.* In the latter, his fate seemed to be sealed as that of the tragic criminal whose crime removes him forever from his family and from his fellow men, destined to be an outcast, abhorred though perhaps pitied by everyone. In the former he dies as a man surrounded by two loving daughters and by new friends whose benefactor he has become, not with a feeling of guilt but with a conviction of his right, not as an outcast but as one who has eventually found his home—with the earth and the goddesses who rule there. The tragic guilt that had pervaded *King Oedipus* has now been removed, and only one conflict has remained as bitter and unsolved as ever—that between father and son.

The conflict between the patriarchal and matriarchal principles is the theme of the third part of the trilogy, *Antigone*. Here the figure of Creon, which has been somewhat indistinct in the two former tragedies, becomes colorful and definite. He has become the tyrant of Thebes after Oedipus' two sons have been killed—one by attacking the city in order to gain power, the other defending his throne. Creon has ordered that the legitimate king should be buried and that the challenger's body should be left unburied—the greatest humiliation and dishonor to be done to a man, according to Greek custom. The principle that Creon represents is that of the supremacy of the law of the state over ties of blood, of obedience to authority over allegiance to the natural law of humanity. Antigone refuses to violate the laws of blood and of the solidarity of all human beings for the sake of an authoritarian, hierarchical principle.

The two principles for which Creon and Antigone stand are those which Bachofen characterized as the patriarchal as against the matriarchal principle, respectively. The matriarchal principle is that of blood relationship as the fundamental and indestructible tie, of the equality of all men, of the respect for human life and of love. The patriarchal principle is that the ties between man and wife, between ruler and ruled, take precedence over ties of blood. It is the principle of order and authority, of obedience and hierarchy.

Antigone represents the matriarchal principle and thus is the uncompromising adversary of the representative of patriarchal authority, Creon. Ismene, in contrast, has accepted the defeat and given in to the victorious patriarchal order; she is a symbol of women under patriarchal domination. Sophocles makes her role very clear by having her say to Antigone, who has decided to defy Creon's command:

> And now *we* in turn—we two left all alone—think how we shall perish, more miserably than all the rest, if, in defiance of the law, we brave a king's decree or his powers. Nay, we must remember, first, *that we were born women, as who should not strive with men*; next, that we are ruled of the stronger, so that we must obey in these things, and in things yet sorer. I, therefore, asking the *Spirits Infernal* to pardon, seeing that force is put on

> me herein, will hearken to our rulers; for 'tis witless to be over busy.

Ismene has accepted male authority as her ultimate norm; she has accepted the defeat of women "who should not strive with men." Her loyalty to the goddesses is expressed only in begging them to forgive her who has to yield to the force of the ruler.

The humanistic principle of the matriarchal world, with its emphasis on man's greatness and dignity, finds a beautiful and forceful expression in the chorus's praise of the power of man:

> Wonders are many, *and none is more wonderful than man*; the power that crosses the white sea, driven by the stormy southwind, making a path under surges that threaten to engulf him; and *Earth, the eldest of the gods*, the immortal, the unwearied, doth he wear, turning the soil with the offspring of horses, as the ploughs go to and fro from year to year.

The conflict between the two principles unfolds in the further development of the play. Antigone insists that the law she obeys is not that of the Olympian gods. Her law "is not of today or yesterday, but from all time, and no man knows when they were first put forth"; and, we may add, the law of burial, of returning the body to Mother Earth, is rooted in the very principles of matriarchal religion. Antigone stands for the solidarity of man and the principle of the all-embracing motherly love. " 'Tis not my nature to join in hating but in loving."

For Creon, obedience to authority is the supreme value; human solidarity and love, if in conflict with obedience, have to yield. He has to defeat Antigone in order to uphold patriarchal authority and with it his virility.

> *Now verily I am no man, she is the man,* if this victory shall rest with her, and bring no penalty.

Creon lays down the authoritarian, patriarchal principle in unequivocal language:

Yea, this, my son, should be thy heart's fixed law—in all things to *obey thy father's will.* 'Tis for this that men pray to see *dutiful children* grow up around them in their homes—that such may requite their father's foe with evil, and honour, as their father doth, his friend. But he who *begets unprofitable children*—what shall we say that he hath sown, but trouble for himself, and much triumph for his foes? Then do not thou, my son, at pleasure's beck, dethrone thy reason for a woman's sake; knowing that this is a joy that soon grows cold in clasping arms—an evil woman to share they bed and thy home. For what wound could strike deeper than a false friend? Nay, with loathing, and as if she were thine enemy, let this girl go to find a husband in the house of Hades. For since I have taken her, alone of all the city, in open disobedience, I will not make myself a liar to my people—I will slay her.

So let her appeal as she will to the majesty of kindred blood. If I am to nurture mine own kindred in naughtiness, needs must I hear with it in aliens. *He who does his duty in his own household will be found righteous in the State also. But if any one transgresses and does violence to the laws, or thinks to dictate to his rulers, such a one can win no praise from me. No, whomsoever the city may appoint, that man must be obeyed, in little things and great, in just things and unjust; and I should feel sure that one who thus obeys would be a good ruler no less than a good subject,* and in the storm of spears would stand his ground where he was set, loyal and dauntless at his comrade's side.

But disobedience is the worst of evils. This it is that ruins cities; this makes home desolate; by this, the ranks of allies are broken into headlong rout; but, of the lives whose course is fair, the greater part owes safety to obedience. *Therefore, we must support the cause of order, and in no wise suffer a woman to worst us. Better to fall from power, if we must, by a man's hand; than we should be called weaker than a woman.*

Authority in the family and authority in the state are the two interrelated supreme values for which Creon stands. Sons are the property of their fathers and their function is to be "serviceable" to the father. "Pater potestas" in the family is the basis for the ruler's power in the state. Citizens are the property of the state and its ruler, and "disobedience is the worst of evils."

Haemon, Creon's son, represents the principles for which Antigone fights. Although he tries at first to appease and persuade his father, he declares his opposition openly when he sees that his father will not yield. He relies on reason, "the highest of all things that we call our own" and on the will of the people. When Creon accuses Antigone of being tainted with the "malady of disobedience," Haemon's rebellious answer is "Our Theban folk, with one voice, denies it." When Creon argues, "Am I to rule this land by other judgment than mine own?" Haemon's answer is "That is no city which belongs to one man. Thou wouldst make a good monarch of a desert." Creon brings the argument again to the crucial point by saying, "This boy, it seems, is the *woman's* champion." And Haemon points to the matriarchal goddesses by answering, "And for thee, and for me, and for *the gods below.*"

The two principles have now been stated with full clarity, and the end of the tragedy only carries the action to the point of final decision. Creon has Antigone buried alive in a cave—again a symbolic expression of her connection with the goddesses of the earth. The seer Teiresias, who in *King Oedipus* was instrumental in making Oedipus aware of his crime, appears again, this time to make Creon aware of his. Stricken by panic, Creon gives in and tries to save Antigone. He rushes to the cave where she is entombed, but Antigone is already dead. Haemon tries to kill his father; when he fails, he takes his own life. Creon's wife, Eurydice, upon hearing the fate of her son, kills herself, cursing her husband as the murderer of her children. Creon recognizes the complete collapse of his world and the defeat of his principles. He admits his own moral bankruptcy, and the play ends with his confession:

> Ah me, this guilt can never be fixed on any other mortal kind, for my acquittal! I, even I, was thy slayer, wretched that I am—I own the truth. Lead me away, O my servants, lead me hence with all speed, whose life is but as death! . . .

> Lead me away, I pray you; a rash, foolish man; who have slain thee, ah, my son, unwittingly, and thee, too, my wife—unhappy that I am! I know not which way I should bend my gaze, or where I should seek support; for all is amiss with that which is in my hands,—and yonder again, a crushing fate hath leapt upon my head.

We are now in a position to answer the questions we raised at the beginning. Is the Oedipus myth as presented in Sophocles' trilogy centered around the crime of incest? Is the murder of the father the symbolic expression of a hate resulting from jealousy? Though the answer is doubtful at the end of *King Oedipus,* it is hardly doubtful any more at the end of *Antigone.* Not Oedipus but Creon is defeated in the end, and with him the principle of authoritarianism, of man's domination over men, the father's domination over his son, and the dictator's domination over the people. If we accept the theory of matriarchal forms of society and religion, then, indeed, there seems to be little doubt that Oedipus, Haemon, and Antigone are representatives of the old principles of matriarchy, those of equality and democracy, in contrast to Creon, who represents patriarchal domination and obedience.[5]

[5]No less a thinker than Hegel saw the conflict represented in Antigone in the same light many years prior to Bachofen. He says of Antigone: "The gods, however, which she worships are the gods below, the gods of Hades, the inner gods of emotion, of love, of blood, and not the gods of the day, of the free and self-conscious life, of the nation, and the state" (Hegel, *Aesthetik,* II, 2, Absch., Ch. I; compare also *Philosophy of Religion,* XVI, p. 133). Hegel in this statement is so much on the side of the state and its laws that he defines Creon's principle as that of "the free life of the people and the state" in spite of the undeniable evidence that Creon does not represent freedom but dictatorship. In view of this one-sided sympathy of Hegel's, it is all the more significant that he states so clearly that Antigone stands for the principles of love, of blood and emotion, which later on Bachofen found to be the characteristic principles of the matriarchal world. While Hegel's sympathy for the patriarchal principles is not surprising, one does not expect to find it in Bachofen's writings. And yet Bachofen's own attitude to matriarchal society has been quite ambivalent. It seems that he loved matriarchate and hated patriarchal principles, but inasmuch as he was also a religious Protestant and a believer in the progress of reason, he believed in the supremacy of the patriarchal principle over matriarchate. In a great part of his writings his sympathy with the matriarchal principle finds expression. In other parts, and this holds true of his brief interpretation of the Oedipus myth (Bachofen, 1926, pp. 259–266), he, like Hegel, sides with the victorious Olympian gods. To him Oedipus stands on the

Our interpretation, however, needs to be supplemented by another consideration. Although the conflict between Oedipus, Antigone and Haemon, on the one side, against Creon, on the other, contains a memory of the conflict between patriarchal and matriarchal principles, and particularly of its mythical elements, it must also be understood in terms of the specific political and cultural situation in Sophocles' time and of his reactions to that situation.

The Peloponnesian war, the threat to the political independence of Athens, and the plague that ravaged the city at the beginning of the war had helped to uproot the old religious and philosophical traditions. Indeed, attacks against religion were not new, but they reached a climax in the teachings of Sophocles' Sophist adversaries. He was opposed particularly to those Sophists who not only proclaimed despotism exercised by an intellectual elite but also upheld unrestricted selfishness as a moral principle. The ethics of egotistical supermen proclaimed by this wing of the Sophists and their amoral opportunism were the very opposite of Sophocles' philosophy. In Creon, Sophocles created a figure representing this school of sophism, and Creon's speeches resembled the Sophist pattern even in style and expression.[6]

In his argument against the Sophists, Sophocles gave new expression to the old religious traditions of the people with their emphasis

---

frontier between the matriarchal and the patriarchal world. The fact that he does not know his father points to a matriarchal origin in which only the mother but not the father is certain. But the fact that he discovers eventually who his real father is, according to Bachofen, marks the beginning of the patriarchal family in which the true father is known. "Oedipus," he says, "is connected with the progress to a higher level of existence. He is one of those great figures whose suffering and pain lead to a more beautiful form of human civilization; one of those still rooted in the old order of things who are at the same time sacrificed and thus become the founders of a new epoch" (p. 266). Bachofen stresses the fact that the dreaded mother-goddesses, the Erinyes, have subordinated themselves to the Apollonian world and that the connection between Oedipus and them marks the victory of the patriarchal principle. It seems to me that Bachofen's interpretation does not do justice to the fact that Creon, although he is the only one who survives physically, symbolizing the victory of the patriarchal world, is the one who is morally defeated. It may be assumed that Sophocles intended to convey the idea that the patriarchal world was triumphant, but that it would be defeated unless it adopted the humanistic principles of the older matriarchal order.

[6]See Callicles in Plato's *Georgias* and Thrasymachus in his *Republic*.

on love, equality, and justice. "The religious attitude of Sophocles . . . is primarily concerned not with the official religion of the state but with those helpful secondary powers which always were closer to the faith of the masses than the aristocratic Olympians and to whom the people turned again in the dangers of the Peloponnesian war" (Schmid, 1934). These "secondary powers," which were different from the "aristocratic Olympian" gods, are easily identified as the goddesses of the matriarchal world.

We see, then, that Sophocles' views, expressed in the Oedipus trilogy, are to be understood as a blend of his opposition to contemporary sophism and of his sympathy for the old, non-Olympian religious ideas.[7] In the name of both he proclaimed the principle that the dignity of man and the sanctity of human bonds must never be subordinated to inhuman and authoritarian claims of the state or to opportunistic considerations.[8]

REFERENCES

Bachofen, J. J. (1926), *Der Mythus von Orient und Okzident*, ed. M. Schroeder. Munich: Beck.

——— (1861), Mutterrecht und Urreligion. Leipzig: Alfred Kroener (1926).

Briffault, R. (1927), *The Mothers*. New York: Macmillan.

Eckermann, J. P. (1830), Gespräche mit Goethe in der letzen Jahren seines lebens. von Johann Peter Eckermann. (Neue Ausg. Hrsg. von Fritz Bergemann) (Wiesbaden) Insel (1955).

(Conversations with Goethe by J. P. Eckermann selected with an introd. and annotated index by Hans Kohn. Translated by Gisela C. O'Brien. New York: F. Ungar Pub. Co. 1964.)

Freud, S. (1900), The interpretation of dreams. In: *The Basic Writings of Sigmund Freud*, trans. A. A. Brill. New York: Modern Library, pp. 308.

Fromm, E. (1934), Zur Rezeption der Mutterrechtstheorie. *Zeitschrift fur Sozialforschung*, 3:196.

——— (1948), The Oedipus complex and the Oedipus myth. In: *The Family: Its Function and Destiny*, ed. R.N. Anshen. New York: Harper.

[7]It is interesting to note that the same blend between progressive political ideas and a sympathy with mythical matriarchal principles is to be found again in the nineteenth century in Bachofen's, Engel's, and Morgan's work (see Fromm, 1934).

[8]See Nestle (1910). The problem of hostility between father and son was also of great personal significance in the life of the poet. Iophon, the son, sued his aged father and wanted the court to deprive him of the right to manage his own business affairs, a suit from which Sophocles emerged victorious.

Morgan, L. H. (1871), *Systems of Consanguinity and Affinity*. Chicago: Charles H. Kerr.

——— (1877), *Ancient Society*. Chicago: Charles H. Kerr.

Nestle, W. (1910), Sophokles und die Sophistik. *Classical Philology*, 5:129–157.

Oates, W. J., & O'Neill, E., Eds. (1938), *The Complete Greek Drama*, trans. R. C. Webb. New York: Random House.

Robert, C. (1915), *Oedipus*. Berlin: Weidemann.

Schmid, W. (1934), Geschichte der Griechischen Literatur. In: *Handbuch der Altertumswissenschaften*, vol. I, ed. W. Otto. Munich.

Schneidewin, F. W. (1852), Die Sage von Oedipus. *Abhandlung der Geschichte der W. z. Gott*, 5.

9

Sociopolitical Functions of the Oedipus Myth in Early Greece

GEORGE DEVEREUX

[1963]

The psychoanalytic study of social and cultural phenomena seeks to translate subjective, unconscious, psychological processes into objective sociocultural data. This problem was first broached by psychoanalysts primarily in terms of paleopsychological speculations regarding the origins of culture, relatively little information being then available regarding concrete examples of the manner in which—under pressures of stress—unconscious conglomerates of impulses and fantasies are transformed into myths or customs.

As the oedipal myth is, from the psychoanalytic point of view, the nuclear example of this transformation of a subjective complex into a cultural phenomenon, it is proposed to discuss the probability that this myth—as distinct from the oedipus complex—may have been evolved in response to certain sociopolitical stresses resulting from the

---

Reprinted with permission from *Psychoanalytic Quarterly*, vol. 32, pp. 205-214.

ultimately successful pressure of the Sky-God-worshiping Hellenic invaders to impose patrilineal descent and patrilineal inheritance laws and practices upon the but half-conquered, Earth-Goddess-worshiping, matrilineal, pre-Hellenic inhabitants of Greece.

It is, of course, clearly understood that the oedipus complex is a universal, developmental human phenomenon, wholly independent, in all its essential aspects, of the specific nature of the society and culture into which an individual is born. It is unnecessary to appeal to highly speculative paleopsychological arguments to provide a biological basis for the oedipus complex, since there exists an observable biological fact, which readily explains the universality of the oedipus complex in man, and only in man (Devereux, 1956b).

The human female is unique in being sexually receptive even during pregnancy and lactation. She is therefore hormonally and psychologically the only female capable of experiencing simultaneously both sexual and maternal emotions. It has been shown elsewhere—both by analysis of the Oedipus myth (Devereux, 1953b) and by clinical data fully confirming my interpretation of it (Devereux, 1960)—that it is most efficient and economical to derive the Oedipus complex from parental counteroedipal impulses. The simultaneous presence of sexual and maternal attitudes in the human female entirely suffices to explain why the oedipus complex is a universal and, indeed, a species-characteristic complex of mankind only. Freud stated that it is the pivot of man's differentiation from animals and of the development of the human psyche and of human culture (Freud, 1913), which, as I have shown, must be viewed as coemergents (Devereux, 1953a).

This conception of the oedipus complex fully dovetails with Lowie's cogent argument (1933), that apes cannot possibly commit incest, because kinship is a psychocultural concept that has no meaning for the ape. The biological fact that a given female happens to be his mother, daughter, or sister has no psychic significance for the ape and therefore no motivational force for the male ape who finds himself in the presence of his sexually receptive mother, daughter, or sister; hence, it can neither impel him to reject "virtuously" nor seek "neurotically" or "criminally" sexual cohabitation with his female relatives.

The demonstration that the genesis of the Oedipus myth—as distinct from the oedipus complex—had certain sociopolitical determinants in ancient Greek society therefore strengthens, rather than weakens, the Freudian position regarding this complex and its nuclear importance in human psychology. What we propose to discuss here are simply the factors which cause a subjective (and partly unconscious) psychic constellation of impulses and fantasies to erupt into consciousness, and—as a defense against this return of the repressed—to become depersonalized and incorporated into culture, by the transformation of subjective fantasies, for which one has a personal feeling of responsibility, into a culturally sanctioned myth for which one does not feel responsible (Devereux, 1956a, 1956b).

The Sociopolitical Setting

Despite wide divergences in the appraisal of details, many classical scholars affirm that the principal problem confronting the Hellenic invaders of Greece was the incompatibility of the Earth-Goddess-worshiping, matrilineal culture pattern of the pre-Hellenic inhabitants of Greece with the Sky-God-worshiping, patrilineal culture pattern of the conquerors.

Considerable effort was required to syncretize the female deities of the pre-Hellenic people with the male deities of the Hellenes; to define the relationship between them; and to impose the view that the ancient local goddess Hera, for example, in marrying the invading Sky-God Zeus became subject to his authority according to the Hellenic pattern, instead of retaining her hegemony which, according to the ancient local pattern, mother-goddesses exercised over their boy-son lovers, who were designated by the term *paredros*. It is permissible to speculate that the innumerable references in Homer and in many other sources to constant bickerings between Hera and Zeus may represent remote echoes of this forcible blending of two pantheons. An even more striking echo of this struggle for power between Zeus and Hera is the birth of Athena and, to a lesser extent, that of Dionysus, and of Typhon and Hephaestus.

In various versions of the myth we find that Zeus and Hera

entered into a contest of parthenogenetic parenthood. Hera managed to give birth parthenogenetically to Typhon and, perhaps, also to Hephaestus, after being angered by Zeus' giving birth to Athena. Regarding Athena's birth, two versions exist. In one, Zeus causes Metis to become pregnant with Athena, and then either swallows the pregnant Metis, or else transfers the already conceived Athena into his own belly. In another version Athena is born, clad in full armor, from the head of Zeus. A less specific pregnancy and birth is exemplified by the myth of Dionysus. After killing his pregnant mistress, Semele, Zeus rescues his unborn son, Dionysus, by slitting open his own thigh and placing the fetus into this substitute womb. Surely a male god would not have "demeaned" himself to the point of seeking to become a mother had the absolute supremacy of male over female been fully established at the time this myth came into being.[1] It is an important fact that Athena—originally herself a local pre-Hellenic goddess—subsequently becomes an obedient tool of her father Zeus' will.

The struggle for supremacy between male and female deities swayed back and forth for a long time. According to one etymology, the name Poseidon simply means Husband of the Lady, suggesting that Poseidon was not granted at once supremacy over his spouse.

On the human level, the conflict assumed its most acute forms in connection with the transmission of royal powers. Graves's extreme views apart (1955), the findings of conservative classical scholars suggest that in pre-Hellenic Greece kingship was not inherited by the king's son, but by the one who at specified intervals ritually killed the current king and married the queen. In the transitional period there appear to have been instances—such as the violent death of Oenomaus when his daughter married Pelops—where the successor was the man who killed the king and married his daughter.

A lingering echo of this tradition is found in the *Odyssey*. Although Odysseus was a just, well-established, and beloved king, not without great difficulties was he able to bring his bride Penelope to his own kingdom of Ithaca, instead of assuming a matrilocal residence, as did so many of the early kings. His son, Telemachus, found it quite

[1]One is reminded in this context of such primitive practices as the couvade (Reik, 1931), and of Róheim's analysis of the Australian "father-with-a-vagina" complex (1932).

impossible to enlist the support of the Ithacans against the suitors who sought to become the heirs of Odysseus by marrying his supposed widow, Penelope. This lack of support for Telemachus' claim can only be viewed as the result of a still altogether insufficient acceptance of the principle of patrilineal succession to the throne. This simple fact is partly obscured by the many references in the Odyssey to the number and power of the suitors and by its description of Telemachus as weak, young, and like Hamlet in his vacillations (Jones, 1949; Devereux, 1957a). Paradoxically, Telemachus' sole support is the originally pre-Hellenic goddess Athena, now a faithful adherent of the new system. She lends her assistance to Telemachus in his claim to kingship by right of patrilineal inheritance. This supports the interpretation that Telemachus' practical difficulties are rooted in the conflict between two traditional modes of inheritance. Indeed, although Telemachus' claim is based on the patrilineal principle, he seeks to obtain sovereignty with the help of a pre-Hellenic goddess, Athena. To restate this important distinction, his abstract claim is based on the principle of patriliny; his method of seeking to gain his inheritance is, however, related to the ancient principle of kingship acquired with the help of, and in a manner agreeable to, a goddess. This distinction is crucial. A correct interpretation of the social function of the Oedipus myth necessitates that a distinction be made between the principle in terms of which inheritance is claimed, and the accepted means for gaining possession of it.

The Succession of Oedipus to the Throne

The crucially relevant episode of the Oedipus myth is that Oedipus does inherit his kingship from his father in accordance with the Hellenic principle of patrilineal succession, but gains possession of it in accordance with a pre-Hellenic ritual: he kills a king who is his father, and marries a queen who is his mother. Anthropologically, the accession of Oedipus to the kingship by means of a traditional rite, whose ideological basis is already in jeopardy or even obsolete, accords with the principle that rituals often outlive their ideological basis and are placed in the service of a new ideology.[2]

[2]A familiar example is the rite of the Christmas tree. It is one of the many pagan rituals incorporated into Christian practice.

Curiously enough, echoes of this duality are found in the lost sequel to the *Odyssey*, which reports that Odysseus was eventually killed by Telegonus, his son by Circe, whereupon Telegonus, together with Penelope and Telemachus, goes to the island of Odysseus' erstwhile parmour, Circe, where Telemachus marries Circe while Circe's son marries Penelope! (Roscher, 1884–1937).

These observations help us view the tragic majesty of the Oedipus myth as the product of an attempt to syncretize patrilineal principles of inheritance with matrilineal techniques of gaining possession of the inheritance. It clarifies the sociopolitical function of the Oedipus myth in the transition from pre-Hellenic to Hellenic society. Thus, the Oedipus myth, even though it arouses an Aristotelian "horror and pity," is, in the last resort, also a "cautionary tale" of immense proportions and scope. Some champions of the old system seem to say: "You wish the kingship to be inherited by the king's son? Very well then! Since only the old, matrilineally oriented ritual of accession validates kingship, you must anticipate and accept the slaying of the father by the son and the subsequent marriage of the son with his mother. That is what Oedipus did. Behold the consequences!"

The thesis that the Oedipus myth has a major political significance is supported by the myth of Theseus. Like Oedipus, he was exposed to death, albeit for the public weal: he was sent to Crete, as part of Athens' tribute to Minos. Having seduced Ariadne, the daughter of Minos, he killed the monstrous Minotaur with her help. On his return to Athens, he "forgot" to hoist the white sail, which was to have signaled to his royal father his safe return, whereupon the king committed suicide, thereby "accidentally" vacating the kingship for his son.

In this myth, marriage between mother and son is transposed to the next generation. Theseus' wife, Phaedra, falls in love with Theseus' bastard son, Hippolytus, who rejects her advances, because, being a devotee of chaste Artemis, he is presumably impotent, as Phoenix became impotent after committing incest with his father's favorite concubine (Devereux, 1955). The frustrated Phaedra thereupon hangs herself, after falsely accusing Hippolytus of having raped her: Jocasta, it may be recalled, hanged herself after truthfully accusing Oedipus of having married her or, according to an earlier version, of having also raped her as soon as he had killed Laius in combat

(Devereux, 1953b). The deceived Theseus curses his son who, as a result, is killed under dramatic circumstances.

These parallels are not mere coincidences. Theseus plays a crucial role in establishing the supremacy of the male in Hellenic Greece. He accomplished this mainly by his daring convocation of the Athenian Areopagus, which absolved Orestes of the crime of matricide and freed him from persecution by the pursuing Erinyes—a judgment which established, once and for all, that a son was more closely related to his father than to his mother. This celebrated deed tends to obscure the fact that, in befriending the blind and homeless Oedipus, in providing him with a retreat at Colonus, and in giving him a hero's burial, Theseus also broke another lance on behalf of the new system of patriliny. He gave protection and honor to the man who acceded to his father's kingship in accordance with the new law of patrilineal inheritance, albeit by means of the ancient ritual of killing the king and marrying the queen.

Another notable parallel is that, having become kings "accidentally" by causing the death of their respective fathers, Oedipus and Theseus both established dynasties which rapidly went down in chaos. The struggle for Oedipus' succession led to the War of the Seven, and then to the War of the Epigoni against Thebes. Theseus' direct succession, too, ended in chaos in the very next generation, power being wrested from his sons by his distant nephew, Menestheus. These aftermaths of the "irregular" manner in which both Oedipus and Theseus succeeded their fathers—comparable to the troubles of Telemachus—show that the old system was reluctant to relinquish its hold on the imagination of the people. Homer sidestepped the issue simply by bringing back Odysseus, thereby leaving the rule of succession in Ithaca undecided. The Telegonia also leaves the problem undecided as regards Ithaca, but clearly returns to the ancient system in Circe's country by having Odysseus' two sons marry their respective stepmothers. The myths of Oedipus and of Theseus bring the issue to a head, and seemingly resolve it in favor of patriliny, though the new system leads to chaos in the very next generation. The case of Phoenix is even more extreme. He commits incest with his stepmother and becomes impotent; hence, the problem of his founding a patrilineal dynasty does not even arise (Devereux, 1955).

A few words should be said here about the concept of hero in ancient Greece. First, nearly all the cities made famous by the deeds of heroes were pre-Hellenic settlements. They were the cities where the struggles between the conquered pre-Hellenic population and the conquering Hellenes took place (Dodds, 1951). Second, the conduct of most of the mythical heroes was anything but virtuous. Now, broadly speaking, even though all heroes were guilty of countless crimes by ordinary standards, the Greeks tended to differentiate between primarily meritorious heroes such as Oedipus, Theseus, Heracles, etc., and truly villainous heroes, such as Aegisthus (slayer of Agamemnon and paramour of Clytemnestra), Salmoneus, Tantalus, etc. This distinction would be understandable and transparent enough, were it not for two curious facts, cogently highlighted by Harrison (1955). The first is that, according to Greek belief, the worship of heroes did not necessarily involve the expectation of receiving positive benefits from the sacrifices offered them. Some of these sacrifices were perhaps more in the nature of bribes to induce the heroes to refrain from harming the donors. This attitude is not unique. The sacrifices offered by the Sedang Moi of Indochina to the Thundergods are, likewise, solely intended to avert harm, and not as inducements to grant benefits (Devereux, 1940); moreover, as Angelo Brelich, Professor of the History of Religions in the University of Rome, kindly pointed out to the author, sacrifices to the Olympians were afterward partly eaten, because one may share sacrifices with the living gods, whereas those offered to the heroes of the past and to chthonian deities were entirely given over to the flames because one may not share a banquet with the dead. In other words, both "good" and villainous heroes were dangerous. Often the sole benefit one derived from their cult was that they could be induced not to cause harm.

The most perplexing problem, however, is one specifically analyzed by Harrison (1955). The paradoxical epithet, "blameless," is apparently given only to villainous heroes like Aegisthus or Salmoneus. According to Harrison, this curious epithet underscores the fact that the villainous heroes were not simply antisocial. Their deeds were largely motivated by their adherence to the ancient, pre-Hellenic ways. Unlike the "heroic" heroes, they are the heroes of the conquered. They are held in qualified admiration by the conquerors, somewhat in the manner in which, in contemporary America, the Indian "villains" of the nineteenth century—Geronimo the Apache, Sitting Bull the Sioux—have become heroes of American history. Oral tradition and imagination—even in Hollywood—after decades of heroic-cowboy versus wicked-Indian plots, is beginning to turn out Westerns in which the roles are reversed.

All these elements and many others suggest that the great crisis of Greek society—far exceeding in importance the Trojan War, the Persian Wars, and the Peloponnesian War—was the struggle for the supremacy of the patrilineal system over the matrilineal, which led to the attempt to blend the two cultures into a functional whole. One decisive element in this syncretistic conflict is the emergence of the Oedipus myth as a traditional cautionary legend, or as a conservative political manifesto, which played an important role in the gradual shaping of the Homeric Greek state.

These findings do not call for a modification, or for a so-called neo-Freudian "culturalization" of the oedipus complex. On the contrary, they illuminate the tremendous role which the oedipus complex in its classical form plays in all human affairs, be they subjective or sociocultural. No realistic conception of man as a phenomenon *sui generis* is possible without assigning a nuclear position to the oedipus complex in social science as well as in psychology.

REFERENCES

Devereux, G. (1940), Religious attitudes of the Sedang. In: W. F. Ogburn & M. F. Nimkoff, *Sociology*. Cambridge, MA: Houghton-Mifflin.

——— (1953a), Cultural factors in psychoanalytic therapy. *J. Amer. Psychoanal. Assn.*, 1:629–655.

——— (1953b), Why Oedipus killed Laius: A note on the complementary Oedipus complex in Greek drama. *Internat. J. Psycho-Anal.*, 34:132–141. Chapter 7, this volume.

——— (1955), A counteroedipal episode in Homer's *Iliad. Bull. Phila. Assn. Psychoanal.*, 4:90–97.

——— (1956a), Normal and abnormal. In: *Some Uses of Anthropology, Theoretical and Applied.* Washington, DC: Washington Anthropological Society.

——— (1956b), *Therapeutic Education.* New York: Harper & Bros.

——— (1957a), Penelope's character. *Psychoanal. Quart.*, 26:378–386.

——— (1957b), Psychoanalysis as anthropological field work. *Transactions of the NY Acad. Sciences,* Series II, 19:457–472.

——— (1960), Retaliatory homosexual triumph over the father. *Internat. J. Psycho-Anal.*, 41:157–161.
Dodds, E. R. (1951), *The Greeks and the Irrational.* Berkeley: University of California Press.
Freud, S. (1913), Totem and taboo. *Standard Edition*, 13:1–161. London: Hogarth Press, 1955.
Graves, R. (1955), *The Greek Myths.* 2 vols. Baltimore: Penguin.
Harrison, J. (1955), *Prolegomena to the Study of Greek Religion.* New York: Meridian.
Jones, E. (1949), *Hamlet and Oedipus.* New York: Norton.
Lowie, R. H. (1933), The family as a social unit. *Papers of the Michigan Academy of Science, Arts and Letters*, 18:53–69.
Reik, T. (1931), *Ritual.* New York: Norton.
Róheim, G. (1932), Psychoanalysis of primitive culture types. *Internat. J. Psycho-Anal.*, 13:1–224.
Roscher, W. (1884–1937), *Ausführliches Lexicon der griechischen und römischen Mythologie.* 6 vols. in 9 tomes. Leipzig: Teubner.

10

On Interpreting the Oedipus Plays

MARK KANZER

[1964]

The Oedipus myth is frequently analyzed on the basis of the *Oedipus Tyrannus* of Sophocles, as though the latter represented an age-old, spontaneous, and unitary fantasy of the human race, a universal dream that had been captured intact by the Greek dramatist. Similarly, the personality and even developmental stages in the life of the hero have been expounded from this same material as though it represented, in fact, the experiences of a particular individual who became somehow the allegorical representative of the male's unconscious sexual strivings everywhere and in all times. Sophocles, however, was not a dispassionate or scientific recorder of myths and, in the *Oedipus Tyrannus,* he was expressing highly personal views on political, religious, and military problems of his own time (Gassner, 1940; Grene and Lattimore, 1959). As an ordained priest and an aristocrat, he had little taste for upstart tyrants like Oedipus who came to power because of their individual intellects and achievements, rather than a royal background and the will of the gods.

Reprinted with permission from *Psychoanalytic Study of Society,* vol. 3, pp. 26–38.

Moreover, Sophocles was submitting his play with an eye to winning the annual award of the Athenian drama critics. In this respect, it may be noted, the *Oedipus Tyrannus* was not a success. Some felt that the fault lay in a poor production, since the playwright was not able to find wealthy backers. Others were upset by sensational aspects which were regarded as an offense to good taste. For example, Sophocles employed a mask which showed blood streaming from the eyeless sockets of his hero. The Greeks, after all, may not have been closer to the unconscious than the Elizabethans, as has been suggested (Freud, 1900). The latter did not object when the eyes of Gloucester were torn from his head in full view of the audience. In any event, the Oedipus that emerges from the Sophocles classic was a dramatic hero, in many respects a contemporary sophisticated Athenian, and scarcely a universal dream that had acquired life.

There was a distinctly different version of the Oedipus myth in Homer's epics some six hundred years before Sophocles. Here there was no reference to the Sphinx; Oedipus was not blinded nor was he exiled, but lived on as ruler of Thebes, afflicted by the Furies as the result of a curse by his dying mother. Ultimately, he was killed in combat and buried with honor in his own country; the version by Sophocles permits the legendary hero to die in Colonus, a suburb of Athens, where the dramatist himself had been born. Several intriguing ideas suggest themselves at this point, but we shall mention just one: the noteworthy parallel to the story of Orestes, the mother murderer, who was also afflicted by the Furies (a euphemism presumably for psychosis), and who found a haven and cure in Athens. Orestes may be regarded as representative of the negative Oedipus complex, the deeper and recessive aspect of the Oedipus myth itself. The parricidal trends appear overtly in the chronicle; the matricidal and homosexual wishes must be hidden, as through the symbolism that conceals the mother behind the figure of the Sphinx (Kanzer, 1948).

Sophocles, it appears, used as his source of information a ninth century B.C. narrative about the Kings of Thebes and the civil wars between the sons of Oedipus, which were dramatized in other plays of the Oedipus cycle (Grene and Lattimore, 1959). In these conflicts, the greatest in Greek history before the Trojan War, Oedipus himself was assigned something of the role of an allegorical spirit, an ancestor like

Adam, whose sins continued to live on and demand expiation even from his descendants. Nevertheless, it is by no means improbable, in the light of modern archeological and historical research, that a factual basis for the Theban legend exists (Reik, 1920). Velikovsky (1960), in a work which is none too convincing, suggests that Oedipus was identical with the Egyptian King Akhnaton. More substance seems to adhere to his endeavors to link the Greek and the Egyptian cities of Thebes, a matter to which we shall also give some attention.

The original chronicle of the Theban kings that Sophocles used has not been preserved. The dramatist is supposed to have adhered to it rather faithfully, though his own account about Oedipus is manifestly filled with contradictions (Grene and Lattimore, 1959). The studies of Carl Robert (1915) suggest a derivation of the hero from a demigod, son, and lover of the earth goddess Demeter. Shrines of an Oedipus cult existed in several Greek cities, the oldest probably at Eteonos, near Attica. The story of Oedipus thus becomes linked with one of the most ancient forms of worship, the spring vegetation rites which are frequently associated with matriarchal regimes and the slaying of the Winter King, real or symbolic, by the Summer King. The relationship between the kings is recognized overtly or tacitly as that between father and son.

Certain universal roots of the Oedipus legend, arising in this way, may be discovered in the play of Sophocles, which was presented in honor of the feast of Dionysus, a similar vegetation demigod and reputed in mythology to be a kinsman of Oedipus. The drama perpetuates and sublimates in art what was originally human sacrifice to procure bread and wine. It was the breakthrough of blood into the artistic mask which horrified the Greeks, not the artfully presented oedipal themes of incest and parricide, which could more readily serve for catharsis of drives that were already attenuated. The plague that the sins of Oedipus drew on Thebes were those that would be disastrous in an agricultural community; along with the inability of women to conceive or give birth, there were corresponding blights on livestock and flocks. Apollo, the god of the sun, had somehow been offended; only the advent of a fertile and blameless new king could remedy the situation. The procession of the seasons was thus linked by a nature myth with that of the human generations.

The role of Oedipus as the traditional dying god, demigod, or king, and his rebirth as the new ruler, parallel the crucifixion of Jesus and his resurrection, as aspects of a similar spring ritual. In both instances, the father is ultimately a god or king, Jehovah or Apollo, Herod or Laius, in the tradition of the family romance. The coming of the son is associated with oracular warnings to the father (renascent memories of his own infantile oedipal strivings), which lead to his efforts to dispose of the infant. The Cross derives from the sacred tree (mother) on which the old king is immolated to insure a new blossoming; the nails through the feet of Jesus correspond with those through the feet of Oedipus; the finding of the newborn child by the shepherd is a birth fantasy that belongs both to springtime and the sexual theories of children.

In the opinion of Robert (1915), this spring ritual aspect of the Oedipus legend must be separated from the narrative of the Sphinx, which seems to accrue to the myth from other sources. The slaying of a monster does belong to the spring ritual and has totemistic antecedents; he is the Winter King. The Sphinx not unnaturally presents some special riddles. It apparently originated in Egypt, where the earliest versions were masculine and without wings (Roscher, 1912). In Crete, we encounter the first female winged Sphinxes; these seem however to be secondary fusions of an imported Sphinx with local monsters, like the harpies, half human, half animal, who represented the mother goddess. The winged birdlike element in the Cretan Sphinx and the harpies bespoke, according to tradition, oracular powers and the solution as well as the propounding of riddles; the priests made prophecies by observing the flight of the birds (Robert, 1915).

The lion's body, which the Greek Sphinx shared with some of the several Egyptian varieties, invites attention to the legend of Cadmus, ancestor of Oedipus, and of his sister Europa. The Cretans, who claimed descent from Europa, and the Thebans, who claimed descent from Cadmus, both contributed to the Sphinx cult. The symbol of Cadmus was a lion; he and his sister were Phoenicians and their father Agenor was reported to have come from Egypt to the land of Canaan some five centuries before Moses traversed the same pathway (Graves, 1955). The name Cadmus itself derives from a Semitic root, *Queddem*, "the easterner." There are many curious parallels between Cadmus and Moses; both shared with Oedipus the fate of offending the gods and therefore being compelled to end their days as homeless wanderers.

Cadmus, the wandering Phoenician, is thus a legendary link between the Sphinx of Egypt and that of Greece. He is also a vehicle of familiar Semitic traditions; like Moses, he was guided by the gods to a promised land, where he proceeded to found a city for his descendants. It was the Egyptian Thebes that was the center of the Sphinx cult and its queen was the consort of the gods—a role that was often equivalent to reposing by the highway, like the Sphinx, and selecting her mate from passersby who after a year of kingship were sacrificed to the gods. In the course of transition to patriarchy, the queens wed their own brothers—providing further material for the Oedipus myth. The Egyptian Thebes of the hundred gates was contrasted by Homer with the Greek Thebes of seven gates—in fact, the Greek name was conferred secondarily on the older Egyptian city. Quite possibly the links were furnished by migration, symbolized by Cadmus, just as legendarily Troy was linked with Rome through Aeneas.

The civic emblem of the Greek Thebes was a monster, half lion, half snake, a figure representing two familiar components of the Sphinx (Graves, 1955). Cadmus, the lion, was reputed to have been turned into a snake in his later years as punishment for having killed a serpent sacred to the natives among whom he came to found his city. Behind this myth apparently rests a history of conflict between patriarchal Phoenicians and local snake-cult matriarchies during the second millennium before Christ. The blind Teiresias, who figures in the Oedipus legend, was originally a snake god or priest (Robert, 1915); the curse of Jocasta against Oedipus was fulfilled by the Furies, archaic winged and snaky-haired representations of the mother goddess; the fate of Oedipus was induced through the prophecies and plagues sent by Apollo, the Python god, who thus doomed the descendant of the conquering Eastern lion to be driven like his ancestor from the land belonging to the snake people. There is in this myth, with its totemistic traditions, a calendar allusion: the lion and the snake were for the Thebans the symbols of the waxing and the waning portions of the year respectively; the transformation of Cadmus from a lion to a snake would coincide with a sacrifice to denote the changing of the seasons.

The transition from lion to snake also expresses fantasies about sexual change and castration. Teiresias, who plays the part of an oracle and sage in many Greek legends and whose name ("he who delights in signs") indicates that he too was a solver of riddles, was apparently introduced into the Oedipus story only secondarily. Here he was made into an alter ego of the hero, to whom were displaced his outer blindness and his inner understanding, characteristic symbols of the internalization of character development as the oedipal phase succumbs to superego formation with the onset of the latency period. At some point in the development of the Oedipus myth, as Robert (1915) points out, the physical conquest over a monster was succeeded by a psychic victory. A symbolic parallel may be found in the traditions about Teiresias, who was reputed to have seen snakes in copulation. In a subsequent sequence of events, he was granted bisexual capacities to enjoy sex alternately as male and female. But he offended Hera, queen of the gods, and was condemned by her to a blindness that was mitigated through his ability to foretell the future events that he would not be able to see.

It was also Hera, offended by the bisexuality of Laius, father of Oedipus, who sent the Sphinx to terrorize the people of Thebes until the monster was subdued by the intellect of the parricidal son. One may make the interpretation that homosexual dispositions of the oedipal period (rivalry with Hera), subdued by castration anxiety and superego formation, were granted a sublimated outlet during adolescent development—the subsequent regression being the point of departure for the oedipal tragedy. A cluster of myths condenses about the Teiresias-Laius theme—the rape of Ganymede by Zeus, for example, finds its parallel in the misconduct of Laius with a youth. As Reik (1920) in particular has emphasized, there is a conspicuous and unlikely duplication of events in the Oedipus narrative—two separate plagues sent down on Thebes, two different encounters of Oedipus on the road to Thebes (with Laius and with the Sphinx), and it is not improbable that (as with two dreams of the same night) there is a split which depicts first the heterosexual and then the homosexual aspect of the hero's lovemaking.

Our endeavor to establish the background of the Oedipus myth as distinct from the dramatized version presented by Sophocles broadens into the typical patterns which develop when a manifest content is traced through the tangles that lead to the latent content. Historical events emerge like day residues; many lands and many cultures made their contributions to the finished product for which the genius of Sophocles provided the facade of a secondary elaboration. The Oedipus myth may be viewed as a poetic chronicle of real historical value, like the Bible or the *Odyssey*; the experiences of individuals and of nations, the records of wars, migrations and social customs, have found their way into it. Cadmus is reputed by legend to have introduced the Semitic alphabet into Greece. A recent archeological and linguistic achievement seems to confirm this: the decoding of a mysterious language which suggests that the Phoenicians did in fact invade Greece and introduce their alphabet at about the time Cadmus and Europa made their appearance on the mythological scene (*New York Times*, 1961). Roscher (1912) is among the authorities with the complementary view that the Phoenicians of this period brought over the Sphinx from the Near East and ultimately from Egypt.

If myths are to be compared to the dreams of young nations (Freud, 1908), it is perhaps because dreams as well as myths deal integratively with external reality as well as with a structural hierarchy of men's wishes to which reality relates. Each dream is stimulated by immediate realistic experiences which evoke real memories of the past. It is the pattern of these memory constellations and the functions which they serve that distinguishes the dream from the myth and places both within a spectrum of problem-solving thoughts. Both the dream and the myth create symbols which expedite the transition between inner and outer reality. The dream symbol mobilizes memories which facilitate the transition to inner reality and autoplastic solutions; the myth is more of an intermediate toward outer reality and alloplastic solutions. External reality is accepted conditionally, provided there are still sufficient elements of denial admissible to safeguard the omnipotence of the ego and fulfill the wishes of the unconscious. Typical stages of myth formation indicate their early use in rituals to insure success in hunting and in planting crops. These food-procuring activities tend to become day residues for repressed impulses which threaten realistic success and must be diverted by ritual and mythmaking. Thus the myth finds its place between the oral hallucinatory satisfactions afforded by dreams and the oral mastery techniques which are part of the development of reality testing; regressively, it serves to conceal and gratify the nascent sexual drives.

The function of the myth in binding repressed instinctual impulses makes it of inherent importance in superego formation for the needs both of the individual and of the group. Where the dream represents the demands of the instincts, the myth tends to perpetuate and represent the demands of society on the mental apparatus for symbolization and acceptance. Different forms of culture evolve their own characteristic myths, and in that of Oedipus may be found deposits of the fantasies of totemistic hunting tribes, nomadic sheep tenders, agricultural matriarchies, and city-founding military chiefs. The Sphinx herself is no simple nightmare figure compiled by primary process thought from infantile memories and anxieties; she is also a consciously devised emblem and ideographic description of momentous events among mature peoples.

The latent content of the Oedipus myth thus becomes truly universal. Perhaps it is possible to trace in the development of Oedipus himself that of a universal man, because the stages of individual growth find parallels among the social formations which left their fossil-like imprints among the various strata of the myth. The tribal hunt presents analogies to the oedipal stage of development and the phobias that go with it; the agricultural ritual, with seasonal death and resurrection, compares with the latency period and superego formation; the reemergence of the sexual impulses, as these become manifest in the Oedipus drama, may be considered closer to puberty and to paranoia.[1]

In previous studies I have discussed such individual and maturational aspects of the Oedipus legend as are recorded in the plays of Sophocles (Kanzer, 1948, 1950). His Oedipus trilogy presents in essence a record of psychosocial problems from birth to death—from the actual abandonment of the newborn infant to his token sacrifice (death) and readoption (rebirth) in the circumcision rite that was symbolized by the laming of the hero. His growth is portrayed through a complex of characters who represent different dispositions

[1]"The oedipus complex too may have had stages of development and the study of prehistory may enable us to trace them out" (Freud, 1919a).

and phases during his personality development—Teiresias, Theseus, Creon, even Antigone—until at Colonus his death revives ancient traditions of the slaying of the Winter King in the sacred grove of the mother goddesses.

Thus, in the Oedipus myth as depicted by Sophocles we find that the diverse roots and fragments have been synthesized into a pattern and parable of human life generally. The very fact that so many men in so many cultures participated in the growth of the myth, each permitting it to pass through and be enriched by his own unconscious, each poet among them passing it on to other men in the idiom of his own time, insured in the end its impersonal representation of the basic drives of mankind, illustrating paradigmatically two of Freud's observations about myths: (1) that they provide an externalization of the inner mental processes themselves and (2) that through them the individual emerges from the group (Freud, 1921). The most unique feature of the Oedipus legend and the one that distinguishes it from all others is the ability to represent in the manifest content such deeply rooted personal and social taboos as the drives toward incest and parricide. To be sure, these may emerge on condition that they are represented as a fate unwittingly undergone. The introspective insights and projective universalizations of paranoid thought would probably be contributory here—especially as the manifest content still wards off homosexual and more deeply regressive preoedipal fantasies which are permitted symbolic representation only, as in the episode of the Sphinx.

Insofar as the Oedipus of the myth is a prototype of all men, he may be said to have no special personality. He is an externalization of the intellectual processes wrestling to control the oedipal conflicts in a social setting that requires their resolution according to established form. He must serve as a scapegoat, openly presenting to the community the desires it dares not fulfill or even acknowledge consciously, and providing it with a catharsis through the suffering of the hero and the horror that the spectator may hypocritically express. The poet gives the Oedipus of an era his own special features—e.g., Shakespeare's Hamlet, the Oedipus of Voltaire, Ivan Karamazov, Don Quixote. It was the special contribution of Sophocles that he developed the Oedipus legend itself beyond its previous limits in terms of psychosocial maturation and made it a vehicle for the prevailing Greek philosophy, "know thyself!"

Where the hero had advanced with the centuries from a monster-slayer, in the externalizing tradition of a totemistic culture and the counterphobic psychotherapeutic measures that it encouraged in adolescence, and had become a more introverted and thoughtful riddle-solver, Sophocles recognized that the riddle lay not in the outer universe but within man himself. Instead of seeking to explain fate as the will of the gods (with aggression internalized through religious institutions against which the Oedipus of Voltaire rebelled), the Greek dramatist advanced toward insight into the fact that fate lies in character, in the interaction between parents and children, and in the dispositions that we now call the Oedipus complex. To that extent, he implanted his own self and that of his contemporaries on the timeless features of the hero. His very innovations in the technique of the drama, such as reducing the importance of the chorus and introducing a third actor, gave greater scope to the role of the individual man emerging from myth and ritual (Gassner, 1940). The third actor, if we may risk an interpretation, was Sophocles himself in the guise of Oedipus.

Freud (1900) pointed out that the play unfolds like an analysis, and it was actually analysis that carried the Oedipus legend to its ultimate development—not only to recognize the meaning of the riddle, but to resolve it permanently, as the catharsis provided by Sophocles could not. With analysis, the myth—with its need to invoke a denial of reality—loses its function. It is interesting to consider how, even in the earliest delineation of the Sphinx, antecedent to all subsequent elaborations and modifications, the message of self-analysis as the key to the riddles of fate and the universe is depicted. Roscher (1912) indicates that there was at first no name for the Sphinx; its origin was in preverbal visual imagery, like the dream. The earliest Sphinxes seem to have been portraits of dead kings superimposed upon the body of a lion and set before their tombs to guard their remains and treasures against intruders. In effect, King Oedipus, confronting the Sphinx, encounters his own image as a mystery to be unraveled. The situation is familiar to the analyst from mirror dreams and the phenomenon of the double, with which man seeks to preserve his identity in the face of forces like castration and death that threaten to impinge upon his ego boundaries (Freud, 1919b). The sense of the uncanny, which arises under these circumstances, is the affective reaction to the encounter with the Sphinx.

The sense of the uncanny is also elicited in a characteristically oedipal phase of development by the sight of the female organ—the Medusa reaction, with the lost penis displaced upward and represented by a headless body (Freud, 1922). The Sphinx, like the Medusa, is equipped with compensatory signs of masculinity—the lion's body, the serpent tail, the wings, even the breasts (which distract attention from the lower to the upper part of the woman's body and acquire phallic significance). The Greek Sphinx, like the Medusa, is a representation of the phallic mother goddess. She now becomes the "sphincter," the vaginal strangler. We encounter the Sphinx-Medusa in the familiar blank dream with orgasm, in which the moment of visualizing or entering the female organ becomes the occasion for blacking out of the dream image and a defensive orgasm (Kanzer, 1954). The blacking out of the image, reproduced in the blindness of Oedipus and the taboo on looking imposed on Perseus, may be presented in attenuated form in dreams of headless persons. The oral interpretation of the blank dream phenomenon, while valid within its own context, should not distract from the inherent phallic significance of the same events.

It is the challenge of the phallic phase of development to confront the penisless body of the love object; the riddle itself is the female organ. There is an ancient tradition which suggests that the answer to the riddle is somehow contained in the name of the riddle-solver (Robert, 1915). Oedipus' "swollen foot," the sexually excited male, is the correct answer, especially as supplemented by the verbal response "Man," in reply to the phallically symbolic problem of establishing the identity of a creature with a variable number of legs. The subsequent fate of the Sphinx is confirmatory; the victorious Oedipus either stabs (deflowers) her, or she throws herself over a cliff (pregnancy—also the habitual punishment of vestal virgins who had violated their vows of chastity).

The phallic interpretation of the encounter of Oedipus with the Sphinx finds almost detailed corroboration in an ancient Egyptian myth about the sun god Ra (*Larousse*, 1959). He was a god of fertility and his image is found on the tombs of the Egyptian kings, the pharaohs, sons of the sun god, as a promise of life arising again from death. He was not all-powerful, however, for the goddess Isis sent a serpent to bite him so that he suffered cruelly until he consented to reveal to her his true name. Thereafter Isis, the Egyptian Hera, herself became the goddess of the sun and of fertility, represented with the orb of the sun and the horns of a cow on her head. Here again the name seems visibly translated into the male genitals.

However, Isis is also depicted with a cow's head set on a human body (reversing the Sphinx arrangement). The legend avers that she was decapitated by her son Horus for protecting her brother Set, who had murdered the father of Horus, Osiris. Later, he replaced his mother's head with that of a cow. Certainly Horus is the ancestor of Oedipus, of Orestes, and of Hamlet; Isis is the forebear of the Sphinx. The alternating loss and possession of the penis name, the riddle of the Sphinx, is a description of sexual intercourse, mirrored again in the story of the bisexual Teiresias and in the division of the Theban calendar between the lion and the snake. Perhaps ultimately the riddle of the Sphinx, so obviously placed in the phallic phase, is to give a name to that which does not exist—the female phallus, a feat that carries animism back to its ultimate origins in the magic of thought and the use of language as a tool to replace lost objects (Freud, 1913).

Discussion and Summary

The Oedipus plays of Sophocles constitute the traditional psychoanalytic source of knowledge and theorizing about the Oedipus legend and even about myths in general. Moreover, psychoanalysis of the characters tends to treat them as real personalities whose histories and motives can be reconstructed. Nevertheless, factual research indicates that this approach, successful as it has been in producing a rich and stimulating body of literature, must proceed with caution and with a view to certain propositions which emerge from the present review:

1. The Oedipus plays themselves, and especially the personalities involved, leaned upon tradition but were creatively elaborated so

as to possess dramatic appeal and contemporary significance for a particular Athenian audience. They were vehicles for the conscious views and aspirations of the dramatist himself as well as for his specific unconscious fantasies. From the analytic standpoint, the Oedipus plays are to be regarded as a manifest content to be traced to its origins.

2. A sociohistorical pathway toward the latent content indicates that in the case of the Oedipus legend, as in most others, cores of historical truth may be disentangled. These spread out in a time and space continuum that apparently contains residues of different social organizations and psychologies—totemistic, agricultural, nomadic, city-founding—together with their associated customs and traditions. Here a universal origin of the Oedipus myth may be discerned.

3. The Sphinx has often been compared to a nightmare figure, a product of condensation and a recurrence of infantile fears. Analogies in the sphere of social evolution and with respect to myths as the dreams of young nations have been made. Dreams and myths have related but different functions. The dream seeks to dissipate the external reality, the myth to make it more palatable. The Sphinx of the Oedipus legend has certain roots in the nightmare—we cite especially the blank dream with orgasm and the uncanny reaction to the realities that suddenly confront us like dreams which have invaded our waking lives. As prototype, the reaction to the sight of the female genital during the phallic phase may be invoked in connection with Oedipus and the triumphs that destroyed him. The Sphinx can also be traced realistically as an emblem that leads to unknown periods of human civilization—but not necessarily to more infantile psychology than that of contemporary man. The Oedipus legend is a psychosocial record, not merely a psychological progression.

4. The mind of the storyteller is compelled to unify the data that the myth makes available to him, a work of secondary elaboration. He usually has different versions of a myth from which to select; it is ritual that tends to establish standardized and invariable accounts because certain more authentic variants are unacceptable. The myth, or myth group, thus provides scope for a variety of psychosocial experiences and outlooks; moreover, it tends to achieve a secondary autonomy that acquires characteristic developmental patterns of its own (see Freud, 1913).

The universality of the myth's roots and the social stages through which it evolves ultimately eradicate the individual detail and preserve the typical, so that the psychic functions themselves come to be externalized in the characters and action. It is this very universality that makes it possible to "analyze" Oedipus as though he were a real person; moreover the submergence of the individual in the general constitutes the very condition which Freud (1908) postulated for the "mysterious transformation" from personal fantasy to the work of art. Myths, as experience has shown, constitute natural source material for dreams and for the artist, wherein preliminary working through provides an economy of creative activities.

The living progression of the Oedipus myth can be followed from prehistoric times to the epic form with which it was endowed by Homer and the sophisticated dramatization that it received at the hands of Sophocles—each of these poets finding in the legend a mirror for his own personality and era. The psychoanalyst must be aware of similar dispositions within himself, i.e., the countertransference tendency in the interpretation which actually makes each article on Oedipus a reflection not only of the analyst's own personality, but also of the contemporary theories that prevail in metapsychology (oedipal, preoedipal, identity testing, etc.). Analysis ultimately curbs the mythmaking tendency itself; but after all, it is the latter that results in the Oedipus tragedy.

REFERENCES

Freud, S. (1900), The interpretation of dreams. *Standard Edition*, 4/5. London: Hogarth Press, 1953.

——— (1908), Creative writers and daydreaming. *Standard Edition*, 9:143–153. London: Hogarth Press, 1959.

——— (1913), Totem and taboo. *Standard Edition*, 13:1–161. London: Hogarth Press, 1955.

——— (1919a), Preface to Reik's *Ritual: Psycho-Analytic Studies. Standard Edition*, 17:259–263. London: Hogarth Press, 1955.

——— (1919b), The "uncanny." *Standard Edition*, 17:219–256. London: Hogarth Press, 1955.

——— (1921), Group psychology and the analysis of the ego. *Standard Edition*, 18:69–143. London: Hogarth Press, 1955.

——— (1922), Medusa's head. *Standard Edition*, 18:273–274. London: Hogarth Press, 1955.

——— (1954), *The Origins of Psycho-Analysis.* New York: Basic Books.
Gassner, J. (1940), *Masters of the Drama.* New York: Random House.
Graves, R. (1955), *The Greek Myths.* Baltimore: Penguin.
Grene, D., & Lattimore, R. (1959), *The Complete Greek Tragedies.* Chicago: University of Chicago Press.
Homer, *The Iliad,* Book 23:366. New York: Black, 1942.
——— *The Odyssey,* Book 11:159. New York: Oxford University Press, 1932.
Kanzer, M. (1948), The "passing of the Oedipus complex" in Greek drama. *Internat. J. Psycho-Anal.,* 29:131-134. Chapter 5, this volume.
——— (1950), The Oedipus trilogy. *Psychoanal. Quart.,* 19:561-572. Chapter 6, this volume.
——— (1954), Observations on blank dreams with orgasms. *Psychoanal. Quart.,* 23:511-520.
Larousse Encyclopedia of Mythology (1959), Egyptian mythology. New York: Prometheus Press.
New York Times (1961), April 4, p. 45.
Reik, T. (1920), Oedipus and the Sphinx. In: *Dogma and Compulsion: Psychoanalytic Studies of Religion and Myth.* New York: International Universities Press, 1951, pp. 289-332. Chapter 3, this volume.
Robert, C. (1915), *Oedipus.* Berlin: Weidemann.
Róheim, G. (1946), Teiresias and other seers. *Psychoanal. Rev.,* 23:341-342.
Roscher, W. (1912), Sphinx. In: *Ausfuehrliches Lexikon der griechischen und roemischen Mythologie.* Leipzig: Teubner.
Tatlock, J. (1917), *Greek and Roman Mythology.* New York: Century.
Velikovsky, E. (1960), *Oedipus and Akhnaton.* New York: Doubleday.

11

On the Genesis of Acting Out and Psychopathic Behavior in Sophocles' Oedipus: *Notes on Filicide*

ARNALDO RASCOVSKY and

MATILDE RASCOVSKY

[1968]

Sophocles' *King Oedipus*, the most meaningful synthesis of the essential conflicts of human condition, has been approached psychoanalytically from various viewpoints. Freud pointed out its significance in *The Interpretation of Dreams* (1900) and studies which followed this are listed at the end of our paper.

Acting out and psychopathic behavior are so significantly predominant in the oedipal tragedy that we feel the challenge to look for the genesis of both phenomena in this universal plight. As Abraham

An abridged version of the paper read at the Twenty-fifth International Psychoanalytical Congress, Copenhagen, July 1967. Reprinted with permission from *International Journal of Psycho-Analysis*, vol. 49, pp. 390–394.

(1909) has rightly remarked and Van der Sterren (1952) expanded, the major difference between *King Oedipus* and other works lies in the fact that, in Sophocles' drama, oedipal emotions are fully and overtly displayed. This can be understood as the presentation of an unrepressed acting out of the most forbidden drives. Due to this lack of repression, the plot represents the manifest content expressed at early levels when repression is not yet organized. We are now in a position to search for the latent contents which are not repressed but denied in their more archaic stages.

We shall develop this viewpoint stressing that, for the interpretation of the genesis of acting out and the accompanying psychopathic behavior we must—as Rosenfeld (1965) points out—go back to the fixations in the paranoid-schizoid position and to the pathology of splitting that leads to excessive acting out.

Freud (1900) considered the development of *King Oedipus* as "a process that can be likened to the work of a psycho-analysis" (p. 262). We shall deal with Oedipus as a case history since there is enough hereditary, historical, and contemporary material to enable us to probe further into the bases for acting out and psychopathic behavior, resulting from persecutory intensification and the reactivation of the defensive mechanisms prior to repression.

We intend to single out filicide as the fundamental causal factor in the genesis of both phenomena, thus being the latent content underlying parricide and incest. In order fully to understand the pattern that the child shapes of the persecutory characteristics which imply the internalized actual mother, the frequent and serious injuries inflicted upon the infant at an early stage should be emphasized. This encompasses a vast gamut of parental acting out, namely, the traumatic vicissitudes of pregnancy and delivery, circumcision, disturbances in natural or artificial lactation, and especially the qualitative and quantitative variations in abandonment, and so on. These factors increase the initial amount of hostility and inborn envy and consequently the exaggerated configuration of the infant's paranoid-schizoid position. These facts have been neglected in research and only occasionally do they appear in psychoanalytical literature. This may be regarded as an aspect of the universal resistance to acknowledging the mother's filicide drives, undoubtedly the most dreaded and uncanny truth for us to face.

In the oedipal tragedy, Jocasta, the filicidal mother, is disguised and denied by Oedipus throughout all the initial period of acting out. Oedipus faces her in a split way in the Sphinx, following his pattern of excessive splitting, and he is able to free himself of the split and idealized Jocasta only when he gains insight and becomes conscious that it was she, his mother, who had ordered his death.

Oedipus stands out as the most accurate example of acting out with all the general characteristics attributed to this phenomenon, and even with the sociopolitical implications suggested by its widest connotation. This can be applied not only to Oedipus but also to the structure common to all heroes: similar persecutory intensification and regression to primitive mechanisms prior to repression.

Sophocles' tragedy actually begins with the working through of Oedipus' earlier psychopathic acting out. In the course of the play, manic defenses gradually fail—denial, omnipotence, idealization, and disparagement of the object and contempt for it—and the hidden paranoid processes of splitting, identification, and projection emerge.

Oedipus' life starts with a remarkable persecutory factor. His ancestors are strongly filicidal. We may trace this attitude back to Uranus, who killed his children to avoid succession. Laius and Jocasta are the immediate representatives of this tendency. The oracle's omen is announced long before Oedipus' birth. When he is born, his parents not only mutilate him by piercing his feet, but order him to be killed or abandoned when he is three days old. These circumstances give rise to the etiological point of paranoid-schizoid fixation. The mother's breast, the mother, and secondarily both parents are the external factors essential to regulate the inborn hate and envy which succeed in coping with inner persecutory demands through their capacity to take in the infant's initial hostility.

When he experiences his parents' abandonment and the ensuing disturbances of introjection and splitting related to them, the ego loses its capacity to develop defenses which enable the gradual working through of anxiety. An excessive amount of anxiety that threatens the ego with disintegration is then inhibited or counteracted through extreme manic defenses and the ego increases the mechanism of denial so much that there is a failure of organization of the further process of repression.

Since the essential element in the plot consists of his absolute failure to repress patricide and incest that conceal the unsparing hatred for the parents who had abandoned him and which is not counterbalanced by a positive introjection of them, denial is the prevailing mechanism in Oedipus.

To maintain his psychic balance during his early development, Oedipus denies the existence of his bad parents and feeds on a typical family romance through an idealization displaced onto the king and queen of Corinth, Polybus and Merope. This is the first splitting of the couple which persists up to the failure of denial and idealization when Oedipus becomes conscious that Polybus and Merope are not his parents. The threat to his psychic balance thrusts Oedipus back to the paranoid-schizoid fixation points. This is the meaning of his return to Thebes, where he will act out his unrepressed hostility by means of a further denial and the full exercise of his omnipotence. Following his primitive patterns, he identifies himself with the aggressor and, in a true manic triumph, kills his father at the cross-roads. He proceeds on his omnipotent course and after the denied destruction of his father he encounters the displaced image of his mother, embodied in the Sphinx, who kills the young Thebans (a projection of his own self) and whose riddle Oedipus alone in his omnipotence can solve.

The second object-splitting between the persecutory filicidal mother denied in the Sphinx and the idealized image of Jocasta occurs here. This splitting prevents insight, and Oedipus perseveres in his idealized bad object relationship, placing the greater part of his death instincts on the Sphinx and his erotic ones on Jocasta. In this second fundamental splitting, this time not of his parents but only of his mother—thus indicating an intensified regression—he acts out again by marrying her and brings on the subsequent manic defenses which support his balance until the outbreak of the tragedy.

The tragedy starts when the denial of guilt and the manic defenses can no longer operate in such an impoverished ego. This situation appears to be projected in the misery, plagues, and sterility in Thebes. The idealization, omnipotence, and splitting of his own ego, which prevented him from gaining insight of the denied psychic reality, start to weaken. Also, the splitting and disparagement of his objects have reached a climax that render them intolerable. This appears in the plot in the form of supplications of the Theban citizens who besiege Oedipus, and who represent the demanding and pressing external and psychic reality which is also expressed by the plagues and calamities scourging Thebes.

When the inquiry for the discovery of Laius' slayer starts and denial gradually gives way, Teiresias appears on the stage. Róheim (1953) has shown that Teiresias represents Oedipus himself. We believe that Teiresias is the split and projected part of Oedipus' ego capable of perceiving the painful psychic reality which can no longer be denied. This reintegration is carried out in the midst of constant struggles and fleeting persecutory relapses. The struggle to maintain the denial of conflict and guilt urges him to act out, and Oedipus sends Creon to question the oracle. He proceeds in his acting out, searching for real receiving objects in the outer world to make them guilty of the projective identification of his denied criminal parts. This is the reason why, after many vicissitudes, Teiresias finally shows Oedipus that it was he who killed Laius. Oedipus, in new projective efforts, turns the accusation back onto Teiresias, as he will also do to Creon.

But the external and psychic reality increases its pressure and influences his hampered perception. Finally the testimony of reality, which is represented by the messenger from Corinth and the shepherd, can no longer be denied. Oedipus as a child was given by Jocasta to the shepherd, who mercifully gave him to the messenger. It was this same shepherd who years later witnessed Laius' death.

As Oedipus gradually becomes conscious that the man whom he killed was his father Laius, the messenger announces that Polybus, his idealized father, has died. The splitting between the persecutory bad father and the idealized one thus disappears for the moment. Before the undeniable statements of the shepherd and the messenger (another splitting that disappears), Jocasta, confronted with Oedipus' indifference, commits suicide, an indifference that kills her who ordered his death, thus relinquishing the idealized part in the split filicidal mother.

As these defenses break down, and in spite of Oedipus having gained insight, the persecutory guilt and anxiety are so acute that he is urged to another acting out, this time not manic but melancholic: he pierces his eyes. This he does with one of Jocasta's gold brooches, following in this way the pattern of submission to the mother who pierced his feet when he was born. But the removal of his eyes annuls the pathological splitting between Oedipus and Teiresias, and Oedipus thus reintrojects the projected part of his ego which had previously appeared in the form of the blind seer.

The loss of his eyes has been interpreted as a displacement of genital castration. But, at a deeper level, the loss of external vision should be related to the attainment of inner vision—Teiresias' main characteristic. The oedipal plot confirms the later investigations of Greenacre (1957) and Greenson (1957). These writers have stressed visual sensitization and the scoptophilic and exhibitionistic characteristics of acting out and psychopathic behavior. We consider that these elements are constant in manic conditions (Rascovsky and Rascovsky, 1967). This problem is related to the intensified projective identification—a further characteristic of acting out—the main agents of which are the eyes. In a previous paper (1967) we have pointed out that, in manic conditions which lead to acting out and psychopathic behavior, external vision is stimulated at the expense of inner vision. We have also stressed that the scoptophilic enhancement constantly appears as a result of the unsurmountable increase of paranoid anxiety.

When Oedipus disavows his acting out, he also surrenders to the loss of his external eyes and in compensation, just like Teiresias himself, attains inner vision. The alternative and the antagonism between outer and inner vision is another aspect of the excessive splitting of the ego and is expressed in this outstanding point of the tragedy.

We can see here, in the words of the attendant, how the repressive process starts (Watling translation, 1947):

> *The Attendant:* Eyes that should see no longer his shame, his guilt,
> No longer see those they should never have seen,
> Nor see, unseeing, those he had longed to see.
> Henceforth seeing nothing but night. . . .
> To this wild tune
> He pierced his eyeballs time and time again.

When the manic defenses break down, the melancholic self-reproaches start in full swing:

Oedipus: Lead me quickly away
Out of this land. I am lost,
Hated of Gods, no man so damned.

And further on:

Oedipus: Cursed be the benefactor
That loosed my feet and gave me life
For death; a poor exchange.
Death would have been a boon
To me and all of mine.
Chorus: Twice-tormented, in the spirit, as in the flesh,
Would you have never lived to read this riddle.

Oedipus says later:

Oedipus: Now, shedder of father's blood,
Husband of mother, is my name;
Godless and child of shame,
Begetter of brother-sons;
What infamy remains
That is not spoken of Oedipus?

Creon steps in as a substitute father, making an allusion to repression:

Creon: Oedipus, I am not here to scoff at your fall,
Nor yet to reproach you for your past misdeeds.
My friends, remember your respect for the Lord of Life,
The Sun above us—if not for the children of men.
The unclean must not remain in the eye of day;
Nor earth nor air nor water may receive it.
Take him within; piety at least demands
That none but kinsmen should hear and see such suffering.

Oedipus at Colonus continues with the melancholic process. Thebes, as a projection of a split part of Oedipus, cannot overcome her conflicts, overwhelmed as she is by fratricidal strife and by continued misfortune that prevent her from depressive working through. Contrariwise, Athens idealized under Theseus' empire—Theseus was dearly loved by his father, Aegeus—enjoys peace and prosperity, which, according to the oracle, Oedipus will strengthen at his death.

Before Oedipus' death the oracle alters its prophecy. This is what Ismene tells her father:

> *Oedipus:* And did you think the gods would yet deliver me?
> *Ismene:* The present oracles give me that hope.
> *Oedipus:* What oracles are they? What prophecy?
> *Ismene:* The people of Thebes shall desire you, for their safety,
> After your death, and even while you live.
> *Oedipus:* What good can such as I bring any man?
> *Ismene:* They say it is in you that they must grow to greatness
> *Oedipus:* Am I made man in the hour when I cease to be?
> *Ismene:* If the gods, who cast you down, now raise you up.
> . . . .
> *Oedipus:* How can I help them, remaining beyond their borders?
> *Ismene:* If ill befall your grave, it falls on them.

Oedipus must disappear, leaving no trace. The oracle has proclaimed that, from his unknown grave, Oedipus will grant peace and prosperity to the land that receives him. Likewise, filicide, parricide, and incest must be fully repressed to ensure evolutionary peace and prosperity. The Oedipus complex should be buried after it has existed, because every evolutionary possibility is kindled in the emotional forge of filicide, parricide, and incest. Only the positive parental introjection will lead to repression. The Oedipus complex, if repressed, is the main foundation of human development, but if unrepressed, is the basis of excessive acting out and psychopathic behavior.

We can see that the fundamental factor leading to acting out and to the inability to organize repression in Oedipus is the paranoid-schizoid intensification and the pathology of splitting arising from filicide which is not counterbalanced by parental positive introjections but aggravated by an excessive use of manic defenses which disturb the integration of insight.

REFERENCES

Abadi, M. (1960), *Renacimiento de Edipo*. Buenos Aires: Nova.

Abraham, K. (1909), Dreams and myths: A study in folk-psychology. In: *Clinical Papers and Essays on Psycho-Analysis*. New York: Basic Books, 1955, pp. 153-209.

Baranger, W. (1947), El personaje de Edipo en la obra de Sófocles. *Revista de Psicoanal.*, 5:861-873.

Bunker, H. A. (1952), The feast of Tantalus. *Psychoanal. Quart.*, 21:355-372.

——— (1953), Tantalus—a pre-oedipal figure of myth. *Psychoanal. Quart.*, 22:159-173.

Devereux, G. (1953), Why Oedipus killed Laius: A note on the complementary Oedipus complex in Greek drama. *Internat. J. Psycho-Anal.*, 34:132-141. Chapter 7, this volume.

Ferenczi, S. (1912), The symbolic representation of the pleasure and reality principles in the Oedipus myth. In: *Sex and Psychoanalysis*. New York: Basic Books, 1950, pp. 253-269. Chapter 2, this volume.

Freud, S. (1900), The interpretation of dreams. *Standard Edition*, 4/5. London: Hogarth Press, 1953.

Greenacre, P. (1957), General problems of acting out. *Psychoanal. Quart.*, 19:455-467.

Greenson, R. R. (1957), Panel: Some clinical and theoretical considerations on acting out and the impulse disorders. *J. Amer. Psychoanal. Assn.*, 5:138-139.

Jung, C. G. (1912), *Wandlungen und Symbole der Libido*. Vienna: Deuticke.

Kanzer, M. (1948), The "passing of the Oedipus complex" in Greek drama. *Internat. J. Psycho-Anal.*, 29:131-134. Chapter 5, this volume.

——— (1950), The Oedipus trilogy. *Psychoanal. Quart.*, 19:561-572. Chapter 6, this volume.

Mullahy, P. (1948), *Oedipus—Myth and Complex*. New York: Hermitage.

Parcells, F. H., & Segel, N. P. (1959), Oedipus and the prodigal son. *Psychoanal. Quart.*, 28:213-227.

Rank, O. (1912), *Das Inzestmotive in Dichtung und Sage*. Leipzig: Deuticke.

Rascovsky, A., & Rascovsky, M. (1967), El alcance de la regresión en la manía. *Rev. Urug. Psicoanál.*, 8:25 65.

Reik, T. (1920), Oedipus and the Sphinx. In: *Dogma and Compulsion: Psychoanalytic Studies of Religion and Myth*. New York: International Universities Press, 1951, pp. 289-332. Chapter 3, this volume.

Róheim, G. (1934), *The Riddle of the Sphinx*. London: Hogarth Press.

——— (1946), Teiresias and other seers. *Psychoanal. Rev.*, 33:314-334.

——— (1953), Oedipus Rex. In: *The Gates of the Dream*. New York: International Universities Press, pp. 529-544.

Rosenfeld, H. (1965), An investigation into the need of neurotic and psychotic patients to act out during analysis. In: *Psychotic States*. New York: International Universities Press, pp. 200-216.

Van der Sterren, H. A. (1952), The "King Oedipus" of Sophocles. *Internat. J. Psycho-Anal.*, 33:343–350.
Walting, E. F., Trans. (1947), *Sophocles: The Theban Plays*. Baltimore: Penguin.

INTERPRETATIONS OF THE MYTH AFTER 1970

12

The Oedipus Myth, Adolescence, and the Succession of Generations

NORMAN B. ATKINS

[1970]

In the United States and in the world at the present time, there exist concern and anxiety about the apparently growing open rebellion and revolt of a large number of adolescents. In his book *The Vanishing Adolescent*, Friedenberg (1959) describes the current concern over adolescents: "There is an obvious something in adolescence itself that both troubles and titillates many adults. The 'teenager' seems to have replaced the communist as the appropriate target for public controversy and foreboding, for discussions designed less to clarify what is going on than to let people vent their fearful or hostile feelings and declare themselves on the side of order and authority" (p. 176).

In the United States "the establishment" is facing assaults from

An earlier version of this paper appeared in the Twenty-fifth Anniversary issue of the *Revista de Psicoanalisis*, Argentina, 1968. Presented at the Annual Meeting of the American Psychoanalytic Association, Miami, May 3, 1969. Reprinted with permission from *Journal of the American Psychoanalytic Association*, vol. 15, pp. 860-875.

the underprivileged, the minorities, and the adolescent generation. This young adolescent generation openly identifies with the struggles of the minorities in our country and with the "adolescent" emerging nations of the world. Established society tends to view with alarm this identification with the rebellious, realizing it to be an attack on itself.

While the characteristic struggle between emerging young adults and their elders is no new development in the relations of parent and child, older generation and youth, this tendency to insurrection seems to be a part of increasing overt behavior among aspiring and emerging groups throughout the world.

Although these insurrections appear to be contemporary, actually they are a problem that has faced all generations in recorded history. In his play *Oedipus Rex* Sophocles deals with dramatic impact with the conflicts associated with the succession of generations. He has much to say about the crisis of adolescence. A reexamination of the Oedipus story as presented by Sophocles in his tragedy can offer a fresh look at these problems.

When the young adult Oedipus leaves his childhood home in Corinth, we may view him as the disturbed adolescent seeking to find his way. He is attempting to achieve emancipation from his childhood attachments, seeking the final path to identity as the mature individual in society, free to achieve gratification of sexual and aggressive forces within himself.

Oedipus is motivated to leave his family and home by the anxiety aroused in him by the tale of "horror and misery" presaged by the oracle: "How I must marry my mother, and become the parent of a misbegotten brood, an offence to all mankind—and kill my father." This is the anxiety regularly seen during puberty with the upsurge of physiological drives accompanying maturation. The hitherto latent oedipus complex becomes recathected with libido and aggressive drives.

Oedipus recounts the story: "at this I fled away, putting the stars between me and Corinth, never to see home again, that no such horror should ever come to pass."

Historically and in other cultures, a young man sets out on his life's journey at a much younger age than in contemporary Western civilization. In Western culture, where a man achieves his occupational and social identity as a peer of the adult community rather late, this lengthier period from puberty until the successful acquisition of autonomy and separation from parental control is still considered by many as an adolescence—but much delayed and prolonged.

In *Oedipus Rex*, the youthful Oedipus kills his father, Laius, at a crossroads. The event is described by Oedipus in this way:

> When in my journey I was near to those three roads, there met me a herald, and a man seated in a carriage drawn by colts, as thou has described; and he who was in front, and the old man himself, were for thrusting me rudely from the path. Then in anger I struck him who pushed me aside—the driver; and the old man, seeing it, watched the moment when I was passing and from the carriage, brought his goad with two teeth down full upon my head. Yet was he paid with interest; by one swift blow from the staff in this hand he was rolled right out of the carriage on his back; and I slew every man of them.

This encounter at the crossroads may be interpreted as a portrayal of the adolescent male at the crossroads of his life. At this *time*, which in the drama is depicted as a *place*, the adolescent finds himself in a situation where he must deal with the internal and external forces which determine his life's direction. Here those forces reflecting the interfering internal parental representations and the obdurate external parents must be overcome in order for him to establish his identity as an adult.

The toothed goad may be regarded as symbolizing Oedipus' phallic-libidinal and aggressive strivings as well as the oral-sadistic contribution to these strivings derived from his relationship with the pregenital mother, projected onto the parental figure he meets at the crossroads.

Is it possible that this confrontation at the crossroads not only reflects Oedipus' struggle with his projected hatred returning in the form of superego prohibitions, but is also an example of the introjection of parental sadism and restraints manifest toward him from the beginning of his life? This would be primary parental sadism, not just the introjected parental restraints that represent an internalization of parental controls which is part of the repression and resolution of the oedipus complex as we usually understand it. This time the adolescent as a physically mature and mobile young man, Oedipus of Corinth on his way to Thebes, was able to respond to external sadism and restraints with his own newly effective motility and competent aggression.

It was perhaps inevitable that Freud's discovery of the instinctual drives within the child led to a deemphasis on the role that parental attitudes play in the formation and development of the oedipus complex. Discussing the role of the parent in the oedipus complex, Rangell (1955) describes dynamisms and clinical instances seen from the parents' point of view.

The universal theme of parental aggression toward the child, which is self-evident in the unashamed authoritarian world and is consciously utilized by rulers and manipulators of power, is minimized and to a considerable extent denied by psychoanalytic thinkers and writers, with a few notable exceptions. Devereux (1966) suggests that this neglect is "not fortuitous, but represents both psychologically and culturally determined scotomization of the important problem" (p. 114).

Having made the momentous discovery of the unconscious oedipus complex and having revealed the incestual and parricidal child in all of us, psychoanalysis has largely left aside the counterpart of this theme, which has to do with incestual and filicidal impulses and fantasies of the parent. The theme of filicide has a crucial meaning in the Sophoclean tragedy. It is receiving current attention in the medical press as the "battered child syndrome."

One may regard Oedipus as the child victim of the filicidal impulses of his ambivalent parents. He is abandoned on a mountainside with his feet cruelly pierced and bound so that he may not even crawl to safety. He is rescued by the good shepherd, representing the reparative aspects of his parents, and is brought to Corinth to be nurtured back to health and into a vigorous adolescence by a split-off good, idealized version of his parents, represented by the King and Queen of Corinth. At this point he leaves the nurturing parents to return to the original aggressive situation, which he finds at the crossroads when he meets the interfering father, Laius, King of Thebes, who this time is unable to carry through his filicidal intent, unable to enforce his restrictions and demands, and is overthrown.

These are speculative attempts to find in *Oedipus Rex* a description of the family turmoil and *actual* conflicts which occur with the advancement of a child from latency through adolescence. These ideas were stimulated by a series of fascinating and provocative papers delineating the role of parental aggression in a more complete description of the oedipus situation and complex. I am especially indebted to the works of Devereux (1966), Flugel (1935), Berliner (1958), Van der Sterren (1952), and Rascovsky and Rascovsky (1968). They present views of the oedipus situation which demonstrate an intricate interaction between parental (both maternal *and* paternal) hostility and aggression toward the child and in turn the child's aggression toward the parents. It seems to me that it is a moot question whether the parents' or the child's aggression is to be viewed as primary, although some authors regard the activity of parental aggression toward the child as the pathogenic situation stimulating the child's counter-aggression. Although evidence is not clear on this subject, it can be assumed that parental and children's aggressive attitudes toward each other are mutually complementary and provocative.

The Rascovskys write that they consider filicide the fundamental causal factor in the genesis of both acting out and psychopathic behavior and "the mother's filicide drives undoubtedly the most dreaded and uncanny truth for us to face" (p. 390).

Oedipus meets in succession two later sets of interferences with his progress toward manhood and eventual kingship of the city of Thebes. First, in his encounter with Laius, he overcomes his internal and external, sadistic, restraining father in a fit of passion.

The second barrier to his progress occurs at the gates of the city of Thebes. Here he confronts the Sphinx, who sits guard at the gates of Thebes, which is in bondage to her. Sophocles describes her as that "vile enchantress," "the winged enchantress," and "the dog-faced witch." She presented "a riddle too deep for common wits" and destroyed all who tried to pass and could not answer her riddle—"I, ignorant, Oedipus came and stopped the riddler's mouth, guessing the truth by *mother wit* not bird lore." The Sphinx was described in Van der Sterren's thoughtful paper as a bitch with hooked claws who sets a riddle and demands tribute from the youth of Thebes.

Other descriptions elaborate that the Sphinx is a composite creature with a lion's body, wings, talons, and a human head. In Greek mythology the creature is usually female, though in earlier forms such as the colossal Egyptian Sphinx at Giza, it is male. The word Sphinx was derived by Greek grammarians, possibly from the verb *sphingein,* which means to bind or squeeze.

Róheim (1934) envisioned the Sphinx as the parents locked in intercourse—the primal scene. Kanzer (1950) wrote of the Sphinx as a monster that represents the challenge presented by female sexuality. Van der Sterren (1952) associates the descriptions of the Sphinx in the Sophoclean drama with Jocasta. He points out that the threat of death posed by Jocasta, who gave her baby to a shepherd to be *bound,* abandoned, and left to die, is the same as the threat of the Sphinx. Kanzer states that the whole drama is a "repetitious depiction of the duel between Oedipus and the Sphinx" (p. 564).

Van der Sterren (1952) concludes that the oracle prophesied that Oedipus would kill his parents but observes that the line "twas said the child should be his father's death" has a double meaning in Greek and can be interpreted as saying that Oedipus would kill his parents or, conversely, that his parents would kill him.

Where is this reservoir of destructiveness? Can it be found within Jocasta as the bad Sphinx-mother, from whose womb Oedipus emerges?

Encountering the Sphinx, Oedipus is presented with her riddle: "What creature is it that speaks with one voice, but walks on four feet in the morning, two feet at noon and three feet in the evening?" Oedipus solved the riddle by answering, *man,* who crawls on all fours in infancy, walks on two feet when grown, and leans on a staff in old age.

Oedipus' answer to the riddle of the Sphinx seems to be no answer at all, but is as cryptic as the question. There have been many interpretations of the latent meaning of both question and answer. Freud pointed out the sexual curiosity of children evident in the riddle, and Bion (1963) views it as an expression of man's curiosity turned upon himself.

The encounter when Oedipus overcomes the Sphinx, solving her riddle, may be understood as symbolizing *an adolescent rite of passage,* similar to the Bar Mitzvah and other pubertal rites which give recognition to the individual as an adult.

It would seem Oedipus is required in this rite of passage to understand the very meaning of life in order to surmount temporarily the effect of the Sphinx. He must be able to overcome the seductions and the obstructive aggression of the Sphinx, which is depicted as an external threat to Thebes as well as to Oedipus. When the young Oedipus destroys the influence of the Sphinx by understanding the meaning of her mystery, Thebes returns to a period of well-being, under the aegis of the king and then parent, Oedipus.

According to the Theban legend, there passed fifteen years of peace and prosperity—fifteen years, which corresponds to the period before the child emerges into adolescence. Later, when Thebes is again beset by a "tide of death from which there is no escaping," Oedipus is again called upon to solve a riddle. The priest pleads:

> It was you, we remember, a newcomer to Cadmus's town
> That broke our bondage to the vile Enchantress. . . .
> Now, Oedipus great and glorious, we seek
> Your help again. Find some deliverance for us.

The second round at finding answers to questions, this time later in the life of Oedipus, does not yield an overpowering of the external sphinx, but instead the revelation of the internal incest and aggression (parricidal within Oedipus and filicidal within Jocasta and Laius), with the eventual doom for the participants in the drama.

Sophocles's *King Oedipus* has been studied and restudied in terms of its latent and manifest content. I would like to discuss an aspect of this drama which to the best of my knowledge has not been explored psychoanalytically—namely, that having to do with the pain and destructiveness associated with the inevitable succession of generations.

Early in life the developing infant, as the herald of the next generation, encounters parental and particularly maternal ambivalence, depicted in the play by Jocasta's abandonment of Oedipus with feet pierced and bound. The attempt to interrupt the inevitable rise and decline of the generations is expressed on the *pubertal* level by the rites of passage of Oedipus' encounter with Laius at the crossroads and with the riddling Sphinx.

The realization of the inevitability of the generations and the destructive attempts to interrupt or to undo *this* inevitability, expressed in fantasy as well as in deed, may be so painful a perception that humans must blind themselves to it.

It is necessary to distinguish between the child's and the parents' internal situations during the various developmental phases of the child within the family; the actual interactions are always a complex resultant of the two. The interactional crises in which there is a confrontation of parents' and children's narcissism and aggression recur throughout development, beginning with the period of conception, which invokes both maternal and paternal impulses to abort the fetus. The stories of Jesus, Moses, and Oedipus contain elements of the universal myths about infanticide. Actual parental aggression toward the child is expressed in many ways, including circumcision, tonsillectomies, and other, more open forms.

Even the most beloved infant can be experienced unconsciously as well as consciously as an attacker, at least of the mother's narcissism. That filicidal impulses are not more frequently openly expressed as in the case of Jocasta is undoubtedly due to the strength of the opposing maternal love and nurturant ties.

The aggression of infants and children is well known psychoanalytically, and the knowledge of unconscious parricidal fantasies and impulses of the preoedipal and oedipal child is one of the central themes of the Sophoclean drama.

It is into this situation of mutual hatred as well as love we are all born and with which all of us must deal throughout our lives. The child defends himself and progressively binds the primitive sexual and aggressive drives during development and maturation until the onset of adolescence, when this achievement threatens to be undone.

Anna Freud (1958) writes, "It seems to be generally accepted that a strong fixation to the mother, dating not only from the oedipal but from the preoedipal attachment to her, renders adolescence especially difficult." Although a break in the tie to the infantile love objects is a difficult but necessary part of the work of adolescence, she feels that the prior establishment of such a tie is a prerequisite for a coherent personality. She states, "the internal possession and cathexis of such an image seems to be essential for the ensuing normal process of detaching libido from it for transfer to new objects" (p. 266).

It appears that the imago of the Sphinx (the internal mother imago and/or fused and combined parental imagos invested with aggression and danger) continues to live within all of us. This imago represents a seductive tie that binds us to our past and exerts a regressive pull that interferes with development and maturation on the one hand and with good parenting on the other. As an archaic and destructive superego element, the internal Sphinx reflects the introjection of the hostility of the mother or parental couple, based on perception of reality or of an image that has been distorted by projection. Also, in identifying with the aggressor, each of us tends unconsciously to become an ambivalent Sphinxlike parent.

Parricidal impulses and fantasies become repressed and unconscious because they endanger the psychological security of the child during the prolonged period of dependency. On the other hand, filicidal impulses are as dangerous and unthinkable to the parents. During the many years of dependent and relatively weak childhood, while children are at their parents' physical and emotional mercy, such impulses within the parent threaten their very capacity to be a caretaking parent. Parental responsibility and love for their children enables mature adults to contain and neutralize the aggression from within that is present in everyone. The analysis of every patient reveals the presence and activity of the residue of the bad Sphinx-mother who could destroy the child within as well as the external child.

Parental aggression that was held in abeyance as long as the child was helpless, dependent, controllable, and a vessel for parental narcissism tends to become activated and deneutralized, and may break through with the onset of puberty. This may occur when it becomes evident that the children are no longer helpless and weak and are now able to make sexual claims and enforce these and other claims by means of the vigor and strength of youth approaching maturity.

Such a struggle between generations can and frequently does invade the psychoanalytic situation. Here, in the setting based genetically on the caretaking aspect of the mother-child relationship, the patient is invited to relax his defenses and permit himself to be taken care of in a derivative fashion. The patient is expected to relinquish motility and report fantasies, feelings, and urges, but not to engage in any other actions. In this relatively helpless and dependent position, like the little child with his caretaking parent, there is a reliving of the conflicts which surrounded this position earlier in life.

The analyst in the parental role is expected to have resolved in good part the disturbances left over from his own childhood and is properly expected to contain and deal with his own aggressive and libidinal impulses toward the dependent person on the couch. Beyond and unlike the task of good parenting, which permits and expects a considerable amount of interaction with the child, including physical care, the analyst has the additional restraint and responsibility that his caretaking function be expressed only in terms of the structured analytic situation and the analytic tools available to him.

These demands on the analyst represent an ego ideal which is at times approximated but not always met. The arousal of hostile-aggressive impulses toward the patient, in the pattern of the filicidal parent, threatens the analytic caretaking function. Paradoxically, on the basis of envy and jealousy, even the patient's progress may arouse destructive attitudes in an analyst.

It is not surprising that under these circumstances psychoanalysts confronted with the evidence of their maternal aggression in the image of the Sphinx need to blind themselves to this sight, as did Oedipus. There is an inclination for psychoanalysts to deny and underestimate the extent of parental aggression that exists in all adults and to which psychoanalysts despite their own analytic experience are not immune.

The Sphinx remains hidden in everyone and the only way of diminishing her influence on our work is an open admission of her presence and the threat she poses for our functioning as good analysts. To the extent that we blind ourselves to her presence and activity within, through denial, repression, and other defenses, the greater the possibility of her continued uninterrupted activity.

Adolescence can be understood as that phase of development concerned with the task of self-definition that must occur in the transition of the child evolving into the adult. It involves the renewed tasks of separation and individuation and implies a renunciation of childhood dependence and preparation for the caretaking role of the parent.

A similar task of self-definition is involved in the work of analysis, which culminates in the termination phase, in which the analysand relinquishes the caretaking analyst and the analyst renounces the patient as the dependent child. This task is invaded by those regressive transference and countertransference forces which oppose this progressive direction, similar to those elements which are at work in the adolescent and his parents.

These transference and countertransference attitudes are stronger and more difficult to deal with in the analysis of persons in training to become psychoanalysts themselves. These added difficulties derive in part, I believe, from the similarity of the psychoanalytic society to the actual family situation in which analysands in training are preparing actually to succeed the senior generation and with whom they will continue to live their professional lives. Most young psychoanalysts do not leave their Thebes or Corinth but choose to remain in their psychoanalytic family, eventually to succeed their parent analysts.

In his paper "Relations between Psycho-Analysts," Grinberg (1963) points to the "idealized position in which patients are accustomed to place the analyst—on account of the screen quality he possesses for them" and adds that though they systematically reject and interpret this idealization it is difficult for analysts not to submit to it (p. 363). The internal resistance to attempts to overcome such countertransference disturbances arises, I believe, from the universal need to idealize the internal and the external mother.

Grinberg states that the analyst works in a situation of isolation, regression, frustration, and disassociation, with the resultant reactivation of anxieties and exacerbation of conflicts. He feels this leads to heightened tension in the relations between analysts. It seems not at all unlikely that the demands of the analytic situation, which tend to activate parental aggression and yet require containment and neutralization of this aggression, are an important source of this tension, which is displaced and discharged in the relations with one's colleagues.

Erikson (1964) in *Insight and Responsibility* writes: "I think that there is a more 'actual' reason for the fact that man's ruthless striving for competence, mastery, and power has come under psychoanalytic scrutiny only gradually: I mean the understandable reluctance to recognize it in one's professional actuality. . . . the history of psychoanalysis makes it clear that, like any investigative method, it can serve the drive for power and the need for a sharp if seemingly unbloody weapon" (p. 212).

It is apparent that much of the disturbance within analytic societies and institutes arises from the inability of members to deal with their oedipal aggression. It is the task of the teachers and training analysts to help the younger generation contain and neutralize their sexual and aggressive strivings in their dealings with patients and colleagues. But this task cannot be accomplished unless the elders, the parental figures, develop the capacity to acknowledge the reality of the mutually narcissistic and aggressive situation which is involved in the succession of generations.

When the implications of this are denied and not acknowledged by psychoanalytic educators responsible for analyzing younger colleagues, and when the sort of idealization Grinberg describes is permitted to remain unanalyzed, this blindness can only be passed on to future generations of psychoanalysts. This limits the development of analysis on the one hand, and invites the unrecognized, unmastered, warded-off aggression to reemerge in the sort of destructiveness which recurrently plagues psychoanalytic societies as it beset Thebes in the Sophoclean tragedy.

In the Oedipus tragedy, Oedipus in his search to free Thebes insists upon learning the dreadful truth about his past. He proclaims that he "cannot leave the truth unknown," despite his mother's plea that he search no further. The secret of his incestual and parricidal deeds weighs heavily upon him, and he can no longer hide from himself the dreadful truth. But Jocasta also bears a dreadful secret, and when her pleas that the truth be not revealed are disregarded she destroys herself. In response Oedipus blinds himself.

This dreaded truth—what was it?

Shepherd: Must I tell?
Oedipus: You must and I must hear.
Shepherd: It was his child, they said. Your lady inside the palace,

> could tell the truth of it.
> *Oedipus:* She gave it to you?
> *Shepherd:* Yes, master.
> *Oedipus:* To what purpose?
> *Shepherd:* To be destroyed.
> *Oedipus:* The child she bore!

Oedipus then bewails: "Alas! All out. All known, no more concealment! O light may I never look on you again."

[The chorus concludes:]

All the generations of mortal man add up to nothing! Show me the men whose happiness was anything more than illusion followed by disillusion. Here is the instance, here is Oedipus, here is the reason why I will call no creature happy.

[And the last chorus:]

Sons and daughters of Thebes, behold; this was Oedipus
Greatest of men; he held the key to the deepest mysteries,
Was envied by all his fellow-men for his great prosperity:
Behold, what a full tide of misfortune swept over his head.
Then learn that mortal man must always look to his ending,
And none can be called happy until that day when he carries his
Happiness down to the grave in peace.

Is this sight of the inevitability of the rise and decline of the generations with the potential for mutual destructiveness of the participants too much even for psychoanalysts to see? Might not this account for the aversion of psychoanalysts to Freud's discourses on the destructive component of human beings?

Just as revolution must be viewed as an expression of parricide, one final manifestation of parental filicidal aggression comes with the advent of our periodic wars between nations. The opportunity for massacre of the young assumes here its ultimate and most devastating form, and the blind kings of every household have their chance to act out and at the same time deny their own filicidal aggression.

Can we as psychoanalysts be of significant help to a world which persists in destroying its young if we continue in remaining blind to the filicide which resides within all of us? As dreadful as this vision is, the consequences of continuing to blind ourselves, as Oedipus did, can only be a continuation of the destruction which plagues the generations in the beginning of the Oedipus story and has continued to do so. The pestilence of mankind is well described by Sophocles:

> You too have seen our city's affliction, caught
> In a tide of Death from which there is no escaping;
> Death in the fruitful flowering of her soil;
> Death in the pastures; death in the womb of woman;
> And pestilence, a fiery demon gripping the city;
> Stripping the House of Cadmus to fatten hell.

If there be a repetition compulsion, as described by Freud in *Beyond the Pleasure Principle* (1920), is this not the most dread aspect of it, the compulsion to destroy the generations?

Summary

In *Oedipus Rex* Sophocles portrays with dramatic impact the conflicts associated with the succession of generations. He has much to say about the crises of adolescence. A reexamination of the Oedipus story as presented by Sophocles in his tragedy offers a fresh look at these problems.

The encounters of the youthful Oedipus with his father, Laius, at the crossroads, and with the Sphinx at the gates of Thebes, are viewed as portraying the young adult in conflict with both the internal and external parental representations. The problems arising from the mutually aggressive situation between parents and their children are discussed. The threat to the family and society posed by the unconscious filicidal as well as the more well-known parricidal attitudes is examined.

Various psychoanalytic authors in recent years have described the universal and usually unconscious filicidal tendencies revealed in myths, which are especially well delineated in the Oedipus drama. Oedipus is motivated to leave his family and home by the anxiety aroused in him by the tale of "horror and misery" presaged by the oracle: "How I must marry my mother, and become the parent of a misbegotten brood, an offence to all mankind—and kill my father." This is the anxiety regularly aroused during puberty with the activation of the latent oedipus complex and the upsurge of aggressive and sexual instinctual drives.

Parental sexual and aggressive attitudes toward the maturing child also tend at this time to become intensified and may break through previously adequate defenses. Parental hostility in particular becomes activated when it is evident that the child is no longer helpless and weak and is able to make sexual claims and to enforce these and other claims by means of the vigor and strength of youth approaching maturity. Such a struggle between generations can invade the psychoanalytic situation and frequently permeates the atmosphere of psychoanalytic institutes.

This paper concerns the triumphs and pains associated with the inevitable succession of generations, the envy and hatred of the generations as well as the love and mutual respect. It attempts to focus attention on the familial conflicts associated with the succession of generations, which reaches a peak of disturbance with the emergence of the adolescent, who must overcome both internal psychological and external actual obstacles to self-realization.

REFERENCES

Berliner, B. (1958), The role of object relations in moral masochism. *Psychoanal. Quart.*, 27:38–56.

Bion, W. R. (1963), *The Elements of Psycho-Analysis.* New York: Basic Books.

Devereux, G. (1966), The cannibalistic impulses of parents. *Psychoanal. Forum*, 1:114–124.

Erikson, E. H. (1964), *Insight and Responsibility.* New York: Norton.

Flugel, J. C. (1935), *The Psycho-Analytic Study of the Family.* London: Hogarth Press.

Freud, A. (1958), Adolescence. *The Psychoanalytic Study of the Child,* 13:255–278.

Freud, S. (1920), Beyond the pleasure principle. *Standard Edition,* 18:3–64. London: Hogarth Press, 1955.

Friedenberg, E. Z. (1959), *The Vanishing Adolescent.* Boston: Beacon Press, 1966.

Grinberg, L. (1963), Relations between psycho-analysts. *Internat. J. Psycho-Anal.*, 44:362–369.

Kanzer, M. (1950), The Oedipus trilogy. *Psychoanal. Quart.*, 19:561–672. Chapter 6, this volume.

Rangell, L. (1955), The role of the parent in the Oedipus complex. *Bull. Menn. Clin.*, 19:9–15.

Rascovsky, A. & Rascovsky, M. (1968), On the genesis of acting out and psychopathic behavior in Sophocles' *Oedipus*: Notes on filicide. *Internat. J. Psycho-Anal.*, 49:390–394. Chapter 11, this volume.

Róheim, G. (1934), *The Riddle of the Sphinx.* London: Hogarth Press.

Sophocles, *The Theban Plays,* Trans. E. F. Watling. Baltimore: Penguin, 1947.

Van der Sterren, H. A. (1952), The "King Oedipus" of Sophocles, *Internat. J. Psycho-Anal.,* 33:343–354.

13

Adoption Trauma: Oedipus Myth/ Clinical Reality

LUIS FEDER

[1974]

The manifest Oedipus myth is the case history of an adopted child. The ubiquity of both myth and complex is associated with Freud's concept of the "family romance" (1909). The adoption trauma as a concept, as a syndrome, and a universal trend follows the clinical sequence tabulated below. It is identical with Rank's "average myth" (cf. Freud, 1939) and with the Oedipus myth. The 200 cases which form the basis for this paper follow the same typical pattern. The traumatic vicissitudes of adoption as outlined here attempt to integrate (from the points of view of both time sequence and psychological significance) previously neglected, earlier psychogenic components (Feder, 1965a, 1965b; Calef, 1968).

Presented at the Twenty-eighth International Psychoanalytical Congress, Paris, July 1973. Reprinted with permission from *International Journal of Psycho-Analysis,* vol. 55, pp. 491–493.

The Clinical Sequence of the Adoption Trauma

(*i*) Ambivalent, conflictual preconceptive coupling, leading to

(*ii*) unwanted pregnancy, which causes

(*iii*) somatization, abortions (fantasied as well as attempted but frustrated), causing in turn

(*iv*) traumatic birth, resulting from the attitudes of a rejecting, filicidal, feticidal mother. The traumatic impact of this on the child and of the mother's attitudes and subsequent abandonment of the child, leads to

(*v*) an adoption agent (or agency) "romance" which is seldom professional, particularly because of unavailable diagnostic criteria. This often reinforces scotomata toward adoptive motivations, leading to

(*vi*) adoptive parents whose profound motivations are unknown. These motivations fluctuate "pregnancy induction," "sterility reparation," "guilty-submissive" in content. The adoptive parents are often psychotics or perverts engaged in triangular mutual sadomasochistic exploitation, masked by

(*vii*) preadoptive idealization on the part of the adoptive parents, followed by

(*viii*) a post-idyllic period, marked by conflict, and possibly the subsequent returning, substitution, or rejection of the child (with infanticidal wishes). This may bring about, in the child,

(*ix*) an "adopted child" pathology, which can flower into narcissistic character disorder, psychotic episodes, delinquency, homosexuality, fantasied or attempted suicide, incest, homicide, fratricide, murder of one or both adoptive parents, and to patricide or matricide.

The mythical admonitions inherent in the Oedipus myth and reality orientation are equally disobeyed; Jocasta and Laius paid no heed to the oracle and Westerners adhere insufficiently to an anticonceptive orientation. Though the use of the "pill" seems to control and diminish the birthrate in certain sections of the population, there still are and will be high numbers of candidates for adoption: Why?

In two myths, that of Oedipus and the biblical story of Sarah and Abraham, power needs and envy prompt action leading to the breaking up of an inconvenient triangle. In the case of Laius, his relationship with a homosexual partner motivated Jocasta to reject the oracle's advice. In the case of Abraham, Sarah's envy of Agar, the slave that gave Ishmael to Abraham, made her overcome her sterility. My own clinical experience with secondary sterility bears out the existence of such motivations.

A diminishing birthrate has eliminated neither unwanted pregnancies nor the urge to impregnate in order to abort; nor has it reduced unconscious filicidal trends in parents. As a result, the clinical adoption problem is but a visible portion of all that it implies. The adoption trauma as such tinges the lives of the adoption triangle in the family as well as in the social macrocosm.

Insights gained from the pathology surrounding adoption traumata open a perspective which goes beyond that of the clinic, of the penitentiary, and of the psychiatric ward to include victims of war, e.g., the children of those raped by the invader.[1]

The Objects of the Research

First, to study the little available data, according to the nine steps outlined earlier. Second, to demonstrate clinically the correlation between preconceptive "unwantedness," the psychogenesis of adoption, the resulting symptoms, and other *sequelae.* The Oedipus myth joins the complex! This suggests equally the existence of a ubiquitous entity, the equivalence and psychogenic universality of the dynamics and symptoms in adopted children and in natural children who, to the degree that they feel they had been unwanted before birth, will behave and fantasize as if they were adopted. Third, to derive and formulate reliable diagnostic, prognostic, therapeutic, and ultimately preventive criteria in this area. Fourth, to develop, on the basis of all this evidence, more reliable diagnostic clues for adequate adoptive matching.

Since adoption is always a problem, we also need to investigate

[1]William Smitt reports on 200,000 Bangladesh women, rejected by family and society, impregnated by Punjabis who left them and fled. Most aborted, but nevertheless about 20,000 of the illegitimate children remained in hiding. Only 100 were registered and were to be sent to Holland and Denmark for adoption (article in *Excelsior*, Mexico, September 17, 1972).

successful adoptions.[2] Thus, beginning with our 200 cases, it should be possible to establish a tentative diagnostic spectrum of variable severity. In regard to motherhood, we should minimize the effects of idealization: libidinous maternity is as real as filicide.

Freud (1916–1917) asked how many mothers that now love their children wished, at one time, to abort them. We answer: all mothers in varying degree! Present theoretical, clinical, sociological, and statistical evidence substantiates this view (Feder, 1963, 1965a, 1965b, 1967a, 1967b, 1970a, 1970b; Calef, 1968; Rascovsky and Rascovsky, 1968).

Preconceptive filicidal ambivalence fluctuates, manifesting itself through whatever predominates in such conflict. We know that ambivalence does not really discriminate, but only appears to yield, and does not effectively succumb to repression.

Unconscious perception in the child appears as curiosity and is basically used in the search for narcissistic reassurance. Primal scene and family romance merge when the question of the baby's origin appears. This manifest wish in the child hides his more profound concern to discover not only sexual circumstances of his conception, but also how *wanted* he or she was. The stimuli of being sexually overexcited, or of being slighted, may precipitate genetic fantasies. This is exemplified in the family romance which is, most likely, the manifestation of unconscious perception by the child in regard to his rejection. The constancy principle having been disturbed, transitory regression is disturbed and this triggers off unconscious perception mechanisms with paranoid features. It is just as with Oedipus: when the drunk reveals to him that he is a bastard, Oedipus runs away and commits murder. Freud implies that in every fantasy there is "a fragment of *historical truth*" (1937, p. 267). But with the adopted child, the portion of not being wanted is almost the whole. With the natural child it usually remains only a portion, though narcissistic disorders equate the rejection of the adopted and the natural as a preconceptive rejection of equal magnitude.

[2]This paper has emerged from the Adoption Study of the Texas Institute of Child Psychiatry. The coordinator of the study is J. Vick, social worker, and the Director is Dr. I. Kraft. The codirector of the study is Dr. E. Bratteng, in collaboration with the author as theoretician (during the period 1970–1971). Two hundred cases form the sample discussed in this paper. They were gathered over a decade by the Texas Institute of Child Psychiatry as part of the adoption project. Some of these cases have been carefully examined by the author, who has spent over ten years in the psychoanalytic study of preconceptive ambivalence, abortion, and filicide.

The common denominator between the oedipus complex and the manifest aspects of the Oedipus myth may now be traced back to the ambivalent preconceptive conflict where feticide, filicide, and infanticide brought a varying degree of concern for the parents. Research in this area has supplied us with symptomatic manifestations on both the maternal and the paternal side. We see their repercussions through symptomatic and circumstantial evidence in the child's character (such as is evident in the impulse-ridden psychopathic character disorders frequent among adopted children). There is still much to learn in the area of unconscious perception. The adoption trauma is destined to become a "marker" in this area and to provide us with evidence indicating many of the subtleties of unconscious perception in the adoptive triangle.

The least available but most conclusive data could be obtained from the natural mother, e.g., her motivations for impregnation and renunciation, and her refusal to look at her child in order to avoid painful separation anxiety, postpartum depression, and suicidal wishes.

It is not suprising that children from such beginnings become a significant part of the population of our psychiatric clinics, reformatories, penitentiaries, and psychiatric hospitals, and of those who commit or attempt suicide. Often the story of narcissistic blows is renewed. Sartre's *Saint Genet* is an ideal literary example. Sterile parents expect "the perfect product." As a consequence the child is returned to the foster home or agency. Later, this leads to vengeful destructive, incestuous behavior and to inconceivable possessiveness, fugues, delinquency, and actual patricidal, matricidal, and fratricidal acts. These protracted vicissitudes of the adoption triangle make adoption pains stronger than labor pains.

Since external reality does play a significant role, future research must pose many questions bearing on reality. Does the intensity of the rejection correspond to the magnitude of the character disorders of the adopted child? Does the real external team (e.g., agencies, adoptive parents, teachers) have sufficient influence to offset the blows of the initial preconceptive abortive conflict, or is the character damage final? In this we must discount those feticidal attempts, abortions, miscarriages, the effects of drug addiction on the fetus, starvation diets, and other prenatal injuries or forms of neglect that would seriously affect the fetus. Finally, we should look at the therapeutic implications. We must take into account the relation between the negative therapeutic reaction and the adoption trauma. The precipitating moment that impels Oedipus to flee from Merope and Polybus, his adoptive parents, is when he is uncovered as a bastard. Here we may have new light on the negative therapeutic reaction as this is repeated in the transference. The ambivalent patricidal or matricidal destructive (but grateful) patient "saves" his parental surrogate, the analyst, through flight (Feder, 1963). He saves himself, at the height of ambivalent regression, from discovering through painful analysis that like Oedipus he was also not entirely wanted. Had he been entirely wanted, would he be in psychoanalytic treatment?

REFERENCES

Calef, V. (1968), The unconscious fantasy of infanticide manifested in resistance. *J. Amer. Psychoanal. Assn.*, 16:697–710.

Feder, L. (1963), Técnica psicoanalítica y fantasías de salvación. *La Técnica*, Mexico, pp. 60–87.

——— (1965a), El eterno Edipo. *Cuad. Psa.* 1:119–122.

——— (1965b), Los abortos arrepentidos. *Cuad. Psa.*, 1:399.

——— (1967a), Madre-hijo, su encuentro y rencuentro en torno a la hipogalactia: Síndrome de tres traumas básicos. *Cuad. Psa.*, 3:195–225.

——— (1967b), Fantasías maternas preconcepcionales conflictivas: Su trascendencia en el carácter del hijo. Presented at the Sixth National Congress of Psychoanalysis, Mexico.

——— (1970a), Filicidio y poder. In: *El Psiconálisis Frente a la Guerra.* Buenos Aires: Alonso, pp. 52–77.

——— (1970b), La primera sesión psicoanalítica: Fantasías preconcepcionales y contratransferenciales. *Cuad. Psa.*, 6:23–32.

Freud, S. (1909), Family romances. *Standard Edition*, 9:237–241. London: Hogarth Press, 1959

——— (1916–1917), Introductory lectures on psycho-analysis. *Standard Edition*, 15/16. London: Hogarth Press, 1963.

——— (1937), Constructions in analysis. *Standard Edition*, 23:257–269. London: Hogarth Press, 1964.

——— (1939), Moses and monotheism. *Standard Edition*, 23:7–137. London: Hogarth Press, 1964

Rascovsky, A., & Rascovsky, M. W. (1968), On the genesis of acting out and psychopathic behavior in Sophocles' *Oedipus*: Notes on filicide. *Internat. J. Psycho-Anal.*, 49:390–394. Chapter 11, this volume.

14

Oedipus and His Cradle Scars

HENRY ROSNER

[1977]

Why another paper on Oedipus? Is it possible that the voluminous literature on the subject has not fully clarified the meaning of the Oedipus myth or of Sophocles' use of it in his *Oedipus Rex*? The answer must lie in the majesty of Sophocles' tragedy. In Oedipus the Athenian dramatist had created the greatest of all Greek tragic characters. The universality of the myth as retold by Sophocles lends itself to renewed study and interpretation according to the life experiences of the reader. This is one reason why *Oedipus Rex* has been revived perhaps more frequently than any other ancient drama. The stimuli for my writing this paper were clinical experiences with children suffering foot deformities early in life (Rosner, 1975), as well as research into problems of abandonment and adoption (Rosner, 1974). Both subjects led me directly back to Oedipus.

I would like to propose here that Oedipus' oedipal conflicts were related not primarily toward his natural parents, Jocasta and Laius,

---

Presented at the Meeting of the American Psychoanalytic Association, December 16, 1977. Published here for the first time.

but toward his adoptive parents, Merope and Polybus. This possibility has not previously been fully explored. In addition, if we ask whether Oedipus ever wondered about his swollen feet, we can apply ourselves to a study of Oedipus' infancy from the perspectives of abandonment and physical deformity. In this presentation, these early traumas are linked together and referred to as "Oedipus' cradle scars."

The published analytic literature on Oedipus begins with Freud's reference to *Oedipus Rex* in *The Interpretation of Dreams* (1900): "And a factor of this kind is in fact involved in the story of King Oedipus. His destiny moves us only because it might have been ours—because the oracle laid the same curse upon us before our birth as upon him. It is the fate of all of us, perhaps, to direct our first sexual impulse towards our mother and our first hatred and our first murderous wish against our father" (p. 262).

This was not Freud's first comment on this subject. As I will shortly discuss, there was an important earlier reference to Oedipus in a letter to Fliess. In addition, the actual term "oedipus complex" was first used by Freud in his paper, "A Special Type of Choice of Object Made by Men" (Freud, 1910, p. 171).

It is beyond the scope of this chapter to review the voluminous literature that has followed. In general, psychoanalytic writers accept the proposition that Oedipus' "Oedipus complex" was directed toward his natural parents, Laius and Jocasta. Kanzer (1948, 1964), in his publications, has provided a comprehensive study of the myth and of Sophocles' Oedipus cycle. His review of the play is mainly from the phallic-oedipal phase of development and in the tradition of a classical oedipal triangle, again focused on the natural parents.

Van der Sterren (1949) sees Oedipus as struggling with the question, Who are my real parents? He concluded, however, that Oedipus' incestuous feelings were directed at Jocasta. Interestingly, Freud, later in his writings, noted that there were atypical features associated with the Oedipus legend. "The Greek hero killed his father and took his mother to wife. That he did so unwittingly, since he did not know them as his parents, is a deviation from the analytic fact, which we can easily understand and which, indeed, we shall recognize as inevitable" (Freud, 1940, p. 187).

It is this deviation that deserves our attention. As I have suggested, early abandonment and physical deformity skewed Oedipus' infantile relationship to his adoptive parents.

A final note before turning directly to the study of Oedipus. An unexpected finding emerged from a review of Freud's writings that has both historical and analytic significance as regards the topic of early object loss. As is well known, Freud's Catholic nursemaid, who was with him for the first two-and-a-half years of his life, was suddenly dismissed on grounds she was a thief. In letters to Fliess, Freud (1950) repeatedly acknowledged his closeness to her. She repeatedly appeared in his dreams, the understanding of which was a crucial aspect of his self-analysis. Grigg (1973), in discussing Freud and his nursemaid, clarified her role in the origin of his train phobia. Grigg has even suggested that Freud's opening of his office on Easter Sunday, April 25, 1886, was either an act of defiance toward her (and her religion) or an attempt at reunion with her (p. 114).

Of historical note is the fact that Freud first recorded his discovery of the Oedipus complex in a letter written to Fliess in 1897 (Freud, 1950, pp. 223–224). This major revelation comes directly after an attempt at self-analysis of a dream about his nursemaid. In accord with the principle of multiple function (Waelder, 1936), one might wonder whether, in addition to the theme of incestuous childhood feelings toward the nursemaid (a mother surrogate), Freud was not also responding to her sudden dismissal, an emotional abandonment and a possible preconscious link with the story of Oedipus, who lost his natural mother.

There is another clue to the significance of this loss for Freud. When he had to find a pseudonym for his first adolescent patient, who also had abandoned him, he used the name of Dora, which was his nursemaid's name (Freud, 1901).

None of this is to suggest in any way that Freud's formulation of the Oedipus complex was an error or to minimize its significance in psychic development or analytic theory and therapy. Rather, the aim is to explore and discuss earlier developmental trauma, such as abandonment, that can influence the oedipal phase.

The Oedipus Myth

Any study of Sophocles' play must begin with a study of the myth. There is some controversy in the nonanalytic literature whether one need know more than what Sophocles included in *Oedipus Rex* in order to fully appreciate the play. Dodds (1973) argues that one need not know the complete Oedipus legend to appreciate his dilemma, while Knox (1957), Vellacott (1971), and others assume that the intelligent Greek playgoer was familiar with the myth and the Greek saga from which it was derived. It seems logical to assume that Sophocles expected his audience to know, before it even entered the theater, the major elements of the myth, which derives from one of the two major sagas linked with the founding of Thebes. Since I am approaching the Oedipus myth as a patient's life history, genealogy is important. Agenor was the King of Phoenicia. When his daughter Europa was abducted by Zeus (in the form of a bull), he sent his three sons to look for her. It was during their search that Cadmus, one of the three, founded Thebes. Laius, Oedipus' father, was a descendent of Cadmus.

Oedipus was cursed because of an indiscretion committed by his father. Laius was the son of Labdacus, who died when Laius was only a year old. At that time Lykos succeeded Labdacus as leader, or warlord. Eventually Laius was banished from Thebes and took refuge with Pelops, King of Pisa. This relationship abruptly ended when Laius kidnapped Pelops' son Chrysippus, with whom he was homosexually involved. It is not clear from the ancient legends whether it was the homosexuality or his inhospitable behavior that so offended Hera that she cursed Laius' offspring and brought his line to an end in two generations (Tripp, 1970).

The next episode in the Oedipus myth occurs after Laius regains his Kingdom of Thebes and marries Jocasta. Whether because they were childless or because his homosexuality interfered with his wife's sexual pleasure, Laius eventually consulted the Delphic oracle, who informed him that any child born to Jocasta was fated to kill him. Jocasta, sexually frustrated, refused to accept her husband's sexual abstinence and seduced him with the help of a little wine. As a result, nine months later, Oedipus was born. Laius snatched him immediately from the nurse's arms, pierced his feet with a nail, and, binding them together, placed him out on Mount Citharon to die of exposure (Graves, 1955, p. 9). Shepherds found the infant and brought him to Merope, the wife of Polybus, King of Corinth or Sicyon. The childless couple brought the boy up as their own son, naming him Oedipus (Swollen Foot) for obvious reasons. Grown to manhood, the aggressive Oedipus was one day taunted by a drunken companion for not being the true son of Polybus. For some reason, this accusation troubled the young man so deeply that he made a journey to Delphi, to inquire of the oracle if it were true. The Pythia, without waiting to hear his question, drove him from Apollo's shrine, saying that he would kill his father and marry his mother. In horror, Oedipus turned eastward, intending never to return to Corinth.

Not far from Delphi, Oedipus came to a spot known as the Cleft Way, where the road to Daulis divides from that leading to Boeotia. There he met a man in a chariot, whose charioteer demanded that the young man move aside. Oedipus refused. The charioteer urged his horses forward, so that a wheel of the car grazed Oedipus' foot. In passing, either the rider or his servant struck Oedipus on the head with his goad. Enraged, Oedipus killed the rider, the charioteer, and all but one of the retainers who, according to various versions of the story, were with them. Letting them lie where they had fallen, the young man continued on his way.

When he reached Thebes the city was in turmoil. A female monster called the Sphinx had settled herself on the walls of the citadel, or on Mount Phicium, to the north, and was eating the Thebans one by one. The last victim had been Haemon, a son of Creon, who was acting as regent for King Laius, the king having left some time before on a trip to Delphi. Before killing her victims, the Sphinx would ask them a riddle: "What is it that goes on four legs in the morning, two at midday, and three in the evening?" The Thebans had learned from an oracle that they would be free from this plague when the riddle was answered correctly, but no one could solve it. To add to the city's troubles, Damasistratus, King of nearby Plataea, reported that he had found and buried the bodies of Laius and his retinue on the way to Delphi. The Thebans, preoccupied with the

Sphinx, had no time to seek the murderer. Indeed, Creon offered the hand of his sister Jocasta, Laius' widow, and a share in the kingdom to any man who could save the city.

Oedipus undertook the task. He visited the Sphinx and gave this answer to her riddle: "Man, who crawls in infancy, walks upright in his prime, and leans on a cane in old age." The monster, chagrined that someone had at last penetrated her secret, flung herself to her death from the walls of the citadel. Oedipus was greeted as a hero and made king of Thebes. Shortly after, the lone survivor of Laius' retinue made his way back to Thebes. Finding Oedipus reigning, and recognizing him as Laius' murderer, he announced that the king had been killed by several highwaymen and asked to be assigned to duties as a shepherd far from the city. The citizens, rejoicing in their new king, forgot Laius and his unhappy fate. Jocasta had, by her new young husband, two sons, Eteocles and Polynices, and two daughters, Antigone and Ismene. Some say, however, that these were Oedipus' children by Euryganeia, daughter of Hyperphas (Tripp, 1970, pp. 422–423).

Sophocles' Tragic Oeuvre

Most of what we know about Sophocles comes from contemporary anecdotes (Whitman, 1951). Born wealthy in 496 B.C., he died famous in 406 B.C. His youthful beauty and skill in dancing and music brought him early recognition. Later he became a priest. He is said to have composed 123 plays and with these he won 24 victories; *Oedipus Rex* did not win a first prize but placed second.

Aristotle credits Sophocles with a major change in the form of tragedy. He is credited with introducing scene-painting and with enlarging the chorus from twelve to fifteen. But the most significant change was his introduction of a third actor, which allowed an author to increase the scope, the dramatic range, and intensity of his plays. While Sophocles is known for the flexibility and vividness of his tragedies, he is also considered to be one of the most violent of dramatists in describing the evils of life. His plays, in the opinions of others, reflect the Greek spirit and its values of harmony, piety, and self-restraint. Yet, while he is alleged to have all but died of his own "magnificent fame" (Whitman, 1951, p. 6), in his work he repeatedly made the point that man must not try to be a god. For Sophocles, man can come to grief by action, even short of crime. "All action and not merely sinful action, may entail suffering" (Whitman, 1951, p. 41).

As Kott (1974) has pointed out, in all the tragedies of Sophocles, except the last, in which Oedipus chooses the place of his death, heroes are plunged to the lower depths of dispair. Sophocles seemed to prepare for the moment when man realizes he is being crushed and the gods are silent. Only then is one faced with the heroic choice, what today may be called existential quandary, to commit suicide or go on living.

In the seven extant tragedies of "Black Sophocles," as Kott calls him (p. 124), there are six suicides, one attempted suicide, and two calls for death to be hastened (Kott, 1974, p. 44). In his first play, *Ajax*, the protagonist kills himself onstage at high noon and remains onstage throughout the entire second half. By contrast, Jocasta commits suicide toward the end of *Oedipus Rex*. Nor is Jocasta's suicide the most violent. The intelligent Athenian theatergoer would have been familiar with Antigone's suicide by hanging and especially the violent suicide of Deianira, who in *The Woman of Trachis* cuts open her stomach with a double-bladed sword.

This play (c. 437–432 B.C.), which followed *Antigone* (c. 442–441 B.C.) and preceded *Oedipus Rex* (c. 425 B.C.) contains a number of themes that are typical of Sophocles and that seem to anticipate their fuller exposition in *Oedipus Rex*: the concept that the dead can come back to haunt and torment the living; the horrifying cry of the hero; the fatal consequences of the use of magic by a female protagonist; and the open request by a father that his son kill him (patricide).

Just as many students of modern drama might familiarize themselves with the earlier work of a playwright in preparation for viewing a new work, it might be helpful to review briefly some of the themes of *The Women of Trachis*.

Heracles has been absent from Trachis for fifteen months. His wife, Deianira, is fearful that he has come to a bad ending. Deianira sends their son Hyllus in search of his father. A messenger then arrives with the news that Heracles is well and is on his way home—but with a mistress, Iole. Deianira tries to restrain her anger at Heracles, for she is familiar with his weaknesses, but the thought that she must share her house with Iole is unendurable. After some hesitation, she decides to recapture her husband's attentions with a love charm given her by the centaur Nessus. When Nessus was mortally wounded by Heracles after attempting to ravish Deianira, he gave her some of his blood with the instruction that she use it if her husband's affections should ever stray. Deianira, having kept the blood hidden from the light as the centaur had bidden, now smears it on a new robe which she sends to Heracles.

After the gift is dispatched, Deianira has premonitions of disaster, for the tuft of wool with which she daubed the blood on the robe has dissolved to dust and foam upon being exposed to sunlight. Cursing his mother, Hyllus relates on his return that Heracles was wearing the robe as he made an offering to Zeus, and that the warmth and light of the sacrificial flame had caused it to cling to his body and consume his flesh. Half mad with pain and suspicion, he is brought to Trachis, barely alive. Deianira, guilt-ridden, rushes away without a word, and kills herself. Her nurse then tells the audience the gory details of Deianira's death.

Heracles is carried in on a litter. He raves wildly in his pain and expresses bitterness that he should have been cut down by a woman; but Hyllus, who is now aware of Deianira's innocence, explains things to his father. Heracles, realizing that his fate represents the fulfillment of an old oracle that he would be killed by one who dwells in the land of the dead, commands Hyllus to take him to the sacred peak of Mt. Oeta and to gather wood for his funeral pyre, and asks his son to start the funeral fire and kill him to end his suffering. Hyllus refuses to kindle the pyre. He concludes the scene with a rebuke to the gods, who load men with sorrows and view the result with indifference.

Some common themes can be noted between this play and *Oedipus Rex*. Deianira, while basically loving, chooses to use magic, a means of playing god and deceiving men, while Jocasta seduces her husband with wine and deceives him. Heracles, after sacking a city out of lust and revenge, wants to bring back a concubine and thus threaten the sanctity of the family, while Laius, with his homosexuality, represents another danger to the family. And while Heracles does not succeed in convincing his son to commit parricide, Oedipus does commit it, though unwittingly. Finally, the youthful rebellion of Hyllus at the end of the play is matched by old Oedipus' denial of any wrongdoing in *Oedipus at Colonus*: "For not in me, not in myself, could you discover any stain of sin, whereby I sinned against myself and mine" (Sophocles c. 406, ll. 966–968). With this as a background, let us now turn to *Oedipus Rex*.

Sophocles' Oedipus

Oedipus Rex (425 B.C.) was the second of three plays that Sophocles wrote about Oedipus. It was preceded by *Antigone* (442 B.C.) and followed, when Sophocles was an old man, by *Oedipus at Colonus* (409 B.C.). However, its dramatic impact was far greater than that of any of his other plays. Its unique quality of maintaining interest and suspense has been noted with admiration by many critics. "The way in which Sophocles succeeded was not by collusion with the unconscious but, on the contrary, by forestalling any incursions from that region. As has often been noticed, in the construction of this tragedy the sheer artistry of unravelling the crime of Oedipus transfigures the fierceness of the conclusion" (Wind, 1963, p. 179).

As a detective story, the play concerns itself with the overt crimes of parricide and incest. If it is viewed as an analytic case, the crucial question is how Oedipus made his decision to act when confronted with an adolescent identity crisis unique to foundlings. Questions are raised about his paternity in both the myth, by a peer, and in the play, by a drunken guest.

It was because of this incident, and against the advice of both Merope and Polybus, that Oedipus decided to consult the Delphic oracle, hoping to discover the secret of his past. But instead he was told that he would kill his father and sleep with his mother. In the play, Oedipus tells Jocasta that he left Corinth in order to thwart the oracle. That statement makes sense only if he believed that Polybus and Merope were his natural parents. But he had gone to the oracle with good reason to believe that they were not his parents. It might therefore have been safer for him to stay in Corinth.

But he could not stay, in my opinion, because he must have had overt incestuous feelings toward his adoptive mother, Queen Merope. When Oedipus was brought to Corinth from Thebes he was adopted by a middle-aged, childless queen. Clinical experience with adoptees who become the only children of older mothers suggests they are likely to experience an excessive degree of cuddling, sensory contact, and excessive libidinal attachment. In Oedipus' case, his deformity must have been an added reason for undue closeness with his mother. While it is quite possible that later in his life, with ego maturity and reflection, he might have wondered about how it had come about that he had been crippled at birth, in his infancy his libidinal need had priority over cognitive understanding.

Let me cite a recent clinical example involving an adoption unusual by today's standards, in that the mother was middle-aged. In this case, a four-year-old adopted boy was referred for analysis because he was too aggressive in nursery school. He would push and fight with the other children and delight in knocking down their projects. In my office he would build beautifully but the pleasure was all in demolishing his creations. He had been adopted at birth by a well-meaning couple in their late forties who just did not have the youthfulness to be the ideal parents they wished to be. The mother loved to stay in bed in the morning, and up until nursery school her son would join her for breakfast in bed. Naturally, he was not happy to give up these pleasures when he had to go to nursery school, and his destructiveness was directly related to sadness over the loss of his oedipal object. When I asked him about his sadness, he replied, "That's the way the world runs for me." (Another "child of chance?") Most recently, he has begun to identify the projects that he builds and then destroys. He told me that they were graves, "but not for Mommy or Daddy."

For Oedipus, whatever intellectual doubts he might have had that Merope and Polybus were his natural parents, his feelings were never in doubt. The oracle was no help. Fenichel (1954) has noted that the ambiguous meaning of oracular predictions must, by its very nature, have social significance. The priests shirk their responsibility and express themselves equivocally, thereby allowing for all eventualities. But such ambiguity may also meet the needs of the ambivalent oracle seeker, who wants permission to gratify his instinctual needs and expects an unavoidable refusal. He tries to interpret the equivocation as permission but remains unable to rid himself of the feeling that he should interpret it as a prohibition, and as a warning of punishment. "Kris," Fenichel (1954) wrote, "called to my attention the connection between interpretation of the ambiguous prophecies and the solution of riddles. The individual who rejects all knowledge of guilt and represses the significance of his act misunderstands the task. And the wise man who can solve every riddle is not the most intelligent but he who can recognize the hidden truth because he is emotionally free and unhindered by repression" (p. 232).

Oedipus tried to use his intelligence to conceal his incestuous feelings but, though he was successful in solving the riddle of the Sphinx, could never free himself from his incestuous tie to Merope. The assumption that Oedipus' infantile libidinal object was Merope would explain a passage that has mystified many who have studied *Oedipus Rex* (Vellacott, 1971). When Oedipus is informed that Polybus has died of natural causes, he should feel relieved: the oracle has not been (and cannot be) fulfilled. Yet three times he proclaims that still he fears his mother's bed. When asked whose bed he means, Oedipus names Merope, his adoptive mother. He also expresses the idea that abandoning his father, Polybus, might have caused his death from grief. The implication is quite clear that, intrapsychically, his infantile wishes and conflicts were very much attached to the real objects who raised him as his parents.

> *Oedipus:* So he died of sickness, it seems—poor old man!
> *Messenger:* Yes, and of age—the long years he had measured.
> *Oedipus:* Ha! Ha! O dear Jocasta, why should one
> look to the Pythian hearth? Why should one look
> to the birds screaming overhead? They prophesied
> that I should kill my father! But he's dead,
> and hidden deep in earth, and I stand here
> who never laid a hand on spear against him,—
> unless perhaps he died of longing for me,
> and thus I am his murderer. But they,
> the oracles, as they stand—he's taken them

away with him, they're dead as he himself is,
and worthless.
Jocasta: That I told you before now.
Oedipus: You did, but I was misled by my fear.
Jocasta: Then lay no more of them to heart, not one.
Oedipus: But surely I must fear my mother's bed?
Jocasta: Why should man fear since chance is all in all
for him, and he can clearly foreknow nothing?
Best to live lightly, as one can, unthinkingly.
As to your mother's marriage bed,—don't fear it.
Before this, in dreams too, as well as oracles,
many a man has lain with his own mother.
But he to whom such things are nothing bears
his life most easily.
Oedipus: All that you say would be said perfectly
if she were dead; but since she lives I must
still fear, although you talk so well, Jocasta.
Jocasta: Still in your father's death there's light of comfort?
Oedipus: Great light of comfort; but I fear the living.
Messenger: Who is the woman that makes you afraid?
Oedipus: Merope, old man Polybus' wife.
Messenger: What about her frightens the queen and you?
Oedipus: A terrible oracle, stranger, from the Gods.
[Sophocles, c. 425 B.C., ll. 962–992]

Oedipus could not accept Jocasta's request that he ignore his inner reality not to pay attention to his dreams. For some, life may be easier, but for others, who must know who they are and where they came from, the search becomes a passion. Oedipus had to know the truth about his past. Jocasta commits suicide before Oedipus discovers that she is his natural mother. Sophocles has so constructed the play that the viewer could easily lose the exact order of mounting revelations. Oedipus accepts her death as due not to their incestuous relationship but to his having been of low birth.

Oedipus: Break out what will! I at least shall be
willing to see my ancestry, though humble.

Perhaps she is ashamed of my low birth,
for she has all a woman's high-flown pride.
But I account myself a child of Fortune,
beneficent Fortune, and I shall not be
dishonoured. She's the mother from whom I spring;
the months, my brothers, marked me, now as small,
and now again as mighty. Such is my breeding,
and I shall never prove so false to it,
as not to find the secret of my birth.
[Sophocles, c. 425 B.C., ll. 1076–1086].

Oedipus has just spoken to the messenger. From Oedipus' questions about his pain when found, it is clear he must have thought about it previously.

Messenger: Yes, but at least at that time
the man that saved your life, son.
Oedipus: What ailed me when you took me in your arms?
Messenger: In that your ankles should be witnesses.
Oedipus: Why do you speak of that old pain?
Messenger: I loosed you;
the tendons of your feet were pierced and fettered,—
Oedipus: My swaddling clothes brought me a rare disgrace.
Messenger: So that from this you're called your present name.
[Sophocles, c. 425 B.C., ll. 1030–1036]

Vellacott (1971) offers a slightly different translation:

Corinthian: And, my son, your preserver at that time.
Oedipus: What pain had I when you took me in your arms?
Corinthian: The joints of your feet could witness.
Oedipus: Alas, why do you mention that ancient deformity?
Corinthian: It was I who freed you when you had your ankles pierced.
Oedipus: Yes, that was the bitter disgrace that I received by way of birth-tokens.

Corinthian: With the result that you received from this chance the name which you bear now.

Oedipus: In the gods' [name, did I receive this injury] from my mother or from my father? [pp. 66–67]

It is important to note that Oedipus' first question was not about his parents but about his emotional state, his pain.

There are differing translations for the word "spargana" in this passage, ranging from Grene and Lattimore's (1959) "swaddling clothes" to Gould's (1970) "a fearful rebuke" to Vellacott's (1971) "birth-tokens," but the implication is clear. Oedipus must have wondered how he received his wounds. At best, they were ugly and something to be ashamed of; at worst, signs that his parents didn't want him to survive. There is a paucity of literary and anthropological data on foot piercing as a common practice. Laius did not kill his son outright, as he wished to avoid incurring ritual guilt for killing a member of one's family. Instead, putting him out on the mountain provided a high degree of certainty that Oedipus would die of exposure. Vellacott (1971, p. 188) says that this was a common practice and that Oedipus must have grown up thinking he was a foundling—especially after his parenthood was questioned in his adolescence. But Gould (1970) disagrees: "He had obviously never inferred from these marks that he must have been a foundling. The mutilation of the feet of the exposed child is unique in this story; parents who exposed their children usually hoped that they would be found and reared by others" (p. 93).

These considerations are important if we are to understand Oedipus. The analytic literature, in general, considers the foot deformity in a more positive way—either as a circumcision (Kanzer, 1948) or a puberty rite (Devereux, 1963). The implication would be that of a ritualistic substitute for castration as a requirement for entry into a group. If, on the other hand, the foot piercing was a stigma (Haffter, 1968), then it was a warning to that society that the stigmatized person was to be excluded. There may have been some understanding that what was considered dangerous in one city was acceptable to another. Thus, Oedipus, a menace to Laius in Thebes, was acceptable to Polybus and Merope in Corinth.

Thus far, I have tried to highlight both Oedipus' incestuous ties to his adoptive parents and his preoccupation with his origins. This latter point will become even clearer if we turn to his encounter with the Sphinx.

> You came and by your coming saved our city,
> Freed us from tribute which we paid of old
> To the Sphinx, cruel singer.
> [Sophocles, c. 425 B.C., ll. 34–36]

The tribute was the destruction of her younger men. The latest victim, according to the myth, had been Creon's own son. While the versions from antiquity differ as to how the Sphinx died, either at Oedipus' hands or by throwing herself over a cliff or battlement, Sophocles offers us another possibility—that Oedipus killed her with thought, intelligence (l. 398). Knox (1957) makes much of this: "In Oedipus' acceptance of the challenge of the Sphinx, the great qualities of the hero of the play were all displayed" (p. 41).

By giving the correct answer, Oedipus was not only demonstrating his sexual potency, but also expressing openly that man is equal to any task if he uses his intelligence. Any answer less than man, any sign of impotence or feeling of inadequacy, would have resulted in death. According to the earlier version, the Sphinx had been sent by Hera, probably against Laius. In *The Women of Trachis*, Sophocles had used a distant relative of the Sphinx, the Hydra, whose venom killed Heracles. Hera, from her own breast, had fed Hydra, who was Cerberus' sister and aunt of the Sphinx, born of the incestuous union of mother and son. Sophocles wanted to speak out against such incestuous relationships, that is, against matriarchical society. At the same time, he seems to have added a new twist to the older myth. Gould (1970) suggested that Apollo sent the Sphinx to aid Oedipus.

> Whereas the earlier versions of the story had Hera or some other god send the Sphinx against the Thebans for some offence that they or one of their kings (usually Laius) had committed, Sophocles, in his arrangement of the timing of the events . . . leaves us with the strong impression that she was sent by Apollo

> solely for the benefit of Oedipus. She seems to have been in Thebes only for a very brief time, between the departure of Laius for Delphi and the arrival of Oedipus just after he had killed Laius; and the chief result of Oedipus' victory over the Sphinx was to demonstrate to the Thebans that here was the logical successor to Laius, both as king and as the husband of Jocasta. The Sphinx thus becomes Apollo's creature, used by that god to engineer the incest. The close connection between the Sphinx and Apollo is demonstrated by the Naxian sphinxes at Apollo's temple in Delphi—probably the best known representations of this deity in Sophocles' time. Sphinxes also lined the last mile of the road to the temple of Apollo at Didyma. . . . [pp. 19-20]

It would seem from a comparison of the myth and Sophocles' version of it that the play condenses into a short period of time action that in myth might have taken many days. Shakespeare (1595) did something similar in *Romeo and Juliet,* basing his play on an Italian version whose action was spread out over three months. Shakespeare shortened it to three days and enormously increased the dramatic effect. So, in the retelling of Oedipus' adolescent experiences after leaving Corinth, one get the impression of great haste, peril, anxiety, and the ultimate triumph of truth. Oedipus makes it quite clear that with the killing of the Sphinx he had resolved the resurgent oedipal feelings of adolescence:

> But I came,
> Oedipus, who knew nothing, and I stopped her.
> I solved the riddle by my wit alone.
> [Sophocles, c. 425 B.C., ll. 397-399]

Knox (1957) points out that there is another meaning to the name Oedipus besides "swollen foot." The name is derived also from the verb *Oida,* "to know." In other words, Oedipus also means to know one's feet or, by extension, to know one's roots—one's parents. Oedipus, given his early injuries, was the ideal man to solve a riddle about feet. The punning of his name, "know nothing Oedipus," is a defense against acknowledgment of his oedipal feelings for Merope and his aggressive feelings toward Polybus. When the chariot carrying his natural father treads on his foot (a reminder of the original injury), Oedipus feels perfectly justified in killing Laius. To Oedipus, within the confines of Sophocles' play, his success against the Sphinx means he was correct in leaving Merope and Polybus. They were the dangerous incestuous objects. The gods would not so favor a man doomed by prophecy to sleep with his mother and kill his father. Following his victory over the Sphinx, Oedipus calls himself the "son of chance" (l. 1080). This is another attempt, via the notion of universal parenthood, to deny his revived oedipal feelings toward his adoptive parents. Similarly, the search undertaken in adolescence by many adopted children for their natural parents has, as one determinant, the search for a defense against incestuous feelings toward the parents who raised them.

The question can be asked, should Jocasta have known that Oedipus was her son? According to Vellacott (1971), Jocasta was probably a much younger woman than Merope, perhaps only twice Oedipus' age of eighteen (p. 163). Also, besides the fact that there may have been many foundlings in Athens (as in every city before the advent of birth control), Oedipus had just saved the city from death.

Finally, it may also be significant that he showed no other physical signs of royal blood—this was important in antiquity. For example, in another version of the Antigone myth, the principal has a son by Creon's son Haemon. The child is discovered by a birthmark peculiar to the royal family, which brings about her downfall. Oedipus had no such mark. For Oedipus, identity (to know his feet) was destiny. He never acknowledged his incestuous tie to Jocasta or his guilt over killing Laius. His blinding himself is not a confession. The two eyes represented the sun and the moon, which in primitive Greek mythology represented the Gods. Since he believes the Gods played a dirty trick on him, he prefers darkness, as did Ajax in an earlier play by Sophocles (460 B.C.). There Ajax says "You Darkness, my sole light" (l. 304). The blinding is generally considered to be an equivalent of castration, but it is significant in itself.

Oedipus survives. Of all the characters in the Theban trilogy, he is the only one to do so. Teiresias, his archrival, the soothsayer, the believer in prophecies, who was nonetheless unable to solve the riddle of the Sphinx, dies, according to the myth, fleeing Thebes after the war that followed Oedipus' departure. Oedipus eventually wanders to the grove of the Eumenides, the Fates. This is to be his burial place. Thus, "know nothing Oedipus," who became a "child of chance" after killing the Sphinx and finding an identity, dies with true heroic stature (Kanzer, 1948; Golden, 1967).

Conclusion

The dramatic structure of Sophocles' *Oedipus Rex* is unique among extant Greek plays. Over 250 of its lines, a greater proportion than that of any other Greek play known to us, are devoted to a retelling of the main character's early life and adolescence. It thus lends itself to analytic speculation, especially precarious here, as I am dependent on others for research and translation from the original Greek. However, given that *Oedipus Rex* is the story of a foundling, my clinical experience with such children, especially an only child with an older adoptive mother, can usefully be brought to bear on this material. This experience has revealed the intense incestuous relationship that can result in such situations. In the case of Oedipus, his foot deformity was a reminder of his questionable origins and heightened his libidinal attachment to his adoptive mother.

The question can be asked whether these feelings toward his primary reality objects were a defense or screen against incestuous ties to his *natural* parents. We are dealing here with a common problem of adopted children, that of dual parenthood. We must distinguish between the aim of the earliest phases of development, which is the establishment of libidinal ties, and phase-specific attempts to cope with the resolution of the Oedipus complex. During infancy and early childhood, psychic structure is not capable of understanding such concepts as abandonment. It only feels their consequences, which, as I have shown, can affect later life decisions. Even today, when adoptive parents, on the advice of social agencies, tell their one- or two-year-olds that they were "specially chosen" or "adopted," they do not expect the child to understand these words until later on in life. The advice is given mainly to allay the anxieties of the parents. Usually, meaningful concern about parenthood begins with questions about where babies come from. Freud (1900) viewed the riddle of the Sphinx as related to the sexual questions of childhood. It is as a means of coping with oedipal conflicts that these questions become the basis of organized inner fantasies of adoption or other variations of typical family romances. Inner confusion over unresolved oedipal conflicts can provide the background for the adopted adolescent's search for his natural parents. The primacy of infantile libidinal attachments to the adoptive parents should not be forgotten. For the foundling, the search for his "real" parents can be an attempt to escape from an intensely incestuous infancy as well as a realistic search for his heritage.

While my aim here has been to highlight a point insufficiently clarified elsewhere, Oedipus' infantile attachment to his adoptive parents, it is not my intention to reduce Sophocles' play to a case study of an adopted child. Contrary to common belief, Sophocles in *Oedipus Rex* does not present us the picture of a man crushed by his traumatic origins. Rather, he seems to have transcended what has been described as his own pessimistic view of life and presented us the picture of a heroic human being.

REFERENCES

Devereux, G. (1963), Sociopolitical functions of the Oedipus myth in early Greece. *Psychoanal. Quart.*, 32:205–214.

Dodds, E. R. (1973), *The Ancient Concept of Progress*. Oxford: Clarendon Press.

Fenichel, O. (1954), *Collected Papers*. 2 vols. New York: Norton.

Freud, S. (1900), The interpretation of dreams. *Standard Edition*, 4/5. London: Hogarth Press, 1953.

_______ (1901), The psychopathology of everyday life. *Standard Edition*, 6:1–279. London: Hogarth Press, 1960.

_______ (1910), A special type of choice of object made by men. (Contributions to the theory of love). *Standard Edition*, 11:163–175. London: Hogarth Press, 1957.

_______ (1940), An outline of psycho-analysis. *Standard Edition*, 23:144–207. London: Hogarth Press, 1964.

_______ (1950), *The Origins of Psycho-Analysis*. New York: Basic Books, 1954.

Golden, L. (1967), *American Imago*, 24:271–282.

Gould, T. (1970), *Oedipus the King*. Englewood Cliffs, NJ: Prentice-Hall.

Graves, R. (1955), *The Greek Myths*. Baltimore: Penguin.

Grene, D., & Lattimore, R., Eds. (1959), *The Complete Greek Tragedies*. Chicago: University of Chicago Press.

Grigg, M. A. (1973), All roads lead to Rome: The role of the nursemaid in Freud's dreams. *J. Amer. Psychoanal. Assn.*, 21:108–126.
Haffter, C. (1968), The Changeling. *History of the Behavioral Sciences*, 4:55–61.
Hathorn, R. (1967), *Crowell's Handbook of Classical Drama*. New York: Crowell.
Kanzer, M. (1948), The "passing of the oedipus complex" in Greek drama. *Internat. J. Psycho-Anal.*, 29:131–134. Chapter 5, this volume.
——— (1964), On interpreting the Oedipus plays. *The Psychoanalytic Study of Society*, 3:26–38. New York: International Universities Press. Chapter 10, this volume.
Knox, B. (1957), *Oedipus at Thebes*. New York: Norton.
Kott, J. (1974), *The Eating of the Gods*. New York: Random House.
Rosner, H. (1974), What can be worse than being an adopted child? Paper presented at the Midwinter Meeting of the American Psychoanalytic Association, New York, December.
——— (1975), Clinical and prognostic considerations in the analysis of a five-year-old hysteric. *J. Amer. Psychoanal. Assn.*, 23:507–534.
Sophocles (460 B.C.), *Ajax*, ed. D. Grene & R. Lattimore. Chicago: University of Chicago Press, 1957.
——— (c.442 B.C.), *Antigone*, ed. D. Grene & R. Lattimore. Chicago: University of Chicago Press, 1959.
——— (c.437 B.C.), *The Women of Trachis*, ed. D. Grene & R. Lattimore. Chicago: University of Chicago Press, 1959.
——— (c.425), *Oedipus Rex*, ed. D. Grene & R. Lattimore. Chicago: University of Chicago Press, 1959.
——— (c.409 B.C.), *Oedipus at Colonus*, ed. D. Grene & R. Lattimore. Chicago: University of Chicago Press, 1959.
Tripp, E. (1970), *Crowell's Handbook of Classical Mythology*. New York: Crowell.
Van der Sterren, H. (1949), The "King Oedipus" of Sophocles. *Internat. J. Psycho-Anal.*, 30:343–350.
Vellacott, P. (1971), *Sophocles and Oedipus*. New York: Macmillan.
Waelder, R. (1936), The principle of multiple function. *Psychoanal. Quart.*, 5:45–62.
Whitman, C. H. (1951), *Sophocles*. Cambridge, MA: Harvard University Press.
Wind, E. (1963), *Art and Anarchy*. London: Faber & Faber.

15

Adopted Oedipus: A Discussion of Dr. Rosner's Paper

PAUL SCHWABER

[1977]

Let me begin with a story. In the city of Ispahan, in Persia, a certain man's servant came to him and said, "I was in the market place and there I saw Death, and he made a threatening gesture to me." The man said, "Let us flee," and he and his servant set out posthaste for Samarra. No sooner had they entered that city than they encountered Death, to whom the man said, "Why did you threaten my servant in the market place in Ispahan?" Death replied, "My gesture was not one of threat but surprise, for I had an appointment to meet you in Samarra, and I was surprised to learn, from seeing your servant, that you were still in Ispahan."

The similarities between *Oedipus Rex* and this little story leap to

Presented at the Meeting of the American Psychoanalytic Association, December 16, 1977. This piece is indebted to Simon O. Lesser (1967), "*Oedipus the King:* The Two Dramas, The Two Conflicts," *College English*, 29:175-197 and Lionel Trilling (1967), *The Experience of Literature: A Reader with Commentaries*. New York: Holt, Rinehart and Winston, pp. 41-44.

mind: for the human world of this folktale is fated. There are inexorable destinies that cannot be escaped and which immortal creatures plan, for whatever reasons. Like King Oedipus, the central character of the story perceived his fate, feared it, and tried to avoid it. And ironically, by trying to avoid it, he ran directly toward it. However brief and almost jocular the story—for it is a kind of joke on the man from Ispahan who tried to save himself—it has a ghastly ring to it: not only for the overt subject matter, death, but for the escape-free circularity and inevitability—the logic, so to speak—that the pattern of narration underscores.

A fated human world, one from which there is no escape, is King Oedipus' very condition of being. Sophocles' great tragic drama—which so inspired Freud at least in part, one thinks, because of its grim recognition of predestined circumstances, matters over which human beings have no real control but can only live out—poses inevitability in terms of oracles, the certainty of the gods (whom no self-respecting Greek thought of as beneficent). Now there was no hedging about this, from oracles known to be cryptic. There were no conditional clauses such as "If you do so and so, then . . .," or "Unless you do so and so. . . ." Jocasta tells him early on:

> There was an oracle once that came to Laius,—
> . . . and it told him
> that it was fate that he should die a victim
> at the hands of his own son, a son to be born
> of Laius and me.
> [Grene and Lattimore, 1959]

Less than a hundred lines later, Oedipus recalls:

> I went at last
> to Pytho, though my parents did not know.
> But Phoebus sent me home again unhonoured
> in what I came to learn, but he foretold
> other and desperate horrors to befall me,
> that I was fated to lie with my mother,

> and show to daylight an accursed breed
> which men would not endure, and I was doomed
> to be murderer of the father that begot me. [ll. 787-795]

The matter is straightforward and fated.

But there is something more to *Oedipus Rex* than the working out of fate or determinism, and the little Persian folktale, which has no less respect for determinism, helps us to delineate it. The story of Oedipus matters in a different way. It holds our attention and enlists our identifying emotions far more deeply because of the involvement it invites with Oedipus himself: the character, the man. Though he is always—and, we should note, safely—a personage in a highly stylized and traditional dramatic form, he seems to be a living person and an important one. This is only to say differently what Aristotle said in the *Poetics* (Butcher, 1961), that in tragedy both plot and character are crucial: "Tragedy . . . is an imitation of an action that is serious, complete, and of a certain magnitude. . . . The Plot is the imitation of the action, . . . the first principle, and, as it were, the soul of the tragedy" (pp. 61-63). Character is only next in importance. The tragic hero is "a man who is not eminently good and just" (that would be too extreme, unlike you and me), "yet whose misfortune is brought about not by vice or depravity" (again, too extreme), but by some error or frailty (again, like you and me). "He must be one who is highly renowned and prosperous—a personage like Oedipus, Thyestes, or other illustrious men of such families" (p. 76). As such the tragic hero is more than fated, though never less than that. He has areas of freedom for characterizing action. And Dr. Rosner has pointed to one overriding aspect of Oedipus' admirability: his desire to know. He is one of those "who must know who they are and where they came from," one for whom "the search becomes a passion." He had to know the truth about his past. To put it more clearly: Oedipus had no choice about killing his father and marrying his mother. That was his destiny, a given. There was nothing fated, however, in that sense, about his insistence on finding out what had happened or who was what; or on his being a man of a certain social magnitude: a king, and apparently a responsible one most of the time, whose intelligence had long been recognized in Thebes as one of its communal gifts, and whose vulnerability to quick anger—anger that obscures his thought—is manifestly displayed throughout the play and recognized by the other protagonists as typical of him. As we would say, anger is part of his psychological character. Nor is anything fated about his taking his punishment on himself by striking out his eyes.

Dr. Rosner has very interestingly connected Oedipus' desire to know his origins with his being raised as an adopted son. With the help of what he has learned from working with adolescent adopted boys and their families, especially their mothers, he suggests a useful perspective for reconsidering King Oedipus' particular qualities and actions—for example, his continuing fear of encountering Queen Merope, his adoptive mother, which suggests an intense incestuous wish he has tried to combat. The continuing presence of the problem validates Dr. Rosner's speculation that young Oedipus, having consulted the oracle, left immediately to avoid what we would call "oedipal" temptations, that he sublimated the same complex of feelings when solving the riddle of the Sphinx, and that later it fueled his desperate assertion that he is the son of "Chance" or "Fortune"—in other words, of universal rather than human parents. I wish Dr. Rosner had gone further along this line. For there are connections between the constellation of impulses and defenses he adumbrates and other aspects of Oedipus' character we know: his rashness, for example. Not only does he anger quickly, he acts angrily. We learn that having heard the oracle and taken flight—directly toward Thebes—he came across an unusual procession involving an elderly man, old enough to be his father, took umbrage and killed. Arriving in Thebes as its liberator, he simply marries the queen, an older woman—as if in neither instance did knowledge of the oracle inhibit him, though we know he had his doubts about who his biological parents were and had wondered about his "cradle scars." Moreover, he married a woman who was also particularly hospitable to younger men, one capable of saying, under pressure:

> As to your mother's marriage bed,—don't fear it.
> Before this, in dreams too, as well as oracles,
> many a man has lain with his own mother.

At least one mother, we may infer, wished for a young man, perhaps about the age the child she had abandoned would have been.

There are plentiful suggestions of a full-blown unresolved Oedipus conflict in King Oedipus, energized indeed by his circumstances as an adopted son, unsure of his origins, in adolescence. That conflict remains unresolved at the time of the drama, when the plague that has beset Thebes, coupled with word from the oracle, stirs all his curiosity and social responsibility into activity again. He wishes to know—as has repeatedly been emphasized—and that is what is so admirable and courageous about his persistence. But he also wishes *not* to know, and that is part of the suspenseful drama of revelation throughout the play, and part of his magnitude. His quickness to anger proves pivotal. As each of the main protagonists comes on stage, Oedipus manages to become furious at them and to provoke angry revelations from them, revelations which often they do not wish to reveal and that are more than he bargained for. And at each new revelation, he seems to forget other things that have been learned (repression as defense), to delay the awful discovery.

Setting out to solve the mystery of who killed the former king, Laius, Oedipus several times makes slips of the tongue that suggest quite early in the play that he knows something nobody else seems to: that not several robbers or bandits killed Laius, but one man. Creon recalls the sole survivor's report:

> This man said that the robbers they encountered
> were many and that the hands that did the murder
> were many; it was no man's single power.

To which Oedipus replies:

> How could a robber dare a deed like this
> were he not helped with money from the city,
> money and treachery?

Earlier Creon had said, "My Lord, before you piloted the state we had a king called Laius" (l. 104). Oedipus responded, "I know of him by hearsay," then added, quite unnecessarily, "I have not seen him"

(1.105). When the chorus remarks, "It was said that he was killed by certain wayfarers" (1.293), Oedipus says, "I heard that, too, but no one saw the killer" (l. 294). Yet having summoned Teiresias, the blind seer who preferred not to reveal anything, Oedipus becomes furious, threatens him, and provokes him into telling more than who killed King Laius. "You blame my temper," Teiresias says, "but you do not see your own that lives within you" (ll. 337–338). "You are the land's polution" (l. 353), he goes on, and eventually, after being goaded by Oedipus' accusation that *he* was the killer and now conspires with Creon for the crown, Teiresias pronounces:

> You have your eyes but see not where you are
> in sin, nor where you live, nor whom you live with.
> Do you know who your parents are? Unknowing
> you are an enemy to kith and kin
> in death, beneath the earth, and in this life.
> A deadly footed, double striking curse,
> from father and mother both, shall drive you forth
> out of this land, with darkness on your eyes,
> that now have such straight vision. Shall there
> be a place will not be harbour to your cries,
> a corner of Cithaeron will not ring
> in echo of your cries, soon, soon,—
> when you shall learn the secret of your marriage,
> which steered you to a haven in this house,—
> haven no haven, after lucky voyage?
> And of the multitude of other evils
> establishing a grim equality
> between you and your children, you know nothing.
> So, muddy with contempt my words and Creon's!
> Misery shall grind no man as it will you.

It is all spelled out quite early in the play. But Oedipus does not comprehend.

When Creon arrives to deny Oedipus' accusations, the King announces that he wishes not to banish but to kill him. Jocasta intercedes, but Creon knows his man:

> I see you sulk in yielding and you're dangerous
> when you are out of temper; natures like yours
> are justly heaviest for themselves to bear.

To calm Oedipus, Jocasta then tells him of the oracle to King Laius, mentioning that Laius had pierced their son's ankles and cast him forth on the pathless hillside, as well as that Laius had been killed at a place where three roads meet. Oedipus is terrified:

> O dear Jocasta,
> as I hear this from you, there comes upon me
> a wandering of the soul—I could run mad.

That's Oedipus: the impulse is to run—to act. Thereafter, no longer needing to know who killed Laius, he tries not to recognize the issue of kinship—namely, parricide and incest, the whole of the fate predicted for him—but concentrates on the secret of his birth. With each further revelation, he puts other aspects of what he knows or fears on hold—repressing, isolating, projecting, denying—in other words, defending himself against exactly the knowledge he is searching for. It is very analytic.

There is not time to trace this process through the play. One particular sequence, however, deserves special attention, both for what it reveals of Oedipus' character and stature, and because it points the direction of my comments toward posing further questions for Dr. Rosner. After the messenger from Corinth has announced that Polybus is dead and Oedipus has been chosen king, he tells Oedipus that he was *not* his parents' natural child, and hence has nothing to fear from Queen Merope. The messenger, who long before had brought the baby to Polybus and Merope, then mentions Oedipus' ankles. With his exposure brought to the fore, Oedipus asks immediately: "Was this my father's doing or my mother's?" (l. 1037). That is the burning issue of long standing: *how could my parents do such a thing to me?* Jocasta begs him to give up the fearful questioning: "What I am suffering is enough" (l. 1061). She understands, and when he refuses, rushes off to her suicide. But Oedipus gets *angry* at her and pushes on, not seeing. He bizarrely explains that she is afraid of his being found to be baseborn. In the drama, that claim is a red herring, having never been mentioned. But it is psychologically splendid. It aids his denial while denigrating her and her values, suggesting an old anger; it offers a final, desperate way out because, if baseborn, he need not be the son of the man he murdered, the husband of his mother, the brother of his children; nor would he be the baby born of a king and queen who pierced his ankles and left him to die. The latter makes a lovely inversion, for royalty, of the usual family romance—a wish to be baseborn. "She was so hard—its mother?" Oedipus had asked (l. 1175), stunned, when the servant of old Laius had told him—again under pressure of the king's anger—of the child Jocasta had given him to leave on the hillside.

His old anger had to do with having been deserted, with fury that thus underlay and fed the intensity of his attachments, the intensity of his hates, his capacity for murder, and his continuingly choleric tendencies when under strain, as well as his special ability to persist in and solve riddles of origins—like the riddle of the Sphinx (a female deity who killed, a bad mother), and like the riddle of his own birth, despite all his reasons not to. Even in very old age, as he is depicted in *Oedipus at Colonus*—purged, blessed, and with the great rages restructured—he still refuses to return to his mother city, Thebes, though he is begged to, but stays in Athens.

Now I suppose I should make professional noises about limitations of inference we can make about a literary character. Some critics feel that even to talk of the personality or individuality, the freedom of action and fate of a literary character is indulgent, for literature is always and finally a construct of words, a text. Lady Macbeth had no existence prior to the play in which she appeared. Polonius had no early years. And Oedipus, they would say, never was an adopted child. I don't myself have much use for such notions, as you must have gathered. They are literal and true but not imaginative, refusing to acknowledge the illusion of reality, the mimetic function that Aristotle noted, which involves not only imitative processes but the life that is imitated. There *are* limitations of inference, however. For example, I see no reason to justify Dr. Rosner's supposition that Oedipus as an adolescent must have been *overtly* drawn to Queen Merope, based only on his relief at the news of Polybus' death and his continued fear of Merope. But I think the direction of Dr. Rosner's thought, from clinical observations and conclusions to the text, is, like Freud's, entirely appropriate and useful. I wonder, however, whether the move from text to clinical observation—a move that Freud also made—might not be equally fruitful. For example, something like Oedipus' bedrock of anger at having been deserted might be viewed as underlying adolescent experiences of intense incestuous feelings toward the adoptive mother, anger at fathers, and a furious component in the search for true origins among those mentioned by Dr. Rosner, for whom "the search becomes a passion." Another example would be Jocasta's proclivity for younger men and what it implies of the guilt and reparation of mothers who have given their children up for adoption.

In short, there has always been a dialogue between psychoanalysis and great literature. I thank Dr. Rosner both for his specific contribution and for continuing that dialogue so impressively.

REFERENCES

Butcher, S. H., Trans. (1961), *Aristotle's Poetics*. New York: Hill & Wang.

Grene, D., & Lattimore, R., Eds. (1959), *Oedipus the King*, trans. D. Grene. In: *The Complete Greek Tragedies: Volume II. Sophocles*. Chicago: University of Chicago Press, pp. 11–76.

16

Oedipus: History, Legends, Plays, Complexes

MARK KANZER

[1978]

A discussion of "Oedipus Was Not the Son of Laius and Jocasta" by Angel Garma, M.D. The thesis that Oedipus was not the son of the Theban royal pair but of his Corinthian "foster parents" raises questions as to which Oedipus is under discussion—one of several different "historical" and legendary accounts, the hero of the plays of Sophocles, or the synthesized "Oedipuses" of millions of individual and ethnic fantasies. Oedipuses, in whom the particular variant described by Dr. Garma can be discerned, certainly abound and should be included among the many possibilities to be considered.

The Oedipus Rex of Sophocles is usually all too readily identified with the legend of Oedipus and whatever historical basis there may be for this legend. This Athenian dramatist of the fifth century B.C. was not engaged in research into history or sociology. He wished to win the annual award of the Athenian drama critics (he placed only second). His source was an ancient chronicle of the Theban kings set down in written form by Cinaethon three centuries before and pur-

---

Reprinted with permission from *International Journal of Psychoanalytic Psychotherapy*, vol. 7, pp. 326–332.

porting to describe events that had occurred centuries earlier still. How good a historian Cinaethon was we cannot tell since his work disappeared ages ago and many different versions of the tale of Oedipus (on some of which we shall touch) are extant.

We do know that Teiresias, surely a figure of myth, according to Graves (1959), appears as a character as does, in an offstage way, the Sphinx. In a similar fashion, Shakespeare freely added ghosts and witches to rather unreliable chronicles of ancient days. In the summer of 1977, on a tour of Greece which included Delphi, Corinth, and Thebes, the locale of the Oedipus drama, the guide pointed out to me the very fork in the road at which Oedipus encountered Laius, and the shelf of rock where he met and vanquished the Sphinx. We do insist that our myths be factually substantiated. When it is profitable, such substantiation is usually forthcoming. I could not help wondering, however: if such a fork in the road had really been substantiated, would it have affected Abraham's interpretation (1922) of the encounter of Oedipus and Laius at that point as a struggle to pass through the female organ? My own investigations have failed to supply the slightest information as to whether the fork appeared in the chronicle of Cinaethon or was added by Sophocles, in which case Abraham's interpretation might well be applicable to an analysis of the dramatist himself. Let us not omit from the chain of possibilities at this point the opinion of Graves (1959) that the details of the slaying of Laius are typical of legends of solar kings "thrown from a chariot and dragged by the horses" after being vanquished by their successors (Vol. 2, p. 13).

Certainly, any questioning of the credibility of the history of Oedipus, or even the adherence to a legend offered by the Sophocles play, might well begin with an exploration of the drama and the dramatist himself, in which we would find ourselves to a considerable extent within the borderlines of fairly verifiable history. We know that he was an ordained priest, sympathetic to the aristocrats, hostile to the democrats who sought to disturb the established order (like Oedipus the "outsider"), and critical of persons who sought to solve problems through reliance on their intellects instead of faith in the old gods (again like Oedipus). When he referred to the blight that the vengeful gods had brought about in Thebes, the audience in Athens knew he meant the Peloponnesian War, which was in fact undermining the future of the city.

Contemporaneous political and moral lessons were thus being offered his fellow townsmen, with the fate of Oedipus as a test. There is no doubt that the technique of dramatic presentation was very much in his mind: he was an innovator who added a third actor, expanded the chorus, and was guilty of sensationalism (in the minds of some) in equipping the self-blinded Oedipus with a mask which depicted gore streaming from his eye-sockets—a rather graphic appeal to pity and terror. Aristotle, who, in the *Poetics* pronounced Oedipus the ideal hero, stressed that his progression first to success and then to tragedy arose from the same traits in his character; these included self-reliance, quickness of temper, and intellectual acuity. Sophocles centered his interest on the very areas which seem open to the human will to prevail, and where the will of the gods prevails instead. Can the psychoanalyst today evade this problem when he sees the ego and consciousness overwhelmed by the unconscious and the inescapable biological and social limitations imposed by the Oedipus complex? Freud himself acknowledged that the play unfolded like an analysis—a characteristic that we shall have to attribute to the playwright rather than to the history or legend of a King Oedipus.

As for the history and legend of Oedipus, we find ourselves confronted with a rival version by no less reliable an historian than Homer, who flourished at about the time of Cinaethon. He accepts Oedipus as an historical King of Thebes who had ruled at the time of the Trojan War several centuries earlier. The incest motive adheres to the account by Homer that Oedipus was suffering from the curse of a dying mother (pursuit by the Furies as a pseudonym for madness?). However, nothing is said by Homer of parricide, of an encounter with the Sphinx, of self-blinding, or of exile. The Theban King was killed in battle and because of his valor was accorded an honorable burial by his people. This more sober history leaves little material for drama, legend, or universal human experience.

Variants of the Oedipus chronicle increase even more when they verge on legend. The *Oedipus Rex* presents Teiresias as a character with as much convincing detail as it does Oedipus himself, yet mythology indicates that he was a priest of one of the ancient snake cults of Greece, and his legendary adventures couple him with the gods Zeus, Hera, and Athena and with such heroes as Heracles, Odysseus, and Narcissus. His blindness is accounted for by sexual transgressions that point to primal scene voyeurism and to resulting bisexuality. Thus one of the narratives in which he figures has him witness two serpents in intercourse (a forerunner of Aesculapius?). In recompense for his loss of eyesight, he gained greater inner vision—a not uncommon theme of mythology (Odin, Samson) with probable roots in representations of superego formation in the wake of the suppression of the oedipal conflicts. Certainly he may lay claim to belong psychologically to the story of Oedipus and the understanding and warning roles which he plays there.

The distinction between history and mythology becomes more difficult as we proceed. If we are inclined to dismiss the Sphinx as purely mythological, we might well be overlooking nuclei of historical truth which should make us hesitate to accept some analytic interpretations of her as a nightmare figure (though that nightmare qualities adhere to her is not unimportant either). For in her simplified form of half-lion, half-serpent, she was a calendar emblem in Thebes, her two parts signifying respectively the waxing and waning portions of a two-season year. Quite possibly she also records on a deeper level the fusion of a conquering patriarchal "lion" people with an indigenous cult of snake-worshippers.

The legend of Cadmus, a reputed ancestor of Oedipus, fits in with this notion. His ancestry was said to be Phoenician and ultimately Egyptian (his name means "Easterner"). He destroyed a dragon (a local serpent deity?) and ultimately was forced to do penance (accept the claims of the snake cults to power?). When Cadmus founded and named Thebes, was he drawing upon the Egyptian Thebes for this purpose and also introducing the Sphinx and its riddles from his native land? The masculine Sphinx of Egypt may well have blended with such Grecian snake monsters with attributes of the female body as the gorgons, harpies, and furies. The female winged sphinx is said to have appeared first in Crete in the fifteenth century B.C. and was associated with Europa, sister of Cadmus, who was supposedly transported to Crete by Zeus (Graves, 1959; Kanzer, 1964).

The histories, or legend, about Oedipus are indeed diversified and inconsistent. In some instances, he is expelled from Thebes by his brother-in-law and uncle Creon, in others by his grown-up sons. In still others, Jocasta kills herself soon after their marriage and the children are the product of a second marriage. Otto Rank (1952) describes an alternate version of his birth: that he was enclosed in a box, put afloat on the waters, and drawn out by the queen of Corinth, who adopted him. This version of course merges him with Moses, Perseus, and other heroes whose careers follow the family-romance type.

Customs and beliefs typical of matriarchal societies find their way into *Oedipus Rex*, attesting to that extent to its derivation from the mythology of an earlier age, if not from history. The traditional passing of the winter kings and their replacement by younger and more virile summer kings is surely reflected in the blight on the land and the barrenness of women which prevails at the beginning of the play. In such matriarchal societies, the queen is the permanent authority; she is the priestess of the mother-goddess, and the son-lover shares the throne with her for a year (Frazer, 1935). Oedipus was supposedly exposed on Mount Cithaeron and rescued by the shepherds but, as Róheim (1952) has pointed out, Cithaeron was sacred to the earth goddess Demeter, and it was in her grove in Colonus that he found his ultimate rest. The chorus in *Oedipus Rex* wonders about his origins, surmising that his father was a god or nature deity and thus indicating the supernatural element that makes him a demigod. The finding of the baby by the shepherds and the nailing of the feet are obviously reminiscent of the legends of the birth and death of the son of a male god who dies and is resurrected with the vegetation and newborn lambs in the spring.

In a sense, it is a matter of indifference as to whether a king of Thebes was converted into a legendary figure after his death, or a traditional deity found a human representative on earth. Figures of myth, like dream images, blend day residues with the symbols that the unconscious has formed. As Angel Garma (1978) points out in "Oedipus Was Not the Son of Laius and Jocasta," the essential significance of his story and the impact it makes upon us lies in its aspects as a family romance (Freud, 1909; Rank, 1952).

There is much to be said for Garma's argument that the Corinthian foster parents, Polybus and Merope, were the real parents from whom he fled, while the Theban parents were the idealized substitutes provided by the family romance. To be sure, reversed situations can occur, and Freud pictured just such a reversal in the case of Moses, who saw the royal Egyptians who raised him as his real parents. The family romance, in a not too uncommon form, endowed him with humbler parents.

I fail, however, to follow Garma in his appraisal of the strength of the oedipal drives toward incest and parricide as less important in the instigation of neurosis than the guilt feelings they occasion. Rather, there is a continuum in which the oedipal drives themselves may be strong and difficult to bring under control, or guilt may be minimal or excessive depending on a concatenation of factors, constitutional, psychological, or social. The family romance may serve as a means for either gratifying or forming distance from the drives, thus reducing conflicts with the superego. Many years ago (1948, 1950), I suggested that the Oedipus of Sophocles was perhaps the husband of a pregnant woman and that conflicts over this pregnancy stimulated neurotic regression. Ultimately he enters the room in which his wife has hanged herself and reemerges blind and helpless. I have seen this symbolizing an entrance into the womb (the mother hanging from a cord, a reversed prototype of the fetus). In the womb, he gives up his masculinity (puts out his eyes with his phallic sword) as a punishment for his offense against his parents. He is then reborn as an infant—one who will, nevertheless, grow up to repeat the sins of the past, the perennial lot of each human being. The transition from phallic masculinity (the sword) to infantile helplessness is also a depiction of the penis' detumescence.

It no longer appears adequate to associate the oedipus complex with the phallic phase of development alone. We are speaking here of the male, though we might remark in passing that the complex of the female is worthy of an independent label; perhaps Freud rejected the not inappropriate appellation *electra complex* because Jung favored it. Actually, there is not just one complex, there are many, and to view them in their phase-specific development would be helpful.

Freud long ago recognized that a full oedipus complex embraced a negative as well as a positive aspect. There is much to suggest that the Orestes legend, plays, and complex, also rooted in matriarchal-patriarchal social organization, as well as in individual psychology, is in fact the negative form of the oedipus complex in its phallic phase. Homer's report that Oedipus was cursed by a dying mother creates a link to Orestes, whose murdered mother instigated the furies of madness to pursue him. However, we may note evidence of Oedipus' hostility toward his mother in its own right. His meticulous public examination in her presence of his alleged origins makes it apparent that he is torturing her in so doing and that she has discovered, long before her supposedly astute son, the direction that the inquiry is taking. We have argued in the past that the Sphinx is an alternative form of the mother, perhaps a taboo against intercourse with the mother. Oedipus also speculates (and justifiably so) as to whether the nailing of his feet was commanded by the father or the mother. The mothers of both Oedipus and Orestes abandon their sons; the latter reveals a positive oedipus complex by slaying his mother's lover, Aegisthus.

The preoedipal forms of the oedipus complex do not require our commentary at this point, nor do the postoedipal per se. However the family-romance aspect, the return of the warded-off oedipal trends of the phallic phase, points to the periods of latency and adolescence as a second chance to gain oedipal triumphs, establish ego identity, and win social approval by acts of benefit to the community while at the same time sparing the actual parents—indeed such behavior will be a source of pride to them.

I am indebted to Dr. Henry Rosner (1977) for permission to read his paper "Oedipus and His Cradle Scars," which sheds light on particular variations among oedipal reactions and on the Oedipus legend itself. His work among adopted and maimed children highlights the sense of rejection among them and the need to find one's real parents. Nevertheless, the objects of the true oedipal drives are the foster parents who bring them up; the search for the "real" parents is a flight into reality. Thus to Rosner as well as to Garma, Merope and Polybus are the true objects of Oedipus' drives. Rosner supplements this thesis by a further consideration of Queen Merope of Corinth as a middle-aged mother, hitherto childless, who dotes upon and intensifies the "Oedipus" within her only son. Did it give him, I wonder, the intellectual acuity and confidence in success postulated by Freud for the son sure of his mother's love and thus make it possible for him to face up to the dreadful Sphinx? Or was it perhaps the sense of being an "exception" entitled to break the rules that prevail for normal mortals? As Rosner indicates, Oedipus was extremely sensitive about his "cradle scars" (circumcision?) and an element of murderous hostility toward both parents may have had its point of departure here.

In summation, the use of Sophocles' *Oedipus Rex* as an adequately based history of an individual or a transmitted legend is not justified. Nevertheless, essentials of a universal problem are sufficiently caught up within it to have been sensed by Freud—and before him by countless generations—as a key to human motivation both in neuroses and in successful individual and social sublimations of the maturing process. The latter may well be represented by Sophocles himself.

REFERENCES

Abraham, K. (1922), The rescue and murder of the father. In: *Clinical Papers and Essays on Psychoanalysis.* London: Hogarth, 1955.
Frazer, J. G. (1935), *The Dying God.* New York: Macmillan.
Freud, S. (1909), Family romances. *Standard Edition,* 9:235–244.
——— (1939), Moses and monotheism. *Standard Edition,* 23:7–137.
Garma, A. (1978), Oedipus was not the son of Laius and Jocasta. *Internat. J. Psychoanal. Psychother.,* 7:316–325.
Graves, R. (1959), *The Greek Myths.* 2 vols. Baltimore: Penguin.
Kanzer, M. (1948), The "passing of the Oedipus complex" in Greek drama. *Internat. J. Psycho-Anal.,* 29:131–134. Chapter 5, this volume.
——— (1950), The Oedipus trilogy. *Psychoanal. Quart.,* 19:561-572. Chapter 6, this volume.
——— (1964), On interpreting the Oedipus plays. *The Psychoanalytic Study of Society,* 3:26–37. Chapter 10, this volume.
Rank, O. (1952), *The Myth of the Birth of the Hero.* New York: Robert Brunner.
Róheim, G. (1952), *The Gates of the Dream.* New York: International Universities Press.
Rosner, H. (1977), Oedipus and his cradle scars. Chapter 14, this volume.

17

On the Generational Cycle: An Address

ERIK H. ERIKSON

[1980]

I

I first must thank you all for the honor of addressing you, and the Program Committee in particular for the cautiously generous assignment given to me. I was asked to speak on "a topic related to the human life cycle." Since this plenary session is safely anchored, on the one hand, in the panel on transference as related to different stages of life and, on the other, in the final discussion of that subject, let me take the liberty to expand on a number of topics related to the human life cycle and, in fact, roam on its very periphery before returning to its daily, clinical implications. Life cycles are, of course, embedded in *generational* cycles, and generational cycles are experienced in different regions of the world in whatever larger configurations the domi-

Presented at the Thirty-first International Psychoanalytical, Congress, New York, August 1979. Reprinted with permission from *International Journal of Psycho-Analysis*, vol. 61, pp. 213–233.

nant world view sees us moving, whether in heavenly courses of rebirth or in a straight line of secular progress, in natural evolution or in social revolutions. But this immediately raises the question as to the various connotations which in any world view a configuration such as "life cycle" may have in comparison with, for example, "developmental lines," which move in linear fashion from the stages of infantile immaturity to whatever mature stages can be expected to be achieved (to paraphrase Hartmann) in the average expectable adult. Freud (1930) knew well what we are up against with our more encompassing cycles when in a rare metaphor he mused: "Just as a planet revolves around a central body as well as rotating on its own axis, so the human individual takes part in the course of development of mankind at the same time as he pursues his own path in life." (p. 141)

This configurational theme leads me back to the one previous plenary talk I was privileged to give (in the American in 1961). There I proposed (Erikson, 1962) that our sense of Reality is marked by both *Factuality* and (as the German Wirklichkeit denotes so clearly) *Actuality*. Factuality comprises the world of facts which can be jointly recognized and verified at a given stage of cognitive development and in a given technological period; while actuality is the mutual activation, or actualization, of individuals sharing such facts in *re vera*, in truth: for human ego strength depends from the earliest stage to the last—and from generation to generation—upon a network of mutual relations which, in William James' words, "inspire with active properties."

More recently, however, I have added to this duo another aspect of Reality, namely, *Contextuality*, or what Einstein called *Begreiflichkeit:* Comprehensibility. This refers to a principle by which a selection of facts suddenly seem to be, in his words, "really existing," because they appear comprehensible within a compelling context. Certainly, Freud's concept of a stagewise infantile sexuality belongs in this category. But, of course, contextuality can only *suggest* connections which must then be verified with the observational methods at hand and communicated in an activating manner. Thus having first recognized the residues of childhood stages in adult neuroses, psychoanalysis has compared child patients with adult patients and then disturbed and well children with each other. Against the background of the glaringly ambivalent treatment of children in all of previous history, it is not surprising that in this search for origins we have developed various clinical and developmental perspectives which saw the first part of the life cycle alternately as something to outgrow or to fulfill, as a set of near-irreversible first causes of adult vulnerability, or as fundamental potentialities seldom lived up to in later life.

For my own conception of the psychosocial stages of the human life cycle as well as for psychosexuality, I have found the contextual principle called *epigenesis* indispensable. Let me show you an old chart of the psychosocial stages in order to illustrate the principle without going into the (much debatable) details (Figure 1). I am doing this here because over the years I have learned how difficult it is for otherwise well-trained students really to visualize and remember the lifelong interweaving of items which develop in successive stages. Play, for example (and we will surely come back to this), vastly dominates the play age. But (as you can see at the meeting of the ascending lines with the third horizontal) play is an indispensable ingredient in all previous stages; and if a developmental line leads from play to work in the school age, certainly play must continue all along the whole third vertical, and this both as an intrinsic part of workmanship, and in new forms of "legitimate" play—including adult play with playing children. Thus, each item has its critical time of decisive unfolding along the diagonal, while it already existed in some form at earlier stages under the dominance of the then-critical items, and it will be revised and renewed in all subsequent stages in relation to the items as yet to become dominant.

I must now confess that I am reminding you of all this also so that I can show you another picture (Figure 2). This is a weaving done by Joan Erikson, who has worked with me on those stages from the beginning but never felt that theory alone could demonstrate their contextuality. So here is her weaving and here is her message: "One color for each vital strength. In the fringe at the bottom—the warp—you can see them all: dark blue for Trust; orange for Autonomy and dark green for Initiative; yellow for Industry—and so on. And please observe from the start that there are grey threads to represent the dystonic elements (basic mistrust, shame, guilt, etc.) over which the colors must maintain their dominance and brilliance, as well as their

Old Age								Integrity vs. Despair. WISDOM
Adulthood							Generativity vs. Self-Absorption. CARE	
Young Adulthood						Intimacy vs. Isolation. LOVE		
Adolescence					Identity vs. Confusion. FIDELITY			
School Age				Industry vs. Inferiority. COMPETENCE				
Play Age			Initiative vs. Guilt. PURPOSE					
Early Childhood		Autonomy vs. Shame. Doubt. WILL						
	Basic Trust							

Figure 1

Figure 2

Figure 3

essential characteristics. When you study this weaving you no longer doubt that the warp must exist from the start; otherwise the whole would not hang together. Also, you can clearly follow the threads as they continue up the years and add their character to the entire life pattern. In this way, everything is interwoven as, indeed, it is in life itself."

Such a piece of work, then, renders in a sensual context the stages of individual life and the sequence of what Anna Freud (1978) has called the "metamorphoses which qualify infantile elements for becoming integral parts of an adult's character and personality." Beyond that, however, it shows the metamorphoses of adult stages which make them an integral part of the life cycle. This method of representation can, of course, be varied to illustrate other thought-provoking contexts. Here (Figure 3) is another weaving which allows appropriate spaces for the different chronological spans occupied by the successive stages: note, for example, the relative duration of the adult years of generativity. Similarly, one could also vary the different subjective time scales which, (as Pearl King suggested, 1980) govern different stages of life. Yet, our pattern cannot yet illustrate the cyclical renewal which must mark the *interlocking of the generations.* If there are any suggestions as to how this might be done contextually, we would welcome hearing from you.

II

Now, as to Freud's second cycle, the individual's participation in the "course of development of mankind," we may divide it into two tasks, namely, the generational renewal of the interdependent life cycles and the cultural renewal of the generational cycles. Within the life cycle I have postulated a psychosocial stage of *Generativity*, which is concerned with new beings as well as new products and new ideas and which, as a link between the generations, is as indispensable for the renewal of the adult generation's own life as it is for that of the next generation.

If all this sounds rather idealized in view of the everyday conditions under and against which it must maintain itself, I can only say that we are here concerned with human potentials without which we would not exist. We must, in fact, claim for generativity a *procreative drive,* whether we wish to consider it an extension of genitality or a further stage. At any rate, it, too, is rooted back in the pregenital stages when the experience parental care, in addition to a certain degree of instinctual gratification also leads to an anticipatory identification with parenthood.

Benedek, of course, once called parenthood a developmental phase (1959). And, indeed, the middle adult crisis of Generativity vs. Stagnation, which to me characterizes an adult's productive as well as procreative involvement, is the link between the life cycle and the generational cycle. From here on the strengths developed in childhood and adolescence must "count" generationally. This crucial fact sometimes does not seem to have the necessary weight in psychoanalytic theories of development which ever again (if for good *clinical* reasons) look for ever earlier origins of a lifelong solipsistic development. The now almost credal preoccupation with the term "object-relation," of course, owes its original contextual convincingness to its use within the libido theory. When habitually applied, however, to a person's inner attitudes toward essential others, the term "object" fails to connote the *mutual* relation in *actuality* on which, in fact, the life of the generations depends. Similarly, whatever individuation has been experienced by the individual must now join generationally in the *mutual activation* offered by the adult world to young individuals in their process of individuation.

Now, it may seem paradoxical to emphasize procreativity at a time when the technological triumph of birth control at last permits the safe prevention of undesirable procreative involvement. But there is today also a real danger that in the very name of genitality a new kind of repression may become a mark of adult life. We, with our generative profession, can easily underestimate how much some modern persons practicing systematic birth control may need enlightenment in regard to what they are *not* doing. For new generations joining in planned parenthood must sublimate some of their procreativity in such active pursuits as will universally improve the conditions of every child chosen to be born. Actually, some such new generative conscience seems to be awakening in many young adults living in improvised new marriage patterns. But there are others who in their undiagnosed aggravation of a sense of *stagnation* and *self-absorption*—the dystonic counterparts to generativity—need help.

Incidentally, in accordance with our epigenetic patterns, generativity reaches into old age. The final generational closure, because it is somewhat removed from clinical psychoanalysis, may not receive in our deliberations the attention it deserves. I mean the specific affinity of childhood and old age which is marked by the interplay of what, psychosocially, I call Integrity (if not without Despair) at the end of life and Trust (if not without Mistrust) at the beginning. This interplay has been an important ingredient of traditional family life and now—in view of radical ethnographic changes, including the more or less splendid isolation of old people—becomes a communal issue.

III

This brings me to the second aspect of what Freud called "the course of development of mankind" and to the much larger cycles which over the centuries have helped to regenerate generative cycles: I refer to man's world view. Here an international psychoanalytic association will have at its disposal much interesting data concerning the influence of different world views on the experience of individuals and generations.

Let me initiate an eventual discussion of such matters by returning to the specific psychosocial strengths which we have allocated to specific stages of life and to the corresponding instinctual conflicts and crises. When I list them (they are Hope and Will, Purpose and Skill, Fidelity and Love, Care and Wisdom), I am always again reminded of the Austrian Emperor who was asked to inspect the model for a great new baroque memorial to be erected in a Vienna park. He looked at it pensively and then announced his decision: "It needs more Hope, Faith, and Charity in the lower left corner!" Well, it so happens that among our strengths there are three, one each for infancy, adolescence, and adulthood, which are named, respectively, *Hope*, *Fidelity*, and *Care* and thus roughly correspond to the Judeo-Christian virtues of Hope, Faith, and Charity. It is not surprising, of course, that viable world views would prove related to some developmental truths, and vice versa, nor that such truths are reflected in rich linguistic associations. Thus the word Care can mean to "cherish" and to caress what emits signs of despair, and it extends to concerns as universal as *Caritas* and *Cura*. But what happens if the corresponding terms are translated into languages steeped in the values of other world views? I asked Professor Sudhir Kakar—with whom, not long ago, I shared the chairmanship of a seminar on Adulthood in India—for the Hindu term corresponding to Care. He replied (and I paraphrase) that there does not seem to be a single term for Care. Rather, if *Loksangraha*, that is, "the maintenance of the world," is the central task of the "householder" (that is, the third and adult stage of the Hindu life cycle) then the adult fulfills it by the practice of *Dáma* (Restraint), *Dána* (Charity), and *Daya* (Compassion). To Hindus, then, Care is composed of these three strengths. Now, a bit of play with the uses of the word "care" in English shows that these three great Hindu terms can all be expressed in our everyday variations of the word Care: for Restraint implies "to be care-*ful*"; Compassion, to "care *for*"; and Charity, "to take care *of*."

Such similarities can make an interesting beginning in the discussion of linguistic relativities and samenesses. I myself first used (playfully, I thought) the term *basic virtues* for the strengths emerging through the life cycle (Erikson, 1968). Now, Professor Mikihachiro Tatara informs me (and I paraphrase again) that in his translation of some of my work he had difficulties with the word "Bitoku" because it suggested certain feudal values. So he chose another, if less "poetical" term, "Jinkaku teki katsu ryoku," suggesting an activation of strength, which is, indeed, what I have in mind. In the meantime, however, I have abandoned the term virtue, both for similar old-fashioned reasons and for a more modern one: there is simply too much Latin manliness in its roots. And it must be clear that there are no essential sex differences in the qualities of human ego strength.

More difficult to ascertain is what in the Hindu's cosmic milieu and its corresponding sequence and stages of life (among which childhood, incidentally, is not an official stage) becomes of *guilt* which in our Judeo-Christian heritage is the most venerable source of conflict. Some avoidance of a guilt stage may to us seem obvious in what Kakar (1978) reports as one of the ancient codes of conduct relating the life stages to the course of destiny:

> Till a boy is eight years old he is like one newly born and only indicates the caste in which he is born. As long as his upanayana ceremony is not performed the boy incurs no blame as to what is allowed or forbidden.

To which Kakar adds:

> I do not mean to suggest that all, or even most people in India live by a conscious philosophical understanding of the twice-born state. . . . I merely want to emphasize that this view of the nature of a child—a completely innocent being who is a gift of the gods, to be welcomed and appreciated and even indulged for the first few years of life—is so deeply rooted in the Hindu world-image that it influences every aspect of the adults' relationships with children.

Kakar's remark is especially suggestive because he assesses the degree to which an age-old ethos still seems viable in the persons—and this must include the patients—of today, a fact which, in turn, must be registered in transferences—and, indeed, countertransferences. This suggests again that international psychoanalysis, in today's world of universal change and yet also of surprising holdovers of ancient values, has a special opportunity to study transference in terms of historical as well as developmental cycles.

With this task in mind I must now introduce a more recent addition to the inventory of trends and qualities which to me seem to make up the stages of the life cycle. While such strengths as Fidelity, Love, and Care connote positive, unifying, and mutual, or what we might call *sympathic* trends, each is necessarily associated with an *antipathic* counterpart. To list some of these briefly, *Rejectivity* is the antipathic counterpart of Generativity in mature adulthood, while in young adulthood *Exclusivity* is associated with Intimacy, and in adolescence, *Role Repudiation* with Identity. It stands to reason that these antipathic trends are necessary for ego-synthesis as well as for social integration: there can be no identity without some repudiation of unacceptable roles, no intimacy without some exclusivity, and no generativity that does not exclude those whom one does not care to care for. All this is related to man's instinctuality, which has replaced the animal's instinctivity in such matters of attraction and aversion—not, however, without the danger of libidinal and aggressive excess in collective as well as in private life. For the constant antithesis of a sympathic and an antipathic readiness leads to that universal dividedness which in small and big matters makes of man an ambivalent animal. Here I must relate Rejectivity to a concept which may not be familiar to some of you and, even if it is, may invite misunderstandings. I refer to *Pseudo-Speciation* (Erikson, 1966), a term I have used to indicate that humanity is universally inclined to differentiate within itself a variety of subspecies—nations, races, classes, etc.—each of which is inclined to mythologize itself as *the* human race as intended by divinity or history, and others as less- or nonhuman. The word "pseudo," however, does not necessarily connote anything pseudological; rather, as in natural science, it means that something appears to be what it is not—here, a "species." Konrad Lorenz suggested for this concept the German *Scheingattung,* which may, more fortuitously, suggest the term Quasi-Speciation. At any rate, such a sense of specieshood can, sympathically, mean an allegiance which brings out the best in man in terms of loyalty, self-sacrifice, and charity; while antipathically it invites a denial of human identification to groups of outsiders who thus become expendable to the point of inviting annihilation. Therefore, within the borders of any political unit, *ethics* and the *law* must define the bearable limits of exclusion and rejection, while religions have attempted to unite many existing and erstwhile mutually rejective units into a semblance of mankind—almost a prophecy of one specieshood—to which a universal *caritas* is owed. But in intracommunal and intrafamilial life, too, rejectivity can, as history teaches us, periodically lead to cruel and fateful outbursts.

Man, on the other hand, cannot function altogether without antipathic values for which, at every stage of life, convincing causes must be found. For where this is not possible because of an outer or inner confusion of values, the antipathy may turn against the self. Thus, an adult unable to reject anything for the sake of a good cause may become self-rejecting and, indeed, dejected. The younger adult, unable to adhere to a selection of partners in intimacy and love, may end up by excluding the Self, as it were, from its own love; while an adolescent who cannot repudiate any offered roles on ideological grounds may repudiate his own best chances for an identity formation. What must interest us in all this, however, are the ways in which such antipathic trends work upon each other in the interplay of generations—as adult rejectivity, for example, playing on a youngster's repudiation, and vice versa—as is demonstrable in good case histories where typical transferences and countertransferences are duly reported. Let me point to the fact that new professions, too, like any new association, can unite previous strangers in the name of a new truth. But soon, new divisions will emerge from new controversies.

IV

Let me illustrate my overall generational theme by returning to one of the oldest cases in our official repertoire, *Oedipus the King*. This play, in its slow and circumstantial revelation of a series of events which constitute an inadvertent consummation of the "infantile core complex"—crimes against the ever more glaring evidence for which the hero defends himself with one self-deceptive trick after another, certainly follows a pattern repeated in every psychoanalysis. But in our eagerness to see the oedipal "core complex" of psychoanalysis revealed as the origin and cause of the whole dilemma one may be apt to pay too little attention to the story's forceful distribution of themata over the whole life cycle—and all its generational implications. To begin with, the riddle which Oedipus gloriously solves depicts man in three postural positions which mark the main ages of life: What walks on four legs in the morning, on two at noon, and on three in the evening? Only having, as a young man, thus become the savior of his adopted *polis* does Oedipus unknowingly commit the act named after him—the act universally considered evil because it short-circuits the generational cycle by intrafamilial procreation. Consequently, this crime is by no means decried as a sexual act only: Oedipus, in fact, is said to have "ploughed the field where he himself was sown" (Knox, 1957) and again, it is spelled out that he "shall be proved father and brother both to his own children in his house; to her that gave him birth, a son and husband both; a fellow sower in his father's bed . . ." (Grene and Lattimore, 1959). Thus, the communal curse of Oedipus' crime is that the land is barren and that "there are no growing children in this famous land; there are no women bearing the pangs of childbirth." So the pollution of the land and of the *polis* originates and results in the pollution of the womb.

In the end, the sinner-savior has to mutilate and expel himself in order to renew the generational process in the *polis*; while the slow and painful reconstruction of all the fateful events confirms that it all began with Oedipus' own rejection and expulsion by his parents—parents who (and his mother, at the end, most touchingly wonders why) had believed the oracle which made them mistrust their own child. They had, in fact, attempted to make it impossible for him to live at all, most poignantly by pinning his feet together and thus undercutting that hubris by which *homo erectus*, in growing up and standing on his own feet inch for inch usurps a place equal to or superior to the tallest and highest in the older generation. But seemingly outliving and outwitting his fate, Oedipus becomes a savior as well as a king. His very name seems to be a composite of "knowledge" and "swell-foot." Thus marked, he becomes a father-murderer at the entrance to adulthood, and this at a "three ways" crossroads—certainly, a good metaphor for identity confusion.

In *Oedipus Rex*, then, the core theme is meaningfully distributed over the stages of life; and yet the major themes of the *oedipal stage* of childhood do dominate the play. In fact, to come close to the phenomenal meaning of *Oedipus Rex* is possible only by bearing in mind that it is, after all, what we do call a *play*—a ritual which with supreme dramatic inventiveness enacts events awakening in the audience a sense of the all-human core of incestuous fantasy central to the *play age*.

Incidentally, of all people, Shakespeare, the playwright, among his seven ages lists no play age: according to him, the child advances directly from infancy to the school age: from the mewling and puking infant to the whining schoolboy. But then, Shakespeare imperiously calls all the world a stage even as he succeeds in making the stage reflect all the world.

As to Sophocles' Oedipus drama, let me list and apply in all brevity some of the psychosocial themes which belong to what, psychosexually, is—well, the oedipal stage. The strength emerging from the conflict between playful *Initiative* and inhibiting *Guilt* (so we have suggested) is a rudimentary *Purposefulness,* which must as yet learn what intentions are sanctioned by the prevalent morality. *Repression,* of course, is at this stage the normative defense against the infantile fantasies of manifold hubris; aggravated, it can lead to the core pathology of morbid *Inhibition.* Now, all these themes are, in the play, strongly emphasized as dominant personal trends. Oedipus is, of course, a tyrannos, a self-made ruler who from the first lines poses throughout as a man of unfailing initiative. As Knox (1957) puts it:

> The characteristic Oedipean action is the fait accompli. By the time the priest hesitantly suggests an appeal to the Oracle, Oedipus has already acted several days before. 'I have put the idea into action.' By the time the chorus suggests recourse to the blind seer Teiresias, Oedipus has already sent for him, not once but twice: 'I did not leave this to wait for tomorrow either.' 'Swift,' *tachys,* is his word.

In fact, Oedipus seems to outdo himself—and eventually, as it were, to do himself in—by pursuing an unbroken initiative for the purpose of finding Laius' killer. Here he displays also that other characteristic of the play age, undaunted *curiosity,* a passion for finding and finding out, which makes him pose an endless series of questions only to bring to light what others beg him to keep in the dark: thus, he turns into a passionate discoverer of the past. As to Oedipus' sense of *guilt,* the dominant shadow of the play age, the audience can only wonder breathlessly how long this man who was clever enough to solve the riddle of the Sphinx can remain blind to the relentlessly mounting evidence of his having committed the very acts which are at the core of infantile repression and inhibition.

At the height of his fateful search, Oedipus develops what can only be called a kind of *transference* to the blind prophet Teiresias, who so clearly sees his predicament. "You have no eyes but in your mind, you know," Oedipus says to Teiresias and ("prostrate," as he puts it) appeals to him to reveal the murderer of Laius: "Do not begrudge us oracles from birds, or any other way of prophecy within your skill; save yourself and the city, save me." But the moment Teiresias advises caution in this search, Oedipus violently accuses *him* of being (with Oedipus' brother-in-law, Creon) a "complotter" of the murder of Laius—adding, "Had you had eyes I would have said alone you murdered him." While this suspicion is by no means totally irrational, considering the politics of the day, its suddenness and intensity bespeaks a projection of his own dawning sense of guilt on the healer-seer on whom he must now depend, and who finally counters his accusation with a vicious revelation of the truth. But Oedipus does not listen; with redoubled initiative he pursues the search for the killer. Later, when the truth dawns on him, it is first in terms of a recognition of his "resistance" to Teiresias' revelation: "I have a deadly fear that the old seer *had* eyes."

From a generational point of view, then, the play *Oedipus Tyrannos* confronts the audience with the drama of a man who has reached the heights of power and wisdom in his community—accomplishments which in the normative order of individual development and of generational renewal would depend on the sublimation of the oedipal attachments to one's parents in childhood. This very "first among men," however, is seen to discover in scene upon scene—before the onlookers' eyes what has already become obvious to them, namely, that his fate had been radically (and literally) undercut—by his own parents. (We note in passing that this patriarchal play gives no hint as to the woman or women who kept the baby alive.) Having lived out his childhood unknowingly with an adoptive royal couple, he had to flee the same curse for which he had been abandoned as an infant—only to consummate the murder and the incest predicted: a total hubris which, indeed, proves to be the cause of the community's pollution. After his first and total shock, however, this tyrant takes charge of his own sentence and with his old swift initiative blinds himself and, for his own as well as the *polis'* sake, insists on his own exile and beggardom. In his last act, however, he is generatively concerned with the further fate of his children. His successor, Creon, must finally warn him that, somewhere, he must stop trying to manage everything.

I cannot (and I mean I really could not) enlarge on the wider cycles of changing world views in the Hellenic context in which this generational drama is embedded—nor the correspondences of that context to themes which we now ascribe to unconscious psychic processes. But I must add that as we review this "antique" life drama, it is fascinating to comprehend that its original viewers really faced themselves and their own time in the characters depicted. Here, I can only briefly mention the two acutely contending world views, Athenian *modernism* as against what Freud called the play's "theological" affirmation of ancient *prophecy*. Athenian modernism has, of course, become a decisive trend in history: it includes a certain entrepreneurship which we did recognize in Oedipus' personal type of tyranny. But it also includes an active attitude of contemplative inquiry, with Hippocratic elements such as *pronoia*, or foresight, as based on the study of the past and the diagnosis of the present. And it results in some mastery of fate by *self-recognition*. In this pervasive trend, finally, we may well recognize an early antecedent of the psychoanalytic ethos which was eventually to replace the warnings of the oracles with some insight into the unconscious.

V

Having reviewed the generational implications of the classic version in Western tradition of the oedipal stage of life, let me conclude by briefly pointing out how one may look at the developmental logic of this as well as of other stages: for only an understanding of that logic can help us connect our conception of the life cycle to such a basic clinical phenomenon as the appearance and use of transference phenomena in each stage of life. I have emphasized that the medium used to dramatize the oedipal fate was a *stage play*—and that I see an intrinsic significance in this. For there seems to be an extraordinary logic in the fact that the play age harbors the combination of incestuous inclinations most dangerous to social evolution, on the one hand, and the affective and cognitive intensification of human *playfulness*, on the other. In play, many potentially dangerous identifications and personifications can be acted out with a certain serious abandon, and with a developing style of individuation—and all this in workable relation to manageable materials, to meaningful toys, and to responsive peers. At the same time, there can occur a playful variation of sexual roles. The *intrusive* and *inclusive* mode potentials of the genitalia must of course wait until puberty for their full expression and polarization. But their instinctual inauguration in the play age can permit the alternation of both masculine and feminine modes and roles in both sexes. I therefore call this stage the infantile-genital rather than the phallic stage; and, indeed, the play of children of both sexes can reflect the procreative secret contained in the female body—a secret which patriarchic phallus worship attempts to match or outdo. Furthermore, the scheduled arrival of latency and school age permits a maximum of instinctual sublimation and of anticipated identification with work roles. Later, and after the latency stage, the playful role rehearsal of childhood is renewed in adolescence in the form of more or less dramatic social experimentation and ideological anticipation which guides identity development; while in adulthood play reappears (among other phenomena) in the ritual participation in public performances, including the communal experience of dramatic play on a variety of stages. Such shared creative experience enables adults to revive and to keep in touch with the abandoned imagination of childhood—and, of course, to become generative partners in the *interplay* of the generations. As to old age, to this post-procreative stage we assign a potential integration of the past; for the aging human being can become aware—if, indeed, playful memory overcomes a certain fatalistic despair—of the existential relativity of all the stages of life. Such "*wisdom,*" of course, has been prepared, stage for stage, throughout life (all the way up the rightmost vertical of our chart, from infancy to old age). And, indeed, the psychoanalytic treatment of successive age groups counts on some readiness for "wisdom" in each. But if psychoanalysis also counts on some transference in all stages, this (as you might suspect) suggests to me that there is a generational factor at work—that is, an attempt on the part of the patient to involve the analyst as a generative being in the repetition of selected life crises in order to restore the *developmental dialogue.* The dynamics of this clinical encounter of the generations, however, can obviously not be fully clarified except by a study of the typical experiences of the psychoanalyst's countertransference in relation to patients of different ages. For only by remaining consistently open to the way in which the patient's present as well as past stages reverberate in the analyst's experience of the corresponding stages, can the psychoanalyst become more fully aware of the generational implications of psychoanalytic work. I emphasize this in conclusion because I think that in these matters it would be rewarding to compare corresponding experiences of the interplay of transferences and countertransferences between analysands and analysts of given sexes and ages in different cultural and historical settings. For Freud's revolutionary decision to make this interplay of transferences the central issue in the healing situation has made of psychoanalysis (and I do not say this lightly in this year of Einstein's centenary)—it has made of psychoanalysis the prime method for the study of the *developmental* and *historical relativity* in human experience. And only such study can confirm what is, indeed, invariantly human.

Summary

This address expands on some themes of the human life cycle in its intrinsic relation to generational cycles—which, in turn, are experienced, at any given time and place, in the context of wider world events, whether these seem dominated by metaphysical, evolutionary, or historical perspectives. Especially in periods of acute cultural change (and thus, of epidemiological variations in psychopathology) all this must be significant also for transferences and countertransferences observable in psychoanalytic work. In this context, it is instructive to review psychoanalytic theories, too, in the light of their historical origins, and this especially in regard to the significance they allocate to various stages of life. Psychoanalysis, for good clinical reasons, always returns to the earliest and most obscure developmental risks. This trend must be complemented by a systematic emphasis on those developmental strengths which count in intergenerational actuality. The address reasserts (and illustrates) the contextual importance of the developmental principle of *Epigenesis* and then concentrates on psychosocial *Generativity* (the adult preoccupation with progeny, products, and ideas), as well as its negative counterparts, *Stagnation* and *Rejectivity*. It suggests that a theory of psychosexuality demands the assumption of Procreativity, an instinctual drive (reinforced by ancient tradition) which under present conditions of otherwise mandatory birth control, may be repressed or rationalized away. Quantitative changes in libidinal life always call for sublimation in some qualitative ethos—here, the worldwide concern for all children chosen to be born. In conclusion, *Oedipus Tyrannos* is briefly reviewed as a generational tragedy beginning with a parental rejection on oracular grounds, and ending with a procreative hubris which imposes a generative curse on the whole *polis*. The relation of this dramatic play to childhood play is briefly pursued. Finally, the address returns to transference as implying an unconscious appeal for the healing of the generational dialogue.

REFERENCES

Benedek, T. (1959), Parenthood as a developmental phase: A contribution to the libido theory. *J. Amer. Psychoanal. Assn.*, 7:389–417.

Erikson, E. H. (1962), Reality and actuality. *J. Amer. Psychoanal. Assn.*, 10:451–474.

——— (1964), Human strength and the cycle of generations. In: *Insight and Responsibility*. New York: Norton, 1966.

——— (1966), Ontogeny of ritualisation in man. In: "A discussion on ritualisation of behaviour in animals and man." Julian Huxley. *Phil. Trans. Royal Soc. London*, Series B., 251, No. 772, pp. 337–350.

——— (1968), The life cycle: Epigenesis of identity. In: *Identity. Youth and Crisis*. London: Faber & Faber.

Freud, A. (1978), The principal task of child analysis. *Bull. Hampstead Clin.*, 1:11–16.

Freud, S. (1930), Civilization and its discontents. *Standard Edition*, 21:64–145. London: Hogarth Press, 1961.

Grene, D., & Lattimore, R. (1959), *Oedipus the King*, trans. D. Grene. In: *The Complete Greek Tragedies: Volume 2. Sophocles*. Chicago: University of Chicago Press.

Kakar, S. (1978), *The Inner World: A Psychoanalytic Study of Childhood and Society in India*. New Delhi: Oxford University Press.

King, P. (1980), The life cycle as indicated by the nature of the transference in the psychoanalysis of the middle-aged and elderly. *Internat. J. Psycho-Anal.*, 61:153–160.

Knox, B. (1957), *Oedipus at Thebes*. New York: Norton.

18

The Oedipal Conflicts of the Analyst

BÉLA GRUNBERGER

[1980]

A neglected dimension of the Oedipus complex is the narcissistic aspect. The universal oedipal narcissistic injury linked to the developmental inadequacy of the child is crucially traversed only when optimal resolution of narcissistic cravings can be established. Rivalry with the parent of the same sex (the historical oedipus) is more visible than the profound oedipus complex linked to narcissistic injury. Failure to resolve the conflicts of the profound oedipus may have fateful consequences for the psychoanalyst himself. Some of the examples in this article are connected with the present situation of French psychoanalysis.

I

My experience has convinced me that there are special oedipal difficulties for those who prepare themselves for the psychoanalytic profession and that these oedipal problems are more important in training analyses than in therapeutic analyses. The so-called training or didactic analyses develop in a different way; they *are* different from others. They require a supplementary effort (often in vain) tied to the

Translated by Marion M. Oliner, Ph.D. Reprinted with permission from *Psychoanalytic Quarterly*, vol. 49, pp. 606–630.

working through of a specific oedipal dimension which I will describe in this paper. To choose a banal example, some physicians in analysis were helped in the affective, social, and even professional spheres of their lives. Although they essentially possessed the needed attributes to become psychoanalysts, they nevertheless continued to encounter difficulties in conducting their own psychoanalytic work. This difficulty is well known, yet the problem continues to present itself acutely and has an impact on the selection and training of analysts. Some young analysts conclude a therapeutic analysis with particularly favorable signs for their future psychoanalytic careers, but after the analysis is terminated and they start to practice psychoanalysis they face unexpected complications and require "some more analytic work." I have been able to establish further that certain analysts have great difficulty in recognizing and identifying oedipal situations in their clinical work. This is probably due to specific deep-seated structural conflicts which must be detected.

There is a resistance to this "nodal complex of neurosis" which exists in every one of us; and if it manifests itself with an almost indomitable force in some, it survives even in those who may seem to have worked it through and analyzed it exhaustively. In fact, it seems that the ubiquitous resistance to psychoanalysis crystallizes around the negation of the "dirty little family secret," as the authors of *Anti-Oedipus* (Deleuze and Guattari, 1977) call the "father complex" of Freud.[1]

My reflections have led me to consider the central importance of the oedipus complex to psychoanalytic activity. This was Freud's principal discovery, and it issued directly from his working through the mourning he experienced after the death of his father. The analyst must have acquired a solid oedipal dimension in order to develop a specific receptivity based on an oedipal maturation that is as complete as possible. But the oedipus, the center of the complex constellation aimed at assuring the subject his psychosexual equilibrium, is of necessity confronted by the narcissism of the individual. The oedipus is confronted especially by the "solutions" (other than psychoanalytic

[1]See also the colloquium assembled by Chasseguet-Smirgel (1974), dedicated to the study of "The Ways of the Anti-Oedipus," and the work of that name.

treatment) in which narcissism predominates, such as love, religions, or ideologies (attempted sublimations straddling narcissism and the oedipus complex). The avoidance of the oedipus complex may be related to the narcissism of some analysts.

Indeed, if psychoanalysis had to fight at the beginning in order to establish itself, and if the small group of pioneers had to suffer the attacks of its scorners, the battle now continues on the *inside* of the movement, which seems to have secreted its own opposition ever since the beginning. In this paper I will identify certain roots of this opposition.

If the oedipus complex is universal, its open discovery and recognition is contrary to the pleasure principle and necessitates a particular structural receptivity and psychosexual maturity. For the "oedipal discoverer" to be in the world is to be engaged in a dynamic process, a task involving an effort which must be renewed continuously (the "combat with the angel" will be taken up later). This is a task and an orientation which are essentially antithetical to the pleasure principle.[2] In a summary fashion, I shall call "narcissists" those whose conduct seems to be largely governed by the pleasure principle, corresponding to a definition which I have often tried to elucidate.[3]

[2]In "The Symbolic Representation of the Pleasure and Reality Principles in the Oedipus Myth," Ferenczi (1912) treated Oedipus as the representative of the reality principle. The woman (mother) of the hero tries to divert him from his search for the truth and promises him peace and happiness if he can be satisfied with make-believe. Oedipus represents the reality principle, and Jocasta signifies mysticism and illusion, the negation of reality. In *The Ego and the Id*, Freud (1923) stated that the birth of the oedipus complex arises in the child's discovery that the father constitutes an obstacle to the fulfillment of his wishes.

The myth, as it is narrated by Sophocles through the staging of his own fantasy, is above all an oedipal drama in the proper sense of the word, but it also contains references to narcissistic omnipotence on the subject of the origin of the hero, of the intervention of divine powers, and, finally, of the apotheosis of Oedipus (*Oedipus at Colonus*); it is always a matter of two levels in which the two elements become mixed—of the earthly level and the heavenly level, of the narcissistic domain and that of the drives. When Freud described the transference phenomenon, he used the adjective "grotesque," and one can understand perfectly if one thinks that transference is induced by narcissistic regression, which, as a dimension, is absolutely independent of contingencies of reality and materiality.

[3]I have considered narcissism as derived from an absolutely specific elational prenatal coenesthesis, and I have shown the derivatives of this state in the narcissism

What I have just alluded to concerning the history of psychoanalysis in the vertical direction, in terms of permanence and succession of "deviations," can also be discerned in the horizontal direction, probably for the same reasons. The disposition of the oedipus takes place differently according to a certain cultural context, but always within the framework of the dialectic between reality principle and pleasure principle, Oedipus and Narcissus. Originating in central Europe, psychoanalysis has spread throughout the world, but it has taken on different aspects in the Germanic and Anglo-Saxon countries on the one hand and Latin countries on the other; in the Judeo-Protestant milieus and those dominated by Catholicism, and especially beyond the cultural area having a European origin: thus, after a brief classical beginning, the Japanese and Indian psychoanalyses have been entirely transformed and are—in relation to the original model—basically unrecognizable, as far as we know. If the oedipus complex, as Freud has shown us, is at the origin of our moral and sociocultural life, the manner in which the individual tries to arrange his oedipal conflict, to "negotiate" it, is in itself a function of certain cultural factors which, having their own historical evolution, are liable to impose the effects of this evolution and its oscillations on the Oedipus itself and, through it, on psychoanalysis in general.

Before undertaking my demonstration, I shall take up again the

---

of the individual. Narcissus did not love his body ego, since he rejected sexuality (and, of course, autoerotism), that is to say, the postnatal solution, the drive dimension. He could only admire himself narcissistically in an elational way, plunged into this state of felicity, but lacking adequate psychosexual support. "To be absolute" he went astray in the universe of materiality, therefore of finiteness, contrary to his principle, and he could not (nor did he want to) effect the necessary synthesis between the two dimensions which are, in principle, antagonists—narcissism and drives. He could therefore only disappear into absolute regression, which (in his postnatal state) could only be death. It is Resnick who drew my attention to the passage in Ovid which retells the birth of Narcissus: "Cephissus entwined Liriope in his sinuous course, and holding her locked in the middle of his waves, violated her. . . . she conceived and put into the world a child . . . whom she named Narcissus." The myth enlightens us both on the fate of Narcissus, whose return to the maternal bosom (water) coincides in fact with his birth, his two parents being rivers, and with regard to his profound structure being made of vagueness and imprecision, the span of time confusing the present moment with eternity.

study of the concepts in question, from the point of view of a dialectic between narcissism and the oedipus.[4]

his oedipal conflict, to "negotiate" it, is in itself a function of certain cultural factors which, having their own historical evolution, are liable to impose the effects of this evolution and its oscillations on the oedipus itself and, through it, on psychoanalysis in general.

Before undertaking my demonstration, I shall take up again the study of the concepts in question, from the point of view of a dialectic between narcissism and the oedipus.[4]

Since discretion precludes my use of clinical illustrations, I will instead consider Oedipus himself. I shall take as the starting point the opposition between Oedipus and Jocasta, as Ferenczi has interpreted it. I shall adopt this interpretation by considering this conflict as fundamental, a conflict which becomes confused with the one in which Oedipus confronts the Sphinx. Moreover, I shall propose as a working hypothesis a certain analogy between the plague which struck the population of Thebes through the monster and the crisis which prevails in our civilization and particularly in our small psychoanalytic world, a crisis which seems to have adhered to the steps of our young discipline from its birth onward.

In addition, it would be logical to apply this viewpoint—i.e., the opposition between Oedipus and Narcissus—to the individual professional fate (theoretical and practical) of each analyst. Indeed, all of us are subject to cultural influences outside our psychosexual development and to permanent oscillations with regard to our positions. Freud himself was no exception. It would be easy to demonstrate, I believe, the effects on him of a pendular movement between the strict enterprise of the researcher (Oedipus)—he was ridiculed because of his "scientism"—and the yielding to a narcissistic seduction of philoso-

[4]In my first study devoted to this subject (Grunberger, 1957) I considered only the narcissistic factor and how it characterizes especially the initial period of the treatment. Furthermore, my essay had as its theme the analytic process in general and not, as with this present work, the analysis of the future analyst, particularly his oedipal phase. Nevertheless, I implied that narcissism was, in my conception, an essential and quasi-unique factor—the motor of treatment—and I take advantage of the present occasion to complete my position, which exceeded the scope of my earlier discussion.

phic speculation, against which he defended himself desperately, only to succumb to its charms eventually. Research feeds upon imagination and rigor, but if the Freudian undertaking corresponds to this synthetic orientation, then the work of the analyst is made up simultaneously of a succession of sectors stemming from one or the other of these two factors. I regret that I cannot elaborate this point of view in this presentation.

II

I have said that analysis is a global process with a beginning, an unfolding, and an end, having a goal which could be formulated as "the narcissistic fulfillment of the individual." Psychosexual development in its entirety cannot have any other finality, and the individual ultimately achieves this fulfillment through a process of drive maturation which will be narcissistically cathected and vice versa. Treatment consists of a taking up again, a resumption of the maturation process on a new basis. During this *new birth* (cf. Balint's *Neubeginn* [1934]),[5] the analyst helps the analysand to push away from his path, one by one, the obstacles stemming from complexes (coming out of the experience of the repetition compulsion reactivated through analysis). He functions as a support for the analysand in his *existential*

[5]The narcissistic impregnation of the analytic situation and its links with the oedipus complex lend themselves to bringing together the history of Oedipus with the myth of the hero in general, the hero whose birth is always miraculous, triumphing over multiple perils, a sort of second birth, the hero being to a certain extent his own sire. Oedipus triumphs over his father (and his mother) by being born, as it were. He does not have to undergo the maturational processes and, by surviving his exposure at the age of three days, he renders inoperative the filicidal intention of his parents. He makes his real castration null and void without mentioning his later victory (the unconscious does not know succession either in time or space) over the Sphinx (the strangulating one). He causes himself to be born or reborn in an autonomous way, so to speak, which corresponds both to *resurrection* and *immaculate conception*. As we have established, the myth corresponds to the narcissistic fantasy, whereas, as we shall later see, the poetic work of Sophocles includes other "solutions" of the oedipal problem.

Analysis is a self-generation at a certain level, the second existence of the analysand, leading to an image of himself which is more satisfying.

project. It seems that, if the destiny of the subject is not *programmed* in the sense a computer is, the particular facts which govern his fate (his personal equation) can determine its trajectory to a certain extent, and, in any case, it corresponds to his wish: he wishes to complete himself, to be himself. This wish stems from and is directed by his narcissism projected onto the analyst, cathected in an omnipotent manner. The individual restructures himself in this way, and his problem is first of all narcissistic, since it is a problem of identity itself: Who am I?—with the equally narcissistic answer, "I am who I am" (I want to be really who I am virtually). He becomes God in this way, but in order to *realize himself* he must change his perspective, to become a man, that is, to use his bodiliness, the fate of his drives embodying in this way his narcissistic project. This is the whole problem, of which the maturation through the oedipus is the key.[6] Oedipus, adoptive son of Polybus and Merope, reigning couple of Corinth, has doubts about his identity and wants to know who he is. This is how the drama begins.

[6]Maturation occurs in stages, each stage corresponding forcibly to a narcissistic achievement (through ego mastery of the phase-specific drive) but also to a certain degree of frustration with regard to omnipotence and fantasies of spontaneous narcissistic accomplishment. Christ is God, having become man in order to assume his real earthly life with all that maturation involves in terms of suffering experienced in a condensed way in his Passion. As to the tribulations of Oedipus (the real content of the drama), they correspond to the same process, ending with the narcissistic apotheosis in both cases: Christ ascends to heaven, Oedipus descends into the entrails of the earth (the chthonic divinities), and both join divinity in this way.

We often experience aggressive manifestations in analysis, particularly with certain narcissistic depressive subjects. These are repetitive aggressive manifestations that are difficult for us to classify among the reactions to oedipal or preoedipal conflicts. These manifestations seem to correspond to a specific narcissistic reaction and not to impulse frustration but, on the contrary (and this causes them to take on a clearly paradoxical character), to improvements realized on the impulse level, possibly analogous to the negative therapeutic reaction of Freud. They come easily after an interpretation which sticks, after the acquisition of an insight: the patient "reacts strongly" but seeks to erase or minimize it ("Okay," and "Now what?" or "After all that, what good will it do me?"). This expresses aggression and causes depression, and all this despite the amelioration that he or she cannot fail to experience. Every transference analysis will reveal itself inoperative in terms of guilt, or of the desire to castrate the analyst, or of aggression against the self of the patient, and we understand that each step of progress in maturation is bought at the expense of a renunciation of primitive narcissism, of Paradise, which one is thereby progressively led to lose.

As to the paradoxical character of these aggressive manifestations, we meet the same phenomena in certain forms of love, in which a real alteration between

This conception takes into account certain aspects of the quasi-mute role of the analyst, whose presence counts above all else. That presence is necessary to complete, by valuing it, the phase of the process that, at a given moment, touches maturity, which it attains through the often mute confirmation of the analyst. Without this concomitant narcissistic cathexis, every interpretation stays intellectual and can be considered wild analysis. Moreover, the interpretation must follow exactly the maturational process, whose unfolding the analyst must, of course, respect. The analysand, like the child, has the right to his own research, which is an important element of well-tempered timing. Oedipus had left to search for his identity and was on the point of discovering it through a series of conflicts when the oracular instance of Delphi, through its precipitation as a wild interpreter, cut the ground from under his feet.

I have insisted upon stressing the importance of the original narcissistic factor and its ties with the oedipus, psychosexual development, and the analytic transference.

I would like to recall here once more that the child, in being born and projected into the world of drives, must of necessity refind his lost narcissistic equilibrium through his new psychophysiological equipment. I have stressed the role of the mother, on whom falls the task of reproducing, around the child, an approximation of his original milieu and of permitting him to try to complete himself with the help of his *external* milieu (merging narcissism). Here the child profits as if externality did not exist, since the mother is not yet an object. But together with these early narcissistic "developments" (in the sense of a passage or transfer from one state to another), the child brings with him at birth the anlage for an image of the father who procreated his developmental trajectory. This is the father who presided over the programming of his becoming and maturing in the sense of a *funda-*

"honeymoon" and "venom" (in French: *"lune de miel"* and *"lune de fiel"*) can establish itself without being able to evoke (after appropriate analysis) sadomasochism or ambivalence as an appropriate interpretation. It involves, most likely, a narcissistic disappointment which comes after drive gratification, as if happiness in the most perfect love could not lead to the forgetting of narcissistic felicity. One should examine from this angle the problem of drugs, the domestic crises which chase men from their homes in search of alcohol, and gambling which supposedly satisfies the nostalgia of autonomous narcissistic felicity.

mental reorganization of his libidinal economy (and his concomitant narcissistic equilibrium). Since the child is condemned to leave his cocoon and to *integrate himself into the world,* he must acquire a new existential dimension based on drives, on castration, and on the defenses against them. Henceforth frustration and narcissistic mutilation will be his daily bread. This whole maturational process is oriented toward the oedipus for reasons which we will examine further on. This evolution centered on the paternal imago takes a certain time, if only because the neonate insists on holding on to his primitive existence (often his mother also has the tendency to maintain him there) and because the passage to the other shore requires of him a particular effort. (This is where the paternal model can support his progress in an adequate manner.) It is in this profound oedipus that we find foreshadowed the historical oedipus induced by the mother as the support of the first pregenital feelings.

At the end of a certain developmental period, the child usually accepts his new drive orientation and opts definitely for this new maturational direction, although he still runs the danger of keeping a certain fear, that is, a dread of the drives: we know the importance of this problem in psychosexual pathology. Schematically, we can say that it is a *nodal point* which rotates the child in his new universe. His subsequent evolution will, from then on, take place under the sign of the oedipus, and we could paraphrase Freud in this way: where Narcissus was, there Oedipus will be.

But what happens when things take a different course? Then there will be chances that the child will remain blocked at a precocious phase of his development and fixated on the mother in a particular way. On the one hand, he will continue to obtain from her satisfactions derived from narcissistic fusion with her, needing the narcissistic supplies from outside because of his blocking, and he will identify himself with her at the same time in order to benefit from her narcissistic omnipotence. On the other hand, he will begin to fear her precisely because of this evil power—evil, because he will end up projecting on her a reactive primitive aggression, especially since he will be incapable of integrating his aggression due to the lack of an adequate preoedipal development. The anal-sadistic component that is not integrated results in a fragile ego, since it lacks the synthesis between the primitive sadism and the elational narcissism, a circumstance the effects of which will be discussed later. It can touch upon certain psychoaffective sectors of the ego without involving others, particularly, I think, of the intellectual sector itself.

As we know, developmental disturbance of the anal-sadistic component complicates oedipal evolution. Full "genitality" designates a state of integration of paternal power. (One is father on one's own; one is a father among fathers.) The subject is disengaged from the anal-sadistic phase of the conflict, on which certain people remain fixated as a result of the internalized conflict with the introjection of the paternal phallus (the "combat with the angel"). We view this in a certain light as the "reconciliation with the father." Here I suggest that just such intrusions of disturbance in oedipal development may echo in the tendency of the future analyst to approach psychoanalysis from a strictly intellectual angle. Indeed, psychoanalysis—like any other discipline considered from the strictly intellectual angle—can be "learned" as a sort of pidgin-analysis (I borrow this term from J. F. Revel [1978], who writes about pidgin-Marxism). Everything will depend on the integration of this knowledge into the global personality and on the degree of its evolution. One can become an analyst in order to enrich one's *having* (increasing one's acquaintances, acquiring a social position, etc.) or one's *being* (modifying oneself in the sense of an oedipal project).

In general it is the oedipus which opens the analytic treatment in emerging constantly during the session in all modes of psychosexual relations; it functions like a structuring element of the ego and as a source of energy nourishing the process of individuation; as the oedipal strivings must be taken up repetitively during the evolution of the subject in order to flesh itself out, it must be worked through continuously during the treatment. In the absence of this repeated analysis and appropriate timing, the subject may not be able to maintain his oedipal position to the point at which it could really be considered definitely acquired. He will be particularly exposed to a regression to the level of identification with the primal mother.[7] This is particularly

[7]The temptation to refind the state of merger with the mother whose narcissistic seduction is infiltrated with pregenital elements stays very much alive at all times. There is an omnipresent tendency to structure oneself in a perverse relation. According to the conditions of education, the subject is in danger of succumbing to it, for reasons we shall approach later.

valid for the so-called training analysis, a deep didactic treatment, the only guarantee actually at our disposal while we suffer the pressure of the reigning narcissistic, antioedipal, and therefore antianalytic, collective superego and collective ego ideal.

I hear at this point the argument which recalls that the first analysts were often poorly analyzed or not analyzed at all, but were nevertheless good analysts. This is a perfectly valid argument which is at the same time questionable, and we shall discuss it in particular with regard to the difference in the conditions of recruitment then and now. But, in fact, what are we concerned about? The therapeutic analysis can correspond to a whole gamut of treatments, which range from the amelioration of symptoms to real structural modifications. It can fail to accomplish the "revolution" and remain truncated with regard to a theoretical ideal. It has, by the way, a tendency to complete itself by a decathexis after the acquisition of the global therapeutic result, according to the principle, "The Moor has done his duty, the Moor can go." Now, this is never the case for the didactic analysis, for the simple reason that the analyst remains in permanent contact with the unconscious of his analysands and therefore with his own, with its conflicts which have either been resolved or at least sufficiently mobilized as to make their presence known. That is why a didactic analysis cannot remain satisfied with a partial result and must be terminated only after having run a complete trajectory. It will have had to attain and to consolidate a postoedipal position endowed with the particular density mentioned earlier. To remain fixated at a pseudo-oedipus (avoidance), that is, the anal-sadistic phase expressing itself through sadistic tormenting of the father, would be a sign of regression which precisely constitutes the defense against the oedipus.[8]

[8]As for the first analysts, the founders of our discipline, whatever their inevitable therapeutic errors, many of these pioneers possessed a special endowment. They had, from the start, a certain spontaneous oedipal maturity, as is proven by the circumstances of the choice of their vocation, which constitutes a genuine natural selection of absolute value, in my opinion. Without this oedipal maturity, at least in a certain sector, they would never have recognized the value and the scope of the Freudian discovery, against that which was fashionable and against the "beautiful people" of their time, who heaped insults on them. And they would never have been capable of the deprivation and the courage that defending their discipline against a hostile environment demanded of them. Like Oedipus, they were in search of the truth with an absolute determination. They pursued their research undaunted by the narcissistic injuries they suffered. This search was antinarcissistic in the sense of

The study of a certain aspect of narcissism seems to me to be particularly enlightening about the importance of a solid didactic training; it also introduces us to a whole dimension of psychoanalysis which tends to metamorphose these days into a cult of language.

Oedipus was expelled from the maternal womb at birth, which constitutes a narcissistic injury, even though it is the lot of all humans. We have seen, however, that it is incumbent upon the mother to supply the adequate gratification and environment in order to help the neonate accept gradually that which I have called the drive solution. Coming into the world is therefore relatively reparable—relatively, since the wound will always be open to a certain extent. The mother of Oedipus not only failed in her duty of reparation, but inflicted on him a threefold narcissistic injury by radically abandoning her child (expelling him, in a way, a second time), and by afflicting him with a true castration (the swollen foot), a somatic expression of the phallic narcissistic loss. The future king of Thebes was able to undertake the reparation of his initial injury in a narcissistically satisfying way, which is reserved for heroes, but he also had to pass through the crisis of identification with the primal mother in order to complete himself in this sense.

Some years ago there appeared in Canadian and other newspapers an account of how a drunkard behaved badly in a pub, and the owner of the place asked him to leave; in other words, he was "treated like dirt." Afterward, he came back armed with a Molotov cocktail and "blew up the joint." There were no survivors. This can be explained as his desire to make null and void his narcissistic injury by causing all those who were witnesses to disappear.

This mechanism seems to have been perfectly grasped by the dramatist, Peter Schaffer, the author of *Equus*. It is the story of a young man who pierces the eyes of all the horses in a stable (although he adores horses) because they were witnesses of his sexual fiasco with a girl. Of course, a psychoanalyst will immediately think that this is a superficial motive and that behind it is an oedipal story (complete

---

regression (all deviations restructure themselves at a particular narcissistic position by denying the oedipus complex). As to their motivation, it had a profound authenticity—different, in any case, from that of some young analysts who say, "Everyone in my department is in analysis. If I don't do it, what will I look like?"

with primal scene and regression to anal-sadistic coitus). But precisely who, if not the parent, is the most direct witness of the original narcissistic injury, especially of the oedipal narcissistic injury linked to the physiological inadequacy of the little boy confronted with his precocious desire? In addition, I have insisted many times on the role of the oedipal interdiction as a defense against the narcissistic injury expressed in the thought: "I am not impotent; it is the other person who is blocking the road (but when I am like him, I shall be able to marry mother without exposing myself to the repetition of the same narcissistic injury, since I shall be an adult myself)."

I have mentioned witnesses, but the most troublesome witness is, without doubt, the parent who is at the same time the rival, which adds the narcissistic injury of defeat to that of inadequacy. We know, however, how to distinguish between that which relates to the rivalry doomed to fail and that which is imputable to the narcissistic injury proper (inadequacy). Guilt diminishes with expiation, punishment, and repentance, whereas shame does not cease until the witnesses have disappeared. Moreover, things introduce themselves differently to the girl and to the boy, if only because the narcissistic injury of the girl is less dramatic and more profound: on the one hand, she can hide from herself her inadequacy or transform it into a fear of penetration; on the other hand, her injury in the form of penis envy may stretch across her psychosexual life in general. Aside from the further complexities of how matters differ for the boy and the girl, I am here stressing that although the oedipus as rivalry with the parent of the same sex (historical oedipus) may be visibly evident throughout analysis, the profound oedipus linked directly to the narcissistic injury proper is infinitely more difficult to grasp and has a tendancy to resist analysis until the end. We could even say that the former functions as a defense against the latter. The two can easily become intermingled because the oedipus *in general* is repressed. The analyst who has this problem will regularly encounter oedipal situations without being aware of them, or, on the contrary, his historical oedipus will be used, exhibited, and relived (acted out) in order to camouflage the primitive oedipus. The inverse does not exist. In order to grasp the nature of the primitive oedipus we have to reconsider its origin, i.e., the narcissistic injury.

We have seen that the fact that the narcissistic injury has a witness is very important. The testimony of the witness can be external or internalized into the ego. In the most severe cases of narcissistic injury, which end in suicide (cf. Grunberger, 1971), it is the evidence of the projected ego structure which pushes the narcissist to eliminate himself. But this testimony can be fought and injury annulled in various ways. One can either suppress the witness or at least wish for his disappearance; but one can also *project* on him the injury in question, that is, the failure or the insufficiency of which one accuses oneself on the narcissistic level. The latter is a method which is extremely widespread and almost "physiological." Narcissism being a question of value, the narcissist can also *devalue* the witness by covering him with insults, by diminishing him narcissistically, which prevents the injury from being reflected, or by clouding the mirror. We know that this reflection can go very far and that the whole world can suddenly take on the aspect of an immense mirror, causing the injury which has been suffered to stand out. This can result in end-of-the-world fantasies (an apocalypse complex), as if only the total disappearance of all humanity could put an end to the shame which has been suffered. In more modest cases, it is only a matter of causing the psychoanalytic society to which one belongs to disappear.

The father of the fundamentally narcissistic oedipus is not a person, since we are far from the literal oedipus rivalry. This does not involve the historical oedipus but the oedipus principle structuring the world in conformity to its derivatives; it is the paternal function in the wide sense of the term. In the conflict we have, on the one side, the subject in his wounded narcissistic omnipotence and, on the other, the paternal function, the ambient material world, reality, since all this is considered by the narcissist as his antagonist, which must disappear. Their existence reminds him of his failure, of the shame of not having been able to master the complex, and of not having been able to evolve to the level of postoedipal drive organization. In order to apply this view to our specialty, we establish, for instance, that the narcissistic analyst cannot endure the notion of training, since being trained means organization, hierarchy, "establishment," and the notion of difference and maturation without mentioning manipulation by instructors. He is the anointed, whose perfection is already there from the beginning, since he is the heir of the absolute charismatic narcissism.[9] If he becomes involved with the "system" anyway, it is only with his lips and with a mental reservation by inverting the situation, by making a "gift of his person" to the institution. But heaven help the one who puts in doubt his immediate and total adequacy, that is, his uniqueness, who would give him a narcissistic injury in the way of a criticism or a refusal. This is a genuine test which is applicable only when it is already too late. The witnesses to his shame must disappear, the institution which served as a framework for his humiliation must be broken into pieces, the theory itself which served as a basis for the recognition that turned against him must be devalued, all of which results in the annulling of his injury. In fact, if the doctrine, whose representative gave him the injury, is no longer valid and is replaced by another—if possible, by one which is diametrically opposed to it—the criterion by which he was judged is invalidated, and the injury annulled.

The oedipal person reacts to failure as a stimulus to attempt the realization of his oedipal desire with renewed determination, but for the narcissist there is no next time, since he prefers the disappearance of the system in which the injury took place. He will "get out of line" with regard to the system and, in this way, will annul the injury by eradicating the possible bases for the repetition of his shame. He will not try to triumph over the father (to identify with him in order to surpass him later), but will try to abolish the principle of paternity itself and the whole frame of reference of which it was the organizer.

However, this does not mean that in this way he will be assured of total independence with regard to his constellation of complexes. Indeed, he will actually surrender to other instances more absolute and more compelling than the ones of which he thought he was ridding himself. It is this problem that we are going to examine now.

We follow Oedipus on the road to finding his identity, which is a double problem, since it is independent of his identity of origin. The sexual identity of Oedipus also constitutes a problem: Laius, his

[9]We know Christ the child and Christ as an adult, but between the two there is nothing, no maturation. We know the words and the miracles (a purely narcissistic accomplishment without reality), but everything that resembles the life of the drive is projected onto the Jews.

father, is in one sense homosexual,[10] while he, Oedipus, has pierced feet and is therefore the carrier of a certain representation of femininity from the start. On his way, Oedipus meets the Sphinx (I think that in the light of the primary process we can afford to overlook the chronological succession of the episodes), a monster which is half animal and half woman, carrier of masculine and feminine attributes corresponding to what we usually call the phallic mother. We know that she threatens with disaster those victims, mostly young people, who cannot answer her riddles concerning sex. It is the primal mother, who is castrating and seductive at the same time, whom Sophocles calls the "cruel singer" (whereas in another passage in *Oedipus Rex* the monster is referred to as "poet": "How is it that when the bitch recited for you her verses, you didn't issue for these Thebans a word of delivery?") in alluding, no doubt, to the maternal function linked to the learning of language.

This apprenticeship of the infant is preceded by a glossolabial play which uses not only the tongue and the lips but also the mucous membranes of the oral cavity and its contents (air, saliva); thus the infant produces noise and sound. At the beginning this is an oral autoerotic play activity, but the quasi-concrete productions of the child, as well as the rumbling of the bowels transposed to the mouth, evoke the highly cathected activity of the later narcissized and eroticized anal phase (displacement upward). Here the libidinal erotic element involving the child and the mother dominates, to the detriment of the following phase, that of the learning of speech as a vehicle with precise content. The precocious sexualization of this game, in which mother and child participate, can furnish the basis of a perverse duo, the third member being excluded and useless, leading to a general tendency of avoiding the oedipus. At the same time the game paves the way for a clear disequilibrium of the affective charge especially belonging to the glossolabial[11] function itself (it will have the lion's

[10]Laius sexually violated Chrysippus, the son of Pelops (Grunberger, 1971, p. 298).

[11]This whole activity, considering its location, often produces the diphthong "bl," from which is derived the designation of a confused and empty discourse as "bla-bla-bla." The Bible story of the Tower of Babel is undoubtedly linked to the cathexis of this phase of phonation. The construction of the Tower of Babel itself is an anal function, and its aim is eminently narcissistic: to reach the heavens and to be like

share), which will be withheld from the mental functions involved in the oedipal struggle, such as reality testing. The father is the reality which troubles the couple. The father also represents causality in the sense of one fact necessarily begetting another, and the negation of this causality is the destruction of the paternal function. Here I suggest the parricidal implications of confusing such cardinal considerations of causality as the distinction between the essential and the contingent, the true and the false, the primary and the secondary, the perception of the limit of things and their respective position in time and space, etc. Much could be said about the cathexis of lallation becoming, through a kind of pseudosublimation, a "superior twittering," but if I continue in this direction, I will go beyond the limits prescribed for this communication.

The child, seduced and fascinated by the phonic play, could stay fixated at this stage or fall back upon it (it seems that this has been foreseen by Sophocles as a dangerous abuse, a plague, and a genuine castration, since it cuts the road to maturation).[12] Oedipus triumphs, however, over the "maid with the pointed claws," resolves the enigma, and, by discovering its content, revealing its precise theme (which is begetting and the line of descendants), puts the monster out of existence. The enigma is in fact presented in the overloaded esoteric style proper to the oracular language of the period (sufficiently known by the public of Sophocles, so that he took it for granted), and it is the demystification of this language that resulted in the Sphinx's being precipitated into nothingness (which can also represent the interior emptiness of the monster suddenly brought to light by the hero).

---

divinity. Besides "bl" (and "vl," which is similar) there are suggested etymological linkages with the French words *volubile, babiller* (to babble), *blêser* (to lisp), *balbutier* (to stammer), and with the Englishh word, bubble. In his Italian etymological dictionary D. Olivieri (1965) states: " 'Babel' is onomatopoeic in origin and refers to the bla-bla of children." He also cites Greek and Sanskrit words having the same significance. For pejorative implications we may allude to the "bl" in *hâbleur* (boaster); in the Hebrew *hevel* (*hevel havalim*, or *vanitas vanitatum*); the name, Hübelé Balazs designates in Hungarian someone who talks without rhyme or reason. (In Hungarian there is generally a vowel between the two consonants.)

[12]Another hero of Greek mythology, Ulysses, defends himself against the siren song. By asking to be tied to the mast of the ship (to the paternal phallic emblem which protects him), Ulysses resists the fatal regressive temptation.

The episode of the Sphinx lends itself to an interpretation which makes of this combat a confrontation between the oedipal ideal and the fixation to the primal mother, which seems to have been the problem of the great century during which Sophocles lived. As a culturally sensitive, politically experienced public man, Sophocles grasped the impact of the impingement of two civilizations expressed by the superstitious, idolatrous language of the Sibyl in contrast to the voice of Oedipus and the language of clarity and reason. It was, after all, an era of Greek philosophic ascendance. In his fundamental work on matriarchy Bachofen (1861) stresses the importance of the era of Sophocles for the birth of our civilization. Harold Stewart (1961) states: "It has been suggested that the Oedipus story represents the changeover from the matrilineal society . . . to the patrilineal, where the line of descent and influence runs through the males" (p. 428).

The pendular movement of history actually seems to favor the matrilineal tendency with the narcissistic regression which is supported by the primal mother imago. What concerns us is the reorientation, in this respect, of our own discipline, with the inversion of the oedipal tendency and of the principles derived from it and the negation of clinical reality as such. Instead, the cathexis of the narcissistic intellectual activity of the analyst displaces the focus to the regressive and at the same time superficial expression of the psyche in a position which is defensive against the principle of oedipal maturation.

In fact, we know that the combat of Oedipus with the primal maternal imago does not end in this way. If we follow the account we establish that, like the Sphinx, Oedipus will be the cause of a scourge (the pestilence with which the gods will afflict Thebes for leaving a regicide unpunished). And, again like the Sphinx, he will cause the misfortune of his environment by tormenting it with his disquiet and his insidious questioning as well as by the implacable pursuit of his goal, which is a problem finally linked to his own downfall, analogous in a sense to that of the Sphinx. By means of a judicious poetic condensation, Sophocles opens a perspective on the telescoping of the levels and on a simultaneous perception of the different degrees of the evolution of the hero. It is the negative aspect of his story which appears this way, bearing witness to the survival of his fixation, or rather representing it. In fact, by apparently triumphing over the monster, Oedipus has *introjected* it, thereby becoming like it. The monster disappears from the tale without a trace, as if swallowed by Oedipus: it can be found from then on inside, as if Oedipus himself will disappear (miraculously) into the entrails of the Earth Mother, swallowed by divinity. The hero will remain from then on in conflict with his introject and will be torn between his two contradictory tendencies, the paternal and the primal maternal identifications.[13]

At the end Oedipus will succumb, a victim of the introject that persecutes him and of his cruel, sadistic superego, but we can interpret the murder of Laius, whose identity he does not know as his identification with the introjected sadistic mother.[14] As to the scene in which Oedipus penetrates into the palace looking for Jocasta, it has been interpreted by Van der Sterren (1948) as a sadistic version of incestuous coitus. (Oedipus, at the peak of anger, demands a sword, forces the double doors, tears down the curtain, etc.)

In fact, the conclusion we can draw on the subject of the story of our hero is that, if one can say this, he could not resolve his oedipus. (Of course, I consider the play by Sophocles a fantasy creation.) He never completely left his fixation on the early mother. He was king indeed, and he engendered and procreated, but he was in reality neither king nor father.[15] He abandoned the reins of his government to

[13]"The sphinx is the enigma which Oedipus will have to resolve, and the enigma has two possible solutions: either the mother Sphinx or Oedipus the human child" (Róheim, 1934).

[14]According to one version, Oedipus was supposed to recover certain horses belonging to his adoptive father, which had been stolen. This makes the incident banal, while lending it a trivial aspect in the style of a Western. The attack on the occupant of the chariot, who asks permission to pass, is tinged with provocation and projection ("You are the bad one"). The incessant harassing of the father is not the expression of oedipal aggression but a defense against it through identification with the sadistic mother.

[15]This history of Oedipus is not that of a subject's having realized incestuous intercourse. That act generally brings about a strong deterioration of the ego, a psychotic regression, and, in this case, the drama would never have been written. To realize prematurely (before death) the return to the maternal womb would deprive the ego forever of its "narcissistic project" and would take away its whole vital resilience. I once had the privilege of hearing the confession of a mother in the case of a consummated mother-son incest. According to her (she was very ill and died shortly after having told me), she offered herself to her twenty-year-old son; the boy fell asleep as soon as he had penetrated his mother, only to wake up schizophrenic. Oedipus behaves as does a classic neurotic. The whole story of the last segment, i.e., his exile and wandering, his disputes with his sons, and his last talk with Theseus prove it.

his brother-in-law Creon (his uncle as well) and never had the relation of a father with his children. He brought his sons to the point of killing each other, and his relation with his daughter Antigone (undoubtedly his preferred one, compared to her sister Ismene) vacillated between a pseudoincestuous and a homosexual tie. (Pasolini had the role of Antigone played by a young boy, thus yielding to an inspiration which could be justified, in my opinion, as a replica of the homosexual grandfather.) After his fight with the primal mother and the oedipal killing, Oedipus *regresses* by returning to his birthplace (Thebes) rather than joining his family in Corinth. The story is also a regressive movement when considered in a sociohistorical light: "The Oedipus cycle has a definite matriarchal orientation. As in the Jason saga, it describes a world seen through matriarchal eyes. Neither gods nor goddesses populate this world. But its matriarchal sprites and bogies are very much present and figure in events . . . the Sphinx, the Erinyes, and Fate" (Balter, 1969, p. 265).

As I have stated, psychosexual evolution, as it traverses the oedipal phase, is determined by the preoedipal imago of the parental couple. The project of narcissistic completion becomes transferred to the acquisition of impulse mastery, which is a long and complicated process stretching over the whole duration of psychosexual development. I lack the space here to examine these under such headings as "maturation," "guilt," "aggression," "castration," "neutrality" (of the analyst). What we must remember is that in the course of the unfolding of the process the positions become constantly fraught with guilt, not only by reason of the ambivalence stemming from the nature of object relations (in the strictly oedipal framework), but also because of the antagonism between narcissism and impulse life, since the oedipal rival, the father, is at the same time the carrier of the narcissistic projection. Also, we must understand why a perfect mastery of the analytic situation demands from the analyst an equally perfect mastery of the oedipal problem, *the permanent penetration into the unconscious taking on for him (and not for the analysand) a clearly incestuous aspect.*

Moreover, the analysand, i.e., the analytic candidate, faces the "didactic" analyst, who is his father in the transference relation, but who is at the same time his real rival, without speaking of the specific analytic phallus of which he is the bearer.

The failure to recognize the unique character of this position ("there is no difference between the therapeutic and the didactic analysis; there is no didactic analysis") can only be intentional; otherwise, those very persons who would like to confer upon *each* analyst the right to conduct didactic analyses would not be as demanding as they are today, with reference to opening to the same analysts access to the status of senior analyst, conferred in principle on those who can express themselves by producing texts. But in this case, we are facing exactly the antagonism which strangely resembles what we have just described in referring to the difference which separated Oedipus from the Sphinx.

There is an antagonism between the two fundamental and, in fact, contradictory positions: that of the analyst, whom I shall call oedipal (since the adjective "Freudian" has been usurped),* and the analyst for whom treatment, even as an object to be cathected, is negligible. What he retains of analysis is *his* intellectual construction, and he shortens the analytic session to be sure that no specific atmosphere could take shape which would favor the vital emotional engagement of the unconscious of both patient and analyst. Having pushed aside the experience that should be lived through, one could, in a pinch, do without the patient, and analysis could become a philosophy, or even a philosophy on a philosophy, to the extent to which it applies its reflection to a philosophico-grammatico-linguistic construction which is called psychoanalysis.

Oedipal psychoanalysis pursues a scientific method by exploring clinical reality, little by little, by verifying the results in a sufficiently reiterated way. It seeks to understand the clinical situation with the help of the discovery of unconscious motivation and also with the help of working hypotheses. Antioedipal analysis, however, proceeds the opposite way; it is a kind of global and immediate *gnosis*, proceeding from an immovable dogmatic whole, unalterable and definite because it is sacred, that which one imposes on every reality (clinical or not), a scheme to which clinical practice must conform.

Psychoanalysis *applies* its knowledge to all psychic manifestations, whereas the antioedipal doctrine *protests* against this way of

*Editor's note: The author here refers to certain current trends in French psychoanalysis.

doing things and, on the contrary, proceeds in the reverse direction. It is not experience or practice that counts but the mystical initiation. This results in a situation in which a candidate can be "consecrated" an analyst at the end of three to six months, whereas *practically* his analysis can last up to ten or fifteen years or more. Thus the Sphinx expresses herself through enigmas. And thus language becomes the essential element which replaces all the rest for the antioedipal analyst and receives the whole narcissistic cathexis.

Summary

The oedipal dimension of the personality of the psychoanalyst enters profoundly into his functioning as an analyst, and it is possible only for the psychoanalyst who has overcome "the narcissistic allure of the Sphinx" to engage in true combat with his oedipal conflicts in such a way that he will fully help his patients to do the same. A variety of issues given polemical attention in psychoanalysis today seem related to this oedipal dimension, which is so ubiquitously "acknowledged" and so often then ignored. These issues include status, promotion to training analyst, technical modifications, and especially the way in which the analyst uses his theories. The future of psychoanalysis depends on the availability of psychoanalysts who think independently because they are *free* to do so. It is precisely the developmental antagonism between the Sphinx and Oedipus which masquerades behind many controversies in our science.

REFERENCES

Bachofen, J. J. (1861), *Myth, Religion, and Mother Right: Selected Writings of J. J. Bachofen.* Princeton, NJ: Princeton University Press, 1967.

Balint, M. (1934), Charakteranalyse und Neubeginn. *Int. Ztschr. f. Psa.,* 20:54–65.

Balter, L. (1969), The mother as source of power: A psychoanalytic study of three Greek myths. *Psychoanal. Quart.,* 38:217–274.

Chasseguet-Smirgel, J., Ed. (1974), *Les chemins de l'anti-Oedipe.* Toulouse: Privat.

Deleuze, G. & Guattari, F. (1977), *Anti-Oedipus: Capitalism and Schizophrenia.* New York: Viking.

Ferenczi, S. (1912), The symbolic representation of the pleasure and reality principles in the Oedipus myth. In: *Sex and Psychoanalysis*. New York: Basic Books, 1950, pp. 253-269. Chapter 2, this volume.

Freud, S. (1923), The ego and the id. *Standard Edition*, 19:12-66. London: Hogarth Press, 1961.

Grunberger, B. (1957), Essai sur la situation analytique et le processus de guérison. *Revue Francaise de Psa.*, 21:373-458. Reprinted in translation in: *Narcissism: Psychoanalytic Essays*. New York: International Universities Press, 1979, pp. 35-90.

——— (1971), The suicide of the melancholic. In: *Narcissism: Psychoanalytic Essays*. New York: International Universities Press, 1979, pp. 241-280.

Olivieri, D. (1965), *Dictionary of Etymology*. Milan: Ceschina.

Revel, J. F. (1978), *Tentation totalitaire*. Paris: Grasset.

Róheim, G. (1934), *The Riddle of the Sphinx: On Human Origins*. London: Hogarth Press.

Stewart, H. (1961), Jocasta's Crime. *Internat. J. Psycho-Anal.*, 42:424-430.

Van der Sterren, H. A. (1948), *Oedipe: Une étude psychanalytique d'après les tragedies de Sophocle*. Paris: Presses Universitaires de France, 1976.

19

Oedipus Revisited: Laius and the "Laius Complex"

JOHN MUNDER ROSS

[1982]

The son unborn mars beauty; born he brings
pain. divides attention, increases care.
. . . [H]is growth is his father's decline,
his youth his father's envy.
—James Joyce, *Ulysses*

. . . and I shall visit the iniquities of the father
unto the third and fourth generations of
them that hate me.—*Exodus 20*

Presented at the Hampstead Child Therapy Clinic, London. November 25, 1981; and at the Fall meetings of the American Psychoanalytic Association, New York, December 18, 1981. Reprinted with permission from *The Psychoanalytic Study of the Child*, edited by A. Solnit, R. Eissler, A. Freud, and P. B. Neubauer, vol. 37, pp. 167-200 (New Haven: Yale University Press).

In the last decade, research pediatricians, psychologists, and psychoanalysts have become attuned to the developmental importance of fathers and to the evolving psychology of fatherhood itself (Abelin, 1971, 1975, 1977; J. M. Ross, 1975, 1977, 1979a, 1979b, 1979c, 1982a, 1982b; Lamb, 1976; Herzog, 1980, 1982a, 1982b; Gunsberg, 1982; Yogman, 1982). So often exempted in theory and practice from the responsibilities and pleasures of parenthood, nonetheless men reveal their own generative and nurturant strivings. These are now seen to emanate from the inner reaches of their sexual identity and its childhood origins. And their children turn to them, it seems, for various gender-specific supplies during critical periods.

Most recently, for example, theorists have highlighted the preoedipal role of the father in inviting children to separate from mother, discover their individuality, assume their gender identity, and modulate and control the derivatives of their drives, especially their aggressivity. The effort has been to offset the relegation of fathers to the one-dimensional tyrant of oedipal fantasy and to flesh out the shadowy figure on the periphery of the mother-child dyad. He is now seen as a potential nurturer during this early era, and subsequent phases of development: the oedipal period itself, latency, adolescence, and beyond (J. M. Ross, 1977; Colarusso and Nemiroff, 1982; Esman, 1982; Tessman, 1982).

But figures such as these "good fathers," like other conceits of theory, tend to be more responsive to their conceptual antecedents than to the real-life people whose variety they but crudely reflect. Oversimplifications and overcompensations abound, as theorists now underscore the more sunny and hopeful possibilities for paternity.

At least until recently, few authors have attended systematically to pathological features in fathering (Neubauer, 1960; Weissman, 1963; Leonard, 1966), that is, apart from the threat of castration, which can be seen to be basically a product of the child's own imagination and inherent psychology, almost independent of actual paternal influences. And when they have scrutinized specific fathers, these authors have often failed to explore the personalities and specific parental conflicts of the parents involved (N. Ross, 1982; Socarides, 1982) as much as their more manifest pathogenic actions.

There is, however, unmistakably a regressive potential in becoming a father, a "heart of darkness," more or less hidden, in all men to whom the lives of little children are entrusted (Freud, 1913a). In some who do not also have the "good father" within themselves, these more frightening and sinister forces will erupt in a variety of pathological and pathogenic actions. The ways in which such disturbing impulses are enacted (whether, for example, directly in a father's own behavior, or through his influence on the mother's ability to take care of her children) will vary according to a host of individual factors. Some of these include: the father's physical presence and emotional closeness with the child; the child's developmental level and its implications for the nature and intensity of the father's importance to him or her; the mother's impact on the father-child dyad and on the family climate as a whole; and, of course, other more characterological features of the specific man. Their effects will also differ for similar reasons; that is, according to the degree and manner in which a child is primed, both individually and epigenetically, to experience his or her father's presence and to have recourse to other caretakers to fill in for a father who is failing that child. Paternal failures may be active "sins," as it were, of commision, or more "passive" omissions in parenting, as in the notorious epidemiological problem of father absence.

Yet, in one way or at one time or another, in fact or in fantasy, fathers may be guilty of some variant of psychic infanticide, some kind of abuse, or "soul murder," to borrow from Shengold (1978) and from the memoirs of Schreber (1903), brutalized by his father (Niederland, 1959a, 1959b). Laius, Oedipus' father, was one of its first would-be perpetrators. He may be seen as an embodiment of a veritable web of paternal disease and its terrible consequences, offering himself as a prototype or paradigm of the "*bad* father."

It is to Laius' forgotten story, itself embedded in a whole generational history of children betrayed, to which I now turn. At times, I shall seem to treat him as if he were a real person with an unconscious rather than a figure concocted by the collective imagination; for this violation of the metaphor, I hope I may be excused. Nor am I a classicist; my aim is to exploit the myth and make of it a psychological parable of the darker dealings between fathers and sons.

The myth of Oedipus, the son, is also the story of Laius, the father. Laius is destiny's cruel and indeed capricious human agent. Oedipus, the unwitting patricide, has also narrowly escaped infanticide. If Oedipus forces himself to play out the role of prime actor in his tragedy (and he does so initially for noble reasons, for the general good), he has remained the passive victim not only of some abstract fate, but also of his father. Finally, the son Oedipus is himself a father and, generally, a good one. Indeed, the whole legend can be viewed as a portrayal of *parenthood* (Ferenczi, 1912, 1933), both in its aspiring, nurturing, almost selfless aspects (Oedipus himself) and as a breach of deep personal trust, a blind and sinister corruption (Laius). It is a corruption, moreover, born of generations past and continuing on, breeding guilt and fouling the lives of future children (Oedipus' cursed and fratricidal sons, Eteocles and Polynices).

Freud and the Oedipus Myth

Freud drew on Sophocles' *Oedipus Rex*, of course, in illuminating the secrets of neurotic symptoms and dreams. Written within a week of the anniversary of his father's death in 1896, a letter to Fliess conveys Freud's excitement at the discovery of what he later would dub the "oedipus complex" (Freud, 1910, p. 170):

> I have found love of the mother and jealousy of the father in my own case too, and now believe it to be a general phenomenon of early childhood. . . . the gripping power of *Oedipus Rex*, in spite of all the rational objections to the inexorable fate that the story presupposes, becomes intelligible. . . . Every member of the audience was once a budding Oedipus in phantasy. [1950, pp. 223–224]

Two years later, in *The Interpretation of Dreams*, Freud (1900) formalized the casual allusion, discerning in the tragedy a metaphorical rendering of the conflictual fantasies of the child and of the adult's unconscious mental life. He was to make of Oedipus a new myth, the shibboleth on which his future psychoanalysis would stand or fall. He wrote:

Oedipus, son of Laius, King of Thebes, and of Jocasta, was exposed as an infant because an oracle had warned Laius that the still unborn child would be his father's murderer. The child was rescued, and grew up as a prince in an alien court, until, in doubts as to his origin, he too questioned the oracle and was warned to avoid his home since he was destined to murder his father and take his mother in marriage. On the road leading away from what he believed was his home, he met King Laius and slew him in a sudden quarrel. He came next to Thebes and solved the riddle set him by the Sphinx who barred his way. Out of gratitude the Thebans made him their king and gave him Jocasta's hand in marriage. He reigned long in peace and honour, and she who, unknown to him, was his mother bore him two sons and two daughters. Then at last a plague broke out and the Thebans made enquiry once more of the oracle. It is at this point that Sophocles' tragedy opens. The messengers bring back the reply that the plague will cease when the murderer of Laius has been driven from the land. . . .

The action of the play consists in nothing other than the process of revealing, with cunning delays and ever-mounting excitement—a process that can be likened to the work of a psycho-analysis—that Oedipus himself is the murderer of Laius, but further that he is the son of the murdered man and of Jocasta. Appalled at the abomination which he has unwittingly perpetrated, Oedipus blinds himself and forsakes his home. . . .

. . . His destiny moves us only because it might have been ours—because the oracle laid the same curse upon us before our birth as upon him. It is the fate of all of us, perhaps, to direct our first sexual impulse towards our mother and our first hatred and our first murderous wish against our father. Our dreams convince us that that is so. King Oedipus, who slew his father Laius and married his mother Jocasta, merely shows us the fulfilment of our own childhood wishes. . . . The contrast with which the closing Chorus leaves us confronted—

> . . . Fix on Oedipus your eyes,
> Who resolved the dark enigma, noblest champion and most wise.
> Like a star his envied fortune mounted beaming far and wide:

> Now he sinks in seas of anguish, whelmed beneath a raging tide.
>
> —strikes as a warning at ourselves and our pride, at us who since our childhood have grown so wise and so mighty in our own eyes. Like Oedipus, we live in ignorance of these wishes, repugnant to morality, which have been forced upon us by Nature, and after their revelation may all of us well seek to close our eyes to the scenes of our childhood. [1900, pp. 261-263]

And to the sins of our fathers, I would add.

The veracity of Freud's formulations has been attested to repeatedly in clinical practice over the more than eighty years which have followed. Children, sons especially, harbor murder in their hearts, however benign their fathers in actual fact. And, as adults, they suffer anxiety, guilt, and conflict as a consequence of their hidden sensuality and malevolence. Much of the drama's power to move its audience to pity and terror resides in its resonance with the onlooker's own unwanted and repressed childhood wishes and his identification with the hero.

Yet it is remarkable that Freud should have ignored Laius' active part in the drama, and that all but a handful of analytic authors after him (Ferenczi, 1912, 1933; Rank, 1912, 1932; Reik, 1920; Kanzer, 1948, 1950, 1964; Licht, 1952; Devereux, 1953, 1963; Rascovsky and Rascovsky, 1968; Michels, 1971; Rosner, 1977; Erikson, 1980; Grunberger, 1980; Sheleff, 1981) should have failed to fill in the gaps. The blind spots are reminiscent of Oedipus' own assumption of the entire burden of guild for the drama's tragic events, as if exculpating the dead father altogether.

In a note appended to the dream book when he was fifty-five, older and an established father himself, Freud may have touched on these forgotten themes when he remarked on the "constantly gnawing wishes of a man who is growing older. . . . for youth" (p. 476). A dream, eight years later, that his son had been wounded at the front he subjected to "deeper analysis" and discovered the "concealed impulse . . . which might have found satisfaction in the dreaded accident to my son: it was the *envy which is felt for the young by those who have grown old, but which they believe they have completely stifled*"

(p. 560; my italics). Freud had, first of all, to find the unconscious in himself before he would trust its veracity. The trouble is: insights of this kind were not integrated into the general psychoanalytic developmental theory, which remained essentially a psychology of sons and their filial conflicts (Mahl, 1982).

Prehistory

It is clear that even Sophocles' play itself portrays a terrible resonance between Oedipus' deeds and Laius' acts. By extension of the metaphor, the character of Laius and his role in his son's fate imply that a father's motives and actions constitute at least one precondition for, or "releasor" of, the Oedipus complex (Spitz, 1965; Lorenz, 1966), certainly in its most aggressivized and pathogenic forms.

Furthermore, the Greek audience to whom Freud refers would have heard the drama within the context of an oral history of the myth and a series of now-fragmentary written documents (including works by Homer, Hesiod, Pindar, Praxilla, and Aeschylus, and such epics as the *Oedipodeia* and the lost *Thebaid* [Rose, 1928; Licht, 1952; Tripp, 1970; Dover, 1978]). Indeed, the play served as a ritual catharsis for the Greeks, who knew perhaps as much about Laius as about Oedipus. They knew of his genealogy and legacy, his own history of expulsion and suffering, the misdeeds he committed long before Oedipus' appearance on the scene, the *hubris* or trespass for which the oracle was his punishment.

Without its prehistory, Oedipus' story might remain mysterious and apparently unmotivated. Ultimately, behind *Oedipus Rex* lies a generational saga which depicts an ominous convergence of impulses and misapprehensions, an articulation of object worlds between father and son which ends in mutual disaster. From the ethical or moral point of view, the fundamental responsibility for this, the tragedy, must fall on the former, the adult father, as the more sentient and powerful of the two. Taken as analytic allegory, the chronicle portrays the "Oedipus complex" not merely as a four-year-old's psychic fiction but also as an outcome of generations of "bad parenting."

Laius and Oedipus were direct descendants of Cadmus, founder of the city later named Thebes. As in the famed curse upon the House of Atreus, Cadmus' line also had been blighted by crimes against nature. With these as a background, the terrible tragedy which was to consume the father and his legendary son was played out. These original sins involved not fathers at first, but rather mothers and sons. Insofar as they set in relief the relations then prevalent between them, they may help explain Laius' filicidal disposition.

Mount Cithaeron, near the city of Thebes, on whose slopes Oedipus, fresh from the womb, was left to die, had witnessed a breach of parenthood, a crime against nature, long before the infant's birth. King Cadmus had several daughters, among them Semele and Agave. Semele lay with Zeus, their union producing a son Dionysus, the ambisexual sybarite of the Greek Pantheon. The Thebans disputed Semele's claims to divine insemination, and when she was killed by lightning because of her wish to see Zeus, the father, in his true form, her son Dionysus was denied his birthright, the status of a god. Orphaned and forced to wander Greece (like Laius and Oedipus after him), Dionysus returned to Thebes to exact his revenge. His hedonism and demonic charisma infected the city's women, who became his Bacchanalian followers or Maenads.

Among the women was Semele's sister Agave. Agave had a son, the Spartan Prince Pentheus. Straining in his display of martial masculinity, he energetically persecuted Dionysus' crazed disciples in an effort to suppress their bisexuality, lustfulness, and savage abandon. But Pentheus' vain war with instinctuality came to a hideously ironic conclusion. According to Euripides' *The Bacchae*, intrigued by the Dionysian mysteries in spite of himself, dressed in women's clothing, Pentheus spied upon the Maenads. Having mistaken his golden wig for a lion's mane and him for a cub (the paranoid distortion is telling), Agave and the other women murdered him in the glens of Cithaeron, dismembering the body and ripping off Pentheus' head. Hence Thebes first filicide at a mother's hands.

Where Oedipus was able to solve the riddle of the Sphinx, the mystery of life, it seems that Pentheus may have succumbed, despite his masculine protest, because of his ignorance of his own instinctuality, specifically his bisexuality. Disavowing desire, he fell prey to what Kanzer (1964) and Devereux (1953) would later describe as the emasculating, murderous power of the preoedipal and phallic mother. In her grasp, this first son was effeminized, castrated, and destroyed.

But Oedipus escaped her reach only then to fall victim to an indifferent (if oedipal) mother and, above all, to an ignorant, weak, authoritarian, and, by all accounts, homosexual father. He was a father who had much in common with his would-be forebear, Pentheus.

Laius, the Father

As a baby, Laius himself had been subjected to abandonment and persecution. His father, Labdacus, the ruling Theban king, died when he was a year old, leaving Laius to the care of his mother. When his uncle usurped the throne, Laius was expelled and forced to wander Greece before he could return to Thebes to reclaim his kingship. In the meantime, however, he himself seems to have displayed that same constellation of characteristics which modern-day clinicians and researchers associate with father absence. If the anachronisms can be pardoned, Laius' misdeeds and delusions can be taken as "evidence" of: disturbances in gender identity and sexual orientation; problems with impulse control; unmodulated aggressivity; cognitive and intellectual impairment; and pathological narcissism (Biller, 1968, 1969, 1970, 1971, 1974; Stoller, 1968; Santrock, 1970a, 1970b, 1972; Herzog and Sudia, 1973).

First of all, almost all versions of the legend point to the Theban monarch's pederasty, which he was credited with having "invented," according to Licht (1952), Devereux (1963), and Dover (1978). Pedophilia was, of course, a notorious commonplace among the Greeks. It found its way into the gymnasium and those rites of passage which sexualized the older male's dominance of the boy and the latter's induction into masculinity, his infusion of manliness through submission.

Slater (1971) and others have further underscored the sadomasochism and the misogyny implicit in the Greek men's homosexuality, their devaluation of women. Loving boys and men, the Greeks sought to controvert the influence of the pre-Hellenic matriarchy and to escape their embittered mothers and wives (Kanzer, 1950; Devereux, 1963). These women, in their turn, retaliated for their husbands' indifference to and subjugation of them by avenging themselves upon their boys, sexually and aggressively overwhelming them. These sons then responded as their fathers had and fled them for the company of males, where as adults they enacted the abuses suffered passively as their mothers' playthings. Hence, Agave's Dionysian filicide, which figures as the first parental horror in the House of Cadmus, may be symbolic of the relations then prevalent between mothers and sons.

Laius' life as a boy with his mother was an uncharted chapter in the legend, of course. What happened after this, in Laius' adulthood, however, was well known, having been chronicled by poets and dramatists, and indicates that he carried common practice beyond the bounds. While visiting Pisa, Laius kidnapped and sodomized Chrysippus, the beautiful illegitimate son of his host, King Pelops. The erotism of the act, the pedophilia proper, was not a crime in the Hellenic scheme of things; but the overbearingness and violence were; Laius' kidnapping and rape were bona fide transgressions.

They infuriated the father, Pelops. He cursed Laius and, together with the Olympians Zeus and Hera, condemned him to remain for a long time childless and/or then to be both murdered by the son he eventually conceived and replaced by him in his wife's bed. (The versions vary somewhat.) Thus, the famous oracle, sealing the destinies of father and son, did not spring into being as a matter of happenstance. Rather, it bespoke revenge—a retaliation for violations perpetrated by a man so caught up in his sadomasochistic desires that he is oblivious to a boy's needs. Oedipus is fated to *avenge* Chrysippus, his alter ego.

If Pelops' life history is considered as well, then his curse may also be seen as an act of self-vindication; for he was himself aggressively and sexually abused as a child. Tantalus, his father, had chopped him up and served him for dinner to his guests, the gods, who took pity on the hapless boy. Thrown into a cauldron, his body knitted together, all save a shoulder, which had been eaten by Demeter and which was replaced by a beautiful one of pure ivory. The god Poseidon fell in love with young Pelops, with his shoulder especially—always an object of cannibalistic attraction, according to L. Shengold (personal communication)—and abducted and used him sexually. Not once did Pelops the man inveigh against his earthly or his divine patrons, cruel though they were to him as a boy; but Laius' betrayal of his hospitality and analogous indiscretions toward his son excited Pelops' vengeful wrath (Bunker, 1952; Kott, 1974).

Various versions of the myth link Oedipus directly with Chrysippus, the two of them shadowing each other through time. In some, Oedipus also falls in love with the boy and kills his father in a duel for him. In other renditions, the homosexuality may be more latent or, better, implicit. Laius does not simply endure years of barrenness but rather, fearful of the oracle's prophecy, of his own accord abjures intercourse with Jocasta. Sexually starved, her wishes to be a mother also frustrated, she finally intoxicates and then seduces her otherwise abstemious husband, conceiving with him their fateful son.

Whatever the real and symbolic connections between the victims Oedipus and Chrysippus, Laius did intrude pitilessly into the life of his son and in *this* sense "raped" him and robbed him of innocence. Responding to the prophecy of death with abject, self-serving *terror* and self-inflating *sadism*, the father visited upon the child, his heir, an expulsion akin to that which he had suffered, but worse by far in its totality.

When Oedipus was born at last, Laius ordered the infant's ankles to be pierced with a spike. It was a stigma which indicated that there was something *wrong* with the *child*, and one which Oedipus carried with him throughout his life and from which he derived his name ("swell-foot"). Pinioned so that he could not crawl, the baby boy was to be left to the desolation and elemental violence of the mountain where he was to have died. As if a neonate could crawl! If it can be said that Laius is a creature of the "heat-oppressed brain," a fabrication of the oedipal imagination, so too is Laius' representation of his son a "dagger of the mind," a misshapen product of *his* paranoia, bespeaking a hideous projective identification on the part of the father.

Only the "kindness of strangers" saved the infant Oedipus. Jocasta's messenger handed the wounded baby to a shepherd, who brought him to King Polybus and Queen Merope of Corinth—Oedipus' adoptive parents. (The parallels with the deprived rich children of our own times and their redemption through benevolent servants and therapists are striking, as are the ultimate meaning, function, and origins of the family romance implicit in the tale.)

It has been said repeatedly that there can be no sadism without masochism (Freud, 1915). What did it mean for a man who loved boys to torture and kill his own son? In this vein, Devereux (1953) has interpreted the attempted infanticide as a self-castration on Laius' part, a sacrifice of manhood bespeaking his primitive desire to be a woman. Even Oedipus' incestuous liaison with Jocasta, Devereux believes, might represent an erotized access of sorts to Laius' bed and his forsaking affections.

Whatever the masochistic and homosexual submission which may be read into a father's persecution and sacrifice of a son (Abraham and Isaac come to mind), Laius' first cruelty toward his baby remains basically an act of manifest *evil.* In a certain sense, it needs no further interpretation, no psychologizing. In its own right the deed serves to climax an intricate allegory, encapsulating a whole complex of delusion and moral failure.

There is, first of all, Laius' monumental and multidimensional *narcissism,* the psychological bedrock of his *hubris,* as the Greeks called it. Above all, Laius thinks of himself. The oracle has named him as the sole victim of destiny; it is his personal survival alone which is at stake. Thus, the blatant selfishness of the would-be murder contrasts with other near or actual sacrifices of children portrayed in folklore and mythology and manifest in wars, where the collective or individual fathers at least make some pretense to a higher purpose.

Such self-absorption compromises clarity of vision, endowing the world with one's own intentionality and omnipotence. Not only is the intended infanticide self-serving, it is also misguided, again feeding into the fatal trespass which is at the core of the tragedy. Laius reacts to the prediction of his inevitable death as if he could, in fact, defy nature and live forever. Oedipus knows better. He responds to the Sphinx's question, "What walks on four legs in the morning, two in the afternoon, three in the evening?" by answering, "Man, in the morning fresh and joyful of hope, in the evening weak and broken." Man must pass through the life cycle, age, and eventually die. Loveless and prideful, also blind to destiny, Laius fails to understand this intimation of mortality—at least insofar as it applies to him. Yet he becomes, as Licht (1952) put it, just such a deluded "pitiable creature" (p. 135). In this sense, too, he is very different from the son who, unjustly victimized, blinded and maimed though he may be, openly betrayed by his father and his sons, will still find solace in his care for others and an informed redemption in old age and death.

The further, indeed the tragic, irony is that in endeavoring to deny death, Laius hastens and ensures his demise. His egocentricity and brutality make an alien and an enemy of a potentially loving, dutiful son, so that the prophecy of patricide becomes *self*-fulfilling. One might speculate whether Oedipus would *in reality* have slain a father known to him.

It is a biological truism that physical life requires death. Moreover, psychological parricide is also inevitable. In assuming more and more their independent responsibility, their "paternality of self" (Erikson, 1950), children are fated to usurp parental functions and eventually to do away with their parents. Even in social institutions like the Hindu joint family (Kakar, 1978), which are autocratically governed by elders, the realities of obsolescence, senescence, and death find recognition in those ritual disengagements whereby once powerful householders cede their material goods and secular authority for the begging bowl of the wandering holy man.

Greek mythology and drama offer analogous social cautionaries (Devereux, 1963) and promises of spiritual release; but the castration implicit in this accession may be and will have been too much for some men to bear. For them, the blush and promise, the inevitable brashness of youth are excruciating reminders of their own frailty and finitude. Then, as now, men made magical and often tyrannous efforts to undo the passing of the generations by attempting to create an illusion of personal immortality, by acting to render of the young subservient reflections or "clones" of the self, or by simply oppressing or destroying them. Laius does all of this. And notwithstanding his contrasting virtues, Oedipus shows the effects: profound neglect as an infant, and thus as an adult a sense of discontinuity, lost origins, and identity confusion, and these despite his visionary powers.

Along with his profound selfishness, Laius betrays a readiness to *jealousy*, which is probably a legacy of his own (one might say) oedipal childhood (and a by-product of homosexual desires). If the augured murder is the father's, as well as the son's, so too is the incest, projected onto the child and future rival. Laius' refusal to satisfy Jocasta sexually, his apparent impotence and infertility, and, by inference, his horror of women seem to call his masculinity into doubt and may have made him especially vulnerable. After all, as Jocasta later tells Oedipus, "How many men, in dreams, have lain with their mothers? No reasonable man is troubled by such things." But Laius was troubled, profoundly so, not only because of the oracle, one might imagine, but possibly because he remembered his own childish "dreams" and their untimely fulfillment in the death of *his* father and exclusive possession of his mother. And is it her desires and their enactment which he fears, recollecting his mother, and then projecting her onto Jocasta? In this sense, Laius' "Laius complex" may represent a transfiguration of his own childhood "oedipal constellation" and its only half-unwanted realization.

Even more primitive, "oral," and, indeed, preoedipal elements may come into play in a *possessiveness* like that of Laius—the wish of a man to have his woman totally, as if she were the mother of infancy, to devour her and to cast aside all other comers. Unmediated by the presence of a father, such demandingness can remain unrestrained and unchallenged, eventuating in the childishness of an imperious adult. As Freud (1930, 1933) implied, no doubt recollecting his own childhood, the love of a mother for a son (or for any child) is often without parallel. It easily equals in intensity romantic love in its ascendance and, quite probably, surpasses it once infatuation has worn into a more everyday mutuality. If a father of such a child is insecure in his relation to his wife; if, by virtue of narcissism and lovelessness, he is unable to share and derive pleasure from a mother's joy in her children; if he is possessed of an overweening sense of entitlement—such a father may treat a son (or daughter) as a threat. Unable to identify with his father, he cannot discover his love for the dyad of mother and child and assume his role as its guardian. Without a father, he is left with an inadequate awareness of temporality; for he does not recognize that his wife will once again be his, just as the typical mother is seen to reassert her loyalty to her husband, his father, when early childhood comes to a close. Depending on his moral sensibility, an unfathered and infantile father may be moved to deprive mother and child of each other, demanding absolute loyalty and obeisance from the woman, even at the expense of her maternal rights and obligations. Laius, lacking a father and thus a template for the development of conscience, was morally wanting as well.

Another possible current suggests itself in this regard, though this is not so directly evident in the myth itself. This has to do with the rivalry not for mother but rather for the *child* and for the close bond between them, the "dual unity" (Mahler, 1974; Mahler, Pine, and Bergman, 1975). Were Laius a real person rather than a figure of the collective imagination (and how often the analyst errs on the side of literalization!), who knows how he would have reacted to Jocasta's birthing or suckling of her son after years of frustrating abstinence, impotence, or infertility? One may speculate: was the exclusion too much to bear, the last straw which broke him, broke them all? A man's *envy of child and mother*—and perhaps this word "envy" is more apt than jealousy—may take the form of an indiscriminate spitefulness in which everyone loses. As already noted, Devereux (1953) has suggested that the attempted murder of Oedipus represents a rageful self-castration, bespeaking Laius' underlying wishes to be a woman and perhaps, I might add, a mother (Jacobson, 1950; Van der Leeuw, 1958; Herzog, 1982b; J. M. Ross, 1982a).

Whatever the motives which can be inferred, Laius demanded that Jocasta give up her baby. Like so many children today, Oedipus was spiritually and actually deserted by *both* mother and father. The abandonment of him was encompassing, as I have said, an expulsion from the family far exceeding mere "father absence." Were it not for the real-life family romance (Freud, 1909b), Oedipus would not have survived.

Finally, there is Laius' imperious *violence,* his greatest and most pervasive *hubris,* according to Licht and other authors. Initially, Laius tries to disown direct responsibility for his actions, by making other people and the whims of nature the agents of destruction. Thus he commands *Jocasta* to hand her baby to the *servant* for the *mountain* to dispose of. At first his aggression is supposedly motivated by self-preservation, though its excess is without even this justification, as I have indicated in noting the sadism of the act.

Later, in the encounter at the crossing of the highways, the cruelty and domination become undeniably and entirely gratuitous. Even here, Laius would try to escape responsibility as well as the dangers of direct confrontation. Acting out of pride alone, he orders his charioteer and groom to humiliate and strike the first blows against the stranger-son who stands in his way. He engages the youth directly only when he has no choice; for Laius is, throughout, a *coward*. It is this untrammeled, dastardly, and wanton aggression which the hero Oedipus *must* answer, rising to the challenge and at last killing the king, "killing them all."

By and large, boys and men tend to be inherently more aggressive than women. In fact, children, phallic little boys especially, act to elicit what appears to be an almost instinctive aggressive behavior from fathers and other adult men. Challenging and provoking them, inviting them to roughhouse, they seek to enact the competitiveness so necessary to masculine development. Indeed, without this kind of actual aggressive interplay, boys may not know the limits of both their own and their father's durability. Untested, their aggression will intensify and fester into what is experienced as a frightening well of seemingly pure destructiveness. Hence, the unconscious violence and projected castrative urges of so many men deprived of "adequate," strong fathers; hence, perhaps, Laius' own unfettered hostility, fearfulness, paranoia, and sexual uncertainty.

The well-adapted father and other men rein their power and check their inherent pugnacity. They confine expressions of hostility and sadism to teasing and overpower children only when they must, when the genuine demands of discipline and development call for restraint. Love and instinctual inhibition offset and modulate their aggression.

There may even be an instinctive basis to parenting. The mere presence of the young moves many men and women to rise above the past and above character and to be gentle and take care. Oedipus himself is such a man (as I shall show below). Even among animals, it has been established that the foreshortening of the juvenile face and ritualized gestures of submission serve to inhibit attacks on the part of the older males (Lorenz, 1966).

Some men, whose conscience is severe and whose drives are particularly pressing, may overcompensate and become as if inexplicably and excessively guilt-ridden—obsessively remote or perhaps depressed, in order to spare their children (Zilboorg, 1931). But, in others, like Laius, defects in instinctual "neutralization" are compounded by moral deficits. These give rise to intemperance and harsh impulsivity and to frank failures in fatherliness which defy the thrust of adult development. Such men may parade their power to hide their infantile fears and fixations, give vent to their unalloyed hostility, and murder, abuse, ridicule, or otherwise injure their own offspring. The effects here seem almost self-evident.

Oedipus, the Son

Yet, precisely what is the impact on Oedipus of his father's anxious and relentless self-absorption and aggressivity? This proves to be as various and contradictory as human nature is complex. The several versions of the myth each depict, in fact, a different Oedipus, incarnations perhaps of the possibilities inherent in different individual constitutions.

In the more disheartening renditions, Oedipus reenacts the sins of his malevolent and vindictive father. Oedipus' own homosexual rivalry with and ultimate submission to Laius has already been touched on. In other accounts, he is said to have engaged the king openly in a mortal combat for Jocasta's favors, with the implication that the patricide—or at least the regicide—was willful, rather than unwitting. Fragments of a lost epic, the *Thebaid,* and Sophocles' last play, *Oedipus at Colonus,* indicate that Oedipus himself cursed his own sons because they slighted him. Lacking the empathy of Antigone, his generous and self-sacrificing daughter, he doomed them to be fratricides (although Homer, Hesiod, and Pindar do not corroborate this identification with the aggressor [Tripp, 1970]). In the end, there remains the deed. For this, Oedipus, according to the moral absolute, must be condemned.

Yet, there also is the Oedipus of *Oedipus Rex,* with which the modern commentator, like Freud, is more familiar. From the play's beginning to its denouement, untainted or remorseful, Oedipus remains, in the words of the Chorus, "noble, great and powerful," more good than bad, and unswervingly courageous.

He is also a man more "sinned against than sinning." As Jocasta puts it:

> My child was *doomed* to kill him;
> and my child—
> Poor baby!—it was my child that died first.

An error of fact, perhaps, but one whose irony is its emotional truth: Oedipus was cast from innocence as from his mother's arms. What he endured apart from her, what wrenching agony and felt chaos fueled the baby's cries in the wilderness are beyond the adult's empathy, as mysterious as the emotional storms of infancy, and the first elements of failed expectation and miasmic mistrust. The later incest only further undoes the secure relation of mother and child.

In fact, Oedipus rises above fate. As Erikson (1980) seems to imply, he stands at his best as the lofty and poignant opposite of his base father. His tragedy testifies to the resilience of the individual and of that individual's capacities for fidelity, love, and care in the face of fate, of those outer and inner misfortunes and cruelties which threaten his integrity.

Oedipus is a virtuous son. Unsettled by the vague hints of a drunken friend that Merope and Polybus are not his real parents, nonetheless he flees Corinth upon hearing the terrible prophecy lest he happen to harm those whom he loves and to whom he is so grateful. There are, to be sure, unconscious motives to the contrary—evident in his failure to integrate the two pronouncements and his paradoxical decision to eschew the safety of his adoptive home. Like so many adopted children, Oedipus is driven. He is haunted by his severed origins, searches for them, and is inexorably drawn to his past during his adolescence (Blos, 1963; Rosner, 1977).

Perhaps it is Polybus' and Merope's goodness which he has exploited in constructing his own sentience—transmuting their love into personal honor and devotion. As an adult man, Oedipus is as faithful to those with whose care he is entrusted as he was to the "parents" who tended him. "My children" are his and the play's first words, echoed again and again as he attempts to unearth the causes of the plague and to discover the murderer. He owes his first duty not to himself, but to others: Thebes ravaged by disease, the "pallid children laden with death who lie unwept in the stony ways." And Oedipus has assumed their trust not because he simply inherited the city, but rather because he has won it—by virtue of his adult achievements. He is a caretaker, a healer, a man of knowledge.

One of these accomplishments has to do with his grasp of the mysterious paradoxes of life. His is an intelligence foreign to the father. Oedipus' virtue is informed, his search for truth relentless. In every sense, Oedipus, unlike his father, strives to assume the total responsibility for his thoughts and deeds.

But here's the rub, Oedipus' first tragic flaw. Lacking a father, Oedipus must father himself and, in more senses than one, is the "fathering son." His enforced precocity, consequent pride, and inability to depend on others make him refuse any mentorship other than his own, even that of the sage Teiresias, who embodies his fate.

A second and related flaw resides in Oedipus' monomaniacal thirst for knowledge at all cost to himself, the near arrogance implicit in his uncompromising integrity and ultimate self-immolation. He tortures himself with the "flooding pain of memory never to be gouged out." Oedipus, noble and "mighty," perspicacious as he is, does what he chooses, acts from the heart, and would know and see all that he can. There is a certain, perhaps "phallic" narcissism (Edgcumbe and Burgner, 1974), even aggression, in all of this. His virtue is dangerous. It is reminiscent at times of Freud—Freud the conquistador; "hawk" to the "hens" who once tutored him, as Breuer put it (Jones, 1953, p. 242); and of a rationalistic and haughty perfectionism whereby comprehension is believed to conquer all. Oedipus, like Freud, has little regard for those defenses and illusions which protect most men from themselves.

Oedipus' rage, insufficiently modulated and repressed, can overwhelm him. Most of all, however, it is the relentless violence of his *guilt* which destroys him. The harshest consequences are internal and self-initiated. Conscience and filial duty move Oedipus to flee the safety of his adoptive home Corinth—and, paradoxically, bring down the calamity on him. Concern and then guilt, less and less rational, drive his dangerous inquiry. It is his growing, as yet inexplicable, and unbearable guilt and the effort to expel it which provoke Oedipus' most uncharitable moments: his persecutory anxiety with regard to Creon; his character assassination of Teiresias; his selfish relief at the news of Polybus' death; the identification implicit in these acts, and in his later condemnation of his sons, with Laius' paranoia and aggression. And it is the searing white light of the final inescapable revelation of himself as parricide which moves him to plunge into his eyes the dead Jocasta's brooches, which long ago he must have undone, loosening her robes in preparation for their incest.

Oedipus' self-destruction is monumental, his remorse remorseless. Insight, he learns too late from Teiresias, can be *blind*—and the blindness is a "tight cell of misery blank to light and sound . . . a dark agony beyond all recollection."

But is this really so, are the crime and the shame Oedipus'? "Ah, Cithaeron" are the words which conclude Oedipus' self-excoriating utterance. The infanticide is ever present, the original sin. True, Oedipus slew the father and slept with the mother, as must the four-year-old in his imagination and in play; all men, as Jocasta has said, have dreamed such things. The son *is* guilty of dark intentions and bad deeds. But the parents acted of their own volition and not from unwitting impulse alone, raised their hands in deplorable violence, and struck out.

Certainly, Jocasta is condemned: she is an "unspeakable mother" and becomes a suicide. Had she not killed herself, Oedipus might have avenged himself on her. But what of Laius?

In Sophocles' first play, not one word is uttered against him. Perhaps his actual death has been punishment enough. But not one word? Must Oedipus, innocent that he was, bear entirely the culpability? It seems he must. The "sins of the fathers" are indeed his, loosed like demons, detached from their sources, and transfigured as the child's own. "Ghosts," the dramatist Ibsen called them, "the Furies," Erinyes, or Eumenides, according to the Greeks, who further personified, and partly disguised, them as angry female figures from the matriarchal past.

Freud and Oedipus Again

Once more the blind spots of Freud, who seems to have been so identified with Oedipus (Rosner, 1977), are remarkable. Not only did he omit mention of Laius' crimes in his summary of the myth itself, as I have already indicated. Once he ceded his seduction theory, Freud also tended to ignore or to exculpate quite actively his patients' and subjects' fathers in the case histories (Freud, 1905, 1909a, 1909c, 1911). Repeatedly Freud neglected the familial reality lurking behind their psychopathology, ascribing the latter mainly to the workings of fantasy.

As Freud turned his conceptual eye ever inward, he came to see in symptoms the workings of unconscious fantasy. Such fantasy he viewed as essentially predetermined, probably universal, and quite possibly inherited from the collective past (Freud, 1913b, 1918, 1927, 1930). Hence he illumined psychic reality, a momentous discovery whose great truth is still indisputable. But in theory, if fortunately not in practice, Freud and many analysts after him often also tended to overlook the intricacies of the interpersonal climate in which such imaginings take root and grow. If, for example, the imagined genital seductions reported by his late adolescent and adult patients were most often fantastical, nonetheless they probably served to screen other problematic traits, rumored activities, and actual behavior on the part of parents which excited and exploited the *pregenital* sexuality and aggression of the child. These *age-specific* seductions, Freud, lacking the hindsight of another half century of observational and clinical contact with children, failed to account for and accommodate in his developmental theory.

It is also clear that all men, even Freud or the legendary Theban king Oedipus (or King Pelops, for that matter), *need* their gods and fathers. And Freud, indeed, loved his dearly. At times sons and daughters will do almost anything—assume a remorse that is not theirs; emasculate, blind, and kill themselves; sacrifice or exploit their children—rather than dislodge the defensive and self-sustaining idealizations in which these imaginary and real patriarchs are ensconced. Need and guilt conspire in the exoneration of the father—the need for his protection, guilt as his internal proxy and as an ever-present protector. Freud (1933) himself put it this way in his dissection of the religious imperative:

> [The individual] harks back to the mnemic image of the father whom in his childhood he so greatly overvalued. He exalts the image into a deity and makes it into something contemporary and real. The effective strength of the mnemic image and the persistence of his need for protection jointly sustain his belief in God. [p. 163]

So compelling are these forces that they can defy all understanding to the contrary. Kafka, for example, wrote in his *Letter to His Father* of the latter's rasping indifference and helpless stupidity. Yet he could not free himself of its absurd consequences, the abiding and irrational remorsefulness which put him, like his protagonists, forever on trial. How could Oedipus, having glimpsed his father's fate, allow himself to see as well into Laius' murderous *heart?* Rather than embrace his most terrible of revelations, and the ontological upheaval, the despair which it would bring with it, he yielded to an identification with the aggressor's transgressions. He fell prey to the kind of hysterical identification, introjection of guilt, uncompromising self-prohibition, and propitiatory longing for a father's beneficence which, Freud (1909c, 1918) noted, lie at the heart of so much neurotic suffering. One might underscore obsessional neurosis in particular, and those alien yet unyielding obligations within the self which are its hallmark. Perhaps this is Oedipus' most apt "diagnosis."

Discovering the inner sources of the plague is but the first step in Oedipus' drama and purgation. It is only after he has come to recognize the *limits* of his responsibility as well in *Oedipus at Colonus* that he finds inner peace and release from suffering. In the end, self-blinded and self-exiled, nonetheless he is honored and shepherded by his daughters, especially his devoted Antigone.

Ultimately, Oedipus, the old man, is redeemed by none other than Theseus, slayer of the Minotaur to whom the young of Crete were offered up for the slaughter. Theseus, son of his utterly devoted father, Aegeus, King of Athens and himself a founding father of the great democratic tradition, is the civilized opposite of Laius, the fatherless and primitive autocrat. At last, through his grace and authority, Oedipus is freed.

Theoretical and Clinical Implications

Methodological advances in the last twenty-five years have realigned psychoanalytic perspectives on development. Where Freud reconstructed his adult patients' histories on the basis largely of their individual reminiscences, actings-in, and transference phenomena, relying on anecdotal glimpses of children, more modern observers—most of all Mahler—have amplified and refined his notions of development by way of direct systematic observation. Investigators have actually watched children grow within their families.

Babies, Spitz (1965) emphasized, are the only persons in a family without a past. Soon enough, however, they are fitted with one, that of their parents, into whose representational worlds they are assimilated. Children are then responded to according to predetermined images of what they will be and what they "are," in ways that demonstrably influence their behavior and their emerging sense of self. Such inputs become evident long before the consolidation of a child's self-boundaries, his or her demarcation of fantasy and reality, and the establishment of character. Thus, a parent's needs and inevitably distorted perceptions penetrate to the "basic core" (Weil, 1970), which lies at the heart of one's eventually more elaborate individuality. Personality does not come into being simply as a product of the dialectics of danger and desire alone.

In this spirit, other investigators have begun to chart some of the transactions of parent and child from the neonatal period (Brazelton, Yogman, Als, and Tronick, 1978), through infancy (Stern, 1974), toddlerhood (Mahler, Pine, and Bergman, 1970), and into adolescence (Shapiro, Shapiro, Zinner, and Berkowitz, 1977; Colarusso and Nemiroff, 1982; Esman, 1982). In a variety of parent training, early intervention, and outreach programs (Kestenberg, 1975; Samaraweera and Cath, 1982), pathology in the parents has been described along with its manifestation in various "dysparenting" phenomena, including asynchrony, incest (Kaufman, 1982), and abuse (Steele, 1970, 1982).

Such investigative and clinical applications of psychoanalytic principles lend further, dynamic meaning to Freud's conceptualization of the "complemental series" (1916–1917). They point to interaction effects wherein the individual's constitution affects his or her environment, and vice versa, establishing elaborate feedback patterns or resonances between the two. In other words, this work suggests that each particular child has his or her own significant part to play in his or her parents' lives. This role is very much a function of the particular child he or she is: premature or full-term, endowed or damaged, female or male, first or otherwise in the birth order.

This is so, we have also learned, because the parents are vulnerable. Prompted by Erikson's conception of the life cycle (1950, 1959, 1964), a number of psychoanalytic and psychological investigators have arrived at the notion of adult development. If adults develop at a slower rate and with less dramatic revolutions in psychic structure than children, nonetheless individuals evince discernible change, in the sense of both growth and deterioration, as they respond to the successive tasks and crises of adult life.

Critical among the latter are procreation and caretaking. Parenthood has been conceptualized as a developmental phase, or better, the climax—the rather protracted climax—of a lifelong developmental progression (Kestenberg, 1956; Benedek, 1959, 1970a, 1970b; J. M. Ross, 1977, 1979c; Gurwitt, 1982). Responding to the birth of children and to the high pitch of their developmental crises, parents—both mothers and fathers—may find themselves thrown into states of dynamic disequilibrium which awaken the past and thus activate progressive as well as hitherto concealed regressive trends. The potential for an outbreak of psychopathology is great, as indeed Freud (1913a, 1937) noted when he emphasized the vicissitudes of adult misfortunes, specifically, setbacks in procreative capacity, in compromising hitherto adaptive resolutions of neurotic conflict (and good analytic results). Forced to play out major parts in the parental drama, which they may unwittingly have set in motion, children are directly affected by a parent's conflicts and their expression within the family.

Psychoanalytic developmentalists have not surrendered the centrality of unconscious fantasy and intrapsychic conflict to the emphasis on external reality and simple interactionism proposed by the interpersonal school or the family systems advocates. Covertly, perhaps, however, they have been responding to the fruits of other forms of inquiry—notably, object relations theory—in concert with their own research. Thus, some analysts have come to view psychic reality and external transactions between people as repositories for each other. Each realm, "inner" and "outer," reflects, enriches, constrains, shapes the other, while both continue to evolve throughout the life cycle. The correspondences are never exact, of course; for the mediating processes of internalization alter externality according to defensive needs and developmental capacities, while other people accommodate to the individual only insofar as the flexibility of their character structures will allow.

There are few constants in this system of reverberating object worlds, and the theorist has created them mainly because it is taxing and perhaps conceptually impossible to do otherwise. If the more balanced view which has been unfolding lacks the elegant, often surprising, and dramatic simplicity of the original, more "classical" scheme of things, nonetheless it may point to a more "open system" which is truer to life, and thus more descriptively encompassing and accurate. It is less reductionistic, for heuristic conveniences remain poor substitutes for real people.

Perhaps most important are the clinical implications for prevention, for auxiliary work with parents, and for individual adult and child analyses. First of all, outside the analytic situation, in preventive work and collateral consultations with parents of child patients, clinical interventions are in need of more substantial theoretical, technical anchorage. For example, only by considering the interlocking inner psychologies of people close to one another can the clinician begin to identify and contend with the childhood bases, current precipitants, and ongoing consequences of an adult father's inner struggles, manifest problems, and parental failures. As one case in point, father absence need not be treated as a *fait accompli,* but most often can be dealt with as an ongoing dynamic condition in which the adult man's patterns of conflict and defense can be addressed more directly.

An explicit appreciation of parental and specifically paternal conflict and behavior also yields certain technical imperatives. One obvious issue has to do with the degree to which the actual or potential parenthood of our male analysands has been subjected to careful scrutiny. A more subtle but no less important matter is the fact that oedipal interpretations of transference and reconstructions may have been left incomplete and inexact. For example, to return to Laius and Oedipus, when the analyst attributes his patients' hostile images of their fathers *exclusively* to the projection of their own guilt-ridden aggressive urges, he may inadvertently help solidify a defense organization. A resistance is fostered in which genuine neurotic conflict serves to screen the starker, more archaic anxieties which are stirred when an individual discerns or even merely imagines the possibility of a parent's ambivalence toward him. Burdened with abiding guilt, nonetheless analysands may thus be spared the full realization that in the end they live alone in an objectively dangerous or at least inconstant world, and that they must survive unguarded by illusions of perpetual parental omnipotence and unequivocal goodwill. It is an understanding which is generally intolerable in childhood and which may foster all manner of disavowal, self-deception, and deviation, but one which for the adult becomes essential to an assumption of psychological freedom and realistic responsibility. At times, perhaps, the analyst's own double-edged countertransference struggles (Atkins, 1970; Grunberger, 1980) are at work in what may amount to a mutually *defensive* interpreting of oedipal fantasy in the face of the abject horror of intergenerational rivalry.

Even analytic work with children may not be immune from considerations of this kind. As long ago as 1935, Burlingham pointed to the "uncanny," indeed nearly "supernatural," intuition of the child into his or her parent's unconscious. Following her lead, in their paper on the genesis of psychic structure, Hartmann, Kris, and Loewenstein (1946) underscored a problematic responsiveness to a mother's, or father's, concealed hostility. The trouble is: with children, the strategic binds can be nightmarish. Whatever their abilities to extract or fabricate parental nurturance, infants remain relatively helpless. Exposed to their parents' indifference or cruelty, they may have to guard their illusions of protection symptomatically and characterologically. In contrast, the adult man, like Oedipus, a good son striving to be a good father, can begin to make of the past what he will.

Conclusion

As in the beginning, so in the end there remains the deed. For this, according to the moral absolute, Oedipus the parricide, like his filicidal, pederastic father before him, must be condemned. In this paper, I have attempted to interpret the Oedipus myth as a metaphor for the tragic "dialogue of the unconscious" (Ferenczi, 1933), which can take place between fathers and sons. My objective has not been to discharge the individual of responsibility for the more sinister ambitions of childhood, his Oedipus complex. Ultimately, such faults are still in ourselves. Quite the contrary, my aim has been to add to the great weight we must all bear. As adults, another constellation of deadly desire and terror is at work within us, affecting our lives and those with whose care we are charged. I refer to the "Laius complex."

REFERENCES

Abelin, E. L. (1971), The role of the father in the separation-individuation process. In: *Separation-Individuation,* ed. J. B. McDevitt & C. F. Settlage. New York: International Universities Press, pp. 229-252.

_______ (1975), Some further observations and comments on the earliest role of the father. *Internat. J. Psycho-Anal.,* 56:293-302.

_______ (1977), The role of the father in the preoedipal years. In: Panel: Parenthood as a developmental phase, rep. H. Parens. *J. Amer. Psychoanal. Assn.,* 23:154-165.

Anthony, E. J., & Benedek, T., eds. (1970), *Parenthood.* Boston: Little, Brown.

Atkins, N. B. (1970), The Oedipus myth, adolescence, and the succession of generations. *J. Amer. Psychoanal. Assn.,* 18:860-875. Chapter 12, this volume.

Benedek, T. (1959), Parenthood as a developmental phase. *J. Amer. Psychoanal. Assn.,* 7:389-417.

_______ (1970a), Fatherhood and providing. In: *Parenthood,* ed. E. J. Anthony & T. Benedek. Boston: Little, Brown, pp. 167-183.

_______ (1970b), Parenthood during the life cycle. In: *Parenthood,* ed. E. J. Anthony & T. Benedek. Boston: Little, Brown, pp. 185-206.

Biller, H. (1968), A note on father absence and masculine development in young lower class Negro and white boys. *Child Devel.,* 39:1003-1006.

_______ (1969), Father absence, maternal encouragement and sex role development in kindergarten age boys. *Child Devel.,* 40:539-546.

_______ (1970), Father absence and the personality development of the male child. *Devel. Psychol.,* 2:181-201.

_______ (1971), The mother-child relationship and the father-absent boy's personality development. *Merrill-Palmer Quart.,* 17:227-241.

——— (1974), Paternal deprivation, cognitive functioning and the feminized classroom. In: *Child Personality and Psychopathology*, ed. A. Davids. New York: Wiley, pp. 11–52.
Blos, P. (1963), The concept of acting out in relation to the adolescent process. *J. Amer. Acad. Child Psychiat.*, 2:118–143.
Brazelton, T. B., Yogman, M. W., Als, H., & Tronick, E. (1978), The infant as a focus in family reciprocity. In: *The Social Network of the Developing Infant*, ed. M. Lewis & L. Rosenblum. New York: Plenum, pp. 29–43.
Bunker, H. A. (1952), The feast of Tantalus. *Psychoanal. Quart.*, 21:355–372.
Burlingham, D. (1935), Child analysis and the mother. *Psychoanal. Quart.*, 4:69–92.
Cath, S. H., Gurwitt, A. R., & Ross, J. M., eds. (1982), *Father and Child*. Boston: Little, Brown.
Colarusso, C. A., & Nemiroff, R. A. (1982), The father in mid-life. In: *Father and Child*, ed. S. H. Cath, A. R. Gurwitt, & J. M. Ross. Boston: Little, Brown, pp. 315–327.
Devereux, G. (1953), Why Oedipus killed Laius: A note on the complementary Oedipus complex in Greek drama. *Internat. J. Psycho-Anal.*, 34:132–141. Chapter 7, this volume.
——— (1963), Sociopolitical functions of the Oedipus myth in early Greece. *Psychoanal. Quart.*, 32:205–214. Chapter 9, this volume.
Dover, K. (1978), *Greek Homosexuality*. Cambridge: Harvard University Press.
Edgcumbe, R., & Burgner, M. (1975), The phallic-narcissistic phase. *The Psychoanalytic Study of the Child*, 29:161–180.
Erikson, E. H. (1950), *Childhood and Society*. 2nd ed. New York: Norton, 1963.
——— (1959), *Identity and the Life Cycle*. New York: International Universities Press.
——— (1964), *Insight and Responsibility*. New York: Norton.
——— (1980), On the generational cycle. *Internat. J. Psycho-Anal.*, 61:213–223. Chapter 17, this volume.
Esman, A. (1982), Fathers and adolescent sons. In: *Father and Child*, ed. S. H. Cath, A. R. Gurwitt, & J. M. Ross. Boston: Little, Brown, pp. 265–274.
Euripides, *The Bacchae*. In: *Greek Tragedies*, ed. & tr. D. Grene & R. Lattimore. Chicago: University of Chicago Press, 1963, 3:189–258.
Ferenczi, S. (1912), The symbolic representation of the pleasure and the reality principles in the Oedipus myth. In: *Sex in Psychoanalysis*. New York: Basic Books, 1950, pp. 253–269. Chapter 2, this volume.
——— (1933), Confusion of tongues between the adult and the child. *Internat. J. Psycho-Anal.*, 30:225–230.
Freud, S. (1900), The interpretation of dreams. *Standard Edition*, 4/5. London: Hogarth Press, 1953.
——— (1905), Fragment of an analysis of a case of hysteria. *Standard Edition*, 7:3–122. London: Hogarth Press, 1953.
——— (1909a), Analysis of a phobia in a five-year-old boy. *Standard Edition*, 10:3–149. London: Hogarth Press, 1955.
——— (1909b), Family romances. *Standard Edition*, 9:235–241. London: Hogarth Press, 1959.
——— (1909c), Notes upon a case of obsessional neurosis. *Standard Edition*, 10:153–320. London: Hogarth Press, 1955.

_______ (1910), A special type of choice of object made by men. *Standard Edition*, 11:163–175. London: Hogarth Press, 1957.

_______ (1911), Psycho-analytic notes on an autobiographical account of a case of paranoia. *Standard Edition*, 12:3–82. London: Hogarth Press, 1958.

_______ (1913a), The disposition to obsessional neurosis. *Standard Edition*, 12:311–326. London: Hogarth Press, 1958.

_______ (1913b), Totem and taboo. *Standard Edition*, 13:1–161. London: Hogarth Press, 1955.

_______ (1915), Instincts and their vicissitudes. *Standard Edition*, 14:109–140. London: Hogarth Press, 1957.

_______ (1916–1917), Introductory lectures on psycho-analysis. *Standard Edition*, 15/16. London: Hogarth Press, 1963.

_______ (1918), From the history of an infantile neurosis. *Standard Edition*, 17:3–123. London: Hogarth Press, 1955.

_______ (1924), The dissolution of the Oedipus complex. *Standard Edition*, 19:173–179. London: Hogarth Press, 1961.

_______ (1927), The future of an illusion. *Standard Edition*, 21:3–56. London: Hogarth Press, 1961.

_______ (1930), Civilization and its discontents. *Standard Edition*, 21:59–145. London: Hogarth Press, 1961.

_______ (1933), New introductory lectures on psycho-analysis. *Standard Edition*, 22:3–182. London: Hogarth Press, 1964.

_______ (1937), Analysis terminable and interminable. *Standard Edition*, 23:209–253. London: Hogarth Press, 1964.

_______ (1950), *The Origins of Psycho-Analysis*. New York: Basic Books, 1954.

Grunberger, B. (1980), The oedipal conflicts of the analyst. *Psychoanal. Quart.*, 49:606–630. Chapter 18, this volume.

Gunsberg, L. (1982), A selected critical review of psychological investigations of the father-infant relationship. In: *Father and Child*, ed. S. H. Cath, A. R. Gurwitt, & J. M. Ross. Boston: Little, Brown, pp. 65–82.

Gurwitt, A. R. (1982), Aspects of prospective fatherhood. In: *Father and Child*, ed. S. H. Cath, A. R. Gurwitt, & J. M. Ross. Boston: Little, Brown, pp. 275–300.

Hartmann, H., Kris, E., & Loewenstein, R. M. (1946), Comments on the formation of psychic structure. *The Psychoanalytic Study of the Child*, 2:11–38.

Herzog, E., & Sudia, C. (1973), Children in fatherless families. In: *Review of Child Development Research*, ed. M. Caldwell. Chicago: University of Chicago Press, pp. 141–232.

Herzog, J. M. (1980), Sleep disturbance and father hunger in 18-to 28-month-old boys. *The Psychoanalytic Study of the Child*, 35:219–233.

_______ (1982b), Patterns of expectant fatherhood. In: *Father and Child*, ed. S. H. Cath, A. R. Gurwitt, & J. M. Ross. Boston: Little, Brown, pp. 301–314.

_______ Patterns of expectant fatherhood. In: *Father and Child*, ed. S. H. Cath, A. R. Gurwitt, & J. M. Ross. Boston: Little, Brown, pp. 301–314.

Jacobson, E. (1950), Development of the wish for a child in boys. *The Psychoanalytic Study of the Child*, 5:139–152.

Jones, E. (1953), *The Life and Work of Sigmund Freud*. Vol. 1. New York: Basic Books.

Kafka, F. (1919), *Letter to His Father*. New York: Schocken, 1953.

Kakar, S. (1978), *The Inner World: A Psychoanalytic Study of Childhood and Society in India.* New Delhi: Oxford University Press.

Kanzer, M. (1948), The "passing of the Oedipus complex" in Greek drama. *Internat. J. Psycho-Anal.*, 29:131–134. Chapter 5, this volume.

——— (1950), The Oedipus trilogy. *Psychoanal. Quart.*, 19:561–572. Chapter 6, this volume.

——— (1964), On interpreting the Oedipus plays. *The Psychoanalytic Study of Society*, 3:26–38. Chapter 10, this volume.

Kaufman, I. (1982), Father-daughter incest. In: *Father and Child,* ed. S. H. Cath, A. R. Gurwitt, & J. M. Ross. Boston: Little, Brown, pp. 491–508.

Kestenberg, J. S. (1956), On the development of maternal feelings in early childhood. *The Psychoanalytic Study of the Child,* 11:157–191.

——— (1975), *Children and Parents.* New York: Aronson.

Kott, J. (1974), *The Eating of the Gods.* New York: Random House.

Lamb, M., Ed. (1976), *The Role of the Father in Child Development.* New York: Wiley.

Leonard, M. R. (1966), Fathers and daughters. *Internat. J. Psycho-Anal.*, 47:325–334.

Licht, H. (1952), *Sexual Life in Ancient Greece.* New York: Barnes & Noble.

Loewald, H. W. (1979), The waning of the Oedipus complex. *J. Amer. Psychoanal. Assn.*, 27:751–756.

Lorenz, K. (1966), *On Aggression.* New York: Harcourt, Brace & World.

Mahl, G. F. (1982), Father-son themes in Freud's self-analysis. In: *Father and Child,* ed. S. H. Cath, A. R. Gurwitt, & J. M. Ross. Boston: Little, Brown, pp. 33–64.

Mahler, M. S. (1974), Symbiosis and individuation. *The Psychoanalytic Study of the Child,* 29:89–106.

——— Pine, F., & Bergman, A. (1970), The mother's reaction to her toddler's drive for individuation. In: *Parenthood,* ed. E. J. Anthony & T. Benedek. Boston: Little, Brown, pp. 257–274.

——— ——— ——— (1975), *The Psychological Birth of the Human Infant.* New York: Basic Books.

Michels, R. (1971), Student dissent. *J. Amer. Psychoanal. Assn.*, 19:417–432.

Neubauer, P. B. (1960), The one-parent child and his oedipal development. *The Psychoanalytic Study of the Child,* 15:286–309.

Niederland, W. G. (1959a), The "miracled-up" world of Schreber's childhood. *The Psychoanalytic Study of the Child,* 14:383–413.

——— (1959b), Schreber. *Psychoanal. Quart.*, 28:151–169.

Parens, H., reporter (1975), Parenthood as a developmental phase. *J. Amer. Psychoanal. Assn.*, 23:154–165.

Prall, R. C., reporter (1977), The role of the father in the preoedipal years. *J. Amer. Psychoanal. Assn.*, 26:143–162.

Rank, O. (1912), *Das Inzestmotiv in Dichtung und Sage.* Leipzig: Deuticke.

——— (1932), *Modern Education.* New York: Knopf.

Rascovsky, A., & Rascovsky, M. (1968), On the genesis of acting out and psychopathic behaviour in Sophocles' *Oedipus. Internat. J. Psychoanal.*, 49:390–394. Chapter 11, this volume.

Reik, T. (1920), Oedipus and the Sphinx. In: *Dogma and Compulsion: Psychoanalytic Studies of Religion and Myth.* New York: International Universities Press, 1951, pp. 289–332. Chapter 3, this volume.

Rose, H. (1928), *A Handbook of Greek Mythology*. London: Methuen.
Rosner, H. (1977), Oedipus and his cradle scars. Read at the fall meetings of the American Psychoanalytic Association. Chapter 14, this volume.
Ross, J. M. (1975), The development of paternal identity. *J. Amer. Psychoanal. Assn.*, 23:783-817.
_______ (1977), Towards fatherhood. *Internat. Rev. Psycho-Anal.*, 4:327-347.
_______ (1979a), Fathering. *Internat. J. Psycho-Anal.*, 60:317-327.
_______ (1979b), The forgotten father. In: *Psychosexual Imperatives*, ed. M. C. Nelson & J. Ikenberry. New York: Human Sciences Press, pp. 261-303.
_______ (1979c), Paternal identity. In: *On Sexuality*, ed. T. B. Karasu & C. W. Socarides. New York: International Universities Press, pp. 78-97.
_______ (1982a), From mother to father. In: *Father and Child*, ed. S. H. Cath, A. R. Gurwitt, & J. M. Ross. Boston: Little, Brown, pp. 189-204.
_______ (1982b), In search of fathering. In: *Father and Child*, ed. S. H. Cath, A. R. Gurwitt, & J. M. Ross. Boston: Little, Brown, pp. 21-32.
Ross, N. (1982), Domination-submission patterns in the patriarchal family structure. In: *Father and Child*, ed. S. H. Cath, A. R. Gurwitt, & J. M. Ross. Boston: Little, Brown, pp. 523-534.
Samaraweera, S., & Cath, C. (1982), Fostering the consolidation of paternal identity. In: *Father and Child*, ed. S. H. Cath, A. R. Gurwitt, & J. M. Ross. Boston: Little, Brown, pp. 543-556.
Santrock, J. (1970a), Paternal absence, sex-typing and identification. *Devel. Psychol.*, 2:264-272.
_______ (1970b), Influence of onset and type of paternal absence on the first four Eriksonian developmental crises. *Devel. Psychol.*, 3:273-274.
_______ (1972), The relation of type and onset of father absence to cognitive development. *Child Devel.*, 43:455-469.
Schreber, D. (1903), *Memoirs of My Nervous Illness*. London: Dawson, 1955.
Shapiro, E. R., Shapiro, R. L., Zinner, J., & Berkowitz, D. A. (1977), The borderline ego and the working alliance. *Internat. J. Psychoanal.*, 58:77-87.
Sheleff, L. (1981), *Generations Apart*. New York: McGraw-Hill.
Shengold, L. (1978), Assault on a child's individuality. *Psychoanal. Quart.*, 47:419-424.
Slater, P. (1971), *The Glory of Hera*. Boston: Beacon Press.
Socarides, C. W. (1982), Abdicating fathers, homosexual sons. In: *Father and Child*, ed. S. H. Cath, A. R. Gurwitt, & J. M. Ross. Boston: Little, Brown, pp. 509-521.
Sophocles, *The Oedipus Cycle*, trans. D. Fitts & R. Fitzgerald. New York: Harcourt, Brace & World, 1969.
Spitz, R. A. (1965), *The First Year of Life*. New York: International Universities Press.
Steele, B. F. (1970), Parental abuse of infants and small children. In: *Parenthood*, ed. E. J. Anthony & T. Benedek. Boston: Little, Brown, 1970, pp. 449-478.
_______ (1982), Abusive fathers. In: *Father and Child*, ed. S. H. Cath, A. R. Gurwitt, & J. M. Ross. Boston: Little, Brown, pp. 481-490.
Stern, D. N. (1974), The goal and structure of mother-infant play. *J. Amer. Acad. Child Psychiat.*, 13:402-421.
Stoller, R. J. (1968), *Sex and Gender*. New York: Science House.
Tessman, L. (1982), A note on the father's contribution to his daughter's ways of working and loving. In: *Father and Child*, ed. S. H. Cath, A. R. Gurwitt, & J. M. Ross. Boston: Little, Brown, pp. 219-238.

Tripp, E. (1970), *The Meridian Handbook of Classical Mythology*. New York: New American Library.

Van der Leeuw, P. J. (1958), On the preoedipal phase of the male. *Internat. J. Psycho-Anal.*, 39:112–115.

Weil, A. P. (1970), The basic core. *The Psychoanalytic Study of the Child*, 25:442–460.

Weissman, P. (1963), The effects of preoedipal paternal attitudes on development. *Internat. J. Psychoanal.*, 44:121–131.

Yogman, M. (1982), Observations on the father-infant relationship. In: *Father and Child*, ed. S. H. Cath, A. R. Gurwitt, & J. M. Ross. Boston: Little, Brown, pp. 101–122.

Zilboorg, G. (1931), Depressive reactions related to parenthood. *Amer. J. Psychiat.*, 10:927–962.

20

Oedipus and Jocasta: A Re-examination of Freud's Drama of Destiny

MICHAEL BROSS

[1984]

The concept of the oedipus complex occupies a central role in the theory of personality development advanced by Freud. His first speculations on this topic occurred in 1897, just over two years before the appearance of *The Interpretation of Dreams* (Freud, 1900), in a letter to Wilhelm Fliess:

> I have found love of the mother and jealousy of the father in my own case too, and now believe it to be a general phenomenon of early childhood. . . . If that is the case, the gripping power of *Oedipus Rex* . . . becomes intelligible. . . . the Greek myth seizes

---

An expression of gratitude is due to the female students in the "Modes of Expression and Interpretation" seminar in the Liberal Arts College at Concordia University, who, through their energetic enthusiasm for detailed discussion of the female figures in the *Odyssey* and *Oedipus Rex*, provided the stimulus for the reanalysis of Oedipus' mother presented here. A slightly modified version of this paper was read at the First Delphic International Psychoanalytic Symposium, Delphi, Greece, 1984.

> on a compulsion which everyone recognizes because he has felt traces of it in himself. [Freud, 1950, p. 223]

While this formulation actually represented a departure from Freud's earlier theory of parental seduction of children (see Freud, 1914), from here on he never abandoned the view outlined to Fliess and went on to elaborate it into a major component of his system. A more definitive version of it appeared in *The Interpretation of Dreams*:

> In my experience . . . the chief part in the mental lives of all children who later become psycho-neurotics is played by their parents. Being in love with the one parent and hating the other are among the essential constituents of the stock of psychical impulses which is formed at that time and which is of such importance in determining the symptoms of the later neurosis. . . .
>
> This discovery is *confirmed* by . . . a legend whose profound and universal power to move can only be understood if the hypothesis I have put forward in regard to the psychology of children has an equally universal validity. What I have in mind is the legend of King Oedipus and Sophocles' drama which bears his name. . . .
>
> . . . [Oedipus'] destiny moves us only because it might have been ours. . . . It is the fate of all of us, perhaps, to direct our first sexual impulse towards our mother and our first hatred and murderous wish against our father. [pp. 260–262; italics mine][1]

This summarizes the essential view Freud advocated and defended throughout the rest of his career and clearly shows that Freud saw in Sophocles' *Oedipus Rex* the prototypical expression of what he regarded as a universal phenomenon.[2] Indeed, in his later works the

[1]The word used by Freud is not "confirmed" but "supported" *(Unterstuezung)*. This is evidently another instance of an overly positivistic translation of Freud (see Bettelheim, 1982), although it makes little difference for the present argument, which simply establishes Freud's use of Sophocles' drama as evidence for this theory.

[2]The Greek title *(Oedipus Tyrannus)* has been rendered variously into English as *Oedipus Rex, Oedipus the King,* and *King Oedipus,* none of which convey the meaning of the Greek *Tyrannos,* which refers to the ruler and foremost authority of a self-contained political unit *(polis)* and is free of any overtones associated with the

oedipus complex, if anything, can be said to become more important. Thus by 1913 Freud, in the closing section of *Totem and Taboo,* reaches the conclusion "that the beginnings of religion, morals, society and art converge in the Oedipus complex," an insight which he sees as fully harmonizing "with the findings of psycho-analysis, namely, that the nucleus of all neuroses as far as our present knowledge goes is the Oedipus complex" (pp. 156–157). In *Three Essays on the Theory of Sexuality* Freud (1905) is still more definite in that he unequivocally states (in a note added in 1920) that "the Oedipus complex is the nuclear complex of the neuroses, and constitutes the essential part of their content" (p. 226), and in *The Future of an Illusion* (1927) he elaborates on the relationship between religion and the oedipus complex: "Religion would thus be the universal obsessional neurosis of humanity; like the obsessional neurosis of children, it arose out of the Oedipus complex . . ." (p. 43).

Freud's theories and their influence on contemporary thought are far-reaching, and references to them can be found in diverse fields of study. So, too, his conceptualization of the Oedipus legend probably has made more people aware of and familiar with Sophocles' drama than that of any other writer. Not surprisingly, a considerable amount of literature has been generated on the correctness and validity of Freud's theoretical construct of the oedipus complex, a literature ranging from orthodox defenses of Freud's formulation through neo-Freudian revisions to outright rejections of it. This paper will not concern itself with these controversies, but will attempt to reexamine the literary source of Freud's inspiration and interpretation, a source which Freud uses so effectively and endows with the evidential force of having "confirmed" his hypothesis concerning the dynamic relation between parents and children, and to relate the results of this reexamination to some of his writings.

Freud's analysis of Sophocles' *Oedipus Rex* concentrates, like that of most commentators, almost exclusively on the figure of Oedipus, an approach quite understandable for anyone who has read or

English "tyrant." Since *Oedipus Rex* is used in the English translations of Freud, I have consistently referred to it by that name. For the citations from the play the literal translation by Gould (1970) has been used, and all citations have been checked against the standard Greek text (Jebb, 1885).

attended a performance of the play. It is a relatively compact drama of some 1,500 lines and moves at a very rapid pace; the action is constantly focused on Oedipus, so that none of the other three supporting characters—Jocasta, Oedipus' mother and wife; Creon, her brother; and Teiresias, the blind prophet—can compete for attention with the protagonist. Oedipus' relentless search for his true origin and identity while being propelled toward a disastrous end engrosses the audience and leaves little respite for calm and reasoned analysis. This, undoubtedly, is one of the reasons why *Oedipus Rex* has been hailed as one of the most moving and perfect dramas of all time. Another reason for its preeminence can be traced to Sophocles' superb craftsmanship, which has led to such accolades as that it represents a "combination of a faultlessly articulated plot with the profoundest insights into human motive and circumstance" (Watling, 1947, p. 14), and that it is "so consummate . . . that we need not pain ourselves to adjust to any preconceived ideal what a drama should be" (Waldock, 1951, p. 143). Critics from Aristotle to the present are virtually unanimous in describing it as the foremost example of skillful plot construction, outstanding character portrayal, and striking depiction of ineluctable fate.

Notwithstanding the general consensus that Oedipus dominates the play, a reflective examination of the other figures around him shows that for a more complete understanding of the drama's plot and power they, too, demand careful consideration. Freud's approach to the drama especially requires a scrutinizing look at Jocasta and her relationship to Oedipus. She represents the other half of Oedipus' destiny, her fate being inextricably intertwined with his, and it is somewhat puzzling that Freud, aside from passing references, never examined and interpreted her role in the drama vis-à-vis Oedipus. In his only remark concerning Jocasta's state of awareness in her incestuous marriage he describes her as the "deluded mother and wife" (Freud, 1916–1917, p. 330), in effect assigning to her an unsuspecting and inactive role as far as the true foundation of her relationship with Oedipus is concerned.

This is at variance with some of Freud's own observations, which, were they applied to Jocasta, would lead to the conclusion that she must have had some share in the state of affairs between Oedipus and herself. First, Freud states, several chapters prior to his description of Jocasta as the deluded mother-wife, that "parents themselves frequently stimulate the children to react with an Oedipus complex" (p. 207), and further on noted again that parents often awaken the Oedipus complex in a child (p. 333). Second, insofar as the ignorance of Jocasta is concerned, in one of his last remarks on the oedipal situation, Freud (1940) declared that "the ignorance of Oedipus is a legitimate representation of the unconscious state" (p. 191).[3] While this argument does not imply that a state of ignorance is a necessary component of the oedipal situation, if it applies to Oedipus it must apply also to Jocasta: her "delusion" too represents a screen for an unconscious desire or state. This line of reasoning, together with the implicit assumption in Freud's approach to the drama, that Sophocles—consciously or unconsciously—constructed a theatrical representation of oedipal dynamics as Freud interpreted them[4], warrants a detailed analysis of the role of Jocasta as created by Sophocles.

It is unfortunate that of the over one hundred twenty plays Sophocles wrote only seven have come down to us intact; of the others only fragments remain. Three of the complete plays deal with the house of Oedipus: *Antigone* (c.441 B.C.), *Oedipus Rex* (c. 427 B.C.), and *Oedipus at Colonus,* which was presented posthumously (c. 401 B.C.). The Theban legends obviously represented a rich source of material for Sophocles (as they did to all Greek tragedians) and, given the wide acquaintance of the Athenian audience with these stories, he was able to add specific features to these legends (or subtract them) to suit his purposes. Every Greek playwright must have relied on the audience's familiarity with the subject matter of their plays; otherwise it would not have been possible for them to use the technique of *in media res,* to make allusions to thematic interconnections which could exist only if the main outline of the plot was known, and, particularly in Sophocles' *Oedipus Rex,* to present instances of great dramatic irony.

With this in mind, it is of no small importance to note that Sophocles' handling of the story of Oedipus represents, in many

[3]In the original German the semantic identification of ignorance *(Unwissenheit)* and unconscious *(Unbewusstheit)* is much stronger than in English.

[4]See Freud (1900): "In what I have written I have only attempted to interpret the deepest layer of impulses in the mind of the creative writer" (p. 266).

aspects critical to the play, an original treatment of the legend. The earliest version of the Oedipus legend known to us comes from Homer, and there one finds considerable divergence from Sophocles. In the *Iliad* (XXIII:679–680) Oedipus is referred to as having been entombed in Thebes, with funeral games held in his honor, suggesting that he reigned and died in Thebes as king. The *Odyssey* (XI:271–280) provides a capsule summary of the legend:

> I saw the beautiful Epikaste, Oidipodes mother,
> who in the ignorance of her mind had done a monstrous
> thing when she married her own son. He killed his father
> and married her, but the gods soon made it all known to mortals.
> But he, for all his sorrows, in beloved Thebes continued
> to be lord over the Kadmeians, all through the bitter designing
> of the gods; while she went down to Hades of the gates, the strong
> one,
> knotting a noose and hanging sheer from the high ceiling
> in the constraint of her sorrow, but left him who survived her
> all the sorrows that are brought to pass by a mother's furies.
> [Lattimore, 1951]

From these reports in the Homeric epics it is apparent that at least three features differ in the ancient legend and Sophocles' rendering of it: (1) Oedipus was not exiled from Thebes, as in *Oedipus Rex*. Instead he continued to reign, even after the revelation that he and Jocasta were not man and wife but mother and son, and received a royal burial at his death. (2) It is extremely unlikely that he and Jocasta had any children in the original myth, seeing that "the gods soon made it all known." This is supported by another source, Pausanias, who reports that in the epic *Oedipodia* Oedipus had a second wife after Jocasta, a woman named Eurygania who was the mother of his children (Jones, 1965, pp. 195–197).[5] (3) The self-inflicted blinding of Oedipus is absent in Homer, appearing for the first time in Aeschylus' *Seven against Thebes,* where the chorus informs us that "with patricidal

[5]An extensive discussion of the sources of the Oedipus legend is to be found in Graves (1958, pp. 371–377).

hand" Oedipus "reft himself of eyes" (Grene, 1956, p. 118). As Sophocles is said to have studied under Aeschylus, it is a reasonable assumption that he followed Aeschylus on this point. These departures from the original legend, then, constitute innovations made by the dramatist that provided the occasion for the insertion of new material into the plot to demonstrate originality and, perhaps even more so, to evoke specific associations and images in his audience, where the success or failure of this material (and with it the drama) would depend very much on how the audience reacted to it as judged against the traditional sources.

These considerations, which establish that Sophocles intentionally attributed novel features to Oedipus and Jocasta, in conjunction with the analysis of *Oedipus Rex* given below, open up a possible perspective on Jocasta different from the one offered by Freud. While Freud sees in her the deluded mother-wife of Oedipus, I would like to propose that there is a considerable amount of intimation, along with unmistakable clues and hints, in the text and the context of Sophocles' drama to support the thesis that Jocasta must have known all along, or at least have suspected, virtually to the point of certainty, that Oedipus was her son.

In approaching the drama, one is struck by the fact that Sophocles placed three crucial features of the Oedipus legend outside the action on the stage, features related only in the dialogue: his exposure as an infant, the killing of Laius, and his marriage to Jocasta. This makes the drama more compact, but it also places these events outside the audience's immediate focus of attention, preventing any direct confrontation with these features and their implications for the characters and dynamics of the play. Yet, they provide an essential background against which Oedipus and, particularly for the purpose of the present argument, Jocasta must be evaluated.

If one pauses and reflects on the figure of Jocasta at the time of Oedipus' return to Thebes, the following picture emerges: Jocasta as a young bride had had her firstborn and, until her marriage to Oedipus, her only child taken away, its feet pierced, to die of exposure on Mount Cithaeron. What mother would forget this? Then, about eighteen years later a young man comes to Thebes who has pierced feet—a matter of public record in Thebes (ll. 1031-1036)—and who, according to Jocasta, is in appearance "not unlike" Laius (l. 743). This collection of coincidences must surely have stirred Jocasta's memory; what were the probabilities that a stranger would (1) have pierced feet and be called Swollen-foot (Oedipus), (2) look like Laius, and (3) be the age of Jocasta's son had he lived. These circumstances alone suggest that Jocasta should have strongly surmised the possibility that Oedipus was her son. For the audience, because these events are not presented on the stage, no immediate need exists to entertain these implications and they are soon pushed aside, if reflected on in the first place, by the need to concentrate on the continuing action.

The unfolding of the relationship between Jocasta and Oedipus is also revealing. Jocasta is first mentioned in the play during Oedipus' quarrel with Creon (ll. 557–580), where it is made clear that Oedipus is beholden to Jocasta and is ready to fulfill her every wish. As she makes her appearance on stage (l. 634) it is at once established that she is in a position to tell both Oedipus and Creon to break off their argument and go inside:

> Wretched men! What has provoked this ill-
> advised dispute? Have you no sense of shame
> with Thebes so sick, to stir up private troubles?
> Now go inside! And Creon, you go home!
> Don't make a general anguish out of nothing! [ll. 634–638]

Jocasta's opening lines, a rebuke really, set the tone for her relationship with Oedipus. They have an undeniably maternal ring, an impression reinforced by the chorus (ll. 678–679), who evidently too see Jocasta as the authoritative voice; they expect her to settle the argument as a matter of course, through her influence over Oedipus. This aspect becomes still more pronounced further on, when Jocasta repeatedly tries to persuade Oedipus not to believe in oracular predestination; here the nature of her arguments indicate that she expects, perhaps due to similar encounters in the past, to hold sway over Oedipus.

The first time she attempts to convince Oedipus to disregard the oracles occurs after he has told her of Teiresias' accusation that it was he who slew Laius. As proof of the fallibility of oracles she relates the story of Laius' oracle, that he was to be killed by his own son; but since their son was set out to die and Laius was slain by robbers (the plural is important here), clearly the oracle was false (ll. 707–725). When she then goes on to relate to him the account given by the lone survivor of Laius' party, she does so in a way that cannot be true:

> . . . When he returned and saw
> you had the power of the murdered Laius,
> he touched my hand and begged me formally
> to send him to the fields and to the pastures
> so he'd be out of sight, far from the city.
> I did. Although a slave, he well deserved
> to win this favor, and indeed far more. [ll. 758–764]

Now if the servant returned *after* Oedipus had become king, he could not have brought the news of Laius' death *before* Oedipus' arrival in Thebes. But that he actually did return beforehand is indicated by Jocasta herself (ll. 735–737); and, of course, he must have, as Oedipus could have ascended to the throne only if it was known that Laius was dead.

This contradiction in Jocasta's lines can be regarded, as it has by some, as a foreshortening on Sophocles' part,[6] but weighed against his almost universally acknowledged craftsmanship and faultless plot articulation, it seems more likely that we are dealing here with an instance of deliberate misdirection, perhaps for both Oedipus and the audience: Jocasta does not want Oedipus to look too closely into these matters, especially since by now his suspicions that he might have killed Laius have been aroused (ll. 738–748). Her desire to leave this issue as clouded as possible is underscored by the circumstance that she knows all along that the survivor of Laius' escort is the same

[6]Waldock (1951, p. 155), argues that Sophocles compressed the scene because it makes for good drama. One can agree that it is effective drama, but for different reasons. Jebb (1885, p. 85) also comments on this apparent inconsistency in Jocasta's lines and suggests a reading of "when he had come thence, and [afterwards] found *not only* was Laius dead, *but* you were his successor" (ll. 758–759). While this insertion of "afterwards" and the change in inflection would remove the inconsistency in Jocasta's story, it is very difficult to believe that Sophocles would not have written it that way himself had this reading been his intention.

herdsman to whom the infant Oedipus was given to abandon on Mount Cithaeron, a dual identity she never reveals to Oedipus; and when the chorus discloses his double role, she actively tries to convince Oedipus not to pay any attention to this information (ll. 1051–1057).[7] Later on, as it is brought to light through the testimony of the herdsman that he had received Oedipus from her and not from Laius (ll. 1171–1172), the potential of a collusion between Jocasta as a young mother, fearing for the life of her son, and the herdsman in assuring the survival of Oedipus suggests itself. This conjecture would go a long way to explain why Jocasta found the herdsman deserving "indeed far more" and readily sent him away from the city. Implied, too, in these lines is the distinct likelihood that the herdsman had recognized Oedipus as the slayer of Laius, though no indication is given that he told Jocasta.

Here again, these inferences readily follow from the text, but because the audience, or the reader, is by now captivated by Oedipus' dramatic *tour de force,* no time or occasion presents itself to make them.

The second time Jocasta tries to convince Oedipus to abandon belief in prophecy comes after he has told his story up to the time of his coming to Thebes. At this point in the play his only remaining hope that Laius was not the man he killed hangs on the circumstance that the survivor claimed it was robbers and not a single man who committed the deed (ll. 842–846). In reply Jocasta, now clearly concerned that the herdsman might change his testimony, once more renounces the veracity of oracles, for which this time she is forcefully chastised by the choral ode that follows her rejection of prophecy (ll. 848–872).[8]

Perhaps because of the chorus' admonitions, or due to her mount-

[7]This dual identity is likely another dramatic invention by Sophocles; it is found nowhere else. He must have had a definitive purpose in mind for this, as no pressing need exists to assign to the herdsman this double role. Since in Oedipus' questioning of the man no use is made of it, the significance of the dual identity appears to relate to Jocasta. The numerous references throughout the play to Mount Cithaeron would have provided a strong association for the Greek audience with another tragic mother-son legend. It was there that Agave, Jocasta's great-grandmother, partook in the killing of her son Pentheus in a Bacchanalian frenzy.

[8]On l. 855 Jocasta's apprehensions of Oedipus' painful self-discovery are foreshadowed in the Greek text; she refers to him as "dystenos" (poor boy). This is the same name she calls him as she makes her exit (ll. 1071–1072) to kill herself.

ing concern about Oedipus' inquiries, the next scene offers a stark contrast in Jocasta's apparent attitude; she now curries the favors of the gods, appearing as a suppliant, pleading for release from the oracular curse (ll. 911–924). Her motivation at this point seems to be a mixture of fear and opportunism, with one dominant objective: she wants Oedipus to realize the consequences of his persistent queries: "For Oedipus excites his soul too much / . . . he will not judge / the present by the past, like a man of sense." That her entreaties to the gods do not arise out of true piety or conviction becomes obvious the moment the messenger from Corinth arrives with the announcement of the death of Oedipus' adoptive father (Oedipus is still unaware that he had been adopted). Jocasta instantaneously forgets her prayers and, rather than offer thanks, she now discredits the auguries of oracles for the third time, seeming at last to persuade Oedipus of the fallibility of prophecy (ll. 945–ff).

Alas, Oedipus is not totally convinced; he still fears the part of the oracle that foretold that he would share his mother's bed. Jocasta's retort is remarkable:

> What's there for a man to fear? The realm of chance
> prevails. True foresight isn't possible.
> His life is best who lives without a plan.
> This marriage with your mother—don't fear it.
> How many times have men in dreams, too, slept
> with their own mother! Those who believe such things
> mean nothing endure their lives most easily. [ll. 977–983]

This passage warrants close consideration, for it not only discloses important aspects of Jocasta's character and outlook on life but also conveys a sense of her apperception of the situation, and of how she proposes to come to terms with it, urging Oedipus to follow her lead. "Chance prevails," "foresight" is useless, it's best to live "without a plan": these are the utterances of someone who has little regard for convention, displays no reverence for divine ordinance, and is capable of transgressing the limits of ordinary propriety. They express a philosophy of "do as you wish," and since chance rules all, with no just rewards or punishment, Oedipus has nothing to fear, regardless of the truth or falsity of his apprehension concerning his mother.[9] Freud (1900) cites the second part of her statement as an important key to the tragedy and thinks Jocasta is trying to console Oedipus by telling him to pay no heed to dreams of a mother's bed, as such dreams mean nothing (p. 264). In light of the picture of Jocasta that emerges from the present analysis, an alternative, equally plausible interpretation suggests itself: Jocasta is telling Oedipus that even if these things happen, "those who believe such things mean nothing endure their lives most easily."

Her blandishments are, however, of no avail. She realizes from Oedipus' questioning of the messenger that he is going to discover his real origin (ll. 1026–1046). As the crucial last piece to the puzzle, the herdsman and lone survivor of the attack on Laius' party is summoned; as he is about to appear, she makes her last desperate attempts to stop Oedipus from proceeding further. Her pleas leave little doubt that her sole objective at this point is to prevent Oedipus from knowing that he is her son (ll. 1055–1073). But the flow of the action is by now beyond her influence; failing to reverse the inevitable course of events she, like the Sphinx, kills herself as Oedipus solves his riddle.[10]

Sophocles' timing of her death and its aftermath also pose some problematic questions. Would she have taken her life had Oedipus discontinued his investigation? Jocasta commits suicide only when she is absolutely certain Oedipus will learn she is his mother. Were she genuinely overwhelmed by guilt, one would expect she would have killed herself sooner, for even in the overt action of the drama it is clear that she knows the truth well before Oedipus does; but it is only when the shame of public exposure looms that she ends her life. Then, too, what is meant by Oedipus "asking for his spear and for his wife-no-wife" (ll. 1255–1256), after he has realized that Jocasta is his mother? It is left for the audience to wonder, if it can find the time at this emotionally charged moment, whether Oedipus had come to the

[9]The reference to marriage *(nympheumata)* in l. 980 is a presumption. The oracle as Oedipus told it (l. 791) predicted only that he would be his mother's lover (*michthenai*: literally, "to copulate with").

[10]Reik (1920) and Rank (1941) have pointed to several similarities between Jocasta and the Sphinx. Gould (1970) finds that the Greek text of the Oedipus play suggests that the Sphinx killed young men by way of a sexual embrace.

conclusion that Jocasta should have known he was her son, and whether now, shattered by his realization of their incestuous bond, he intends to extract violent redemption.

How far is this interpretation of Jocasta compatible with what Sophocles might have intended? *Oedipus Rex,* like all Greek tragedies, was written for an annual religious festival, and it is a reasonable assumption that Sophocles' primary interest was not the personal fates of Oedipus and Jocasta. Rather, the underlying theme of the drama deals with the attainment of self-knowledge. Apollo's oracle at Delphi, the most important religious shrine in Greece at the time, figures prominently in the play; its most renowned teaching was the command "Know thyself."[11] Oedipus' quest for his true identity exemplifies this precept and is Sophocles' way of showing that the Delphic utterance was an imperative to be obeyed even at the peril of personal suffering and destruction. Not that Sophocles did not have considerable freedom in drawing his characters—on the contrary, it is here that he excels in his penetrating observations of human nature. And he devoted the same assiduous care to depicting his supporting characters that he lavished on his protagonists.

An examination of Sophocles' female characters reveals a great deal of nuance: his heroines are no stock characters but run the spectrum from simple devotion to their male companions, as Tecmessa in *Ajax,* to the all-consuming desire for revenge of Electra. In the case of Jocasta I have advanced the hypothesis that her ostensible role as an unsuspecting mother may well be a facade, that Sophocles embedded enough information and ambiguities in *Oedipus Rex* to allow for this interpretation. A clear hint for the implausibility of Jocasta's ignorance is given by Sophocles when he has the chorus ask the rhetorical question "How, how could your parental/furrows, wretched man,/endure you silently so long?" (ll. 1210–1212). Had he wanted to project her as the deluded mother-wife Freud sees in her, a look at another female in a wifely role, Deianira in *The Women of Trachis,* shows that he could convey the attributes and mannerisms of misguided innocence in a convincing fashion.

[11]An excellent discussion of the religious aspects of *Oedipus Rex,* along with their significance to Sophocles' contemporaries, is found in Knox (1957), a work that provides an outstanding analysis of Athenian society at the time. For a critical examination of the role of oracles in Sophocles' dramas see Kirkwood (1958).

It would be of more than passing interest to see how Sophocles handled similar mother-son motives in other plays. We know that he wrote at least two other dramas that dealt with the topic of the attraction between mother and son, and it is unfortunate that of these only fragments survive. One of them is the *Odysseus Acanthoplex*, in which Telegonus, Odysseus' son by Circe, kills his father and marries Penelope.[12] The other is his *Phaedra*. From this drama a fragment exists that enables us to gain some insight into Sophocles' understanding of the dynamics of mother-son bonds. The fragment reads: "Sons are the anchors of a mother's life" (Pearson, 1917, p. 302). More than 2,000 years later, Freud (1933) echoes this sentiment: "A mother is only brought unlimited satisfaction by her relation to a son . . ." (p. 133).

What remains to be shown is how far the picture of Jocasta delineated here is compatible with Freud's conceptualization of the oedipal situation. Freud had in his earliest writings stressed the role of parents or parent figures as the seductive agents who stimulate the first erotic interests in the child, but then abandoned this view in favor of his formulation of the oedipus complex. As indicated earlier, in subsequent works the Oedipus complex was assigned a pivotal role both in Freud's psychological explanations of individual neuroses and in his metapsychological studies. It was considered the prime mover of virtually all human cultural endeavors. Inasmuch as Freud based his oedipal theory on his self-analysis and what he claimed was confirmatory support from *Oedipus Rex*, a good test of the viability of the hypothesis that the mother figure plays a more active, and perhaps knowing, role in the oedipal drama than Freud allowed would be to examine one of his case histories in which a psychoneurotic state is hypothesized to have been engendered by the oedipus complex.

Among the better known of Freud's case histories is that of Little Hans (1909). Although Freud himself did not psychoanalyze the boy, he reproduced the case history verbatim and provided an extensive introduction together with detailed commentary in his analysis of the case. Freud sees in Hans "a little Oedipus who wanted his father 'out

[12]Bates (1940) discusses the *Odysseus Acanthoplex*. The legend has it that Telemachus, Odysseus' son by Penelope, subsequently marries Circe. It is not known whether Sophocles made use of this disguised situation of double mother-son incest.

of the way' . . . so that he might be alone with his handsome mother and sleep with her" (p. 111). He regards the case history as confirmation for his theory of the oedipus complex, claiming that it represents both "a type and a model" for the origin of neuroses due to infantile complexes (p. 147). Numerous references to this case are found in Freud's writings citing it as a primary instance of empirical support ("irrefutable proof") of his oedipal hypothesis (Freud, 1908, p. 214).

An observant reading of Hans' case history, however, shows unmistakably that Hans' mother exhibited seductive as well as domineering attitudes toward him.[13] It is she who "cannot resist taking him into bed with her," (Freud, 1909, pp. 23, 39, 90), who tolerates his presence in the bathroom (p. 63), and who issues the first threats of castration (pp. 7–8). In discussing the case, Freud is aware on one level of the troublesome role of the mother and points out in a footnote that parents themselves are often responsible for stimulating sexual feelings in their children (p. 23).[14] It is therefore surprising when in his evaluation of her part in the genesis of Hans' neurosis Freud exempts her, like Jocasta, of any culpable interaction with her son:

> We must say a word, too, on behalf of Hans' excellent and devoted mother. His father accuses her, not without some show of justice, of being responsible for the outbreak of the child's neurosis, on account of her excessive display of affection for him and her too frequent readiness to take him to bed. We might as easily blame her for having precipitated the process of repression by her energetic rejection of his advances. . . . But she had a predestined part to play, and her position was a hard one. [pp. 27–28]

This forthright absolution, with its reference to predestination, evokes resonances of Sophocles' drama of destiny and thus closes the circle back to Freud's original source of inspiration.

[13]This case history has been reanalyzed in much greater detail by Fromm (1970, pp. 90–100).

[14]To be sure, the role of the other parent, the father figure in the oedipal situation, a topic on which Freud advanced some strong theories, has been omitted in this paper, as this would require a separate analysis that would take the present argument too far afield.

Given Freud's own identification with Oedipus, together with his tendency to vindicate the role of the mother (notwithstanding his frequent allusions to her potential role as catalyst in the oedipal situation), one would expect that Freud might elaborate on the possible seductive force of an oedipal mother in some of his less technical writings, especially those he regarded as psychoanalytic explorations into areas normally beyond the reach of first-hand documentation, where he would not feel as constricted by the need for strict logical consistency. One instance where we can find such an "uncensored" description of an oedipal mother is in Freud's speculative reconstruction of the psychosexual development of another great figure he identified with, Leonardo da Vinci.[15]

Published just one year after the case history of Little Hans, *Leonardo da Vinci and a Memory of His Childhood* (1910) must be ranked among Freud's more speculative ventures; seldom did he try to adduce so much on so little. Relying on the sole childhood recollection recorded by Leonardo, along with publicly known biographical data (dates, paintings, expense accounts, etc.), Freud wrote this work with the express purpose of demonstrating how his theories were capable of rebuilding from such scanty evidence the psychological make-up of the artist (Freud, 1925a, p. 65). As it turns out, Freud does much more than that; he also reconstructs for the reader, quite conjecturally, many character traits of Leonardo's mother, about whom virtually nothing is known except her probable name (Caterina).

As his point of departure Freud takes the childhood memory of Leonardo, in which a vulture flew into his crib and struck him "many times with its tail against my lips" (p. 82).[16] This reminiscence from the cradle, a fantasy or daydream perhaps, Freud uses to establish, via successive symbol substitutions, the equation of vulture and mother. He then completes his argument by restating Leonardo's recollection as "My mother pressed innumerable passionate kisses on my mouth" (p. 107). On the assumption that Leonardo probably spent the first

[15]The affinities of Freud for great men of the past are legend. Concerning his identification with Oedipus, to give but one example, Puner (1947) tells how Freud early in his career, upon completing an analysis, showed the patient Ingres' picture *Oedipus Solves the Riddle of the Sphinx* (p. 162).

[16]Leonardo's memory actually refers not to a vulture but to a kite. For a discussion of this, see the editorial note preceding the essay.

years of his life alone with his mother, Freud further speculates that he had been left "to the tender seductions of a mother. . . . [and] kissed by her into precocious sexual maturity" (p. 131),[17] this being the determining factor of Leonardo's fate and later privations, a theme Freud develops in his analysis of Leonardo's paintings. Thus, in his discussion of the Mona Lisa Freud endorses the view that her expression is representative of archetypical female sensuality and seductiveness and that the famous smile must have been one of Leonardo's earliest memories of his mother.[18]

To fully convey the extent to which Freud developed the theme of the oedipal mother in Leonardo's essay, one can do no better than to quote him at some length. The emphatic understanding Freud extends to Leonardo's mother at the beginning of the quote indicates that here, too, he readily extenuates his conceptualization of her, just as he had done for Jocasta and the mother of Little Hans.

> In her love for her child the poor forsaken mother had to give vent to all her memories of the caresses she had enjoyed as well as her longing for new ones; and she was forced to do so not only to compensate herself for having no husband, but also to compensate her child for having no father to fondle him. So, like all unsatisfied mothers, she took her little son in place of her husband, and by the too early maturing of his erotism robbed him of a part of his masculinity. A mother's love for the infant she suckles and cares for is something far more profound than her later affection for the growing child. It is in the nature of a completely satisfying love-relation, which not only fulfils every mental wish but also every physical need; and if it represents one of the forms of attainable human happiness, that is in no little measure due to the possibility it offers of satisfying, without

[17]This description of Leonardo's mother is strikingly similar to that of Little Hans' mother: "No doubt the ground [for Hans' phobia] was prepared by sexual overexcitation due to his mother's tenderness . . . " (Freud, 1909, p. 22).

[18]Freud (1910) concurs with the view that the smile of the Mona Lisa is the "most perfect representation of the contrasts which dominate the erotic life of women; the contrast between reserve and seduction, and between the most devoted tenderness and a sensuality that is ruthlessly demanding—consuming men as if they were alien beings" (p. 108).

reproach, wishful impulses which have long been repressed and which must be called perverse. [pp. 116–117]

Freud's unwillingness to implicate the mother figure in the oedipal situation is consistent with his later assertion that there is a difference in the superego and hence in the standard of ethical norms of women and of men. He regarded the female superego as lacking those elements which erect the absolute, impersonal barriers required in order not to be influenced by feelings or to yield to primary affections and commit actions deemed socially unacceptable (Freud, 1925b, pp. 257–258). This view readily lends itself to the generalization that for females the prohibitions surrounding the incest taboo would also be less strongly developed than in the male.

The steadfast reluctance to interpret the role of the oedipal mother with the same diligent emphasis that characterizes Freud's analysis of the oedipal child precluded the integration of these two factors into a more complementary theory of the Oedipus complex, a theory that would not place the paramount psychological focus on the child, with little or no consideration given to the potentiality of an erogenic influence emanating from the mother. One of the great insights provided by Freud into the psychosexual development of children is precisely the observation that the child will invariably make the mother the object choice of its first sexual attachment, but what is lacking is a fully developed theoretical analysis of the obverse case—where the child becomes the erotic object choice of the mother. This reticence has been noted by several commentators. Thus Rieff (1959) notes that Freud's treatment of women suffers in general from a sense of apprehension and that though he was a Jew, "and therefore one for whom, as a son, the relation to the mother must have been specially fraught with meaning, Freud achieved a notable repression of it in his own self-analysis . . ." (p. 203). A similar conclusion was reached by Fromm (1970), who finds that for Freud the "tie to mother could be conceived only in terms of the Oedipus situation when the little boy is already a little man. . . . aside from the repression of his own strong fixation to his mother, Freud's patriarchal bias did not permit him consciously to consider the woman-mother as the powerful figure to which the child is bound" (p. 54).

The reexamination of Oedipus' mother outlined above, together with the case of Little Hans and the essay on Leonardo da Vinci, indicates that a reevaluation of Freud's conceptualizations about the mother figure in the oedipal situation is in order. Freud himself came in his final years to recognize the one-sidedness of his views. In his last work, the unfinished "An Outline of Psychoanalysis" (1940), he takes some tentative steps in that direction by following up his reaffirmation that a child's first erotic object is the mother with the complementary observation that the mother is the first seducer of the child, due to her intimate interaction with it. "In these two relations," he writes, "lies the root of a mother's importance, uniquely without parallel, established unalterably for a whole lifetime as the first and strongest love object and as the prototype of all later love relations . . ." (p. 187). But Freud's later views did not have the influence of his earlier theories, the concept of the oedipus complex having been too firmly established by then to be altered without a major revision on Freud's part.

From the arguments presented it does not follow that the construct of the oedipal situation should be replaced by a "Jocasta situation." Freud's hypotheses concerning the psychosexual development of children remain an enduring contribution to the field of psychology, and so, too, the ubiquity of the oedipal situation, with its inherent potentialities and dynamics. What is suggested is that it appears likely, as the examples cited from Freud's work indicate, and if we take *Oedipus Rex* as seriously as Freud did, that an unfolding of these potentialities entails the presence of a mother figure who, knowingly or not, contributes to the activation and development of the essential nucleus of neuroses Freud described in the metaphor of the oedipus complex. One consequence of this reformulation is that, unless one makes the a priori assumption that all mothers fall into the category of the oedipal mother, it calls into question Freud's insistence that the oedipal situation automatically results in the presence of an oedipus complex in every individual. Within the Freudian paradigm, one benefit arising out of this more restrictive view would be to make the concept of the oedipus complex more precise, thereby increasing its potential explanatory effectiveness in both clinical and theoretical applications.

REFERENCES

Bates, W. N. (1940), *Sophocles: Poet and Dramatist.* New York: Barnes.

Bettelheim, B. (1982), Freud and the soul. *New Yorker,* March 1, pp. 52–93.

Freud, S. (1900), The interpretation of dreams. *Standard Edition,* 4/5. London: Hogarth Press, 1953.

——— (1905), Three essays on the theory of sexuality. *Standard Edition,* 7:130–243. London: Hogarth Press, 1953.

——— (1908), On the sexual theories of children. *Standard Edition,* 9:209–226. London: Hogarth Press, 1959.

——— (1909), Analysis of a phobia in a five-year-old boy. *Standard Edition,* 10:3–149. London: Hogarth Press, 1955.

——— (1910), Leonardo da Vinci and a memory from his childhood. *Standard Edition,* 11:63–137. London: Hogarth Press, 1957.

——— (1913), Totem and taboo. *Standard Edition,* 13:1–161. London: Hogarth Press, 1955.

——— (1914), On the history of the psycho-analytic movement. *Standard Edition,* 14:7–66. London: Hogarth Press, 1957.

——— (1916–1917), Introductory lectures on psycho-analysis. *Standard Edition,* 15/16. London: Hogarth Press, 1963.

——— (1925a), An autobiographical study. *Standard Edition,* 20:7–70. London: Hogarth Press, 1959.

——— (1925b), Some psychical consequences of the anatomical differences between the sexes. *Standard Edition,* 19:248–258. London: Hogarth Press, 1961.

——— (1927), The future of an illusion. *Standard Edition,* 21:3–56. London: Hogarth Press, 1961.

——— (1933), New introductory lectures on psycho-analysis. *Standard Edition,* 22:3–182. London: Hogarth Press, 1964.

——— (1940), An outline of psycho-analysis. *Standard Edition,* 23:144–207. London: Hogarth Press, 1964.

——— (1950), *The Origins of Psycho-Analysis.* New York: Basic Books, 1954.

Fromm, E. (1970), *The Crisis of Psychoanalysis.* Greenwich, CT: Fawcett.

Gould, T., Trans. (1970), *Oedipus the King.* Englewood Cliffs, NJ: Prentice-Hall.

Graves, R. (1958), *The Greek Myths.* London: Cassell.

Grene, D., Trans. (1956), *Seven Against Thebes.* In: *The Complete Greek Tragedies: Volume 2. Aeschylus,* ed. D. Grene & R. Lattimore. Chicago: University of Chicago Press.

Jebb, R., Ed. (1885), *The Oedipus Tyrannus of Sophocles.* Cambridge: Cambridge University Press, 1963.

Jones, W. H. S., Trans. (1965), *Pausanias' Description of Greece.* Vol. IV. Cambridge: Harvard University Press.

Kirkwood, G. M. (1958), *A Study in Sophoclean Drama.* Ithaca: Cornell University Press.

Knox, B. (1957), *Oedipus at Thebes.* New Haven: Yale University Press.

Lattimore, R., Trans. (1951), *The Odyssey.* Chicago: University of Chicago Press.

Pearson, H. C., Ed. (1917), *The Fragments of Sophocles.* Vol. II. Amsterdam: Hakhert, 1963.

Puner, H. W. (1947), *Freud: His Life and His Mind.* New York: Charter.

Rank, O. (1941), *Beyond Psychology*. New York: Dover, 1958.
Reik, T. (1920), Oedipus and the Sphinx. In: *Dogma and Compulsion: Psychoanalytic Studies of Religion and Myth*. New York: International Universities Press, 1951, pp. 289–332. Chapter 3, this volume.
Rieff, P. (1959), *Freud: Mind of a Moralist*. New York: Doubleday.
Watling, E. F., Trans. (1947), *Sophocles: The Theban Plays*. Baltimore: Penguin.
Waldock, A. J. A. (1951), *Sophocles the Dramatist*. Cambridge: Cambridge University Press.

21

Oedipus: The Myth, the Developmental Stage, the Universal Theme, the Conflict and Complex

GEORGE H. POLLOCK

[1983]

> Each man is in each instance in dialogue with his forebears, and perhaps even more and in a more hidden manner with those who will come after him. *Martin Heidegger* (cited in Carroll, 1983, p. 65)

Portions of this essay were presented in Athens, Greece, on October 19, 1983, at the conference on "Oedipus Revisited" sponsored by the Institute for Psychoanalysis of Chicago. This work was in part made possible by the support of the Anne Pollock Lederer Research Fund of the Institute for Psychoanalysis of Chicago and appears, in somewhat different form, in *The Annual of Psychoanalysis,* XIV:77–106, Madison, CT: International Universities Press, 1986.

I begin this essay with Heidegger because his observation, succinctly put, is the major theme of my presentation. It is in a deeper sense one of the fundamental principles of psychoanalysis—the past influences the present and can be a significant determinant of the future.

The oedipus complex, named or not, has been known probably since man first appeared on earth. Manifestations of it appear even in the animal kingdom, studies of which are being actively pursued by ethologists, sociobiologists, and students of animal behavior. At the dawn of history, the myth of Oedipus was known to Homer and his precursors.

Lowell Edmunds and Richard Ingher (1977) have compiled a bibliography of 208 books and papers dealing with the psychoanalytic aspects of the Oedipus legend. Their bibliography is no longer complete, as new essays and reports have appeared in the ensuing decade. They note, however, that the "Oedipus legend" includes all its versions; they do not believe in "elevating one particular version of the legend to the level of . . . one 'true' account. This impulse toward the idea of one authentic Oedipus narrative may lead in one direction to the misleading and often apparently unconscious attitude that all other accounts are essentially 'variants' of the 'real' plot" (p. 375). Perhaps the "real plot" is that of each individual, who must experience the situation in a unique way.

Edmunds' recent book on the Oedipus legend (1985) is a major contribution that considers the narrative from many points of view. His reference to the work of the Russian folklorist V. I. Propp is especially germane, as it supports my contention that the narrative is reflective of aspects of prehistorical stages of human society. The roots of this narrative can be found also. I believe, in the behavior of apes. Edmunds' interpretation and the medieval and modern analogues he presents are very illuminating of what Freud considered a universal developmental constellation. Edmunds' geographical and historical survey, including medieval Europe, the Near East, modern Europe, the Slavic lands, Asia, Africa, and the Western Hemisphere, is most impressive, as is his chapter on the ancient sources for the Oedipus legend (pp. 47–57).

Themes recurrent throughout time and space support the universality of the story. Treatment of the theme in literature, drama, opera, and cinema continues to the present. Philosophers, literary critics, feminist theorists, and psychoanalysts continue to explore various facets of the Oedipus narrative and the oedipal constellation: riddles, detection, spiritual tragedy, crime and punishment, infanticide and abandonment, fantasy and deed. In fact, one might find in the Oedipus tale and its variations almost all aspects of human conflict and dilemma. Edmunds suggests that Freud abolishes the consciousness of Oedipus' awareness of what he has done by pushing it into the unconscious. He suggests further that Oedipus' self-blinding is a way of deliberately refusing to see what he has done. Edmunds points out that Propp saw in the Oedipus legend "traces of the passage from a matriarchal to a patriarchal organization of society" (p. 4).

The ancient Oedipus legend, Edmunds suggests, at least the blinding of Oedipus, may represent a variant of the legend earlier than the mention of Oedipus in Homer's Odyssey. In the fifth century B.C. various accounts existed of the crimes preceding those of Oedipus. One such account told of Oedipus' father, Laius, raping a young boy, Chrysippus. The boy's father, Pelops, cursed Laius, wishing on him that if ever he had a son he would be destroyed by him, a curse that came to fruition. Laius has been called the "father" of pederasty. Outraged at Laius' deed, Hera sent the Sphinx to prey on the young men of Thebes. Euripides mentions the curse upon Laius in *The Phoenician Women*, and Aeschylus in *Seven Against Thebes* suggests that because of Pelops' curse Laius dared not have intercourse with Jocasta, lest he beget a son. Aeschylus goes on to say that one day, overcome by wine, Laius forgot his resolve, and Oedipus was conceived. One might suggest that Laius was homosexual and married Jocasta simply to have a queen. It might be that for this reason he avoided her sexually, despite her wishes for a child. We know that the feet of the child Oedipus were mutilated, and that he was set out on Mount Cithaeron to die. Instead he was rescued, adopted by Polybus and Merope, King and Queen of Corinth. After this ensued the killing of Laius at the crossroads, the visit to the Delphic oracle, the temporary kingship of Creon until Oedipus appeared at Thebes to solve the riddle of the Sphinx, the Sphinx's suicide, Oedipus' marriage to Jocasta in supposed ignorance of their kinship, and either a barren marriage or four children, possibly with a second wife, Eurygone.

Edmunds cites four versions of how Oedipus' identity came to be detected and three versions of the death of Jocasta. In the first, she hangs herself after discovering Oedipus' identity. In the second, she kills herself with a sword over the bodies of her sons during the campaign of the *Seven Against Thebes,* and in the third she is killed by Oedipus. Edmunds refers to the various outcomes as they relate to Oedipus' blinding and his death. He then turns to later analogues of the ancient Oedipus legend, e.g., the Judas folktale and the Pope Gregory folktale, in which parricide is absent, and the Arabic Nimrud story and a Zulu tale, in which it occurs.

Edmunds identifies several later folktales that focus on different aspects of the oedipal narrative: prophecy or forewarning as a reason for infanticide; mutilation, exposure, and feral nursing themes; the "compassionate executioner"; rescue, adoption, rearing, departure from the adoptive or foster home; acts of valor, parricide, and incest; and discovery, penance, and exaltation. Different legends have emphasized one or another of these themes and subthemes.

Freud was less interested in the folkloric or mythic aspects of the Oedipus drama than in its psychological significance—child development, the oedipus complex, the origin of the superego. The Oedipus legend, as Edmunds makes clear, has a number of motifs, but Freud emphasizes only parricide and incest with the mother. These desires are fantasies of the child and can be identified in everyone. Freud (1900) says, "Like Oedipus, we live in ignorance of these wishes, repugnant to morality, which have been forced upon us by Nature, and after their revelation we may all of us well seek to close our eyes to the scenes of our childhood" (p. 263). Oedipus' blinding of himself was, as I have suggested, a way of not "seeing" what he had done, what it was ordained he would do by Nature or psychological development. In *Totem and Taboo* Freud (1913) describes the origin of the incest taboo and also the taboo against cannibalism—one must not eat the symbolic totemic animal. The exaltation of the departed father becomes the ego ideal-superego system of the child.

The development of the Oedipus story parallels the oedipus complex—a universal developmental state. Freud did not invent the oedipus complex; he observed it in himself and in his patients, and named it after the Sophoclean tragic hero. He attributed to its lack of resolution crucial significance as a factor in neurosogenesis. In "An Autobiographical Study" he writes:

> A number of suggestions came to me out of the Oedipus complex, the ubiquity of which gradually dawned on me. The poet's choice, or his invention, of such a terrible subject seemed puzzling; and so too did the overwhelming effect of its dramatic treatment, and the general nature of such tragedies of destiny. But all of this became intelligible when one realized that a universal law of mental life had here been captured in all of its emotional significance. [Freud, 1925, p. 63]

Note that Freud says *a* universal law of mental life, not *the* universal law. Freud recognized the oedipus complex as part of a developmental progression, further details of which have been given us by later psychoanalytic investigators.

But to return to Freud: "Fate and the oracle were no more than materializations of an internal necessity; and the fact of the hero's sinning without his knowledge and against his intentions was evidently a right expression of the *unconscious* nature of his criminal tendencies" (1925, p. 63). He writes that Rank (1912) "in his large volume on the incest theme . . . was able to show how often imaginative writers have taken as their subject the themes of the Oedipus situation, and traced in the different literatures of the world the way in which the material has been transformed, modified, and softened" (Freud, 1925, p. 64). He next compares poetic and artistic creation to neurosis:

> The artist, like the neurotic, had withdrawn from an unsatisfying reality into this world of imagination; but, unlike the neurotic, he knew how to find a way back from it and once more to get a firm foothold in reality. His creations, works of art, were the imaginary satisfactions of unconscious wishes, just as dreams are; and like them they were in the nature of compromises, since they too were forced to avoid any open conflict with the forces of repression. But they differed from the asocial, narcissistic products of dreaming in that they were calculated to arouse sympa-

> thetic interest in other people and were able to evoke and to satisfy the same unconscious wishful impulses in them too. Besides this, they made use of the perceptual pleasure of formal beauty as what I have called an 'incentive bonus.' What psycho-analysis was able to do was to take the interrelations between the impressions of the artist's life, his chance experiences, and his works, and from them to construct his [mental] constitution and the instinctual impulses at work in it—that is to say, that part of him which he shared with all men. [pp. 64-65]

We know that there are different components to the oedipal phase of development and that the traversing of this critical period can result in a normal progression, or in an arrest, fixation, or pathological result, with immediate or later psychopathology. Perhaps we should consider the varied cross-sectional aspects of the oedipal developmental field (Pollock, 1981) and trace each of these from their beginnings to their later unfoldings. In this way we can better understand the complexities of the oedipus complex and avoid a reductionistic formulation.

Myths and Truths

It is a common belief that myths are fictional, or even false, by definition. However, since they do portray patterns and conflicts of life, myths can be seen as narratives that present a picture of reality, or of facets of it. Young children, their parents, and writers of children's stories anthropomorphize animals, e.g., the Mother Goose and Beatrix Potter stories. Aesop did the same in his fables, although these were not primarily written for children and are not myths. Unlike the ancient Egyptians, who animalized their gods, the Greeks saw their gods and heroes as having human characteristics. The divinities took the form of human beings. They had the same passions, desires, hurts, conflicts, pleasures, hates, etc., that are seen in man. Thus the Greek gods were externalizations of human character traits, represented different aspects of mental-emotional activity and different personality types, and mirrored the family and society. The humanization of divinities, though not exclusively Greek, gives us a picture of the ancient Greek scene.

Kirk (1974) has noted that many myths lie beyond interpretation. They are in their nature allusive, their mode of reference tangential, their sequence illogical and often incomplete. Plato was the first writer known to use the word *muthologia.* He meant "talking about, or telling stories." In Greek, *muthos* basically means "utterance," something one says—like an associative account. It has, however, come to mean something else—a form of tale, narrative, or story. Aristotle used the word in his *Poetics* to refer to the plot of a play. *Muthos* was sometimes contrasted with *logos. Mutho-logia,* mythology, implies something like an analytical statement or even a theory (Kirk, 1974, p. 22). When the Greeks, however, talked about *muthoi,* they most often meant tales of gods and heroes. They did not intend to make a statement about the accuracy or falsehood of these tales, although some were regarded as containing important elements of truth. Of course not all stories are myths, for there are also novels, short stories, biographies, and historical narratives. The Homeric tales of the Trojan War are historical, for some of the stories have been verified by archaeologists, and Achilles, Hector, and Helen were not gods or goddesses. But myths, like the Oedipus story, have elements of the folktale. Kirk (1974) suggests that myths are a special kind of tale, "Profound, imaginative, other worldly, universal or larger than life" (p. 25), and universal in the sense that the underlying meaning is applicable to all, from the beginning of time and in all developing beings. The tale or play, passed from one generation to the next, can serve as a cautionary tale—the rules of conduct condoned or prohibited by the family, society, culture, or religion. The tale, originally told by one person, can become a ritual or play, now involving more than one being, more than one voice. Similarly, the analysand performs or attributes to the analyst the varied roles of a dramatized life; these we can understand and invest with meaning, assisting the analysand in the resolution of internal conflicts. This drama is enacted in our consulting rooms.

In sum, a myth is a story with a dramatic structure and a climax; a narrative that succeeds in becoming traditional because of its intrinsic importance to individuals and to society; and a theme that is passed from generation to generation because of its fundamental relevance to an important aspect of life and its role in maintaining equilibrium, both social and individual.

In nonliterate cultures, the tale serves as a means of instructing, communicating, shaping, and regulating tensions between older and younger generations, especially within the family. Myths further fashion basic philosophical ideas, ideals, superego prohibitions, and even ideas of cosmogony. But as Kirk reminds us, tales and myths are products of the psyche—they represent, as Freud noted, externalizations of what goes on in each of us, intrapsychically at present and developmentally over time.

Oedipus Complex and Oedipus Myth: Biological Aspects

Freud's oedipus complex, in its simplest form, arises from the boy's desire to get rid of his father, to kill or castrate him and take his place with the mother—to marry her, sleep with her, impregnate her. Freud derived from this idea his explanations of totemism, taboos, incest barriers, and related symbolic phenomena. Freud arrived at his ideas from his self-analysis, clinical observations, the studies of anthropologists and other social scientists, and works of art and literature. As early as 1932, Zuckermann noted from the careful study of primates in the London Zoo that a "patriarchal" form of society exists among baboons. The "overlords" dominate their own family of females, children, and "bachelor" males in a way very similar to Freud's reconstruction of primitive society based on his understanding of the oedipus complex and totemism. What Freud was suggesting was a phylogenetic basis for the complex and its connection to the "family" triad of father, mother, son. The implications of this in terms of more current animal studies will be elaborated later. Let me suggest that the phylogenetic origins of each developmental stage in man can be observed and that we can consider how in man the phylogenetic evolved into the ontogenetic—not only along the lines of Ernst Haeckel's principle that ontogenesis recapitulates phylogenesis, but seeing also how ontogenesis goes beyond phylogenesis and elaborates upon each stage or phase. Thus the oedipus complex may be viewed as a stage of development, but not as the sole *critical* stage. If the complex is not resolved, developmental arrests, fixations, and later regressions or deviations may result in psychopathology. This is true of all developmental stages. Later stages may be influenced by deviations in earlier ones, but this influence may be less significant than we realize. Some critics have suggested that there is a tendency to overemphasize the importance of early childhood experiences in personality formation. We do know that character can change markedly in later life, and these changes may not always be predictable from earlier life events. Psychoanalytic therapy becomes intimately involved with developmental resolutions or their lack. Through displacements, projections, and transferences from early family life—the demands and needs of the mother, rivalry with siblings, competition with the father and the need for his love—the nursery may, as Flugel (1934) has noted, distort the political and economic judgment of adults. What comes from the nursery and the bedroom can determine the fate of the world.

The role of the family in development, though understood implicitly, is now being examined more carefully. The earliest relations with caretakers—especially the mother—and the transmission of values, prohibitions, standards, morals, etc. through the family—mother, father, siblings, grandparents—are now being addressed in depth. The oedipus complex is a family affair. From studies of animals and myths we can see a development, not only from extrapsychic to intrapsychic, from interpersonal to intrapersonal, but from the earliest forms of life to the highest—human beings. The evolution of intimacy is a fascinating study, one that can shed light on our areas of interest.

De Waal (1982) has noted that "the animal world is rife with sexual rivalry between males" (p. 167). Birds, fish, and other animals establish territories to demarcate their procreational rights.

> There is a definite link between power and sex; no social organization can be properly understood without knowledge of the sexual rules and the way progeny are cared for. Even the proverbial cornerstone of our society, the family, is essentially a sexual and reproductive unit. When I am observing the Arnheim chimpanzees I sometimes feel I am studying Freud's primal horde; as if

> a time machine has taken me back to prehistoric times, so that I can observe the village life of our ancestors. They will accept the *droit de seigneur,* one of the forgotten products of Western culture (an unwritten law allowing the lord to bed the newlywed wife of his serf and spend the night with her).

In his studies, De Waal found the alpha male was alone responsible for about three quarters of all matings in the colony. He monopolized sexual activity in the group until two other males joined forces and revolted against him. While he was not cut into pieces, he could never regain anything like his former share of the sexual activity. Coalitions of males against the top-ranked male are definitely political. High-ranking males were not more virile; they were only incredibly intolerant and chased lower-ranking rivals away from estrous females. "If they catch another male mating, they intervene by attacking either him or his mate. The females are also clearly aware of this risk" (p. 168). De Waal asks why the males are so competitive with each other. He believes that jealousy as an explanation "for sexual rivalry between males" itself requires an explanation:

> A female can only be fertilized by one male. By keeping other males away from her a mate increases the certainty that he will be the father of her child. Consequently children will more often be sired by jealous than by tolerant males. If jealousy is hereditary—and this is what this theory assumes—more and more children will be born with this characteristic, and later they in turn will attempt to exclude other members of the same sex from the reproductive act. [p. 170]

De Waal saw jealousy among females as less marked: "The struggle among females for the attentions of the male occurs almost exclusively in pair-forming species, and then it concerns the long-term tie with the male rather than the sexual contact" (p. 170).

Success in the rivalry between males is reflected in the male's rank. Thus the process of striving for a higher rank or the "hunger for power" increases the probability that more sons will be born with this characteristic. De Waal's theory thus offers an explanation for the origins of ambition; he notes that the connection between rank and sex can be seen in baboons, macaques, and wild chimpanzees. But the act of procreation is only half the job; the children also have to be protected once they are born, and dominant males are in a better position to offer such protection. Could it be that the female accepts or seeks out the dominant male for this reason, and that we thereby have a reciprocal selection?

Poirier (1984), an anthropologist who has studied many primate species, has noted that female primates tend to stay together in one area for life, while males move about from group to group. The females form a

> family-oriented society and may be selecting non-aggressive males as their mates, they seemingly ensure that the genes of non-dominant males may be propagated. Thus we have conflicting interpretations and even observations. However what is to be noted is that the female may be the controlling figure in mating, be it with a dominant or a gentler male. These observations may suggest another aspect of the Oedipal configuration, namely that the mother may have fantasies about her male child or conversely the father about his female child and these play a role in conflict resolution, perpetuation or "pathology." [p. 140]

Berger (1983) presented evidence that invading wild horses induce abortions in females unprotected by their stallions and that these females are then inseminated by the victorious males. He even cites accounts where postnatal killing of the young occurs in primates and carnivores, and where some rodents induce abortions in females fertilized by other males.

Konner (1982) describes sexual competition among male peacocks, seals, deer, and antelope. Successful males in these and other species do not know in any cognitive sense that they have won the right to reproduce and sexually possess the females, but they behave as if they know this. In pair-bonded species, both females and males are mated on a long-term basis, and continue to reproduce the same genes in their progeny. The females here "corral" the males as well as being "corralled" by them. The application to the Oedipus myth becomes clearer.

Jocasta may have been as enamored of Oedipus as he of her. Her wish to mate with a male stronger than Laius may have been as important an element as Oedipus' wish to possess an older queen who could be the replacement for the mother he never knew. Reciprocal choices by male and female may be significant and often involve power. That mothers wish to have their sons for many reasons may be an important aspect of the Oedipus complex that we have overlooked, and fathers may relate to their daughters similarly. Thus incest is very much a mutual situation, much more than previously realized. Nonetheless, society could not condone this practice—it would be too disruptive to "civilized groupings"—and so taboos came into being. Jealousy, competition, and acted-out resolves could destroy the family and society and thereby jeopardize the rearing of the young and the survival of the species. Renunciation, inhibition, repression, exogamy—all were needed for survival in the broad sense, and they evolved functionally.

Crockett (1984), in her field studies of red howler monkey society, observed males attempting to invade a troop to which they did not belong and depose the resident males. "These invasions are highly correlated with infant mortality: there is strong evidence that males that take over troops kill young infants and then mate with their mothers" (p. 62). She observed that more than twenty red howler infants in her study area vanished under circumstances that probably involved infanticide. This was seen when an invading male stalked the group, when new males took over, or when a formerly subordinate male ousted the male that was previously dominant. Crockett and her colleague found that infanticide victims were at just the age to be expected if they were being killed by males seeking a reproductive advantage—namely, under ten months of age. Infanticidal males have greater reproductive success than noninfanticidal males. Females with young try to avoid new males and actually choose interlopers who might kill their infants. A colleague who has studied langurs, Asian monkeys that commit infanticide, believes that females of that species have evolved the strategy of faking estrus in order to deceive new males as to the paternity of already conceived young as a way of protecting them. In other words, a pregnant female langur displays estrous behavior, and as a result the male who mates with her "believes" that the infant born later is his. Species variations undoubtedly exist, but the displacement of the reproductive male by a new male seems to lead to the "wish" or "need" in the latter to destroy the fetus or infant and to impregnate the female with his own sperm.

Recent emphases on child abuse, ranging from physical harm to sexual exploitation to the psychological victimization of the child by parents and siblings, calls attention to the ultimate instance of child abuse and neglect—infanticide. This of course is the deepest dread of the child, one that exists in the deepest layers of the unconscious. The infanticidal intent of the crippling and abandonment of Oedipus by his biological father, despite what I believe to be the opposition of his mother, fits into the pattern. However, infanticide is not exclusively a father-son phenomenon. Hoffer and Hull (1981) have researched infanticide by mothers in England and New England from 1558 to 1803. The abandonment of newborn infants is most frequently the work of mothers, most of them unmarried.

Breiner (1984), comparing child abuse patterns in traditional China and ancient Western cultures, presents evidence that child abuse in one form or another has existed since the earliest recorded history. He emphasizes that there were no laws in Greece or Rome that proscribed infanticide. Child sacrifice was part of the religion of the Celts, Gauls, Romans, Egyptians, Phoenicians, Moabites, and others. Child abandonment was for varying periods of time quite common. We know that the Aztecs sacrificed children, and Breiner's survey indicates how commonly child abuse was practiced in China from 1500 B.C. to A.D. 1644. Warren (1984) has described new excavations and discoveries on Crete which reveal child sacrifices, including the removal of flesh from the bodies. The children were in normal health, and the evidence is that they were deliberately killed. Perhaps the Minoan religious practices in the Bronze Age (2000 B.C.) included ritual cannibalism as part of the sacrificial tradition.

Korbin (1981) has recently edited a volume on the cross-cultural aspects of child abuse, infanticide, and abandonment in New Guinea, Sub-Saharan Africa, South America, India, Turkey, Japan, Taiwan, China, and Polynesia. These various reports all indicate the universality and long history of what we have learned in the Oedipus legend. In another edited volume dealing with infanticide, Hausfater and Hrdy

(1981) point out that infanticide is a biologically significant phenomenon. In addition to its ubiquity in human history and society, we know now that it is widespread in the natural world as well. Ethologists and sociobiologists have been supplying us with observations of infanticide and cannibalism, and even cases of siblings killing siblings in certain species of birds. Thus we can view human infanticide from an evolutionary perspective as well as from psychological, sociological, religious, and economic viewpoints. The biological aspects of oedipal phenomena are thereby highlighted. What we see as a psychological developmental stage may parallel a biological evolutionary development. The authors in the Hausfater and Hrdy collection cover infanticide, siblicide, and cannibalism in birds, fish, amphibians, invertebrates, and mammals (including red howler monkeys, baboons, gorillas, langurs, and rodents) and human infanticide, especially excess female mortality during childhood. And only now are we beginning to obtain endocrinological data that may give us more precise indications of what changes occur during the various developmental phases described by Freud for infant sexuality (Lehrer, 1984).

The abandonment of the threatening male child right after birth has been studied by Rank (1912). It may be that this was a reaction to an earlier cannibalism. Instead of eating the child, it was abandoned to be eaten by wild animals. Later the castration theme entered the picture, and only the penis was eaten, as in the case of Osiris. Still later the castration threat became dominant.

Frazer (1983), in his introduction to *The Poems of Hesiod*, describes the succession myth and how this affected Hesiod's *Theogony*. In these myths we read of the origin of the world. In the *Theogony* three major gods succeed one another—Ouranos, Kronos, and Zeus. But before them were Chaos, then Gaia (Earth), Tartarus (the underworld), and Eros (Love), all of whom came into existence apparently by spontaneous generation. Gaia produced Ouranos (Heaven), with whom she mated to produce the "older" gods, the Titans, of whom the youngest was Kronos. Gaia plotted with Kronos to overthrow his father. Kronos then castrated Ouranos with a long, jagged sickle. The severed genitals floated to sea, and from them rose the beautiful goddess of love, Aphrodite. Kronos and his sister Rhea produced the first generation of Olympians, including Zeus. But Kronos, wishing to rule forever, took to swallowing his children, until Rhea, with the help of her parents, saved the infant Zeus and gave Kronos a stone to swallow. Kronos vomited his other children and Zeus escaped.

Zeus fell in love with Metis, who tried to escape but without success. The god knew from an oracle of mother Earth that if Metis ever gave birth to his son, the boy would dethrone him. To escape such a fate Zeus swallowed Metis before she gave birth to her child, thus outwitting the oracle. Then one day he had a terrible pain in his head. Hephaestos struck Zeus' head and out came Athena in full armor, to the great astonishment and admiration of the assembled gods. Thus, by having a daughter instead of a son did Zeus break the chain of Ouranos and Kronos. (For now we shall emphasize Athena's virgin birth and not tie it to other virgin births of godlike creatures.)

For a long time, the myths tell us, the virgin goddess Athena and her uncle Poseidon, god of the sea, quarreled over who should be the patron of the city destined to become Athens. Finally the inhabitants were told to choose one of the two. Poseidon, to demonstrate why he should be selected, hit a rock on the Acropolis with his trident. Salt water jutted up; his offer was supremacy of the sea. Athena in her turn hit a rock with her spear, and an olive tree shot up. She was offering the people food, light, and wisdom. The men voted for Poseidon, the women for Athena. Since the women outnumbered the men by one, Athena was chosen, and Athens acquired its name. The story continues, however: Poseidon in his fury flooded Athens, and the men, considering the women responsible for their misfortune, reduced their rights. They abolished their right to vote and to give their name to their children. A woman goddess, Zeus' firstborn, became supreme over Athens, but the women of Athens were subjugated to the men.

The parallel to Laius and Oedipus is striking. In the *Theogony* we find the castration of Ouranos, Kronos' nemesis of his children, the escape of Zeus, his subsequent defeat of Kronos, and Zeus' election as king of the gods.

This succession myth has parallels in Oriental mythology which are so striking that a connection is almost incontestable. They occur principally in Hittite, Akkadian, Phoenician, Babylonian, and Hurrian texts, some going back as far as 2000 B.C. The succession myth came to Greece from the East. Hesiod lived around 700 B.C.

In the Hittite texts the defeated god has his genitals bitten off by his competitor. After the castration, gods are born from the severed genitals. The third king also castrates his father. One can begin to infer that the Oedipus myth and the Oedipus complex have a long history—probably one of the oldest myths known to man, one based on primeval practices perhaps with biological determinants.

"In ancient Canaan and Israel, the sacrifice of children to deities was quite common. In grave corporate emergencies, or to accompany the foundation of important temples or cities, the surest way of all to appease the divine power was to sacrifice a human being, especially a son or daughter" of the ruler (Grant, 1984, p. 25).

In many of the Greek tales of infanticide or abandonment, then, we may detect practices which derived from earlier belief systems in the Middle East. A parallel to Jocasta's anger at Laius about the supposed sacrifice of her only child, Oedipus, is found in the story of Agamemnon's sacrifice of his daughter Iphigenia. Clytemnestra, like Jocasta, was furious with her husband for what he had done but, unlike her, proceeded to kill him. In the case of Jocasta, one might suspect that she harbored death wishes toward her older husband and was more than willing to turn to a younger man who, as fate had decreed, turned out to be her own son.

Oedipus Myth to Oedipus Drama

The most famous of all Greek tragedies is Sophocles' masterpiece, *Oedipus the King*. The story is as well known as the fact that Freud used the name of the hero to designate the developmental period that parallels the action of the play. I wish to call attention to one element that occurs before the action of the play begins. The Sphinx, her riddle solved by Oedipus, who thus saves Thebes, kills herself. In gratitude the crown is offered to Oedipus along with the hand of Jocasta, widow of the slain King Laius. The riddle illustrates the progression of human development from infancy through adulthood to old age, a progression that is universal and that sets the stage for our drama. The son succeeds the father, whom he deposes, and then the son has access to the still fertile females—including sisters and mother. Jocasta may have known at some level who Oedipus was, and so was not eager to pursue any investigation into his past. She felt guilt and punished herself only when the unconscious became known.

There were other Oedipus plays, a few of which I shall briefly summarize.

1. The *Oedipus* of John Dryden and Nathaniel Lee was probably first acted in late 1678 or early in 1679. Although borrowing from Sophocles' play, Dryden and Lee also took from Seneca's play the idea of raising the ghost of Laius, who identifies his murderer to the magician Teiresias, an element similar to that of Hamlet. Kallish, MacLeish, and Schoenbohm (1968) note that Dryden and Lee borrowed also from the *Oedipus* of Pierre Corneille, their French contemporary. Sir Walter Scott, in his introduction to Dryden and Lee's play, notes that Aristotle admired Sophocles' masterpiece, that Horace mentioned it, that Lucullus and Julius Caesar wrote about Oedipus, and that Seneca also wrote an *Oedipus*.

2. Hugo von Hofmannsthal (1874–1929) author of *Oedipus and the Sphinx*, felt that each age and each individual must reckon with the past in order to achieve a valid self-comprehension and self-expression. He points out that each important figure in the tragedy has a special problem. Laius, who has condemned the newborn infant to death, is unhappy in his marriage because he is aware that Jocasta is consumed by her longing for a child. Jocasta, who cannot bear the knowledge that her baby is "dead" through the command of her husband, remains silent. Creon, her brother, is jealous and a man without courage.

3. The *Oedipus* of the Roman dramatist Seneca is a poor play in comparison with Sophocles'. Seneca's main interest seemed to be in necromancy, which he described in detail. Creon reports that the ghost of Laius reveals his son's guilt. Jocasta, after calling her son a parricide, suggests he complete his work by killing her. She does the deed herself, however, impaling herself on a sword raised in the upright position of an erect phallus.

4. Oedipus plays were written also by Voltaire (1718), Yeats (1912, 1927), and Cocteau (1934)—his *The Infernal Machine*.

5. Homer, in the *Odyssey*, writes as part of Odysseus' recollection:

I saw the mother of Oedipus, lovely Epicaste,
Who did an enormous deed in the ignorance of her mind,
And married her son. He slew his own father and married her.
The Gods soon made these things known to men.
But he suffered pains in his much-beloved Thebes,
And ruled the Cadmeians through the destructive plans of the gods;
And she went to the place of the mighty gatekeeper Hades.
She hung up a high noose from the lofty roof beam,
Possessed by her grief. For him she left many pains
Behind her, the kind of a mother's Furies bring to pass.

In the story Homer knew, Oedipus continued to reign in Thebes after his guilt is discovered. He was eventually killed in battle and buried with full royal honors.

Homer's naming of Oedipus' mother and wife, Epicaste, is a variation of Jokaste, Iocasta, Jocaste.

6. Euripides

a. *The Phoenician Women*—Jocasta's Prologue.

b. *Oedipus*—a lost play.

In Euripides' version, the soldiers blind Oedipus; this is represented in works of art—an urn in Florence, a bowl in the Louvre—which shows the play was popular but eclipsed by Sophocles' version.

7. H. Kleist's *Der Zerbrochener Krug.*

8. Corneille's *Oedipus.*

9. Schiller's *Die Braut von Messina.*

10. Andre Gide's *Oedipus.* In this play Gide's emphasis is not on horrors, it is an intellectual debate and the realities of physical violence are subordinated to order, design, and the greatest misfortune of Oedipus—the failure of his ambition to make man independent of the gods.

11. Aeschylus—In *Seven Against Thebes,* the issue of the sins of the fathers that can be visited on innocent children is addressed. The sons of Oedipus and Jocasta fall victims to the curse that haunts their house. Aeschylus addresses the moral conflict and deliberately guides the last descendant of the guilty family toward death. Eteocles is to die, but before he does, he saves his city from defeat and slavery. Behind the mournful account of his death we hear the triumphal hymn of

thanksgiving for deliverance. Thus, despite destiny, there is greatness in his tragedy even at the instant of his destruction. The hero, by sacrificing his doomed life to the salvation of his fellow men, reconciles a seeming senseless and needless destruction to a higher value (Jaeger, 1945).

The poets, playwrights, historians, and psychoanalysts have approached the Oedipus story from various points of view. Sophocles has been the prime and best known carrier of the myth but it is a tale of universal significance.

The story is old, strange, and terrible. The childless king and queen of Thebes were told by Apollo that their son would kill his father and marry his mother. When the son was born, the father tried to make sure that the prophecy would not come true. He drove a metal pin through the infant's ankles and gave him to a shepherd with instructions to abandon the baby on a mountainside to die of exposure. But the shepherd pitied the infant and gave him to a fellow shepherd, who came from Corinth, on the other side of the mountain. That shepherd in turn gave the child to the childless king and queen of Corinth, who adopted him and raised him as their own. They named him Oedipus or "swollen foot." He grew up in Corinth as the king's son, with no idea of his parentage. Laius and Jocasta believed their child was dead and the prophecy wrong.

When Oedipus was a young man, he was told by a drunkard at a banquet that he was not the real son of the king of Corinth. Though his adoptive parents assured him that he was their real son, lingering doubts remained in his mind and rumors were spreading. Oedipus then went on his own to Delphi, to the oracle of Apollo, to ask the god who his parents were. All he was told was that he would kill his father and marry his mother. Resolving never to return to Corinth or to his parents, he started off to make a new life for himself. Coming to a narrow place where three roads met, he was ordered off the road and then attacked by the driver of a chariot in which an old man rode. In the ensuing fight, Oedipus killed the old man and his attendants in self-defense—all except one who escaped and fled to Thebes. The old man in the chariot was Laius, king of Thebes, the biological father of Oedipus. Thus was the first part of Apollo's prophecy fulfilled, though Oedipus was not consciously aware of it. Oedipus then came to Thebes, a city in distress. A monster, the Sphinx—part bird, part lion, part woman—was killing the young men of the city and refused to go away until someone answered her riddle. Many tried; all failed and met their death. The Thebans offered the throne of Thebes, and the hand of Jocasta, their widowed queen, to anyone who could answer the riddle. Oedipus, taking up the challenge, succeeded in ridding Thebes of the Sphinx. He then married Jocasta and became King of Thebes. The prophecy was fulfilled, but he did not realize it. For many years he ruled Thebes well, an admired and just king. He had two daughters and two sons. And then a plague broke out. The people of the city died, the cattle died, the crops rotted. The temples were filled and a delegation of priests came to Oedipus, begging him to save them. It is here that Sophocles' play begins.

The Life of Sophocles

Lefkowitz (1981) notes that virtually nothing can be known about the lives of the Greek poets. There are no records, no diaries, no letters, no archives, and no ancient poet had a Boswell. Almost all the material in the ancient lives of the poets is fiction, and what little factual information they contain comes from the literary works of their subjects. For this reason, Lefkowitz contends, the retrieval of biographical information requires imagination and discrimination.

What seems certain is that Sophocles was an Athenian by birth. The son of a slave-owning father, he was well-educated, raised in comfortable circumstances, and later involved in government and diplomacy. He was born in 495 or 494 B.C., seven years after Aeschylus and twenty-four before Euripides. He trained in both wrestling and music, and won prizes in each. He learned about tragedy from Aeschylus and was responsible for innovation in the dramatic competitions. He wrote one hundred thirty dramas, and competed against Aeschylus, Euripides, and others, including his son Iophon. In general he used Homeric vocabulary and took plots from Homer's works, especially the *Odyssey*.

Sophocles played the lyre, and his character was said to be so charming that he was loved everywhere and by everyone. The Athenians elected him a general when he was sixty-five years old, seven years before the Peloponnesian war began. Sophocles was very pious, was a member of the priesthood, and established a shrine to Heracles.

At some point he brought a suit against his son Iophon, whose mother was Nicostrate. He had another son, Ariston, whose mother was Theoris. He was especially fond of Ariston's son, who was named after his paternal grandfather. Once in a drama he portrayed Iophon as being envious of him, as making accusations to his clansmen that his father had become demented in his old age. The poet is supposed to have said, "If I am Sophocles, I am not out of my mind; if I am out of my mind, I am not Sophocles." And then he produced the *Oedipus*. After his death, in 406 B.C. at the age of almost ninety, the Athenians honored his memory with a yearly sacrifice. *Antigone* was produced in 442 B.C., when he was fifty-three, *Oedipus Rex* between 430 and 425 B.C., and *Oedipus at Colonus* posthumously, in 401 B.C.

It may be noted here that the *Iliad* is filled with oedipal themes. The stolen wife who agrees to leave her husband to be with her lover, the irate husband who mobilizes his forces to retrieve his Helen and punish his sexual rival, the actual reference to Oedipus and his mother-wife—all suggest that Sophocles may well have found Homer's work a stimulus for writing *Oedipus Rex*.

If we may speculate, it might be suggested that Sophocles' problems with Iophon may well have been an additional stimulus. For a more certain instance of family issues stimulating creativity, recall that Freud discovered the Oedipus complex in himself following the death of his father in October 1896. In a letter to Fliess dated October 15, 1877, the first anniversary of his father's death, Freud (1950) writes that "I have found love of the mother and jealousy of the father in my own case too, and now believe it to be a general phenomenon of early childhood . . ." (p. 223). He goes on:

> The gripping power of *Oedipus Rex,* in spite of all the rational objections to the inexorable fate that the story pre-supposes, becomes intelligible. . . . the Greek myth seizes on a compulsion which everyone recognizes because he has felt traces of it in himself. Every member of the audience was once a budding Oedipus in phantasy, and this dream-fulfilment played out in

> reality causes everyone to recoil in horror, with the full measure of repression which separates his infantile from his present state. [pp. 223–224]

Freud's self-analysis and his reading of *Oedipus Rex* gave rise to his idea of the universality of the complex.

The first hint of the formulation of the oedipus complex appears in Draft N, dated May 31, 1897. There Freud (1950) observes, undoubtedly in reference to himself, that the death of one's parents results in grief and in self-reproach or melancholia. The identification with the dead parent, however, has another root: "in sons [there is] a death-wish . . . directed against their father and in daughters against their mother" (p. 207).

In the preface to the second edition of *The Interpretation of Dreams*, Freud (1900, p. xxvi) writes that after he completed this work, in the course of his self-analysis, he discovered the significance of his father's death and the role it apparently played in his discoveries. In the text proper, he discusses Sophocles' drama in the context of his discovery (pp. 261–263), but the term "oedipus complex" seems to make its first appearance in 1910 (Freud, 1910, p. 171).

Let me turn briefly now to Freud's relations with his sons, the other side of the equation, so to speak. In 1915 two of his sons, Martin and Ernst, were in the Austrian army. "Freud had several dreams about calamities to his sons, which he interpreted as envy of their youth" (Jones, 1955, p. 180). It was not by accident that Freud turned to Sophocles and the Oedipus myth to explain his discovery and to then apply this label to it, further immortalizing both Sophocles and his tragic hero.

Jackson (1982) has observed that all major Western epics tell of some form of confrontation between an established ruler and a younger hero. The ruler often shows weakness, either in his handling of a situation (Laius' inability to deal with the Sphinx) or in his character (Laius' guilt over ordering his son's death, especially after his wife had such difficulty conceiving and bearing a child). The ruler is in danger of being supplanted by a challenging hero. Oedipus can be considered as the savior of Thebes, preventing its sociopolitical and economic disintegration. But this was possible only after he followed a set path. Youth supplants age—the riddle of the Sphinx is the oedipal dilemma. Son succeeds father and in his unconscious mates, reproduces, and has a son who wishes in turn to supplant him. This conflict is seen over and over again, however varied in its depiction by creative writers, playwrights, and poets. Epics have strong social overtones, but they spring from very different societies throughout recorded history. Nonetheless, the underlying theme is the same—conflict between king and hero, between father and son.

Heilbrun (1982) has commented on Oedipus' self-blinding as an act of self-castration, equating eyeballs with "balls" or testicles. This, as we know, occurs when he realizes he has killed his father, married his mother, and had children with her. For this antipaternal crime (and I add antimaternal crime, as Oedipus involves Jocasta in his activities), Oedipus tears out his eyes in order to punish himself, not only for patricide but for incest. And his four children suffer as well for the "crimes" of their father and mother.

The Universality of the Oedipus Complex

Myths appears to be fictional but, as I have tried to show, they often seem to parallel life. The Oedipus myth, in particular, offers a definition of reality and, from our contemporary vantage point, a developmental reality. In this concluding section I will discuss the Oedipus myth over time and as it has appeared in other cultures.

As I have shown above, the phenomena associated with the Oedipus myth have been described in antiquity by Hittites, Phoenicians, and Babylonians. The myth has been viewed cross-culturally. Heisaku Kosawa, a Japanese therapist, has proposed the Ajase complex as being more applicable to his nation than the oedipus complex.

> In ancient times, the myth goes, the young prince Ajase, feeling betrayed by his mother because of her sexual feelings towards his father, killed the older man. Ajase had planned to murder his mother as well but could not bring himself to do it. Ajase then broke out in suppurating sores so offensive that no one would help him. But his mother, despite her horror at her son's deed,

> cared for him, and he was so moved that they reconciled. [*Time*, 1983, p. 67]

In prerevolutionary Russia, the myth forms the basis of Dostoyevsky's *The Brothers Karamazov.* Among Russian royalty there were several instances in which fathers killed their sons in order to maintain their thrones: Ivan the Terrible, Peter the Great. Other writers have given us pictures of how this theme relates to their cultures, for example, D. H. Lawrence's autobiographical novel, *Sons and Lovers.* In real life, Lawrence acted on his oedipal longings when

> he convinced a pretty, lively, unhappily married woman, who was certainly as devoted to her children as most mothers are, that she must . . . abandon her children, humiliate her husband, scandalize her aristocratic German relatives—in short risk everything—for an unknown writer of two febrile novels, a few first-rate short stories, and some interesting if often rough-hewn verses. Lawrence offered Frieda nothing except his intense . . . conviction that they were to love and cleave to each other. He had no money and no social or professional status. [Moynahan, 1963, p. 2]

Frieda von Richtofen Weekley returned to Germany to deal with her parents. She and Lawrence then had a prolonged European "honeymoon" until they married. Frieda was grief stricken over the loss of her children but married Lawrence despite her great anguish.

Spiro (1982) has noted that the oedipus complex represents "a pivotal event in the human career which has far-reaching consequences for our understanding of society, culture, and human nature" (p. ix). His focus is on reexamining the Trobriand controversy which occupied anthropologists following the publication of Malinowski's work more than fifty years ago. Malinowski argued that the Oedipus complex could not be found in the Trobriand archipelago and that it was a product uniquely of the West, its institutions, and its "patriarchal" family structure. Spiro challenges this thesis and uses as data his reanalysis of Malinowski's own data. He concluded that the oedipus complex is stronger in the Trobriands than in the West and argues very persuasively that this pivotal complex is universal.

The cross-cultural variability observed in the oedipus complex is not a refutation but a substantiation of its universality. The idea of multiple independent origins, based on the limited alternatives encountered by people in different cultures and life situations, makes it possible to appreciate the fact of separately evolving lines stemming from a central matrix. The oedipus complex is such a matrix, and man in his unique ability to symbolize, fantasy, displace, condense, and transform has done this intrapsychically and extrapsychically in the social, cultural, and religious spheres.

I have followed several paths in this presentation. Traversing it has taken us through many disciplines and a great deal of data. Nonetheless, there is a convergence, and a fundamental conclusion: the oedipus complex exists, is universal, has significance for all of humankind, is of clinical relevance, has biological antecedents, gives us insights into the human drama and the many creative works that stem from it, and allows us to appreciate the genius of Freud in the theater of the mind and Sophocles in the theater of Greece and of the world.

One occasionally reads or hears of oedipal enactments occurring in everyday life. Two dramatic reports have recently appeared which bear upon this facet of everyday life. A French brother and sister had a child together and asked permission to marry. In France it was noted that incest itself is not a crime, but that a marriage between brother and sister is not legal and the child of such a union may not be registered under the names of both parents (Van Biema, 1985). In a recent report of a mother-son marriage, the son was given up for adoption when he was three. When the son was eighteen, he asked who his mother was. When he obtained her name and address, the son visited the woman, who "denied being his mother" (*Washington Post*, 1984, p. A2). They began to date and then began to live with one another. Eventually they were married, but the son, on finding out that in fact she was his mother, attempted to have the marriage annulled. He indicated he had had no physical relations with her once he found out who she was. The mother refused her son's entreaties to end their marriage. She wrote to him that she loved him like no other could love him. She also indicated that she could not stand to lose her son a second time and that it had hurt her very deeply to have to put him up for adoption because she could not support him. The mother was charged with criminal incest and if convicted faces five to twenty-one years in prison. This modern Oedipus tragedy suggests that mother and son were mutually involved with each other and that patricidal impulses were secondary to the enactment of the developmental crises.

Additional Notes, Observations, and Issues

1. Stages of human psychological and biological development are probably universal despite cultural, social, and economic determinants. These stages probably evolved from lower forms of life, and deal with the rhythms of aging. The oedipal period is one such stage and the riddle of the Sphinx was the riddle of normative developmental progression through the course of life.

2. Grossvogel (1979) has drawn interesting comparisons between the Oedipus legend and the modern detective story. The crime, the detective, the clues, the questioning, the unmasking of the guilty, the motives, the punishments, and the social responses are all clear and parallel. One might say the oedipal mystery in some ways is the prototype of all later mystery and detective stories.

3. Slotkin (1947) has noted that despite the fact that all societies have exogamic regulations, the violation of which is by definition incest, data exist which question the truth of this proposition in regard to ancient Iran. Slotkin calls our attention to the writings of the ancient Persians in which marriage and cohabitation with mothers, daughters, and sisters was permitted to sons and fathers. Incest among the ruling families of Egypt and Hawaii is also well known. Probably at some level this was a way of keeping political and economic power within the immediate family. In more recent times, it might also be the reason for the practice of royalty marrying only royalty, though these marriages occur between the royal families of different countries. Slotkin suggests that the Iranian sources not only do not prohibit incest but actually advocate "the preferential mating of next-of-kin" (p. 617)—for all and not merely for priests and rulers.

Rossi (1978) has noted that the function of any family system is human continuity through reproduction and child rearing. This is related to Freud's earlier views on the need for species preservation as well as individual immortality through actual or symbolic descendants. Thus the encouragement of incestuous mating might have been a means of insuring both family and individual perpetuity and only later was prohibited when it threatened family and social continuity and integrity. Perhaps issues of envy, jealousy, rivalry, and power within the family led to this endogamic prohibition. Freud's suggestions in *Totem and Taboo* (1913) might be one scenario for the incest taboo. We know that oedipal development takes place in a social context. However, what psychoanalysis has shown is how the resolution of this normative crisis gives rise to the superego, the ego ideal, values, controls, and creative activities that are harmonious and ego-syntonic.

Davis (1978) has written of how the Church in early modern France established laws of kinship. As late as the thirteenth century, one could not marry within the seventh degree, that is, any of the descendants of one's great-great-great-great-great grandparents. At the Lateran Council of 1215, this was changed to the fourth degree; that is, one was forbidden to marry any of the descendants of one's sixteen great-great grandparents. The prohibition extended to the relatives of one's spouse in the case of remarriage, and even of a person with whom one had had intercourse (pp. 101–102). "There was also a prohibition established among 'spiritual relatives,' that is among all the godparents at a baptism, their own children, and their godchildren. Intercourse or marriage under any of these circumstances was incest, though the sin was worse the closer the relative, and any marriage so contracted was null" (p. 102). Davis notes that parish priests would keep charts and diagrams and would inquire about relationships before marriages could be performed. However, "couples wanting to marry within the third and fourth degrees sought and paid for dispensation from the Church. Couples or parents wanting to end a union could also discover such hindrances to marriage at a convenient moment" (p. 102). This "abuse" may have been a major reason for reducing the prohibition from the seventh degree to the fourth, but it could still be seen as an option for wealthy families and not for illiterate impoverished groups. In the late sixteenth century, the Jesuit Emond Auger indicated that "our carnal desires are by nature strongest toward those closest to us and would be boundless if we married them" (cited in Davis, 1978, p. 102), and so more formal prohibitions continued. For Protestants, however, this complex mechanism of illicit degrees of marriage and dispensation was seen as another example of "papal tyranny and priestly trafficking. The Calvinists simply prohibited marriage in the immediate family, uncle-niece, aunt-nephew, and between first cousins. In the Church of England, the prohibition did not even extend to first cousins. . . . No dispensations were allowed. All other marriages, including those involving godparents, were not incestuous" (p. 103). Further research in the actual reasons for endo-exogamy is needed. This should include studies of economic factors as well as the traditional psychological and social issues.

In Lieu of a Conclusion

Let me conclude with some clinical material. A female adult patient told me a dream: "I was standing with my son. A tall, slender man in a very lavish hotel room. Two beds. We'd just arrived. My son said, 'It was very expensive, the hotel. Why didn't we share the room together?' I said nothing." That was the dream. The patient then went on and said, "Share the room?" I speculated when the question was posed, "Was it worth the money to get another room?" "I would never share a room with my son. We would just not be comfortable," she replied. So what did this seem to mean? The patient laughed and said, "It's the oldest story in the world." I said, "What's that?" She said, "Incest. Mother-son. You know what it's all about." She then went on and elaborated and told me that she had always been very careful when he was a little boy and he'd crawl into the bed next to her. She would always move him to the other side, next to her husband. She said, "I had a real concern about seductive mothers. I never even kissed him on the lips. Never." And, after a pause, she went on to say, "I did see in a number of friends who really seduced their sons what happens, not overtly as far as I could tell, but it was obvious to me." She proceeded to associate to this, that one of these young men had become homosexual, the other was a failure at school and in work, and she elaborated on the details of their situations. When she said, "There's a fine line between seduction and affection," I asked her why she thought she had had the dream when she did. She said, "My son, who lives out of town, is coming to visit me, and I feel uneasiness when we are together, especially since my husband is away." Whereupon she looked around the room (she was lying on the couch) and said, "Come to think of it, there's only one couch in this room." And she laughed and said, "This must have something to do with what's going on inside of me. But the facts are that I still never kissed him on the lips and I would never be comfortable with him in bed. Oh, by the way, did you see the movie *Murmur of the Heart?*"

Another account is from a father who was in analysis with me. The father reported that he was going up to his bedroom to do something. His little girl, who was two years old, immediately volunteered that she wanted to go up with him to the bedroom and do things with him. She then turned to the patient's wife and said, in a very cute way, "And I want you to stay here." A little later, the mother decided that she had to do something on the second floor and began to go upstairs. The little girl came out of the room, stamped her foot, and said, "Stay there. Don't come up."

Another little vignette: a three-and-a-half-year-old boy decides he has to use the toilet while his mother is taking a shower. His father volunteers to help him. He yells at his father, "I don't need your help," pointing to the shower, "she can take care of me if I need her to, and she can come out and then she can go back into the shower."

My last clinical illustration is not mine; it comes from Freud (1919) from the very famous case of Little Hans, who had a phobia for horses as well as some very strong sexual impulses. At age four he said, after his bath and as his mother was powdering around his penis and taking care not to touch it, "Why don't you put your finger there?" His mother insisted that such an action would be disgusting. Hans laughingly replied, "But great fun."

Hans quickly developed a strong attraction to many other females, including the landlord's fourteen-year-old daughter, Mariedl, who played with him. One evening as he was being put to bed, he said, "I want Mariedl to sleep with me." When told this was not possible, he replied, "Then I'll just go downstairs and sleep with her." Hans picked up his clothes and went toward the staircase to go and sleep with her, but naturally his parents stopped him. We encounter such situations repeatedly despite the fact that some say we no longer see these things.

The oedipal situation is a biological, a psychological, and a social situation in which issues are crystallized on a developmental scale. These are internal as well as external and involve both resolutions and persistent conflicts, as well as such later concerns as choice of mate, identification, incest, child abuse, neurosis, homosexuality, misogyny, misanthropy, sexual dysfunction, and such positive components as sexual pleasure, intimacy, and the wish to have children. I wish to remind the reader that part of this is wanting either to give a baby to one of the parents or wanting to receive a baby. And this does play an important role as we are beginning to discover the whole area of parenting and of reproduction, mating, parenting, and then we get into more adult functioning. Again, I am giving an overview, but this leads into the whole issue of sexual role, of gender role, which is somewhat different though it does deal with sexual identity, as well as with personality identity, with issues of masculinity and femininity which are separate from gender, with issues of the sexual apparatus and orgastic or release patterns, and also with issues of maternality and paternality. All of these that I have just listed can be differentiated and one can again begin to see how they are emerging in the young being who is confronted by all sorts of things in the world. In addition, we find such factors and problems as envy, jealousy, rivalry, and some of these have earlier antecedents and they also have later consequents. I am not suggesting that all of this comes from this particular developmental period, but I am saying that it is one of the nodal periods in the developmental unfolding—not the only one, but one that deserves more consideration than has been given heretofore.

The role of fantasies, the role of creativity, and how this is actually played out, must be considered. When I had an opportunity to once again see *Carmen*—the movie, and also the opera—I was struck by the oedipal theme, the triadic situation: the jealousy, the humiliation, the esteem, even the symbolism of the killing of the bull and the use of the knife. The opera *Tristan and Isolde* is yet another oedipal drama, as is Rossini's *Semiramide*: "The libretto of *Semiram-*

ide was written by Gaetano Rossi after Voltaire's tragedy *Semiramis*. The plot, based more on the mythical rather than the real events in the life of the Assyrian Semiramis (about 800 B.C.), is similar to that of the Greek drama in which Agamemnon (Ninus) was killed by his wife Clytemnestra (Semiramide) and Aegisthus (Assur). There are further Oedipus-like complications: Semiramide falls in love with a young hero who turns out to be her own son" (Parsons, 1984, p. W5).

I have attempted to examine various aspects of the oedipus complex, and the pathways I have followed and the many I hope to pursue, lead, like those found in ancient cities, in many directions. The oedipus complex was not invented by Freud. It existed for centuries before him, and probably long before Sophocles as well, and has been seen the world over. The story is old, and yet, like Freud, we can experience and discover it anew in ourselves. Freud was able to recognize, identify, and universalize the developmental complex in both normal and psychopathological situations. In doing this he was able to formulate a theory about the genesis of psychoneurosis and how the oedipus complex may be identified in the clinical situation through analyzing the transference.

The integration of the many threads of the oedipus complex and the weaving of all of these into a fabric that has utility and aesthetic and scientific validity has been my objective. Many themes touched on here are deserving of further exploration: filicide and infanticide; the role of fantasy in development, neurosis, and therapy; and—an idea that struck me only recently—Oedipus, Scapegoat of Fate, and his later successor, Sigmund Freud.

Oedipus solved the riddle of the Sphinx and this opened up a new world for him. He did not marry Jocasta after slaying Laius. He was offered her after freeing Thebes from the Sphinx. But Oedipus has to pay for the crimes of his ancestors and becomes the focus of ambivalence. Praise the King—Love the King—Blame the King—Kill the King—The King must die—as did Jesus and a host of other legendary heroes.

Freud, too, solved the riddle of the Sphinx, the riddle of psychic development, and discovered a new world for himself and for all of us. But in many ways he too was a Scapegoat of Fate. He died in a foreign land, and many beloved members of his family were destroyed, as he was in many ways, by the Nazis. His children and disciples fought among themselves, and there are some who would sacrifice him still, though he is no longer here.

REFERENCES

Berger, J. (1983), Induced abortion and social factors in wild horses. *Nature,* 303:59–61.

Breiner, S. J. (1984), Child abuse patterns: Comparison of ancient Western civilization and traditional China. Presentation to the Wednesday Research Series of the Institute for Psychoanalysis, Chicago, November 14.

Carroll, D. (1983), The alterity of discourse: Form, history, and the question of the political in M. M. Bakhtin. *Diacritics,* 13(2):65.

Crockett, C. M. (1984), Family feuds. *Natural History,* 93:54–63.

Davis, N. Z. (1978), Ghosts, kin, and progeny: Some features of family life in early modern France. In: *The Family,* ed. A. Rossi, J. Kagan, & T. Hareven. New York: Norton, pp. 87–114.

De Waal, F. (1982), *Chimpanzee Politics: Power and Sex Among Apes.* New York: Harper & Row.

Edmunds, L. (1985), *Oedipus: The Ancient Legend and Its Later Analogues.* Baltimore: Johns Hopkins University Press.

——— & Ingher, R. (1977), Psychoanalytical writings on the Oedipus legend: A bibliography. *American Imago,* 34:374–386.

Flugel, J. C. (1934), *Men and Their Motives.* London: Kegan Paul, Trench, Trubmer.

Frazer, R. M., Trans. (1983), *The Poems of Hesiod.* Norman, OK.: University of Oklahoma Press.

Freud, S. (1900), The interpretation of dreams. *Standard Edition,* 4/5. London: Hogarth Press, 1953.

——— (1909), Analysis of a phobia in a five-year-old boy. *Standard Edition,* 10:3–149. London: Hogarth Press, 1955.

——— (1910), A special type of choice of object made by men. *Standard Edition,* 11:163–175. London: Hogarth Press, 1957.

——— (1913), Totem and taboo. *Standard Edition,* 13:1–161. London: Hogarth Press, 1955.

——— (1925), An autobiographical study. *Standard Edition,* 20:7–70. London: Hogarth Press, 1959.

——— (1950), *The Origins of Psycho-Analysis.* New York: Basic Books, 1954.

Grant, M. (1984), *The History of Ancient Israel.* New York: Scribner.

Grossvogel, D. I. (1979), *Mystery and Its Fictions: From Oedipus to Agatha Christie.* Baltimore: Johns Hopkins University Press.

Hausfater, G., & Hrdy, S. B., Eds. (1984), *Infanticide: Comparative and Evolutionary Perspectives.* New York: Aldine.

Heilbrun, C. G. (1982), *Towards a Recognition of Androgyny.* New York: Norton.

Hoffer, P. C., & Hull, N. E. H. (1981), *Murdering Mothers: Infanticide in England and New England: 1558–1803.* New York: New York University Press.

Jackson, W. T. H. (1982), *Critique of Scientific Reason.* Chicago: University of Chicago Press.

Jaeger, W. (1945), *Paideia: The Ideals of Greek Culture: Volume I. The Mind of Athens.* 2nd ed. New York: Oxford University Press.

Jones, E. (1955), *The Life and Work of Sigmund Freud.* Vol. 2. New York: Basic Books.

Kallish, M., MacLeish, A., & Schoenbohm, G., Eds. (1968), *Oedipus: Myth and Drama.* New York: Odyssey Press.

Kirk, G. S. (1974), *The Nature of Greek Myths.* Harmondsworth: Penguin.

Konner, M. (1982), *The Tangled Web.* New York: Holt, Rinehart & Winston.

Korbin, J. E., Ed. (1981), *Child Abuse and Neglect: Cross-Cultural Perspectives.* Berkeley: University of California Press.

Lefkowitz, M. R. (1981), *The Lives of the Greek Poets.* Baltimore: Johns Hopkins University Press.

Lehrer, S. (1984), Modern correlates of Freudian psychology. *Amer. J. Med.,* 77:977–980.

Moynahan, J. (1963), *The Deed of Life: The Novels and Tales of D. H. Lawrence.* Princeton: Princeton University Press.

Parsons, A. (1984), Overture to *Semiramide.* Program Notes, Chicago Symphony Orchestra, October 1984.

Poirier, X. (1984), Female apes and monkeys mate with unaggressive males. *Geo,* September 1984, p. 140.

Pollock, G. H. (1981), Aging or aged: Development or pathology. In: *The Course of Life: Volume III. Adulthood and the Aging Process,* ed. S. I. Greenspan & G. H. Pollock. Washington, DC: U.S. Government Printing Office, pp. 549–585.

Rank, O. (1912), *Das Inzest-Motiv in Dichtung und Sage.* Leipzig & Vienna: Franz Deuticke.

Rossi, A. (1978), A biosocial perspective on parenting. In: *The Family,* ed. A. Rossi, J. Kagan, & T. Hareven. New York: Norton, pp. 1–31.

Slotkin, J. S. (1947), On a possible lack of incest regulations in old Iran. *Amer. Anthropologist,* 49:612–617.

Spiro, M. E. (1982), *Oedipus in the Trobriands.* Chicago: University of Chicago Press.

Time (1983), On Japan. Volume 122, No. 5, p. 67, August 1, 1983.

Van Biema, D. (1985), Jacqueline and Andre are sister and brother—and mom and dad. *People,* pp. 97–103.

Warren, P. (1984), Knossos: New excavations and discoveries. *Archaeology,* 37:48–55.

Washington Post (1984), Tennessean unwittingly was wed to his mother. September 12, 1984, p. A2.

Zuckermann, S. (1932), *The Social Life of Monkeys and Apes.* Century Bookbindery.

22

How Culture Influences the Interpretation of the Oedipus Myth

SAMUEL WEISS

[1985]

Samuel Novey (1968) in his seminal work, *The Second Look,* noted that there is a universal tendency to assume that history refers to matters that had existence only in the past. But, he continued, many historians have emphasized that history is always a matter of the present; only the subject matter—the actual event—is of the past. Piaget too commented that we reconstruct the past as a function of the present (Bringuier, 1980, p. 120).

Novey elaborates the point further by quoting W. H. Walsh, the historian:

> The suggestion I am making is that historians approach the past each with his own philosophical ideas, and that this has a decisive effect on the way they interpret it. If I am right, differences between historians are in the last resort differences of philosophies. . . . When I try to put myself in the place of an ancient Greek or a medieval cleric or a Victorian parent, in order to write

> the history of the ancient world or the medieval church or the Victorian family, I must certainly put aside, so far as I can, the moral and metaphysical preconceptions of my own time. But I cannot escape, if I am to make any sense of my material, making some general judgments about human nature, and in these I shall find my own views constantly cropping up. . . . And however much I tell myself to eschew my own prejudices and concentrate on understanding what actually happened, I shall not succeed in carrying out the injunction to the letter, since understanding itself is not a passive process but involves the judging of evidence by principles whose truth is independently assumed. [Novey, 1968, p. 21]

A work of art reflects its time. A forgery attempting to imitate a period other than its own invariably gives itself away by virtue of techniques, materials, etc. proper to its own era. So too the reconstruction of a piece of history, be it of Ancient Greece or of an individual, will necessarily reflect the present perception of the past event and thus contribute an imaginative, creative addition to that event.

Freud took the Oedipus myth, as presented by Sophocles in *Oedipus Rex,* as an important representation of the internal state of all human beings. It is probable that Freud was acquainted with earlier versions of the myth, the Homeric, for example, yet he chose to ignore them, focusing instead on Sophocles' version. And even here he was highly selective in what he chose to emphasize. It would appear then that he was using this data not so much for the purpose of discovering some universal truth as to corroborate a hypothesis already arrived at. He might also have been attempting to solve an emotional problem as well as an intellectual one.

Freud had already made the brilliant discovery of the concept of a latent content behind what was manifest. But curiously, he abandoned this approach when he dealt with the ancient Greeks. Certainly he must have known that the Greeks were a highly cultured, sophisticated people who would be adequately defended against unacceptable impulses. Nonetheless, he took the manifest content to be the same as the latent content—in effect, nothing was hidden.

My contention is that there is a latent content behind the manifest content of Sophocles' drama and that that content is incest—not between son and mother, but between father and son.

Sophocles himself was very likely bisexual. In the Oedipus drama we are informed retrospectively that Oedipus had saved Thebes by answering the riddle of the Sphinx, a phallic female creature that had been terrorizing the community. The Thebans were so grateful to Oedipus that they offered him the crown and the king's widow as his queen. No explanation is offered why the Sphinx had descended on the city.

In other versions of the myth this is made clear. Laius, Oedipus' father, had seduced and raped Chrysippus, the illegitimate son of King Pelops. Bowman (1918) sums it up this way: "One day while teaching Pelops's son, Chrysippus, the art of chariot driving, Laius seized this opportunity to bear him away; for he was filled with an unnatural love for the boy . . . This was the first example of knabenliebe among the Hellenes . . . Later this unnatural passion became more common" (pp. 18–19). In almost all versions of the legend, Laius is credited with having invented pederasty.

This act of Laius provoked the goddess Hera to such a rage that she condemned Laius to be murdered by his own son and to be replaced by him in his wife's bed. Later she sent the Sphinx to terrorize Thebes.

In any review of sexuality in ancient Greece (see Licht, 1952), what is most focused on is the phenomenon of bisexuality; women were available for procreation, but a man's real love was directed toward beautiful young boys. Homosexuality was not so much that of man to man but rather of man to boy. What I am suggesting is that what was not acceptable was a sexual love between father and son. I am suggesting that Laius, because of strong homosexual tendencies directed toward young boys, did not want to have children, by way of defending against these impulses. But in any event, Jocasta got Laius drunk and seduced him. The result was her pregnancy with Oedipus. In the several versions of the myth, Laius was impotent, avoided sex with Jocasta because of Hera's curse, or was simply not interested in women sexually.

It is most interesting that Freud ignored this part of the story. As Ross (1982) points out, it was within a week of the anniversary of

Freud's father's death in 1896 that he wrote a letter to Fliess, conveying his excitement at the discovery of what he was later to call the "oedipus complex."

Homer's version of the Oedipus myth, written some 600 years before Sophocles, did not include a Sphinx; neither was Oedipus blinded or exiled. Rather, as Kanzer (1964) notes, he lived on as ruler of Thebes, afflicted by the Furies as the result of a curse laid on him by his dying mother. Ultimately he died in combat and was buried with honor in his native city. Sophocles, by placing his hero's last years and death in Colonus, a suburb of Athens (the playwright's own birthplace), revealed his own interests and those of his time. Kanzer (1964) notes that in his use of myths Sophocles "was expressing highly personal views on political, religious, and military problems of his own time" (p. 26).

Other versions of the myth reflect how they, too, spring from a social and historical context. For example, in one version Laius did not expose Oedipus on a mountainside but rather locked him in a chest, which was then lowered into the sea by a ship. This chest then drifted ashore where Merope or, according to Graves, Periboea, Polybus' queen, was supervising the royal laundry. She quickly retired to a thicket and pretended to give birth to this baby. The story bears a remarkable resemblance to that of Moses.

In another version, the name of Labdacus (Oedipus' grandfather) refers to the torchlight arrival of a divine child, acclaimed as a son of the goddess Brimo. And the piercing of Oedipus' feet with a nail occurs at the end of the story rather than at the beginning. This version bears a remarkable resemblance to the story of Jesus and his crucifixion.

And in nineteenth-century Vienna, too, Freud's Vienna, the rendering of material, whether mythical or clinical, was determined by the needs and problems of a specific place and time. In his autobiography, Stefan Zweig (1943, pp. 61–78) emphasized that this was a society completely preoccupied with the thought of sex; the very fact that it was never to be discussed openly insured that it was always on one's mind.

In Vienna every part of the female anatomy had to be concealed by clothing so cumbersome that it was impossible to dress oneself without assistance. It also required that women adopt a rather artificial manner of movement. For men, the problem was different. Middle-class marriage required a gentleman to be established, both financially and socially; this meant that men were not marrying until they were in their middle or late twenties. If a man was to find a sexual outlet, he had to turn to prostitutes, for sexual relations with a girl of "good breeding" was entirely out of the question (Janik and Toulmin, 1973).

Freud, of course, was a product of this Vienna. And though with daring insight he could see the latent, sexual content behind the manifest, there appears to be evidence of some distortion and selectivity on his part in support of his hypothesis.

In the case of Little Hans, for example, Freud (1909) reports that Hans, at the age of three-and-a-half, was found with his hand on his penis. His mother threatened him in these words: If you do that, I shall send for Dr. A. to cut off your widdler. And then what'll you widdle with? With my bottom, he answered (p. 8). It appears in the text as a casual encounter in which both mother and child seemingly knew that nothing was going to happen to the child's phallus.

It reminds me of one of Bruno Bettelheim's stories, of the mother who angrily yells at her child, I'm going to kill you. And Bettelheim stresses that both mother and child know that nothing is going to happen and thus the heated outburst is not experienced as traumatic. And this seems to be the case with Hans. But Freud says no, that this was the occasion of Hans' acquiring the castration complex. And in a note added to the text in 1923 he goes on to say, "Anyone . . . will of course find difficulty in ascribing its origin to a chance threat . . .; he will be driven to assume that children construct this danger themselves out of the slightest hints, which will never be wanting" (p. 8). At this point Freud makes no clear decision as to the respective roles of fantasy and reality. It is also quite interesting that Freud decided that the blinding of Oedipus symbolizes castration, although there was plenty of evidence that the Athenians did not hesitate to speak of castration, even depict it, whenever they needed to. Freud mentions in the note that his analytic students and colleagues had come up with a great many things that they took as evidence of the "castration complex"—withdrawal of the breast, defecation, the act of birth itself.

Putting a brake on this exuberance, he insisted that talk of the castration complex be restricted to "excitations and effects . . . bound up with the loss of the penis" (p. 8). Apparently he had not formulated this caveat when, in a note added to *The Interpretation of Dreams* in 1914, he referred to Oedipus' blinding as a castration (1900, p. 398).

Ross (1982) reminds us that Freud largely ignored the role of Laius in the oedipal drama; in fact, because he sees Laius as the primary culprit and the ultimate bad parent, he adds a new complex to our nomenclature: the "Laius complex." Ross goes on to suggest that Freud needed to protect his own father from accusation, by attributing hostile impulses to himself which were then projected onto his father. Ross thus revives the so-called seduction theory as a viable alternative to the revised Freudian theory.

Colman and Colman (1981) are among those who emphasize that the story of Oedipus begins not with the hero killing his father and marrying his mother, but rather with the father's attempt to kill his son.

Schorske (1981) points out that a major crisis in Freud's life in the nineties was personal, centering on the death of his father, as Ross has also suggested. "The most important event, the most poignant loss of a man's life," was the way Freud characterized the death of his father (p. 186). His father's death in 1896 came at a time when it could only reinforce Freud's other difficulties. His dreams and their analysis make plain to Schorske that his psychological crisis over his father's death unfolded as if it were a crisis of professional failure and political guilt.

Schorske continues: "In most of the other great creative Viennese who were Freud's contemporaries, the generational revolt against the fathers took the specific historical form of rejection of their fathers' liberal creed. . . . Not so Freud, at least not consciously. He defined his oedipal stance in such a way as to overcome his father by realizing the liberal creed his father professed but had failed to defend" (p. 191).

In the final scene of the Revolutionary Dream, Freud (1900, pp. 208–219, 431–435), found himself on the platform in the company of a blind man, whom he recognized in his analysis as his dying father. He held a urinal for the helpless old man. Freud then recalled that he had been reprimanded for urinating in his parents' presence as a child. His father had said, "This boy will come to nothing." In the dream, Freud reverses the situation and it is the helpless father who is urinating.

Freud's task now was to draw theoretical deductions from the experience of the patricidal impulse he had found in the dream. Schorske notes: "This he did by identifying a mythic archetype, the myth of Oedipus, to give form to his findings that 'the death-wish against parents dates back to earliest childhood.' He appropriated the Oedipus myth in such a fashion as to bring out the sexual dimensions (a preoccupation of nineteenth-century Vienna) it contains." He thus went from the personal infantile experience to the childhood of the human race.

The father's impulse to harm the son Freud constructed as a projection. It was his own fantasy, which then got externalized onto the father and aimed back at him, the son. And then it was generalized to the status of archetype. He could in this way avoid blaming first his father and then himself.

In his consideration of the Oedipus myth, Freud similarly avoided any notice of Laius' misdeeds. In my construction, this defense against awareness of the father-figure's hostile impulse was itself a defense against the homosexual love of father and son. Parenthetically, it is interesting to note that the blind Oedipus, in *Oedipus at Colonus,* was cared for by his devoted daughter Antigone. In the dream, it is Freud (the daughter?) who cares for the blind old man. This aspect of Freud's relationship with his father could be expressed quite openly by Freud as long as it was desexualized and he could convince himself that this expression was in fact a defense against a patricidal impulse. This supports my view of the circular and reciprocal relationship between impulse and defense, by which an impulse, once made conscious, can serve as a defense against another impulse, affect, or need. It is also interesting to note that Freud, like Oedipus, was cared for by his daughter in his old age.

In my work with children I am profoundly impressed how often parents are in fact inimical to their children. Surprisingly, the children themselves find it almost universally necessary to support an idealization of the parents as good, bountiful, protective, and loving. At all costs they must avoid the awareness of the parents' badness or wrongdoing.

I think that one may justly state that Freud's concept of the complementary series belongs here too. The father's hate and the father's love, the son's hate and the son's love, each in turn requiring defensive maneuvers against both recognition and realization.

I have suggested that Freud's ideas about the oedipus complex were an expression of a need on his part to solve an internal problem within the framework of his time and place. Perhaps it is a mark of his genius that he could resonate with universal themes. But some universal themes, like incest between father and son, or the hostile wishes between them, he had to defend against.

What has happened to the Oedipus myth in our own time? The major thrust has been toward the preoedipal. In one such trend, the father has virtually been eliminated as a factor in the child's development. The entire focus has been on the mother as the primary or sole person in the child's formative years. When we talk about empathy, a holding environment, dyadic relationships, libidinal object constancy, we are invariably talking about the mother-child relationship.

Although Freud did pursue a developmental model, psychological life for him did not begin until the oedipal phase. He did not attend to infant development. That was left to child analysts and later to infancy researchers. People like Anna Freud, Melanie Klein, Erikson, Spitz, Winnicott, and Bowlby revolutionized much of our understanding of early childhood.

The findings of much of this research have made us aware that infancy is somehow the crucial determinant in development, particularly as we began to pay more and more attention to narcissistic, preoedipal, and borderline disturbances. People in these categories are generally seen to have deficits in their psychological structure, and to have dyadic rather than triadic object relations. Thus has evolved a theory that emphasizes the crucial role of the early mothering figure. The mother and father of the oedipal period are relegated to an increasingly insignificant role, while bonding and empathy—clearly the province of the early mother—become the central determinants in development. In our theories up to this point, no role was ascribed to the father prior to the phallic-oedipal phase of development. If he had an earlier role, it was usually considered that of a surrogate mother. Even Therese Benedek saw the father's role during the child's infancy as that of simply supporting the mother in her motherliness.

But if we do concentrate on the role of the mother, why has there been so little attention paid to Jocasta and her role in the attempted sacrifice of Oedipus? (cf Bross, Ch. 20) Paralleling that, what was Sarah's role in Abraham's attempt to sacrifice Isaac? Is the mother so weak she cannot protest? Is she compliant, even collusive? Or does the story basically exclude the mother and involve only the love-hate homosexual relationship of father and son? In one version of the myth, the slaying of Laius is the result of both Laius and Oedipus being enamored of Chryssipus and competing for him. At the oedipal phase of development, there is no conceptualization of the mother as an actor in the drama. And, of course, there are no preoedipal phenomena in an oedipal drama.

Yet in Greek mythology the female is very powerful. Pentheus is murdered by his own mother. Medea kills her own children in revenge against her husband. It is Hera, a goddess, who sends the Sphinx, generally seen as a phallic woman, to terrorize Thebes. In describing the fate of Pentheus, Ross (1982) says that "he fell prey to . . . the emasculating, murderous power of the preoedipal and phallic mother. In her grasp, this first son was effeminized, castrated, and destroyed" (p. 177).

Blos (1979) notes the following: "I have come to the conclusion that castration anxiety in relation to the phallic woman is not only a universal occurrence of male preadolescence but can be considered . . . its central theme" (p. 109). Kanzer (1964) adds: "Perhaps ultimately the riddle of the Sphinx, so obviously placed in the phallic phase, is to give a name to that which does not exist—the female phallus . . ." (p. 35).

In still another version of the myth (Graves, 1955), Oedipus tried to substitute a patrilineal succession for a matrilineal one. Is it possible that Sophocles, based on his own homosexual orientation, was in fact attempting to eliminate the influence of women altogether?

The threatening, castrating father was seen by Freud as the child's invention; he was simply projecting his own castrating impulses onto the father. Freud, much less concerned with developing a psychology of women, paid less attention to the issues involving the mother's role. It was therefore less clear whether he saw the *mother's* castrating impulses toward the son as merely the son's projections. His explanation had more to do with the mother's penis envy. This so-called phallic mother was generally ignored until resurrected by Blos.

Freud had primarily written about the phallic mother in relation to a girl's development. We all seem to be much more comfortable with the mother of nurturance—or of an oedipal mother as an object of desire but not as having wishes and motives of her own. Is the phallic-mother the mother with a phallus? Or is the phallic-mother the mother of the so-called phallic period of development—a phase that spans or is a bridge between the dyadic and triadic levels of object-relationships? It is no longer fashionable to talk about such things as vagina dentata, for example. Although the Greeks did conceptualize a female with a phallus, our own proclivity has been to identify a female wish for a phallus as a wish to be a male. But there are alternate ways of looking at that.

And if we continue to focus on the importance of the nurturing mother, can we continue to ignore Jocasta, the mother of abandonment? We need to remember that this was part of the oedipal myth as well. The current trend is to pay a lot of attention to the mother of abandonment and to largely ignore the mother of the oedipal phase. In this model the father has ceased to exist as a major factor in child development.

But another trend has of late been developing that makes the father a much more significant force in the child's early life, while still minimizing his role at the oedipal level. This is still a model of preoedipal development. Along with the greater emphasis on the father comes deemphasis of the mother. For example, the concept of self-righting tendencies suggests that, except in extreme situations, most children will arrive more or less at the same place in development at about the same time, and that environmental input becomes significant only after eighteen to twenty-four months. There has been research suggesting that bonding with the mothering figure may be far less significant than originally thought. The idea of discontinuities in development takes issue with the critical period theory of development (which stresses the role of the mother and the ensuing deficits for subsequent development if timely and adequate passage through a phase does not occur; in this model there is no catching up). This tendency to minimize the role of the mother has aided or even permitted the conceptual entry of the father into early development, in which he is no longer simply acting as a mother surrogate.

The role of the preoedipal father has been focused on by Abelin (1978), Benedek (1970), Blos (1984), Herzog (Ch. 26), and Ross (Ch. 23), among many. Most of these authors have focused on the positive paternal role. Blos has emphasized the importance of resolving the preoedipal love of father and son as a precondition to making a satisfactory heterosexual adjustment.

Lance Morrow (1984), in a recent biographical account of his relationship with his famous father, Hugh Morrow, writes:

> From time to time I have felt for my father a longing that was almost physical, something passionate, but prior to sex—something infantile, profound. It has bewildered me, even thrown me into depression. It is mysterious to me exactly what it is I wanted from my father. I have seen this longing in other men—and see it now in my own sons, their longing for me. I think that I have glimpsed it once or twice in my father's feelings about his father. Perhaps it is some urge of Telemachus, the residual infant in the man still wistful for the father's heroic protection. One seeks to return not to the womb, which is enclosing, a warm, passive oblivion, but to a different thing, a father's sponsorship in the world. A boy wants the aura and armament of his father. It is a deep yearning, but sometimes a little sad—a common enough masculine trait that is vaguely unmanly. What surprises me is how angry a man becomes sometimes in the grip of what is, in essence, an unrequired passion. [p. 6]

This statement is a remarkable confirmation of the preoedipal attachment of son and father, a phenomenon previously neglected. What is it in our current cultural milieu that permits such remembrances, when previously they had either been taboo or had needed to be defended against? Why is research on the father coming so late compared to the work on the mother of infancy?

I have seen this same theme operate in the clinical area. In one adolescent patient an early attachment—the patient reports how as a little boy he would try to dress like father and walk like father and take on father's interests and shadow him—became a major stumbling block in resolving the adolescent phase and prevented his going on to age-appropriate heterosexual attachments. Once I would simply have taken these early attachments and identifications to the father as necessary and phase-appropriate rather than seeing them both as necessary and as obstacles to subsequent development. Blos' idea that an early object relationship with the father can interfere with a later object relationship with the mother (at the oedipal level) is very new to our understanding. It is not the same as the negative Oedipus, but the earlier preoedipal relationship does provide a greater access to this kind of solution.

What is it in our society, at any one time, that triggers off a particular kind of search and research, an introspection that gives a new meaning and a new direction to issues that have always been there?

Perhaps Kanzer (1964) sums it up best:

> the storyteller is compelled to unify the data . . . , a work of secondary elaboration. . . . it is ritual that tends to establish standardized and invariable accounts because certain more authentic variants are unacceptable. The myth . . . thus . . . tends to achieve a secondary autonomy that acquires characteristic developmental patterns of its own.
>
> The living progression of the Oedipus myth can be followed from prehistoric times to the epic form with which it was endowed by Homer and the sophisticated dramatization that it received at the hands of Sophocles—each of these poets finding in the legend a mirror for his own personality and era. The psychoanalyst must be aware of similar dispositions within himself, i.e., the countertransference tendency in the interpretation which actually makes each article on Oedipus a reflection not only of the analyst's own personality, but also of the contemporary theories that prevail in metapsychology. . . . [pp. 36–37]

I would add that these are not flaws but potentially valuable insights into ourselves and into our times, so long as we are aware of what *we* contribute to myth, legend, and history. But perhaps our creative imagination should be used more in understanding myths than in making them.

REFERENCES

Abelin, E. (1978), The role of the father in the preoedipal years: A panel report. *J. Amer. Psychoanal. Assn.,* 26:143–162.

Benedek, T. (1970), Fatherhood and providing. In: *Parenthood: Its Psychology and Psychopathology,* ed. Anthony & Benedek, pp. 167–183.

Blos, P. (1979), *The Adolescent Passage.* New York: International Universities Press.

——— (1984), Son and father. *J. Amer. Psychoanal. Assn.,* 32:301–324.

Bowman, H. N. (1918), *The Crimes of the Oedipodean Cycle.* Boston: Richard G. Badger.

Bringuier, J.-C. (1980), *Conversations with Jean Piaget.* Chicago: University of Chicago Press.

Colman, A. & Colman, L. (1981), *Earth Father/Sky Father. The Changing Concept of Fathering.* Englewood Cliffs, NJ: Prentice-Hall. A Spectrum Book.

Freud, S. (1900), The interpretation of dreams. *Standard Edition,* 4/5. London: Hogarth Press, 1953.

——— (1909), Analysis of a phobia in a five-year-old boy. *Standard Edition,* 10:3–149. London: Hogarth Press, 1955.

Graves, R. (1955), *The Greek Myths.* Baltimore: Penguin Books.

Janik, A. & Toulmin, S. (1973), *Wittgenstein's Vienna.* New York: Simon & Schuster.

Kanzer, M. (1964), On interpreting the Oedipus plays. *Psychoanalytic Study of Society,* 3:26–38. New York: International Universities Press. Chapter 10, this volume.

Licht, H. (1952), *Sexual Life in Ancient Greece.* New York: Barnes & Noble.

Morrow, L. (1984), *The Chief. A Memoir of Fathers and Sons.* New York: Random House.

Novey, S. (1968), *The Second Look. The Reconstruction of Personal History in Psychiatry and Psychoanalysis.* Baltimore: Johns Hopkins Press.

Ross, J. M. (1982), Oedipus revisited: Laius and the "Laius Complex." *The Psychoanalytic Study of the Child,* 37:169–200. New Haven, CT: Yale University Press. Chapter 19, this volume.

Schorske, C. (1981), *Fin-De-Siecle Vienna. Politics and Culture.* New York: Vintage Books.

Walsh, W. H. (1958), *Philosophy of History: An Introduction.* New York: Harper & Brothers.

Weiss, S. (1981), Reflections on the psychoanalytic process, with special emphasis on child analysis and self-analysis. *Annual of Psychoanalysis,* IX:43–56. New York: International Universities Press.

Zweig, S. (1943), *The World of Yesterday: An Autobiography.* London: Cassell and Company,

CLINICAL, CULTURAL, AND DEVELOPMENTAL IMPLICATIONS

23

The Darker Side of Fatherhood: Clinical and Developmental Ramifications of the "Laius Motif"

JOHN MUNDER ROSS

[1984]

Preamble

In a tape made by Columbia's Psychiatric Educational Research Division in conjunction with the St. Luke's Parents' Center, fathers are being interviewed with their babies. One of them, a gentle and mildly bearish young man with ministerial beard and Midwestern twang, concludes his segment by lifting his six-month-old boy by the right foot and swinging the dangling and inverted baby in sweeping arcs. The audience, marveling perhaps at what has become for them the long-lost vestibular complacency of the infant, his look of matter-of-fact pleasure, breaks into laughter. But then again, the scene may

---

Reprinted with permission from *International Journal of Psychoanalytic Psychotherapy*, vol. 11, pp. 117–144.

evoke other responses as well, for one of its members, a renowned female child psychiatrist, remarks that no *mother* ever handles her baby in this manner.

In another videotape, this one made by Michael Yogman under the auspices of T. Berry Brazelton's Child Development Unit at Harvard, a beetle-browed father, a sort of young, intellectual John L. Lewis with Boston drawl, zeroes in on his two-month-old, whom he calls a "young man." Asking whether he has been "good to his mother," and whether he has eaten his "dinner of beef," he taps the propped infant's abdomen vigorously as his animated face dives repeatedly toward that of his first-born son—wide-eyed, alert, high-keyed, and excited. It is a pattern—the intrusion, the tapping, the high-keyed stimulation—typical of fathers in interaction with their babies during the first six months, according to Yogman (1982). It is, moreover, distinctly different from the more enveloping and equilibrating dialogues that transpire between mothers and infants. Once again, when confronted with this particular spectacle, audiences of analysts, pediatricians, and laymen alike typically roar with laughter.

Introduction

There is a good deal more to the dealings between fathers and sons than the mutual and fearful murderousness about which I shall shortly speak. The two generations of males can and most often do love each other (see Ross, 1977, 1979a, 1979b, 1979c). Nevertheless, I am compelled to advance a most stark and terrible thesis. Loving them, fathers also want to rape, abuse, and kill their sons. It is an ugly, repulsive, hateful notion, but I now know that it is a truth of the human heart and, as a psychoanalytic thinker, am compelled to give it credence and utterance. The statistics, certainly, even in this age of enlightened attention to childhood, attest to its crude, real-life manifestations. According to the Statistical Abstract for the U.S. for 1985, there were approximately 200 reported infanticides a year between 1960 and 1980 and 600,000 to 925,000 cases of child abuse and neglect. In 1983, 88 percent of the persons arrested for "offenses against family and children" were male, and of the offenders, 62.7 percent were between 25 and 44 years old—typically the "age of fatherhood" in a man's life. And perhaps the victims are more numerous. According to Steele (1982), are abused, while 2,000 to 3,000 die of neglect and injuries sustained at adult, mostly male, hands.

At other times a father's aggression may even promote adaptation. Subject to primal repression, paternal violence may emerge in the form of aggressive interactions—teasing, roughhousing, discipline—which then enhance a child's, and especially a boy's, development in a variety of ways and along various lines. I will return to this dimension of my subject in closing, in the meantime focusing on its pathological and pathogenic manifestations.

To continue: psychoanalysts partly disavow this intergenerational hostility when they attribute to imagination and intention alone their patients' intuition into the darkness of the parent's heart. Truth after all is proverbially stranger, eerier than fantastical fiction and can be a good deal scarier and more unsettling. Filicide, unwanted or premeditated, is everywhere. Witness the flurry of popular novels and films which have as pivotal events inadvertent, premeditated, attempted, or actual child murder. *The World According to Garp, Sophie's Choice, The White Hotel, The Changeling, The Shining, Total Abandon,* and a good many others all portray the killing of children. The theme permeates not only the popular media but also our legacy of Greek mythology. The stories, for instance, of Uranus, Kronos, and Zeus, Agamemnon and Iphigenia, Heracles, and Medusa and Perseus, and Andromeda all chronicle the sacrifice of the young, as does the legend of Oedipus himself—a personification of the conflictual inner truths on which Freud's brainchild and our subsequent discipline has been said to rest. (Kakar [1978] has suggested that the Hindu mythology lays a similar stress on intended infanticide, more so than parricide.) In this last, the Oedipus narrative, as in the others, it is the children who bear the brunt of the parents' cruelties and indiscretions, and, most disturbingly, the apparent culpability for generations of parental misdeeds. In a sense, every patient has suffered such abuse, subtle or obvious, glimpses of which the analyst tends to interpret according to the transference of the moment.

Fathers Good and Bad: Freud, Oedipus, and Laius

It took me some time to appreciate more fully these sinister currents in all fathers. For nearly a decade, having responded to the limitations of existing theory and prompted by feminism to heed the variegations and vicissitudes of a man's sexual identity, I underscored a good or "good enough" father's optimal or ideal functions and functioning. Emphasizing male nurturance and generativity, I strove to counter the prevailing emphasis on the paternal castration threat. Notwithstanding the realities of hate and hostility in the relations between father and children, these are, I concluded, counterbalanced and neutralized by the equally potent presence of fatherly care and mutual love. *Agape* mitigates violence, real and imagined (see Kestenberg, 1975; Ross, 1975, 1977, 1979a, 1979b, 1979c).

But soon a number of other factors began to impinge on this rather sunny prospective: the sadistic power-posturing of world leaders by the close of the decade and their malignant neglect of the young and needy; pervasive authoritarianism; the struggles of myself and my supervisees to engage fathers clinically; the struggles of adult analytic patients to contend with their parents' mistreatment of them, the persistence of their idealizations of them and of the analyst; the tenacity with which even as sentient and insightful adults they cling to outworn guilts. I was struck by my own relative blindness and the purblindness of those before me, the partial disavowal of self-evident interpersonal truths on the part of the analytic community.

Beginning with the new decade, then, my attention turned more and more to the sex-specific rivalry and hostility besetting and potentially compromising a man's paternal capacity. Cognizance of these themes had seemed to assert itself in the analytic literature only then to lapse into obscurity, requiring repeated rediscovery. Like a man's aspirations to an unrequited motherhood, a father's filicidal urges occasioned resistances to which psychoanalysts themselves proved vulnerable.

Along with authors like Rosner (1977), Erikson (1980), Atkins (1970), and, most of all, Devereux (1953), I returned to the Oedipus myth, and to Freud's reading of it. Freud's rendition of Oedipus' life story, I found, was as remarkable for its single-mindedness and omissions as for its abiding veracity (Ross, 1982d). To summarize what I learned:

In *The Interpretation of Dreams* Freud (1900) discussed Sophocles' *Oedipus Rex,* discerning in the play's evocative power themes which he would eventually formalize as basic tenets of psychoanalysis (see also Freud, 1950). His synopsis of the plot and its parallel with the psychoanalytic process are familiar to most analysts as a paradigmatic statement about the unwanted nature of *self*-discovery, of *in*sight. In time Oedipus would become not only an analytic parable but a prototype for a universal "complex" (Freud, 1910), eventually engendering a whole language peculiar to psychoanalysis. In the meantime, Freud's central thesis was simply that the play's ability to stir its audiences through the millennia resided in its abiding resonance with the onlooker's unwanted and repressed *childhood* wishes.

So, having penetrated the secret of sons, could Freud look as well into the soul of the father? Indeed, it is the intrapsychic, the inner world of intentionality, which is truly at issue; less compelling are the possibilities of literal, sensational transgressions and their manifestations, for example in Freud's own life, as those who would revive the seduction theory in its initial crude form would have us believe. The point is this: for reasons about which one can but speculate, Freud reversed himself and demurred rather than impugn the actions and more or less defended urges and proclivities of fathers in general, Laius included. In theory at least, Freud seems to have overcompensated for his earlier literalness by underplaying certain subtle misbehaviors on the part of his patients' parents, notably fathers. It was a trend that seems to have influenced Freud's clinical judgment and handling of transference phenomena, as is evident in the major case histories (Ross 1979a, 1982d).

Freud's initial version of Oedipus' story was wanting, based as it was solely on the one play of Sophocles, excluding even the tragedy of the dramatist's old age, *Oedipus at Colonus.* His classicism notwithstanding, Freud's knowledge of the many variants of the Oedipus legend remains uncertain (Kanzer, personal communication). In any event, whether because of forgetfulness or because of ignorance, Freud overlooked the crime, the trespass, on the part of Oedipus' father which had set the whole family tragedy in motion (Ross, 1982d). Laius failed to appreciate his son's emergent and ultimately greater promise, power, and fortitude. It is interesting that in the myth he acts to harm his son at two junctures which do not correspond with the "oedipal period": at the infant's birth, when there is great personal upheaval, regression, and a reorganization, for better or worse, of the representational world; and during adolescence, when the succession of the generations becomes a reality, as Freud himself noted in 1909 (see also Blos, 1980; Esman, 1982). Thus, for example, Wainwright (1966), Jarvis (1962), and before them Zilboorg (1931) described the pathogenic potential of biological paternity, with a particular stress on depressive phenomena in prospective and new fathers.

One young man in analysis reported a series of reactions during the delivery by emergency caesarian section of his firstborn son. Waiting while his wife was rushed into the operating room, he imagined her giving birth to a dead girl. Later, enraptured by his healthy and bawling male infant, he found himself impressed by the boy's flailing arms and seemingly mythic vital powers and, withal, simultaneously enraged at the damage which, he fantasized, had been done to his wife's beautiful, youthful, and sexually affirming body. Cradling the child, he stared into the boy's beloved and, to him, utterly unspoiled and beatific face, only, in a parapraxis, to call him "my father."

The theme of generational succession was inescapable during these few hours, as it was for another analysand, described by Colarusso and Nemiroff (1982), who uncovered his envy of his *adolescent* son's sexual exploits, his penis, and the simple promise afforded by youth. What, these men wondered, had their fathers felt toward them? The braggadocio and phallic pretenses of the oedipal son may seem somehow more "knowable" and therefore more easily encompassed and subdued than are the vulnerability of the infant and the novelty of a fatherly role or the departure into adulthood of the adolescent in all his "omnipotentiality."

Whatever motives may be read into the successive events of the Oedipus narrative, its mythologized "facts," it remains clear that in discovering his own inadvertent misdeeds Oedipus also uncovers the willful sins of his father. Embracing his culpability, he nonetheless averts his gaze from the more heinous abuse done to him. For all his phallic and prideful narcissism, easy rage, arrogance, and moralism,

Oedipus the son, having killed his cruel father, does not inveigh against him when he finds out the truth—at least not in *Oedipus Rex*. He does call Jocasta an "unspeakable mother"; but about his tyrannical father, not a word. He succumbs instead to his own excruciating guilt, assuming total responsibility for the tragedy and blinding himself. Why? Overdetermined as it was, the analyst might speculate, Oedipus' "oedipal guilt" also may serve to obscure the crimes of the father, rendering Laius' wrongdoing as the son's own and thereby perpetuating an illusion of undying benevolence and patronage.

Clinical Realities: The Laius "Complex" or Motif and Its Implications

Analysts must proceed beyond mythic metaphors to clinical realities to support conjecture. Even before researching the various versions of the Theban chronicle, I found myself becoming more and more attuned to the gender-specific conflicts experienced by even the most caring men in their parenting and intuited by their children. These include: man's inherent aggression toward other males and children, as seen in all primates; *rivalry* for wife and mother—a possessiveness that is in origin sibling, oedipal, conjugal, patriarchal, and otherwise; bisexual, maternal envy and competitiveness, leading fathers to prevent mothers from mothering on one pretext or another; aggressivized and defensive power-posturing and abuse to conceal the feminizing implications of these wishes to be a mother; exclusion from the mother-infant dyad and subsequent rage; pure and simple pathological narcissism and imperious grandiosity. Indeed, a whole *constellation* of paternal conflicts, with the psychic organization this implies, can emerge in more or less benign or malignant forms, all of this bespeaking destructive aggression toward the child.

The father's "Laius complex," or for the sake of terminological parsimony, "Laius *motif*," includes both filicidal and pederastic trends. It is instigated partly in reaction to the child's own successive developmental demands but seems inherent in the adult himself. It represents a transfiguration of the adult father's childhood oedipal constellation, including both his competition with his father and his identification with the latter's felt or perceived paternal aggression. But it is also a phase- or age-specific response to the succession of generations and to his own predestined demise, and the utter narcissistic blow inherent in our mortality. This may be compounded by conflicts in sexual identity, with hostile, sadistic, and phallic displays serving to defend against bisexual and infantile trends. Thus, a father's history and "preparental" character structure figure in his capacity for child rearing. But parenthood is further influenced by the child's unique characteristics and the marital and family context. Jocasta can abandon her baby or fight back, for instance, asserting her prerogative and cementing the "ties that bind." Oedipus' is thus also a family tragedy.

The behaviors in which the Laius motif becomes manifest range from storytelling, roughhousing, discipline, and teasing, all more or less appropriate, to more blatant and pernicious expressions of possession with regard to a man's wife, to the outright neglect, abuse, or even murder of the children. Present to some degree in all fathers, however "repugnant" to most, the Laius complex can give rise to a variety of pathological and pathogenic postures, from an excessive neurotic inhibition of impulses on the part of depressive or obsessively remote fathers, to quasi-transference psychoses in which the child is the central object in the projection of the adult's unneutralized aggression. Aggressive interchanges may be either wanting or excessive. Whether brutalized by fathers or shortchanged by their faintheartedness, however, children at some level sense and respond to the latent communications involved in the paternal behavior.

In fact, these communications of paternal impulses serve as dynamic preconditions or releasors of the son's negative and positive oedipus complex—universally, I believe. The adult man's inevitable intrusion and domination invite a more or less sexualized submission, his oppression and "interruptions of activity" exciting narcissistic and possessive hostility. Indeed, there is a feedback system of sorts between the adult's Laius and the son's Oedipus constellations. Present in its own right, the would-be imperiousness of the child can itself assume either a pathological and destructive or an adaptive and assertive form of expression, depending on a father's manifest actions and reactions, and on the delicate balance between his empathy and mature love and his communications of unconscious hostility and selfish desire. Long ago Burlingham (1935) and Hartmann, Kris, and Loewenstein (1946)—and, more recently, Stern (personal communication)—marveled at the child's "uncanny" and even seemingly "supernatural" intuitions into a parent's unconscious, particularly, they emphasize, his (or her) more destructive urges toward his own offspring, whether blatant or insidious.

There are many implications for all levels of intervention to be derived from an awareness of the "Laius" present to some degree in all fathers, and of intergenerational hostility in general. First of all, therapeutic work with fathers of child and adolescent patients must be attuned to these phenomena and to resistances to them. Noteworthy is the male parent's typical posture of indifference, with denial and avoidance constituting a defense against potential hostility, and at the same time a representational void and thus a distorted expression of psychic murder. The de facto exclusion of fathers from the treatment situation often bespeaks a collusion, a fearful glimpse on the part of all involved into the realities of paternal aggression. It is a perception that becomes exacerbated by male and, to some extent, female clinicians' identifications with the child, unconscious remembrances and their projections of awesome power as well as their own murderous and castrative urges onto the patient's father (see Ferholt and Gurwitt, 1982). In this climate, the clinician, the child, and the father himself may accede to images propagated by many mothers to the effect that fathers are alternately dangerous, indifferent, incompetent, and irrelevant—"hopeless nonparents."

Second, the problem of father absence has been treated as a fait accompli to which the clinician accedes helplessly. It is, rather, a dynamic process in which intervention may be possible and beneficial. Related to this issue are the conflicts of divorced fathers. There is according to Wallerstein and Kelly (1982), no way of predicting the postdivorce relationship on the basis of what has taken place in the past. The pain of loss commingles with resentment in the face of old hurts and new burdens. Much can be done to confront the denial, the avoidance, and the reassertion of lost youth plaguing fathers who are in *the process of becoming absent.* Nor, as the analyst well knows, will exhortation or instruction suffice.

B.D., a thirty-five-year-old journalist, sought treatment in the wake of an unhappy love affair. Bereft, deprived, beset by fantasies of vengeance toward his old girlfriend and especially her new flirtation—he responded to the question posed over the phone as to when he would prefer his first appointment, "Yesterday." He had left his older wife and son Eric, when the boy was eighteen months old, for this younger and ostensibly sexier woman, only to find her withholding and, in the end, unabashedly rejecting.

After the dust of the crisis settled, enabling him to scrutinize and disengage from Billi, B.D. became immersed in intensive psychoanalytic therapy. Among the many issues which emerged were the man's formerly intense involvement with his young son as an infant and toddler and subsequent detachment from and avoidance of him following the divorce when the boy was two-and-a-half. His and his former wife's schedules had been such that during the day he had functioned as their child's primary caretaker, embracing the role wholeheartedly. It gradually became apparent that B.D.'s loss and severed dependency had as much to do with the boy as with the errant Billi.

Fears of femininity and a strong maternal identification, along with a horror of associated homosexual trends (which became clear within the transference as well), we learned, had moved B.D. to flee his son and his fatherhood. He became preoccupied with parading his manly body before the new girlfriend, whose own phallic attributes were to be explored in the analysis (she had also energetically rejected his son).

Ignored by his once loving father and relegated by his hardworking mother to the care of babysitters, B.D.'s son became increasingly timid and evidently rather schizoid, requiring evaluation and treatment. His learning disabilities, reminiscent of the patient's problems as a child, added to the difficulties and compounded B.D.'s increasingly undeniable disappointment in and guilt toward the son. All the while he was at pains to disavow any hostility toward Eric.

At one point, however, he began to speculate about the therapist and the therapist's children, particularly an imagined son, in the context of complaining about his more limited life and about the prospect of growing old. He had long ago surpassed his father, while having identified with the old man's plaintive, embittered, and self-defeating posture as a sort of atonement for his better lot in life. Now he recalled the father's herniated scar from abdominal surgery and remarked on how small, set against his bulk, his father's penis had once seemed to him when he caught sight of it in the shower. In contrast he imagined the therapist to be more powerful, fit, and well-muscled, in addition to being smarter, kinder, and more fatherly. He envied his intact family. He thought that the therapist's son, in contrast to

Eric, must be similarly well-endowed and a source of pride. He remembered holding his pet dog before the vet put her to sleep. And then with great shock, B.D. uncovered his wish to rid himself of a boy, who, once his darling, had become basically a burden and a disappointment. Failing to solace him with the promise of self-perpetuation, Eric merely reminded B.D. of his limitations and failures as well as his inescapable mortality. Avoiding him served to prevent the fits of anger he now confessed to when presented by the child's sloppy appearance, slowness, and preoccupation with "little people." In effect, it served to do away with him: out of sight, out of mind, out of existence. With these insights B.D. was enabled to rediscover his deep love for Eric. Whereas in the past he might not see him for a month or more at a time over vacations, he now rearranged his scheduled and living space to accommodate him three days a week, further contending with a new wife's jealousy of her stepson.

A third point involves work with adults. Therapists and analysts must be aware of the actual, prospective, and potential parenthood of their analysands. Often relatively absent fathers themselves, by virtue of their own long training in midlife, male clinicians, analysts especially, have tended to overlook or underestimate the paternal conflicts of their male patients. When these do not emerge in treatment, for example, many clinicians fail to interpret the resistance. Conversely, when a patient does discuss his would-be or actual fatherhood, one reflexive tendency is to relate this material to the transference neurosis and to *filial* pretension and competitiveness. Parental inclinations toward the therapist are further treated as reaction-formations and other defensive distortions.

A colleague offered the following report:

H.L., a twenty-nine-year-old man, had been in analysis five times weekly for four-and-a-half years when he was finally able to propose to and marry his girlfriend of one year. He had initially presented a panphobic picture, compounded by compulsive symptoms, along with infantile tendencies, paranoid trends, and structural impairment, notably his profound failures in affect and drive modulation. Work on oscillating preoedipal and rather dramatic oedipal conflicts, wherein intense castration anxiety commingled with fears of object loss (leaving, the analyst took his penis away with him, he once said) revealed a problematic constellation of primary objects.

The patient had been terrorized by a controlling, explosive, strap-wielding mother whose aggressivity confounded his evident incestuous impulses toward her—"it's tough when the hand that hits is the hand that loves," as he put it—and, pervasively and repeatedly, injured his masculinity. He devalued his generally more loving and gentle but also inadequate father, resenting his lack of self-respect and, with this, his inability to control the patient's mother, who eventually left him when the patient was seventeen. Initially, he had wanted his father to act as a disciplinarian, to hit him, subsequently playing this wish out in an overobvious oedipal transference neurosis.

More precise reconstruction unearthed the father's aggressivity and fits of sadism. Rather than roughhouse or wrestle or instruct him, he played the "flinching game" with his dangerously asthmatic and easily startled son—sadistically and to excess. Perhaps, the patient later mused, this was one of the sources of his compulsion to look over his shoulder while walking down the street. Similarly, the mother's initial timidity, self-doubt, and overprotection were also clarified, as he reflected on the motives for her mistreatment of him. H.L. discovered to his dismay that his mother, devalued and narcissistically deflated by her father, had exacted her revenge on his grandson, beating him and commenting on how small his penis was. Once again, analysis demonstrated the complex layering and multiple determination of a patient's manifest infantile objects, especially the fact that a patient's parents are also children.

In his parents' stead he clung to his maternal great-aunt and great-uncle. He cherished his enveloping and somewhat alarmist and overly cautious nana, with whom he lived when he began analysis. He virtually worshiped his great uncle, who had died of abdominal cancer two years after the divorce, at which point the patient had moved in with the nana. He had found the powerful old man authoritarian and therefore awesome, "a real man," idealizing him utterly. Only with great pain, remonstration, and repeated defensive regressions could the patient allow himself to see the man's defects and indiscretions, specifically the way in which such compulsivity, tyranny, and misogyny had been responsible for his hapless plight at his mother's hands. His fiancé, later his wife, was experienced as being like his great-aunt, motherly and loving rather than vicious. When he wed her, H.L. softened the "challenge to the gods" (his most problematic phobia had involved thunder and lightning) by using the grandfather's wine cup at the wedding.

Obviously the analysis was extremely complex, volatile, and arduous. For example, I have elsewhere elaborated on how H.L.'s phallic posture served to defend against a strong maternal, bisexual identification (Ross, 1982b). As this fell away, exposing his intense parental interest in a younger brother born when he was six, the patient was better able to experience tenderness and sexual intimacy with a woman and to entertain the prospect of fatherhood. Even the analyst was often subjected to parental concern in what the patient called a "role reversal."

During the course of the analysis, H.L.'s phobias were gradually replaced by a variety of psychosomatic symptoms, representing a sort of way station en route to genuine internalization (and the subjective representation of conflictual affects), troublesome as they became in their own right. Prior to his marriage, for example, H.L. developed upper abdominal gastric and duodenal pains, which he associated to his father's gall bladder condition. Following the ceremony and a Latin American honeymoon, the symptoms shifted, becoming reminiscent of the ominous signs of his grandfather's cancer. Now he complained increasingly of lower left quadrant gastrointestinal pain, eventuating in a spastic colon and moving him to subject himself first to a sigmoidoscopy and finally a colonoscopy—the latter undertaken without anesthesia because of his history of asthma. At last acknowledging the psychogenic and subsequent hypochondriacal elements of his physical illness, the patient began to own and to explore more fully his parental ambitions, his pregnancy fantasies, and the act of homosexual submission obvious in what had amounted to a sort of colossal rape. He was, as Gurwitt (1982) has put it, "getting ready" in his idiosyncratic way for fatherhood—even to the extent of inuring himself to the "shit" which once appalled him. Among the many issues to be worked on was the patient's identification with his mother, whose aggression and inaccessibility stood in sharp contrast to his wife's warmth and care, the felt maternal transference, and the empathy inherent in the analyst's emotionally precise interpretations. He thus punctuated his frenzy over the state of his body with bouts of weeping and rage at the violence he had suffered at his mother's hands. He was further terrified that in becoming a father he would be like her, repeating her cruelties out of envy for the better parenting his children potentially might have. An avid urban botanist, he loved his plants dearly, he said, even though they "stole" his light from him.

The gastrointestinal distress abated finally and then disappeared only to be temporarily replaced by a transient headache. He dwelt on this for a week, concluding his complaints with the following rather poignant Friday session:

I have a score to settle with my boss and Dr. L. (the first consultant)—just like my mother.

He associates to a suicide, the Rosenberg man in the paper who was caught stabbing his wife, and to a man on the West Coast who set his son on fire because of a custody battle.

They're upper class.

They are Rastafarians who put kids in the oven to get the devil out of them. But that's just ignorance and superstition. It's crazy we harbor these crazy instincts in us. Horrible.

My wife's parents brought back a present. I dislike getting valuable gifts 'cause of a fear of worrying about them. I don't want them to get ripped off or up.

I remember buying different clothes when I moved out—a way of getting away from her. My mother bought me white socks. They were ridiculous.

(And the gift of a child?)

I have a lot of concerns about children, and I would need to differentiate from her—from my mother. My mother set up rules, but she wasn't loving—although I guess she was overprotective when we were young. I might—I put a cover on my wife when she went to sleep—I reprimanded her—I'd probably do that too with kids.

Having a child is a risky proposition. Anything can happen. With me too. There are no guarantees. It depends on stresses.

(You're afraid of . . .?)

Running out of patience, getting angry. Like with toilet training for example, if the kid kept making a mess in his pants. I wouldn't succumb to peer pressure, but still I'd get furious.

I feel sorry for my friend M. with his hyper kid—he takes after the mother, not him; I don't know how he can stand it.

(Afraid of hurting, killing?)

Hitting, yes. It might erupt. It's not conscious—something spontaneous. Like the way I keep waking up in the early morning. Frustration. Like the old foot banging. If the kid was being disobedient. If he played games with me, like wanting toilet training and then he craps in his pants. What are you doing, fucking with me! Or an ugly kid, I joke about gassing kids or sedating them. I'm—It sounds cruel and inhuman. In order to raise a child, you have to be understanding and stable. I am understanding now, but I'm not so sure I'm stable. (pause) Somewhere along the line I have to decide about the headache (he's had it for a week). I'll have to go to the doctor.

(You're talking about children being headaches.)

Yeah, but not acting out.

(You're torturing yourself ahead of time because these wishes vie with your wish to mother babies and also make you guilty.)

Yeah, but you have to recognize there are certain energies to do harm.

You can't delude yourself. That's why I was quizzing you yesterday about the kids coming here. It's the parents who screw up the kids.

With S. (his wife), I don't like the way her mother treats her father. She kept taking over the stories he told about their trip—like he had nothing valuable to say. Like making fun of him.

You wanna know a Freudian slip I made last night? Her mother brought back twigs from South America. S. said it's like my mother, who collects rocks. I said it's like for her husbands. You know what I mean. She whittles them down and puts them on the mantel piece. The association is between rocks and balls—like the slang. That's why I hate these women. Come to think of it, put the sticks and rocks together and you've got the whole thing.

(That's why you'd be moved to attack a child. To avenge yourself on your mother in displaced fashion and make yourself feel like a big man.)

I wonder, does it matter? What sex it is—a boy or a girl.

My mother was put down by her father. I'd get even with a daughter, like she was a little twat. I think the only difference between men and women is a man has a penis. I know you disagree with that stuff about the insides. The estrogen's the mainline. Cut off the balls, and you lose the testosterone and the man turns into a woman . . . (H. L. gives more details about biology).

I always viewed it as the haves and the have-nots. Girls are fucked up because they are the have-nots. I used to think the doctor slipped during circumcision. That was the going joke, later. But I believed it.

My mother's behavior robbed me of a feeling of masculinity. She stripped me of it. Even if you had a dick or they cut off your balls, you feel like a woman if your mother acts that way. (Laughs.) Like a whimpering cock, unmasculine. If you get whipped into submission, big deal you have a cock, because you can't use it.

I guess I did see women as powerful, and I hated strong women. . .

(The abuse you fear you would commit has to do with your fighting to be a man rather than a woman.)

Or, better—or defective. Castrated. It would be a constant struggle. I can't relax myself. Even today I can't make myself sleep. In order to relax you have to be trusting and realize if you wake up you can defend yourself. You have to let your guard down to sleep. Uncle Mervin could. And S.'s dad. This aunt of mine and my uncle Sam. That son of a bitch Rachel destroys him. He's a tyrant in her presence. Like he needs to do it. He walks around with a stiff dick.

(And you?)

Yeah, it's the same, all that Hulk and Superman stuff.

(You felt overwhelmed and abused by your mother and were moved to identify with her cruelty and her femininity.)

It's unconscious. You make it conscious in analysis, but then you have conflict. There's an overhead to saying you want to smack a kid and know it's morally wrong—rather than just acting on it.

(The overhead now being a headache.)

Yeah.

Finally, interpretations of the oedipal dilemma have often been left incomplete and inexact by virtue of an exclusive focus on the intrapsychic conflicts of the patient as a child, as if excluding and exempting parents from the pressures of psychic life and its systematic scrutiny. In this vein, representations of destructive fathers have most often been ascribed basically to the workings of projection, with their bases in reality glossed over. Images of a father's domination and cruelty have been seen as reflections of the child's own cruel intentions, which serve to externalize and thus to alleviate the tension which is engendered by intrapsychic conflict and guilt. Transference distortions underscore the unreality of the patient's anticipation of murder and mutilation in the analytic situation and are used to clarify the "internal" nature of his conflicts.

This is true enough, of course; but, left at this level, such constructions, and implicit reconstructions, may serve to further invalidate the patient's observation of or intuition into the father's either obvious or unconscious wish to kill his offspring. In blinding himself, in embracing fate, guilt and absolute responsibility, Oedipus would close his eyes forever to his parent's cruelties (only then, in his dependent weakness, to compromise *his* children's well-being, identifying willy-nilly with Laius' and Jocasta's abdication of parenthood). In some instances, conflicts over oedipal rivalry can provide a whole defense *organization* (Hoffer, 1954), screening longings and dangers of a more primitive or primal order. Guilt, constriction, and abiding submission may act as a father's internal proxy, as slavemasters obscuring the recognition of the parent's "human frailty," vulnerability to impulse, and unpredictability, and softening the terror these provoke.

The need for a father's protection (of the child and the dyad) is, as Freud (1929) wrote, perhaps the most pressing condition of childhood, an imperative around which a great variety of neurotic edifices are constructed. Without it, one, all, is lost. In childhood especially, the ontological upheaval of a life alone is, quite simply, too great to bear. The little boy or girl must be and feel sustained and secure in his or her idealization of parental guardians. Challenging even the most brittle of these images is, technically, a risky undertaking when treating a child, no matter how transparent the parents' deficits or malevolence, and notwithstanding the compromising of various ego functions necessary to buttress such denial.

But as an adult, when he or she is cognitively equipped and socially and physically independent, it should be more possible for a patient to face the dangers and solitude of being on one's own. This aloneness is also what Oedipus' story, his journey—heroic, sublime, foolhardy, and agonizing and relieving by turns—is all about; it is, as Freud implied, what must be the ultimate work of analysis.

Thus, in the termination phase, E.D., a thirty-two-year-old woman, described a gnawing sense of solitude even as her interpersonal horizons widened and object relations deepened. The aloneness had to do with the revival of rapprochement struggles, to be sure, but also bespoke the final conquest of oedipal guilt. In laying to rest the voice of conscience which had plagued her symptomatically and then served to obscure the erotic transference that dominated the middle phase of her analysis—in giving up her mother's voice, that is—she found herself bereft of her infantile objects and their protection. I, the analyst, had lost my magic, my awesomeness, and some of my lustre as she made me her own (see Loewald, 1979).

It is a questionable venture, verging on wild analysis, to analyze in absentia a patient's parents, and this is not what I am advocating. But liberating the patient's convictions and perceptions about them and their motives is, quite the contrary, a most important undertaking, one which dissipates irrational guilt in favor of greater responsibility and initiative. The patient's poignant understanding of his parents' personhood, seen initially through insight into his own conflicts and imperfections, fosters personal freedom and genuine compassion. Possibly this is what is meant when analysts refer to "modifications of the harsh and archaic superego" and the "strengthening of the ego" which ensues. Blos (1962, 1980) describes the process more developmentally when he lays stress on overcoming persistent negative oedipal trends which seriously interfere with the individual's completion of adolescence and entry into adulthood.

A clinical vignette reveals with particular poignancy the presence of the sins of the fathers, in the more everyday psychopathology of the perversions:

The patient (*B*) is a 41-year-old man who has been in analysis for three years. His homosexuality was not the original reason for starting analysis but recently has been a major focus. After an intense effort to establish a close heterosexual relationship he has retreated. He has returned to homosexual or pederastic preoccupations, though trying to avoid seductions of boys which have been, he has decided, harmful to them and dangerous to him. His alcohol abuse and pathological narcissism have been major factors in the work, which in part characterized his father as well. His father often said that he (the father) was no longer the king of the roost. He was instead a rooster pushed aside in his own home. *B* didn't want that, though he had a large stake in it. After all, he (*B*) was just a little boy and didn't know how badly his parents hated and hurt each other (indeed, until very recently in the analytic work, he had seen as his early mission in life the bringing together of his parents, with himself as the healer of the breech). "My mother was the safest place and I clung to her to be protected." They were big people at war, and the child was like a small boat in a raging sea. He could understand his father's rage at him (*B*) for the possession of his mother (they often slept together until the patient was fifteen). But how could his father have dropped him one day, when he was very small, on his head? Father Leo (a priest friend of the family) was visiting, and they all were sitting in the kitchen. He (*B*) apparently bolted unexpectedly and fell off his father's lap onto the floor. His father was frightened—he hadn't really wanted to kill *B*. It was a minor incident, and he knew his father knew the distinction between thinking and wishing people harm and actually doing it. "But getting rid of me must have been so real in his thoughts that it (the incident of the fall) scared him." He doesn't now think his father really tried to kill him "but a part of him wanted to." And it was that part he was afraid of. When his father was drunk at night, angry at his mother or him, he was sometimes out of control. It was awesome and terrifying. There is a nursery story about a boy who dares to do something wrong. A monster comes and devours him. Only his shoes and pants are left. *B* recalls being terrified by that story, but he also found it erotic as he wondered about the little boy's penis. He also recalls having fantasies, as a boy, about robbers coming to the house. He was afraid of them at first but they liked him and let him feel their penises. They hid out in his room and stayed close. They became afraid of him because he might call the police or his parents, but as long as they were nice and let him feel their penises it would be O.K. and they could rely on each other. It was all so frightening and exciting at the same time.

The analyst interprets B's recent tending to claim weakness and lack of structure as reasons for his inability to deal with real threatening events in his neighborhood as a continuation of the pact with burglars past. It also is a disguise for exercising power and control. *B* is thoughtful, silent. He feels discovered, as if a hidden secret is revealed. He is also the malicious burglars at the same time, though he tries on the role of a tender warm father when he seduces boys, homeless and bad boys—exiles and wanderers.

To ascribe to fantasy alone this driven man's fearful and tenuous glimpse into his father's darker aspect would be to perpetuate a sort of consensual, pseudoauthoritative denial. Oblivious to one of life's most agonizing facts, to the actuality of his past, he would be forever doomed to repeat it, compromising in turn the next generation at the height of its vulnerability and plasticity. Similarly to dismiss as a disguised positive oedipal construction the acts of castration on the part of H.L.'s strap-wielding mother would be to acquiesce once again in the manner of his weak and perhaps covertly sadistic father.

Perhaps, as analysts Atkins (1970) and Grunberger (1980) have suggested, it is the underpinnings of their own intergenerational countertransference reactions, often passing unperceived by them, that prevent many clinicians from contending with these issues. As a result, they fail to fully analyze their patients, and to free them from an irrational deference to erstwhile and evermore ephemeral figures of authority and from the authoritarianism that derives from this. No analysis is exhaustive, and we all remain prisoners to some degree of our dependent pasts as well as our unwanted mortal destinies. It is man's fate which Oedipus anticipates and finally welcomes; hence his transcendence of it.

I would like to offer a brief case in point of a more subtle countertransference acting in. More obvious examples I leave to the collective "conscience of the analysis."

A twenty-eight-year-old male patient had been in intensive three-day-a-week psychotherapy for four years. Having decided on his profession relatively late, he then dallied within it, contenting himself with a lackluster and bureaucratically constraining job on the pretext of his vague left-wing convictions, sentiments without, he conceded, a clear ideological base. He wished, he said, to help the poor. Reflecting on his "underachieving," after much thought he concluded that he would like to remain an adolescent after all, with the "omnipotentiality" (Pumpian-Midlin 1969) and dependency afforded by this status. He saw his passivity and his relationship with his parents as further problems.

He spoke about his aggressive, overbearing mother, with whom he had an unwanted "conspiratorial" and seductive relationship. She complained to him about her husband "incessantly and inappropriately." His father was a weak, debilitated, passive man who had had a stroke when the patient was sixteen. Soon after this happened, he remembered, he then found himself inexplicably masturbating, as if in triumph, he concluded retrospectively and to his horror. He did remember wrestling with his father as a boy. But he lamented his "old man's" abiding accession to weakness and ineffectuality, a self-indulgence which grew after the stroke (beyond what the damage warranted), and his lack of interest in his son's high school academic, athletic, and political successes. Memories surfaced in which the father's loss of control and indeed his sadism became clear as well. Helping with homework, he exploded at his son. While wrestling, he had sometimes hurt the boy, just as now the prematurely old man punctuated his general vacuousness with outbursts of rageful religiosity or embarrassing lapses into sleep during conversations in the company of friends and potential in-laws.

Basically heterosexual, the patient had had fantasies of being enslaved and used erotically by women—"slave fantasies." Explicit homosexual dreams and fantasies involving his father and emerging during treatment gradually revealed the disguised "father hunger" underlying these sexualized but still heterosexual constructions.

In a related process, the transference came more and more to assume a frankly homosexual or negative oedipal cast. Initially, the therapist was seen as a "straight," more "conventional" older brother of sorts, advocating bourgeois achievements such as marriage, money, and hard work. The patient "argued his case" to the contrary, typically resisted fee increases at the close of the year and often withheld the fee for more than a month. But the fighting, both verbal and silent, was also a provocation with other aims, of course. These became conscious, and the transference shifted from defiance to a somewhat idealizing and certainly tender, warm, and increasingly erotic interest in the therapist. He had been, he remarked, "wrestling with an angel."

Working genetically and transferentially, the patient made great strides. He shed his passive, sleepy demeanor along with a beard and wrinkled shirts and, with his handlebar mustache and more alert look, suddenly seemed alive in and outside his hours. He later described how he no longer sank into the waiting room's soft sofa but chose instead a hard chair with a straight back. More important, he found and took a better job, one that provided him not only with more money and power but with the authority and opportunity to exercise his "commitment" to helping the helpless, the "underdog." No longer a grudging underling, he was a boss now, a role which had once connoted being "snakelike." He became less withholding with his girlfriend of eight years and with the therapist, whom he paid promptly and gratefully. Finally, he began to talk more and more about wanting to be a father and, with this, about the prospect of terminating therapy, that is, once he was certain that the inner strength and the gains that derived from it were "really" his own.

Consciously, the therapist was entirely pleased with his patient's progress. Aware at the same time of pangs about the separation to come, of the fact that in treatment closeness and collaboration portend loss, he privately foresaw another nine to twelve months of work. It was a time, incidentally, when many of his somewhat younger male patients seemed to be approaching termination on the basis of self-possession, symptomatic improvement, and the handling of life's major milestones—autonomy in work, marriage, and fatherhood.

He then made an uncharacteristic error. On one month's bill, he failed to count one of the sessions and undercharged his patient. Though, as the patient confessed, he had toyed with the idea of "cheating," he called the error to the therapist's attention. It was the first time he had noticed such a mistake, and it surprised him. Perhaps, he added significantly, the therapist had somehow charged him the lower and long superseded fee (though, even then, the therapist told him, the figures would not have totaled the way they did). Having said this, the patient proceeded to describe an uncomfortable weekend visit with his parents. He had felt ashamed of his father, who exploded foolishly at a waitress. The next day, wandering through a beach club, he and his girlfriend decided to hide themselves in a cabana, prepared to make deliciously illicit love. For some reason, however, they masturbated each other instead, she "touching" him first, as he put it with an uncharacteristic recourse to euphemism. Moreover, while she did, he had had a fantasy of anal penetration reminiscent of his "old self." Scrutinizing himself, he interpreted his trial or "mini" regression as a guilty reaction to his rage and shame at yet another demonstration of his father's fallibility.

The therapist was not satisfied with this conclusion; it was incomplete.

Having scanned and contemplated his own error and the realities and inner motives behind it (it had been a month in which his scheduling had been disrupted more than usual), the therapist brought his own intrusion back into the transference. He and the patient remarked on the patient's telling distortion in reinstating the old fee. They noted his guilty temptation to cheat, to take advantage of the therapist's weakness, and a further error in which the patient called the bill the "check." What they concluded was this: the patient had regressed in the face of the therapist's evident imperfection in order to atone for the hostility excited by his vulnerability and to keep him ensconced in an ideal position whose glorious and warming presence the patient could continue to bask in. He was not really independent yet, he sighed, and "how fragile the human psyche is! I know you make mistakes, you're not perfect. But still!"

Privately, his therapist thought about his inadvertent gift, the seductiveness as well, and realized the intuitive truth of the patient's attributing the error not to a missed hour (perhaps the one where he had wondered about finishing up) but to the old fee. The gift had been a Trojan horse, a killing with kindness. He did not want his "son" to complete his adolescence, after all. Rather, he would undermine and diminish him in order to remain the young man's rescuer, to borrow from Blos (1962). Having prided himself on his patient's growth in masculinity, unconsciously the therapist had invited the man's homosexual submission. He had feared and resisted becoming outdone, obsolete, forgotten.

The Aggressive Dialogue: Developmental and Adaptive Dimensions

Together with Herzog, I have underscored an optimal aggressive dialogue between fathers and their children, sons especially (see Herzog, 1980; Ross and Herzog, 1985.) Fathers may err on the side of commission or omission, either excessive or insufficient aggressive stimulation making for pathogenic situations. A father's aggressivity seems, moreover, to be gender-specific. More aggressive by nature than mothers (Mitchell, 1981), the male is further exploited by children in this vein and represented as such in their mind's eye. This is one aspect of what Abelin has called the "father principle" (1971, 1975, 1980). Such aggressive interchanges, I have suggested, must also be state- or age-appropriate in quantity, quality, or modality. Indeed, the father's aggressivizing function tends to run parallel to that of the mother with regard to early sexual excitation. On the one hand, too little libidinal input on her part during infancy seems to engender apathy or even marasmus, compromising neurophysiological maturation, as Spitz (1965) and later researchers have demonstrated. On the other, clinicians beginning with Freud (1905; see also Greenacre, 1971a) have shown that somewhat later too much disposes the child to become perverse or severely psychoneurotic.

In "The Economic Problem of Masochism," a paper that followed the development of his early version of the dual instinct theory and of the structural hypothesis and that anticipated the concept of signal affects, Freud reformulated the pleasure principle, discarding, in fact, the absolutes and notions of discharge characterizing his earlier economics. A rhythmicity, he now suggested, a tempo, an ebb and flow of endopsychic and external stimuli rather than sheer quantities, or even optimum but constant levels, determined the phenomenology of pleasure and pain. Analogous processes may be inherent in aggressive excitations taking place within the father-child *dialogue.*

Furthermore, because the drives are stirred and subsequently organized within an object-relational context, the doses are interpersonally meted out, titrated, received, aborted, interpreted, and articulated according to the caretakers' attunement to the child and according to the child's own state or arousal, receptivity, and communicative capacity. The model of a feedback system between two individuals rather than isolated cauldrons of impulses toward constant objects and their representations may best capture the unfolding, dovetailing, and often unconscious communication of object relations.

The aggressive interactions of fathers and children and their intrapsychic sequelae are stimulated or contained by the nature of the father's relation to his wife. With this, the woman's capacity to empathize at once with his struggles and with the needs of her child is a crucial factor, informing their images of each other and the quality and intensity of drive expression transpiring between them. Again, at a more general theoretical level of discourse, what is implied is a more open system, with greater variability than earlier developmental models imply, though with diminishing degrees of freedom as the life cycle progresses. One aspect of one object relation reverberates throughout the personality and through development.

In this vein Herzog has described a "Kamikaze" mode of play between fathers and sons beginning with the second year (Herzog, 1982). In such interactions, fathers incite aggressive displays and then, often prompted by mothers, abruptly act to constrain the consequences of the impulses they have evoked. As far as the child's drive organization is concerned, a father thus helps establish a template for what will emerge later as the individual's capacity to "change gears or states."

In 1979, based on a study of fathers which I had originated at Judith Kestenberg's Child Development Research Project, I reported related observational findings of interactions during the third year, when these seemed most age-appropriate and facilitative, more so than earlier or later. I further suggested that these father-child exchanges serve to anticipate or to usher in development, that the father guides the child toward the future on the basis of his past and present. In other words, the father helps "release" the oedipus complex during the boy's transitional third year. As with his older infant or toddler, a son especially, a man continues to love and stimulate his child in characteristically fatherly fashion, for example, tossing the boy up into the air:

> Jake and his son Richard, aged two-and-a-half years, sit at the table where they and the other fathers and children in the observation center are in the midst of hammering sundry pieces of wood, plastic, and metal into objects. Like the other fathers, Jake does not face his son but sits to the side and slightly in back of him. . . . For that matter, they do not seem to say all that much to each other—with notable exceptions, of course—choosing to interrelate through various more inanimate media.
>
> Richard wants his nail to protrude perpendicular to the side of his construction, and when his father affixes it in a less patently phallic manner, the boy yowls in disgusted rage, a yowl, that culminates in half an obscenity hissed through pursed lips. With mock sternness and a transparent glee, Jake scolds the boy, who frowns. Momentarily, his father hoists him, end over end, heaving the compact little body up toward the ceiling, where it arcs barely short of it. Richard squeals and squeals, as the onlookers witness the ritual, silently aghast at all the near misses, until finally the boy is somersaulted and rolled across his father's chest and landed safely in his seat once again.

Between two and three years, a little boy's relationship with his father will reflect the transitional stage between his earlier love affair with him, and the world in general, and the growing sense that they are both males who will become engaged in a rivalry for the mother's love. A father like Jake, sensitized at some level to the urges and fears abating and awakening in his boy, will respond in kind to his son's silent "ambitendencies" toward him. In addition, he will impose on his son certain of his own conflicts, left over from oedipal and postoedipal developmental phases, and thus point the way toward the future.

In this instance, we might speculate that Jake's tendency not to position himself face-to-face with Richard springs from his sense of the boy's impetus toward increasingly autonomous functioning, which the father encourages as indicative of a budding masculinity. At the same time as he adjusts to his son's needs, Jake defends against his own more problematic temptations, avoiding face-to-face and thus genital-to-genital contact, with all its aggressive as well as increasingly homosexual implications. It is safer for the two males to communicate through impersonal if also rather phallic activities, which further assure both participants that they are acting as two males together. . . .

Paternal love, previously expressed more easily is not entirely submerged, of course. Rather it is left unstated, physicalized. Indeed, other fathers, who found it harder than Jake to talk with their boys or to participate in their activities, would nevertheless fondle them.

In this instance, too, Jake continued to love and stimulate Richard in characteristically fatherly fashion, tossing the boy up into the air. But this act now conveyed another opposing meaning. It was also a statement of limits, a demonstration of phallic power, exciting identification and affording pleasure to his son, if at the cost of a certain submission on his part, betrayed indeed by the boy's squeals of delight tinged with anxious and helpless defiance. Invited to be manly, a boy is enjoined by his father to go only so far, else he crash into the ceiling and fall to the floor. Remember, the father seems to say, ever so playfully, it was Icarus the son, not Daedalus the father, whose wings melted in the heat of their mutual overreaching, who plummeted to earth. One day you may fly like this, but on your own—one day, but not now. My love for and authority over you are one, a benevolent despotism. (See Weissman, 1963, on the meaning and impact of father-son play.)

Granted certain common trends, the variations were also striking among fathers in terms of which elements of this complex communication are to be exaggerated and which suppressed. One father simply ignores his son, four months older than Richard, letting the boy bump and thrust wildly about until his efforts end in a lonely crash, accompanied by screams of enraged pain. Another hovers about his son, watchful of his every move, both proud and cautious. A quiet, rather sad man, disappointed in his work life, he retreats from the group with his son into corners where the two mumble together, intimate with each other and apart from others. Yet another man appears and disappears without notice, hardly greeting his two-and-a-half-year-old boy verbally, but simply settling in behind him, caressing the child while his gaze wanders off to spaces beyond the room. [Ross, 1979b]

Conclusion

There is always choice, along with analysis and the prevailing zeitgeist, and, in fact, a certain parental instinctiveness. Victims like Laius need not victimize. Despite being creatures of character, adults, more than children, have discretion at their disposal. Even infrahuman primates have access to wellsprings of love which, with felicitous circumstance, flow forth and submerge inherent hostility toward youthful usurpers.

The ethologist and anthropologist are familiar with the principles of territoriality and dominance hierarchies that govern mammalian groups and simple societies. To them survival is all, the infanticidal or filicidal impulse therefore a commonplace, and the substance of a paper such as this self-evident. Furthermore, the universality of male aggressivity, whatever its wellsprings, is a well-established fact (see Mitchell, 1981). In this vein, Robin Fox (1981) has recently elaborated on the manner in which older hominid males have attempted to control the access of juveniles to the sexual usage of females and all the generational prerogatives that derive from this.

At the same time, however, instinctive or societal mechanisms serve fairly universally to inhibit intraspecific or intrafamilial expressions of destructive hostility—automatic regulatory schema which have tended to be attenuated because of man's evolving cortical ascendancy, concomitant volition, and social plasticity (Lorenz, 1966). As far as intergenerational hostility is concerned, Lorenz stressed, it is the foreshortened juvenile face, in concert with a submissive exposure of the abdomen, hindquarters, or jugular area, which inhibits potentially lethal attacks on the part of dominant males. For instance, rhesus monkeys, those nasty little gnomes who otherwise gobble at and abuse their offspring, treat them tenderly when they witness birth and are given the opportunity to bond to them. Presence can serve to make the heart grow mutually fonder, tapping sentiments of care otherwise forgotten.

REFERENCES

Abelin, E. (1971), The role of the father in the separation-individuation process. In: *Separation-Individuation,* ed. J. McDevitt & C. Settlage. New York: International Universities Press, pp. 229-252.

_______ (1975), Some further comments and observations on the earliest role of the father. *Internat. J. Psycho-Anal.,* 56:293-302.

_______ (1980), Triangulation, the role of the father and the origins of core gender identity during the rapprochement subphase. In: *Rapprochement: The Critical Subphase of Separation,* ed. R. Lax, S. Bach, & J. A. Burland. New York: Aronson, pp. 151-169.

Atkins, N. (1970), The Oedipus myth, adolescence, and the succession of generations. *J. Amer. Psychoanal. Assn.,* 18:860-875. Chapter 12, this volume.

Blos, P. (1962), *On Adolescence.* New York: Free Press.

_______ (1980), The life cycle as indicated by the nature of transference in the psychoanalysis of adolescents. *F. J. Psychoanal.,* 61:145-52.

Burlingham, D. (1935), Child analysis and the mother. *Psychoanal. Quart.,* 4:69-72.

Colarusso, C. A., & Nemiroff, R. A. (1982), The father in mid-life. In: *Father and Child,* ed. S. H. Cath, A. R. Gurwitt, & J. M. Ross. Boston: Little, Brown, pp. 315-327.

Demos, J. (1982), The changing faces of fatherhood. In: *Father and Child,* ed. S. H. Cath, A. R. Gurwitt, & J. M. Ross. Boston: Little, Brown, pp. 425-445.

Devereux, G. (1953), Why Oedipus killed Laius. *Internat. J. Psycho-Anal.,* 34:132-141. Chapter 7, this volume.

Erikson, E. H. (1980), On the generational cycle: An address. *Internat. J. Psycho-Anal.,* 61:213-233. Chapter 17, this volume.

Esman, A. (1982), Fathers and adolescent sons. In: *Father and Child,* ed. S. H. Cath, A. R. Gurwitt, & J. M. Ross. Boston: Little, Brown, pp. 265-274.

Ferholt, J., & Gurwitt, A. R. (1982), Involving fathers in treatment. In: *Father and Child,* ed. S. H. Cath, A. R. Gurwitt, & J. M. Ross. Boston: Little, Brown, pp. 557-568.

Fox, R. (1982), Les conditions de l'évolution sexuelle. In: *Communications,* No. 35, Sexualités Occidentales Paris: Seuil, pp. 2-13.

Freud, S. (1900), The interpretation of dreams. *Standard Edition,* 4/5. London: Hogarth Press, 1953.

_______ (1905), Three essays on the theory of sexuality. *Standard Edition,* 7:130-243. London: Hogarth Press, 1953.

_______ (1909), Family romances. *Standard Edition,* 9:235-241. London: Hogarth Press, 1959.

_______ (1910), A special type of choice of object made by men. *Standard Edition,* 11:163–175. London: Hogarth Press, 1957.
_______ (1924), The economic problem of masochism. *Standard Edition,* 19:159–170. London: Hogarth Press, 1961.
_______ (1929), Civilization and its discontents. *Standard Edition,* 21:64–145. London: Hogarth Press, 1961.
_______ (1950), *The Origins of Psycho-Analysis.* New York: Basic Books, 1954.
Greenacre, P. (1971a), *Emotional Growth.* 2 vols. New York: International Universities Press.
_______ (1971b), Problems of overidealization of the analyst and analysis: Their manifestations in the transference and countertransference relationship. In: *Emotional Growth,* Vol. II. New York: International Universities Press, pp. 743–761.
Greenson, R. (1968), Disidentifying from Mother: Its special importance for the boy. In: *Explorations in Psychoanalysis.* New York: International Universities Press, 1978, pp. 305–312.
Grunberger, B. (1980), The oedipal conflicts of the analyst. *Psychoanal. Quart.,* 49:606–630. Chapter 18, this volume.
Gurwitt, A. R. (1982), Aspects of prospective fatherhood. In: *Father and Child,* ed. S. H. Cath, A. R. Gurwitt, & J. M. Ross. Boston: Little, Brown, pp. 275–300.
Hartmann, H., Kris, E., & Loewenstein, R. (1946), Comments on the formation of psychic structure. *The Psychoanalytic Study of the Child,* 2:11–38.
Herzog, J. (1979), Attachment, attunement, and abuse. Unpublished manuscript.
_______ (1980), Sleep disturbance and father hunger in 18- to 28-month-old boys: The Erlkonig Syndrome. *The Psychoanalytic Study of the Child,* 35:219–233.
_______ (1982), Patterns of expectant fatherhood. In: *Father and Child,* ed. S. H. Cath, A. R. Gurwitt, & J. M. Ross. Boston: Little, Brown, pp. 301–314.
Hoffer, W. (1954), Defensive process and defensive organization. *Internat. J. Psycho-Anal.,* 35:194–198.
Jarvis, W. (1962), Some effects of pregnancy and childbirth on men. *J. Amer. Psychoanal. Assn.,* 10:689–700.
Kakar, S. (1978), *The Inner World: A Psychoanalytic Study of Childhood and Society in India.* New Delhi: Oxford University Press.
Kestenberg, J. (1975), *Children and Parents.* New York: Aronson.
Loewald, H. W. (1979), The waning of the oedipus complex. *J. Amer. Psychoanal. Assn.,* 27:751–756.
Lorenz, K. (1966), *On Aggression.* New York: Harcourt, Brace & World.
Mitchell, G. (1981), *Human Sex Differences: A Primatologist's Perspective.* New York: Van Nostrand Reinhold.
Nabokov, V. (1966), *Speak, Memory.* New York: Perigee.
Pumpian-Midlin, . (1969), Omnipotence, omnipotentiality, conformity and rebellion (abstract) *Bull. Assn. Psychoanal. Med.,* 8(3): pp. 31–34.
Rosner, H. (1977), Oedipus and his cradle scars. Chapter 14, this volume.
Ross, J. M. (1975), The development of paternal identity: A critical review of the literature on nurturance and generativity in boys and men. *J. Amer. Psychoanal. Assn.,* 23:783–817.
_______ (1977), Toward fatherhood: The epigenesis of paternal identity during a boy's first decade. *Internat. J. Psycho-Anal.,* 4:327–347.

_______ (1979a), Fathering: A review of some psychoanalytic contributions on paternity. *Internat. J. Psycho-Anal.*, 60:317-327.
_______ (1979b), The forgotten father. In: *Psychosexual Imperatives*, ed. M. C. Nelson & J. Ikenberry. New York: Human Sciences Press, pp. 261-303.
_______ (1979c), Paternal identity. In: *On Sexuality: Psychoanalytic Observations*, ed. T. B. Karasu and C. W. Socarides. New York: International Universities Press, pp. 78-97.
_______ (1982a) Beyond the phallic illusion. Presented to the Yale Department of Psychiatry, New Haven, April, and The American Psychiatric Association, Toronto, May.
_______ (1982b), From mother to father. In: *Father and Child*, ed. S. H. Cath, A. R. Gurwitt, & J. M. Ross. Boston: Little, Brown, pp. 189-204.
_______ (1982c), Mentorship in middle childhood. In: *Father and Child*, ed. S. H. Cath, A. R. Gurwitt, & J. M. Ross. Boston: Little, Brown, pp. 243-252.
_______ (1982d) Oedipus revisited: Laius and the "Laius complex." *The Psychoanalytic Study of the Child*, 37:169-200. Chapter 19, this volume.
_______ & Herzog, J. (1985), The sins of the father. In: *Parental Influences in Health and Disease*, ed. E. J. Anthony & G. H. Pollock. Boston: Little, Brown, pp. 477-510.
Spitz, R. (1965), *The First Year of Life*. New York: International Universities Press.
Steele, B. (1982), Abusive fathers. In: *Father and Child*, ed. S. H. Cath, A. R. Gurwitt, & J. M. Ross. Boston: Little, Brown, pp. 481-490.
Wainwright, W. H. (1966), Fatherhood as a precipitant to mental illness. *Amer. J. Psychiat.*, 123:40-44.
Wallerstein, J., & Kelly, J. (1982), The father-child relationship: Changes after divorce. In: *Father and Child*, ed. S. H. Cath, A. R. Gurwitt, & J. M. Ross. Boston: Little, Brown, pp. 451-466.
Weissman, P. (1963), The effects of preoedipal paternal attitudes on development and character. *Internat. J. Psycho-Anal.*, 44:121-131.
Yogman, M. (1982), Observations on the father-infant relationship. In: *Father and Child*, ed. S. H. Cath, A. R. Gurwitt, & J. M. Ross. Boston: Little, Brown, pp. 101-122.
Zilboorg, G. (1931), Depressive reactions related to parenthood. *Amer. J. Psychiat.*, 10:927-962.

24

The Complete Oedipus Complex

GERTRUDE BLANCK

[1984]

The purpose of this paper is to show that the complexities of the oedipal situation can be more broadly comprehended by combining the theories of psychosexual maturation, structuralization, and conflict, with the object relations theory derived from ego psychology. I believe that this will enrich our conceptual thinking about the manner in which sexuality (from drive theory) and love (from developmental object relations theory) connect at the oedipal position. The implications of emphasizing this dramatic convergence are broad. They are especially enlightening in their contribution to understanding the incompetent oedipal arrangements of the less adequately structured personalities (the so-called borderline and narcissistic personalities). In these relatively less-than-neurotic structures an incomplete or distorted oedipal position is reached because of the very failure of convergence of drive with corresponding level of object relations.

Freud was not unaware of object relations even when he wrote his

---

Reprinted with permission from *International Journal of Psycho-Analysis*, vol. 65, pp. 331–339.

classic paper on drive theory, "Three Essays on the Theory of Sexuality" (1905). There he says:

> In view of the importance of a child's relations to his parents in determining his later choice of a sexual object, it can easily be understood that any disturbance of those relations will produce the gravest effects upon his adult sexual life. [p. 228]

My attempt to contribute to further understanding of the complete Oedipus complex by combining psychoanalytic object relations theory with the first developmental theory of psychoanalysis, psychosexual maturation, is not new. Those who preceded me were remarkably successful despite the fact that they lacked the knowledge of object relations which we possess today. It is for that reason that those contributions must now be updated. I have no doubt that future discoveries will necessitate revision of my contribution too, and so I present it not as finite, but as a link in a long chain of thought that will continue into the future. In order to make a coherent presentation, it will be necessary to repeat some concepts that are generally known.

Although Freud had object relations in mind from the beginning of his work, the importance of preoedipal object relations and their effect upon oedipal formation was noted by Ruth Mack Brunswick in 1940. Freud's earlier statement on object relations was elaborated upon by Lampl-de Groot (1952). She shows that differences in the nature of the early mother attachments manifest themselves not only in the oedipal relationships, but also in adult object relationships. She referred to the oedipus complex as the final product of preoedipal development and, most pertinent to the theme I shall develop, she emphasized that disturbances in the preoedipal phase can cause abnormal shapes and weaknesses in the oedipal constellation.

Gitelson (1952) was also interested in the effect of preoedipal life upon the oedipus complex, although he referred to it as *pregenital* because he wrote in a period of psychoanalytic theory construction when *pregenital* and *preoedipal* were terms that theorists tended to use interchangeably, not yet making clear-cut distinction between a level of psychosexual maturation and a level of object relations. I believe that Gitelson meant to say *preoedipal* because he went on to make the exceedingly important point that, in borderline and psychotic conditions, not more than a vestigial oedipal position can be reached because "object relations were destroyed, root and branch, at an earlier period, or because such relations never existed at all" (p. 353). (The tendency to confuse *pregenital* with *preoedipal* persists to the present. Lebovici [1982, p. 205] refers to "pregenital organization in object relationships.")

To attain my objective of describing the confluence of drive and level of object relations, especially as it pertains to the complete oedipus complex, I extend Spitz's concept of critical periods (1959). Spitz was concerned with the first eighteen months of life. However, the concept itself is equally valuable in contributing to a more thorough understanding of the convergence of psychosexual maturation and object relations at the oedipal level, because that developmental phenomenon also fits Spitz's definition of a critical period. In a parallel extension of Spitz's work, Rangell (1972) applies the concept of organizers of the psyche to the oedipal level; he suggests that the oedipus complex is the fourth in the series of organizers of the psyche.

Freud (1924a) introduced the hyphenated term "phallic-oedipal" to indicate his view that the phallic phase is contemporaneous with the oedipal position. He believed that the genital phase is not attained in the infantile period, but that sexual maturation is interrupted by latency, and that genitality is reached after that.

While that formulation was adequate for its time, it seems desirable now to regard the phallic phase as pregenital and to think that a first approach to genitality which we (Blanck and Blanck, 1979) have termed *genital interest* is made in the infantile period. This reasoning is central to my thesis, namely that genitality and object love are the essential components of the oedipus complex. We suggested that genital interest, a precursor of true genitality, has the status of the fourth psychosexual phase of the infantile period. At this level, the same bodily organ as is used in the phallic phase now becomes cathected in a new way, no longer for narcissistic pleasure, but for object-related pleasure. We say:

> a position not based solely upon anatomy would include psychological development as well as physical maturation. Then, dis-

> covery of the genitalia *and* of autonomous functioning can be seen as constituting determinants of identity formation and simultaneously as furthering the separation process, the complementary track of the individuation process. From this we may conclude that interest in one's genitals at the so-called phallic phase represents, for both sexes, a beginning culmination of the connection to the symbiotic object and to symbiotic need. It is at this point in development that aggressive drive comes into dominance as a separating and individuating force. That part of the anatomy that will later be used by the libidinal drive to seek connection is used also by the aggressive drive to preserve ego boundaries by establishing gender interest and gender difference. [p. 85]

This formulation preserves and highlights the object relations aspect of the oedipal situation, which is lost when the oedipal position is hyphenated with a pregenital psychosexual phase. Perhaps even more important is that the role of autonomous functioning in development is stressed. This may contribute toward filling in one of the "blank spaces" in psychoanalytic theory by proposing a solution to the puzzle of the shift in the object at the oedipal level, especially for the girl. It implies that both boy and girl find their heterosexual destinies in the progressive development of autonomous functioning, which joins the nonhostile aggressive drive to propel the individual toward ever higher levels of development. The shift in the object has been stressed in the literature as essential for the girl if she is to attain the oedipal position. But as we consider that the shift is not from the real object but from the object representation, and that it includes shifting from the passive to the active mode in relation to the object, it is evident that the boy, too, has to make an important shift in the juxtaposition of self- and object representations. That the object in reality is the same person for the boy at both the oedipal and preoedipal levels is merely an external fact.

The phallic phase, on the other hand, more resembles the pregenital phases that precede it in that the drive need dominates over object relations need. Yet it is inaccurate to speak of dominance of drive need in absolute terms, for it has a fluctuating quality throughout the phases of pregenitality as the child learns to tame drive needs to conform with developing levels of object relations. Tension between drive need and object relations need is first experienced late in the oral phase, but acquires greater power in the anal phase, forcing the child to tame the drive in order to please the object. A reversal takes place in the phallic phase where narcissistic needs are at a height. Then drive need once again dominates, temporarily, over object relations need. I shall return to this important theme shortly.

First I wish to acknowledge the priority of Edgcumbe and Burgner (1975), who recognize the theoretical incompatibility of joining the phallic phase with the oedipal position. They point out that the assumption that the oedipal child is at the same time a phallic child is a legacy from the historical growth of psychoanalytic theory. They say:

> Our examination of the literature disclosed a tendency to assume that entry into the phallic phase is accompanied by the *simultaneous development* of oedipal relationships, so that the terms phallic, oedipal, and phallic-oedipal are often used synonymously. *Yet close scrutiny of clinical and observational material reveals distinct differences in the forms of drive derivatives and in the nature of the child's relationships in the preoedipal phallic phase as compared with the phallic-oedipal phase.* [p. 162]

I agree with them in recognizing the awkward theoretical contradiction in equating phallic and oedipal, but I find the solution they suggest—to postulate that there are two phallic phases, one oedipal and the other preoedipal—equally awkward. The suggestion that approach to genitality does not await termination of latency to make its first appearance seems to me to be not only a more logical solution, but also one that is subject to clinical validation.

Galenson and Roiphe (1976) as well as Edgcumbe and Burgner question altogether whether there is a phallic phase in girls. Although the issue is not resolved, it is clear from newly discovered knowledge about female psychology that the girl's phallic phase, if it exists, must be quite different from that of the boy. Jacobson (1964), borne out by the later investigation of Galenson and Roiphe, shows that awareness of anatomical difference is forced upon the child's attention, not at the phallic phase as Freud thought, but in the second year of life. This finding necessitates consideration of the resonating effect of that dramatic discovery upon the phallic phase proper when that phase is reached. The phallic phase proper must be appreciably shaped and influenced by the earlier discovery of anatomical difference and by the quality of recovery from the impact of it.

The long and continuing process of organization begins in the oral phase and includes organization of erotic need with experience of gratification. Images of a gratified self merged with a gratifying object begin to be formed in order later to differentiate (Jacobson, 1964). This is an elaboration upon what Freud (1905) already knew, and it became a tenet of psychoanalytic theory long before ego psychology that the first affective experiences of a gratified self become the template for future gratification. The dimension added by Jacobson and other ego psychologists is that of formation of self- and object images out of experience. That brings object relations squarely into the picture and implies that drive gratification is only one side of a complex phenomenon involving the entire process of organization.

Quickened by maternal stimulation in the oral phase, the pleasure-seeking aims permeate subsequent psychosexual phases as these mature in conjunction with ego development, orchestrated by the organizing process. Organization becomes increasingly complex as psychosexual maturation and ego development proceed. By the anal phase, self- and object images are more differentiated than before; object relations have expanded to include father, siblings, and others; motor skills have increased and fall under the control of the total ego organization. Transfer of erogeneity from the oral to the anal zone brings the child into a situation in which gratification of drive need and of object relations need come into opposition. The child must learn to subordinate the drive in order to comply with the wishes of the much needed object.

This is well known. What I wish to add is that here exists the first precursor of genitality—where zonal need is conjoined with object love. The second precursor will be established when drive need and object relations need coincide at the oedipal level. But it is at the anal level that the pattern for combining psychosexuality with object love is established by means of suppression of direct discharge which, in the oral phase, was carried out without regard for the object. Later, reaction-formation supersedes suppression, as drive opposition for the purpose of complying with object relations need becomes part of structure and even acquires secondary autonomy (Hartmann, 1958). The ego functions of anticipation, delay, and intentionality were begun to be acquired in the oral phase. When capacity for sphincter control is added, intentionality broadens in scope to become volition. Then the child becomes capable of the exercise of ego autonomy, which begins with the well-known "No" (Spitz, 1957). "Yes" becomes possible when identification with the aggressor undergoes a change in function, making it possible to agree without loss of autonomy. The very style of achieving pleasure begins to shift from self-directed to object-directed. However, if this is not to be pathologically altruistic, there must be a gratifying return. Thus, while still in the anal phase, the child discovers that pleasure can be attained by the use of the body to please the object, and that that pleasure can be greater than that of pleasing oneself alone. In well-conducted training the child is, of course, not required to abandon zonal gratification entirely, only to bend it to the wishes of the object. Thus the pleasure-seeking attitude first acquired in the oral phase gains reinforcement in the next phase and continues, despite regression during the phallic phase, through the psychosexual progression. With this major shift from drive dominance to compromise of drive need with object relations need in the anal phase, the form and direction of object relations alters. From that time on, the wish to give pleasure while receiving begins to enter the character. Ruth Mack Brunswick (1940) recognized the element of giving and receiving that begins in the anal phase but, unfortunately, confused it with the boy's and girl's wishes for a baby and, paradoxically, with intensification of aggression.

At the phallic phase the capacity for compromising drive need with object relations need appears to undergo regression. Cathexis of the erogenous zone once again dominates, subordinating the object relations factor. I believe that this is analogous to rapprochement; return to a more narcissistic cathexis of the body is an essential step toward consolidation of bodily integrity before the child can once again, as in the anal phase, subordinate drive needs by effecting a compromise between them and regard for the object. By this apparent regression in the phallic phase, the self-representations are more firmly secured and the child can then proceed to distribute cathexis more evenly between the self- and object representations. Only then can transfer to that which we have termed genital interest combine with object love to move the child into the oedipal position proper.

While this is taking place on the side of the drives, ego development is proceeding. Especially in the practicing subphase of the separation-individuation process, which is simultaneous with the anal phase, are certain personality characteristics acquired which also contribute to later oedipal competence. I am proposing that traits such as venturesomeness, initiative, courage, and even ambition are developed in an adequate practicing subphase, that these predispose to ability to enter the oedipal conflict, and, in favorable circumstances, even to conquer it. Traits such as indecision, hesitancy, timidity, fearfulness—consequences of an inadequate practicing subphase—impair ability to deal with the oedipal crisis. Special emphasis needs to be given to ambition because, despite our better judgment, we tend to regard it pejoratively. Brutus wept for Caesar's love, rejoiced for his fortune, honored him for his valor, but slew him for his ambition. Can this attitude toward ambition stem from our own oedipal rivalry—fear that our children can defeat us?

In normal sequential development, the oedipal position is attained after or in coincidence with psychological birth as described by Mahler, Pine, and Bergman (1975), that is, when the rapprochement subphase has given way to the phase that they have termed "on-the-way-to-object-constancy." Then interpersonal relationships are superseded by intrasystemic negotiations (between self- and object representations), and structuralization has proceeded far enough to make intersystemic conflict possible. Pursuing my theme that the oedipal level is a critical period, representing convergence of drive maturation and ego development, one has to think about it as occurring over a span of time, even in the first round. The entry point, middle phase, and temporary cessation of oedipal wishes that takes place with entry into latency differ in quality and intensity. (While this appears to state the obvious, it is important to the proposal I shall make regarding the negative oedipal position.) That oedipal wishes revive again in adolescence, early adulthood, and parenthood, has been pointed out by several authors (Benedek, 1959; Blos, 1962; Blanck and Blanck, 1968).

Freud (1923a) describes the complete Oedipus complex:

> One gets an impression that the simple Oedipus complex is by no means its commonest form, but rather represents a simplification or schematization which, to be sure, is often enough justified for practical purposes. Closer study usually discloses the more complete Oedipus complex, which is twofold, positive and negative, and is due to the bisexuality originally present in children: that is to say, a boy has not merely an ambivalent attitude towards his father and an affectionate object-choice towards his mother, but at the same time he also behaves like a girl and displays . . . a corresponding jealousy and hostility towards his mother. [p. 33]

Although he worded this as though it is an interpersonal conflict, it is understood that this conflict exists in internalized form, not between oedipal child and parent but, intersystemically between id and superego, and intrasystemically between self- and object representations.

I shall now reconsider the complete oedipus complex for the purpose of refining our understanding of the negative oedipal position in the light that contemporary theory throws upon it. This task requires revision of the universally accepted diagram of an equilateral triangle. That diagram is misleading, not only because it suggests that the three participants in the oedipal drama are on equal terms, but also because it fails to depict the negative as well as the positive position with the accuracy now made possible by contemporary theory. I am aware that diagrams cannot do justice to the complex psychological constructs we attempt to illustrate with them, but they do aid in conceptualization if we do not take them too literally. Therefore I propose that we try to visualize a straight line instead of a triangle, with one parent representation at either pole, while the oedipal child moves along the line flexibly; this makes it possible to visualize her or him closer to one parent representation at one psychological moment, to the other parent representation at another moment, and in the very middle of the conflict at still another time. These variations in position depict the negative as well as the positive oedipal situations. If we wish to be even more precise, we may imagine a calibrated line which can tell exactly where the self-representation of the oedipal child stands in relation to both object representations at any given psychological moment.

At the point of entry the oedipal strivings have a fleeting quality because they are in a state of flux before coming firmly into the oedipal position proper. The developing child may at one moment "touch" the oedipal position and may at another moment regress to a preoedipal level of object need. Whether regression is along the psychosexual line as well—that is, to phallic, anal, or even oral levels, can only be determined in individual cases. These fluctuations are directed by the state of object need and, where there is defensive regression, by the level of anxiety. The child, whether boy or girl, may at one moment be in the position of experiencing the object in one representational form, as an oedipal object, and at another moment of needing the same person in the entirely different representational form of the object of a lower level of object need.

For those reasons, the concept of the negative oedipal position calls for reexamination. My thesis is that the oedipal position is competently reached when the level of object relations and the coinciding psychosexual level converge to form the complete oedipus complex. This implies that the child cannot be in a passive position in relation to either parent if it is to be said that she or he is in the oedipal position proper. Clinical observation appears to refute this. In the course of an analysis, one sees the patient in an apparently passive position in relation to the parent of the same sex under the stress of oedipal anxiety. This poses neither a theoretical nor a clinical dilemma. Clinically, the determination is made according to the nature and quality of that special object relationship that we call transference, the reflection of infantile object relations. Careful attention to the level of object relations as they appear in the transference contributes to clinical precision in interpretation by distinguishing between that which is truly oedipal and that which is preoedipal, and, in addition, whether the position is a defensive one. Despite the fact that object relations theory was not available to her at that time,

Lampl-de Croot (1946) came very close to stating that the negative "oedipal" position is in fact preoedipal. She says:

> The analytic exploration of such cases shows that the continuation of the passive relation to the father is due to a fixation in the negative oedipus complex. In prolonged analysis we reach the earlier history of this fixation, and we are able to observe the residues of the original passive attachment to the mother. We may therefore say that the passive feminine relation to the father is with the male a second edition of his primitive passive love relation to the mother, in a similar way as with the girl. [p. 77]

As I see it, the so-called negative oedipal position exists at the border between preoedipal and oedipal object relations. Since the shift from passive to active is in the very process of being effected it is quite vulnerable and easily constitutes a point, not only of fixation, but of regression in the face of oedipal anxiety. Where the courage to venture is weak, the individual may hover around this border, seeking refuge in the preoedipal position, venturing forward, retreating to the safety of passivity, venturing forth again, and on. This is a fine point in diagnosis. When we say that the oedipal position has been reached, do we mean that the heart of the crisis is approached, or that the individual has ventured one small step across the border while retaining the opportunity for rapid retreat to the haven of preoedipal passivity when anxiety threatens?

That which we designate as the negative oedipal position resembles the structure of obsessional neurosis in reverse. In that neurosis, regression is along the psychosexual line to the anal position, while the foothold in the oedipal position of object relations is retained. In the negative oedipal position, the drive position remains at the oedipal level while, under the pressure of anxiety, partial regression is along the object relations line. Thus the clinical appearance is an oedipal wish combined with cathexis of a preoedipal object representation. Whether this be a representation of the parent of the same or of the opposite sex, the self-object experience is a passive one, such as the need for a protector. But since the drive component remains at the more advanced level, the passive object need contains a genital sexual tinge. It is well known in the analysis of adults that preoedipal object need is often expressed in sexual terms.

I turn now to the myth as dramatized by Sophocles. Van der Sterren (1952) analyzed it as one would a dream, to expose the latent content. But his purpose was to show that Oedipus was motivated by hostility toward his mother for having abandoned him. One can agree with that. To be added are the affective tones of the oedipal situation, especially the split affects and split object images. There is the image of a destructive father, as well as images of a loving father in the forms of the shepherd and the foster father. Quantitatively, the distribution between positive and negative object images is that the negative images are in preponderance. This is not because of projection of the child's hostility, for the neonate is a blank slate so far as object images are concerned. Yet, in the myth, the negative father images abound. These always have a prehistory, as Ross (1982) points out in describing Laius' own history of abandonment and persecution. Yet I see Jocasta as the guiltier parent because of the importance of the preoedipal mother in the mother-child dyad during the separation-individuation process. Jocasta was not even willing to enter the dyad, but complied with Laius' plan to have the child destroyed. Neither was she an adequate oedipal mother, for she failed to maintain the generation gap and the incest taboo.

Although Freud applied the Oedipus myth to the normal family, it does not describe a normal family constellation. The normal oedipal situation requires that there shall have been a preoedipal family life in which preponderantly positive self-representations and positive representations of both parents develop out of positive affective experiences. These attenuate the murderous wishes of the oedipal phase. One questions whether the normally developing child can wish unambivalently to kill the parent of the same sex with whom she or he has built up positive cathexes over the preoedipal years. Murderous wishes have to be transient, not even necessarily restricted to oedipal wishes, but more broadly attributable to normal quantities of negative affect. I am not persuaded that the oedipal wish can overthrow all that went before, although I acknowledge its power. Also, it is usually insufficiently emphasized that the oedipal child has acquired a sense of time which includes the fantasy of "when I grow up." That fantasy, too, yields to the phase-specific sense of reality that develops in later years. Jacobson (1964) describes how love for the parent of the same sex results in identification as a mechanism for resolution of the oedipal conflict.

Many hostile-appearing behaviors are construed as such because of the confusion between aggression (a drive) and hostility (an affect) (Freud, 1940; Blanck and Blanck, 1979). With regard to all developmental thrusts, including the oedipal one, we have to distinguish between those that represent object-directed hostility and those that emanate from the growth-promoting aspects of the aggressive drive. The oedipal child who wishes to supplant the parent of the same sex is expressing wishes of the same nature and quality as the younger child at an earlier developmental level who wishes to take over a parental function. A developmental thrust is taking place that can be mistakenly interpreted as destructively object-directed. It is true that the developing child can become quite hostile in an object-directed way out of normal negative affect, and especially so if the developmental thrusts are impeded by an unattuned parent. This has to be distinguished from the thrust itself, which is powered by normal, nonhostile aggression. There is a normal progression in development whereby the functions of the object representations are continuously being transferred to become part of the self-representation (R. Blanck, 1982). This process is in operation at the oedipal as well as at all other developmental levels. But the oedipal level is, by Freud's very designation, more complex than earlier levels for three reasons: (1) triadic object relations, begun in the second year of life (Abelin, 1971) become the established mode; (2) drive needs must combine with object relations to achieve a comfortable equilibrium; and (3) the child is not yet physiologically equipped to carry out oedipal wishes.

Loewald (1980) points out that many terms have been applied to the puzzle of how the oedipus complex is surmounted. The Riviere translation of the *Collected Papers* (Freud, 1924b) refers to the passing of the oedipus complex. The *Standard Edition* translates it as dissolution. More commonly, one speaks of resolution. Sometimes it is referred to as destruction. Loewald uses the more felicitous term "waning," to encompass the contemporary view that it never disappears altogether. Sometimes one hears of the child's oedipal defeat. In the case of a genius, such as Picasso, one hears of the father's defeat by the son. But it is, of course, fallacious to regard victory or defeat in the oedipal situation in externalized or interpersonal terms. If the outcome of the oedipal conflict were to be a defeat in reality, it would result in passivity and fear to venture ever after. In fact, all of the traits that I have suggested as the consequence of adequate practicing subphase experience would be lacking later in life—not venturesomeness alone, but initiative, ambition, and courage. But since the conflict is intrapsychic, victory builds structure. The outcome, at least, is the compromise of neurotic formation. At best, ego and superego gain strength from having joined forces. The victory, of course, is structuralization.

Loewald believes, as do I, that understanding preoedipal issues will contribute to a broader insight into oedipal issues. He, however, regards the waning of the oedipus complex within the broader context of a death instinct. Thus he concludes that each step away from the parent represents an act of parricide. This is different from the developmental point of view, which describes the processes of selective identification (Jacobson) and of transfer of functions of the object representations to the self-representation—processes which internalize rather than destroy the object representations. I see this as the opposite of parricide. In the developmental position that I am pursuing, each step away from the parent representations takes an aspect of those representations along. Aggression and libido operate in concert as the separating, nonhostile and nondestructive aggressive thrusts result in libidinal connection at the next higher level of internalization.

The oedipus complex wanes after the first round, only to wax again in subsequent developmental phases. At each adult developmental phase there is internalization of new, nonincestuous object representations which promotes advancement away from primary object representations. Thus the scope and influence of the primary object representations diminish. This process, begun in childhood, continues and even accelerates. By adulthood, need for the primary object has receded. The parricidal ideation of childhood, as an aspect of primary object need, atrophies. Establishment of new libidinal connections at adult levels now satisfies object need.

Summary

The "complete oedipus complex" is shown to be a critical period in Spitz's sense of convergence of drive maturation with ego development. It is proposed that competence to venture into the heart of the oedipal conflict is acquired in the practicing subphase of the separation-individuation process where traits such as venturesomeness, courage, initiative, and the like become part of the self-representations.

Also proposed is that tension between drive need and object relations need at the anal phase results in compromise that establishes a pattern for taming the drive because of object relations considerations.

The so-called negative oedipal position is seen as a regression to a preoedipal level of object need that is tinged with sexual wishes carried back from the oedipal position.

Finally, the waning of the oedipus complex is regarded as another developmental thrust terminating in identification with and love for the parent of the same sex, with transfer of functions of the object representations to the self-representations, which results in diminution of primary object need and frees the individual to make new libidinal connections at adult levels of object need.

REFERENCES

Abelin, E. L. (1971), The role of the father in the separation-individuation process. In: *Separation-Individuation*, ed. J. B. McDevitt & C. F. Settlage. New York: International Universities Press, pp. 229–252.

Benedek, T. (1959), Parenthood as a developmental phase. *J. Amer. Psychoanal. Assn.*, 7:389–417.

Blanck, G., & Blanck, R. (1968), *Marriage and Personal Development*. New York: Columbia University Press.

_______ _______ (1979), *Ego Psychology II: Psychoanalytic Developmental Psychology*. New York: Columbia University Press.

Blanck, R. (1982), The functions of the object representations. Unpublished paper read at the Second Annual Conference on Psychoanalytic Developmental Psychology sponsored by the Department of Psychiatry, Beth Israel Medical Center, New York.

Blos, P. (1962), *On Adolescence: A Psychoanalytic Interpretation*. New York: Free Press.

Brunswick, R. M. (1940, The preoedipal phase of the libido development. *Psychoanal. Quart.*, 9:293–319.Edgcumbe, R., & Burgner, M. (1975), The phallic-narcissistic phase: A differentiation
Edgcumbe, R., & Burgner, M. (1975), The phallic-narcissistic phase. A differentiation between preoedipal and oedipal aspects of phallic development. *The Psychoanalytic Study of the Child*, 30:161–180.
Freud, S. (1905), Three essays on the theory of sexuality. *Standard Edition*, 7:130–243. London: Hogarth Press, 1953.
——— (1923a), The ego and the id. *Standard Edition*, 19:12–66. London: Hogarth Press, 1961.
——— (1923b), The infantile genital organization. *Standard Edition*, 19:141–145. London: Hogarth Press, 1961.
——— (1924a), The dissolution of the Oedipus complex. *Standard Edition*, 19:173–179. London: Hogarth Press, 1961.
——— (1924b), *Collected Papers*, trans. J. Riviere. London: Hogarth Press.
——— (1940), An outline of psycho-analysis. *Standard Edition*, 23:144–207. London: Hogarth Press, 1964.
Galenson, E., & Roiphe, H. (1976), Some suggested revisions concerning early female development. *J. Amer. Psychoanal. Assn.*, 24 (Suppl.): 29–57.
Gitelson, M. (1952), Re-evaluation of the role of the Oedipus complex. *Internat. J. Psycho-Anal.*, 33:351–354.
Hartmann, H. (1958), *Ego Psychology and the Problem of Adaptation*. New York: International Universities Press.
Jacobson, E. (1964), *The Self and the Object World*. New York: International Universities Press.
Lampl-de Groot, J. (1946), The pre-oedipal phase in the development of the male child. *The Psychoanalytic Study of the Child*, 2:75–83.
——— (1952), Re-evaluation of the role of Oedipus complex. *Internat. J. Psycho-Anal.*, 33:335–354.
Lebovici, S. (1982), The origins and development of the Oedipus complex. *Internat. J. Psycho-Anal.*, 63:201–215.
Loewald, H. (1980), *Papers on Psychoanalysis*. New Haven: Yale University Press.
Mahler, M. S., Pine, F., & Bergman, A. (1975), *The Psychological Birth of the Human Infant*. New York: Basic Books.
Rangell, L. (1972), Aggression, Oedipus and historical perspective. *Internat. J. Psycho-Anal.*, 53:3–11.
Ross, J. M. (1982), Oedipus revisited: Laius and the "Laius complex." *The Psychoanalytic Study of the Child*, 37:169–200. Chapter 19, this volume.
Spitz, R. A. (1957), *No and Yes*. New York: International Universities Press.
——— (1959), *A Genetic Field Theory of Ego Formation*. New York: International Universities Press.
Van der Sterren, H. A. (1952), The *King Oedipus* of Sophocles. *Internat. J. Psycho-Anal.*, 33:343–350.

25

Is the Oedipus Complex Universal?

MELFORD E. SPIRO

[1985]

The Motivational Disposition to Incest

In the previous chapters I attempted to achieve two separate, but related, goals. First, I attempted to demonstrate that its empirical foundation is too weak to support Malinowski's argument that a matrilineal complex exists in the Trobriands. Second, I attempted to show that the evidence indicates to the contrary that an unusually strong oedipus complex exists in the Trobriands. In this (the final) chapter I wish to examine the implications of these Trobriand findings for human societies in general.

Malinowski and those who follow his lead have argued that the male oedipus complex is culturally relative because it is produced not by the boy's experience in the family in general, but by his experience in the "patriarchal" family uniquely. Since, so they argue, it is the authoritarian father—the nineteenth-century European father being

Reprinted with permission from *Oedipus in the Trobriands*, pp. 144–180 (Chicago: University of Chicago Press).

paradigmatic of the class—who arouses filial hostility, matrilineal societies whose family structure does not conform to the "patriarchal" type—the Trobriands being paradigmatic of the class—would not be expected to produce an oedipus complex.

In a sophisticated and perceptive explication of that argument, Campbell and Naroll (1972, p. 437) quite properly observe that in principle the boy's hostility to the father may be motivated either by his rivalry with him for the love of the mother (as Freud claimed) or by the father's punitive authority (as Malinowski claimed). Freud, they argue, confounded these two motives in his construction of the oedipus complex because, in his European patient population, the father was both the authority figure and the mother's lover. Since in the Trobriands, however, these roles are performed by different persons rather than by one and the same person, and since the boy's hostility, according to Malinowski, is directed to the authority figure (mother's brother) rather than the mother's lover (father), the hostility dimension of the Western oedipus complex is brought about not by the son's sexual rivalry with the father, they argue, but by his resentment of the latter's authority.

That argument can now be faulted on three grounds. First, there are no a priori grounds for assuming that hostility to the father cannot be motivated by both sexual rivalry and resentment against his authority. Indeed, that is the view I have adopted here in distinguishing between oedipal and nonoedipal grounds for filial hostility. Second, there are no evidential grounds, as we observed in chapter 2, for claiming that in the Trobriands the jural authority of the mother's brother is exercised either frequently or punitively. Hence, even if the boy's *conscious* hostility is directed toward the mother's brother, it cannot be a function of the latter's punitive authority. Third, the findings presented in the last two chapters demonstrate rather conclusively that in fact it is the father who is the prime target of the boy's hostility in the Trobriands, and moreover his hostility is oedipal in motivation, i.e., it is motivated by his rivalry with him for the love of the wife-mother.

Even, however, without that empirical demonstration, the claim that the male oedipus complex would not be expected in matrilineal societies because the father is not an authority figure can be faulted on theoretical grounds alone. In order to sustain that claim, it would have to be demonstrated that in matrilineal societies it is the case not only that the father is not an authority figure for the son (however important that might be for the nonoedipal dimensions of the father-son relationship), but that the mother is not a love-object for him. For if it is the case that the son has a libidinal attachment to the mother in matrilineal as well as in "patriarchal" societies, the contention that he would nevertheless not be hostile to the father—or anyone else that he perceived to be the rival for her love—would be warranted only on the assumption that hostility to a rival is a phenomenon which is restricted to patriarchal societies. That assumption, however, is easily refuted, if only by the abundant evidence to the contrary reported by Malinowski for the Trobriands. That being the case, unless it were demonstrated that a libidinal attachment to the mother is restricted to boys in patriarchal societies, then, all things being equal, it would be no less likely for the oedipus complex to be found in matrilineal societies than in patriarchal ones.

Malinowski, who waffled on this issue of the boy's relationship to the mother—on the one hand he claimed that in the Trobriands the young boy has a "passionate" attachment to his mother, on the other that this attachment disappears spontaneously prior to the normally expected onset of the oedipus complex, a point to which we shall return—nowhere adduced any structural feature(s) peculiar to matriliny that might account for the absence of a libidinal attachment to the mother in matrilineal societies. Unless such a feature can be identified, it seems judicious to go along with the large body of evidence which suggests that a motivational disposition to nuclear family incest in general, and to mother-son incest in particular, is a panhuman characteristic. Since Lindzey (1967) has brought together much of the evidence pertaining to incest in general, our discussion of that topic will take its departure from his excellent paper, following which we shall turn to mother-son incest, which is our primary concern here.

The evidence marshaled by Lindzey can be classified into two categories, indirect and direct. Beginning with the former, we might mention in the first place the abundant social-psychological findings which suggest that "personal attractiveness and interpersonal choice are mediated, or determined, by similarity in attitudes, values, needs, and background factors," and that "positive social choice is strongly facilitated by physical or geographic proximity" (Lindzey, 1967, p. 1056). When these social-psychological findings are combined with the sociological findings concerning homogeneity of mate selection and the demographic findings concerning assortative mating (which indicate that the grounds for preferential choice in nonsexual domains apply to the sexual domain as well), their cumulative force suggests that in the absence of countervailing factors (most notably, incest taboos) sexual choice within—but not restricted to—the nuclear family would be a likely outcome.

That suggestion is supported by the direct evidence regarding the motivational disposition to nuclear family incest. Consider, first, the psychiatric findings concerning the existence of incestuous wishes at least in clinical populations. Consider, again, the psychological findings concerning the frequency of incestuous wishes, both overt and covert, in the dreams of normal populations. Consider, moreover, the anthropological findings concerning the near-universal incidence of the incest motif in myths, legends, and folktales, as well as the universality of nuclear family incest taboos. Consider, in addition, the sociological findings concerning the prevalence of incestuous behavior: in the United States, for example, one out of every twenty persons questioned in 1970, according to an authoritative estimate, had had an incestuous experience (Justice and Justice, 1979, p. 17). Consider, finally, the ethological findings (Bischof, 1975) which indicate a near-universal motivation to incest in infrahuman mammalian societies.[1] If, then, we consider the cumulative force of these various kinds of evidence, it is hard to avoid the conclusion that the existence of a panhuman motivational disposition to incest is a highly probable

[1]Despite their motivational disposition, incestuous behavior is infrequent in mammals because of a variety of structural constraints—most notably the formation of all-male adolescent groupings, adolescent extrusion, and dominance structures—which are summarized by Bischof (1975) in his admirable survey of the mammalian evidence. Although Bischof, a zoologist, shows that in the absence of these structural arrangements incest would be prevalent in mammalian societies, and although he argues that these arrangements are the evolutionary result of a selection process to constrain its occurrence, he then, strangely, concludes that the infrequency of mammalian incest indicates the absence of motivation to incest. It is hard to account for this non sequitur in an otherwise exemplary study.

hypothesis. This hypothesis, I hasten to add, does not entail the conclusion that nuclear family members are the strongest objects of sexual desire—though that too may sometimes occur—but only that they, among others, are members of that class.

Although almost all anthropologists, representing the entire range of anthropological thought, accept this conclusion, it has always had its opponents. If, so their counterargument goes, incest behavior is rare in human societies, it is not because of social or cultural pressures, most notably the implementation of incest taboos, which lead to its inhibition (as the proponents of the incest hypothesis argue), but because (to quote a recent statement of a distinguished critic) "human beings are 'naturally' non-incestuous" (Fox, 1980, p. 14). (Fox's view is much more complex than this quotation suggests, as will become apparent when we return to it below.) Hence, before turning to the motivational disposition to incest in the mother-son dyad, which is our concern in this book, it is necessary to examine this counterargument especially since prominent findings from China and Israel have been recently adduced on its behalf.

Various of its proponents base the counterargument to the incest hypothesis on different theoretical grounds, but they all agree with Westermarck (who first proposed it) that sexual indifference or aversion, rather than attraction, develops between any persons (including family members) who live together from an early age. It is this naturally developing aversion that then accounts for the relative infrequency of incestuous behavior (Westermarck, 1906–1908, vol. 2, p. 368). In order to fully grasp this counterargument it must be emphasized that none of the proponents of the incest hypothesis argue that—except for young children—members of the nuclear family have a conscious wish to take one another as sexual partners. They, no less than Westermarck, are fully aware that, consciously, most individuals are either indifferent or aversive to having sexual relations with family members. For them, however, sexual indifference or aversion is a consequence not of childhood propinquity but, rather, of the internalization of incest taboos and the consequent repression or extinction of the incestuous wishes.

Although Westermarck's theory has been persistently rejected by social scientists, most particularly on the grounds—first adduced by

Frazer (1887, vol. 4, p. 97 ff.)—that the universality of nuclear family incest taboos implies that the motivational disposition to incest is also universal, it has recently been defended on the basis of two sets of findings, one from China, the other from Israel. Since these findings, both confined to the question of sibling incest, have been widely heralded as constituting conclusive support (see Bischof, 1975; Demarest, 1977; Wilson, 1978; Fox, 1980, Chapter 2; Money, 1980) for Westermarck's theory, it is important to examine them rather carefully.

The Chinese case, which has been extensively studied by Wolf (1966, 1968, 1970) and by Wolf and Huang (1980), concerns a type of marriage known as *simpua* marriage. In this marriage type, a boy's parents choose as his future bride a young girl, often orphaned or from a poor and socially inferior family, who is adopted as a daughter, who lives in the family household throughout childhood, and whom he subsequently marries at the appropriate age. In short, prior to their marriage the structural relationship between the boy and his chosen bride is little different from that of biological siblings raised in the same family. According to Wolf's findings, the adultery and divorce rates found in *simpua* marriages are higher and the fertility rate is lower than those found in regular Chinese marriages. Taking these rates as a measure of sexual dissatisfaction, Wolf argues that the greater sexual dissatisfaction in *simpua* marriages is a consequence of the sexual aversion that develops between the boy and girl in childhood, which supports Westermarck's theory that propinquity leads to sexual aversion.

Convincing as it might seem, Wolf's argument, I believe, is invalid on both empirical and theoretical grounds. Empirically, Wolf's findings regarding *simpua* marriage do not sustain the conclusion that children who live together typically develop a sexual aversion for each other, for although these marriages are characterized by higher rates of divorce and adultery and a lower rate of fertility than regular marriages, it is nevertheless the case that the great majority of them do not display these characteristics. If it is then claimed that these findings indicate that there is a greater likelihood for childhood propinquity to lead to sexual aversion, even this lesser claim can be sustained only on the dubious assumption that adultery, divorce, and low fertility are necessarily (as Wolf takes them to be) measures of sexual dissatisfaction. Surely, other factors also contribute to these forms of behavior in China—in regular and *simpua* marriages alike—as we know to be the case elsewhere.

But even accepting the assumption that sexual dissatisfaction is the sole determinant of divorce, adultery, and low fertility, Wolf's ethnographic data cast considerable doubt on his contention that the postulated sexual dissatisfaction found in *simpua* marriages is primarily determined by the sexual aversion that, putatively, the couple develop as a result of their living together in childhood.

Consider in the first place that the boy, according to Wolf, feels cheated and frustrated by a *simpua* marriage because it deprives him not only of honor and prestige—these marriages are viewed as "vulgar and inferior" and are therefore "socially despised"—but of a dowry, affinal alliances, and other advantages of a regular marriage, as well. Considering all of these disadvantages, it is hard to credit Wolf's contention that although the boys "resent their having their best interests sacrificed by their parents," their resentment is nevertheless "not likely to disrupt permanently their relationship as husband and wife" (Wolf, 1970, p. 506). I would assume, on the contrary, that their resentment would have that effect precisely.

Consider, again, that a girl adopted for a *simpua* marriage is an object of "abuse" by her adoptive family; indeed, such girls are treated so badly that they are the very "symbol of the life of misery." Consider, too, that (presumably as a result of this treatment) the girl is hostile to the members of her adoptive family, including her "brother" (and future husband), of whom she is jealous and toward whom she displays "sibling" rivalry. It is again hard to credit Wolf's contention that these factors do not importantly affect the girl's subsequent relationship with the boy when she becomes his wife. It is also difficult to believe that the girl's abusive treatment by his parents does not affect the boy's perception of her as an inferior person, one who is unworthy of esteem and affection. Indeed, since the main reason for a *simpua* marriage is the wish of the boy's mother to have a subordinate daughter-in-law, one who will not be a rival for her son's affection (as is the case in regular marriages), it would seem not unlikely that she goes out of her way to prevent her son from establishing an affectionate relationship with his "sister."

In short, given all of these considerations, it is hard to credit Wolf's claim that the boy's "resentment" and the girl's "misery" have no influence on their feelings for each other, and that these feelings, in turn, have no effect on their subsequent relationship as husband and wife, most especially their sexual relationship. Indeed, everything that we know about the influence of emotional attitudes on sexual desire and performance supports the contrary assumption. Hence, even if it were the case that the differences in the rates of fertility, divorce, and adultery in regular and *simpua* marriages are exclusively determined by a higher incidence of sexual dissatisfaction in the latter marriages, it is hard to believe that all of these social and cultural factors have no influence on that dissatisfaction. Indeed, given those factors it is a wonder that these marriages do not display a much greater degree of dissatisfaction.

When, then, to these social and cultural impediments to a satisfactory sexual relationship that are contained in Wolf's data we add the observation that in *simpua* marriage the boy and girl must marry each other even if, being sexually unattractive, they would not have married had they been raised separately; and when to that we add the additional observation that almost everywhere divorce in early marriages is higher than in later ones, so that the higher divorce rate of *simpua* marriages (in which twice as many couples marry before seventeen than in regular marriages—44 as against 22 percent) would be expected as a function of the couple's age at marriage—when these observations are also taken into account, I would then submit that Wolf's contention that the case of *simpua* marriage proves Westermarck's theory that childhood propinquity leads to sexual aversion rests on a very shaky foundation.

Let us then turn to the second ethnographic case that allegedly proves Westermarck's theory, the Israeli kibbutz movement. In 1958 I reported that in the kibbutz I had studied none of the children who had been reared together from birth had married each other, and that to the best of my knowledge none had had sexual intercourse with each other (Spiro, 1958, pp. 347-348). These findings were replicated in a later study by Talmon (1964) in three kibbutzim. Still later, based on a study of the marriage records of kibbutz children in all kibbutzim—2,769 marriages in all—Shepher (1971) reported that in not one case had there been a marriage between children reared together from birth through the age of six years. Shepher also reported that, so far as he was able to ascertain, this finding also applied to love affairs, those at least that were publicly known.

Now what makes these three reports of considerable interest is that no marriages (and probably no love affairs) have taken place among members of the same peer groups *despite the fact that such marriages are not prohibited.* It is understandable, therefore, that these findings have aroused a great deal of attention.

I interpreted my own findings as indicating that members of the kibbutz peer group repress their sexual feelings for each other. This interpretation was based on two sets of data. First, with one exception they themselves attributed the absence of marriage within the peer group to the sexual indifference which, they explained, arose from their perception of each other as "siblings." Second, the data regarding sexual behavior and socialization in these peer groups, to which I shall advert below, suggested rather strongly that their sexual indifference did not develop spontaneously.

Some (but hardly all) incest theorists, especially those acquainted with Shepher's subsequent large-scale report, interpreted the kibbutz findings, as did Shepher himself, as supporting Westermarck's theory that children reared together in childhood (whether or not they are siblings) develop a sexual aversion for each other. Since the latter interpretation, however, was offered without giving any consideration to (what I believe to be) the crucial data on sexual socialization, in order to evaluate these competing interpretations it is necessary to summarize those data for the particular historical period—because much has changed since then—for which the marriage findings were reported (for details see Spiro, 1958, Chapters 9, 11, 13, 14).

In that period, consistent with the kibbutz ideology of sexual freedom, young children were almost entirely free to engage in sexual play without interference or punishment by their caretakers. Since, therefore, boys and girls of the same age not only lived together in one dormitory, but also slept and showered together and had frequent other opportunities to see each other in the nude, it is not surprising that they also engaged in (childlike) sexual behavior and that they displayed little sexual shame (Spiro, 1958, p. 219–228). An important change in their behavior occurred, however, around eleven or twelve, when girls, who were beginning to show the first signs of puberty, refused to shower together with the boys, and in general began to display overt signs of sexual shame. At the same time, sexual behavior no longer occurred, and was replaced by a great deal of bickering and hostility between the sexes. Although the bickering and hostility gradually disappeared, sexual shame, including the avoidance of mixed showers, persisted throughout high school, and there was no return to the sexual play that characterized early childhood, nor was there an assumption of sexual behavior of a more mature form.

With this brief behavioral description, we may now examine the cultural and structural factors associated with these behavioral changes. First, despite their differential physical maturation at puberty, boys and girls of the same peer groups continued to live and sleep together. This meant that physically immature boys continued to be the roommates of girls who may have begun to menstruate, and whose secondary sexual characteristics—the development of breasts, the growth of pubic hair, and the like—were becoming prominent. Hence, although the girls were beginning to experience the sexual tensions of puberty and a concern with the physical changes in their bodies, the boys remained physically immature. It is not surprising, then, that the girls displayed no interest in the boys, and that in some cases the latter were put off—even frightened—by the girls, while others (outsiders) were sexually aroused by them.

Even at a later age, however, when the boys' maturation caught up with the girls', two other factors intervened. First, in the case of the older children—beginning around prepuberty and continuing until the end of high school—the permissive ideology of the kibbutz regarding the sexual play of young children was replaced by a strong prohibition on sexual behavior. The introduction of such prohibitions at this age was not based—not, at least, officially—on sexual puritanism, but on the assumptions that sexual behavior disrupts the learning process, that intellectual development is enhanced when the sex drive is sublimated in intellectual pursuits, and that pair bonding, which often results from sexual behavior, interferes with the intensive group interaction and group identification that the kibbutz viewed as paramount values. Hence, at this age strong pressure was exerted on the children to defer all sexual encounters until graduation from high school, and especially to avoid the formation of permanent liaisons. The latter in particular were the objects of strong social sanctions.

Second, despite these sexual prohibitions and their attendant sanctions, kibbutz educators believed that to encourage children to develop a wholesome attitude to sex and a "natural" attitude to the body and its functions, it was important that boys and girls live together not only in early childhood but throughout their educational careers until graduation from high school. Beginning, however, in the seventh grade the group of approximately sixteen age peers, who had previously shared one barracks-like dormitory room, was divided into groups of four—two males and two females—each group sharing one bedroom.

Here, then, I would submit, is a classic example of incompatible demands. On the one hand, we have a group of teenagers, at a physiological developmental stage of maximum sexual tension, who are exposed to persistent sexual stimulation induced by living in close quarters with members of the opposite sex, who dress and undress in one another's presence—though it was expected that they avert their eyes during this process—and who sleep in adjacent beds. At the same time, these same teenagers are expected to comply with a cultural norm which prohibits sexual behavior between them on pain of serious social sanctions. Such a contradiction, I would submit, can only result in intolerable conflict and unbearable sexual frustration. Edith Buxbaum, a child therapist, highlights this contradiction in her discussion of a fifteen-year-old kibbutz boy who could not sleep because of his urge to touch a girl, and who was advised to seek psychiatric help for his "problem." It seems paradoxical, Buxbaum (1970, p. 286) writes,

> that people should consider it abnormal for a fifteen-year-old boy to want to touch a girl with whom he sleeps in the same room. Indeed, it would be extraordinary if he did not want to. Yet, this is what kibbutz educators expect and the children expect of them-

selves. They are not supposed to have these feelings, or if they have them, they are not supposed to act on them.

That, however, only a small percentage of these teenagers required professional help to cope with the tensions induced by this contradiction suggests that the majority managed to erect strong psychological barriers against them. These barriers, as I suggested above—and as Buxbaum (1970, p. 285-290) and Bettelheim (1969, pp. 235-240) have suggested elsewhere—could only have consisted in the repression of their sexual wishes (which would explain how they might have consciously become sexually indifferent to each other) and, if that were not sufficient, in the formation of a reaction against them (which would explain how they might have consciously developed a sexual aversion for each other).[2]

There are three reasons, I would submit, for preferring this interpretation of these kibbutz findings to that of Westermarck's followers. First, the early sexual play of kibbutz children for the period under discussion was replaced by sexual abstinence only after the sexual permissiveness of childhood was replaced by the sexual prohibitions of adolescence. This suggests, pace Westermarck, that their sexual aversion for each other—if that is what it was—did not develop endogenously. Second, the sexual abstinence of the adolescents applied not only in regard to the members of their peer group—the group with whom they lived as children—but to other groups as well—those

[2]If correct, this analysis confutes Fox's attempt to salvage Westermarck's theory. The latter theory, according to Fox (1980, Chapter 2), only applies to children who not only live together but also engage in intense physical interaction. Since, he argues, their physical contacts lead to sexual arousal, and since immature children have no means of physiological discharge, their painful frustration leads to a consequent sexual aversion for the children (later adults) who are responsible for their pain. If, however, children who live together have no physical interaction and, therefore, no history of painful sexual frustration, Westermarck's theory does not apply. The kibbutz case, according to Fox, supports this argument because it involves physical interaction in childhood followed by aversion at adolescence.

According to my analysis, however, it is not the physical interaction in childhood, but the sexual prohibition at adolescence in the face of powerful sexual stimulation that leads to sexual aversion in the kibbutz. By my argument, the sexual stimulation leads to sexual arousal, which is frustrated by sexual prohibitions, and the resulting painful tensions are defended against by repression and reaction-formation which, if effective, lead to sexual aversion.

with whom they did not live as children. Third, and most important, this interpretation is supported by the recent findings of Kaffman (1977), a psychiatrist employed by the kibbutz movement, regarding sexual behavior in the kibbutz.

Although Kaffman's findings regarding peer-group marriage do not disagree with the early findings reported above, those regarding love affairs are at variance with them. "There is hardly a kibbutz," Kaffman writes, "without its report of heterosexual relationships between adolescents brought up together from infancy" (Kaffman, 1977, p. 216). Such relationships, he claims, "may not be typical, but [they are] not all that rare either" (p. 216). Kaffman also reports that whereas in an earlier study of seventeen-year-old kibbutz children, 66 percent of the sample were opposed to sexual relations, in 1973 only 7 percent of the males and 11 percent of the females voiced opposition.

How, then, are the discrepancies between Kaffman's report and the earlier reports to be explained? And what light do these discrepancies shed on the conflicting interpretations of the earlier reports? Kaffman's findings are based on studies conducted some few years after two major changes had begun to take place in the kibbutz movement. In the first place, many kibbutzim changed the living arrangements in the high school dormitories from mixed to unisexual bedrooms. In many of them, too, the prohibition on teenage sexual behavior has been informally if not formally abolished. According, then, to my interpretation of the earlier findings, Kaffman's findings are exactly what one would expect from such changes: no longer suffering the severe sexual tensions aroused by a contradiction between their living arrangements and sexual norms, adolescents in those kibbutzim which had undergone these changes had no need to create psychological barriers (repression and/or reaction-formation) to their sexual feelings. As more and more kibbutzim make these structural and cultural changes, we would then expect the sexual changes reported by Kaffman to become more widespread. It is difficult, however, to accommodate Kaffman's findings to Westermarck's theory. Since, according to that theory, sexual aversion results from joint living in childhood, and since no changes in the children's living arrangements were associated with the sexual changes reported by Kaffman, his data are clearly inexplicable by that theory.

If, then, my interpretation of the earlier reports is correct, why is it that the structural and cultural changes pointed to above have not had an even greater effect on the incidence of intragroup love affairs and marriage? There are at least two answers to that question. In the first place, the fact that individuals who live together in childhood (whether they are siblings or nonsiblings) acquire sexual wishes for each other does not mean, as I observed above, that these are their strongest sexual wishes. When we consider, then, that kibbutz peer groups, as Kaffman observes, are small and the range of sexual choice limited, and when we consider too the differential maturation rates of boys and girls, we would not expect a surge of sexual behavior within the peer group despite those changes. In the second place, since sexual attractiveness is hardly the only basis for marriage, we would not expect all couples who are sexually attracted to each other to wish to enter into a marriage.[3]

I would conclude, then, that the kibbutz case no more than the Chinese constitutes proof for the Westermarck theory. Indeed, if my analysis is correct, the kibbutz case provides strong support for the contention of the vast majority of incest theorists that individuals who live together (whether they are family or nonfamily members) do indeed develop and retain sexual feelings for each other unless they are inhibited by countervailing social and cultural pressures.

This analysis of the Israeli case is supported by yet another case, one which was reported only some few years following the claim that the kibbutz and Chinese cases support the Westermarck theory. This case, which has already been mentioned in a previous chapter, consists of brother-sister marriage in Roman Egypt. For two centuries, brother-sister marriage, according to Hopkins (1980, p. 310), was a "frequent practice" in Roman Egypt. According to second century census returns, for example, 23 of 113 recorded marriages were

[3]Those incest theorists—the so-called alliance theorists—who see the unchecked motivational disposition to incest as a barrier to the formation of interfamily alliances have primitive and prehistoric families as their model. Since the latter (hunting and gathering) families are frequently isolated from other families in their bands, mating with a family member is much more likely—unless it is checked by incest taboos—than in families in which a wide range of sexual partners, in addition to family members, are available. Physical isolation of the family, as we have previously observed, is an important condition for incest in modern families as well.

between brother and sister. More important for the terms of this discussion is that these marriages, which were considered to be entirely "normal"—hence, not prohibited by an incest taboo—were based not on economic or other practical considerations, but on "love and sexual passion." Hence, when such marriages came to an end in the third century, it was not because love and passion between brothers and sisters came to an end, but because Egypt came under Roman law, which prohibited incest.

If, then, the Chinese case does not refute the generalization that siblings who are reared together develop incestuous feelings for each other, and if the kibbutz and Egyptian cases offer strong support for that generalization, we may now turn to the question of incestuous feelings in the dyad that is relevant to the oedipal problem, the mother-son dyad.

There is nothing in the evidence summarized above regarding the existence of a motivational disposition to nuclear family incest which suggests that the boy's incestuous feelings for his mother are less strong than those for his sister. Indeed, given the nature of the mother-son bond in humans, it is reasonable to assume that, typically, his incestuous feelings for the mother are stronger by far than those for his sister, and that this generalization holds even when the mother is not seductive, as she is (according to my argument) in the Trobriands. Moreover, given the nature of the mother-child bond in humans, the incestuous feelings for the mother in our species, so I shall argue below, are much stronger than those found in any other species. In short, contrary to most incest theorists, I shall argue that if the (mother-son) incest taboo represents the transition from the state of nature to that of culture, it is because the intensity of the incestuous attachment to the mother is much stronger in human (culture) than in animal (nature) societies. A comparison of human with infrahuman primate societies—for convenience' sake this discussion will be restricted to primates, our closest animal relatives—can reveal why this is the case.

For obvious biological reasons it is the mother with whom any primate infant, human or infrahuman, sustains its most intimate emotional and physical relationship. It is she primarily who suckles, trains, and plays with him. It is her voice, her body, and her face that the infant knows best, and it is she whom above all others he seeks out for pleasure, protection, and comfort. As a consequence, it is the mother who is the primary object of the infant's emotional attachment. If, then, even the infant—as we observed in Chapter 4—is a sexual creature and capable of sexual arousal, it is not unreasonable to assume that the early attachment to the mother has important libidinal overtones, and that the mother, therefore, is the object of the earliest libidinal attachment. Despite these similarities between humans and other primates, the incestuous attachment to the mother is much stronger and especially problematic in humans because of two important biological characteristics that are unique to humans: the suppression of estrus and prolonged infantile dependency.

Among infrahuman primates there is an incompatibility between sexuality and mothering because at the height of estrus, when the females are in a state of sexual "mania" or "frenzy," as the primatologists call it, they have little interest in mothering or, for that matter, in any other activity except sex. Hence, mothering can only occur during anestrus—the period in which the female is not sexually receptive—which, apart from the normal sexual cycle, begins immediately following pregnancy and continues until the end of lactation. When, at the end of lactation, estrus returns, the juvenile is already weaned, and since typically infantile helplessness does not extend beyond weaning, the mother's indifference to her offspring during estrus does not endanger their welfare since they are no longer dependent upon her for care and nurturance. Indeed, at the conclusion of weaning the juvenile's relationship with the mother is typically and abruptly severed. Thus, in those primate societies consisting of mother-child families, the juvenile is usually driven off by the mother when, at the conclusion of weaning, she enters estrus, while in those with biparental families, he is usually driven off by her consort. In either case, he usually joins a group of juveniles who, with some few exceptions, are permanently "peripheralized" (as the primatologists say).

Since, then, mother and son are separated following weaning, and since their separation is socially enforced at least until the son achieves maturity—when, in a few cases, he may force himself upon the dominant adult male(s)—there is no opportunity for his early attachment to the mother to become intensified by a continuing relationship with her. (For a more extensive treatment, see Chance and Jolly, 1970; Rowell, 1972; Bischof, 1975; Lancaster, 1979; Fox, 1980.)

Among humans, the mother-child relationship is very different. Since infantile helplessness is prolonged, and cultural acquisition complex, it is necessary that the child remain dependent upon the mother (or mother surrogate) long after the completion of weaning. And since, with the suppression of estrus, the human female is not characterized by sexual mania, her interest in sex, though continuous, does not interfere with her motivation or ability to care for her young children. Since, then, there is no incompatibility between mating and mothering among humans, human offspring live with and remain dependent upon their mothers for many years, not excluding the "phallic" period (when the early libidinal attachment to the mother receives strong reinforcement) and puberty (when sexuality may erupt explosively).

In short, since the son's relationship with the mother may persist throughout childhood and even into puberty, thereby intensifying his early emotional attachment to her, and since that attachment is based on *both* libidinal and dependency feelings, it is reasonable to expect the incestuous attachment of the son to the mother to be much stronger in humans than in primates. For the same reason, one would expect the attachment to the mother to be much stronger than the incestuous attachment to the sister. Although brother and sister live together, they never have—indeed, they are prohibited from having—the intimate physical relationship that the son has with his mother.

Strangely enough, Malinowski (unlike most of his followers) fully recognized the strength of the boy's incestuous attachment to the mother, as well as the critical challenge that it posed for his contention that the oedipus complex is confined to "patriarchal" families of the Western type. Indeed, in a long rhapsodic passage he expatiates in concrete detail on the erotic feelings of the young boy for his mother (1927, pp. 212–214). At the same time he also observes that since lovers employ the same organ zones and behavioral modes in their physical interaction with each other that mother and child employ in their interaction, the male's later induction into the "erotic life" may arouse in him "disturbing memories" of the relationship with his mother, because she "remains in the foreground of [his] emotional interests throughout his life." That being the case, Malinowski continues, before the boy reaches sexual maturity it is necessary that "all sensuality felt toward the mother become repressed." That is achieved by inculcating in the boy emotions of "reverence, dependence [and] respect" toward the mother so that if a "subconscious temptation of incest" is aroused when he is mature, it is muted by its "blending" with these nonsexual emotions.

The above analysis represents Malinowski's conception of what happens to the early incestuous attachment to the mother in the West (and some other societies), but it is not what happens (according to him) in matrilineal societies, in which the "passionate" attachment of the infant to the mother spontaneously disappears by the time the boy reaches the "phallic" stage of development, the very stage when genital love for her is normally expected to appear. Unfortunately, however, his argument on behalf of this claim, as was indicated in Chapter 2, is less than convincing. In a nutshell, Malinowski nowhere indicates how or why the spontaneous disappearance of the boy's passionate attachment to the mother occurs. *That* it occurs, however, he is quite sure on the grounds (it will be recalled) that, when he asked the Trobriand men whether they wished to have intercourse with their mothers, they ridiculed the very suggestion. Such a response, he argued, proves that a "repressed Oedipus complex" cannot possibly exist in the Trobriands.

Although I have already dealt with this "proof" in Chapter 2, it is nevertheless worth repeating because most other critics of the notion that incestuous motives might be repressed adduce exactly the same argument. Briefly, the argument is invalid on three counts. First, although it now seems unlikely that the boy's incestuous wishes in regard to the mother are ever—to use Freud's metaphor—"smashed" in childhood (as a result of castration anxiety), it does seem to be the case that in some individuals and in some societies those wishes do undergo a gradual process of extinction, coordinate with the cessation of childhood sexuality (sexual "latency"). Second, even in those individuals and societies in which incestuous wishes regarding the mother persist into adulthood, it is rare that the adult mother is the object of these wishes. Rather, it is the mother of childhood—or, rather, his mental representation of her—on whom the son's incestuous wishes remain fixated. In the latter event—to come to the third reason—the son's fixation cannot be discovered by the mere asking because, typically, it is not in conscious awareness, which is precisely what is meant—to use Malinowski's expression—by a "*repressed* Oedipus complex." To that extent Westermarck and his followers are correct when they argue that incest taboos do not have the function of prohibiting incest (with mother or anyone else), not because incestuous wishes (as they contend) do not exist, but because typically the implementation of the incest taboos in childhood has achieved its intended function. In short, from this perspective, the function of incest taboos is not to signal to *adults* that their incestuous wishes must be inhibited, but rather to banish such wishes from *children* before they become adults.

If, then, the implementation of the mother-son incest taboo (a subject to which we shall return) typically results in the disappearance of the incestuous attachment to the childhood mother—as a result either of extinction, on the one hand, or of repression and reaction-formation, on the other—to challenge the universality of such an attachment on the grounds that in some society (or societies) adults do not consciously experience any sexual feelings for the mother is clearly misguided. By that criterion, such an attachment does not exist in any society, whether "patriarchal" or matrilineal, not at any rate in its "normal" members. In short the evidence for the universality of a motivational disposition to mother-son incest remains unaffected by this challenge.

Since, then, that evidence is very strong, and since (as we argued above) the existence of the incestuous dimension of the oedipus complex renders its aggressive dimension all but axiomatic, the only appropriate response to the question, "Is the oedipus complex universal?" is "How could it possibly not be?" Even in those primate societies in which females have no permanent consorts—the multi-male societies of trooping monkeys—and in which, therefore, there can be no rivalry between son and father, powerful rivalry nevertheless exists between the peripheralized young males as a group and the dominant males who monopolize the females (Chance and Jolly, 1970). In single-male primate societies, on the other hand, whether those of the monogamous gibbon (Carpenter, 1940) or the polygynous hamadryas baboon (Kummer, 1968), the rivalry is directly and explicitly between father and son.

In sum, there is only one obvious retort to the above riposte. If there were a human society in which mothers did not have male consorts—so that the son had no adult rival for the love of the mother—in such a society the oedipus complex (by definition) would not exist. So far as we know, however, no human society of that type exists, or has ever existed. The "matrifocal" households—widely prevalent in the Caribbean (Smith, 1956) and among lower-class American blacks (Rainwater and Yancey, 1967)—do not constitute an exception to that generalization because typically a husband-father is intermittently present or else the mother brings a series of temporary lovers into the household. That being the case, although there is no evidence one way or the other, I would also expect these New World matrifocal households to produce an oedipus complex. This expectation is supported by the findings of Gough (1953) that an oedipus complex is found among the Nayar, an Indian caste of the Malabar Coast, despite the fact that Nayar women typically take a series of lovers rather than living with a permanent consort.

That the oedipus complex, according to this analysis, would be expected to be universal does not imply, I hasten to add, that it would also be expected to be cross-culturally uniform. On the contrary, since we know (from Western data) that the oedipus complex is variable within societies, we would then expect that it would exhibit a wide range of variability across societies. That is the thesis I want to explore in the following section.

Cross-Cultural Variability in the Oedipus Complex

Since the oedipus complex may be said to have three important dimensions—structure, intensity, and outcome—in principle at least it could be expected to display cross-cultural variability in all three. Let us begin with its structure. By the "structure" of the oedipus complex I mean the members—in addition to the boy himself—who make up the oedipal triangle and who are the objects, therefore, of his sexual and aggressive wishes.

If in the classical oedipus complex it is the boy's biological parents who are the objects of those wishes, that is not to be explained, surely, by the closeness of their genetic relationship, nor again by some instinctual vectorial dimension of the sexual and aggressive drives. Rather, that particular oedipal triangle is best accounted for by the sociological fact that the boy and his biological parents, typically constituting a social group and inhabiting a common household, sustain certain modes of social relationships with each other. It is these relationships that account for the biological parents, specifically, becoming the objects of his sexual and aggressive wishes. Hence, variability in these relationships could be expected to result in corresponding and predictable variability in the structure of the oedipal triangle. Thus, for example, if there were a society in which, rather than belonging to a common residential household, parents and children were distributed in different households, it might then be expected that the child's mother-surrogate (rather than his biological mother) would be the focus of his libidinal wishes, and that her consort (rather than his biological father) would be the focus of his aggressive wishes. At the moment, however, such a society is not known.

If, then, there is no theoretical reason why the adult members of the oedipal triangle must consist of the boy's biological mother and father, it might well be the case that in some society this triangle consists of the boy, his sister, and his mother's brother. Malinowski's claim that this is the case in the Trobriands was rejected (in Chapter 2) not on theoretical, but on empirical grounds: neither the composition of the Trobriand household nor the social relationships that obtain within the nuclear family display the characteristics that might expectably produce that particular structural variant of the classical oedipus triangle. For exactly the same reason neither this nor any other structural variant of the classical oedipus triangle has been reported at a total societal level for any other society, which does not mean that such a variant or variants may not occur in individual cases or in certain subgroups in some societies, or that some variant may not be reported in the future for some (as yet unknown) total society.

Although the structure of the oedipus complex, while variable in principle, seems to be universal in fact, this is not the case in regard to its two other attributes—its intensity and outcome—in which cross-cultural variability is not only a theoretical expectation but an ethnographic fact. Since variability in the intensity of the oedipus complex was discussed in the previous chapters, we shall focus here on variability in its outcome, especially since the latter attribute has important social and cultural consequences. Moreover, since the implementation of the incest taboo is a major determinant of its outcome, we shall limit our discussion to that determinant alone.

Since libidinal desires for the mother may be present, as we have seen, in the nursing infant, the implementation of the incest taboo may be said to begin with weaning, which is also the time when the child is usually banned from the mother's bed and when, in general, he is discouraged from continuing those more intimate forms of physical contact with the mother that she had previously permitted, if not actively encouraged. The diminution, if not cessation, of these intimate forms of bodily contact with the mother during this—the preoedipal—period does not, of course, lead to the extinction of the boy's libidinal desires for her, especially since those desires are intensified when he enters the "phallic" stage of psychosexual development. At the latter stage, therefore, the mother-son incest taboo is implemented in all societies by still other means which (in varying degrees) result in its internalization, i.e., in the acquisition of a motivational disposition on the part of the boy to comply with the prohibition. These means and the process of internalization are conceived of differently by different theorists.

For cognitive theorists, the implementation of the mother-son incest taboo, like the implementation of any other cultural prohibition, is achieved by the usual processes of enculturation, i.e., by verbal instruction, including instruction in the punitive consequences attendant upon its violation. For social learning theorists that kind of instruction is not sufficient to achieve the internalization of the taboo unless it is accompanied by various socialization techniques—techniques of positive and negative reinforcement—which provide the boy with important incentives for complying with the taboo. Psychoanalytic theorists, who also stress the importance of socialization, emphasize the signal importance of castration anxiety as the motivational basis for compliance with the taboo. As they see it, the threats (negative reinforcement) which are used to sever his incestuous attachment to the mother lead to the son's fantasized expectation of castration as the punishment for incest with the mother.

Whether it is achieved by the one means or the other, if the implementation of the incest taboo leads to its internalization, compliance with the taboo is achieved either by the extinction of the boy's incestuous desire for his mother or by its repression, the latter often being accompanied by a reaction-formation against the desire, i.e., by an emotional aversion to sexual contact with the mother. In sum, if the taboo is internalized, the boy's incestuous attachment to the mother either disappears entirely (extinction) or, although persisting unconsciously (repression), disappears from conscious awareness. Why the internalization of the taboo results in the one consequence rather than the other is a question concerning which there are many, but few satisfactory, answers.

Extinction and repression, however, are not the only possible outcomes of the incestuous attachment to the mother. If, for example, the implementation of the incest taboo by any of the processes mentioned above is only partially successful in promoting its internalization, the son's libidinal attachment to the mother is not extinguished, and although it may be repressed, it undergoes only weak or incomplete repression. In Bengal, for example, mother and son—so Roy (1975, p. 125) observes—remain "highly cathected libidinal objects [for] . . . a lifetime." (For other parts of India, see also Carstairs, 1956 and Kakar, 1978.) Similarly, the typical male in the Mexican town of San Juan, according to Hunt (1971, p. 129), "has never been able to transfer his libidinal energies from his mother to an outsider," thereby manifesting a "typical Mediterranean pattern." (For other parts of Mexico, see also Bushnell, 1958.) That such an outcome is a "Mediterranean pattern" is readily discerned, for example, from Parsons' (1969) description of the mother-son relationship in Italy (Naples). The same pattern is also found, however, in East Asia. In Japan, for example, as Tanaka (1981, p. 16) observes, the mother-son relationship is characterized by the "continuous presence of unresolved libidinality." In many societies in which the incestuous attachment to the mother is incompletely repressed, other means than those mentioned above are used for the implementation of the incest taboo, as we shall see below.

Let us first, however, turn from the incestuous attachment to the mother to briefly comment on the possible outcomes of the boy's hostility to the father, the other dimension of the oedipus complex. Since, as we have seen, the boy's hostility to the father sustains a correlative relationship with his love for the mother, the outcome of his oedipal hostility is systematically related to the outcome of his oedipal love. In short, it is the entire oedipus complex whose outcome may variously take the form of extinction, repression, or incomplete repression.

While all three outcomes may be found in a single society, as we know from clinical evidence in the West, it is usually the case (as I have been suggesting) that one of them is dominant. Since, however, the dominant outcome (as I have also been suggesting) is not the same in all societies, we may now say that this—the second dimension—of the oedipus complex is cross-culturally variable not only in principle but in fact.

Although of some interest in itself, the cross-cultural variability in the outcome of the oedipus complex is anthropologically important because its outcome has social and cultural consequences. Since, then, the differences in the psychological characteristics of these three outcomes are nontrivial, the differences in their variable social and cultural consequences are likewise nontrivial. The latter differences are especially marked when we compare societies in which extinction and repression are the dominant outcomes with those in which incomplete repression is dominant.

Operationally defined, a "weak" or "incomplete" repression of the oedipus complex is one in which repression is insufficiently powerful to preclude the conscious arousal of the boy's incestuous wishes for the mother (and hence his hostile wishes toward the father) under conditions of incestuous temptation. Hence, those societies in which incomplete repression is the dominant outcome of the oedipus complex are societies in which the implementation of the taboos on mother-son incest and father-son aggression by the enculturation and socialization techniques described above is not entirely successful in achieving their internalization. This being the case, rather than relying on the boy's own psychological resources—extinction, repression, and reaction-formation—to ensure compliance with those taboos, many of those societies achieve compliance by means of social and cultural resources, as well.

In short, so far as their social and cultural consequences are concerned, the first notable difference between societies in which extinction and repression are the dominant outcome of the oedipus complex and those in which incomplete repression is its dominant outcome is that the latter societies (much more often than the former) practice child extrusion and painful initiation rites. These customs (as was noted in a previous chapter) ensure compliance with the twin oedipal prohibitions by reducing the opportunities for incestuous and aggressive temptation or by strengthening the incomplete repression of the boy's sexual and aggressive oedipal wishes. Let us briefly examine each of these customs, beginning with child extrusion.

When boys—and, in some societies, girls too—are extruded from the parental household, their subsequent residence, as the cross-cultural record indicates, is highly variable. It may be an age-graded dormitory, a men's house, a children's village, some other household, a boarding school, or the like. Whatever the conscious motives for these practices may be—depending on the society, they include the reduction of the son's rivalry with the father (Wilson, 1949; Spiro, 1958), the prevention of his witnessing the primal scene (Elwin, 1968), economic apprenticeship (Aries, 1962), educational advancement (Gathorne-Hardy, 1977), the economic advantage of adoption (Powell, 1957), and others—they have the consequence (among others) of separating the son from his parents, thereby reducing the opportunities for the arousal of his sexual and aggressive oedipal wishes. When, at some later age, more frequent interaction with the parents is once again resumed, his libidinal and aggressive impulses have typically been rechanneled. Son extrusion in human societies has its analogue, it will be recalled, in the peripheralization of male juveniles in primate societies. By the latter process, the juveniles are deprived of the opportunity of acting upon their sexual and aggressive impulses toward their mothers and adult males, respectively.

The second consequence of the incomplete repression of the oedipus complex—which, like the first, constitutes a cultural resource for enhancing the compliance with the taboos on mother-son incest and father-son aggression—is the practice of painful initiation rites. Although the conscious, culturally constituted explanations for these rites only infrequently relate them to the oedipal issue we have been addressing here, the ethnographic descriptions of these practices and of the initiates' psychological reactions to them provide strong evidence for the thesis that these rites, like child extrusion, constitute an important cultural resource for ensuring compliance with the taboos on incest with the mother and aggression toward the father.[4]

If, however, child extrusion achieves this end by removing the son from the locus of oedipal sexual and aggressive temptation, initiation rites achieve the same end (according to some theorists at least) by removing these oedipal wishes from the son. That is, by hazing, isolation, physical torture, ordeals, and phallic mutilation (circumcision, subincision, and superincision), these rites arouse in the boys intense fear and anxiety—often, in my view, castration anxiety—regarding the father and/or the father-figure initiators (Fox, 1980, p. 159), thereby serving to break the boys' incestuous attachment to their mothers (Hiatt, 1971, p. 81) and inhibit their aggression to their fathers. In sum, these rites, I am suggesting, serve to strengthen the (incomplete) repression of the boys' oedipal (sexual and aggressive) wishes, and in some cases they might perhaps lead to their extinction. That these painful and often brutal rites also provide a culturally sanctioned (and ritually limited) opportunity for men to express their complementary oedipal hostility to boys—rationalized, of course, by the ideology of helping them achieve social and cultural maturity—seems equally obvious, as Reik (1919) suggested some years ago.

I must hasten to say, however, that an oedipal interpretation of these rites not only is *not* obvious to other commentators, but has typically been rejected by anthropologists (see Langness, 1974) and psychoanalysts (see Lidz and Lidz, 1977) alike. Since I believe that rituals, like most other cultural activities, have multiple meanings, I have little difficulty in accepting most of the sociological and psychological meanings that other commentators have attributed to these rites. But I have great difficulty in ignoring their oedipal and complementary oedipal meanings, which, in the light of recent descriptions (see footnote 4), are just too blatant to overlook. Indeed, from these descriptions I would argue that societies which practice initia-

[4]For four superb descriptions of these rites and of the emotional reactions of the initiates in New Guinea, I especially recommend Read (1965), Tuzin (1980), Herdt (1980, 1982), and Poole (1982).

tion rites of the ferocity found in—and perhaps confined to—New Guinea and Australia are societies in which the incomplete repression of the childhood oedipus complex is most pronounced.

As an illustration of their "blatant" oedipal and complementary meanings, consider Herdt's (1982) description of the boy's initiation rite among the Sambia of Papua New Guinea. The first stage of the rite, which consists of forcible nose-bleeding, administered by the men on boys of seven to ten years, is a "violent assault whose effects are probably close to producing authentic trauma," the boys themselves referring to their fright by such expressions as "'I feared they were going to kill me.'" If the boys resist the men and cry, as they often do, the men "have little pity" for them, and they are "severely dealt with by prolonging the action and thereby brutalizing it." Herdt is hardly exaggerating in calling it "an act of raw aggression." Similarly, in the third stage, performed for boys thirteen to sixteen, a line of warriors, appearing as ghosts and enemies, surround them and, plucking bows and arrows, hooting, and shouting, they again forcibly nose-bleed the boys, who are now in a state of "terror."

That this aggression both gratifies the complementary oedipal complex of the men and is intended to contain the oedipal wishes of the boys is indicated by Herdt's comments. Nose-bleeding is described by the Sambia as "punishment" for the boys for their insubordination to their fathers and elders. That this insubordination includes oedipal insubordination is reflected both in the warning given the boys that they may never again so much as touch, hold, talk with, eat with, or look at their mothers and in the conscious and unconscious symbolic equation of nose and penis in Sambia thought and culture. Because of their early and exclusive attachment to them, Herdt comments, the boys "must be traumatically detached from their mothers and kept away from them at all costs." In later stages of the rite, those following puberty, references to the mother drop out, and, instead, the boys are admonished by the initiators to avoid other women, especially married women; should they disobey, they are warned, they will be killed. Indeed, beginning with the separation of the boys from their mothers at the first stage of the initiation rite until their marriage following the last stage, males are never again alone with a woman, and throughout that period ritual aggression is used by the older males to "instill [in them] fear and obedience" so that their avoidance of females will be maintained.

Although the Sambia begin their first stage of initiation in early childhood, it is important to note that there are important cross-cultural differences in the age at which these rites, as well as child extrusion, occur. In some societies they take place in childhood, in others not until puberty. Insofar, then, as these customs are (among other things) cultural resources for the implementation of the taboos on mother-son incest and father-son aggression, it may perhaps be assumed that those societies in which they do not take place until puberty are societies in which the boy's repression of his incestuous and aggressive wishes, though incomplete, is sufficiently strong to prevent them from passing through the repressive barrier throughout childhood, and that it is only at puberty, with the eruption of his sexual urges, that his own psychological resources are inadequate to that task. If that assumption is correct, it then follows that, conversely, those societies in which these cultural resources are already brought into play in childhood are societies in which the boy's psychological resources for coping with his oedipal wishes are inadequate from the very beginning.

Whether the one or the other, however, if the oedipus complex is incompletely repressed in childhood, there is a special urgency for containing the boy's oedipal wishes either before or at the time he reaches puberty, for it is then that he is physiologically capable of acting upon his sexual wishes and physically capable of acting upon his aggressive wishes. That is the time, in short, by which it is especially urgent that cultural resources be brought into play either to strengthen the incomplete repression of his oedipal wishes (painful initiation rites) or to reduce his opportunities for acting upon them (extrusion).

If, then, son extrusion and painful initiation are most likely to be practiced in societies in which the oedipus complex is incompletely repressed, and least likely in those which exhibit the two other outcomes, we can now see that differences in the outcome of the oedipus complex have other important consequences as well. Since, for example, societies in which the oedipus complex is extinguished or fully repressed are unlikely to practice child extrusion, the family is more likely to remain an intact residential group than in those in which, as a consequence of the incomplete repression of the oedipus complex, the son is extruded from the household. But not all intact family households are the same; among other things they vary importantly in their emotional texture. Thus, the emotional texture of the family in which the oedipus complex is extinguished and in which, therefore, children can live together with parents in emotional comfort, without suffering intrapsychic conflicts regarding their sexual and aggressive oedipal wishes, is very different from the emotional texture of the family in which the oedipus complex is repressed and in which, therefore, the integrity of the family household is purchased at the cost of persistent unconscious struggles with oedipal wishes. These differences, of course, are much more pronounced during puberty than during childhood.

Differences of another type distinguish societies which, because of incomplete repression of the oedipus complex, practice painful initiation rites from those which, because of its extinction or full repression, have no need to practice them. Thus, in many tribal societies, initiation rites can be of unimaginable complexity, extending over a period of many years, and consuming a large proportion of their social and economic resources. Indeed, in many of these societies—most notably those of New Guinea—these rites may be said to dominate the lives of the members of the group, constituting the main focus of their interests and action (see Read, 1965; Herdt, 1980; Tuzin, 1980). A funnel for so many social and economic resources, and for so much emotional energy, a cultural focus of this type has still other consequences. For example, it is significantly limits the options of these societies for choosing alternative (and perhaps more productive) cultural means for the investment of emotional energy and the allocation of social and economic resources. Moreover, inasmuch as a cultural focus of this type is both a highly elaborated magical response to unconscious wishes and fears, as well as a stimulus for the arousal of still others, it may serve to reinforce the skewed ratio of magical to realistic thinking found in many of these tribal societies. If so, this would account not only for the high proportion of magical (alternatively, primary-process, prelogical, animistic) thinking that, in my view, is one of their singular psychological characteristics, but also for their seeming inability to evolve an alternative cultural focus (or foci) based on realistic (alternatively, secondary-process, logical, nonanimistic) thinking.

There are, of course, many other social and cultural consequences attendant upon the variability in the outcome of the oedipus complex which, since their explication would require a separate book, can only be mentioned here. Thus, in societies in which unconscious oedipal conflicts require persistent repression for their containment, the oedipus complex may undergo structural transformations as a result of defensively motivated projections and displacements which importantly affect other social relationships and institutions. That, indeed, is Jones' (1925) contention regarding the boy's hostility toward the mother's brother in the Trobriands, which, so he argues, represents the displacement of his oedipal hostility for his father. Gough (1953) interprets the nephew's hostility toward the mother's brother among the Nayar in the same manner.[5]

Kin relationships, however, are not the only social relationships in which repressed oedipal conflicts are projected and displaced. Political (Lasswell, 1960), religious (Erikson, 1958), and economic (Brown, 1959) institutions, to mention only a few, constitute some of the larger social arenas for the symbolic expression of a repressed oedipus complex. Thus, to advert to its hostility dimension, rebellious attitudes toward authority figures often have their psychodynamic source in repressed oedipal hostility, the former being a vehicle for the displacement or sublimation of the latter (see Erikson, 1963; Feuer, 1969; Rothman and Lichter, 1982). The same process occurs in regard to the sexual dimension of the oedipus complex. Thus, for example, the strong male involvement in the Marian cult in southern Italy (Parsons, 1969) and Mexico (Bushnell, 1958) is often interpreted as a sublimation of the repressed oedipal attachment to the mother.

Since religion (because, perhaps, of its frequent use of family idioms) like politics (for the same reason) is an especially important cultural domain for the expression of repressed oedipal conflicts, it

[5]Structural transformations in the initial formation of the oedipus complex are also found in its symbolic expression in myth, as Paul (1980) has shown in his perceptive analysis of the hostility dimension of the oedipus complex in Greek, Judaic, and Christian oedipal myths.

might be added that other differences between societies in which the oedipus complex is repressed in contrast to those in which it is extinguished may also be seen in such diverse religious phenomena as ritual circumcision and clitoridectomy, ascetic abstinences and self-torture, sexualized goddesses and witches, celibate priests and priestesses, mystical and trance states, and many others.

Although further examples would require a monograph, this brief discussion has perhaps been sufficient to suggest that the continuing debates over the oedipus complex are debates not merely about a passing episode in the psychological development of the child. Rather, they are debates about a psychological constellation which, as this discussion has attempted to show, has pervasive cultural, social, and psychological consequences.

The Making of a Scientific Myth

In the previous two sections I argued that although the universality of the oedipus complex is rendered highly likely by the child's potentiality for sexual and aggressive arousal, inasmuch as the intensity and distribution of sexual and aggressive wishes are each a product of the social relationships that the child sustains with those adults who constitute his "significant others," in principle we would expect to find cross-cultural variability in the oedipus complex as a function of the variability in those relationships. That this expectation is most probably actualized, however, in regard only to the intensity and outcome, but not the structure, of the oedipus complex is not surprising. Since the classical oedipal traingle—consisting of mother, father, and son—is determined by the twin facts that the child's early mothering figure is the first and most important object of his sexual wishes, and that his perceived rival for her love is the consequent object of his hostility, cross-cultural variability in this structure would be expected if, but only if, there were some range of variablity in the social recruitment to the mothering role. Since at the *societal* level, however, it is the biological mother who is the child's central (if not exclusive) early mothering figure, and the biological father his most salient rival for her love in all known societies, it is understandable that the structure of the oedipus complex, although cross-culturally variable in principle, is most probably invariant in fact.

This, of course, brings us back to our point of departure, the controversy over the Trobriand oedipus complex. For the very nub of Malinowski's contention that the structure of the nuclear complex (as he preferred to put it)[6] is culturally variable not only in principle, but also in fact, consists of his claim that although the biological mother is the primary mothering figure in the Trobriands, it is the sister who is the primary object of the boy's libidinal desires. Since that paradoxical claim was already shown in Chapter 2 to be refuted by Malinowski's own evidence, there is no need to repeat that demonstration. Rather, in this final section, I wish to address the remarkable fact that this paradoxical claim has been accepted with almost no skepticism or critical inquiry for fifty years.

Given the powerful evidence (discussed earlier in the chapter) for the universality of the motivational disposition to mother-son incest, if it were reported that in some society the mother is not an incestuous object for the son, such a report would, of course, be rather surprising. But since the history of science is a history of persistent refutations of well-established generalizations, there would be no reason to greet such a report with special skepticism. In claiming, therefore, that it is a "remarkable fact" that Malinowski's report of such a finding in the Trobriands has not been greeted with sufficient skepticism, it is not because that report challenges an established generalization, but because in the context of Trobriand culture the absence of an incestuous attachment to the mother is twice anomalous.

The first anomaly consists in the fact that of the three types of incestuous desire that might, in principle, be found in any male, the desire of the son for the mother is, alone, reported to be absent in the Trobriands, while that of the father for the daughter is reported to be as strong as it is purported to be in the West, and that of the brother for the sister stronger by far. This gestalt is all the more anomalous since

[6]Since, for Malinowski, the oedipus complex is a cultural product, he used "nuclear complex" as a cover term for all possible cultural variants, reserving "oedipus complex" for that particular variant in which mother and father are the objects, respectively, of the child's sexual and aggressive impulses.

typically the boy's incestuous attachment to the mother is, if anything, much stronger than the other two; and it becomes still more anomalous when it is recalled that the incestuous attachment of the Trobriand daughter to the father, unlike that of the son to the mother, is reported to be of normally expected oedipal intensity.

In claiming that because it is anomalous Malinowski's report should have been greeted with skepticism, I am by no means suggesting that its truth or accuracy should therefore have been impugned. If "anomaly" is glossed as "puzzle," and if we follow Kuhn (1962, Chapter 4) in viewing science as a puzzle-solving enterprise, then, rather than impugning the accuracy of an anomalous finding, scientific skepticism merely signals the existence of yet another puzzle to be solved. In the case of this Trobriand puzzle, one simple solution immediately suggests itself. Since, as has already been observed, it is their physical and emotional intimacy that accounts for the son's incestuous attachment to the mother, part of the Trobriand puzzle would be solved if it were the case that the most intimate relationship of the young boy is with some woman (or women) other than the biological mother. If, moreover, it were also the case that this structural arrangement did not affect the relationship of the male to either his sister or his daughter, the other parts of the puzzle would be solved, as well, and the skepticism could be laid to rest.

Unfortunately, however, the ethnographic facts are the very opposite of this proposed solution. As we have seen in the previous chapter, all the conditions that highlight the mother-son relationship as the primary arena for the boy's most intense incestuous struggles in the "normally expectable" family are present in the Trobriands as well—and then some! In short, there is nothing in Malinowski's account that might solve the puzzle of why it is that in a family and socialization system of the Trobriand type the sister and daughter are the objects of the male's incestuous desires, whereas the mother is not. That, indeed, is why I characterized Malinowski's claim as anomalous.

Perhaps, however, the solution to this anomaly might be found by taking another tack. For just as the problem of inflation can be tackled from either the supply or the demand side of the market, the solution to an ethnographically anomalous finding can sometimes be found not in an antecedent, but in a consequent condition. Specifically, if the reported absence of a normally expectable incestuous attachment to the mother were accompanied by the absence of a normally expectable mother-son incest taboo, the former report would not then constitute an anomaly (although the absence of such an attachment would still have to be explained by some as yet unknown, and theoretically unexpected, antecedent condition). Unfortunately, the ethnographic reality is once again the reverse of the proposed solution: the mother-son incest taboo is, in fact, present in the Trobriands. Moreover, the presence of this taboo not only leaves the anomaly unresolved, but creates yet another: if the boy has no incestuous desire for the mother, why should there be a taboo prohibiting incest with her? This second anomaly, of course, could be resolved by simply rejecting the assumption on which it is based, viz., that taboos exist to prevent the practice of the tabooed actions. But that requires at least a brief discussion of the historical debates regarding incest taboos.

It was Frazer (1887, vol. 4, p. 97 ff.) who first converted the above assumption about the function of taboos into the generally accepted theory of incest taboos. Since, following from that assumption, the function of incest taboos is the prevention of incest with their stipulated targets, the existence of these taboos, so Frazer argued, implies the existence of incestuous desire for those very targeted persons.[7] This theory, however, has had its opponents from its very inception. Most of them, following Westermarck's (1906–1908, vol. 2, p. 368) view that sexual aversion develops between family members who live in proximity to each other from an early age, argue that incest taboos are merely the institutionalized expression of sexual aversions.

Although the acceptance of this theory would resolve the anom-

[7]Why it is that all societies have wanted to prevent incest at least within the nuclear family is a question that has been variously answered, but all the proposed answers point to one or more of the following maladaptive consequences of the widespread practice of nuclear family incest which are precluded by compliance with incest taboos: (1) biological impairment attendant upon inbreeding (see Lindzey, 1967), (2) collapse of the family authority structure, because of the sexual rivalry between father and son, with the attendant difficulty of cultural transmission (see Malinowski, 1927, p. 216), (3) structural breakdown of the family attendant upon role confusion (see Parsons, 1954), (4) breakdown of social alliances attendant upon family endogamy (see Lévi-Strauss, 1949, Chapters 4 and 29).

aly of the reported co-occurrence in the Trobriands of a mother-son incest taboo and the absence of an incestuous desire for the mother, there are powerful grounds for rejecting it as invalid. One could point, for example, to the evidence in support of the motivational disposition to nuclear family incest which was summarized earlier in this chapter. Again, one could point to Lindzey's reformulation of Frazer's hypothesis in terms of the adaptive framework of evolutionary biology, a reformulation which, in my view, is unimpeachable. "It seems unlikely that there would have been universal selection in favor of such a taboo if there were not widespread impulses toward expression of the prohibited act" (Lindzey, 1967, p. 1055). Rather, however, than evoking these general empirical and theoretical grounds in refutation of Westermarck's theory, it is enough—and in this context much more relevant—to refute it on specific Trobriand grounds.

The latter grounds consist of evidence that proclaims loudly and clearly that rather than sexual aversion, at least some Trobrianders who live in close propinquity develop strong sexual feelings for each other. That is how Malinowski, at any rate, describes the relationship between brothers and sisters in the Trobriands, and (to a lesser degree) between fathers and daughters. At the same time there are taboos in the Trobriands which both prohibit and (as Malinowski makes quite clear) are intended to prevent incest between the members of these dyads. For the Trobriands, then, there can be no doubt about the functional relationship between incestuous desires and incest taboos, so far at least as these two dyads are concerned. Hence, for the Trobriands the co-occurrence of the mother-son incest taboo and the absence of incestuous desires for her is clearly an anomaly, not because it violates a (disputed) theoretical assumption, but because in the Trobriand cultural configuration their co-occurrence is incongruous.

If, however, it were still contended that this finding is not anomalous—because the anomaly now derives from merely another theoretical assumption, that of pattern consistency—this contention would convert an unresolved anomaly into an unresolved dilemma. For if it were held, on the one hand, that the taboo on incest with the mother does not imply the existence of incestuous wishes for her, what possible explanation might then be offered for the taboos on incest with the sister and daughter which, in fact, do correspond to known incestuous wishes for them? And if it were held, on the other hand, that the taboos on sister and daughter incest are explained by known incestuous wishes for them, how could it then be contended that it is invalid to infer the existence of incestuous wishes for the mother from the taboo prohibiting incest with her?

Malinowski, himself a leading proponent of Frazer's theory of incest taboos, was keenly aware of this dilemma, and, it will be recalled, he attempted to resolve it by holding to both of its horns. That is, while he held that incest taboos are valid measures of incestuous wishes, he also held that in the Trobriands the taboo on mother-son incest is "weak." Hence, he argued, just as the strong incestuous desire for the sister in the Trobriands is reflected in a "strong" brother-sister taboo, the weak desire for the mother is reflected in a "weak" mother-son taboo. Unfortunately, however, the facts (see above) are otherwise: there is simply no evidence for the putative weakness—whether absolute or relative—of the mother-son taboo. In short, despite Malinowski's attempt to resolve it, the second anomaly in his reported absence of an incestuous attachment to the mother in the Trobriands remains—like the first—unresolved.

The fact, then, that neither of these anomalies can be resolved—or, to put it more cautiously, that neither has been resolved thus far—must surely constitute sufficient reason to be skeptical of the report that the Trobriand son has no incestuous attachment to the mother. That this report, then, has not received the skeptical reception that normally greets an anomalous scientific report is not only, as I said above, a remarkable fact, but one which itself constitutes an intriguing intellectual problem. Since its solution could shed important light on the influence of scientific paradigms on the acceptance and persistence of scientific ideas, it is to be hoped that an investigation of the problem might some day be undertaken by an intellectual historian or a historian of science.

Although the causes for the unskeptical reaction to this anomalous report are still to be discovered, its consequence—with some notable exceptions—has been an uncritical acceptance of the putative Trobriand matrilineal complex. I would suggest, then, that if this report had been subjected to the probing scrutiny to which anomalous scientific findings are usually subject, the matrilineal complex would have been rejected (on the grounds adduced in Chapter 2) as empirically unsupported rather than achieving the status of an incontrovertible finding of anthropological science. Nevertheless, it is not its weak empirical foundation that led me to characterize the Trobriand matrilineal complex a "scientific myth." This characterization stems, rather, from the uncritical acceptance of the reported finding—the absence of an incestuous attachment to the mother—on which its plausibility hangs, despite the fact that this finding is not only once, but twice, anomalous.

A myth, Malinowski taught us, enjoys uncritical acceptance because it serves important functions for those who believe it to be true. It would be well, therefore, if our hoped-for historian were to address yet another question in the course of his investigations: what functions might have been served by the acceptance of *this* myth? Indeed, since the role of the "will to believe" in the acceptance of scientific ideas is as prominent as the role that William James attributed to it in the acceptance of religious doctrines, it is entirely possible that the answer to this second question might simultaneously provide the answer to the first.

REFERENCES

Aries, P. (1962), *Centuries of Childhood.* New York: Knopf.

Bettelheim, B. (1969), *The Children of the Dream.* London: Macmillan.

Bischof, N. (1975), Comparative ethology of incest avoidance. In: *Biosocial Anthropology,* ed. R. Fox. London: Malaby Press, pp. 37–67.

Brown, N. O. (1959), *Life against Death.* Middletown, CT: Wesleyan University Press.

Bushnell, J. (1958), La Virgen de Guadalupe as surrogate mother in San Juan Atzingo. *Amer. Anthropologist,* 60:261–265.

Buxbaum, E. (1970), *Troubled Children in a Troubled World.* New York: International Universities Press.

Campbell, D. T., & Naroll, R. (1972), The mutual methodological relevance of anthropology and psychology. In: *Psychological Anthropology,* ed. F. L. K. Hsu. Cambridge, MA: Schenkman, pp. 435–463.

Carpenter, C. R. (1940), A field study in Siam of the behavior and social relations of the gibbon. (*Hylobatis lar*). *Comp. Psychol. Monographs,* 16:1–212.

Carstairs, G. M. (1956), *The Twice Born.* Bloomington: Indiana University Press.

Chance, M. R. H., & Jolly, C. J. (1970), *Social Groups of Monkeys, Apes, and Men.* New York: Dutton.

Demarest, W. J. (1977), Incest avoidance in human and nonhuman primates. In:

Primate Bio-Social Development, ed. S. Chevalier-Skolnikoff & F. E. Poirier. New York: Garland, pp. 323–342.
Elwin, V. (1968), *The Kingdom of the Young*. Oxford: Oxford University Press.
Erikson, E. H. (1958), *Young Man Luther*. New York: Norton.
——— (1963), *Childhood and Society*. New York: Norton.
Fenichel, O. (1945), *The Psychoanalytic Theory of Neurosis*. New York: Norton.
Feuer, L. S. (1969), *The Conflict of Generations*. New York: Basic Books.
Fox, R. (1980), *The Red Lamp of Incest*. New York: Dutton.
Frazer, J. G. (1887), *Totemism and Exogamy*. London: Macmillan, 1910.
Gathorne-Hardy, J. (1977), *The Public School Phenomenon, 597–1977*. London: Hodder & Stoughton.
Gough, E. K. (1953), Female initiation rites on the Malabar Coast. *J. Royal Anthropological Soc.*, 85:45–80.
Herdt, G. H. (1980), *Guardians of the Flutes: Idioms of Masculinity*. New York: McGraw-Hill.
——— (1982), Fetish and fantasy in Sambia initiation. In: *Rituals of Manhood*, ed. G. H. Herdt. Berkeley: University of California Press, pp. 44–98.
Hiatt, L. R. (1971), Secret pseudo-procreation rites among the Australian aborigines. In: *Anthropology in Oceania*, ed. L. R. Hiatt & C. Jayawardena. San Francisco: Chandler, pp. 77–88.
Hopkins, K. (1980), Brother-sister marriage in Roman Egypt. *Comparative Studies in Society and History*, 22:303–354.
Hunt, R. C. (1971), Components of relationships in the family: A Mexican village. In: *Kinship and Culture*, ed. F. L. K. Hsu. Chicago: Aldine, pp. 106–143.
Jones, E. (1925), Mother-right and the sexual ignorance of savages. *Internat. J. Psycho-Anal.*, 6:109–130.
Justice, B., & Justice, R. (1979), *The Broken Taboo*. New York: Human Sciences Press.
Kaffman, M. (1977), Sexual standards and behavior of the kibbutz adolescent. *Amer. J. Orthopsychiat.*, 47:207–217.
Kakar, S. (1978), *The Inner World*. New Delhi: Oxford University Press.
Kuhn, T. S. (1962), *The Structure of Scientific Revolutions*. Chicago: University of Chicago Press.
Kummer, H. (1968), *Social Organization of Hamadryas Baboons*. Chicago: University of Chicago Press.
Lancaster, J. B. (1979), Sex and gender in evolutionary perspective. In: *Human Sexuality: A Comparative and Developmental Perspective*, ed. Herant A. Katchadorurian. Berkeley: University of California Press, pp. 51–80.
Langness, L. L. (1974), Ritual power and male domination in the New Guinea highlands. *Ethos*, 2:189–212.
Lasswell, H. D. (1960), *Psychopathology and Politics*. New York: Viking.
Lévi-Strauss, C. (1949), *The Elementary Structures of Kinship*. London: Eyre & Spottiswoode, 1969.
Lidz, R. W., & Lidz, T. (1977), Male menstruation: A ritual alternative to the oedipal transition. *Internat. J. Psycho-Anal.*, 58:17–31.
Lindzey, G. (1967), Some remarks concerning incest, the incest taboo, and psychoanalytic theory. *Amer. Psychologist*, 22:1051–1059.
Malinowski, B. (1927), *Sex and Repression in Savage Society*. New York: Meridian, 1955.

Money, J. (1980), *Love and Love Sickness.* Baltimore: Johns Hopkins University Press.
Parsons, T. (1954), The incest taboo in relation to social structure and the socialization of the child. *Brit. J. Sociol.* 5:101-117.
_______ (1969), *Belief, Magic, and Anomie.* New York: Free Press.
Paul, R. A. (1980), Symbolic interpretations in psychoanalysis and anthropology. *Ethos,* 8:286-294.
Poole, F. J. P. (1982), The ritual forging of identity: Aspects of person and self in Bimin-Kuskusmin male initation. In: *Rituals of Manhood,* ed. G. H. Herdt. Berkeley: University of California Press.
Powell, H. A. (1957), Analysis of Present-Day Social Structure in the Trobriands. Doctoral dissertation, University of London.
Rainwater, L., & Yancey, W. L. (1967), *The Moynihan Report and the Politics of Controversy.* Cambridge: MIT Press.
Read, K. E. (1965), *The High Valley.* New York: Scribner.
Reik, T. (1919), *Ritual: Four Psychoanalytic Studies.* New York: Grove Press, 1946.
Rothman, S., & Lichter, S. (1982), *The Radical Impulse.* New York: Oxford University Press.
Rowell, T. E. (1972), Female reproduction cycles and social behavior in females. *Advances in the Study of Behavior,* 4:69-105.
Roy, M. (1975), *Bengali Women.* Chicago: University of Chicago Press.
Shepher, J. (1971), Mate selection among second generation kibbutz adolescents and adults: Incest avoidance and negative imprinting. *Arch. Sexual Behav.,* 1:293-307.
Smith, R. T. (1956), *The Negro Family in British Guiana: Family Structure and Social Status in the Villages.* London: Routledge Kegan Paul.
Spiro, M. E. (1958), *Children of the Kibbutz.* Cambridge: Harvard University Press.
Talmon, Y. (1964), Mate selection on collective settlements. *Amer. Sociol. Rev.,* 29:491-508.
Tanaka, M. (1981), "Maternal" authority in the Japanese family. Paper presented at the International Symposium on Religion and the Family in East Asia, National Museum of Ethnology, Osaka, August 30-September 7, 1981.
Tuzin, D. F. (1980), *The Voice of the Tambaran.* Berkeley: University of California Press.
Westermarck, E. (1906-1908), *The Origin and Development of the Moral Ideas.* London: Macmillan, 1924-1926.
Wilson, E. O. (1978), *On Human Nature.* Cambridge: Harvard University Press.
Wilson, M. (1949), Nyakyusa Age Villages. *J. Royal Anthropological Inst.,* 79:21-25.
Wolf, A. P. (1966), Childhood association, sexual attraction, and the incest taboo: A Chinese case. *American Anthropologist,* 68:893-898.
_______ (1968), Adopt a daughter-in-law, marry a sister: A Chinese solution to the incest taboo. *American Anthropologist,* 70:864-894.
_______ (1970), Childhood association and sexual attraction: A further test of the Westermarck hypothesis. *American Anthropologist,* 72:503-515.
_______ & Huang, C. (1980), Marriage and adoption in China, 1845-1945. Stanford: Stanford University Press.

26

Preoedipal Oedipus: The Father-Child Dialogue

JAMES M. HERZOG

[1985]

This is a paper about the developmental precursors and foreshadowings of the Oedipus complex. King Oedipus, we now realize, was a baby once, with parents, parents who were quite remarkable in their treatment, or mistreatment, of a hapless son. In this sense, too, he serves as a prototype for budding Oedipuses at all times and places. All children have mothers and fathers who lay the groundwork in early life for the internal drama that comes to the fore later on and that comes to dominate the transferential and reconstructive work of most adult analyses. Here, based on my applied analytic observations of parents and toddlers and my efforts at early intervention when parenting and emotional growth have gone awry, I will survey some of the broad strokes that are later refined into the exquisite fantasies of the

---

An earlier version of this paper was presented in Dublin, Ireland, at the Tenth International Congress of the International Association for Child and Adolescent Psychiatry and Allied Professionals, July 1982.

oedipal era proper. Because they have been so neglected in the past, and because I have made a point of studying them, I shall focus on fathers in particular.

I propose a somewhat complicated scaffolding as a way of setting the stage for presentation of the various kinds of data used by a variety of observers and students of fathers, fathering, and father-child and father-mother-child interaction. To do this, I shall present three levels of investigation that figure in my own thinking: the research-clinical, the research-observational, and the research-psychoanalytic. In each stratum I shall employ the clinical model—that is, the case method. In each case the same set of questions organize the investigation: What is the father's role in the development of his child? How are we to understand the impact of his behavior, personality, role, and relationships on what we perceive or infer with the methods being used? Are there general or nomothetic issues and influences as well as idiographic aspects of the father-child relationship to be elucidated? Can we treat complexity as a given rather than as a complication?

In the clinic we watch Jamal. He is just three, but big for his age. Jamal plays with his mother, twenty, who is lying on the floor next to him. Each time Jamal makes a move his mother says, "No, don't do that, Jamal, stop." She conveys the impression of being afraid of what her son will do next. After observing mother and son together, I enter the room. Jamal will not leave. His mother retreats and suggests that I take charge. Jamal begins to throw some blocks in my direction. He then lunges toward me, striking me with his fists and then his feet. The mother says that this is how Jamal is. She has a lot of trouble with him; he is so angry and aggressive. Jamal's parents are not married. His father calls often but comes around rarely. We arrange to see the father the following week.

Our first view of Jamal's father is quite dramatic. He is at least six feet four and is wearing his belt around his neck. He tells us that Jamal listens to him better when his belt is around his neck rather than around his waist. We watch Jamal and his mother and father together. It looks to us as though his mother is trying to incite Jamal to anger or naughtiness. Each time he responds, his father touches the leather necklace and Jamal seems to get the message. We observe Jamal and his father alone. The tension is markedly decreased. They play nicely together. When I enter the room, the father takes his belt from his neck and threads it through the loops of his pants. He grins and says that his mother always wore the belt around her neck when he needed reminding. It helps Jamal "to listen better," he states. The following week, Jamal's father is not present. Jamal and I play together. The play centers on a giraffe baby and his mother. The baby is always hungry. It does not have a long enough neck to reach the tender shoots at the tops of the trees. The giraffe mother gives her baby some leaves, but not enough. She seems nervous and skittish around him. She brings the leaves down and then jerks them away. It is sort of fun for the little giraffe but not really. He wants more. I wonder if we should get another big giraffe to help; two leaf pickers are better than one, I suggest. "No," says Jamal. He points to another giraffe in the corner and calls it Daddy. I bring the giraffe over and Jamal has the mommy and the daddy fight. Meanwhile the baby giraffe cries. He is getting nothing and still needs more. Jamal then takes the mother giraffe and throws her hard against the wall. I wonder what will happen now, now that the mother has been thrown out and the daddy and the baby are together.

"Baby gets, gets it, gets more," Jamal says, "he wants more." His affect is calm. Then he puts his head down and looks sad. Suddenly he kicks out at me, stares at me, and then looks away. He seems to be concentrating diligently again on the play. Shortly thereafter, when his mother rejoins us, Jamal gets quite agitated again. He flashes the light on and off, throws blocks, and starts hitting. After one well-aimed blow delivered to me, I enclose him in my arms, acting as a kind of human straitjacket. Jamal relaxes perceptibly. I can feel the tension reduction as he begins to smile.

In this short clinical vignette I try to illustrate the interaction among an actual father and child, mother and child, and father, mother, and child. The observations are coupled with a play sequence and a report of two interactions with the participant observer. Although the interactions and the play are rich and dramatic and tell us something of the dynamics of the family and of the nature of Jamal's pain, they do not tell us very much about the general question of the father's role in preoedipal development, nor of the relevance of the father-mother relationship to the father's role. There are hints and only hints, even with the kind of caricature seen in the father's leather necklace, that Jamal needs his father for something—possibly help with the control of aggression. The play tends to confirm our notion, of needing more, not getting enough, although here it seems perhaps a more oral or alimentary nutriment that is required; and something is conveyed that suggests that when mother and father are together this need is subverted or not met, that it becomes part of some ongoing sexual or other interpersonal passion of the parents. In his interactions with me, Jamal provokes and actually hurts. He seems pleased, almost gratified, when his jabbing secures physical restraint by me.

When we watch such a series of interactions, we see something of the way in which a child interacts with his parents and they with him. A portrait is drawn of what Meissner (1979) has called the object *relatedness* of an individual—a picture of his social relationships and the things that *actually happen* between him and the people in his personal world. The relationship between this portrait and the child's object *relations* is never clear. By object relations I mean, again after Meissner, the *internal representations* of self and others and what transpires between them. The connection between object relatedness and object relations is the process of internalization. Through incorporation, imitation, introjection, and identification occur transformations, transmutations, and transfigurations leading to the establishment of psychological structure. Shafer (1968) has stated that "internalization refers to all the processes by which the subject transforms the real or imagined regulating interactions with his environment, and real or imagined characteristics of his environment into inner regulation and characterization" (p. 9).

Only in the giraffe sequence might we see something of what Rapaport (1957) has called the inner world, a sort of intrapsychic map of the external world and only here may we glimpse something of what he called the internal world, the organization and interpretation of intrapsychic situations that compose the psychic apparatus.

In order to learn more about the actual interactions between young children and their fathers and about the nature of their object relatedness (as well as to learn something about the beginning of this object relation), I undertook a home-based naturalistic observation of eight children in the second year of life. My intention was to observe and describe father-child interactions. I also planned to conduct play interviews with the children when they were between twenty and twenty-four months old, looking in the play for evidence of representation of self and father so that I might examine what transpired between them. Each of the families in the study consisted of a father, a mother, and an only child between twelve and twenty-four months of age. There were four girls and four boys. The families, all volunteers, were of the professional middle class. Observations were conducted on weekend days when both parents were at home, and after I had become quite well known to the children. Each of the parents was intensively interviewed at the conclusion of the study.

Let me tell you about one family. Remember, however, that these data represent the results of only fifty hours of observation and interview as compared to the five hundred or more typical of an analysis. Daniel was the firstborn son of thirty-year-old parents, both of whom were psychiatric residents. At the time of his birth, David and Miriam had been married for three years. They described their relationship as close and growing. The pregnancy had been planned and had proceeded smoothly. The delivery had been uncomplicated, and the 7-pound, 12-ounce Daniel was welcomed, seemingly without ambivalence. Miriam went back to work when Daniel was three months old. She worked part time until he was nine months and then decided to stay home full time, arranging a leave of absence from her residency program. "He will only be a baby once and I want to be here," she explained. Miriam seemed warm and friendly toward her husband and toward her son, though she was occasionally critical of the former's indecisiveness. She was a careful, mildly obsessional woman who was clearly very invested in her mothering. David seemed even more obsessional than his wife. When I began my Sunday afternoon visits, he seemed quite nervous. He would advance very strong opinions and then, under his own scrutiny or that of his wife, reconsider them. He felt that someone interested in fathers might find fault with his fathering. By my third visit, however, he had noticeably relaxed. A typical observation follows.

Danny is seventeen months old. He and Miriam are sitting on the floor. They are playing with some blocks. Miriam is following Danny's lead. He is sort of arranging the blocks. Some are placed on top of one another, some next to one another. Miriam tries to be the assistant contractor-engineer. David is on the phone. He hangs up and comes barreling over. Danny looks up. David gets down on his hands and knees. He tousles Danny's hair and says, "No, no, come on, let's go." He pushes over the assembled blocks. Danny squeals with laughter. Miriam's face breaks into a smile. Now Danny starts to hit the blocks. Both father and son are pushing them around. About a minute later Danny picks up a block and throws it. It doesn't travel very far. Miriam says, "Oh no!" David says, "Stop it, Dan." A second block is picked up. "I said stop it now. That's dangerous," his father says. He speaks more quietly than his more raucous play voice. His voice is very serious. Danny puts down the block. He smiles, as do his parents. Less then thirty seconds later David gives the blocks another jab. Round two has begun, and almost immediately Danny is again convulsed by giggles and squeals of delight.

Other kinds of interaction were observed subsequently, but the pattern described above was often repeated. David would disrupt what Danny was doing. Danny would welcome this assault and his spirits would rise dramatically as the exciting play commenced. Often the intensity of his affect would escalate to the point where he would lose control. At this point his father, who had initiated the sequence, would bring it to a close. Whereas at seventeen months most second and third rounds were initiated by David, by twenty-four months successive rounds were initiated by Danny himself.

To place these observations on the David-Danny interactions in context, let me cite an earlier paper (Herzog, 1980), which provides an overview of this undertaking. There I observed that fathers of both boys and girls interacted with their children in a more physical, rough-and-tumble way than did mothers. This interaction involved large motor activity, pushing, shoving, tickling, and other "aggressive" behaviors. There were, of course, many libidinal and nurturing interactions as well, but the behavior that differentiated fathers from mothers was in the "aggressive" realm. Noteworthy in this regard was the fact that fathers would often initiate this sort of interaction. The child might be playing quietly and his dad would zoom in, imitating a kamikaze pilot, and really jazz things up. In no instance, and there are some forty discrete episodes in which such a sequence occurred, did the child resist these blunt and seemingly unmodulated advances. In no instance did the child evidence displeasure or distress at the beginning of the episode. I specify beginning, because there was one father-daughter pair in which the father did not seem to know when to let up. The daughter, Tammy, would become very distressed and disorganized when her father's tickling continued beyond a minute or two. The father, Frank, seemed genuinely amazed at this development and would respond with efforts to tone down his play and to soothe her. These were almost always successful and perhaps explained why Tammy was always excited and eager at the inception of each new episode (an equally possible response would have been for her to be leery and avoidant of such interactions). Interestingly, Tammy's mother, Grace, never interrupted this rather aggressive tickling. By contrast, in the other families one might hear such phrases as "Easy does it" or "I think we're having an earthquake" when fathers and children would escalate to a certain point. Careful analytic interviewing of Frank and Grace has confirmed the impression that this lack of sensitivity to Tammy's limits is part of a larger problem for her father. His rigid obsessional character style is punctuated by unmodulated outbursts that require much undoing and making of amends on his part. His relationship with his wife is as compromised in this regard as is his interaction with his daughter. In fact there was rather suggestive evidence that the heat—the tickling heat—was turned on under Tammy just when the situation was most strained between the parents, an instance of the proposition I have advanced that adult-adult interaction predicts adult-child interaction and that what cannot be contained, titrated, and expressed within the caretaking dyad may spill over and exert an inappropriate and deleterious effect on the child. This concept of the adult protective shield (or stimulus barrier) has proved quite useful clinically. In another communication I shall specify dynamic constellations in the fathers that appeared either to enable or to curtail this interactive style.

To return to normative observations, another pattern of father-child interaction was repeated in these subjects. As I have noted, fathers would often initiate rough-and-tumble behavior with their children. Fathers of boys were rougher with their children than were fathers of girls (of course, these observations did not permit us to compare the same father with both a boy and a girl). But boys' fathers differed from girls' fathers in another interesting way. Not only would the father evoke a higher level of tumult and excitement in the boy than in the girl, but he (and the mother) would allow it to continue longer. It seemed that fathers not only turned on the rough-and-tumble, but also turned it off. At a certain point, when the proceedings were becoming too raucous, too noisy, or too destructive (or when the mother made an "earthquake" comment) the father would say "No" or "Stop," not infrequently administering a whack to the child's bottom. This point was always recognizable by the transition in the father's affect. The first "no" would be delivered playfully, almost in fun. The second one would be less playful, and by the third injunction the father's voice and demeanor would be serious, sometimes even angry. The child's affect seemed to follow the father's and often would reflect an appraisal of how the mother regarded the proceedings. Frequently this limit setting to exuberance and dyscontrol would be followed by a second or third round. Whereas children at twelve months always reacted to initiation of the sequence by the father, at eighteen months they often initiated round two or three on their own. Fathers of girls brought these exciting and pleasurable interactions to a close sooner than did fathers of boys. Mothers of girls said "Easy does it" more frequently than did mothers of boys. The number of rounds was fewer for the father-girl interactions and the number of second and third rounds initiated by daughters was smaller at eighteen to twenty-four months than the number of such rounds initiated by boys.

Now, back to Danny. At twenty-three months he played out the following scenario with me. Dada bear growled. Baby bear growled back. Mama bear laughed. Baby bear said "play, play." He went over to the daddy and he pretended to be something that made a great noise. The father bear made a lot of noise back. They jumped up and down together. At one point he had the daddy bear invite the mother bear to play too. She did. Then the baby bear said no, very loudly and distinctly. Everything stopped. "Who said that?" I asked the baby bear. "Me," Danny had the bear say. "Who are you?" I asked the baby bear; "I'm new here, I don't know you" (I was animating another bear, child-size). "I'm Dada," Danny had the little bear say. He roared with laughter. "You look awfully little to be a daddy," I had my bear say. "I do Dada things," the little bear said. To be difficult, I said "I think those are Mommy things." "No," said Danny, "I do Dada things. No, no, come on, let's go." He took the little teddy bear and had him start to tousle the daddy's head. This behavior was identical to the way David had initiated the play interactions with Danny which I had observed, and the words too were identical. Then Danny had the little bear say, "I, Dada, Danna a Dada," and he then growled exactly as the big bear had growled at the beginning of the play.

I took this material to represent in displacement the emergence of a definitive internal image of a daddy, as distinct from the internal image of a mommy. Similar material was obtained from all the children from about nineteen months onward. That this is the time when such representations emerge is not demonstrated by this fact, however. They may or may not have been present earlier. This is, however, the time when these eight children began to elaborate syntactical play of the sort I've described. It is a case of a method becoming available to assess the presence or absence of an internalized object. The relation between the capacity to elaborate syntactical play and the capacity to have an internalized representation of the father (not the same as object constancy), however, is not clear.

Moreover, the fact that this representation mirrored an actual and quite specific set of father-child interactions seemed most significant. It is as if interactions become interactional representations which become the basis for object representations. To paraphrase Piaget, action precedes thought and leads to the development of a new schema. Clearly much elaboration, and idiographic associative meaning, is imparted to this representation and becomes an ever more significant aspect of it.

We see something, but certainly not all, of the elaborations in the play episode from Jamal with which I opened my discussion. There, a seriously convoluted familial situation provided the context for anxiety provoking interactions, affects, and behaviors. Jamal's internal representations of himself and his father would be expected to reflect these disturbances, though not in any one-to-one way. Block (1982), in a critical review of Piagetian cognitive theory, has pointed out the inadequacy of a model of personality development that does not take into account the role of anxiety. Certainly we must expect that anxious, disappointing, painful, alarming, or frightening actual object relatedness must affect ensuing representations and object relations.

Now let me say something of what I made of this observation. The first point I have perhaps already made in excessive detail. The father is present intrapsychically as a distinct object representation by the end of the second year. This representation is in all likelihood not in a final form, but it is there, and its form has, as at least one determinant, a kind of interaction that is disruptive rather than homeostatic, and fatherlike rather than motherlike, at least in the families I observed. Whether fathers play this role because they are men or because they are secondary rather than primary caretakers is a question of interest but perhaps not overwhelming importance.

The second point is that in the action mode fathers seem to be introducing experience with intense affect—its escalation, toleration, diminution, and cessation. Is the father the modulator and organizer of an intense affect system? Or is this aspect of the father's role critical to the further elaboration of elation, sexual excitement, anger, or other strong feelings? Do fathered children have a greater freedom in regard to the intensity gradient of emotion? Certain preliminary observation on children raised by a mother alone suggest that they are less able to modulate intense affect in peer situations than children with two caretakers. A single caretaker may not be as free to be disruptive as may a secondary caretaker father. And it is by being disruptive, perhaps, that a paradigm is constructed for the experience and control of intense affect.

And something else is going on here too. When the father zooms in, he disrupts the status quo, and a radical changing of gears is called for. The child must change from the more reciprocal mother channel to the more hyped-up father channel. Something accrues from this having to change channels, I think, some increased capacity to change perspective, to be resilient and not get stuck.

In my study, fathers "kamikazied" more with boys than with girls. Boys get more practice in this mode. Block (1982) has suggested that girls favor the assimilative mode in their affective-cognitive style while boys prefer the accommodative. Roughly speaking, this means that girls fit new pieces of information or new challenges to existing schemas or models, whereas boys are likely to ditch a current conceptualization and move on to something new. Obviously these broadly based sexual differences have many determinants, some perhaps biological. It seems plausible to me, however, that father-child interactions and the paradigm of intense affect followed by a changing of gears that I am describing figures prominently in this outcome.

Finally, something about disruptive and destructive action—aggression—is being negotiated. In these interactions I never saw an angry child, but the fathers in their limit setting and roughhousing occasionally verged on anger or even hurt a child, though unintentionally. These interactions were not hostile; on the contrary, they were fun and were enjoyed by the child, but the fathers' mode of exciting intense affect and then limiting it was intrusive, disruptive, aggressive, and occasionally inadvertently painful. In other settings I have noted the father's role as modulator and organizer of aggressive drive and fantasy. Something paradigmatic, I think, is going on in these interactions in this regard. Jamal, whose father was absent most of the time, struck out repeatedly at his mother, at children in the preschool, and at me. He had not learned to modulate and organize his aggressivity in his father's absence and was perhaps incited toward dyscontrol when both parents were present. He was more organized and composed, at least in terms of his object relatedness, when his father was physically present and displayed the leather necklace.

In our observations of children from fatherless families, the amount of unprovoked and unbridled aggression is significantly greater than in matched children from two-parent families, although the Jamal case suggests a whole taxonomy of familial disorders in which a paternal or father-mother interactive style may seriously disorganize a child's functioning.

If we are to regard the Jamal case as an example of the research-clinical level of exploration and the Daniel vignettes as an example of the research-observational, we are still left with the question of what can be learned at the research-psychoanalytic level. Here we have the addition of the transference, defined by Kris (1982) as (1) the direct operation of an unconscious memory of a relationship; (2) the unconscious re-creation of this old relationship so that thoughts, feelings, wishes, sensations, and images are directed toward the analyst and the analysis in place of the person or, less frequently, the nonhuman partner (e.g., an animal or an institution) involved in the original relationship; and (3) a tendency to disrupt the agreement for analysis, to reject the constraints of verbal free association, to affirm the misperceptions of the analyst as reality, to redress old injuries, and to seek gratification rather than reexperience old frustrations. It is a process which affords an extraordinary window on the meaning of events—not in the sense, suggested by Nelson and Greundel (1979) or Shank and Abelson (1977), of social scripts or the factual representation of events, but in the object relations sense as defined by Meissner. Here one must deal with the advantages and disadvantages occasioned by the fact that the data being presented are processed, reconstructed, metabolized, experienced, and interpreted by both analyst and analysand. A new level of information is now available. In analytic exploration there is both greater temporal scope and a collapse of temporality, an alliance and an adversarial relationship—the expectation of understanding and the hope for amelioration and change. What does this third level of inquiry show us about the father's role in early development? Can it or should it be integrated with the research-observational and research-clinical levels?

I will now present three analytic vignettes.

Gabriel is referred to me for analysis by his mother's therapist. I begin by meeting with his parents, a distinguished neurophysiologist and a musician. Gabriel, I am told, has major trouble at school. Although he has an IQ of 154, he cannot master the third-grade curriculum in his progressive private school. The recommendation that he repeat the year seems imminent. Also, his parents tell me, Gabriel confabulates. He exaggerates, embellishes, and dramatizes every experience. I am struck by his father's eloquence and charm. He confides that he has always spoken extensively to Gabriel, his firstborn, about his dreams, his dilemmas, his goals, and his ghosts. Could this be part of the problem, the father wonders? The mother is less effusive, and somewhat more pugnacious. She has many complaints about the school and its faculty. She has dabbled in behavioral psychology and is almost on the verge of a point system which will ensure that Gabriel finishes his homework.

When I finally meet Gabriel, after three months of meeting with his worried parents, I am struck by his petiteness and physical beauty.

Neither feature has been mentioned by mother or father. Gabriel complains about the fact that he has had to wait so long to see me. He is impatient to begin. I am introduced to a Chinese warlord—drawn by him in exquisite detail—who hates women, whips slaves, and dissects brains. We spend many weeks making the further acquaintance of Dr. Fu Manchu. His most diabolical experiments are with dogs. Gabriel creates a menagerie of cross-breeds and half-breeds featuring split brains which cannot coordinate and brains which are disconnected from the viscera. Fu Manchu is the architect of these anatomical anomalies. As the analysis unfolds, layers of Fu Manchu's motivation appear—some of his experimental results are by design, some quite by happenstance. Fu's childhood is revealed to have been quite unhappy. It featured a traumatic relationship with a dog named Noodles, and there are hints that he is extracting a convoluted and problematic revenge on his canine cadre. The dogs, half-breeds, cross-breeds, and occasionally one with a pedigree (a very rare creature according to Gabe), all display one very curious feature. They are all utterly devoted to Dr. Fu Manchu, a mystery that takes us many months to unravel. It appears that Fu whispers many things into their ears. He talks to them in a language which they can never quite understand, and this makes their brains whir, though with delight, to be sure. We now begin to explore these whirring brains. To do so, complicated models must be constructed to depict the brains. Fu coos into the brain's ear—it bounces and jumps. Gabe is very excited. "He is throwing him up into the air!" he shrieks. "But Dr. Fu is not touching him," I observe. "No silly," says Gabe, "he does it with words. Dr. Fu's words make the half-breeds' brains jump and wiggle and dance." And indeed they do; in the transference, too, my words are potent and kinetic. Often I am asked to be quiet by Gabe, lest I upset the applecart. Controlling my words—being able to shut them out with other words ("Please don't talk")—was an important first step for Gabe in being able to begin to keep his own brain from dancing so that he could concentrate and attend and limit the intrusive and disorganizing fantasies to which he fell prey.

Gabe's father was a good man and a very smart man. He told me in one of our initial meetings that he overstimulated Gabe. That this aspect of his relationship with his son might lead to Gabe's representation of the father-son dyad as mad doctor and dissected dog was the furthest thing from his mind. Of course, he did volunteer the information that his wife hated to hear about his work; he guessed that was why he told Gabe so much about it. They would go to his lab together, and Gabe would want to bring one of the experimental dogs home. "I think," said the father, with pride in his voice, "he wanted to take good care of them—because I was taking such good care of him."

Is Gabe's organizational dilemma the result of a particular kind of excessive kamikaze-ing, verbal rather than physical? Is there perhaps an overutilization of the accommodative mode, which becomes inimical to learning in a structured setting? Obviously any analyst would want to know more about the intensity of Gabe's inner endowment, about his drives, defenses, susceptibilities, and fixations. Why the extreme libidinization of the father? Why the predilection for aggressive fantasy development rather than a more expectable erotic elaboration? Where is the mother in all this? But for present purposes let us say that Gabe's father is reconstructed and experienced in the transference as a very, very present father who was very stimulating, very Kamikaze-ish, but in a particular and quite idiographic way.

Matt is eleven and has entered analysis after a year-long psychotherapy with another clinician. He has deeply distressed his liberal middle class parents by desecrating a local NAACP building with racist slogans. As the analysis unfolds, elaborate plans for world conquest are revealed. In addition to a grandiosity that seems defensive, there is a markedly aggressive coloration to Matt's fantasy. Over time it becomes clear that much of this anger is aimed at his mother, who is perceived as a strident, castrating bitch, yet who in her strength, militancy, and devotion is clearly the more interesting of Matt's parents. She undoubtedly loves her son and is loved in return. The question of my responsivity and my disappointing Matt then emerges. Matt writes a very gory, sexually explicit and perverse story for his sixth-grade English class. He reads it to me. Will I stop him from handing in this novella about Clytemnestra, a witch who whips and anally rapes with her long Lady Godiva–like hair, he wonders? I try to help him explore the pros and cons. Matt thinks that this is helpful. He tells me that his father has also been asked to read the story. His father has commented on the literary style, but neither on the content nor the consequences. Matt feels disappointed in him.

Matt's disappointment in his father becomes a central theme in the transference, in dreams, and in his discussion of daily events. It appears also in the sexual and aggressive dramas he plays out in his world conquest schemes, which continue, but confined now to analytic sessions. We learn something about the circumstances of Matt's father's reserve and nonavailability. His therapist tells me of his chronic depression and constriction in the sexual sphere, in the work sphere, and in his relations with his own parents. Matt begins to talk about killing a fly with a cannon and the lack of correspondence between the intensity of his anger and that of his fantasied response and its attempted implementation. He says he needs to learn to modulate his anger and to learn more about turning it on and off—setting the thermostat. He thinks he is doing that in analysis. There is perhaps a connection here between the normative findings of my observational studies and these intrapsychic sequelae of a certain kind of mother-father-child interaction in the second year of life, in a case in which the father is incapable of functioning in the "kamikaze" mode.

Arthur is a thirty-eight-year-old graduate student in physics. He is stuck. He can neither finish his dissertation nor agree to his wife's fervent wishes that they conceive a child. They have been married fifteen years and his psychiatrist wife at last gets him to agree to undertake psychoanalysis.

Arthur is extremely erudite, controlled, polite, and obsessional. He tries to teach me a great deal about a mathematical model of interpersonal interactions. He tells me that there was very little overt emotion in his family and that he finds it hard to be the live wire his wife would like. To his considerable surprise and distress he begins to have vivid dreams. A recurrent one focuses on a character or series of characters with the name Liebermann. Arthur thinks that the name is rather like mine—German, Jewish. He translates it eventually as dear man. It means nothing to him. Arthur plays a game. Although he could find out a great deal about me from his wife's colleagues, he prefers to be a detective—not that he is interested—right here at the scene of the crime. He will find out what needs to be known. There are then more dreams about Herzog, hearses, and Hirsches, and then about fawning, and does (dough)—money. What it costs. What happens if one bucks or doesn't buck, fucks or doesn't fuck—does or doesn't doe. Arthur and I think he is still talking about deer or dear men, perhaps dead. The fawns and the money, the bucks and the does, are all frolicking. They are playful. Much to his surprise Arthur cries and speaks about his father. His father has been dead for almost twenty years—a nice man, but not there. He worked around the clock. Arthur and his mother and sister, who was born when he was two, were the triumphant trio. The father floated on the periphery - beneficent, provident, but noninvolved. No kamikaze pilot he, but a very nice man, nonetheless; a dear man, but not playful.

Arthur and I explore his stuckness. He wonders if I will spar with him. Someone has told him I have a keen mind and am good at repartee, not that he has seen it in the analysis. He experiences me as floating (free floating attention, he adds with a laugh) at a considerable distance above the fray.

No analysis is reducible to a single explanatory tenet; no person is understandable by reference to a single complex, developmental dilemma, or other formula. No father can be defined by a single way of being. Yet, I think, as we piece together data, admittedly and unapologetically selected data from three levels of inquiry, differing ways of looking at a particular developmental need—its origins, parameters, mode of delivery, excesses, deficiencies, and ways of being experienced, represented, and expressed—are encountered. The father is or can be experienced as a state-transforming caretaker who, rather than returning the child to a level of reduced tension directly, may instead introduce levels of heightened affectivity and tension and by so doing, if all goes well, teach methods for the organization, modulation, control, and utilization of these intense affects. His way of doing this has a nomothetic, perhaps gender-specific determinant and a whole host of idiographic components—past history, current relationships—which influence his libidinal and aggressive availability. If we heed E. M. Forster's instruction at the beginning of *Howard's End*—"only connect"—and apply it to the various levels of data available to us as developmentalists, as clinicians, and as analysts of both children and their caregivers, we significantly increase our capacity to understand such complex questions as the father's role in the development of his child and the sequelae, both normative and pathological, to be encountered in individual cases.

Furthermore, our knowledge of developmental process in the

preoedipal years heightens our appreciation of the equipment the child brings to the oedipal situation. Intense affect toleration, gear shifting, and the modulation of aggressive drive and fantasy are all constituents of the child's armamentarium as he negotiates his love of the opposite sex parent and his love of and rivalry with the same sex parent. Careful attention to developmental progressions antedating the oedipal crisis increases our capacity to anticipate, understand, and reconstruct this fateful landmark in psychological development. We are able to trace continuities and discontinuities as these are evident in the realm of observational reality (what the camera would see), interrogative reality (conscious secondary processing), and personal meaning (dreams, associations, unconscious meaning). These continuities and discontinuities in each realm may in turn guide hypothesis formation, data gathering, and clinical application in a variety of settings.

REFERENCES

Block, J. (1982), Assimilation, accommodation and the dynamics of personality development. *Child Development,* 53:281-295.

——— (1983), Differential premises arising from differential socialization of the sexes: Some conjectures. *Child Development,* 54:1335-1354.

Herzog, J. (1980), Father child interaction in the 2nd year of Life. Presented at the The American Academy of Child Psychiatry, Chicago, IL.

——— (1981), Libidinal and aggressive availability. Aspects of the father-child dialogue. Presented at the International Psychoanalytic Congress, Helsinki, Finland.

Kris, A. (1982), *Free Association.* New Haven: Yale University Press.

Meissner, W. W. (1979), Internalization and object relations. *J. Amer. Psychoanal. Assn.,* 27:345-360.

Nelson, K., & Greundel, J. M. (1979), From personal episode to social script. Paper presented at the biennial meeting of The Society for Research in Child Development.

Rapaport, D. (1957), A theoretical analysis of the superego concept. In: *The Collected Papers of David Rapaport,* ed. M. M. Gill. New York: Basic Books, 1967, pp. 685-709.

Shafer, R. (1968), *Aspects of Internalization.* New York: International Universities Press.

Shank, R. C., & Abelson, R. (1977), *Script, Plans, Goals and Understanding.* Hillsdale, NJ: Erlbaum.

27

Oedipus and Insight

ROBERT MICHELS

[1986]

Insight and *Oedipus Rex*

The prototype for the psychoanalytic story of the human life cycle is of course the story of Oedipus. The first psychoanalytic readings of the Oedipus myth emphasized the dual themes of patricide and incest, the so-called oedipal dynamics. More recent interpretations of the story have broadened and enriched this early reading, inviting us to consider the psychodynamics of Jocasta and Laius as well of as their son, Oedipus, and the family constellation that evolved among them. Oedipus was physically abused and then abandoned as an infant. Rescued and then adopted, he came to compensate for his disability,

---

Portions or earlier versions of this paper were presented as the Sandor Rado Lecture of the Association for Psychoanalytic Medicine, New York, March 4, 1986; at Duke University Medical Center, Department of Psychiatry, Durham, North Carolina, March 13, 1986; as the Sandor Feldman Lecture of the Western New York Psychoanalytic Society, Rochester, April 19, 1986; as the Editha and Richard Sterba Lecture of the Michigan Association for Psychoanalysis, Detroit, April 26, 1986, and at Dallas Psychoanalytic Society Founders Day, Texas, October 2, 1986.

but throughout his life he remained impulsive and prone to attacks of narcissistic rage. In other words, he suffered major preoedipal trauma and his most salient psychopathology was of the type we associate with preoedipal dynamics. Of course all of this relates to one particular version of the Oedipus story. Most of us today first learned of the Oedipus myth through Sophocles' great tragedy, *Oedipus Rex*, and many of us have come to understand that tragedy in the light of Freud's interpretation of it. In other words, what we think of as the "classical" story of Oedipus is Freud's specific reading of Sophocles' unique rendition of an ancient myth. Each of them creatively transformed the raw material of the myth. Sophocles deleted the events that preceded Oedipus' birth—the story of the curse upon Laius, stemming from his homosexual attack on Pelops' son, Chrysippus. Freud further deleted Jocasta's role, clear in both myth and play, as seducer of Laius and abandoner of Oedipus. Thus, in our usual version of the story, Laius and Jocasta are relegated to background roles, father and mother to Oedipus, significant only in terms of the meanings he attaches to them.

Sophocles' tragedy in fact does not depict all of even this truncated story; many events are referred to only retrospectively. The actual events of the play take place in a single day in the life of the mature Oedipus, the day on which he comes to know the story of his origin and acquires the insight that has such dramatic impact on the rest of his life. If the *myth* of Oedipus is the prototype of the psychoanalytic model of development, many have thought that the *play* provides a prototype for a model of the psychoanalytic process, particularly for the role of insight in that process. Freud was the first to suggest this, when he wrote in *The Interpretation of Dreams*, "The action of the play consists in nothing other than the process of revealing . . . a process that can be likened to the work of a psychoanalysis" (1900, pp. 261-262).

The play begins with King Oedipus troubled by a blight on his nation; the land and the people are barren. His subjects implore him to find a solution to their problem, as children turn to their father when they feel overwhelmed. He is, of course, famous for his problem solving ability; he had become king after solving the riddle of the Sphinx, the mystery of human development. As he proudly describes it, "I came, Oedipus, who knew nothing, and I stopped her. I solved the riddle by my wit alone" (Grene and Lattimore, 1959, ll. 396–399; this translation is cited throughout). In the past his keen intelligence had always been directed outward, and once again he identifies the problem as outside himself; he seeks an external solution. He must find and banish the man who killed King Laius. Oedipus seeks advice from someone known for his wisdom, the blind seer Teiresias, who may not have eyes with which to see out but who does have the ability to see within—perhaps the prototype of the psychoanalyst. The chorus reminds us, "What the Lord Teiresias sees, is most often what the Lord Apollo sees" (ll. 284–285), and Oedipus adds, "You have no eyes, but in your mind you know" (ll. 302–303). Teiresias knows that each thing has its place, and that knowledge is not always desirable; that is, he understands the dangers of wild analysis. He warns, "How terrible is wisdom when it brings no profit to the man that's wise" (l. 316); but Oedipus cannot tolerate frustration or delay. He attacks Teiresias, threatening him, and in so doing nearly reenacting his fateful struggle with a father figure. Teiresias recognizes Oedipus' character pathology, and even his defensive projection, "You blame my temper but you do not see your own that lives within you; it is me you chide" (l. 338). Finally, angry and provoked, Teiresias ignores his own warning and tells Oedipus the hidden truth: "You are the land's pollution" (l. 353). Oedipus—and this comes as no surprise to a psychoanalyst—does not understand. "I did not grasp it. . . . Say it again" (l. 361). If Teiresias is the prototypical psychoanalyst, we have here the prototypes of countertransference, premature and partial interpretation, and resistance.

The story as we know goes on to suggest that insight is a powerful tool, that it occurs in life as well as in psychoanalysis, and that it can lead to harm as well as to good. We will return to these issues later.

The Meaning of Insight

The term insight originally suggested a seeing within, with the mind's eye. It came to mean seeing beneath the surface or understanding the inner meaning of things. This continues to be its most common meaning today. Psychiatry has used the term in a special way, referring to a patient's awareness that he is sick, or that his mental disturbances are pathological. In most discussions of mental status, insight is paired with judgment, the patient's awareness of social norms and expectations. I have taught, half humorously, that insight refers to a patient's agreement with the psychiatrist's view of the patient, while judgment refers to his agreement with the psychiatrist's view of everyone else.

The meaning of insight in psychoanalysis is derived from both the general and the psychiatric meanings. The English translation of Freud's work (the *Standard Edition*) uses the term 192 times. Most often Freud used it in the general sense. An example is the famous sentence in the 1931 preface to *The Interpretation of Dreams*: "Insight such as this falls to one's lot but once in a lifetime" (Freud, 1900, p. xxxii). The term is used similarly in the Rat Man case, where Freud speaks of his own "insight into the nature of the malady" (1909, p. 197). Less often, he uses the term in its psychiatric sense, as when he says that a patient had "a clear insight into his delusion" (1907, p. 28) or refers to "a case of severe obsessions accompanied by complete insight" (1900, p. 457).

However, we see hints of an emerging psychoanalytic meaning as early as Freud's chapter on psychotherapy in *Studies on Hysteria*: "It happens particularly often that, after we have laboriously forced some piece of knowledge on a patient, he will declare: 'I've always known that, I could have told you that before!' Those with some degree of insight recognize afterwards that this is a piece of self-deception . . ." (Freud and Breuer, 1893–1895, p. 299). The implication is similar in "On the History of the Psycho-Analytic Movement," where he speaks of bringing pressure to bear on patients in order "to induce them to get insight into their resistances" (1914, p. 24). In these passages, as in most contemporary psychoanalytic writings, the term refers to the patient's knowledge and understanding of something inside himself—some subjective experience or psychological mechanism (I will return to this distinction later) rather than to the patient's or the analyst's awareness of a general truth about human nature, or to the patient's recognition that he has a specific type of deviance.

We most often think of a person's insight into himself, but a person can also have insight into the psychic life of another. When Freud discussed insight into the psyche, he was usually referring to his own insight into his patient's psyche. His model was of an analyst who first developed insight into the patient and then imparted it to the patient, as in a teacher-student relationship. A common suggestion about the difference between psychoanalysis and psychotherapy is that while both the analyst and the therapist strive to develop insights into the patient, the analyst does so with the primary goal of sharing these with the patient while the therapist does so in order to use them in helping the patient, at times by sharing them, but at other times by using them as strategic guides in attempts to influence the patient therapeutically, in ways that do not necessarily enlighten him.

The word insight is itself a double metaphor. It refers to a kind of knowing, using the metaphor of sight, and also to a domain of what is known, using the spatial metaphor of "inner." Both the figure of the blind seer Teiresias and Oedipus' blinding of himself are dramatic elements that use the sight metaphor. But why seeing, rather than hearing or some other sense? I suspect this has to do with the quality of knowing that we associate with insight. Seeing is immediate, personal; it carries conviction. Seeing is believing, and one picture is worth a thousand words, while hearing is hearsay, and may be false. In fact, if we don't yet see something that will later develop into insight, we may at first feel it, the most internal and, we believe, the least fallible of our perceptions. One understands what one sees at an earlier age than one understands the spoken word. Further, one hears words, units of meaning in sequence, but one sees patterns, configurations, relationships synchronously. To hear everything at once is to hear a jumble, noise, but to see everything at once is to see things clearly, in their proper relationship. The content of insight like that of vision—is immediate, convincing, and configurational. Finally, one can avoid seeing; many have suggested that closing one's eyes is the prototype of denial, but there is no way to shut out sound.

Vision is also the most distant, the least inner of our perceptions. We can touch, smell, feel, and even hear the inside of our body, but never see it. Vision is also the metaphor for knowledge of the future, long-term adaptation, and wisdom. Teiresias was a seer not because of his actual powers of sight, but because of a metaphorical capacity to see the future. Of course, a central tenet of psychoanalysis is that our personal future is shaped by our psyche, that character is destiny, and that to see the future requires first that one see one's self. But why is the self viewed as being inside? Considering that no one has ever really seen or found his self, why are we all so certain where it is located? There are obvious reasons for locating our appetites in our abdomens and pelvises, and our thoughts in our heads, just as our emotions and passions seem to belong to our chests—the thorax lies between the site of our thoughts and the seat of our desires and contains our hearts and lungs, organs whose rhythms are so sensitive to our feelings. Certainly the self must include our appetites, thoughts, and passions, and these are all "inside." However, there is, of course, one powerful argument against locating the self inside: the self is our favorite thing and we would like to protect it from the corruption, decay, death, and eventual destruction that threatens the body. The Greeks solved this dilemma of self or soul by identifying it with the air we breathe (the original meaning of "psyche" is breath), inside yet capable of rapid escape. Today, as ologists, iatrists, or analysts of the psyche, we continue this verbal equation of breath and soul.

Perhaps the most important implication of the spatial metaphor, however, is that it dichotomizes the domain of what we know. Inside is not outside, and knowledge of the one is not knowledge of the other. Oedipus, like so many people today, knew a great deal about the world, but very little about himself. Indeed, the capacity to understand, as reflected in knowledge about the world, is probably a prerequisite for being an analytic patient, with the analyst's task being to direct that capacity inward, to encourage insight as well as outlook. A central question of modern psychoanalytic theory is to what extent this involves not only a change in the direction of attention, but also a fundamentally different kind of knowing. Seeing is only a metaphor for knowing and understanding, but some would go further and argue that knowing and understanding the outer world is only a metaphor for knowing and understanding oneself—that the mental activity in one is quite different from that involved in the other, even though we may use the same words for both. Freud did not think so, but many have since questioned his view, and the issue is basic to contemporary discussions of psychoanalytic theory and technique, of explanation and understanding, empathy and inference.

Metaphorically we see, and metaphorically in rather than out, but see what? Oedipus saw forgotten or repressed memories, stories of his childhood, and the forbidden wishes that were revealed both by the events themselves and by his need to forget them. The term insight often refers to the patient's developing a conscious awareness of hitherto unconscious mental content—feelings, fantasies, memories. Thus we might speak of a patient's developing insight into her anger at her mother, into her envy at her brother and her desire to be a boy, or even into the helpless despair she experienced when her parents left her in a summer camp at age eight and she tried to run away. Bibring (1954) even uses the term to refer to a clear comprehension of previously conscious but amorphous experiences. A different type of insight, perhaps the other end of a spectrum, perhaps a later stage, perhaps qualitatively distinct, is illustrated by the patient who develops an understanding of internal psychological patterns or mechanisms, as the man who developed insight into how his recurrent attempts to please depressed women stemmed from his experience with a depressed mother who had relied on him to cheer her up, or the woman who recognized that her constant struggles with her adolescent daughter were related to an unconscious equation of the daughter with her own envied and hated younger sister. These instances involve not only the recovery of memories or experiences the patient knew or experienced directly, consciously or unconsciously, but also the understanding, with personal conviction, of theories or explanations accounting for the experiences. The distinction is not between conscious and unconscious experience, but between experience and understanding. The former involves a clearer and more conscious focus on what has previously been registered and encoded internally, a recovery of what has been lost, the latter a more profound theoretical grasp of experiences that before had been unconnected, fragmentary, or meaningless: in short, the construction of a new creative synthesis.

Insight and Psychoanalysis

Insight occupies a special place in our theory of the mechanism of the therapeutic action of psychoanalysis. Abreaction, suggestion, manipulation, identification, education, and transference are part of psychoanalysis and may be of therapeutic value, but they are found also in other dynamic psychotherapies and are often more important there. Insight is different. In psychoanalysis it is central; if other mechanisms are employed, we regard them as disruptions that must themselves be treated with insight. Without some suggestion that insight is involved, we question whether a psychoanalysis has truly occurred. When new modifications of psychoanalytic technique are proposed, emphasis is often placed on the continued importance of interpretation and insight, as though to demonstrate that the treatment is still "psychoanalytic." In other therapies insight may be relevant, but even when its role seems rather significant we may wonder whether it is only a corollary, a vehicle for more important but nonspecific factors, rather than itself the primary therapeutic agent. Of course, the same question has been raised with regard to psychoanalysis, but while the role of insight in psychotherapy is a problem for research, its role in psychoanalysis is the question of whether psychoanalysis exists at all as a distinct treatment modality.

It is an old psychoanalytic maxim that insight never cured anything but ignorance. This reminds us that insight, narrowly defined as the acquisition of knowledge about oneself, is a technique or a means in psychoanalysis, not its goal. However, two qualifications must be made lest we accept the principle too casually. First, while insight is a means rather than an end, psychoanalysis, when properly prescribed and conducted, is the only psychotherapy that is carried out *as if* insight were the goal. That is, patients and situations are selected so that the pursuit of insight is the appropriate means to the goals of therapy, and any divergence from that pursuit is both resisted and examined for the insight it might provide. While insight is not its ultimate goal, psychoanalysis does involve selecting and creating situations within which insight is the goal. It is much like playing a game. Winning need not be the ultimate goal of participating, but if one does participate, then winning is the goal within the game.

The second qualification is that while we say that insight is a means rather than an end, it may be that the knowledge acquired in insight is not the critical factor but only a corollary of something more important. I am referring not to the powerful nonspecific therapeutic factors present in all psychotherapy, insight-oriented or not, but rather to the *process* of acquiring insight (as distinct from the knowledge that is its *product*). Aspects of this process include the collaborative work between patient and analyst, the mode of thinking, the direction of attention inward, and the conviction that there is something there to be seen that is both interesting and important. The importance of process may well explain the efficacy of the different, at times conflicting, conceptual models that inform the insights of various analysts and their patients. In other words, the process of seeking insight might work its therapeutic effect by making the patient more psychologically minded rather than by making him more psychologically knowledgeable. Insight may cure not ignorance but inner blindness—or, better, the state of having one's inner eyes tightly closed. Students can be well educated by being taught theories that are later discarded as false, and patients may be well analyzed by systematically and carefully pursuing self-knowledge that may have little validity, if in the process they develop an interest in their inner life and become more insight-oriented, if not more insightful. A patient's pursuit of historical data regarding his past usually has far more significance in these terms than as an aid to the reconstruction of childhood events.

Insight, like most everything else in psychoanalysis, may well have its greatest significance in relation to transference and resistance rather than the patient's growing self-knowledge. Psychoanalysts believe that insight is important, and patients quickly learn what their analysts believe to be important. Recently a colleague met a new patient of mine at a cocktail party. My colleague later told me that he had congratulated my patient for his good fortune at having me as his analyst, and had offered him two pieces of advice—to tell me everything, and to try to remember his dreams. Since then, my patient has made a considerable effort to tell me all about himself, has virtually flooded us with dreams, and has worked insightfully and constructively at exploring and understanding everything—his dreams, his life, and the relationship between them. However, he has not told me quite everything about himself. He has not yet mentioned his conversation with my colleague, though my knowledge of it has probably led me to probe more than I otherwise might. At times, especially early in an analytic process, what appears to be insight may more properly be seen as a transference bribe that allows more uncomfortable associative pathways to be avoided. In time, no doubt, my patient will develop insight into this as well, as his current insight comes to be reframed. He is beginning to recognize that his life has been a series of quests for kind and powerful male protectors, and will eventually see that both his acceptance of my colleague's advice and his very formulation of that genetic insight in the analysis are recent episodes in that quest.

One developmental forerunner of the transferential role of insight can be seen in the common pattern of relationship between students, teachers and learning. In the beginning most students learn in order to please and earn approval from their teachers. The knowledge that results from this learning is real, but the process of learning survives the end of formal schooling only if it becomes secondarily autonomous from the transference relationship with the teacher. This sometimes happens, and an important criterion in evaluating an educational experience is the extent to which it fosters this secondary autonomy of the learning process, as opposed to the extent to which it facilitates the immediate acquisition of knowledge. An analogous argument can be made for psychoanalysis and the interpretive process: the encouragement of an autonomous interest in insight and psychological awareness is more important than any specific piece of insight or self-knowledge.

Insight, like every other mental phenomenon, can be understood in psychoanalytic theory as a compromise. That is, while our most characteristic formulation emphasizes its adaptive and rational role, insight can also gratify infantile wishes, allay unconscious fears, and reflect underlying patterns of psychic organization. Put in other terms, self-knowledge is never fully determined by the self as the object of knowledge, for there are always many possible ways for the self as knower to know the self as object. The selection among those possibilities will be responsive to the psychological advantages and disadvantages of the various options. The insight that provides the best set of compromise satisfactions will be the most attractive. Oedipus could have focused on his discovery of his infantile victimization or on the recurrent tragedies that resulted from his family's overidealization of the oracles and the gods. However, he selected instead the theme of his oedipal transgressions and thereby satisfied his masochistic quest for self-punishment and proof of his guilt. (Similarly, we might speculate that Sophocles, who spent his latter years embroiled in litigation with his son, preferred a version that expunged Laius' transgressions, while Freud, with his special intimacy with his mother, ignored Jocasta's culpability.) The insight that Oedipus acquired tells us something about the Oedipus he came to know, but his selection of that specific insight tells us a great deal about the Oedipus who set out on that search, the inner needs the discovery was designed to gratify, and thus why he chose to make this discovery rather than another. Reformulating this in a more clinically relevant way, our patients in psychoanalysis have insight to start with; we seldom provide insight where there was none before. We do, however, provide alternative insights and examine with our patients why they might choose to select one rather than another. Indeed, an interest in acquiring insight into one's choice of insights is one of the most fundamental characteristics of psychoanalysis, one that differentiates it even from other insight-oriented psychotherapies.

Insight and Development

There are several models of the mechanism of action of psychoanalysis. One, as we have noted, emphasizes the central role of insight in facilitating new resolutions of old conflicts and shifts in the configuration of psychic structures. Another model employs developmental metaphors and considers psychoanalysis an opportunity for the resumption of an interrupted or arrested developmental course, or perhaps a new chance to negotiate a developmental challenge that somehow went awry. These two models are frequently regarded as competitive, if not contradictory, but this view implies a prejudice regarding the role of insight in normal development. If we believe that insight into one's inner life and psychological processes is not unique to psychoanalysis but rather is a widespread occurrence in human experience, if we believe that when psychoanalysis attempts to create an opportunity for insight to develop it is facilitating a normal process, not producing an artificial one, then the transformations that stem from insights in psychoanalysis may be viewed as continuous with the developmental transformations that result from other insights in the course of life. In other words, insight and its psychological sequelae are a normal psychic phenomenon, not a special therapeutic event; insight is a food, not a drug. There may be individuals who have special needs for assistance in achieving insight, individuals suffering from insight deficiency syndromes, for whom psychoanalysis makes normal development possible, but the mechanisms by which insight operates can be sought in the effects of insight in life outside the consultation room. The view that psychoanalysis operates by means of insight does not contradict the view that it operates by allowing the resumption of arrested development, for insight is itself a normal developmental process.

This calls attention to a deficiency in our current theory of insight. There have been a number of attempts to develop a theory of how insight operates in psychoanalysis—how it comes about and what effect it has. There has even been discussion of the developmental aspects of insight in psychoanalysis, addressing such issues as the prerequisites for insight, the ages at which they appear, and the forms of insight that are possible at each developmental stage. However, little attention has been directed to the role of insight in normal development. The problem was clearly formulated by Anna Freud in her 1981 paper on insight, but after that formulation little was said. Psychoanalytic theories of development have focused on the earliest years of life, while we are more likely to think of insight as a later acquisition. Motives and drives have been emphasized rather than cognition, and when the latter has been discussed capacities and interferences have been emphasized rather than the content of self-knowledge and its effect on personality development. We speak as if children grow and mature emotionally, and in the course of doing so blind themselves to certain kinds of awareness and understanding, but we fail to consider the developmental impact of whatever awareness and understanding does occur. Piagetian psychology addresses the development of cognitive functioning but has little interest in the impact on other aspects of the personality of the knowledge acquired through that development.

What would such a theory of insight entail? It would recognize that psychological development is a story not only of organismic cravings, fears, relationships, patterns of mental functioning, perceptions of self and others, and understandings regarding the world, but also of evolving understandings and awarenesses of the self. Psychological development proceeds throughout the life cycle, and different perspectives may be helpful in organizing our understanding of different developmental epochs. A period that is relatively "latent" from the point of view of drives may be crucial from the perspective of insight. Drives and fears are central in our understanding of infancy, while self-knowledge is central in our understanding of the second and third decades of life. This is particularly important to psychoanalysts, because not only are these themes part of their patient's histories, they are often the background of the patients' contemporary life during the analysis. Furthermore, the technique of psychoanalysis includes major efforts to revive the themes of potentiality and self-reflection that normally characterize these epochs. The psychoanalytic situation may be designed to frustrate infantile drives, but it certainly strives to elicit and enhance the patient's interest and curiosity regarding himself.

If self-knowledge were not influential in shaping the outcome of normal development, we would hardly expect insight to have much impact during psychoanalysis, and the central assumptions of our theory of technique would be without foundation. The theory that guides us to the meanings of our inner experiences and that informs our interpretations may best be regarded as a hermeneutic system, a meta-metaphor. However, the theory that explains why the insight that results from such interpretations makes a difference, why meanings influence lives, is a special case of a more general scientific theory of the role of insight in psychological development.

Oedipus Revisited

Oedipus was a difficult case. He presented in midlife, following a successful career and an apparently satisfactory marriage, troubled by a mysterious sense of doom that threatened his world and a deep foreboding that somehow he might bear responsibility for it. There was evidence of significant character pathology; he was impulsive, stubborn, arrogant, quick-tempered, and repeatedly provoked conflicts with older men. Despite his great intelligence he seemed to have little insight into his own dynamics, and had forgotten major segments of his earlier life. As the history unfolded, it was clear there had been much to forget. It is important to separate what Oedipus did not consciously know about his past into two categories: (1) that which he knew but was desperately disavowing (his murder of his father Laius and his marriage to his mother Jocasta, both of which occurred well after he must have registered them mentally) and (2) major traumas that occurred before he could possibly have remembered or registered them (his abandonment by his parents, his physical mutilation, and his adoption). Oedipus may have been preoccupied with his oedipal sins, as have we, but it was these *pre*oedipal traumas that shaped his character pathology. Oedipus gained insight into his oedipal dynamics—he learned or, to be more accurate, he finally accepted what he always knew, that he had killed his father and married his mother. However, he never came to understand the link between his preoedipal and oedipal experiences, or his early experiences and his adult character, or, for that matter, even the nature of that adult character. Jocasta, who as mother and wife knew him well, recognized the risks of insight for a man of such character. After he rejected Teiresias' warning, she tried once more to soothe him and to divert him from his quest: "Best to live lightly, as one can, unthinkingly. As to your mother's marriage bed, don't fear it. Before this, in dreams too, as well as oracles, many a man has lain with his own mother. But he to whom such things are nothing bears his life most easily" (ll. 977–983). Jocasta was hardly a neutral observer, of course, and had much at stake. She might well represent, in fact, the very prototype of familial interference and resistance to the psychoanalytic process of uncovering.

However, Oedipus rejected Jocasta just as earlier he had rejected Teiresias. He fought with Creon and then with the messenger and the herdsman, just as years earlier he had fought with Laius, never recognizing his own contribution to these struggles and never gaining insight into the origins of his quest for insight. Ultimately, he used his newly found knowledge in the most narcissistic and masochistic way possible. If *Oedipus Rex* is the prototype of psychoanalysis and Oedipus' discovery is the prototype of insight, then certainly the climax of the drama is the prototype of a most horrifying negative therapeutic reaction.

What might have been different? When Oedipus first confronted Teiresias with his demand for knowledge, Teiresias responded to the content of the request, but not to the form. He addressed *what* Oedipus wanted to know, but not *why* or *when*, or *how* he went about seeking knowledge. Oedipus came to grief not because his curiosity was so broad but because, in the end, it was too narrow. Teiresias ignored contemporary reality, the precipitating situation, and the transference. He did warn Oedipus that knowledge can do more harm than good, but then in anger he made his revelation.

Teiresias could have said, "Oedipus, calm down. You demand that I answer your questions, and I am willing to do so. But first look at what you already know, and what you hope to find out by looking further. You imagine some horrible discovery that you fear to voice. You hope that I will deny it while you dread that I will confirm it. You threaten my life, an old blind man, and seem to feel no guilt or responsibility for what you do, claiming that it is the will of the gods. What can we learn from your fears, and from the way you treat me, for if we do not start first with these things, with your world today, and learn what your questions mean and why they arise now, if we answer your questions but do not address mine, the consequences will be disastrous." (And this would have been the prototype of an overly long and intellectualized interpretation!)

Oedipus might have come to understand not only his incestuous and patricidal wishes, but also the context in which they had developed, the severe parental failures that preceded his dramatic transformation of universal fantasy into most unusual action, and the features of his current life that had reawakened them. He might have regarded his new knowledge differently, and responded to it more adaptively. The play ends with Jocasta dead and Oedipus blind, holding his young daughters Antigone and Ismene. He utters his final words: "Do not take them from me" (l. 1523). We know that he goes on to spend the rest of his life with his daughters. His quest for insight, triggered by their adolescence, has led to self-knowledge, but self-knowledge of a restricted and restricting sort. In the end he only shifted from his mother's bed to his daughters' arms, repeating his incestuous destiny.

Oedipus Rex is a tragedy because we see Oedipus differently than he sees himself; we understand the behavior for which he can only blame himself; and we recognize that his quest for truth leads him only to blind repetition. Viewed as a psychoanalysis, his quest must be considered a failure, for while Oedipus acquires insight, it is insight without context, insight that provides ammunition for his unconscious guilt but not an understanding of the need to feel that guilt, insight that fails to change the basic pattern of his life. The tragedy of *Oedipus Rex* is that while he acquires insight, it is insight in the service of justification and repetition. He never learns what Sophocles makes apparent to us, and as a result he changes neither his character nor his destiny.

REFERENCES

Bibring, E. (1954), Psychoanalysis and the dynamic psychotherapies. *J. Amer. Psychoanal. Assn.*, 2:745–770.

Freud, A. (1981), Insight. *Psychoanalytic Study of the Child*, 36:241–249.

Freud, S. (1900), The Interpretation of Dreams. *Standard Edition*, 4/5. London: Hogarth Press, 1953.

——— (1907), Delusions and dreams in Jensen's *Gradiva*. *Standard Edition*, 9:7–95. London: Hogarth Press, 1959.

——— (1909), Notes upon a case of obsessional neurosis. *Standard Edition*, 10:155–318. London: Hogarth Press, 1955.

——— (1914), On the history of the psycho-analytic movement. *Standard Edition*, 14:287–359. London: Hogarth Press, 1957.

——— & Breuer, J. (1893–1895), Studies on Hysteria. *Standard Edition*, 2. London: Hogarth Press, 1956.

Grene, D., & Lattimore, R., Eds. (1959), *Oedipus the King*, trans. D. Grene. In: *The Complete Greek Tragedies: Volume II. Sophocles*. Chicago: University of Chicago Press, pp. 11–76.

Name Index

Subject Index